'Antony Beevor's *D-Day: The Battle for Normandy* has all the qualities that have made his earlier works so successful: an eye for telling and unusual detail, an ability to make complex events understandable, and a wonderful graphic style of writing'
Ian Kershaw, *Guardian*, Books of the Year

'A brilliantly organized, eye-opening epic' *Observer*, Books of the Year

'Utterly absorbing' Craig Brown, *Mail on Sunday*, Books of the Year

'Revivified by Beevor's expert grasp of complex detail'
Financial Times, Books of the Year

'Powerful, compelling' *The Times*, Books of the Year

'Will surely stand as the definitive account for years'
Daily Telegraph, Books of the Year

'Beevor does battle history consummately, but he does something more than battle history . . . It is not so much the face of battle as the very pores. The texture comes from the testimony he noses out, truffle-like, from the archives . . . Beevor is well-nigh unbeatable'
Alex Danchev, *Independent*

'He succeeds, to a quite remarkable degree, in catching that sense of scale that marked out one of the decisive campaigns of history'
Richard Holmes, *Evening Standard*

'Excellent. Written with tremendous verve and flair . . . Beevor is the consummate military historian'
Roger Moorhouse, *Independent on Sunday*

'Invaluable' *Spectator*

ABOUT THE AUTHOR

Antony Beevor's books and awards include *Crete – The Battle and the Resistance* (Runciman Prize); *Paris After the Liberation, 1944–1949*; *Stalingrad* (the Samuel Johnson Prize, the Wolfson Prize for History and the Hawthornden Prize for Literature); *Berlin – The Downfall* (Longman–*History Today* Trustees' Award); and *The Battle for Spain* (La Vanguardia Prize). *D-Day: The Battle for Normandy* (Prix Henry Malherbe and the RUSI Westminster Medal) was an international number one bestseller in hardback. His *The Second World War* was also an international number one bestseller. His books have appeared in thirty foreign editions and sold more than six million copies.

D-DAY

THE BATTLE FOR NORMANDY

Antony Beevor

PENGUIN BOOKS

For Miles, my oldest friend

PENGUIN BOOKS

Published by the Penguin Group
Penguin Books Ltd, 80 Strand, London WC2R 0RL, England
Penguin Group (USA) Inc., 375 Hudson Street, New York, New York 10014, USA
Penguin Group (Canada), 90 Eglinton Avenue East, Suite 700, Toronto, Ontario, Canada M4P 2Y3
(a division of Pearson Penguin Canada Inc.)
Penguin Ireland, 25 St Stephen's Green, Dublin 2, Ireland (a division of Penguin Books Ltd)
Penguin Group (Australia), 707 Collins Street, Melbourne, Victoria 3008, Australia
(a division of Pearson Australia Group Pty Ltd)
Penguin Books India Pvt Ltd, 11 Community Centre, Panchsheel Park, New Delhi – 110 017, India
Penguin Group (NZ), 67 Apollo Drive, Rosedale, Auckland 0632, New Zealand
(a division of Pearson New Zealand Ltd)
Penguin Books (South Africa) (Pty) Ltd, Block D, Rosebank Office Park, 181 Jan Smuts Avenue,
Parktown North, Gauteng 2193, South Africa

Penguin Books Ltd, Registered Offices: 80 Strand, London WC2R 0RL, England

www.penguin.com

First published by Viking 2009
Published in Penguin Books 2010
This edition published with a new foreword in Penguin Books 2014

001

ISBN: 978-0-241-96897-0

www.greenpenguin.co.uk

Contents

Contents

List of Illustrations and Maps

MAPS

List of Illustrations and Maps

Glossary

To help clarify the distinction between German and Allied divisions in the text, I refer on the one hand to the 352nd Infanterie-Division (German) or on the other to the 90th Infantry Division (American). The German version here is, of course, a slight hybrid – in German it would be the 352. Infanterie-Division.

When it comes to regiments, it should be remembered that references to a British or Canadian regiment imply a single battalion. An American or German regiment, on the other hand, usually included three battalions and was the size of a brigade.

BCRA	Bureau Central de Renseignements et d'Action: General de Gaulle's secret and special operations service, led by Colonel André Dewavrin, known by his nom de guerre of 'Passy'.
bocage	dense Norman countryside of small fields surrounded by large hedgerows on thick banks, often with sunken lanes in between.
DUKW	US amphibious transport vehicle built by General Motors.
FFI	Forces Françaises de l'Intérieur: organization of the Resistance into the semblance of an army under the command of General Koenig in London.
Fifi	slang for a member of the FFI.
FTP	Francs-tireurs et Partisans: Communist-led part of the Resistance.

Hiwi	German abbreviation of *Hilfsfreiwillige* or volunteer: mainly Soviet prisoners of war who had been coerced through starvation in camps to serve the German army as auxiliaries. A few became passionately loyal to their German masters. Those captured by the Allies were returned to Stalin. Some were shot, but most died in labour camps.
Jäger	German Army equivalent of light infantry or chasseurs.
Jedburgh	American, British and French three-man teams, consisting of two officers and a radio operator, parachuted into France before and during the battle for Normandy, their task being to train and advise Resistance groups.
Kübelwagen	Made by Volkswagen, this was the Wehrmacht's slightly larger and heavier counterpart to the Jeep.
LCT	landing craft tank.
LST	landing ship tank.
Landser	German equivalent of a GI or ordinary soldier, but usually indicating an experienced front-line infantryman.
Luftlande	(as in 91st Luftlande-Division) German air-landing division trained to land in gliders in support of a drop by Fallschirmjäger or paratroop units.
OB West	Oberbefehlshaber West, or Commander-in-Chief West: designation of the headquarters of Generalfeldmarschall Gerd von Rundstedt (and later Generalfeldmarschall von Kluge) at Saint-Germain-en-Laye, just outside Paris.
OKH	Oberkommando des Heeres: the Supreme Command of the Army, which in practical terms was responsible for the eastern front.
OKW	Oberkommando der Wehrmacht: the Supreme Command of the Wehrmacht, which directed all other theatres, especially OB West, during the battle for Normandy.
ORA	Organisation de Résistance de l'Armée: the most conservative wing of the Resistance, stemming from those French troops permitted by the Armistice who set up

	their own groups following the German reoccupation of the demilitarized zone in November 1942.
OSS	Office of Strategic Services: American counterpart to SOE.
Ost-Battalion	a battalion formed from *Osttruppen*.
Osttruppen	'Eastern troops': former Red Army prisoners of the Germans, mostly from General Vlasov's ROA, who served in German uniform under German officers and NCOs in France.
Panzerfaust	the simple and effective shoulder-launched anti-tank rocket-propelled grenade mass-produced for German infantry.
'Peep'	slang for Jeep.
PIAT	Projector Infantry Anti-Tank: the inferior British equivalent of the bazooka.
ROA	Rosskaya Osvoboditel'naya Armiya: Russian Liberation Army of former Red Army soldiers, led by General Andrei Vlasov.
SAS	Special Air Service: British special forces, organized into two brigades for the invasion of Europe, but including French and other national units and sub-units.
SHAEF	Supreme Headquarters Allied Expeditionary Force.
SOE	Special Operations Executive: the organization set up by Churchill in 1940 to promote resistance in German-occupied Europe.

For a table of comparative ranks between the American, British and German armies, as well as the Waffen-SS, see www.antonybeevor.com.

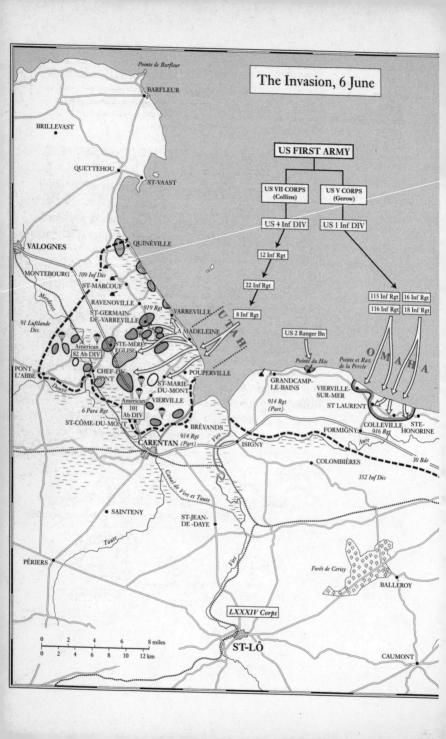

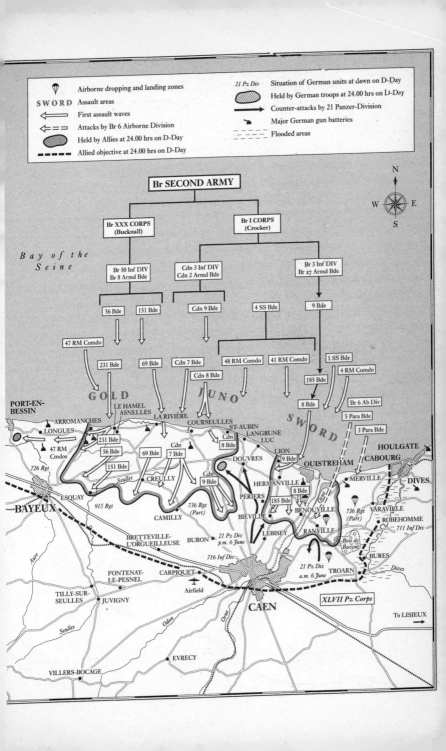

D-Day: A New Foreword

Seventy years have now passed since the Allied invasion in June 1944 that began the liberation of western Europe from Nazi occupation. One might have expected interest to diminish with the passage of time and the death of participants, yet there are more museums in Normandy and more visitors than ever before.

As family groups stand on the bluffs above Omaha beach and look out across the great Baie de la Seine, the largest amphibious landing in history still grips their imagination. You cannot help but try to put yourself in the place of the Allied soldiers coming ashore in their landing craft under heavy fire, sick with fear, and thrown around by the waves. Others try to share the feelings of a German defender in one of the positions nearby, as they first caught sight of the vast invasion armada in the grey dawn. But the great emphasis on the landing beaches distracts the casual visitor from a brutal truth. Even with the horrors of Omaha beach, casualties on D-Day were far fewer than had been expected. The real carnage came later, and further inland, during the battle for Normandy.

The planning for Operation Overlord was meticulous. Nothing was left to chance. The instructions issued by staff ran to many hundreds of pages. In true British style, nervousness was camouflaged with jokes. Operation Overlord became known as Operation Overboard. A spoof set of instructions circulated just before the invasion. It defined the objectives as:

a. To provide some employment for a very great number of officers.

b. To prove that the cardinal principles of administration, movement and common sense may all be disregarded or overcome by improvisation.

c. To re-establish the NAAFI firmly on the Continent of Europe.

With so much at stake, all the American and British planners suffered from 'D-Day jitters', as they were known. But one of General Omar Bradley's staff officers, the wonderfully named Colonel Charles Bonesteel III, observed later: 'The British had a much greater fear of failure.' This was indeed true, after the evacuation from Dunkirk and the disastrous raid on Dieppe in 1942, to say nothing of manpower shortages and a war-weariness.

The British Army had other more systemic flaws. Perhaps even more than the United States Army, the British Army had been marked by the social and political tensions of the interwar years. Soldiers and NCOs had become far more politicized than their father's generation in the First World War. As a result, a trade-union mentality influenced attitudes as to what could be expected of them. American and Canadian observers were amazed by the British soldier's expectation of regular tea and smoke breaks.

On D-Day itself, an astonishing number of soldiers, who felt tired after wading ashore, believed that they had earned a rest simply for having survived the landing. An American liaison officer reported: 'There was also a feeling amongst many of the men that having landed, they had achieved their object, and there was time for a cigarette – and even a brew up – instead of getting on with the task of knocking out the enemy defences and pushing inland.' 'The British Army couldn't fight for three and a half minutes without tea,' a Canadian Glengarry Highlander remarked with cheerful exaggeration. A week later, when part of the 7th Armoured Division attacked Villers-Bocage, troops stopped for a break in the town before throwing out reconnaissance patrols or taking up fire positions, with disastrous results when the 'panzer ace' Michael Wittmann charged into the town with his Tiger tank.

The other British failing came from a demarcation mentality, of not doing anything that was not strictly your job. Sappers, as a Canadian observed, did not believe it was their task to fire at the enemy when not engaged on an engineering task, and infantry refused to help 'fill a crater or get a vehicle out of difficulties'. There was little of that attitude in either the German or the American Army.

The main drawback of the British regimental system was its reluctance to face major structural reform. It was incapable of adopting a German panzergrenadier or American armoured infantry organization to work closely with tanks. In fact, the systematic introduction of armoured personnel carriers took another twenty years. They finally reached the British Army of the Rhine in 1965. Infantry battalions and tank regiments were attached in armoured brigades, and sometimes worked very well together, but, with the notable exception of the Guards Armoured Division, they never integrated on a divisional basis. Only armoured reconnaissance regiments had their own mounted infantry as an integral part of the unit.

The Germans quickly observed that the British and Canadians were very brave in defence, but often over-cautious in attack. There are numerous reasons for this. British military myths had always focused on heroic defence: the retreat to Corunna, the squares at Waterloo, the sieges of Lucknow and Delhi, and Rorke's Drift. Glorification of the attack had been much rarer. It must also be remembered that in 1944 the country had been at war for nearly five years, so there was a considerable war-weariness. And, as the end of the war came in sight, men wanted to survive. They became reluctant to take risks, especially those who had fought through North Africa and Italy. Britain and Canada also had started to suffer from a severe shortage of manpower, and this was one of the reasons for Montgomery's caution. Churchill was afraid, with the very heavy casualties during the battle for Normandy, that the British would not have much of an army left by the time they reached Berlin, and would thus lose what little influence they had when it came to the peace settlement.

Most of the United States Army divisions involved in the invasion may have lacked combat experience and faced many problems, but they usually proved quick to learn. They shared tips on how to deal with nasty German tricks, mostly learned on the eastern front. But the US Army, like the British, was woefully unimaginative when it came to sending in 'replacements' to make up for battle casualties. Unlike the troops who had trained for the invasion, these young men, some still teenagers, were pathetically unprepared for the shock of battle.

Nobody knows what their own behaviour in battle will be until they experience it. Combat creates the most volatile emotions imaginable. In fact, the study of warfare should focus on fear and the suppression of fear, because that, paradoxically, is probably the greatest source of violence. I have gone into the question in some detail in the book because of the very high number of those who suffered from battle shock, otherwise termed combat fatigue.

The psychological casualties on the Allied side during this battle of attrition were very high indeed – some 30,000 cases in the US First Army alone – and it is interesting to see the different ways of dealing with this immense problem. Significantly, both American and British army psychiatrists were later struck by the fact that comparatively few German prisoners appeared to be suffering from combat fatigue, in spite of the shelling and bombing which they had had to endure. This, they concluded, was due partly to the effects of Nazi propaganda over the last eleven years and to the fact that the German Army simply did not recognize the condition.

General Barton, the American commander of the 4th Division, wrote: 'The Germans are staying in there just by the guts of their soldiers. We outnumber them 10 to 1 in infantry, 50 to 1 in artillery and an infinite number in the air.' He wanted unit commanders to convince their men 'that we have got to fight for our country just as hard as the Germans are fighting for theirs'.

The Germans were also far more professional, mainly as a result of their training system, their experience on the eastern front and their doctrine of *Auftragstaktik*, which was a commander's obligation to achieve an objective on his own initiative. This gave them a much greater flexibility of response. The Allied armies were essentially civilian armies, and they could not exert the same sort of pitiless discipline to overcome fear. Also the Germans were deeply influenced by the idea promoted through propaganda that they were fighting to defend their country from annihilation, while the Americans and British just wanted to get the war over with and return home.

In a corps intelligence summary of 8 September 1944, soon after the battle for Normandy was over, British officers observed on the basis of prisoner interrogations that the officers of the 3rd Fallschirmjäger Division were almost entirely diehard Nazis and that these German paratroop units were the closest in the Wehrmacht to the Waffen-SS. (On the other hand, German paratroop units, unlike the Waffen-SS in Normandy, were not guilty of large-scale massacres of civilians or prisoners.) A ruthless professionalism was no doubt true of the 3rd Fallschirmjäger Division and the 6th Fallschirmjäger Regiment commanded by Oberstleutnant von der Heydte (although Heydte claimed strenuously later that he was not a Nazi), but the more junior Fallschirmjäger divisions were not nearly so effective. This was because they were manned largely by Luftwaffe ground crew and even trainee pilots whose courses had been cancelled due to fuel shortages.

The important point is that we should always be wary of any generalization. In their book *Soldaten*, Sönke Neitzel and Harald Welzer write: 'It is high time to stop overestimating the effects of ideology.' They rightly argue that 'soldiers could murder Jews without being anti-Semites and fight fanatically for the fatherland without being committed National Socialists'. Nevertheless, many German soldiers were deeply influenced by propaganda. Particularly in the Waffen-SS, they believed that Germany would still destroy the western Allies and then defeat the Red Army.

Much has been written about the fighting qualities of armies in the Second World War, especially the difference between the armies of democracies and the armies of dictatorships. You could not have expected the average citizen from a western democracy to have fought in the same way as a member of the Wehrmacht or the Red Army. Americans, Britons and Canadians alike did not regard it as shameful to give up after a certain level of suffering or hopelessness was reached. Phrases like 'Fight to the last man!' were seen as rhetorical, not literal. And we today would be most uneasy if they had fought in Normandy in the same way as the Waffen-SS.

Much less has been said, on the other hand, about the similarities if one studies the performance of average, as opposed to elite, troops. The evidence indicates that only a small proportion of front-line forces truly engage in combat. An initial study in the British Army was carried out in Italy by Major Lionel Wigram. Wigram estimated that in most platoons only a small handful of men really did the fighting. Another small group of men were likely to run away at the first opportunity. Those in the main group in between would follow the fighters, if things went well, or the potential deserters if they went badly. General Montgomery was so horrified by the report that he had it suppressed.

The Germans divided their soldiers' combat performance into four categories, which were essentially the same as Wigram's breakdown except that they split the main group in the middle in two:

Die Einsatzfreudigen – those who enjoy fighting
Die Einsatzwilligen – those prepared to fight
Die Einsatzgehemmten – those reluctant to fight
Die Einsatzflüchtigen – those who will flee from their duty.

The American combat historian Brigadier General S. L. A. Marshall went into the subject in much greater detail soon after the war. And even though some of his research has been shown to be very dubious, there can be little doubt about the overall conclusion that only a minority of soldiers in a conscript army actually shoot at the enemy. The Red Army was no different, as I found in the Russian archives. Soviet officers argued during the war that a weapons inspection should be carried out immediately after an engagement with the enemy. All those found to have clean barrels should be executed immediately as 'deserters'.

British, Canadian and American armies all shared one belief. To reduce their own losses, they would always rely on a massive artillery bombardment, and on several occasions heavy aerial bombing. The battle for Normandy led to the deaths of 35,000 French civilians and the serious wounding of probably 100,000 more. The terrible paradox about democracies at war is that because of the pressure at home from the press, public opinion and parliament, commanders will try to reduce their own casualties by any means. That usually leads to an excessive reliance on high explosives, both bombs and shells, in an attempt to neutralize the enemy without exposing their own men. This is bound to lead to heavy civilian casualties, and Normandy unfortunately provides an outstanding example.

All one can say, as French historians have been the first to recognize, is that the martyrdom of Normandy at least spared the rest of France from similar destruction. And as the warmth of the welcome still afforded to Allied veterans in Normandy amply testifies, as we see every June, the courage and the sacrifice of those Allied soldiers who fought there can never be doubted.

Antony Beevor
London, November 2013

I

The Decision

Southwick House is a large Regency building with a stucco façade and a colonnaded front. At the beginning of June 1944, five miles to the south, Portsmouth naval base and the anchorages beyond were crowded with craft of every size and type – grey warships, transport vessels and hundreds of landing craft, all tethered together. D-Day was scheduled for Monday, 5 June, and loading had already begun.

In peacetime, Southwick could have been the setting for an Agatha Christie house party, but the Royal Navy had taken it over in 1940. Its formerly handsome grounds and the wood behind were now blighted by rows of Nissen huts, tents and cinder paths. Southwick served as the headquarters of Admiral Sir Bertram Ramsay, the naval commander-in-chief for the invasion of Europe, and also as the advanced command post of SHAEF, the Supreme Headquarters Allied Expeditionary Force. Anti-aircraft batteries on the Portsdown ridge were positioned to defend it as well as the dockyards below from the Luftwaffe.

Southern England had been enjoying a heatwave compounded by drought. Temperatures of up to 100 degrees Fahrenheit had been recorded on 29 May, yet the meteorological team attached to General Dwight D. Eisenhower's headquarters soon became uneasy. The group was headed by Dr James Stagg, a tall, lanky Scot with a rather gaunt face and a neat moustache. Stagg, the leading civilian weather expert in the country, had just been given the rank of group captain in the RAF to lend him the necessary authority in a military milieu unused to outsiders.

Since April, Eisenhower had been testing Stagg and his team by demanding three-day forecasts delivered on a Monday which were then checked against the reality later in the week. On Thursday, 1 June, the day before the battleships were due to sail from Scapa Flow off the north-west tip of Scotland, weather stations indicated some deep depressions forming over the North Atlantic. Rough seas in the English Channel could swamp the landing craft, to say nothing of their effect on the soldiers cramped on board. Low cloud and bad visibility presented another great threat, since the landings depended on the ability of the Allied air forces and navies to knock out German coastal batteries and defensive positions. General embarkation for the first wave of 130,000 troops was under way and due to be completed in two days' time.

Stagg was plagued by a lack of agreement among the different British and American meteorological departments. They all received the same reports from the weather stations but their analysis of the data simply did not match up. Unable to admit this, he had to tell Major General Harold R. Bull, Eisenhower's assistant chief of staff, that 'the situation is complex and difficult'.

'For heaven's sake, Stagg,' Bull exploded. 'Get it sorted out by tomorrow morning before you come to the Supreme Commander's conference. General Eisenhower is a very worried man.' Stagg returned to his Nissen hut to pore over the charts and consult the other departments yet again.

Eisenhower had other reasons for 'pre-D-Day jitters'. Although outwardly relaxed, with his famous open smile for everyone whatever their rank, he was smoking up to four packs of Camel cigarettes a day. He would light a cigarette, leave it smouldering in an ashtray, jump up, walk around and light another. His nerves were not helped by constant pots of coffee.

Postponing the invasion carried many risks. The 175,000 soldiers in the first two waves risked losing their fighting edge if cooped up in rough weather on their ships and landing craft. The battleships and convoys about to head down British coasts towards the Channel could not be turned round more than once without needing to refuel. And the chances of German reconnaissance aircraft sighting them would increase enormously.

Secrecy had always been the greatest concern. Much of the southern coast was covered with elongated military camps known as 'sausages', where the invasion troops were supposedly sealed off from contact with the outside world. A number of soldiers had, however, been slipping out under the barbed wire for a last drink at the pub or to see sweethearts and wives. The possibilities of leaks at all levels were innumerable. An American air force general had been sent home in disgrace after indicating the date of Operation Overlord at a cocktail party in Claridge's. Now a fear arose that the absence from Fleet Street of British journalists called forward to accompany the invasion force might be noticed.

Everyone in Britain knew that D–Day was imminent, and so did the Germans, but the enemy had to be prevented from knowing where and exactly when. Censorship had been imposed on the communications of foreign diplomats from 17 April, and movement in and out of the country strictly controlled. Fortunately, the British security service had captured all German agents in Britain. Most of them had been 'turned' to send back misleading information to their controllers. This 'Double Cross' system, supervised by the XX Committee, was designed to produce a great deal of confusing 'noise' as a key part of Plan Fortitude. Fortitude was the most ambitious deception in the history of warfare, a project even greater than the *maskirovka* then being prepared by the Red Army to conceal the true target of Operation Bagration, Stalin's summer offensive to encircle and smash the Wehrmacht's Army Group Centre in Belorussia.

Plan Fortitude had several aspects. Fortitude North, with fake formations in Scotland based on a 'Fourth British Army', pretended to prepare an attack on Norway to keep German divisions there. Fortitude South, the main effort, set out to convince the Germans that any landings in Normandy were a large-scale diversion to draw German reserves away from the Pas-de-Calais. The real invasion was supposedly to come between Boulogne and the Somme estuary during the second half of July. A notional '1st US Army Group' under General George S. Patton Jr, the commander the Germans feared the most, boasted eleven divisions in south-east England. Dummy aircraft and inflatable tanks, together with 250 fake landing ships, all contributed to the illusion. Invented formations, such as a 2nd British Airborne Division, had been created alongside some real ones. To increase the illusion, two fake corps headquarters also maintained a constant radio traffic.

One of the most important double agents to work for British intelligence on Fortitude South was a Catalan, Juan Pujol, who had the codename 'Garbo'. With his security service handler, he constructed a network of twenty-seven completely fabricated sub-agents and bombarded the German intelligence station in Madrid with information carefully prepared in London. Some 500 radio messages were sent in the months leading up to D-Day. These provided details which together gradually made up the mosaic which the Double Cross Committee was assembling to convince the Germans that the main attack was to come later in the Pas-de-Calais.

Subsidiary deceptions to prevent the Germans moving troops to Normandy from other parts of France were also dreamed up. Plan Ironside conveyed the impression that two weeks after the first landings a second invasion would be launched on the west coast of France directly from the United States and the Azores. To keep the Germans guessing, and to prevent them moving the 11th Panzer-Division near Bordeaux north into Normandy, a controlled agent in Britain, known as 'Bronx', sent a coded message to her German controller in the Banco Espirito Santo in Lisbon: '*Envoyez vite cinquante livres. J'ai besoin pour mon dentiste.*' This indicated 'that a landing would be made in the Bay of Biscay on about the 15th June'. The Luftwaffe, clearly fearful of a landing in Brittany, ordered the immediate destruction of four airfields close to the coast. Another diversion, Operation Copperhead, was mounted in late May when an actor resembling General Montgomery visited Gibraltar and Algiers to suggest an attack on the Mediterranean coast.

Bletchley Park, the highly secret complex about fifty miles north-west of London which decoded enemy signals, adopted a new watch system for Overlord from 22 May. Its experts were ready to decrypt anything important the moment it came in. Thanks to these 'Ultra' intercepts, they were also able to check on the success of Fortitude disinformation provided by the main 'Double Cross' agents, Pujol, Dusko Popov ('Tricycle') and Roman Garby-Czerniawski. On 22 April, Bletchley had decoded a German signal which identified the 'Fourth Army', with its headquarters near Edinburgh and two component corps at Stirling and

Dundee. Other messages showed that the Germans believed that the Lowland Division was being equipped for an attack on Norway.

Ultra decrypts revealed in May that the Germans had carried out an anti-invasion exercise, based on the assumption that the landings would take place between Ostend and Boulogne. Finally, on 2 June, Bletchley felt able to report: 'Latest evidence suggests enemy appreciates all Allied preparations completed. Expects initial landing Normandy or Brittany followed by main effort in Pas-de-Calais.' It looked as if the Germans really had swallowed Plan Fortitude.

Early on 2 June, Eisenhower moved into a trailer hidden in the park at Southwick under camouflage nets. He dubbed it 'my circus wagon', and when not in conference or visiting troops, he would try to relax by reading westerns on his bunk and smoking.

At 10.00 hours that Friday, in the library in Southwick House, Stagg gave Eisenhower and the other assembled commanders-in-chief the latest weather assessment. Because of the continuing disagreement among his colleagues, particularly the over-optimistic American meteorologists at SHAEF, he had to remain Delphic in his pronouncements. Stagg knew that by the evening conference he must produce a firm opinion on the deterioration of the weather over the weekend. The decision to proceed or to postpone had to be made very soon.

At the same meeting, Air Chief Marshal Sir Trafford Leigh-Mallory, the air commander-in-chief, outlined the plan 'to establish a belt of bombed routes through towns and villages thereby preventing or impeding the movement of enemy formations'. He asked whether he was free to proceed 'in view of the civilian casualties which would result'. Eisenhower announced his approval 'as an operational necessity'. It was decided to drop leaflets to the French to warn them.

The fate of French civilians was just one of many worries. As supreme commander, Eisenhower had to balance political and personal rivalries, while maintaining his authority within the alliance. He was well liked by Field Marshal Sir Alan Brooke, the Chief of the Imperial General Staff, and by General Sir Bernard Montgomery, the commander-in-chief of 21st Army Group, but neither rated him highly as a soldier. 'There is no doubt that Ike is out to do all he can to maintain the best of relations between British and Americans,' Brooke wrote in his diary, 'but it is equally clear that he knows nothing about strategy and is *quite* unsuited to the post of Supreme Commander as far as running the war is concerned.' Monty's characteristically terse judgement on Eisenhower after the war was: 'Nice chap, no soldier'.

These opinions were certainly unfair. Eisenhower demonstrated good judgement on all the key decisions over the Normandy invasion and his diplomatic skills held a fractious coalition together. That alone represented a considerable feat. Brooke himself acknowledged that 'national spectacles pervert the perspective of the strategic landscape'. And nobody, not even General George S. Patton, was as difficult to deal with as Monty, who treated his supreme commander with scant respect. At their very first meeting he had ticked off Eisenhower for smoking in his presence. Eisenhower was too big a man to take such things badly, but many of his American subordinates felt he should have been tougher on the British.

General Montgomery, despite his considerable qualities as a highly professional soldier and first-class trainer of troops, suffered from a breathtaking conceit which almost certainly stemmed from some sort of inferiority complex. In February, referring to his famous beret, he had told King George VI's private secretary, 'My hat is worth three divisions. The men see it in the distance. They say, "There's Monty", and then they will fight anybody.' His self-regard was almost comical and the Americans were not alone in believing that his reputation had been inflated by an adoring British press. 'Monty,' observed Basil Liddell Hart, 'is perhaps much more popular with civilians than with soldiers.'

Montgomery had an extraordinary showman's knack which usually radiated confidence to his troops, but he did not always receive a rapturous response. In February, when he told the Durham Light Infantry that they were to be in the first wave of the invasion, a loud moan went up. They had only just returned from fighting in the Mediterranean and had received little home leave. They felt that other divisions which had never left the British Isles should take their place. 'The bloody Durhams again' was the reaction. 'It's always the bloody Durhams.' When Montgomery drove off, all ranks were supposed to rush to the road to cheer him on his way, but not a man moved. This caused a good deal of angry embarrassment among senior officers.

Monty had been determined to have seasoned troops to stiffen the untried divisions, but this idea was greeted with a good deal of resentment by most of his desert veterans. They had been fighting for up to four years abroad and considered that it was now the turn of others, especially those divisions which had not yet been committed in any theatre. A number of former Eighth Army regiments had not been home for six years, and one or two had been away for even longer. Their resentment was strongly influenced by wives and girlfriends at home.

The US 1st Division, known as the 'Big Red One', also grumbled when picked yet again to lead the way in a beach assault, but its experience was badly needed. A major assessment report on 8 May had rated almost every other American formation allocated to the invasion as 'unsatisfactory'. American senior officers were stung into action and the last few weeks of intensive training were not wasted. Eisenhower was encouraged by the dramatic improvement, and privately grateful for the decision to postpone the invasion from early May to early June.

There were other tensions in the Allied command structure. Eisenhower's deputy supreme commander, Air Chief Marshal Sir Arthur Tedder, loathed Montgomery, but he in turn was deeply disliked by Winston Churchill. General Omar Bradley, the commander of the First US Army, who came from poor Missouri farming stock, did not look very martial with his 'hayseed expression' and his government-issue spectacles. But Bradley was 'pragmatic, unruffled, apparently unambitious, somewhat dull, neither flamboyant nor ostentatious, and he never raised hackles'. He was also a shrewd commander, driven by the need to get the job done. He was outwardly respectful towards Montgomery, but could not have been less like him.

Bradley got on very well with Eisenhower, but he did not share his chief's tolerance towards that loose cannon, George Patton. In fact Bradley barely managed to conceal his intense distrust of that eccentric southern cavalryman. Patton, a God-fearing man famous for his profanity, enjoyed addressing his troops in provocative terms. 'Now I want you to remember,' he once told them, 'that no bastard ever won a war by dying for his country. You win it by making the other poor dumb bastard die for *his* country.' There is no doubt that without Eisenhower's support at critical moments, Patton would never have had the chance to make his name in the coming campaign. Eisenhower's ability to keep such a disparate team together was an extraordinary achievement.

The most recent dispute produced entirely by D-Day jitters came from Air Chief Marshal Leigh-Mallory. Leigh-Mallory, who 'made everyone angry' and even managed to rile Eisenhower, suddenly became convinced that the two US airborne divisions due to be dropped on the Cotentin peninsula faced a massacre. He repeatedly urged the cancellation of this vital element in the Overlord plan to protect the western flank. Eisenhower told Leigh-Mallory to put his concerns in writing. This he did, and after careful consideration Eisenhower rejected them with Montgomery's full support.

Eisenhower, despite his nervous state and the appalling responsibility heaped upon him, wisely adopted a philosophical attitude. He had been selected to make the final decisions, so make them he must and face the consequences. The biggest decision, as he knew only too well, was almost upon him. Quite literally, the fate of many thousands of his soldiers' lives rested upon it. Without telling even his closest aides, Eisenhower prepared a brief statement to be made in the event of failure: 'The landings in the Cherbourg–Havre area have failed to gain a satisfactory foothold and I have withdrawn the troops. My decision to attack at this time and place was based on the best information available. The troops, the air and navy did all that bravery and devotion to duty could do. If any blame or fault attaches to the attempt it is mine alone.'

Although neither Eisenhower nor Bradley could admit it, the most difficult of the five landing beaches was going to be Omaha. This objective for the American 1st and 29th Infantry Divisions had been closely reconnoitred by a British team from COPP, the Combined Operations Beach Reconnaissance and Assault Pilotage Parties. In the second half of January, the midget submarine X-20 had been towed close to the Normandy coast by an armed trawler. General Bradley had requested that, having checked the beaches selected for the British and Canadian forces, COPP should also examine Omaha to make sure that it was firm enough for tanks. Captain Scott-Bowden, a sapper, and Sergeant Bruce Ogden-Smith of the Special Boat Section swam ashore, each armed only with a commando knife and a Colt .45 automatic. They also carried an eighteen-inch earth auger and a bandolier with containers into which they put their samples. The sea was unusually flat and they only just escaped discovery by German sentries.

The day after his return, Scott-Bowden was summoned to London by a rear admiral. He arrived at Norfolk House in St James's Square just after lunch. There, in a long dining room, with maps covered by curtains along the walls, he found himself facing six admirals and five generals, including General Bradley. Bradley interrogated him carefully on the beach-bearing capacity. 'Sir, I hope you don't mind my saying it,' Scott-Bowden said to him just before leaving, 'but this beach is a very formidable proposition indeed and there are bound to be tremendous casualties.' Bradley put a hand on his shoulder and said, 'I know, my boy, I know.' Omaha was simply the only possible beach between the British sector on the left and Utah beach on the right.

As soon as the invasion troops moved off for embarkation, the civilian population rushed out to wave goodbye. 'When we left,' wrote a young American engineer who had been billeted on an English family, '[they] cried just as if they were our parents. It was quite a touching thing for us. It seemed like the general public seemed to know pretty much what was going on.'

Secrecy was, of course, impossible to maintain. 'As we passed through Southampton,' wrote a British trooper in an armoured regiment, 'the people gave us a wonderful welcome. Each time that we halted we were all plied with cups of tea and cakes, much to the consternation of the Military Police escorting the column, who had strict orders to prevent any contact between civilian and soldier.'

Most troops were moved in army trucks, but some British units marched, their hobnailed ammunition boots ringing in step on the road. Old people, watching from their front gardens often with tears in their eyes, could not help thinking of the previous generation marching off to the trenches in Flanders. The helmets were a similar shape, but the battledress was different. And soldiers no longer wore puttees. They had canvas gaiters instead, which matched the webbing equipment of belt, yoke, ammunition pouches and pack. Rifle and bayonet had also changed, but not enough to make a noticeable difference.

The troops had sensed that D–Day must be close when twenty-four-hour leave passes were offered. For the less enthusiastic soldier this provided a last chance to disappear or get drunk. There had been many cases of soldiers going absent in the pre-invasion period, but relatively few cases of outright desertion. Most had returned to duty to be 'with their mates' when the invasion was on. Pragmatic commanding officers did not want to lose men to a military prison. They left it up to the individual to redeem himself in battle.

Soldiers noticed that officers had suddenly become much more solicitous of their men. Film shows were laid on in the closed camps. A more generous ration of beer was available and dance music played from loudspeakers. The more cynical spotted that quartermasters had suddenly become generous, an ominous sign. The poet Keith Douglas, a twenty-four-year-old captain in the Sherwood Rangers Yeomanry, wrote to Edmund Blunden, that poet of the previous war, 'I've been fattened up for the slaughter and am simply waiting for it to start.' Douglas was one of a number of men who harboured a strong sense of imminent death and spoke to their closest friends about it. It is striking how many turned out to have been right, and yet perhaps such a belief somehow turned into a self-fulfilling prophecy. Douglas went to church parade on the last Sunday. He walked afterwards with the regimental padre, who recorded that Douglas was reconciled to his approaching death and not morbid about it. In the view of a fellow officer, he was fatalistic because he felt that he had used up his ration of luck in the desert war.

Almost everyone hated the waiting and longed for the worst to be over. 'All are tense and all are pretending to be casual,' commented an American infantryman. 'Bravado helps,' he added. Many thought of their girlfriends. Some had married them in haste to make sure that they would benefit from a pension if the worst happened. One American soldier bundled up all his pay and sent it to a jeweller so that his English fiancée could select a ring ready for their wedding on his return. It was a time of intense personal emotion. 'The women who have come to see their men off,' noted a journalist shortly before, 'nearly always walk to the very end of the platform to wave their elaborately smiling goodbyes as the train pulls out.'

A few men cracked under the strain. 'One night,' recorded a member of the US 1st Infantry Division, 'one of the soldiers put on two bandoliers of ammunition and his hand grenades, grabbed a rifle, and took off. Nobody had seen him do this, but the moment they became aware, a search party was formed. The search party found him. He refused to give up, so he was killed. We never did know whether he just didn't want to die on the beach, or he was a spy. Whatever he did, it was dumb. He was a sure dead man versus a maybe.' Perhaps he had had a premonition of what lay ahead on Omaha.

While tanks and troops were still being loaded on to landing ships that Friday evening, Group Captain Stagg conferred again over secure landlines with the other meteorological centres. He had to give a firm report at the conference due to start at 21.30 hours, but there was still no agreement. 'Had it not been fraught with such potential tragedy, the whole business was ridiculous. In less than half an hour I was expected to present to General Eisenhower an "agreed" forecast for the next five days which covered the time of launching of the greatest military operation ever mounted: no two of the expert participants in the discussion could agree on the likely weather even for the next 24 hours.'

They argued round and round until time ran out. Stagg hurried to the library in the main house to present a report to all the key commanders for Overlord.

'Well, Stagg,' Eisenhower said. 'What have you got for us this time?'

Stagg felt compelled to follow his own instinct and overlook the more optimistic views of his American colleagues at Bushey Park: 'The whole situation from the British Isles to Newfoundland has been transformed in recent days and is now potentially full of menace.' As he went into detail, several of the senior officers glanced out of the window at the beautiful sunset in slight bewilderment.*

After questions about the weather for the airborne drops, Eisenhower probed further about the likely situation on 6 and 7 June. There was a significant pause, according to Tedder. 'If I answered that, Sir,' Stagg replied, 'I would be guessing, not behaving as your meteorological adviser.'

Stagg and his American counterpart, Colonel D. N. Yates, withdrew,

---

* It was still light because they were operating on double British summertime.

and soon General Bull came out to tell them that there would be no change of plan for the next twenty-four hours. As they returned to their tented sleeping quarters, the two men knew that the first ships had already left their anchorages. Stagg could not help thinking of the black joke made to him by Lieutenant General Sir Frederick Morgan, the initial chief planner of Overlord. 'Good luck, Stagg. May all your depressions be nice little ones, but remember we'll string you up from the nearest lamp post if you don't read the omens aright.'

Early the next morning, Saturday, 3 June, the news could hardly have been worse. The weather station at Blacksod Point in western Ireland had just reported a rapidly falling barometer and a force six wind. Stagg felt 'all but physically nauseated' by the weather charts and the way the teams still analysed the same data in different ways. That evening, at 21.30 hours, he and Yates were summoned. They entered the library, its shelves emptied of books. Mess armchairs were arranged in concentric arcs, with commanders-in-chief in the front row and their chiefs of staff and subordinate commanders behind. Eisenhower, his chief of staff, General Walter Bedell Smith, and Tedder sat on three chairs facing the audience.

'Gentlemen,' Stagg began. 'The fears my colleagues and I had yesterday about the weather for the next three or four days have been confirmed.' He then launched into a detailed forecast. It was a gloomy picture of rough seas, winds up to force six and low cloud. 'Throughout this recital,' Stagg wrote later, 'General Eisenhower sat motionless, with his head slightly to one side resting on his hand, staring steadily towards me. All in the room seemed to be temporarily stunned.' Not surprisingly, Eisenhower felt compelled to recommend a provisional postponement.

It was not a good night for Eisenhower. His aide, Commander Harry Butcher, came to him later with the news that Associated Press had put out a tape stating, 'Eisenhower's forces are landing in France.' Even though the agency cancelled the story twenty-three minutes later, it had been picked up by CBS and Radio Moscow. 'He sort of grunted,' Butcher noted in his diary.

When Stagg went off to his tent at about midnight, having heard of the provisional postponement, it was strange to look up between the trees and see that 'the sky was almost clear and everything around was still and quiet'. Stagg did not attempt to sleep. He spent the early hours of the morning writing up detailed notes of all discussions. When he had finished the forecast was no better, even though outside all remained calm.

At 04.15 hours on the Sunday, 4 June, at yet another meeting, Eisenhower decided that the twenty-four-hour postponement provisionally agreed the night before must stand. Without maximum air support, the risks were too great. The order went out to call back the convoys. Destroyers set to sea at full speed to round up landing craft which could not be contacted by radio and shepherd them back.

Stagg, who had then gone back to his camp bed exhausted, was taken aback when he awoke a few hours later to find that the sky was still clear and there seemed to be little wind. He could not face the other officers at breakfast. But later in the day he felt a certain shamefaced relief when the cloud and wind began to increase from the west.

That Sunday was a day of endless questions. Surely the tens of thousands of men could not be kept cooped up on their landing craft? And what of all the ships which had put to sea and had now been ordered back? They would need to refuel. And if the bad weather were to continue, then the tides would be wrong. In fact, if conditions did not improve within forty-eight hours, Overlord would have to be postponed for two weeks. Secrecy would be hard to maintain and the effect on morale could be devastating.

2

Bearing the Cross of Lorraine

Eisenhower was far from being the only one to be awed by the enormity of what they were launching. Churchill, who had always been dubious about the whole plan of a cross-Channel invasion, was now working himself up into a nervous state of irrational optimism, while Field Marshal Sir Alan Brooke confided to his diary that there was 'an empty feeling at the pit of one's stomach'. 'It is very hard to believe that in a few hours the cross Channel invasion starts! I am very uneasy about the whole operation. At the best it will fall so very very far short of the expectation of the bulk of the people, namely all those who know nothing of its difficulties. At the worst it may well be the most ghastly disaster of the whole war.'

'The British,' observed a key American staff officer, 'had a much greater fear of failure.' This was hardly surprising after the long years of war, with bitter memories of Dunkirk and the ill-fated Dieppe raid. Yet whatever their reasons, they were right to have refused to invade the Continent any earlier. An overwhelming superiority was necessary, and the US Army had had many harsh lessons to learn in North Africa, Sicily and Italy.

Churchill once remarked that the Americans always came to the right decision, having tried everything else first. But even if the joke contained an element of truth, it underplayed the fact that they learned much more quickly than their self-appointed tutors in the British Army. They were not afraid to listen to bright civilians from the business world now in uniform and above all they were not afraid to experiment.

The British showed their ingenuity in many fields, from the computer which decoded Ultra intercepts to new weapons such as Major General Percy Hobart's swimming tanks and mine-clearing flails. Yet the British Army hierarchy remained fundamentally conservative. The fact that the special tanks were known as Hobart's 'funnies' revealed that inimitable blend of British scepticism and flippancy. The cult of the gentleman amateur, which Montgomery so detested, would continue to prove a considerable handicap. Not surprisingly, American officers regarded their British counterparts as 'too polite' and lacking a necessary ruthlessness, especially when it came to sacking incompetent commanders.

Churchill himself was a great gentleman amateur, but nobody could accuse him of lacking drive. He took a passionate interest in military operations – in fact rather too much, in the view of his military advisers. A stream of ideas, most of them utterly impractical, poured forth in memos that produced groans and sighs in Whitehall. General 'Pug' Ismay, Churchill's military adviser, had to deal with the Prime Minister's latest inspiration at this historically symbolic moment. Churchill wanted to 'display some form of "reverse Dunkirk" for Overlord with small [civilian] boats landing infantry to follow up and supplement proper assault troops after beaches have been cleared'.

The Prime Minister's obsessive desire to be close to the centre of action had prompted him to insist that he sail with the invasion fleet. He wanted to watch the bombardment of the coast from the bridge of the cruiser HMS *Belfast*. He did not warn Brooke, knowing that he would disapprove, and tried to justify his demand on the grounds that he was also Minister of Defence. Fortunately the King dealt with this in a masterly letter on 2 June: 'My dear Winston, I want to make one more appeal to you not to go to sea on D-Day. Please consider my own position. I am a younger man than you, I am a sailor, and as King I am the head of all the services. There is nothing I would like better than to go to sea but I have agreed to stay at home; is it fair that you should then do exactly what I should have liked to do myself?'

Churchill, in a 'peevish' frame of mind at being thwarted, ordered up his personal train as a mobile headquarters to be close to Eisenhower. Brooke wrote in his diary, 'Winston meanwhile has taken his train and is touring the Portsmouth area making a thorough pest of himself!' There was one bright moment on that eve of D-Day. News arrived that

Allied forces under General Mark Clark were entering Rome. But Churchill's attention was about to be taxed with an almost insoluble problem. General Charles de Gaulle, the leader of the Free French, who used the Cross of Lorraine as his symbol, had arrived in London that morning. Pre-D-Day jitters, combined with political complications and de Gaulle's patriotic egocentricity, were to lead to an explosive row.

The central problem of relations with de Gaulle stemmed from President Roosevelt's distrust. Roosevelt saw him as a potential dictator. This view had been encouraged by Admiral Leahy, formerly his ambassador to Marshal Pétain in Vichy, as well as several influential Frenchmen in Washington, including Jean Monnet, later seen as the founding father of European unity.

Roosevelt had become so repelled by French politics that in February he suggested changing the plans for the post-war Allied occupation zones in Germany. He wanted the United States to take the northern half of the country, so that it could be resupplied through Hamburg, rather than through France. 'As I understand it,' Churchill wrote in reply, 'your proposal arises from an aversion to undertaking police work in France and a fear that this might involve the stationing of US Forces in France over a long period.'

Roosevelt, and to a lesser extent Churchill, refused to recognize the problems of what de Gaulle himself described as 'an insurrectional government'. De Gaulle was not merely trying to assure his own position. He needed to keep the rival factions together to save France from chaos after the liberation, perhaps even civil war. But the lofty and awkward de Gaulle, often to the despair of his own supporters, seemed almost to take a perverse pleasure in biting the American and British hands which fed him. De Gaulle had a totally Franco–centric view of everything. This included a supreme disdain for inconvenient facts, especially anything which might undermine the glory of France. Only de Gaulle could have written a history of the French army and manage to make no mention of the Battle of Waterloo.

Throughout the spring, Churchill had done his best to soften Roosevelt's attitude, knowing that the Allies had to work with de Gaulle. He encouraged Roosevelt to meet him. 'You might do him a great deal of good by paternal treatment,' he wrote, 'and indeed I think it would be a help from every point of view.'

Roosevelt agreed to see him, but he insisted that de Gaulle must request the meeting. To issue an official invitation would imply recognition of de Gaulle as France's leader. The President stuck to his line that the Allied armies were not invading France to put de Gaulle in power. 'I am unable at this time,' he wrote, 'to recognise any Government of France until the French people have an opportunity for a free choice of Government.' But since elections could not possibly be held for some time, this would mean that the administration of liberated areas would be carried out by AMGOT, the Allied Military Government of Occupied Territories.

This acronym represented a deadly insult, both to de Gaulle and to the Comité Français de Libération Nationale in Algiers. On 3 June, the day before de Gaulle flew to Britain, the CFLN declared itself to be the Gouvernement Provisoire de la République Française. This announcement was immediately seen by Roosevelt as a deliberate provocation. He had already forbidden Eisenhower to have any contact with the French administration in waiting.

Eisenhower was permitted to work only with General Pierre Koenig, whom de Gaulle had appointed as commander of the Resistance, known as the Forces Françaises de l'Intérieur, or the FFI. Yet even then Eisenhower was told not to trust Koenig with details of the invasion, because he would be obliged to report back on them to his political masters. These contradictions resulted in 'acute embarrassment', as Eisenhower admitted in a report to Washington. 'General Koenig feels very keenly the fact that he is denied even the most general knowledge of forthcoming operations although French naval, air and airborne units are to be employed, and much is expected from [the] French resistance.'

Churchill had meanwhile been urging Roosevelt to accept 'a working arrangement' with the French Committee, principally because the Allies needed the Resistance to play its part in the invasion. He had also helped persuade the Americans to send to England the French 2nd Armoured Division (known as the 2ème DB for Division Blindée), which they had armed and equipped in North Africa. Commanded by General Philippe Leclerc, it would form part of Patton's Third Army later in the Normandy campaign. Yet to the amused resignation of British officers, one of the first ceremonies which Leclerc's Division organized after its arrival in Yorkshire was an official mass in honour of Joan of Arc, whom the English had burned at the stake some five hundred years earlier.

Allied troops, on the other hand, were warned not to offend French sensibilities after they landed. A pamphlet told them to avoid any reference to France's humiliating defeat in 1940. 'Thanks to jokes about "Gay Paree" etc.,' it added, 'there is a fairly widespread belief that the French are a gay, frivolous people with no morals and few convictions. This is especially not true at the present time.' But official briefings were unlikely to have much effect on those gripped by excited speculation over 'French mademoiselles'.

Churchill's War Cabinet realized that the Free French leader had to be invited to Britain to be briefed on D-Day. Despite 'all the faults and follies of de Gaulle,' the Prime Minister wrote to Roosevelt, 'he has lately shown some signs of wishing to work with us, and after all it is very difficult to cut the French out of the liberation of France.' The President, however, had insisted that in 'the interest of security' de Gaulle must be kept in the United Kingdom 'until the Overlord landing has been made'.

The weakness of Free French security stemmed not from Vichy spies infiltrating the Gaullist network but from the unsophisticated French codes. Exasperation within the Special Operations Executive, especially after the massive Gestapo infiltration of the Resistance the year before, prompted the chief SOE cryptographer, Leo Marks, to go round to the Gaullists' office in Duke Street in central London. He asked their cipher officers to encode any message they wanted, then he took it from them and broke it 'under their astonished noses'. 'This did not endear the British to the French,' wrote the official historian with dry understatement. Yet Gallic pride still prevented the Free French from using British or American code systems. Just before D-Day, 'C', the head of the Secret Intelligence Service, warned the Prime Minister that the French must not be allowed to send any messages by radio, only by secure landlines.

Churchill sent two York passenger aircraft to Algiers to bring back de Gaulle and his retinue. But de Gaulle was reluctant to come, because Roosevelt would not permit a discussion on French civil government. Churchill's representative, Duff Cooper, argued with him for an hour on 2 June, trying to persuade him to back off from this brinkmanship. If de Gaulle refused to come, then he would be playing into Roosevelt's hands, Duff Cooper told him. He should be present in England in his role as military leader. Above all, Duff Cooper warned him, he would finally lose the regard of the Prime Minister, who would decide that he was an impossible man to deal with. De Gaulle agreed only the next morning, when the two Yorks were already waiting for them on the airfield to take them on the first leg of the journey to Rabat in French Morocco.

After flying through the night from Rabat, de Gaulle's plane touched down at exactly 06.00 hours on 4 June at Northolt. After all the secrecy imposed on their journey, Duff Cooper was surprised to find a large guard of honour drawn up and an RAF band playing the 'Marseillaise' as they descended the steps. A very Churchillian letter of greeting was handed to de Gaulle. 'My dear General de Gaulle,' it read. 'Welcome to these shores! Very great military events are about to take place.' He invited him down to join him on his personal train. 'If you could be here by 1.30 p.m., I should be glad to give you dejeuner and we will then repair to General Eisenhower's headquarters.'

Duff Cooper was mystified by the notion of Churchill's 'advance headquarters' on a train, which they finally found in a siding at a small station near Portsmouth. He considered it 'a perfectly absurd scheme'. His heart sank much further when he found that Field Marshal Smuts, the decidedly Francophobe South African, was in the Prime Minister's entourage. Then Churchill opened the conversation with de Gaulle by saying that he had brought him over to deliver a speech on the radio. To make matters even worse, he made no mention of discussing civil affairs in France, the subject of greatest interest to de Gaulle.

When Anthony Eden, the Foreign Secretary, turned the conversation to 'politics', which basically meant Roosevelt's continued refusal to recognize de Gaulle and his provisional government, de Gaulle's anger erupted. His resentment was inflamed by the Allied currency printed in the United States and issued to their troops. He said that this currency, which he considered '*une fausse monnaie*', was 'absolutely unrecognized by the government of the Republic'. This was an important point which does not appear to have occurred either to the American authorities or to the British. If no government was prepared to back these rather unimpressively printed banknotes – American troops compared them to 'cigar coupons' – then they were worthless.

Churchill flared up, demanding how the British could act separately from the United States. 'We are going to liberate Europe, but it is because the Americans are with us. So get this quite clear. Every time we have to decide between Europe and the open sea, it is always the open sea that we shall choose. Every time I have to decide between you and Roosevelt, I shall always choose Roosevelt.' De Gaulle coolly accepted that that was bound to be the case. Tempers calmed as they sat down to lunch. Churchill raised his glass: 'To de Gaulle, who never accepted defeat.' De Gaulle raised his in reply: 'To Britain, to victory, to Europe.'

Afterwards, Churchill accompanied de Gaulle over to Southwick House. There, Eisenhower and Bedell Smith briefed the French leader on the plan for Overlord. Eisenhower was charming and concealed the turmoil he was going through as a result of the weather. Before de Gaulle left, however, Eisenhower showed him a copy of the proclamation he was to make to the French people on D-Day. Although he had softened Roosevelt's peremptory tone, the speech did not recognize the authority of the provisional government in any way. In fact, it even instructed the French to obey the orders of the Allied command until 'the French themselves should choose their representatives and their government'. For de Gaulle this confirmed his worst fear of an Anglo–Saxon occupation of France. He kept his temper, however, and simply said that he 'wished to suggest certain changes in General Eisenhower's message'. Eisenhower agreed to consider them, since there might be time to make alterations.

On his return to London, de Gaulle heard that his suggested amendments could not be approved in time, as the Joint Chiefs of Staff would need to agree them. De Gaulle then refused to speak to the French people on the BBC the next morning after Eisenhower and the leaders of other occupied countries. De Gaulle also announced that he was ordering the French liaison officers allocated to British and American divisions not to accompany them because no agreement had been reached on civil administration. When Churchill received the news during a meeting of the War Cabinet he exploded in a terrible rage.

That night, Eden and de Gaulle's emissary, Pierre Viénot, engaged in shuttle diplomacy between the two furious leaders to repair the damage. De Gaulle raged at Viénot, saying that Churchill was a 'gangster'. Viénot then went to see Churchill, who accused de Gaulle of 'treason at the height of battle'. He wanted to fly him back to Algiers, 'in chains if necessary'.

Even with all these dramas, the most important event on that evening of Sunday, 4 June, took place in the library at Southwick House. During the afternoon, Stagg and his colleagues had seen that the approaching depression in the Atlantic had concentrated, but also slowed down. This indicated that a sufficient gap in the bad weather was emerging for the invasion to go ahead. At 21.30 hours the conference began and Stagg was summoned. Few of those present felt optimistic. Rain and wind were battering the windows, and they could imagine what conditions were like for the tens of thousands of soldiers on the landing ships and craft anchored along the coasts.

'Gentlemen,' said Stagg, 'since I presented the forecast last evening some rapid and unexpected developments have occurred over the north Atlantic.' There would be a brief improvement from Monday afternoon. The weather would not be ideal, was the gist of his message, but it would do. Searching questions followed and an earnest discussion began.

'Let's be clear about one thing,' Admiral Ramsay broke in. 'If Overlord is to proceed on Tuesday I must issue provisional warning to my forces within the next half-hour. But if they do restart and have to be recalled again, there can be no question of continuing on Wednesday.'

Leigh-Mallory again expressed concern about sufficient visibility for his bombers, but Eisenhower turned to Montgomery, who was wearing his unconventional uniform of a fawn pullover and baggy corduroys.

'Do you see any reason why we should not go on Tuesday?'

'No,' replied Montgomery emphatically in his nasal voice. 'I would say – *Go.*'

Outside in the hall, staff officers were waiting with sheaves of orders ready to be signed by their chiefs. Two sets had been prepared to cover both alternatives.

In the early hours of Monday, 5 June, further data came in to confirm the break in the weather. At the morning conference, Stagg was able to face his intimidating audience with much greater confidence. The tension eased and 'the Supreme Commander and his colleagues became as new men', he wrote afterwards. Eisenhower's grin returned. Further details were discussed, but everyone was impatient to leave and the room emptied rapidly. There was much to be done to get the 5,000 ships from nearly a dozen different nations back to sea and on course down pre-established shipping lanes. A small fleet of minesweepers in line abreast would then proceed in front of them to clear a broad channel all the way to the beaches. Admiral Ramsay was particularly concerned for the crews of these vulnerable craft. They expected very heavy casualties.

Now that the great decision had been taken, Eisenhower went to South Parade Pier in Portsmouth to see the last troops embarking. 'He always gets a lift from talking with soldiers,' his aide, Harry Butcher, noted in his diary. At lunchtime, they returned to Eisenhower's trailer at Southwick Park and played 'Hounds and Fox' and then checkers. Butcher had already arranged for the supreme commander, accompanied by journalists, to go to the airfield at Greenham Common that evening to visit the American 101st Airborne Division. They were due to take off at 23.00 hours for the mission which Leigh-Mallory had predicted would be a disaster.

Unlike the infantry and other arms, who had been enclosed in the barbed-wire 'sausages', the airborne troops had been driven directly to the airfields from where they were to take off. The 82nd Airborne Division had been based around Nottingham, while the 101st was spread around the Home Counties west of London. For five days they had been quartered in aircraft hangars and provided with rows of cots with aisles in between. There, they stripped and oiled their personal weapons time and again, or sharpened their bayonets. Some had bought commando knives in London, and several had equipped themselves with cut-throat razors. They had been instructed how to kill a man silently by slicing through the jugular and the voice box. Their airborne training had not only been physically rigorous. Some of them had been forced 'to crawl through the entrails and blood of hogs as part of getting toughened up'.

To take their minds off the oppressive wait extended by the postponement, officers provided gramophones which played songs such as 'I'll Walk Alone' and 'That Old Black Magic'. They also organized projectors to show movies, especially ones starring Bob Hope. Many paratroopers had also been listening to 'Axis Sally'* on Radio Berlin, who played good music as well as transmitting vicious propaganda on the programme *Home Sweet Home*. Yet even when she said on repeated occasions before D-Day that the Germans were waiting for them, most regarded it as a joke.

There were also Red Cross doughnut and coffee stands run by young American women volunteers. In many cases they slipped soldiers their own cigarette ration. The food provided, including steak, chips and ice cream, was a luxury which inevitably prompted more black jokes about being fattened up for the kill. The 82nd Airborne had acquired a taste for fish and chips in the Nottingham area as well as many local friendships. They too had been touched by the population rushing out to wave them off, many of them in tears, as convoys of trucks drove the paratroopers to their airfields.

A large number of men took their minds off what lay ahead with frenetic gambling, first with the dubious-looking invasion money and then with saved dollars and pound notes. They were shooting dice and playing blackjack. One man who had won $2,500, a very considerable sum in those days, deliberately played on until he lost the lot. He sensed that if he walked away with the money, the fates would decree his death.

Paratroopers looked over their main chutes and reserves to make sure that they were in perfect order. Others wrote last letters home to families or girlfriends in case of their death. Sometimes precious photographs were taken from their wallet and taped on the inside of their helmet. All personal papers and civilian effects were collected up and packed to be held until their return. Chaplains held church services in a corner of the hangar and Catholics took confession.

In this time for individual reflection, no greater contrast could have come than from some of the regimental commanders' pep talks. Colonel

* 'Axis Sally' was the name given by the US forces to Mildred Gillars (1900–1988), a failed American actress originally from Portland, Maine, who had moved to Germany in 1935 and become an announcer on Radio Berlin. She broadcast music as well as Nazi propaganda designed to undermine Allied morale. She was tried for treason in 1949 and served twelve years in prison.

'Jump' Johnson, who led the 501st Parachute Infantry Regiment, drove into the hangar in his Jeep and leaped on to the calisthenics platform. Johnson, who had acquired his nickname from wanting to throw himself from almost any flying object, wore pearl-handled revolvers on each hip. The 2,000 men from his regiment gathered round. 'There was a great feeling in the air; the excitement of battle,' noted one paratrooper. After a short speech to arouse their martial ardour, Johnson swiftly bent down, pulled a large commando knife from his boot and brandished it above his head. 'Before I see the dawn of another day,' he yelled, 'I want to stick this knife into the heart of the meanest, dirtiest, filthiest Nazi in all of Europe.' A huge, resounding cheer went up and his men raised their knives in response.

General Maxwell Taylor warned his men in the 101st Airborne that fighting at night would be highly confusing. They would find it hard to distinguish their own side from the enemy. For that reason they should fight with their knives and grenades during darkness, and use firearms only after dawn. According to one of his men, 'he also said that if you were to take prisoners, they handicap our ability to perform our mission. We were going to have to dispose of prisoners as best we saw fit.'

Brigadier General 'Slim Jim' Gavin of the 82nd Airborne was perhaps the most measured in his address. 'Men,' he said, 'what you're going to go through in the next few days, you won't want to change for a million dollars, but you won't want to go through it very often again. For most of you, this will be the first time you will be going into combat. Remember that you are going in to kill, or you will be killed.' Gavin clearly created a strong impression. One of his listeners said that, after his quiet talk, 'I believe we would have gone to hell with him.' Another commanding officer decided to adopt shock tactics. He said to his men lined up in front of him, 'Look to the right of you and look to the left of you. There's only going to be one of you left after the first week in Normandy.'

There can be little doubt about the very high level of motivation among the overwhelming majority of the American airborne troops. The most effective way for officers to enforce discipline for some time had been to threaten a soldier that he would not be allowed to join the invasion drop.

*

Eve of battle rituals included shaving heads, to make it easier for the medics to deal with head wounds, but a number of men decided to leave a strip of hair down the middle in Mohican style. This contributed to the German idea, influenced by Hollywood gangster films and later whipped up by Wehrmacht propaganda detachments, that American airborne troops were recruited from the toughest jails in the United States and came from the '*übelste Untermenschentum amerikanischer Slums*' – 'the nastiest underclass from American slums'. Faces were also blackened up, mostly with soot from the stoves, although some used polish and others added streaks of white paint in a competition over who could make their face look the 'most gruesome'.

Their jump suits carried their divisional emblem on the left shoulder and an American flag on the right. One soldier, who had been given two extra cartons of Pall Mall cigarettes by a Red Cross helper, slipped one down each leg. But for those who found themselves dropping into flooded areas, this choice of hiding place was likely to produce an extra disappointment. Boots and straps were fastened as tightly as possible, as if they constituted a form of armour to protect them in the fighting to come. Paratroopers also went back for extra ammunition, overloading themselves. The greatest fear was to face an enemy with an empty gun. Bandoliers were slung crossways over their chests 'Pancho Villa style', canteens were filled to the brim, and pouches packed with spare socks and underwear. The camouflage-netted helmets had an aid kit fixed to the back with bandages, eight sulfa tablets and two syrettes of morphine – 'one for pain and two for eternity'.

Pockets and pouches bulged, not just with 150 rounds of .30 ammunition, but also D-Ration chocolate bars, which possessed a texture akin to semi-set concrete, and a British Gammon grenade, which contained a pound of C2 explosive in a sort of cotton sock. This improvised bomb could certainly be effective against even armoured vehicles (paratroopers called it their 'hand artillery'), but it was also popular for other reasons. A small amount of the fast-burning explosive could heat a mug of coffee or K-Rations without giving off any smoke from the bottom of a foxhole.

Dog tags were taped together to prevent them making a noise. Cigarettes and lighters, together with other essentials, such as a washing and shaving kit, water-purifying tablets, twenty-four sheets of toilet paper and a French phrase book, went into the musette bag slung around the neck, along with an escape kit consisting of a map printed on silk, hacksaw blade, compass and money. The largesse of the issued equipment amazed poor country boys more used to make-do and mend at home.

On top of all these smaller items came an entrenching tool and the soldier's personal weapon, usually a carbine with a folding stock partially disassembled in a bag known as a 'violin case' which was strapped across their chest. Others were armed with a Thompson sub-machine gun. Bazookas were broken down into their two halves. Together with several rounds of anti-tank grenades, they were packed in leg bags which would dangle during the descent. The leg bags alone often weighed up to eighty pounds.

Paratroopers had their own superstitions. A number of them also foresaw their own death. One soldier remembered a 'tow-headed kid' named Johnny. 'He was standing there, staring into space. I went over to him and I said, "What's the matter, Johnny?" He said, "I don't think I'll make it." I said, "Nah, you'll be alright." I sort of shook him because he was like in a daze. As it turned out, he was one of the first men killed in Normandy.'

When Eisenhower arrived at Greenham Common in his Cadillac staff car, followed by a small convoy of pressmen and photographers, he began to chat with paratroopers of General Maxwell Taylor's 101st Airborne shortly before they emplaned. It must have been hard not to think of Leigh-Mallory's dire prediction that they were almost all going to their deaths. Yet Eisenhower's 'informality and friendliness with troopers' amazed even his aide. A Texan offered the supreme commander a job after the war roping cows. Eisenhower then asked airborne officers if they had any men from Kansas. He hoped to find someone from his home town of Abilene. A soldier called Oyler was sent over to meet him.

'What's your name, soldier?' Eisenhower asked him.

Oyler froze in front of the general and his friends had to shout his name to jog his memory.

Eisenhower then asked him where he was from.

'Wellington, Kansas,' Oyler replied.

'Oh, that's south of Wichita.'

The supreme commander proceeded to ask him about his education and service and whether he had a girlfriend in England. Oyler relaxed and answered all his questions about their training and whether he thought the other men in his platoon were ready to go.

'You know, Oyler, the Germans have been kicking the hell out of us for five years and it is payback time.'

Eisenhower went on to ask him if he was afraid and Oyler admitted that he was.

'Well, you'd be a damn fool not to be. But the trick is to keep moving. If you stop, if you start thinking, you lose your focus. You lose your concentration. You'll be a casualty. The idea, the perfect idea, is to keep moving.'

Movement at that moment was the paratroopers' biggest problem. They were so loaded down with kit that they could only waddle to the waiting planes lined up beside the runway.

The ground crews of their C-47 Skytrains (the British called them Dakotas) had been working hard. All invasion aircraft were painted at the last moment with black and white stripes on the wings and fuselages to identify them more clearly to all the Allied ships below. Some paratroopers were taken aback at the sight. 'We were surprised as dickens to see the big wide stripes painted on the wings and also on the fuselage. You thought they would be up there like sitting ducks for every ground gunner to try his luck on.'

The danger of 'friendly fire' was a major preoccupation, especially for airborne forces. During the invasion of Sicily in July 1943, US Navy anti-aircraft gunners had shot at both American transport aircraft and those towing gliders. In their desperation to escape the fire, pilots of tow aircraft had let loose their gliders, leaving them to crash into the sea. More than a dozen had been lost in the disaster. This time, to avoid flying over the invasion fleets, the routes planned for the drop on to the Cotentin peninsula would take the two airborne divisions on a wide sweep to the west, making their final approach from over the Channel Islands.

Many of the C-47s, which paratroopers referred to as 'goony birds', had names and symbols painted on the side of the nose. One, for example, had a picture of a devil holding up a tray on which sat a girl in a bathing suit. The inscription underneath was 'Heaven can Wait'. A less encouraging aircraft name was 'Miss Carriage'.

It took forty minutes to load the planes, for heavily burdened para-troopers needed help to get up the steps, almost like knights in armour trying to mount their horses. And once they were in, a large number needed to struggle out again soon afterwards for another 'nervous pee'. The pilots of the troop carrier squadrons became increasingly worried about the weight. Each aircraft was to carry a 'stick' of sixteen to eighteen fully laden men and they insisted on weighing them. The total made them even more concerned.

A sergeant mounted first to go to the front of the plane and the platoon commander last, as he would lead the way. The sergeant would bring up the rear so that he could act as 'pusher' to make sure that everyone had left and nobody had frozen. 'One trooper asked the sergeant if it was true that he had orders to shoot any man that refused to jump. "That's the orders I've been given." He said it so softly that everybody became quiet.'

The 505th Parachute Infantry Regiment of the 82nd Airborne Division received a nasty shock during loading. A Gammon grenade exploded inside one fuselage, killing a number of soldiers and setting the plane on fire. The survivors were simply switched to a follow-up detail. Nothing was allowed to delay the schedule for take-off that night.

Their engines 'growling', the heavily laden C-47s began to trundle in a seemingly endless sequence down the runway at Greenham Common. General Eisenhower stood there, apparently with tears in his eyes, saluting the paratroopers of the 101st as they took off.

Churchill, on that night of problems with de Gaulle, was also thinking of their powerful ally in the east. He had been trying to persuade Stalin to coincide his summer offensive with the invasion of Normandy. On 14 April he had signalled, 'We ask you to let us know, in order to make our own calculations, what scale your effort will take.'

The year before Stalin had begun to despair of the western Allies ever launching the invasion of northern Europe, a development which they had been promising since 1942. Churchill had always preferred an indirect, or peripheral, strategy in the Mediterranean, to avoid another bloodbath in France like the one which had slaughtered the youth of his generation. He was right in the end to have delayed the invasion, albeit for the wrong reasons. The Anglo-American armies had simply not been ready, either materially or in trained manpower, to attempt such an operation before. A failure would have been catastrophic. Yet none of the excuses or genuine reasons had placated Stalin, who never ceased to remind his allies of their commitment. 'One should not forget,' he had written to Churchill on 24 June 1943, 'that on all this depends the possibility to save millions of lives in the occupied regions of western Europe and Russia and reduce the colossal sacrifices of the Soviet armies, in comparison with which the losses of the Anglo-American troops could be considered as modest.' More than 7 million members of the Soviet armed forces had already died in the war.

At the Teheran conference in November, Roosevelt, to Churchill's dismay, had gone behind his back to tell Stalin that as well as the landings in Normandy, they would also invade the south of France with Operation Anvil. Churchill and Brooke had been resisting this plan ever since the Americans dreamed it up. Anvil would drain the Allied armies in Italy of reserves and resources, and this would wreck Churchill's dream of advancing into the northern Balkans and Austria. Churchill had foreseen the consequences of the dramatic Red Army advances. He dreaded a Soviet occupation of central Europe. Roosevelt, on the other hand, had convinced himself that by charming Stalin instead of confronting him, a lasting post-war peace was a real possibility. It would be based on the United Nations Organization which he intended to create. The President felt that Churchill was guided far too much by reactionary impulses, both imperial and geopolitical. Roosevelt believed that once Nazi Germany was defeated with American help, then Europe should sort herself out.

Stalin had been pleased during the Teheran conference to have the firmest assurances so far that the cross-Channel invasion would take place in the spring. But then he became deeply suspicious again when he heard that a supreme commander had not yet been appointed. Even after Eisenhower's nomination, Stalin still remained sceptical. On 22 February, he received a signal from Gusev, his ambassador in London: 'We have heard from other sources, mainly English and American correspondents, that the dates for the opening of the Second Front which had been fixed in Teheran, can probably change from March to

April and maybe even to May.' And when Roosevelt finally wrote with the date, Stalin's foreign minister, Vishinsky, summoned the American chargé d'affaires in Moscow to demand what the 'D' stood for in 'D–Day'.

On the eve of the great undertaking, Churchill sent a signal to Stalin with the feeling that the blood debt which the western Allies owed the Soviet people was being paid at last: 'I have just returned from two days at Eisenhower's headquarters, watching the troops embark ... With great regret General Eisenhower was forced to postpone for one night, but the weather forecast has undergone a most favourable change and tonight we go.'

3

Watch on the Channel

While the Wehrmacht awaited the invasion, Hitler remained at the Berghof, his Alpine residence on the mountainside above Berchtesgaden. On 3 June, as the Allied ships were loading, a wedding had taken place in these rarefied surroundings. Eva Braun's younger sister, Gretl, married SS-Gruppenführer Hermann Fegelein, Himmler's representative at Führer headquarters. Guests wore their best clothes or dress uniform. To mark the solemnity of the occasion, Hitler, who hated to be photographed in formal civilian attire, joined the party in white tie and tails like the other guests. Hitler, assuming the role of father of the bride, did not object to the abundance of champagne being served and he allowed them to dance to an SS band. He left the bridal party early to let them celebrate late into the night. Martin Bormann became so drunk on schnapps that he had to be carried back to his chalet.

Hitler was in a confident mood. He longed for the enemy to come, certain that an Allied invasion would be smashed on the Atlantic Wall. The Reich propaganda minister, Joseph Goebbels, even implied that the Allies would not dare to cross the Channel. His great slogan at the time was: 'They are supposed to be coming. Why don't they come?'

Hitler had convinced himself that defeating the invasion would knock the British and Americans out of the war. Then he could concentrate all his armies on the eastern front against Stalin. The casualties the German armies in France would suffer in this great defensive battle did not concern him. He had already demonstrated what little attention he paid to loss of life, even in his own guard formation, the

1st SS Panzer-Division *Leibstandarte Adolf Hitler*. Yet he sent the men Christmas boxes each year containing chocolate and schnapps, but no cigarettes since that would be bad for their health. Himmler had to make up this deficiency from SS resources.

The Atlantic Wall, which supposedly stretched from Norway to the Spanish frontier, was more a triumph of propaganda for home consumption than a physical reality. Hitler had once again fallen victim to his own regime's self-deception. He refused to acknowledge any comparisons to France's Maginot Line of 1940 or even listen to complaints from those responsible for the coastal defences. They lacked sufficient concrete for the bunkers and batteries, because Hitler himself had given priority to massive U-boat shelters. The Kriegsmarine had lost the battle of the Atlantic, but he still believed that the new generation of submarines being developed would destroy Allied shipping.

Generalfeldmarschall Gerd von Rundstedt, the Commander-in-Chief West, regarded the Atlantic Wall as 'just a bit of cheap bluff'. Like many senior officers, the elderly Rundstedt did not forget Frederick the Great's dictum 'He who defends everything defends nothing.' He believed that the Wehrmacht should abandon Italy, 'that frightful boot of a country', and hold a line across the Alps. He also disagreed with the retention of so many troops in Norway, whose strategic importance he considered 'a purely naval affair'.*

Almost all senior German officers were privately scathing about Hitler's obsession with 'fortresses'. The ports of Dunkirk, Calais, Boulogne, Le Havre and Cherbourg on the Channel coast, and Brest, La Rochelle and Bordeaux on the Atlantic, had each been designated a *'Festung'* to be held to the last man. Hitler also refused to contemplate bringing in the strengthened division based on the Channel Islands because, judging the British by himself, he was certain that they would want to take back the only piece of their territory that he had managed to occupy.

Hitler had convinced himself that his 'fortress' orders, both in the east and in the west, provided the best way to hold back the enemy and

---

* Rommel also wanted to abandon Italy and withdraw troops from the south of France and the west coast to reinforce the Channel, but this was rejected by Führer headquarters.

prevent his own generals from permitting retreats. In fact it meant that the garrisons – 120,000 men in the case of northern France – would not be available later to help defend Germany. His policy was contrary to every traditional tenet of the German general staff, which insisted on flexibility. And when Rundstedt pointed out that, with their guns and concrete emplacements facing seawards, they were vulnerable to attack from the landward side, his observation was 'not favourably received'.

Yet even many experienced officers, and not just the fanatics of the Waffen-SS, looked forward to the approaching battle with some confidence. 'We considered the repulse at Dieppe as proof that we could repel any invasion,' Generalleutnant Fritz Bayerlein told his American interrogators later. An urge to get to grips with the enemy on the ground was widespread. 'The face of the war has changed dramatically,' a lieutenant wrote just five days before the landings. 'It is no longer like it is in the cinema, where the best places are at the back. We continue to stand by and hope that they're coming soon. But I'm still worried that they're not coming at all, but will try to finish us off by air.' Two days after the invasion he was killed by Allied bombers.

The key question, of course, was where the Allies would attack. German contingency planning had considered Norway and Denmark, and even landings in Spain and Portugal. Staff officers of the OKW, the Oberkommando der Wehrmacht, looked carefully at the possibilities of attacks against France's Mediterranean coast and the Bay of Biscay, especially Brittany and also around Bordeaux. But the most likely areas would be those well within range of Allied airbases in southern and eastern England. This meant anywhere from the coast of Holland all the way down the Channel to Cherbourg at the tip of the Cotentin peninsula.

Hitler had given the task of improving the Channel defences to Generalfeldmarschall Erwin Rommel, the commander-in-chief of Army Group B. Rommel, a former Hitler loyalist, had become dejected by the effects of Allied air superiority in North Africa. The energetic panzer commander who had been made a national hero now referred cynically to Hitler's mesmerizing pep talks aimed at depressed generals as 'sun-ray treatments'. But Rommel never slackened in his attempts to improve the coastal defences.

The most obvious target of all was the Pas-de-Calais. This offered the Allies the shortest sea route, the greatest opportunity for constant air support and a direct line of advance to the German frontier less than 300 kilometres away. This invasion, if successful, could cut off German forces further west and also overrun the V-1 launching sites, which would soon be ready. For all these reasons, the main defences of the whole Atlantic Wall had been concentrated between Dunkirk and the Somme estuary. This region was defended by the Fifteenth Army.

The second most likely invasion area consisted of the Normandy beaches to the west. Hitler began to suspect that this might well be the Allied plan, but he predicted both stretches of coast so as to make sure that he could claim afterwards that he had been right. The Kriegsmarine, however, bizarrely ruled out the Normandy coastline in the belief that landings could be made only at high tide. This sector, running from the Seine to Brittany, remained the responsibility of the German Seventh Army.

Rommel chose as his headquarters the Château de la Roche-Guyon, which lay on a great bend of the River Seine, which marked the boundary between his two armies. With chalk cliffs behind and a ruined Norman stronghold on the heights above, it looked down across the parterres of a famous herb garden to the great river below. The Renaissance entrance set in medieval walls seemed entirely fitting for the seat of the Rochefoucauld family.

With Rommel's permission, the current duke and his relations kept apartments on the upper floor of the great house. Rommel seldom used the state rooms apart from the grand salon, with its magnificent Gobelin tapestries. There he worked, looking out over a rose garden not yet in flower. His desk had been the one on which the revocation of the Edict of Nantes had been signed in 1685, a measure which had sent the Huguenot ancestors of many Wehrmacht officers to seek new lives in Prussia.

Rommel seldom spent daylight hours at the château. He usually rose at five, breakfasted with Generalleutnant Hans Speidel, his chief of staff, then set out immediately on tours of inspection in his Horch staff car, accompanied by no more than a couple of officers. Staff conferences were held in the evening on his return, then he dined frugally with his closest entourage, often just Speidel and Konteradmiral Friedrich Ruge, Rommel's naval adviser and friend. Afterwards, he would continue the discussion with them outside, strolling under two huge cedar trees. They had much to talk about in private.

Rommel was exasperated by Hitler's refusal to bring the Luftwaffe and Kriegsmarine under a centralized command for the defence of France. Encouraged by Göring and Admiral Dönitz, Hitler instinctively preferred to maintain rival organizations which only he could control from the top. Speidel argued that the Luftwaffe had more than a third of a million ground staff and signals personnel in the west, all part of Göring's empire building. To make matters worse, the Reichsmarschall refused to put his flak corps at the service of the army, which his own aircraft could not defend from Allied air attack.

Whenever Rommel complained of the uselessness of the Luftwaffe, Führer headquarters would try to impress him with the prospect of a thousand new jet fighters and countless rockets to bring Britain to its knees. Not only did he refuse to believe these promises, he knew that his hands were tied operationally. Ever since the Battle of Stalingrad, Hitler had not allowed a flexible defence. Every inch of ground must be held.

Speidel, a member of the army's resistance movement, recorded that Rommel himself bitterly quoted Hitler's own dictum in *Mein Kampf* from the days of the Weimar Republic: 'When the Government of a nation is leading it to its doom, rebellion is not only the right but the duty of every man.' Rommel, however, unlike Speidel and the plotters in Berlin motivated by Oberst Claus Schenk Graf von Stauffenberg, did not believe in assassination.

The elderly Rundstedt, on the other hand, while constantly referring in private to Hitler as 'that Bohemian corporal', would never have contemplated revolt. If others were to remove the Nazi 'brown band', then he would not stand in their way, but he would certainly not commit himself. His ambivalence went deeper. Rundstedt had accepted massive amounts of money from Hitler and must have felt compromised as a result. But even Speidel underestimated the depths to which Rundstedt would sink after the attempted revolution against Hitler failed.

Rundstedt had become almost as much a figurehead of the army and nation as Generalfeldmarschall von Hindenburg after the First World War. The British regarded 'the Last Prussian' as nothing more sinister than a reactionary Guards officer and failed to appreciate that he shared many of the Nazis' murderous prejudices. Rundstedt had never objected to the mass murders of Jews by the SS Einsatzgruppen on the eastern front. He had then spoken of the advantages of using the Russian slave labourer in France. 'If he does not do as he is told,' he said, 'he can quite simply be shot.'

Rundstedt's dismay over Hitler's disastrous conduct of the war had turned into a lethargic cynicism. He showed little interest in the theory of panzer tactics and held himself aloof from the fierce debate over the best way to fight the invasion. This was conducted mainly between Rommel on the one hand, who wanted a forward defence to defeat the Allies as they landed, and the two leading proponents of a massive armoured counter-attack on the other: Generaloberst Heinz Guderian, the inspector-general of panzer troops, and General der Panzertruppen Leo Freiherr Geyr von Schweppenburg.

Geyr, a former military attaché in London who bore a certain resemblance to Frederick the Great, was rather more cultivated than many of his contemporaries. His intellectual arrogance, however, made him a number of enemies, especially within Führer headquarters and the SS, who suspected his loyalty to the regime. As commander-in-chief of Panzer Group West, Geyr believed with Guderian that a panzer army should be assembled in the forests north of Paris ready to smash the enemy back into the sea.

Rommel, who first made his name as a bold panzer leader in 1940, had since been profoundly influenced by his experiences in North Africa. And now that the Allies had achieved total air supremacy over north-west Europe, he believed that panzer divisions held back from the front for a counter-attack would never be allowed to reach the battle in time to ensure a decisive result. Predictably, a bad compromise was the result of Hitler's insistent meddling and the confused command structure. Neither Geyr nor Rommel had control over all the panzer divisions, because Hitler would only permit them to be deployed with his approval.

Increasingly convinced that the Allies might well land in Normandy after all, Rommel visited the coastal defences there frequently. He thought that the long curving bay which the Allies had designated as Omaha beach was similar to Salerno, where they had landed in Italy.

Certain that the outcome would be decided in the first two days, Rommel was tireless in his efforts. Turrets from French tanks captured in 1940 were fixed to concrete bunkers. They were known as 'Tobrouks', from the battle in North Africa. French labourers and Italian prisoners of war were drafted in to erect large posts to thwart glider landings on the most likely sites identified by German paratroop officers. These forests of stakes were nicknamed 'Rommel asparagus'.

The Army Group commander's energy produced mixed feelings in many unit commanders. All the time spent on improving the defences had left fewer opportunities for training. They also suffered from a shortage of ammunition for range practice, which may well have contributed to the generally bad marksmanship of many German units. Rommel also insisted on a dramatic increase in the number of minefields. A British officer heard later from prisoners that many of the dummy minefields had in fact been marked out on the orders of German officers purely to impress their demanding commander-in-chief. They had assumed that he would not poke about too much to check that they were real.

In theory, Rundstedt's command included one and a half million members of the Wehrmacht, although he had no control over the Luftwaffe and Kriegsmarine. The army units, with 850,000 men all told, were of very mixed quality. Of the thirty-six infantry divisions, just over half had no transport or mobile artillery. These were mainly the formations allotted for coastal defence. Some even included 'ear and stomach battalions', composed either of soldiers who had suffered stomach wounds or – a truly surreal notion when it came to giving orders in battle – of those who had lost their hearing.

Many of the Germans in other infantry divisions in France were either comparatively old or else very young. The writer Heinrich Böll, then an Obergefreiter in the 348th Infanterie-Division, wrote, 'it is really sad to see these children's faces in grey uniforms'. The infantry had also suffered, because the best recruits were sent to the SS, the Luftwaffe paratroop divisions or the panzer corps. 'No good replacements were ever sent to the infantry divisions,' observed General Bayerlein. 'That is one reason why good panzer units had to be kept in the front line for an excessive time.'

Numbers on the western front had also been made up with conscripts from Alsace, Lorraine and Luxembourg, as well as those defined as Volksdeutsch. These included men deemed to be of German extraction born in central Europe from the Baltic to the Black Sea, even though few of them spoke or understood the language. Poles had also been forcibly conscripted.

Around one-fifth of the troops in the Seventh Army command were Poles by birth or *Osttruppen* – eastern troops recruited from Soviet prisoners of war. Many had volunteered only to save themselves from starvation or disease in German camps. Their deployment on the eastern front had not been a great success, so the Nazi regime had withdrawn them gradually, to be incorporated into General Andrei Vlasov's ROA, or Russian Liberation Army. Most had then been sent to France. They were organized in battalions, but the German attitude to Slav *Untermenschen* changed little. As in the occupied territories of the Soviet Union, they were often used in anti-partisan operations. General-feldmarschall von Rundstedt approved of the idea that their presence and tendency to loot would create an 'apprehensive impression about the invasion of France by the Soviet army'.

German officers and NCOs who commanded them were anxious about being shot in the back by their own men once the fighting started. A number of these *Osttruppen* deserted to French resistance groups. Many surrendered to the Allies at the first opportunity, but a second change of side would not save them from Stalin's revenge at the end of the war. In any case, German attempts to stiffen their morale with hatred of the western Allies – the '*Plutokratenstaaten Amerika und England* '– proved a failure. Only a couple of units, such as the Ostbataillon Huber, were to fight effectively in the battle to come.

For French civilians, the *Osttruppen* presented an unusual sight. A citizen of Montebourg on the Cotentin peninsula, a town which was to experience heavy fighting, watched in amazement when a battalion of Georgians marched down the main street behind an officer mounted on a grey horse. They were singing an unfamiliar song, 'very different to the usual "Heidi–Heidi–Hos" which had rung in our ears since 1940'.

The French, who sometimes referred to the Volksdeutsche as 'booty Germans', showed most sympathy towards the conscripted Poles. One woman in Bayeux heard from Poles in the German army that word had spread secretly from Warsaw that they should surrender to the Allies as soon as possible and then transfer to the Polish army of General Anders, fighting with the British. These Poles also spread word to the French of the SS extermination camps. Their existence was not always believed, particularly if accompanied by garbled details, such as a story that Jewish corpses were rendered into sugar. These Poles also foresaw the fate of their own country as the Soviet armies advanced. 'You will be liberated,' they said to the French, 'but we will be occupied for years and years.'

In stark contrast to the weak infantry divisions were the panzer and panzergrenadier divisions of the Waffen-SS and the army. Generalleutnant Fritz Bayerlein, one of Rommel's officers from North Africa, commanded the Panzer Lehr Division, whose cadres were based on the staff from the armoured training establishments. When he took over, Guderian told him, 'With this division on its own you must throw the Allies into the sea. Your objective is the coast – no, not the coast – it is the sea.'

Other full-strength armoured divisions which would fight in Normandy included the 2nd Panzer-Division under Generalleutnant Heinrich Freiherr von Lüttwitz, a tubby man with a monocle. Rommel trusted him enough to open negotiations with the Allies, if the need arose. The armoured formation closest to the Normandy coast was the 21st Panzer-Division, which would face the British in front of Caen. Equipped with the Mark IV tank, rather than the latest Panthers or Tigers, a sixth of its personnel consisted of Volksdeutsche. According to their commander, Generalleutnant Edgar Feuchtinger, they 'could hardly understand orders and could hardly be understood by their NCOs and officers'. Feuchtinger was a convinced Nazi who had helped organize the Berlin Olympics of 1936. Unadmired by his colleagues, he was also a philanderer. On the night of the invasion, he was with his mistress in Paris.

Those fighting in Normandy, especially in the British sector on the eastern flank round Caen, would see one of the greatest concentrations of SS panzer divisions since the Battle of Kursk. There would be the 1st SS Panzer-Division *Leibstandarte Adolf Hitler*; the 12th SS Panzer-Division *Hitler Jugend*, which contained the youngest and most fanatical troops of all, and then later, when they were transferred from the eastern front, the 9th SS Panzer-Division *Hohenstaufen* and the 10th SS Panzer-Division *Frundsberg*. British armour would also encounter two SS Tiger battalions, with devastating consequences. The American forces to the west would find themselves facing only the 17th SS Panzergrenadier-Division *Götz von Berlichingen*, the weakest and worst trained of all the Waffen-SS formations in Normandy, and the 2nd SS Panzer-Division *Das Reich*, which was soon to become even more infamous for its brutality. But the Americans would come up against many more infantry divisions. Of these, General der Fallschirm-truppen Eugen Meindl's II Paratroop Corps would prove the most formidable.

The commander of LXXXIV Corps, which controlled the Normandy sector, was General der Artillerie Erich Marcks, a highly respected and intelligent leader. Thin and wiry, he had lost one eye in the First World War and a deep scar ran across his nose and cheek. The bespectacled Marcks had also lost a leg earlier in the Second World War. 'He was of Spartan-like, old Prussian simplicity,' wrote one of his admiring officers. On one occasion, when whipped cream was served at dinner, he said, 'I do not wish to see this again as long as our country is starving.'

Marcks was indeed an exception. Since its defeat in 1940, France had been seen as 'a conqueror's paradise', according to Rundstedt's chief of staff, General Günther Blumentritt. As a posting, the country represented the complete antithesis of the Russian front. In fact unmarried officers on leave from the war in the east tried to obtain passes for Paris instead of spending it in an austere and heavily bombed Berlin. They far preferred the prospect of sitting in the sun outside cafés on the Champs-Elysées, then dining in Maxim's and going on to nightclubs and cabarets afterwards.

Even the idea of civilians helping the Allies did not seem to disturb them too much. 'The enemy will certainly be well informed because it is easy to conduct espionage here,' wrote a technical officer from the 9th Panzer-Division on leave in Paris. 'There are signposts everywhere and generally relationships between soldiers and the fair sex are very close. I have spent wonderful days here. One really has to have seen and experienced Paris oneself and I'm glad I had the opportunity. You can get everything here in Paris.'

Formations transferred from the eastern front, especially Waffen-SS divisions, believed that the soldiers garrisoned in France had become soft. 'They had done nothing but live well and send things home,' commented one general. 'France is a dangerous country, with its wine, women and pleasant climate.' The troops of the 319th Infanterie-Division on the Channel Islands were even thought to have gone native from mixing with the essentially English population. They received the nickname of the 'King's Own German Grenadiers'. Ordinary soldiers, however, soon called it 'the Canada Division', because Hitler's refusal to redeploy them meant that they were likely to end up in Canadian prisoner of war camps.

Members of the German occupation army in France indeed led an easy life. This had been helped by the correct behaviour demanded by their commanders towards the civilian population. In Normandy, the farmers above all had simply wanted to get on with their lives and their work. It was usually the arrival of SS units or *Osttruppen* in a neighbourhood during the spring of 1944 which led to outbreaks of drunken violence, with shooting in the streets at night, occasional incidents of rape and frequent examples of robbery and looting.

Many German officers and soldiers had struck up liaisons with young Frenchwomen in the provinces as well as in Paris, and for those without a girlfriend there was an army brothel in Bayeux. This had been established in the quiet little town along with an army cinema, a military dental practice and other facilities attached to the Maison de la Wehrmacht. German soldiers in France, especially those quartered amid the rich farmlands of Normandy, availed themselves of another advantage. Those going home on leave went back with wooden boxes packed with meat and dairy produce for families having to survive on ever-diminishing rations. As Allied air attacks against rail communications intensified in the spring of 1944, Norman farmers had found it increasingly difficult to market their produce. Ordinary German soldiers known as '*Landser*' and NCOs were able to swap their cigarette ration for butter and cheese, which they would then send back to Germany. The only problem was that the air attacks on transport also made the Feldpost less reliable.

One senior NCO spent a night before the invasion in a dugout with his company commander, discussing how people back in Germany would react when it came. He was, however, preoccupied by another problem. 'I have here more than four kilos of butter,' he wrote to his wife, Laura, 'and I very much want to send it to you, if I only get the opportunity.' He presumably never did, because a few days later he 'gave his life *für Führer, Volk und das Großdeutsche Reich*', according to the standard formula which his company commander used in a letter of condolence to his wife.

One soldier in the 716th Infanterie-Division defending the coast was asked by a French storekeeper how he would react when the invasion came. 'I will behave like a mussel,' he replied. Many, however, thought of their patriotic duty. 'Don't be too concerned if I am not able to write in the near future or if I am in action,' a senior NCO with the 2nd Panzer-Division wrote home. 'I will write to you as often as I can, even if sparks really begin to fly. One cannot rule out the possibility that the great blow against the Fatherland, of which our enemies have been dreaming for so long, will now be struck. You can be sure though that we will stand firm.'

During those first days of June, there were numerous contradictory indications of the expected invasion. According to Rommel's naval adviser, Konteradmiral Ruge, an imminent attack was discounted because of the weather. German meteorologists, who lacked the information available to the Allies from weather stations in the western Atlantic, believed that conditions would not be right before 10 June. Rommel decided to seize the opportunity to return to Germany for his wife's birthday and to see Hitler at Berchtesgaden to ask him for two more panzer divisions. He clearly showed great confidence in the forecasts, for he had not forgotten his absence from the Afrika Korps due to illness when Montgomery launched the Battle of Alamein, nineteen months earlier. Generaloberst Friedrich Dollman, the commander-in-chief of the Seventh Army, also decided on the basis of the weather forecasts to hold a command post exercise for divisional commanders in Rennes on 6 June.

Others, however, seemed to sense that something might be happening this time, even after all the false alerts that spring. On 4 June,

Obersturmführer Rudolf von Ribbentrop, the son of Hitler's foreign minister, was returning from a 12th SS Panzer-Division radio exercise when his vehicle was machine-gunned by an Allied fighter. He was visited the next day in hospital by a member of the German embassy in Paris. The diplomat said as he was leaving that, according to the latest report, the invasion was due to start that day.

'Well, another false alarm,' said Ribbentrop.

'The fifth of June is not quite over yet,' his visitor replied.

In Brittany, an increase in Resistance activity aroused suspicions. North-east of Brest, an airdrop of arms to the local network had landed almost on top of the 353rd Infanterie-Division's headquarters. 'Couriers and individual soldiers were waylaid' and its commander, General Mahlmann, only just survived an ambush with automatic weapons. His aide was killed in the attack and his staff car was found afterwards to have twenty-four bullet holes. Then, on 5 June, Oberst Cordes, the commanding officer of the 942nd Grenadier-Regiment, was killed. The no doubt brutal interrogation of a member of the Resistance captured at the beginning of June also obtained results. He is said to have 'made statements about the beginning of the invasion in a few days'.

The bad weather on 5 June did not stop an exercise with blank ammunition in the streets of Montebourg on the Cotentin peninsula, but the Kriegsmarine decided that it was not worth sending out naval patrols into the Channel that night. As a result the flotillas of Allied minesweepers were able to advance in line abreast towards the Normandy coast completely unobserved.

During the early evening, one of the BBC's 'personal messages' in code to the Resistance aroused suspicions. Rundstedt's headquarters passed on the information at 21.15 hours as a general warning, but only the Fifteenth Army in the Pas-de-Calais implemented 'Alert Stage II'. At the Château de la Roche-Guyon, General Speidel and Admiral Ruge had guests to dinner. They included the writer Ernst Jünger, an ardent nationalist who had now become a member of the German resistance. The party went on until quite late. Speidel was about to go to bed at 01.00 hours on 6 June when the first reports came in of airborne landings.

4

Sealing off the Invasion Area

The French resistance movement, which had grown up from isolated beginnings in the darkest days of the war, was bound to prove fragmented and unregimented. Bringing so many groups of widely differing political views together had proved a difficult and dangerous task. Many brave men, of whom the most famous was Jean Moulin, had died or risked death in their attempts to coordinate the Resistance. In February 1944, some form of unity was achieved under the Conseil National de la Résistance, and Georges Bidault was elected its leader. Bidault, who later became de Gaulle's minister of foreign affairs, proved acceptable to both Communists and non-Communists.

In the most general terms, French politics in 1944 split three ways, with people identified by their opponents as Pétainist, Communist or Gaullist. This is not, of course, how they would necessarily have seen themselves. Large parts of the Resistance worked with de Gaulle, without necessarily being Gaullist. The ORA, the Organisation de Résistance de l'Armée, took de Gaulle's orders, but its leaders never quite shed their suspicions of him. Led by General Revers and other officers, the ORA emerged from the ruins of Vichy's Armistice army, which had been disbanded by the Germans after they marched into the unoccupied zone in November 1942. The Communists regarded them as no better than turncoat Pétainists infiltrating the Resistance. Yet the Communists, working behind the scenes, were the most proficient infiltrators of all, using their classic tactics of 'entryism'. Many tricks were used to get their representatives, often in a disguised role, on to the key Resistance committees. They would then take them over from the inside, while leaving an appearance of political unity on the surface.

The French Communist Party had found itself in an indefensible position during the Nazi–Soviet pact. But since Germany's invasion of the Soviet Union, radical and determined young Frenchmen and women became enthusiastic recruits. The immense sacrifices of the Red Army and partisans had proved a powerful inspiration which owed little to the Stalinism of the pre-war period. Some in the armed wing of the French Communist Party, the FTP (Francs-tireurs et Partisans), believed that the fight against Vichy and the German occupation should become a political insurrection as well as a battle of national liberation. Untrained in Stalinist discipline and lacking instruction from Moscow, they had no idea that the last thing the Kremlin wanted was a revolution in France breaking out behind the Allied front lines. Until Germany was finally defeated, Stalin needed all the American assistance he could get in the form of Lend-Lease trucks, food and steel. In addition, his worst fear was that the western Allies might be tempted to make a separate peace with Germany. He certainly did not want any trouble from local Communists which might give them an excuse.

French Communists in the Resistance knew nothing of this, and not just because of communication difficulties. In Moscow, the International Section of the Central Committee, which had replaced the Comintern, received little guidance from above. Stalin had washed his hands of France. It appears that he could not forgive her collapse in 1940, which, contrary to all his calculations, had left the Soviet Union suddenly vulnerable to the Wehrmacht.

The Special Operations Executive in London, which was in radio contact with 137 active stations, estimated that by the spring of 1944 the strength of the Resistance approached a total of 350,000 members. Around 100,000 may have had serviceable weapons, yet only 10,000 had ammunition for more than a single day of combat. The main contribution which the Resistance offered to the success of Overlord lay not in guerrilla action, but in intelligence and sabotage, contributing to the isolation of Normandy from the rest of France.

Résistance Fer, the organization of railwaymen, played a considerable part in both these fields. The strength of divisions could be estimated by the number of trains used to move them. For example, the 12th SS Panzer-Division *Hitler Jugend* was known to be close to maximum strength because the railwaymen, known as '*cheminots*', had reported that eighty-four trains were needed. A 'Plan Vert', or Plan Green, covered sabotage. Working with other Resistance groups, the French *cheminots* helped derail trains in tunnels, from where it was difficult to extract them. Heavy lifting cranes became a priority target for both sabotage and air attack. Engines were wrecked in marshalling yards and railway tracks constantly blown up.

In Burgundy and eastern France up to the German border, rail traffic came to a halt. Altogether thirty-seven railway lines were cut around Dijon just before the invasion. French railwaymen suffered heavy German reprisals. Several hundred were executed and another 3,000 deported to German camps. Engine drivers also faced the perpetual danger of attacks by Allied fighter-bombers. Typhoon pilots delighted in targeting trains with rockets and cannon to see the engines explode in a cloud of steam. On a less dramatic level, the *cheminots* became expert in delaying German troop trains, often by sending them down the wrong line. The Germans had been forced to bring in 2,500 of their own railwaymen, but the sabotage continued.

Apart from the obvious reasons for preventing the movement of German troops and supplies by rail, there was an added advantage in forcing movement on to the roads. Tank tracks had only a limited mileage, and as a result of the American Eighth Air Force bombing oil plants and refineries, the Wehrmacht was desperately short of fuel. Their lack of rubber for tyres also provided another very easy target for Resistance groups. Tacks and glass scattered on roads used by supply vehicles proved very effective in hampering road traffic, which was the point of 'Plan Tortue', or Plan Tortoise.

'Plan Violet' was assigned to members of the French telephone and telecommunications organization, the PTT. This concentrated on cutting the underground cables which the Germans used. Although they did not know it, this had the added advantage of forcing the Germans to use radio communications, which could then be decoded through Ultra. 'Plan Bleu', meanwhile, focused on sabotaging electric power lines.

In the Norman *départements* of Calvados and La Manche, the Resistance was not a major force. The most militarily active of the small networks was the Surcouf group at Pont-Audemer. There were some 200 members in and around Bayeux, as well as some fishermen in the little ports along the coast. Further inland, where the conditions were more favourable, weapons were hidden ready for the moment. In the Orne, which offered the concealment of forests, the Resistance could call on 1,800 men and women, of whom a third possessed weapons.

The small number of action groups in Calvados did not mean a lack of assistance to the Allies. A stream of information had been passed back to London. German divisions in the region were identified in laundries by the numbers inscribed on the collars of their tunics. Many of the details which enabled the British to seize the bridge over the Orne at Bénouville in a highly successful glider operation came from members of the Resistance. And two men who worked in the Organisation Todt offices, which supervised the construction of coastal defences, had copied plans and maps. One of them, Monsieur Brunet, was caught and condemned to death. Minefields, both real and fake, were identified, and attempts were made to estimate the calibre of the guns covering the beaches. This was difficult, since workers were evacuated before the coastal artillery was installed, but the depth of the zone forbidden to fishing craft during firing practice gave a useful indication.

While General Koenig and his staff coordinated Resistance activities from London, SHAEF planned the operations of the special forces groups to be parachuted in to work with the Resistance. SHAEF envisaged that the SOE groups already in place would attack rail targets principally in the interior. The 2,420 Special Air Service troops, on the other hand, would be dropped closer to the coast. In Bradley's First US Army headquarters, the conventional 'straight-legs' of the regular army were sceptical of the SAS, whom they regarded as 'nothing more than highly trained parasaboteurs'. 'The purpose,' ran the report on the subject, 'is to drop SAS people very close to the area and have them do little bits of killing here and there in addition to such things as putting water in gas tanks, letting air out of tires and generally playing around.' The US Army would become rather more appreciative of their efforts later on, especially in Brittany.

The unit tasked for Brittany, the 2ème Régiment de Chasseurs

Parachutistes of the SAS Brigade, was to be the first French unit in action on the soil of France since 1940. Wearing the maroon beret of the British Parachute Regiment with the Cross of Lorraine as a badge, its advance detachments took off in Halifaxes from Fairford on the night of 5 June. By the end of July, the French SAS had a force of over 30,000 Breton *maquisards* in action.

Since March 1943, other groups had been training to parachute into France to assist and train the Resistance in key areas. The most important were the three-man 'Jedburgh' teams, usually consisting of a British or an American officer, a French officer and a radio operator. Altogether, eighty-three teams briefed by Koenig's staff would be dropped in uniform, but many of them arrived too late to be useful.

Rommel was well aware of the threat to his lines of communication, not just from the Resistance, but above all from the Allied air forces. 'We will undergo the same experience with supplies in the invasion battle as we had in North Africa,' he had told General Bayerlein on 15 May. 'The supply lines will be destroyed and we will get nothing across the Rhine as we got nothing across the Mediterranean.'

The Allied plan, however, was not to seal off the battlefield at the Rhine. SHAEF aimed to cut off Normandy and Brittany by smashing rail communications and destroying all the bridges along the River Seine to the east and the Loire to the south. But 'Transportation', as the operation became known, proved very hard to launch, because of British anxieties and personal rivalries.

Eisenhower's deputy, Air Chief Marshal Tedder, was the main proponent of the plan. In February, Air Marshal Harris of Bomber Command and General Spaatz of the Eighth Air Force received warning that preparations for Overlord would require their heavy squadrons to be diverted from the strategic bombing offensive against Germany. Harris, who believed obsessively that his bomber force was on the point of bringing Germany to its knees, objected strenuously. He wanted his aircraft to continue smashing German cities to rubble. There should be only 'minimum diversions' from the task of 'reducing the enemy's material power to resist invasion', he wrote to Air Chief Marshal Sir Charles Portal, the chief of the air staff.

Above all, Harris fiercely resisted the idea that he should be told what to bomb. Because of weather variations, he must have 'full discretion'. As for targets in France, he was prepared to offer only Halifax and Stirling squadrons, as they did not have the range of the Lancaster for deep penetrations into Germany. Spaatz also showed great reluctance to change targets. He wanted to continue attacking oil refineries and German fighter production. Their objections were overruled by Eisenhower at a major meeting on 25 March, but they still tried to get their own way.

Spaatz also pointed out the dangers of killing large numbers of French civilians. This was a matter of immense concern to Churchill. He wrote to Roosevelt, arguing that the Luftwaffe 'should be the main target'. He feared 'the bad effect which will be produced upon the French civilian population by these slaughters, all taking place so soon before Overlord D-Day. They may easily bring about a great revulsion in French feeling towards their approaching United States and British liberators. They may leave a legacy of hate behind them.' Roosevelt firmly rejected his plea on 11 May. 'However regrettable the attendant loss of civilian lives is, I am not prepared to impose from this distance any restrictions on military action by the responsible commanders that in their opinion might militate against the success of Overlord or cause additional loss of life to our Allied forces of invasion.'*

Tedder, however, still faced considerable opposition from the antagonistic Harris. Bomber Harris was at odds with the Air Ministry, he loathed Leigh-Mallory and he had become increasingly difficult with Portal, his direct superior as chief of the air staff. 'The RAF was a house divided,' observed a senior American staff officer afterwards. 'The air side stank beyond belief.' Facing opposition from both Harris and Churchill, Tedder went to Eisenhower. 'You must get control of the bombers,' he told him, 'or I must resign.' The supreme commander did not waste time. He threatened to take the matter to the President and both Churchill and Harris were forced to give way. According to Portal, Churchill simply could not believe that the bombing campaign might succeed in isolating the battlefield.

This rebuff did not stop Churchill's anxieties about the French. He

---

* French civilian casualties reached 15,000 killed and 19,000 injured in 1944 before the invasion.

had tried to set a limit of 10,000 civilian casualties, at which point he wanted the bombing to cease. He kept asking Tedder whether the figure had been reached. He also suggested that SHAEF should consult the French on targets. 'God, no!' came the appalled reply.

Civilian casualties were indeed heavy, and so too were those of the bomber crews. The bombing programme also had to hit targets further afield in such a way as to prevent the Germans from deducing the site of the invasion. But Harris's claim that his heavy bombers would not be effective against tactical targets, such as railways and bridges, proved very mistaken. Rommel's fears were realized even before the invasion began in earnest.

The first warning to the Resistance to prepare had been transmitted by the French service of the BBC on 1 June. The announcer read these 'personal messages' in an emphatic tone. Defying the usual security measures for codes, the message could not have been clearer: '*L'heure du combat viendra*' – 'The moment of battle is approaching.' The signal to be sent in the event of cancellation was slightly more veiled: '*Les enfants s'ennuient au jardin*' – 'The children are getting bored in the garden.' During the first days of June, members of the Resistance all over France leaned closer to their wireless sets to be certain of what they heard. So too did the German Abwehr and Sicherheitsdienst. Others not in on the secret also listened in fascination. An intellectual living near Lisieux described his wireless as this 'insolent little sphinx emitting baroque messages on which the fate of France depended'.

Finally, in the early evening of 5 June, personal messages sent the Resistance all over France into action. The Allies deemed this necessary because they could not risk identifying the main landing areas. That evening, the Resistance in Normandy heard the announcer say, '*Les dés sont sur le tapis*' – 'The dice are down.' This was their order to start cutting cables and telegraph wires immediately. It was followed by '*Il fait chaud à Suez*', the signal to attack all lines of communication.

5

The Airborne Assault

During the hour before midnight on 5 June, the roar of hundreds of aircraft engines in a constant stream could be heard over villages near airfields in southern and central England. People in their nightclothes went out into their gardens to stare up at the seemingly endless air armada silhouetted against the scudding clouds. 'This is it' was their instinctive thought. The sight evoked powerful emotions, including painful memories of the evacuation from Dunkirk four summers before. Some went back inside to kneel by their beds to pray for those setting forth.

Three airborne divisions were taking to the air in over 1,200 aircraft. The British 6th Airborne Division was headed for the east of the River Orne to secure Montgomery's left flank. The American 101st and 82nd Airborne Divisions would be dropped on the Cotentin peninsula to seize key points, especially the causeways across the flooded areas inland from Utah beach.

The first group to take off was D Company of the 2nd Battalion, Oxfordshire and Buckinghamshire Light Infantry. They left even before the pathfinder detachments sent ahead of the main force to mark dropping zones. This company, commanded by Major John Howard, was flown in six Horsa gliders towed by Halifax bombers. Officers and soldiers all had blackened faces and wore round paratroop helmets with camouflage netting. They were armed with a mixture of rifles, Sten sub-machine guns and several Bren guns. The Halifaxes took them over to the east of the invasion fleet and aimed for the seaside resort of

51

Cabourg, where there was a gap in the German flak defences. The gliders were at an altitude of 5,000 feet when the tow lines were cast off. Howard told his men to stop their songs, which had been bellowed out for most of the way across the Channel. From then on there was no noise apart from the rushing wind. The pilots banked, turning the flimsy craft westwards. After losing height rapidly, they flattened out at 1,000 feet for the approach.

Their objectives were two bridges close together, one over the River Orne and the other over the Caen Canal. They had to seize them before the Germans guarding them could blow demolition charges. Howard, who had positioned himself opposite the door on the first glider, could see the gleam of the two parallel waterways below. As his Horsa swept in, the men braced themselves for the shock of landing. The two pilots brought the cumbersome glider in with astonishing accuracy. After bumping and leaping and skidding across the field, the nose of the glider came to a halt penetrating the barbed-wire entanglement. The two pilots were knocked unconscious in the crash, but they had achieved a landing within fifty feet of the pillbox beside the bridge.

Some of the plywood Horsa gliders – unaffectionately known as 'Hearses' – broke up on impact, so soldiers scrambled out through the broken sides as well as the door. Within moments, the first men out of Howard's glider had hurled grenades through the slits of the pillbox on the west side of the Caen Canal. The rest of the platoon did not wait. Led by Lieutenant Den Brotheridge, they were already charging across the bridge. Howard had made sure they were at the peak of fitness with cross-country runs. But by the time Brotheridge's platoon reached the other side, the German guards had got themselves together and opened fire. Brotheridge was mortally wounded from a shot through the neck and died soon afterwards.

Another platoon arrived led by Lieutenant Sandy Smith, although he had broken his arm badly in the landing. After a fierce but mercifully brief firefight, the bridge over the Caen Canal was secured. Howard was concerned at having heard nothing from the platoon ordered to take the bridge over the Orne, a few hundred yards beyond, but then a message arrived to say that they had secured it without the defenders firing a shot. Its commander, Lieutenant Dennis Fox, took a certain pleasure in greeting the next platoon to arrive, panting heavily since

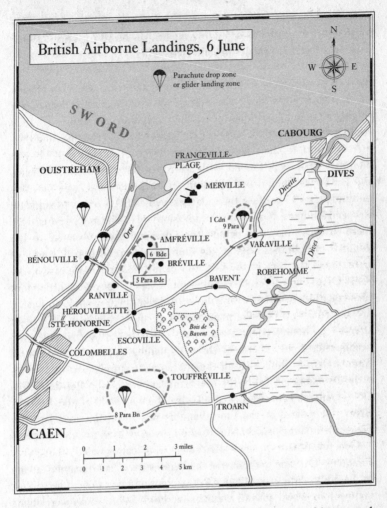

they had landed half a mile off target. When asked how things stood, he replied, 'Well, so far the exercise is going fine, but I can't find any bloody umpires.'

Howard immediately ordered an all-round defence and sent Fox's platoon out in fighting patrols to probe the nearby village of Bénouville. The curious choice of success signal for the two bridges – 'Ham and Jam' – was sent off by radio. Howard could hardly dare believe that such a tricky operation had gone entirely according to plan, but then at 01.30 hours the platoons defending the bridges heard the unmistakable noise of armoured vehicles beyond Bénouville.

By then paratroopers were landing all over the place. German officers in command posts along the Normandy coastline were desperately ringing regimental headquarters on field telephones. In some cases they could not get through because the Resistance had cut the lines and they had to resort to their radios. To increase confusion, the RAF had mounted Operation Titanic, with a force of forty Hudsons, Halifaxes and Stirlings. They dropped dummy parachutists and 'window' aluminium strips to confuse the radar, as well as SAS teams to simulate airborne landings away from the invasion area. The SAS teams were there to cause mayhem behind the lines and give substance to the dummy parachutists. Some 200 dummies were dropped south of Carentan at the base of the Cotentin peninsula, fifty more east of the River Dives and fifty to the south-west of Caen. They were little more than rough scarecrows, with a device to make them explode and catch fire on landing. The Germans called them '*Explosivpuppen*'. Soon after 01.30 hours, teleprinters began chattering in corps and army headquarters, but reports of these 'exploding puppets' caused most commanders to think that all the attacks were simply part of a large-scale diversion, probably for the main landing in the Pas-de-Calais. Only Generalmajor Max Pemsel, the chief of staff of the Seventh Army, recognized at the time that this was the major invasion, but Generalleutnant Speidel at La Roche-Guyon refused to believe him.

Generalleutnant Joseph Reichert, who commanded the 711th Infanterie-Division to the east of the Orne estuary, had remained talking in the officers' mess until late. On the point of going to bed, he and his companions heard aircraft engines overhead. 'The planes were flying so low that we had the feeling they might almost touch the roof,' he wrote later. Reichert and his companions went outside to have a look. 'It was a night of the full moon. The weather was fairly stormy, with low-hanging black clouds, but in the gaps between them several low-flying planes could be distinctly observed, circling the divisional command post.' Reichert went back inside to grab his pistol, then heard the shout of 'Parachutists!' Paratroopers were coming down all round his divisional headquarters. The 20 mm quadruple flak guns on the main strongpoint opened fire.

While his operations officer alerted the division, Reichert rang LXXXI Corps headquarters at Rouen. By this time the guns had stopped firing, leaving an uneasy calm. Reichert, who had been sceptical about the whole invasion, now sensed that it really was starting, even if this attack was only a feint. Two captured British paratroopers were brought in, but they refused to answer questions. The accuracy of the maps found on them shook Reichert. They showed almost every gun emplacement. He deduced that the French Resistance had been even busier than the Germans had imagined. Not all prisoners were so fortunate. Elsewhere in the sector, a Hauptfeldwebel in Reichert's division executed eight captured British paratroopers, probably in obedience to Hitler's notorious *Kommandobefehl*, which demanded the shooting of all special forces taken on raids.

South of Evreux, Brigadeführer Fritz Witt, the commander of the 12th SS Panzer-Division *Hitler Jugend*, had been enjoying a late drink with staff officers in front of a log fire when the first reports of dummy parachutists came in. They dismissed these as yet another of the false alarms which had taken place that spring. But almost as soon as they went to bed, they were woken with more insistent warnings. Witt rang 1st SS Panzer Corps headquarters, but found that they had heard nothing. On his own authority, he ordered the alert for the *Hitler Jugend*, with the codeword 'Blücher'. Yet, to their intense frustration, most of his men would spend many hours waiting in their armoured vehicles until Führer headquarters finally agreed to release them for action. Witt nevertheless permitted the 25th SS Panzergrenadier-Regiment to move towards Caen and sent ahead part of his reconnaissance battalion in their six-wheeler armoured cars and BMW motorcycles with sidecars.

Of the British airborne operations that night, Howard's success with the two bridges was about the only one which went according to plan. Brigadier James Hill, the commander of 3rd Parachute Brigade, had warned his officers before their departure, 'Gentlemen, in spite of your excellent training and orders, do not be daunted if chaos reigns. It undoubtedly will.'

Major General Richard Gale, the commander of the 6th Airborne Division, had formulated a sound plan. To secure the left flank of the landings, his force needed to occupy and defend the area between the River Orne and the River Dives five miles further east. By destroying five bridges on that eastern side, he could make use of the Dives and the flood plain around it, which the Germans themselves had inundated, as a barrier against armoured counter-attacks. He could then concentrate the bulk of his forces facing southwards to hold off an expected counter-attack from the 21st Panzer-Division. For this they needed anti-tank guns, which would be brought in with the first glider force two hours later.

Another important objective for the 6th Airborne Division was the battery at Merville, on the far side of the Orne estuary from Ouistreham. RAF air reconnaissance had monitored the preparation of these emplacements for coastal artillery. Large-calibre guns there could wreak havoc on the fleet and the landing ships, as well as Sword beach, the most easterly landing sector. Their massive concrete construction made them virtually impervious to bombing. Lieutenant Colonel Terence Otway's 9th Battalion of the Parachute Regiment therefore received orders to capture the site and destroy the guns. The barbed-wire defences, minefields and machine-gun positions around them made this an awesome assignment. A bombing raid by Lancasters to soften up the defences was due to go in just before the battalion jumped, then four Horsa gliders carrying an assault group were to land inside the wire and on top of the battery.

Otway's men had practised the attack many times over on mocked-up positions back in England, but chaos was destined to reign, as their brigade commander had warned. The battalion was dropped all over the place. This was partly due to their aircraft taking evasive action when the flak opened up, but also because the pathfinder group's Eureka homing devices to guide in the main force had broken on landing. Many paratroopers fell into the flood plain of the River Dives. One of Otway's men was sucked into a bog and drowned in mud despite efforts to save him. The airborne soldiers had been equipped with duck calls to try to find each other in the dark, but the battalion was so spread out that these could not be heard. Fewer than 160 men out of 600 reached the rendezvous point.

Two sticks of the 9th Battalion had failed to join Otway because they were dropped at Saint-Pair, sixteen miles too far south. They could not believe the silence of the night. Their officer went to a nearby house and woke up the inhabitants to find out where they were. Horrified by the news, he told the men to break up into small groups and try to make their way back to join the battalion, but many of them would be captured on the way. Altogether 192 of Otway's battalion were still unaccounted for at the end of the battle for Normandy.

Colonel Otway could not wait any longer. He had to complete the mission and send the success signal before 06.00 hours, when the six-inch guns of the light cruiser HMS *Arethusa* would open fire. To make matters worse, much of their kit had been lost in the jump. Otway's men had no mine detectors and only a few Bangalore torpedoes for blowing gaps in the barbed-wire entanglements. Otway nevertheless decided to carry on, with only a quarter of his force. His soldier servant, a former professional boxer, proffered a small flask. 'Shall we take our brandy now, sir?' he said.

The next blow was to find that the Lancasters coming to soften up the battery had missed their target. Otway had to abandon the set plan completely, above all because the Horsa gliders which were to land on the battery never reached their objective. A young officer and a sergeant crawled ahead through the minefield to mark the way, then the attack went in. The force of 160 men suffered seventy-five casualties in a matter of minutes, but they still seized the emplacements. To their bitter frustration they found only 75 mm guns, not the anticipated 150 mm heavy coastal artillery. Using the plastic explosive which each man carried, they blew the breeches and retired as best they could with their wounded to be out of range before the *Arethusa* was in position to open fire.

The other seven parachute battalions of Gale's division were also to be dropped between the rivers Orne and Dives. After the bridges between Bénouville and Ranville had been secured by Howard's company, the next objective was to destroy the bridges over the Dives to protect the east flank. This was the task of the 3rd Parachute Squadron Royal Engineers, assisted by the battalions dropping on that flank. After the bridges were blown, the 8th Battalion took up positions in the south-east of the area, in and around the Bois de Bavent.

Almost all the battalions dropping that night lost a large amount of kit. Bren guns and PIAT anti-tank launchers suffered damage on landing. In many cases, the jump bag attached to a paratrooper's ankle was so heavy because of the extra ammunition that either the webbing attachment broke or the bag buried itself deep in the mud of marshy ground. Some soldiers drowned in the ditches of flooded areas adjoining the River Dives. Brigadier James Hill, the commander of the 3rd Parachute Brigade, dropped not far from Cabourg into flooded marshland there. The water was only waist deep, but this did not save him from one minor disaster. All the tea bags which he had brought stuffed inside his trouser legs were ruined. He soon suffered a far more serious blow, when British bombs exploded nearby. As he threw himself sideways, landing on another officer, Hill was wounded in the left buttock. He then saw to his horror a blown-off leg lying in the middle of the path, but it was not his. It belonged to Lieutenant Peters, the man on whom he had fallen. Peters was dead.

Hill's brigade had suffered the most from inaccurate drops. Low cloud had made navigation difficult and pilots had tried to avoid the flak. Some were also confused because the River Dives, swollen by flooding, looked like the River Orne, and they dropped men on the wrong side. The 1st Canadian Parachute Battalion, bound for the same drop zone as Otway's 9th Battalion, was also scattered widely for the same reasons. Many of its men fell into the flooded surrounds of the Dives and two sticks were even dropped on the west side of the Orne. Only a small force reached Varaville, where the bridge was to be destroyed. Part of a company helped the 9th Battalion withdraw from the Merville battery, while other detachments, guided through the night by a French girl they met, seized and held the bridge at Robehomme until sappers arrived to destroy it.

One of the Canadian officers noted just before departure that his men were all in a 'very suggestible state'. This may have been made worse by their Catholic padre. Appalled to hear that the paratroopers had been issued with condoms, he had ranted in his sermon before take-off that they should not be going to meet their deaths with 'the means of mortal sin' in their pockets. At the end of the service, the ground was apparently littered with discarded packets. But as soon as the Canadian paratroopers were in action, particularly during the fierce fighting for the village of Varaville, they showed no lack of courage. They also had confidence in their commander, Brigadier Hill, showing a rare respect among Canadians for a senior British officer.

The 5th Parachute Brigade dropped just to the east of the two captured bridges. It was while their battalions were still sorting themselves out that Major Howard's men heard the clanking and grinding of tracked vehicles approaching from Bénouville. The only anti-tank weapon available was a PIAT launcher and two rounds. Sergeant Thornton ran forward with this hefty apparatus. Knowing that the weapon was useless except at close range, he took up a firing position next to the road. Fortunately, the oncoming tracked vehicle turned out to be a half-track rather than a tank. Thornton knocked it out with the first round and the following vehicle retreated rapidly. He and his men captured several survivors from the half-track, including the local German commander, Major Schmidt, who was coming from Ranville to see if the bridges really had been taken.

Shortly afterwards, Howard's little defence force was relieved by the 7th Battalion, commanded by Lieutenant Colonel Pine-Coffin, whose name alone qualified him for a place in an Evelyn Waugh novel. These reinforcements were able to increase the bridgehead considerably by occupying more of the surrounding area on the west bank of the canal, including most of the village of Bénouville. Meanwhile the 12th Battalion took up defensive positions along the low ridge beside the Orne. The 13th Battalion moved into Ranville ready for a counterattack, while one of its companies began to clear the landing zone for the gliders.

Soon after 03.00 hours, Major General 'Windy' Gale and his divisional headquarters landed near the bridge at Ranville. Tall and heavily built, the unflappable Gale, with his military moustache, was a welcome sight to those from the first wave, reassuring them that the invasion was proceeding as planned. Gale, for his part, admitted to a private glee at being the first British general back in France since 1940.

Other gliders brought in Jeeps and the anti-tank guns to strengthen the defences. Chester Wilmot, the BBC reporter, accompanied this wave. 'The landing went just like an exercise and was a most wonderful sight,' he reported, perhaps optimistically, considering the state of most of the crash-landed gliders. But then another unexpected threat to the bridge at Bénouville appeared in the form of German gunboats, armed with 20 mm flak guns, coming down the canal from Caen. Once again a PIAT round hit the target, and the boats behind fled past to the open sea, not knowing that they were sailing right into the muzzles of the Royal Navy.

The newly arrived forces wasted little time digging in. Explosive charges planted into the ground accelerated the process greatly. Their positions appeared to be under mortar fire, as one trench after another was prepared. But real mortar bombs had also started to fall, as the panzergrenadiers from the 21st Panzer-Division started a series of counter-attacks.

The most important bridge, the one just beyond the small town of Troarn on the main road from Caen to Pont-l'Evêque, had not yet been blown because of the scattered drops. Major Roseveare, the officer in charge, gathered a small force, accumulated enough explosives and seized a Jeep and trailer from a protesting medical orderly. They fought their way through a couple of German roadblocks, then Roseveare had to drive their overloaded vehicle down the main street of Troarn, while the other paratroopers on board fired back at the Germans shooting down at them from houses on either side. They reached the bridge, having lost only the Bren gunner on the back. They set their charges and within five minutes the centre span had collapsed into the Dives. Having ditched the Jeep, Roseveare managed to lead his small party on foot through the marshes and back across the Dives to rejoin the main force late in the afternoon. The left flank at least was secured. The threat now lay to the south.

The two American airborne divisions, the 82nd and 101st, had taken off about the same time as the British paratroopers. The pilots of their troop carrier squadrons had cursed and prayed as they pulled their 'grossly overloaded' C-47 Skytrains off the ground. Closing into their V formations, the matt-olive transport aircraft then streamed out over the Channel. The sky control officer on the cruiser USS *Quincy* observed that 'by this time the moon had risen, and although the overcast was still fairly solid, it lighted the clouds with a peculiar degree of luminosity . . . The first Skytrains appeared, silhouetted like groups of scudding bats.'

Their aircraft could not have felt very bat-like to the sticks of sixteen or eighteen men inside, as they endured the thundering roar and vibration from the over-strained engines. A number held their helmets ready on their laps, but most vomited straight on to the floor, which was to make it slippery at the crucial moment. Catholics fingered their rosary beads, murmuring prayers. The pilots had already noticed that the mood was significantly different from what it had been on exercise drops in England. One observed that they were usually 'cocky unruly characters', but this time 'they were very serious'. The aircrew were also far from relaxed about the mission. Some pilots at the controls wore goggles and a steel helmet in case the windscreen was shattered by flak.

Paratroopers in the main formations envied the pathfinders who had gone ahead with the radar beacons. They would already be on the ground, having jumped shortly after midnight, before the Germans realized what was happening. Many men feigned sleep, but only a few managed to doze off. General Maxwell Taylor, the tall commander of the 101st Airborne, even took off his harness and stretched out on the floor with some pillows. He looked forward to the jump with keen anticipation. It would be his fifth and thus gain him his wings.

As the aircraft reached the Channel Islands, German flak batteries on Jersey and Guernsey opened fire. One paratrooper remarked that it was ironic to get such a welcome from 'two islands named after nice moo cows'. A Royal Navy motor torpedo boat, MTB 679, signalled the point where the aircraft were to turn east for their run over the Cotentin peninsula to their drop zones. Once the French coast was in sight, pilots passed back the warning that they had less than ten minutes to go. On General Taylor's plane, they had trouble waking their commander and getting him back into his harness. He had insisted on being first out of the door.

Once the aircraft reached the coastline, they entered a dense fog bank which the meteorologists had not predicted. Paratroopers who could see out were alarmed by the thick white mist. The blue lights at the end of each wing became invisible. The pilots, unable to see anything, were frightened of collision. Those on the outside of the formation veered off. Confusion increased when the aircraft emerged from the fog bank and came under fire from flak batteries on the peninsula. Pilots instinctively went to full throttle and took evasive action, even though this was strictly against their orders.

Because they were flying at little more than 1,000 feet, the aircraft were within range of German machine guns as well as flak. Paratroopers were thrown around inside the fuselage as their pilot weaved and twisted the plane. Bullets striking the plane sounded 'like large hailstones on a tin roof'. For those going into action for the first time, this provided the shocking proof that people were really trying to kill them. One paratrooper who suffered a shrapnel wound in the buttock was made to stand so that a medic could patch him up right there. General Taylor's order that no paratrooper would be allowed to stay on board was taken to the letter. Apart from a dozen who were too badly wounded by flak to jump, there appear to have been only two exceptions: one was a paratrooper who had somehow released his emergency chute by mistake inside the aircraft, the other a major who suffered a heart attack.

On the USS *Quincy*, the sky control team at the top of the cruiser's superstructure watched in dismay. 'Often, a yellow ball would start glowing out in the middle of a field of red tracers. This yellow ball would slowly start to fall, forming a tail. Eventually, it would smash into the black loom of land, causing a great sheet of light to flare against the low clouds. Sometimes the yellow ball would explode in mid-air, sending out streamers of burning gasoline. This tableau always brought the same reactions from us sky control observers: a sharp sucking-in of the breath and a muttered "Poor goddamn bastards".'

The red light by the door went on four minutes from the drop zone. 'Stand up and hook up!' came the shout from the dispatcher. Some of the heavily burdened men had to be hauled to their feet. They clipped their static line to the overhead cable running the length of the fuselage, then the order was yelled to check equipment and number off. This was followed by the command, 'Stand in the door!' But as the aircraft continued to jink or shudder from hits, men were thrown around or slid on the vomit-streaked floor. The flak and tracer were coming up around them 'in big arcs of fire', the wind was roaring in the open door, and the men watched, praying for the green light to come on so that they could escape what felt like a metal coffin. 'Let's go!' many shouted impatiently, afraid that they might be dropped in the sea on the east side of the peninsula.

The planes should have reduced speed to between ninety and 110 miles an hour for the jump, but most did not. 'Our plane never did slow down,' remembered one paratrooper. 'That pilot kept on floor-boarding it.' As soon as the green light came on, the men shuffled in an ungainly way towards the exit to jump. One or two made a hurried sign of the cross as they went. With all the shooting outside, it was easy to imagine that they were about to jump straight into crossfire from machine guns or land on a strongly defended position. Each paratrooper, as he reached the door, carried his leg pack, which would dangle below from a long strap as soon as he jumped. Weighing eighty pounds or more, many broke off during the descent and were lost in the dark. If any men did freeze at the last moment, then presumably the sergeant 'pusher' kicked them out, for there are hardly any confirmed reports of a man refusing to jump. As they leaped into the unknown, some remembered to shout 'Bill Lee!', the paratrooper's tribute to General Lee, the father of the US Airborne.

Most suffered a far more violent jerk than usual as the parachute opened, because of the aircraft's excessive speed. Those who fell close to German positions attracted heavy fire. Their canopies were riddled with tracer bullets. One battalion commander, his executive officer and a company commander were killed immediately, because they had landed among an advance detachment of Major Freiherr von der Heydte's 6th Paratroop Regiment. Another officer, who landed on top of the command post, was taken prisoner. An Obergefreiter in the 91st Luftlande-Division wrote home, 'US parachute troops landed in the middle of our position. What a night!'

The natural instinct, when dropping under fire, was to pull your legs up almost into a foetal position, not that it provided any protection. One man literally exploded in mid-air, probably because a tracer bullet had hit his Gammon grenade. In some cases the pilots had been flying below 500 feet and the parachutes barely had time to open. Many legs and ankles were broken, and a few men were paralysed with a broken back. One paratrooper who landed successfully was horrified when a following plane dropped its stick of eighteen men so low that none of the chutes opened. He compared the dull sound of the bodies hitting the ground to 'watermelons falling off the back of a truck'. The men of another stick which had been dropped too low along a small ridge were found later in a long line, all dead and all still in their harnesses.

As the Germans had flooded large areas around the River Merderet and inland from the beaches, many paratroopers fell into water. A number drowned, smothered by a soaked chute. Others were rescued either by buddies or, in a number of cases, by a French family who had immediately launched their rowing boat. Most who landed in water up to their chest had to keep ducking under the surface to reach their trench knife to cut themselves free. They cursed the American harness and envied the British quick-release system. Similarly, those whose chutes caught on tall trees had to strain and stretch to cut themselves free, knowing all the while that they presented easy targets. A number were shot as they struggled. Many atrocity stories spread among the survivors, with claims that German soldiers had bayoneted them from below or even turned flame-throwers on them. A number spoke of bodies obscenely mutilated.

Those coming down into small pastures surrounded by high hedges were reassured if they saw cows, since their presence indicated that there were no mines. But they still expected a German to run up and 'stick a bayonet' in them. To land in the dark behind enemy lines with no idea of where you were could hardly have been more disorientating and frightening. Some heard movement and hurriedly assembled their rifle, only to find that their arrival had attracted inquisitive cows. Men crept along hedgerows and, on hearing someone else, froze. Colonel 'Jump' Johnson, whose determination to knife a Nazi had led him to bring a veritable arsenal of close-quarter combat weapons, was nearly shot by one of his own officers, because he had lost his 'damn cricket'. These 'dime-store' children's clickers were despised by many in the 82nd Airborne. They resorted to the password 'Flash', to which the reply was 'Thunder': these two words were chosen because they were thought to be difficult for a German to pronounce convincingly.

The sense of relief to find another American was intense. Soon little groups formed. When an injured paratrooper was found, they gave him morphine and marked his position for medics later by sticking his rifle with the bayonet in the ground and the helmet on the butt. The most bloodthirsty went off 'Kraut-hunting'. Tracer gave away the position of German machine-gun positions, so they stalked them with grenades. Most paratroopers followed the order to use only knives and grenades

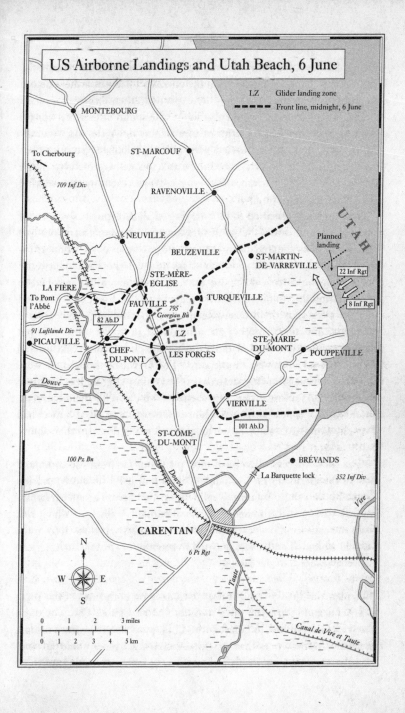

during darkness. But one who did fire his rifle noticed afterwards the torn condom hanging loosely from the muzzle. 'I had put it there before the jump to keep the barrel dry,' he explained, 'then forgot about it.'

The 'Kraut-hunters' would also follow the sound of German voices. In some cases they heard Germans approaching down the road, marching in formation. After hurried whispers, they lobbed grenades over the hedge at them. Some claimed to be able to smell Germans from the strong odour of their tobacco. Others recognized them by the creaking of all their leather equipment.

German troops seemed to be hurrying in all directions as reports of landings up and down the peninsula came in. A couple of pilots had become so disorientated from the fog and taking evasive action afterwards that they had dropped their sticks near Cherbourg, some twenty miles from the correct dropping zone. The captain with them had to go to a farmhouse to find out where they were. The French family tried to help by giving them a simple map of the Cotentin torn from a telephone directory. Another airborne officer, however, observed that the unintended dispersal of units during the chaotic drop had proved an unexpected advantage in one way: 'The Germans thought we were all over creation.' But the paratroopers were only slightly less confused themselves. As a lost group approached a well to refill their canteens, an old farmer appeared from his house. One of them asked him in bad French, 'Ou es Alamon?' He shrugged and pointed north, then south, east and west.

The most successful ambush took place not far from the command post of the German 91st Luftlande-Division near Picauville. Men from the 508th Parachute Infantry Regiment opened fire on a staff car bringing the divisional commander, Generalleutnant Wilhelm Falley, back from the command post exercise in Rennes. Falley was thrown from the vehicle wounded and, as he crawled to retrieve his pistol, an American lieutenant shot him dead.

The plan was for the 82nd Airborne to drop on both sides of the River Merderet and secure the town of Sainte-Mère-Eglise. This would cut the road and rail link to Cherbourg. They were also to capture bridges over the Merderet so that the forces arriving by sea could advance rapidly across the peninsula and cut it off, before advancing north on the port of Cherbourg. The 101st, dropping closer to Utah beach, would seize the causeways leading to it across the flooded marshes and also take the bridges and a lock on the River Douve, between the town of Carentan and the sea.

Several platoons of the 82nd Airborne dropped in and around Sainte-Mère-Eglise as planned. One paratrooper's chute caught on the church tower, where he hung helplessly, pretending to be dead while the bells deafened him. They were ringing in alarm because a house on the square by the church had caught fire and the townsfolk were passing buckets of water in a human chain. The scene below was chaotic. Soldiers from the local anti-aircraft unit under the command of an Austrian officer were firing in all directions as paratroopers dropped. Many Americans were riddled with bullets before they reached the ground. Those caught in trees stood little chance. One paratrooper dropped straight on to the blazing house. But with great determination, other rapidly formed groups who had landed outside the town began to advance towards its centre, dashing from cover to cover. Within an hour they had forced the Germans to withdraw. Sainte-Mère-Eglise was thus the first town in France to be liberated.

Sainte-Mère-Eglise became a focal point for many scattered detachments. One member of the 82nd Airborne was amazed to see two troopers from the 101st come riding bareback down the road on horses they had taken from a field. Another appeared driving a captured half-track motorcycle. Only a small number of paratroopers lost in the countryside appear to have been inactive. A few bedded down in ditches wrapped in their chutes, waiting for the dawn to find their bearings. The large majority, however, could not wait to get into the fighting. With nerves still taut after the jump, their blood was up. A trooper in the 82nd remembered his instructions only too clearly: 'Get to the drop zone as fast as possible. Take no prisoners because they will slow you down.'

The fighting became pitiless on both sides; in fact that night probably saw the most vicious fighting of the whole war on the western front. One German soldier, justifying the annihilation of an American platoon which landed on his battalion's heavy-weapons company, said later, 'They didn't come down to give us candies, you know. They came down to kill us, to fight.' German soldiers had certainly been lectured by their officers about the 'criminals' recruited to the US Airborne forces and their fears were transformed into violence. But it is hard to establish the accuracy of horror stories about German soldiers mutilating paratroopers caught in trees.

Whether or not these accounts were true, American paratroopers sought revenge. There seem to have been a number of cases of soldiers shooting the prisoners taken by others. Apparently, a Jewish sergeant and a corporal took a captured German officer and non-com from a farmyard. Those present heard a burst of automatic fire and, when the sergeant returned, 'nobody said a thing'. It was also said of another Jewish paratrooper that 'you didn't dare trust him with a PoW out of sight'. A soldier in the 101st recounted how, after they had come across two dead paratroopers 'with their privates cut off and stuck into their mouth', the captain with them gave the order, 'Don't you guys dare take any prisoners! Shoot the bastards!'

One or two men appear to have enjoyed the killing. A paratrooper recalled having come across a member of his company the following morning and being surprised to see that he was wearing red gloves instead of the issued yellow ones. 'I asked him where he got the red gloves from, and he reached down in his jump pants and pulled out a whole string of ears. He had been ear-hunting all night and had them all sewed on an old boot lace.' There were a few cases of brutal looting. The commander of the 101st Airborne's MP platoon came across the body of a German officer and saw that somebody had cut off his finger to take the wedding ring. A sergeant in the 508th Parachute Infantry Regiment was horrified when he found that members of his platoon had killed some Germans and then used 'their bodies for bayonet practice'.

On occasions, the killing of prisoners was prevented. About 02.30 hours, a handful of paratroopers from the 101st, including a lieutenant and a chaplain, were standing in a farmyard talking to the French inhabitants. They were astonished when around a dozen troopers from the 82nd came in at the run, herding a group of very young German orderlies, whom they then told to lie down. The terrified boys pleaded for their lives. The sergeant, who intended to shoot them all, claimed that some of their buddies caught in trees had been turned into 'Roman candles' by a German soldier with a flame-thrower.

The sergeant pulled the bolt back on his Thompson sub-machine gun. In desperation, the boys grabbed the legs of the lieutenant and the chaplain as they and the French family shouted at the sergeant not to shoot them. Finally, the sergeant was persuaded to stop. The boys were locked in the farm's cellar. But the sergeant was not put off his mission of vengeance. 'Let's go and find some Krauts to kill!' he yelled to his men, and they left. The members of the 101st were shaken by what they had witnessed. 'These people had gone ape,' a senior non-com remarked later.

As the scattered groups coalesced during the night, officers were able to exert control and concentrate on objectives. Soldiers who could not find their own units attached themselves to any battalion, even if it was from the other division. General Maxwell Taylor, the commander of the 101st, had accumulated a group of thirty men, which included four colonels as well as other officers. This prompted him to parody Churchill, with the comment, 'Never before in the annals of warfare have so few been commanded by so many.' Another group of troopers were sighted pulling the regimental commander of the 502nd Parachute Infantry Regiment, Colonel George Van Horn Mosely Jr, around on a machine-gun cart because he had broken his leg on the jump.

Several soldiers and officers who had broken an ankle on landing just strapped it up and hobbled on, gritting their teeth. Those who could not walk at all were left to guard prisoners. The bravery of the overwhelming majority of men cannot be doubted. Apart from a single battalion commander in the 508th Parachute Infantry Regiment who spent the night hiding in a ditch, there were few cases of nervous collapse.

There appear to have been considerably more examples of battle shock on the German side. A soldier called Rainer Hartmetz went back to his company command post for more ammunition. There he found two men in deep shock: 'They couldn't talk. They were trembling. They tried to smoke, but they couldn't get the cigarette to their lips.' And the company commander, a captain who had apparently been brave on the eastern front, was lying in a foxhole drunk. Whenever anybody appeared with a message from the forward positions, he waved his pistol and muttered, 'I should execute every man who runs back.'

*

A mixed force of some seventy-five paratroopers attacked the village of Sainte-Marie-du-Mont. The officer who took command had no idea how many Germans were there, but their training paid off. With machine guns on the flanks to cover them, squads leapfrogged forward. A bazooka team rushed out into the main street and fired at the door of the church with an anti-tank round. A dozen German soldiers, with their leader waving an improvised white flag, appeared out through the smoke and dust with their hands in the air. The village was cleared in less than an hour. Most of the defenders had fled down the road towards Carentan.

Other groups moved to secure the causeways over the flooded areas behind Utah beach. A handful of paratroopers came across fifteen Germans transporting ammunition in three horse-drawn carts. They forced them to surrender and then made them march ahead down the road. A German speaker told them that if they came under fire they were not to move. A short time later a German machine gun opened up. The paratroopers took cover in the ditches. One of the Germans began to run, but was shot down immediately. 'We threw him in the cart,' one of the paratroopers recorded. 'He died later that morning. From then on, we had no problem with the prisoners remaining erect in the road, under any conditions.' This practice was, of course, a flagrant breach of the Geneva Convention.

As with the British airborne forces, one of the tasks of the paratroopers was to clear and secure the landing zone for the Waco gliders bringing in reinforcements and heavy equipment. But their landing near Sainte-Mère-Eglise was not to pass off so smoothly. 'After a short march,' wrote one paratrooper assigned to this duty, 'we arrived at the field and encountered a small group of Germans who were guarding it. They were quickly routed after a brief firefight. The field was nothing more than a large clearing surrounded by woods and several farmhouses. We were quickly assigned to squads and formed a perimeter defense around it. There was nothing more to do but wait.'

At the appointed moment signal lamps were switched on. 'We could hear the sounds of planes in the distance, then no sounds at all. This was followed by a series of swishing noises. Adding to the swelling crescendo of sounds were the tearing of branches and trees followed by loud crashes and intermittent screams.' The gliders were coming in rapidly, one after the other, from different directions. Many overshot the field and landed in the surrounding woods, while others crashed into nearby farmhouses and stone walls. The gliders had been loaded with Jeeps, anti-tank guns, and other weapons too large to drop by parachute. The cargo was strapped down and secured to plywood floors. Pilots and glider troops alike had only canvas and light wood to protect them.

In a moment, the field was complete chaos, with gliders ploughing in all directions. Equipment broke away and catapulted through the front of the plane when it hit the ground, often crushing the pilots. Bodies and bundles were scattered the length of the field. Some of the glider troopers were impaled by the splintering wood of the fragile machines. 'We immediately tried to aid the injured,' wrote one of the paratroopers who had prepared the landing zone, 'but knew we would first have to decide who could be helped and who could not. A makeshift aid station was set up and we began the grim process of separating the living from the dead. I saw one man with his legs and buttocks sticking out of the canvas fuselage of a glider. I tried to pull him out. He would not budge. When I looked inside the wreckage, I could see his upper torso had been crushed by a jeep.'

British gliders, which were larger, carried the field guns of the 320th Glider Field Artillery Battalion. They were even more dangerous than the Waco gliders. On a hard landing the front wheel structure would smash up through the plywood floor, causing considerable injury. A lot of the crashes were caused by confusion and too many planes coming in at the same time. A number were shot down by ground fire from nearby German positions. 'The troop-carrying gliders came like a swarm of ravens,' wrote the Obergefreiter from the 91st Luftlande-Division, 'and then the war really got started.' Among the casualties was Brigadier General Pratt, the assistant divisional commander of the 101st Airborne. He too was killed by a Jeep smashing through the front of the aircraft when it came to an abrupt halt on hitting a tree. Within twenty minutes, enough glider troops had landed to allow them to start caring for their own injured. Medics were working frantically, administering morphine, sulfa pills and whatever bandages they had.

A number of the gliders missed the landing zone altogether. One came down on a landmine and blew up. Some came in on the flooded areas, which at least softened the landing. Pilots had to remember to take off their heavy flak jackets before cutting their way out through the side panels. The water could be deep in places.

Glider infantrymen were extremely vulnerable at this moment if within range of German positions. 'Upon landing,' wrote one pilot, 'we discovered the source of the ground fire which nearly got me. It turned out to be a bunker containing about a dozen conscripted Polish soldiers with one German in charge. After the glider infantrymen from several gliders, including ours, directed a hail of rifle-fire at the bunker, the resistance ceased. There was silence in the bunker, and then a single shot. Then there were shouts and laughter, and these Poles emerged with their hands held high. They weren't about to fight the Americans so they simply shot the Kraut sergeant.'

Reactions among the French civilian population could also be unpredictable. While many made omelettes or crêpes for the paratroopers and offered them swigs of Calvados, others were frightened that this operation might just be a raid, and that the Germans would return afterwards to take revenge. But such fears did not stop farmers' wives from rushing out into the fields and grabbing as many parachutes as possible for their silk. Not surprisingly, the rather stolid Norman farmers, who seldom travelled far from their own villages, were confused by this extraordinary intrusion. A trooper in the 101st recounted that when they stopped to talk to three Frenchmen, one of the farmers said to his companion, pointing to the blackened face of a paratrooper, 'You've now seen an American negro.'

Despite the intensely vicious skirmishes, the fighting had hardly started. As dawn approached, the paratroopers knew that the Germans would launch counter-attacks in strength. Their prime concern was the possible failure of the main invasion. If the 4th Infantry Division did not secure Utah beach and break through across the causeways to join them, then they would be abandoned to their fate.

After seeing the 101st Airborne take off from Greenham Common, General Eisenhower had returned to his nickel-plated trailer at 01.15 hours. He had sat there in silence for a while smoking. His aide, Harry Butcher, did not know then that the supreme commander had already written a statement assuming all responsibility if Overlord turned out to be a disaster.

A few hours later, Air Chief Marshal Leigh-Mallory, the very man who had warned of catastrophe on the Cotentin airborne operation, telephoned through a preliminary report. Butcher immediately went to Eisenhower. Unable to sleep, the supreme commander was reading a western in bed and still smoking. Only twenty-one of the 850 transports carrying the American airborne troops had been destroyed. British losses were even lighter, with just eight missing out of around 400 aircraft. Leigh-Mallory was already composing an apology in writing which managed to be both grovelling and handsome at the same time: 'I am more thankful than I can say that my misgivings were unfounded . . . May I congratulate you on the wisdom of your choice.' But they all knew that the airborne operation had been just the first step. Everything depended upon the seaborne landings and the German response.

6

The Armada Crosses

As those who set forth in the convoys of warships and landing craft looked over Southampton Water on the evening of 5 June, the invasion fleet seemed to stretch to the horizon. Many wondered what the Germans would think when they caught sight of this armada, by far the largest fleet that had ever put to sea. Nearly 5,000 landing ships and assault craft were escorted by six battleships, four monitors, twenty-three cruisers, 104 destroyers and 152 escort vessels, as well as the 277 minesweepers clearing channels ahead. Most were British, American and Canadian, but there were also French, Polish, Dutch and Norwegian warships.

On the landing ship carrying Lord Lovat's commandos in the 1st Special Service Brigade, his personal piper, Bill Millin of the Cameron Highlanders, stood on the bow in battledress tunic and kilt, playing 'The Road to the Isles'. The sound carried across the water and the crews of other ships began to cheer. Captains of several warships had the same idea. Two Hunt-class destroyers played 'A-hunting We Will Go' at full blast over their tannoys and Free French destroyers responded with the 'Marseillaise'. Their sailors leaped about on deck, waving in joy at the prospect of a return to France after four years.

Convoys converged from all directions on the assembly area south of the Isle of Wight dubbed 'Piccadilly Circus'. Admiral Middleton, on board the battleship HMS *Ramillies*, which had sailed down the west coast, recorded that 'the traffic got thicker and thicker' after they rounded Land's End. In 'strong winds and lumpy seas', the *Ramillies* ploughed on through the slower convoys. He described it as 'an exciting sport, especially at night', but it must have been alarming for the crews of small ships which found the battleship bearing down on them.

The feelings of the 130,000 soldiers approaching the French coast by sea that night were turbulent. Field Marshal Lord Bramall, then a young lieutenant, described 'a mixture of excitement at being part of such a great enterprise and apprehension of somehow not coming up to expectations and doing what was expected of us'. This fear of failure seems to have been especially strong in young, unblooded subalterns. An old sweat had come up to him and said, 'Don't you worry, sir, we'll look after you.' But Bramall knew that in fact 'many of them had already had too much of a war'. His own regiment, the 60th Rifles, had fought throughout the desert campaign and the strain had told. At the back of many British and Canadian minds was also a fear that the whole operation might turn out to be a murderous fiasco like the raid on Dieppe two years before. Many wondered whether they would return. Some, just before leaving, had picked up a pebble from the beach 'as a last reminder' of their native land.

Almost everyone at every level was acutely conscious of taking part in a great historical event. Headquarters of the American V Corps heading for Omaha beach recorded in its war diary, 'The attempt to do what had been contemplated by all the great military leaders of modern European History – a cross channel invasion – was about to commence.'

The main question in most minds was whether the Germans already knew what was afoot and would be waiting for them. Planners of Operation Neptune, the cross-Channel phase of Overlord, had spent months considering possible threats to the invasion fleets: submarines, mines, E-boats, radar and the Luftwaffe. Every precaution was taken.

Mosquito squadrons were patrolling the French coast all night, ready to down any German aircraft which might sight the approaching fleets. Aircraft equipped for radio counter-measures were also aloft to jam the frequencies used by German night-fighters. Large-scale radar-jamming operations were carried out by British and American aircraft over the Channel. And for several weeks, rocket-firing Typhoons had attacked German radar sites all along the Channel coast from the Netherlands to Brittany.

In Operation Taxable, Lancaster bombers of 617 Squadron dropped 'window', aluminium strips to simulate on radar screens an invasion convoy approaching the coast at Cap d'Antifer, north-east of Le Havre. This was assisted by a naval deception using motor launches and torpedo boats towing reflector balloons, which would look like large ships on radar. A similar deception plan, Operation Glimmer, consisted of Stirling bombers dropping 'window' opposite Boulogne. Mines were also dropped round Cap d'Antifer.

One of Admiral Ramsay's greatest concerns was a mass attack on the invasion fleet by German U-boats from their bases in Brittany. Naval anti-submarine forces were deployed, but the main task of covering the south-western approaches fell to 19 Group of Coastal Command mainly flying B-24 Liberators and Sunderland flying boats. The group included one Czech, one Polish, one New Zealander, two Australian and three Canadian squadrons. Even the RAF's own 224 Squadron was a mixed bag of nationalities, with 137 Britons, forty-four Canadians, thirty-three Anzacs, two Americans, a Swiss, a Chilean, a South African and a Brazilian.

Their crews faced long missions day and night, constantly patrolling the western Channel in box patterns from southern Ireland down to the Brest peninsula. When their radar picked out any submarine on the surface, the aircraft would dive, the front gunner trying to kill and wound as many as possible on the conning tower to impede a crash dive, then the aimer would release the depth charges. In Operation Cork, aircraft from 19 Group attacked forty submarines. One of 224 Squadron's Liberators piloted by the twenty-one-year-old Canadian, Flying Officer Ken Moore, made naval history by sinking two U-boats within twenty-two minutes on the night of 7 June. To the embarrassment of Großadmiral Karl Dönitz and the high command of the Kriegsmarine, not a single U-boat penetrated the English Channel. Other Allied aircraft attacked German destroyers to prevent them from engaging the invasion fleet. Only fast German E-boats and later midget submarines managed to inflict any losses.

On board the landing ships, soldiers whiled away the time. Some tried to sleep, some attempted to learn a little French from their phrase books, some read their Bibles. Many attended improvised church services, finding comfort in religion. On the British ship *Princess Ingrid*, however, God had appeared to be in a less reassuring mood when the bosun piped 'Hands to church' the previous afternoon. 'Although attendance was entirely voluntary,' wrote a forward observer with the 50th Division, 'every soldier on board seemed to be at the service which was held on the upper boat deck. In the bows stood an Army chaplain behind a table covered by a table cloth on which stood a small silver cross. As we waited for the service to begin, the wind started to increase in vigor. A sudden gust flipped up the table cloth, the cross slipped to the deck and broke in two. Utter consternation in the congregation. What an omen! For the first time I realized what "fear of God" really was. All around, men were looking absolutely shattered.'

On American landing ships, dice and poker games began, with bets made mostly in the new Allied occupation currency which General de Gaulle so abhorred. Aboard the USS *Samuel Chase*, war correspondents, including the photographer Robert Capa and Don Whitehead, joined in enthusiastically. 'All are tense and all are pretending to be casual,' remarked one soldier. 'Bravado helps.'

In contrast to the riotous gambling parties, there were many who said little. 'Even though huddled together and cramped,' noted Lieutenant Gardner Botsford with the 1st Infantry Division, 'one felt very *private*.' A number had discussed 'who was going to make it once we landed and who wasn't'. 'My thoughts turned to home and family,' one soldier recounted, 'and I wondered how they would take the news of my death. I consoled myself with the fact that I was insured for the maximum amount of the GI insurance plan, and that my parents would at least have ten thousand dollars to compensate them for my death.'

The men of the 116th Infantry Regiment heading for Omaha found it hard to forget the address of their commanding officer, Colonel Charles D. Canham. He had predicted that two out of three of them would never return home. He finished off his warning in a pronounced southern drawl: 'Anyone who has *butterflize* in the *bellah*, speak up now.' A senior British officer on the *Empire Broadsword* provided an equally discouraging envoi when he finished his pep talk with the words: 'Don't worry if you do not survive the assault as we have plenty of back-up troops who will just go in over you.'

On the USS *Bayfield*, a young officer wrote in his diary of his sense of 'approaching a great abyss – not knowing whether we are sailing into one of the world's greatest military traps or whether we have caught the enemy completely off guard'. Another man observed that there was little hatred of the Germans, but everyone sensed that it would develop after the first casualties.

The captain of the USS *Shubrick* ordered his crew to shave, shower and dress in clean clothes to reduce the chance of infection if they were wounded. Soldiers of the 4th Infantry Division headed for Utah beach also shaved their heads, some leaving a V of hair, but more opted for the Mohican fashion like the paratroopers. The sobering thoughts prompted by these precautions were offset when ships' captains read Eisenhower's message to the invasion troops over the public address system: 'Soldiers, sailors and airmen of the Allied Expeditionary Force! You are about to embark upon the Great Crusade, towards which we have striven these many months. The eyes of the world are upon you. The hope and prayers of liberty-loving people everywhere march with you. In company with our brave allies and brothers in arms on the other fronts, you will bring about the destruction of the German war machine, the elimination of Nazi tyranny over the oppressed peoples of Europe, and security for ourselves in a free world.' Many admitted to getting 'goose bumps' on listening to the stirring words. Before midnight, US Navy ships went to 'general quarters' and the Royal Navy to 'action stations'.

On more than 100 airfields in England, bomber pilots from both the RAF and the USAAC were being roused from their beds for breakfast and an early briefing. Most guessed that something big was up, but they were not sure what. The pilots of the American 388th Bomber Group at Thetford were apparently unprepared for the 'dramatic announcement' of the briefing officer on the platform. 'As he drew back the white sheet that covered the operational map, he said, "Gentlemen, today the Allies invade the Continent". Pandemonium broke loose as the briefing room exploded with cheers and whistles and shouts.' He then went on to tell them that 'everything in the Eighth Air Force that could fly' would be taking off that morning. The bomb groups, once assembled in the air, would stretch for miles and miles as they streamed over towards their targets on the Normandy coast. Formation and fire discipline was vital. 'Any individual plane flying in the opposite direction, that is, against traffic, once we left the coast of England, would be shot down.'

The reaction at British briefings appears to have been more subdued, mainly out of awe at the magnitude of the whole operation. 'The preparations were staggering,' wrote Desmond Scott, a New Zealander who commanded a wing of four Typhoon squadrons. 'The airborne assaults, the quantity and variety of shipping, the number of army divisions, the tremendous weight of the air offensive. The scale and the precision of it all made our past efforts look insignificant. When the briefing was over there was no conversation, no laughter. No one lingered and we filed out as though we were leaving church. Expressions remained solemn. The task ahead outweighed all our previous experiences and sent a shiver down the spine.'

The RAF was putting up a maximum effort that night. Apart from the aircraft on deception and airborne missions, 1,000 bombers took off to attack ten coastal batteries during darkness with more than 5,000 tons of bombs. Spitfire squadrons scrambled to provide air cover over the beaches, along with American P-38 Lightnings. Their task was to prevent any Luftwaffe incursions over the invasion area, while the longer-range Mustangs would sweep deeper into France to attack any German fighters attempting to take off from airfields closer to Paris. American P-47 Thunderbolts and RAF Typhoon fighter-bombers, meanwhile, would hunt inland along the approach routes, ready to strafe any columns of German troops advancing to reinforce the coast.

The D-Day air offensive was another multinational operation. It included five New Zealander, seven Australian, twenty-eight Canadian, one Rhodesian, six French, fourteen Polish, three Czech, two Belgian, two Dutch and two Norwegian squadrons. Other units from these Allied countries were assigned to 'anti-Diver' missions, attacking the V-bomb launch sites in northern France.

The air chiefs' lingering fears about visibility were justified. The cloud ceiling was about 4,000 feet and their aircraft normally bombed from over 10,000 feet. The mission of the American heavy bombers attacking at dawn was twofold: to destroy their targets, but also to make bomb craters on the beaches 'to provide shelter for ground forces who followed us in'.

Soon after 01.00 hours, the assault troops were given breakfast. The US Navy was generous to a fault. On the *Samuel Chase*, the cooks gave them 'as much steak, pork, chicken, ice cream, and candy' as they could eat. Other ships provided 'wieners, beans, coffee and doughnuts'. Royal Navy ships offered little more than corned-beef sandwiches and a tot of rum from a great big earthenware jar, 'as if it were Nelson's navy', observed a major in the Green Howards. Many sailors volunteered their own rations for the soldiers going ashore. On the *Prince Henry*, taking the Canadian Scottish regiment, sailors made sure that the soldiers had an extra two hard-boiled eggs and a cheese sandwich to take with them. Wardroom staff, attending on Royal Navy officers, saw no reason why standards should slip at such a time. Ludovic Kennedy, on board the headquarters ship HMS *Largs*, was surprised by the impression that 'we might have been alongside the jetty in Portsmouth. The white tablecloth was laid, and then along came a steward saying "porridge or cereal this morning, Sir?".'

As soon as breakfast was over, soldiers in the first wave began to get their kit together. American troops cursed the fatigues with which they had been issued. They had been impregnated with a foul-smelling chemical which was supposed to counteract the effects of gas. American GIs called them 'skunk suits'. But the main problem was the weight of all their equipment and ammunition. They felt almost as ungainly as the paratroopers when they were called forward. The overloading of soldiers in the first wave to hit the beaches was to prove fatal for many. Sailors, who did not envy them their fate, joked away to keep their spirits up. They made ribald remarks about the condoms fastened round the muzzles of their rifles to keep them dry. One US Navy officer wrote of soldiers 'nervously adjusting their packs and puffing on cigarettes as if that would be their last'.

Having cleared channels to the landing beaches, the screen of mine-sweepers turned back, making the signal 'Good luck' to the destroyers which passed them to proceed towards their bombardment positions. It seemed miraculous that the fragile minesweepers, whose likely losses had so concerned Admiral Ramsay, should have achieved their task without a single casualty. An officer on the Hunt-class destroyer HMS *Eglinton* wrote, 'We crept still further in, amazed at the relative silence of the proceedings.' Ahead of them were two midget submarines, X-20 and X-23, ready to provide markers for the British beaches. The postponement of the invasion to 6 June had forced them to stay submerged for a long time in appallingly cramped conditions.

An officer of the US Rangers stayed on the bridge of HMS *Prince Baudouin*, a Belgian cross-Channel steamer. He had posted two of his snipers, one on each side. Their task was to watch for floating mines as they approached the French coast. Around 04.00 hours, the captain announced over the tannoy, 'Attention on deck! Attention on deck! British crews report to their assault boats.' The Ranger officer decided that he preferred the British 'Attention on deck!' to the US Navy's 'Now hear this!'

Inevitably, such a huge fleet could not remain unseen for long. At 02.15 hours, the headquarters of the German 352nd Infanterie-Division, which was spread along the coast, had received a call from the Seekommandant Normandie in Cherbourg stating that enemy ships had been sighted seven miles north of Grandcamp. But the confusion caused by all the paratroop drops seems to have distracted attention away from the main threat to the coast. The dropping of the exploding parachute dummies had even led to a whole regiment from the 352nd Infanterie-Division being sent off on a wild-goose chase. It was not until 05.20 hours that the garrison on the Pointe du Hoc reported the presence of twenty-nine ships, of which four were large, perhaps cruisers.

Task Force O off Omaha, which they had sighted, in fact included the US battleships *Texas* and *Nevada*, as well as the monitor HMS *Erebus*, four cruisers and twelve destroyers.* Two of the cruisers, the *Montcalm* and the *Georges Leygues*, formed part of the Forces Navales Françaises Libres. *Montcalm*, the flagship of Contre-amiral Jaujard, flew the largest tricolore battle ensign that anyone had ever seen. The

---

* One of these ships, the anti-aircraft cruiser HMS *Bellona*, remained ready to protect the capital ships from air attack, but it never fired its guns during the day.

only British influence on the bridges of French cruisers came in the form of duffel coats and steaming mugs of cocoa as their officers tried to study the shore through binoculars. For French sailors, as for French airmen, the idea of bombarding their own country was deeply disturbing, but they did not shrink from their task.*

The Eastern Task Force off the three British and Canadian beaches, Sword, Juno and Gold, consisted of the battleships *Ramillies* and *Warspite*, the monitor HMS *Roberts*, twelve cruisers, including the Polish warship *Dragon*,† and thirty-seven destroyers for close support. When they opened fire, 'the whole horizon appeared to be a solid mass of flames,' wrote Generalleutnant Reichert of the 711th Infanterie-Division, watching from the coast.

The Western Task Force lost a destroyer, the USS *Corry*, to a mine, and the Eastern Task Force suffered a similar loss, but to a torpedo attack from a German E-boat. At 05.37 hours, while the smaller vessels headed towards their bombarding positions, the Norwegian destroyer *Svenner* was hit amidships. A small flotilla from Le Havre had approached under cover of the smokescreen laid by Allied aircraft to the east of the fleet to shield it from the Le Havre batteries. The *Svenner* broke in half, its bow and stern halves lifting out of the water, forming a V, then she sank rapidly. Five other torpedoes ran on, narrowly missing the *Largs* and the *Slazak*, both of which managed to take avoiding action just in time. Two warships raced to rescue the crew from the water. HMS *Swift* alone took on sixty-seven survivors, but thirty-three men had been killed in the explosion. *Swift* herself was sunk by a mine in the same waters eighteen days later.

The landing ships also moved in to their offshore positions. A US Navy lieutenant who commanded an LST (landing ship tank) headed

---

* The French destroyer *La Combattante* assisted in the bombardment of Ouistreham in support of the French commando detachment. Other French warships involved in Operation Neptune also included frigates guarding convoys, *Aventure*, *Découverte*, *Escarmouche* and *Surprise*, while the corvettes *Aconit*, *Renoncule*, *Roselys* and *Estienne d'Orves* were on anti-submarine duty. Other old French ships, including the battleship *Courbet*, were used to create the breakwaters for the Mulberry harbour.

† In addition to the cruiser ORP *Dragon*, the Polish destroyers ORP *Krakowiak* and *Slazak* took part in the beach support operation, while the destroyers ORP *Blyskewica* and *Piorun* were employed as part of the covering force.

for Gold beach with British troops slipped below for a moment to look at the radar plot. 'The screen was literally filled all over with little pinpoints of light,' he wrote, 'ships everywhere 360 degrees from the centerpoint of where we were.' When he returned, the senior British officer on board put a hand on his shoulder just before he addressed the ship's company over the tannoy. 'Most of my men,' this colonel said, 'have seen the worst of desert warfare and a good many of them were in France and evacuated through Dunkirk. So I'd advise you to go easy, go quick, and don't get dramatic or emotional.' The young American followed his lead and 'made a very simple announcement'.

At 04.30 hours on the *Prince Baudouin*, the waiting soldiers heard the call: 'Rangers, man your boats!' On other landing ships there was a good deal of chaos getting the men into the landing craft. Some infantrymen were so scared of the sea that they had inflated their life jackets on board ship and then could not get through the hatches. As they lined up on deck, an officer in the 1st Division noticed that one man was not wearing his steel helmet. 'Get your damn helmet on,' he told him. But the soldier had won so much in a high card game that his helmet was a third full. He had no choice. 'The hell with it,' he said, and emptied it like a bucket on the deck. Coins rolled all over the place. Many soldiers had their field dressings taped to their helmet; others attached a pack of cigarettes wrapped in cellophane.

Those with heavy equipment, such as radios and flame-throwers which weighed 100 pounds, had great difficulty descending the scramble nets into the landing craft. It was a dangerous process in any case, with the small craft rising and falling and bouncing against the side of the ship. Several men broke ankles or legs when they mistimed their jump or were caught between the rail and the ship's side. It was easier for those lowered in landing craft from davits, but a battalion headquarters group of the 29th Infantry Division experienced an inauspicious start a little later when their assault craft was lowered from the British ship, HMS *Empire Javelin*. The davits jammed, leaving them for thirty minutes right under the ship's heads. 'During this half-hour,' Major Dallas recorded, 'the bowels of the ship's company made the most of an opportunity which Englishmen have sought since 1776.' Nobody inside the ship could hear their yells of protest. 'We cursed, we cried and we laughed, but it kept coming. When we started for shore, we were all covered with shit.'

The US Rangers, whose principal task was to scale the cliffs at Pointe du Hoc to the west of Omaha beach, were less heavily burdened. Most were armed with little more than a Thompson sub-machine gun, a .45 automatic and a quarter-pound of TNT attached to their helmet. The ship's captain bade them farewell over the public address system: 'Good hunting, Rangers!'

One engineer about to land on Utah with the 4th Infantry Division later described in a letter the lowering of the assault boats as 'the loneliest time' of your life. 'With a slap that jars everyone aboard, the craft hits the water. We chugged away and in a few seconds the large mother ship became just a darker blob in a world of darkness and then disappeared from view entirely.'

As the first flotillas of landing craft took up formation, two Ranger officers jumped on hearing a tremendous explosion. They looked around to see what had caused it. 'That, sirs', a British petty officer informed them pedantically, 'is the battleship *Texas*, opening the barrage on the Normandy coast.' The men on the landing craft felt the shock waves of the heavy shells from the battleships and cruisers firing over their heads. The other bombarding ships of the Western Task Force for the two American beaches of Utah and Omaha also opened up with their main armament. Unlike the Royal Navy, which fired their turrets in sequence, the American battleships *Texas*, *Arkansas* and *Nevada* fired broadsides with all their fourteen-inch guns at once. The sight made some observers think for a moment that the ship had blown up. Even at a distance, the concussion could be felt. 'The big guns,' noted Ludovic Kennedy, 'make your chest feel that somebody had put their arms around you and given you a good squeeze.' The passage of the heavy shells created a vacuum in their wake. 'It was a strange sight,' wrote a staff sergeant in the 1st Division, 'to see the water rise up and follow the shells in and then drop back into the sea.'

Many, however, were suffering dreadfully from seasickness as the flat-bottomed boats pitched and rolled in and out of the five-foot waves. 'The other landing-craft,' wrote a private, 'could be observed sinking and reappearing in their troughs.' As he looked around, he observed that 'the sky and the sea and the ships were all the colour of pewter'.

Soaked in spray, British and American soldiers alike regretted their 'hearty breakfast for the condemned man'. Many 'started throwing up chunks of corn beef' from their sandwiches. The damp seasickness bags which they rapidly filled fell apart and some resorted to vomiting into their helmets, then rinsing them out over the side when a wave came along. The Royal Navy forward observer attached to the 50th Division was faintly amused when a senior officer, sitting majestically in his Jeep, became furious after soldiers were sick over the windward side and the results were blown back over him. The effects of seasickness, however, were far from funny. Men were exhausted by the time they reached the beaches.

Others who had good reason to feel queasy from fear were the crews of tanks about to launch into the sea. These were specially adapted and waterproofed DD, or duplex-drive, Shermans, with propellers and inflatable canvas screens. The idea of this new invention was to surprise the Germans by landing tanks at the same time as the very first wave of infantry. Unrecognizable in the water, they would emerge to provide fire support against bunkers and gun emplacements. DD tanks had not been designed for sea conditions as rough as this and some soldiers, terrified by their training back in England with the Davis escape apparatus designed for submarines, had refused 'to be a bloody sailor in a bloody tank'. Only the commander, standing on the engine deck behind the turret, was above water level. The rest of the crew remained inside and the driver could see nothing but a grey-green murk through his periscope.

The original plan had been to launch them from tank landing craft at 8,000 yards from the shore, out of the range of German guns, but the sea was so rough that this was reduced. Major Julius Neave of the 13th/18th Hussars received instead the order: 'Floater, five thousand!' But the Sherwood Rangers Yeomanry launched their tanks much closer to the beaches. Even so, five tanks foundered out of their two swimming squadrons. Most crews managed to get out and were rescued, but a number of men drowned. The American tank battalions swimming in were to face even greater difficulties, partly because of the currents further west, but mainly because one of them received the order to launch much too far out.

*

The grey dawn began to reveal to the German defenders the huge fleet lying offshore. The headquarters of the 352nd Infanterie-Division began to receive frantic calls on the field telephones. At 05.37 hours the 726th Grenadier-Regiment reported, 'Off Asnelles [Gold beach] numerous landing craft with their bow towards the coast are disembarking. Naval units begin to deliver fire on beaches from their broadsides.' A few minutes later the divisional commander called his superior, General Marcks, the commander of LXXXIV Corps. He suggested that 'in the light of new developments' he should bring back the task force of three battalions commanded by Oberstleutnant Meyer which had been sent to investigate the '*Explosivpuppen*'. Marcks agreed. At 05.52 hours, the 352nd Infanterie-Division's artillery regiment reported, '60 to 80 fast landing craft approaching near Colleville [Omaha beach]. Naval units on high seas too far off for our own artillery.'

As soldiers on the landing craft started to see the coast more clearly, the last phase of the bombardment began with rocket ships. These were specially adapted tank landing craft, with 1,000 racks welded to the open deck. Each rack was armed with three-foot fused rockets with another 1,000 below deck in reserve. The rockets created a terrifying sound when fired in salvoes. One soldier in the Hampshires, approaching Gold beach, indicated the torrent of shells and rockets and shouted to a neighbour, 'Fancy having that lot on your breakfast plate.' One Royal Navy officer in command of a rocket ship had frozen in horrified disbelief when he had opened his secret orders. His allotted target at the mouth of the River Dives was the elegant seaside resort of Cabourg. As a Francophile and a devoted Proustian, he was appalled. Cabourg was Marcel Proust's 'Balbec', the setting for *A l'ombre des jeunes filles en fleurs*.

The fearsome sight of the rocket salvoes raised the spirits of soldiers going in, but those on assault craft approaching Omaha were unable to see that the rockets 'missed the target entirely. All the rounds fell short and in the water.'

Just as the first waves went in, General Eisenhower contemplated the good news from Leigh-Mallory about the far lighter losses than expected on the airborne operation. Ramsay's headquarters staff were also deeply relieved at the way the naval operation had gone. They could still hardly believe their luck, that the minesweeper force had escaped unscathed seemed like a miracle. Eisenhower wrote a quick report for General George C. Marshall back in Washington, then prepared a communiqué with his staff. The Germans, however, made the first announcement, but to the pleasant surprise of SHAEF headquarters it stated that the landings had taken place in the Pas-de-Calais. Plan Fortitude and the deception activities in the eastern Channel seemed to have worked.

It was six months to the day since Roosevelt had turned to Eisenhower in the staff car on Tunis airfield and said, 'Well, Ike, you are going to command Overlord.' But the 'longest day', as Rommel was to call it, had only just begun. Extremely worrying news soon came in from Eisenhower's great friend General Gerow, the commander of V Corps, which was assaulting Omaha beach.

7

Omaha

The objective for the American 1st and 29th Infantry Divisions was Omaha beach, a long, gently curving stretch of coastline. Approaching from the sea, the beach ended on the right with massive cliffs. Four miles further round to the west was the Pointe du Hoc promontory. This was where a battalion of Rangers had to scale a sheer cliff to silence a German battery.

The main strip of beach rose gently to a bank of shingle up against a low sea wall. Beyond the sea wall was a short stretch of marshy grassland and just above that stood a steep sandy bluff covered in seagrass. These bluffs, ranging from 100 to 150 feet in height, dominated the whole bay. Along this low escarpment from left to right lay three villages, Colleville-sur-Mer, Saint-Laurent-sur-Mer and Vierville-sur-Mer. The heights were accessible through five steeply rising valleys, or 'draws'. These offered the only places where vehicles could be driven off the beach, and the entrances to the openings were covered by German strongpoints and gun emplacements. This was why Captain Scott-Bowden had warned General Bradley that Omaha was a formidable position to attack.

General Leonard T. Gerow, the commander of V Corps, had wanted to begin the operation at low tide, under cover of darkness. Rommel had ordered the construction of the most fearsome system of underwater obstacles against landing craft, with mined stakes, hedgehogs made out of steel girders and rectangular constructions known as 'Belgian gates'. Gerow argued that combat engineers and naval demolition teams should have time to clear channels to the beach at low tide without being under

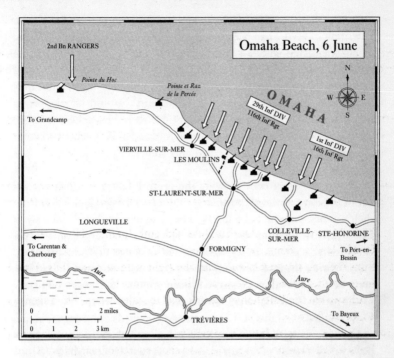

direct fire. He was supported by his most senior subordinates and Admiral John L. Hall, who commanded the task force. But Eisenhower, Montgomery and Bradley all insisted on an attack at 06.30 hours, half an hour after dawn. The assault would be preceded by a massive aerial and naval bombardment. The invasion commanders believed that this combination would achieve tactical surprise and overwhelm the defenders. In any case, they could not risk the assault on one beach starting several hours before the others.

Gerow's original plan was to assault Omaha with two divisions, the 1st Division on the left and the 29th Division on the right, under his command. Bradley, however, had much greater confidence in the 1st Division, the 'Big Red One', and in its outstanding commander, General Clarence R. Huebner. Their experience and combat effectiveness from opposed landings in the Mediterranean were unequalled. So Bradley made Huebner the commander and simply attached the 116th Regimental Combat Team from the 29th Division.

Bradley felt that 'Gee' Gerow, who had not yet commanded a large formation in battle, had been given command of the corps only because of his friendship with Eisenhower. Gerow, however, feared that the bombing and naval bombardment might not work, and he remained unconvinced even after Eisenhower assured him that 'the greatest fire-power ever assembled on the face of the earth' would be supporting him. Events were to prove Gerow right. He shared his concerns before the invasion with the military analyst Basil Liddell Hart 'about whether the importance of the unexpected was sufficiently considered in our planning'.

The first landing craft carrying the 116th Infantry Regiment of the 29th Division and the 16th Infantry of the 1st Division had set off from their mother ships at 05.20 hours. They had over an hour's journey in heavy seas to land on the beach at H-Hour. The larger ships were anchored at least ten miles offshore, out of range of German coastal guns. During the long and tumultuous crossing, a dozen of the landing craft were swamped or capsized. Fifteen minutes later, two companies of the 741st Tank Battalion, which were to support the 1st Infantry Division, launched their DD Shermans 5,000 yards out from the shore.

Captain Scott-Bowden, as Bradley had promised in January, was back in an assault pilotage role with Sergeant Ogden-Smith. Scott-Bowden's pilot boat had a crew of three, a US Navy lieutenant, a coxswain and a Mexican-American sailor manning a quadruple pom-pom gun. The lieutenant on Scott-Bowden's craft suddenly drew his attention to the fact that the LCTs had stopped at 5,000 yards out to launch their tanks. Scott-Bowden was horrified. 'It's far too rough,' he said. 'They should go right in.' He later described the decision to launch the 741st Tank Battalion's Shermans at that distance as 'absolutely insane'.

Twenty-seven of their tanks out of thirty-two foundered and sank. Only two reached the beach through the water. Three more could not be launched because the ramp jammed, so the landing craft took them all the way in to the beach. Altogether thirty-three tank crewmen drowned. The rest were rescued later. Those of the 743rd Tank Battalion who reached the shore owed their survival to the fact that both army and navy officers decided to take the rest of them all the way in. Major General Percy Hobart, the mastermind behind the amphibious tank, told Liddell Hart ten days later that 'the Americans bungled their use'. But whether the DD tank was the right answer to the problem of infantry support on the restricted space of Omaha remains a matter for debate.

When still some way offshore, Scott-Bowden and the crew became aware of the 329 heavy American bombers coming in from behind them. To their dismay they saw that the bombs were falling well beyond the top of the ridge. None hit the beach or the German positions guarding the beach exits. 'That's a fat lot of use,' Scott-Bowden said angrily to the lieutenant. 'All it's done is wake them up.' In the thirty minutes preceding H-Hour, the Liberators and Fortresses of the Eighth Air Force dropped 13,000 bombs, but none fell on Omaha beach.

The US Army Air Corps had made wildly optimistic claims about their 'precision bombing'. Unfortunately Montgomery, who grabbed at any opportunity which might save the lives of his ground troops, accepted the idea without question and abandoned the British doctrine of night landings. Both he and Bradley seemed oblivious to the fact that the heavy bombing formations remained incapable of dropping the majority of their load within a five-mile radius of their target.

The bomber formations appeared at 06.05 hours. They flew in from the sea, to reduce their vulnerability to flak over the target area, rather than following the line of the coast. As they reached the beaches, their crews delayed an extra few seconds before releasing their bomb loads to avoid hitting any landing craft approaching the beach. As a result all the ground commanders' over-optimistic hopes that the attack would destroy barbed-wire entanglements, minefields and some of the defensive positions were utterly dashed. 'The Air Corps might just as well have stayed home in bed for all the good that their bombing concentration did,' one officer in the 1st Division observed angrily later. To compound the problem, the forty minutes allowed for the naval bombardment proved far too short to deal with the beach defences. Montgomery and Bradley's plan had achieved neither local surprise nor overwhelming force.

The Germans had hardly needed waking up, even before the naval bombardment started at 05.50 hours. All the batteries along that stretch of the coast were already preparing for gunnery practice. The local Feldkommandantur had instructed the Préfet of Calvados to warn all fishing boats to avoid the area early on that morning of 6 June. The French inhabitants of Vierville-sur-Mer, however, had certainly been jolted awake by naval gunfire straddling the village. One shell destroyed the bakery, killing an employee and the baker's baby. But although a number of houses were destroyed – the mayor's wife was relieved to find her false teeth in the ruins of their house – casualties remained miraculously light. To their huge relief, the bombers flying inland missed Vierville entirely. Other villages and farms were not so fortunate.

In a bunker designated as Widerstandsnest 73 near the Vierville-sur-Mer exit, an Obergefreiter of the 716th Infanterie-Division was shaken by the sight which dawn revealed. 'The invasion fleet was like a gigantic town on the sea,' he wrote afterwards. And the naval bombardment was 'like an earthquake'. Another soldier manning a machine-gun position in a 'Tobrouk' near the Colleville exit had also been shaken at dawn by the sight of the fleet 'stretching in front of our coast as far as the eye could see'. During the thunder of the naval bombardment, he found himself praying desperately out loud. But as soon as the landing craft could be sighted approaching the beach, he heard cries of '*Sie kommen!*' from comrades in nearby positions and knew that they too had survived the shelling. He loaded his MG 42, the rapid-fire German machine gun, and waited.

The German ability to recover rapidly was impressive. At 06.26 hours, the 352nd Infanterie-Division's headquarters heard that, although the 'heavy bombardment' had buried some of the 716th Infanterie-Division's guns under rubble, 'three of them have been set free again and re-emplaced'. One of the myths of Omaha is that the German defenders possessed numerous 88 mm guns. In fact the 716th Infantry Division had just one in Widerstandnest 72 and another elsewhere on their sector. Most of the German artillery at Omaha consisted of far less accurate Czech 100 mm guns.

Another misunderstanding arose in post-war years over the forces that the Americans faced at Omaha. Allied intelligence had under-estimated German strength in the sector, but not to the degree which many historians have since implied. SHAEF intelligence had long known of the low-quality 716th Infanterie-Division, which included three *Ost* battalions made up from Red Army prisoners. This static defence formation was responsible for the forty miles of coast from the

Vire estuary to the River Orne. It is true that SHAEF headquarters had assumed unwisely that the more powerful 352nd Infanterie-Division would still be in the area of Saint-Lô, half a day's march to the south. Yet only two of its integral infantry battalions and a light-artillery battalion were positioned close to Omaha, certainly not the whole division, as many historical works have stated.

The rest of Generalmajor Dietrich Kraiss's division was spread in depth over 250 square miles between the mouth of the River Vire and Arromanches. If Oberstleutnant Meyer's battlegroup, representing nearly half of Kraiss's infantry strength, had not been sent off in the night to investigate the 'exploding puppets' dropped south of Carentan during Operation Titanic, then the German defence at Omaha might indeed have been formidable.* That diversion and Kraiss's ill-chosen deployment of his forces truly saved the Allies from disaster in this central sector of the whole invasion. None of this, of course, diminishes the still-formidable defensive positions which the 1st and 29th Divisions at Omaha were about to face.

The first wave of troops in their landing craft had been deeply impressed by the heavy guns of the battleships. Many compared the huge shells roaring over their heads to 'freight cars'. At a given moment, the landing craft, which had been circling offshore to await H-Hour, then headed in towards the beach. The absence of fire at that stage aroused hopes that the navy and air force had done their work as planned. The infantrymen were so tightly wedged that few could see much over the helmets in front of them and the tall landing ramp at the front. One or two, however, noticed dead fish floating on the water, killed by the rocket fire which had fallen short. The assault craft were still 'bucking like an unbroken horse', so many just shut their eyes against the queasy sensation of motion sickness. By then the landing craft 'reeked of vomit'.

Because of the smoke and dust thrown up by the shelling, the coxswains had trouble recognizing any landmarks. One landing craft

---

* Kampfgruppe Meyer, the 352nd's divisional reserve, consisted of the whole of the 915th Infanterie-Regiment as well as the 352nd Fusilierbataillon. Based south-east of Bayeux, Generalmajor Kraiss had ordered it at 03.15 hours towards the Vire estuary, as a result of a call five minutes before by LXXXIV Corps reporting a threat to Carentan.

with men of the 1st Division beached near Port-en-Bessin, over ten miles down the coast. Many of the landing craft were manned by Royal Navy crews. Several misleading accounts have suggested that they were young, inexperienced and frightened, and in a couple of cases were ordered at gunpoint to take the craft in closer. More reliable sources from eye-witnesses have in fact testified to their skill and courage. A number of them had worked with the Americans in amphibious operations in the Mediterranean.

'Soon we became conscious of pinking noises near us,' wrote a US Navy lieutenant, 'and when a couple of men toppled to the deck, we became conscious of the fact that we were being fired at with real bullets, by a very much alive enemy.' Some officers still hoped to inspire their soldiers. 'Make it look good, men,' one shouted as their landing craft jammed on a sandbar just short of the beach. 'This is the first time American troops have been here in 25 years!'

When the ramps were dropped, the German machine-gunners concentrated their fire on the opening. In all too many cases, the landing craft had come to a halt on a sandbar short of the beach. The water appeared shallow, but ahead there were deep runnels. The more experienced coxwains, both from the US Coast Guard and the Royal Navy, knew how to cut their engine at just the right moment and allow the back wash to carry the landing craft over a sandbar. Those that did managed to land right on the beach.

'As the ramp went down we were getting direct fire right into our craft,' wrote a soldier in the 116th on the western part of Omaha. 'My three squad leaders in front and others were hit. Some men climbed over the side. Two sailors got hit. I got off in water only ankle deep. I tried to run but the water suddenly was up to my hips. I crawled to hide behind the steel beach obstacle. Bullets hit off of it and through my pack missing me. Others hit more of my men.'

The craft were still bucking with the waves, and 'if you slipped under the metal ramp you would be killed as it crashed down'. In some places men leaped off and found the water over their heads. Many did not know how to swim at all. In desperation, the majority who fell into deep water dropped their weapons and wriggled out of their equipment to survive. Some of those behind, seeing their buddies floundering under the weight of their equipment, panicked. 'Many were hit in the water, good swimmers or not,' wrote the same soldier. 'Screams for help came from men hit and drowning under ponderous loads . . . There were dead men floating in the water and there were live men acting dead, letting the tide take them in.'

One soldier, who jumped into five feet of water, found that 'bullets were splashing right in front of my nose, on both sides and everywhere. Right then and there I thought of every sin I'd committed and never prayed so hard in my life.' A member of the 1st Battalion, 116th Infantry, watched the fate of a devout non-com, Sergeant 'Pilgrim' Robertson. He 'had a gaping wound in the upper right corner of his forehead. He was walking crazily in the water without his helmet. Then I saw him get down on his knees and start praying with his rosary beads. At this moment the Germans cut him in half with their deadly crossfire.'

The prospect of crossing the stretch of beach in front of them seemed impossible. Any idea of trying to run through the shallows, carrying heavy equipment and in sodden clothes and boots, seemed like a bad dream in which limbs felt leaden and numb. Overburdened soldiers stood little chance. One had 750 rounds of machine-gun ammunition as well as his own equipment. Not surprisingly, many men afterwards estimated that their casualties would have been halved if the first wave had attacked carrying less weight.

There were cries in all directions: 'I'm hit! I'm hit!' A soldier from the 1st Infantry Division who had jumped into water up to his neck waded in slowly. He felt so exhausted that he lay down in a foot of water to rest. 'Everything seemed like slow motion, the way the men moved under all their equipment. Overloaded we didn't have a chance. I was so tired I could hardly drag myself along.' Only nine men out of thirty-one in his platoon survived.

Machine-gun fire criss-crossed the beach and, 'as it hit the wet sand, it made a "sip sip" sound like someone sucking on their teeth'. One soldier saw a fellow GI running from right to left, trying to get across. An enemy gunner shot him as he stumbled. 'He screamed for a medic. An aid man moved quickly to help him and he was also shot. The medic lay next to the GI and both of them were screaming until they died a few minutes later.' Some continued to shelter behind the beach obstacles as bullets clanged off them, but others realized that their only hope was to make it to the shelter of the sea wall. Company A of the 116th Regiment, landing opposite the heavily defended Vierville draw at the western end of Omaha, suffered the worst casualties.

While the German machine-gunners turned the foreshore and surf into a killing zone, their artillery fired at the landing craft. As the V Corps report later acknowledged, the concave curve of the beach allowed the Germans both 'frontal and enfilade' fire. A staff sergeant in the 1st Division on the eastern side of Omaha saw a direct hit on the neighbouring assault boat. Several of the men on board were blown 'fifty or sixty feet in the air'. Few of the first tanks to land survived for long, but their burning hulls at least provided something to shelter behind.

Under heavy fire, men of the Navy combat demolition units started on their task. 'We went to work,' wrote one, 'laying plastic explosive bags on the various obstacles, running from one to the other and connecting the group with primacord, an instantly exploding fuse. Some of the obstacles had GIs sheltering behind them. We told them to move forward or they would be blown up with it. As the tide rose, we raced from one to another.' They cleared a 100-foot gap for the following landing craft to come in, but the rising tide forced them out of the water. 'Only three out of sixteen gaps were cleared that morning.' With water beginning to cover the mined obstacles, the coxswains in the succeeding waves had an even more dangerous task. General Gerow's worst fears had been proved right.

With many of their officers and non-coms among the first casualties, soldiers recovering from the shock of their reception realized that they had to get across the beach, if only to survive. A soldier from Minnesota in the 1st Division wrote home later describing how he had dashed forward in thirty-yard sprints: 'I've never in all my life prayed so much.' He looked back at the remnants of his squad. 'It was awful. People dying all over the place – the wounded unable to move and being drowned by the incoming tide and boats burning madly as succeeding waves tried to get in . . . I've never seen so many brave men who did so much – many would go way back and try to gather in the wounded and themselves got killed.' Those who had made it were not even able to help with covering fire. 'At least 80% of our weapons did not work because of sand and sea water.' In their desire to be able to fire back as soon as they landed, most soldiers had made the mistake of stripping the waterproof covering from their gun before reaching the shore. Almost all the radios failed to work as a result of sea water, and this contributed greatly to the chaos.

The better organized ran in squad columns to minimize their exposure to the arc of machine-gun fire. A lieutenant in the 121st Combat Engineer Battalion ran back with a sergeant to fetch a man with a shattered leg. It was difficult to drag him, so the sergeant picked him up. He was then mortally wounded and the lieutenant was hit in the shoulder. Other soldiers ran out and pulled them up to the relative shelter of the low sea wall. The first combat engineers to arrive had to act as infantry. They had lost almost all their demolition stores on landing. Enemy fire was far too intense to do anything until armoured bulldozers arrived.

As the follow-up wave approached, survivors from the first wave watched with a sick sensation from the bank of stones under the sea wall. 'Some men were crying, others were cursing,' recalled a young officer in the 116th Infantry. 'I felt more like a spectator than an actual participant in this operation.' He had a dry mouth from fear yet still wanted a cigarette. As the ramps dropped and the machine guns opened fire, wrote a sergeant from Wisconsin, 'men were tumbling just like corn cobs off of a conveyor belt'. A few men at the back of the craft tried to seek shelter and several in the water tried to climb back on to escape. Shells exploding in the water made 'large geysers'.

An officer in that second wave recorded that, at 300 yards off the beach, there was too much smoke to see what was happening, but they could hear all the firing. They too had assumed that Allied air power had done its job. 'Some of our boys said: "The 29th is on the ball: they are really going to town". But when they reached the beach, they realised that it was the Germans who were firing.'

Another officer in the 116th Infantry said that in some ways it felt like just one more landing exercise, 'another miserable two day job with a hot shower at the end'. Unsure whether they had come to the right beach, his company commander said to the naval officer of their landing craft, 'Take us on in, there's a fight there anyway.' But as they came closer, they recognized the draw by the hamlet of Les Moulins and knew they were hitting the right beach. 'We kept the men's heads down so that they would not see it and lose heart. The tanks were still at the water's edge, some still firing and some were on fire. Men from the assault companies were taking shelter around these tanks and in the water. The majority of these were wounded and many dead were floating in with the tide.'

Captain McGrath of the 116th Infantry, when he arrived at 07.45 hours, saw that the tide was coming in very fast and that the base of the sea wall was crowded with men. He and other officers attempted to get them moving. 'We talked to them and tried to get them to follow us. None of them however would come along. Many of them seemed to be paralyzed by fear.' A ranger saw a lieutenant from the 116th Infantry stand up and turn his back to the firing. He 'yelled down at the troops that were huddled up against the seawall, cowering, frightened, doing nothing and accomplishing nothing, "You guys think you're soldiers?!" He did everything he could, trying to organize the troops of the 116th [sheltering behind] the seawall, but to no avail.' An artillery officer, Captain Richard Bush, who had landed ahead of the 111th Field Artillery, described the soldiers he saw: 'They were beat up and shocked. Many of them had forgotten that they had firearms to use.' Battalion and company officers ordered their men to clean their weapons and told those without them to collect them from the dead. Some of the wounded were also put to work making weapons serviceable.

Captain Hall, an assistant surgeon with the 1st Division, observed the different reactions of men under extreme stress: 'I saw a man coming to the boat in a "Fugue" state – screaming and yelling, waving his arms. He had thrown all his equipment away . . . Many were hit in the water and the wounded were drowned by the rising tide. I yelled to some and urged them to crawl in and some of them did. Many did not seem to be functioning at all mentally. Just sitting and sprawling around. [They] could move their limbs, but would not answer or do anything. Several officers started to go and get them, but [more senior] officers yelled at them to come back.' A few of the wounded clasped on to the end of a beached landing craft as the water rose. 'They toppled off one by one and drowned. [I] saw one with a chest wound and water eventually covered his face . . . One boy waded casually up the sand – strolling. Some one yelled to him to get down as a burst of machinegun fire made a circle of sand bursts all around him, but he came in safely.' But a young engineer driven crazy by terror 'started running up and down the beach' until 'a bullet killed him'.

The doctor, who was wounded by the time he reached the bank of shingle, wrote that they 'lay on wet pebbles, shaking with cold and fear'. With astonished admiration, he watched one of his medical orderlies: 'Corporal A. E. Jones, who was always puny – 105 lbs and 5' 5" high – was the last one to expect anything spectacular of. In all this fire when one would hardly have a chance to go down the beach and back to live, he went out six times and brought men in.' On one occasion, he went to examine one of the wounded, came back to Captain Hall to describe the wound and asked what he should do.

The infantry were not the only ones to be traumatized. Landing on the Fox Green sector of the beach, one tank commander, a sergeant, suffered a nervous breakdown and ordered the crew to abandon the tank. A private took command. The sergeant disappeared into a fox-hole and cowered there the whole day. A major later asked the private why he had not shot him. Another Sherman, hit on landing and immobilized, continued to fire at targets until the rising tide forced the crew to abandon the tank. German artillery concentrated its fire on the Shermans, especially tanks with dozer blades. No fewer than twenty-one of the 743rd Tank Battalion's fifty-one Shermans were knocked out. Those tanks that ran out of ammunition moved up and down the beach in relays to give shelter to infantrymen crossing the killing ground. 'What saved us were the tanks,' a private in the 1st Division acknowledged.

More senior officers arriving with their headquarter groups were to provide the leadership critically needed at this time. Much of the chaos, as the V Corps report later put it, came from landing craft coming in at the wrong place and breaking up units as a result. Some sectors of the beach 'were crowded, others not occupied'. The command group of the 116th Infantry under Colonel Charles Canham and Brigadier General Norman D. Cota, the deputy commander of the 29th Division, swam and waded ashore on Dog White beach soon after 07.30 hours. They sheltered behind a tank, then ran to the sea wall.

Cota, who had shared Gerow's doubts about the excessive reliance on the bombardment, was well aware of the potential disaster they faced. He had seen waves swamp the DUKW amphibious trucks carrying the 105 mm howitzers of the 111th Field Artillery Battalion. Eleven out of thirteen foundered, most of them when still circling in the rendezvous area. The 1st Division's artillery had fared no better. Cannon Company of the 16th Infantry lost all six of its 105 mm howitzers in DUKWs. The 7th Field Artillery Battalion did not manage to land any guns, most of them also sunk in DUKWs.

Closer in, the obstacles had still not been cleared. The engineers of the 146th Special Underwater Demolition Battalion had been landed over a mile east of their appointed landing place, mainly because of the cross-current. Cota and Canham held a hurried discussion. Not only battalions, but even companies and platoons had been broken up in the landings. What they needed to do was to force the men, once they had cleaned their weapons, to start breaking through the wire and minefields on to the bluffs behind to attack the German positions.

At 08.00 hours, while Cota searched for a point to break through the wire towards the Les Moulins draw, a terrible scene took place. Just as a large landing craft, the LCIL 91, approached the beach, an artillery shell exploded on board, apparently hitting the fuel tank of a soldier carrying a flame-thrower. 'He was catapulted clear of the deck, completely clearing the starboard bulkhead, and plunging into the water. Burning fuel from the flame-thrower covered the foredeck and superstructure of the ship . . . The LCIL, which was the 116th's alternative headquarters, continued to burn for more than 18 hours, during which her stores of 20 mm ammunition for the Oerlikon anti-aircraft guns continually exploded.' Ten minutes later the LCIL 92 suffered a similar fate. Many badly burned engineers had to be dragged under heavy fire up to the lee of the sea wall.

Cota decided to carry out a reconnaissance to the right, while Canham went to the left to find an exit from the beach. Shortly afterwards, Canham was shot through the right wrist, but he just had it bandaged and carried on. One of his soldiers spotted 'Old Hatchetface' with his 'right arm in a sling and clutching a .45 Colt in his bony left hand'. Canham, 'tall and thin, with wire-rim glasses and a pencil thin mustache', was the southerner who had warned his men that two-thirds of them would be killed. He was shouting for officers to get their men off the beach. 'Get these men the hell off this beach! Go kill some goddamned Krauts!' A lieutenant colonel sheltering from the mortar barrage shouted back, 'Colonel, you'd better take cover or you're going to get killed!' 'Get your ass out of there!' Canham screamed back. 'And get these men off this goddamned beach.'

On the eastern side of Omaha, Colonel George Taylor, the commander of the 1st Division's 16th Infantry Regiment, acted in the same manner. The 1st Division's lack of armoured support after the disaster launching the 741st Tank Battalion too far out makes their achievement even more impressive. Captain Hall, the wounded doctor, watched as Taylor moved from one officer to another. 'We've got to get off the beach before they put the 88s on us,' he told them. 'If we've got to get killed, we might as well kill some Germans.' With Colonel Taylor was a British naval officer with a big beard who, 'sitting on his haunches and smoking, just looked bored'. Taylor also made the famous remark to his men: 'The only people on this beach are the dead and those that are going to die – now let's get the hell out of here!'

In fact the first breakthrough on Omaha had already taken place when part of the 2nd Battalion of the 16th Infantry landed between Saint-Laurent and Colleville. They crossed the beach with only two casualties. At 07.35 hours, the German 352nd Infanterie-Division had reported to General Marcks's headquarters, 'North-east of Colleville enemy forces of 100 to 200 men have penetrated our lines.' The Germans were clearly concerned. One battalion of 'Task Force Meyer' was told to deal with the breakthrough near Colleville, but according to its divisional headquarters, it could not be expected to arrive 'within one and a half hours'. In fact Allied air attacks prevented it from arriving until late afternoon.

Generalmajor Kraiss, however, soon saw that he could not divert any more forces to Omaha. As the American official history pointed out, the British 50th Division, which was landing on Gold beach some miles to the east, provided 'the gravest immediate threat for the Germans'. Even though their H-Hour had been fixed an hour later than the American assault, 'the British assault cracked through the coast defenses in some places during the first few hours'. The left flank of the 352nd Division was completely exposed and the bulk of Meyer's *Kampfgruppe* was redirected towards Crépon to face the British. Meyer himself was killed later that day fighting the British at Bazenville. Only ninety of his men out of nearly 3,000 rejoined the division.

While one company of the 2nd Rangers had landed with disastrous losses alongside Company A of the 116th at the western end of Omaha, the rest of the battalion had as its main objective the battery on the Pointe du Hoc, much further round the headland. But these Rangers too were to be plagued by bad luck.

Lieutenant Colonel James E. Rudder, the commanding officer of the 2nd Rangers, when heading for the Pointe du Hoc, realized that the Royal Navy coxswain was taking them in much too far to the east, almost on to Omaha beach. Half an hour was then lost beating against the current round to the Pointe du Hoc. Once the boats were in position under the cliff, rocket-fired grappling irons invented by British commando forces were used. Many fell short, partly because the ropes were heavy from sea water, but several took hold and the first men began to scale the cliff. Some London fire brigade ladders were also used. The Germans could not believe that the grappling irons were coming up from the landing craft under the cliff. The 352nd Infanterie-Division headquarters were informed that 'from warships on the high sea the enemy is firing special shells at the cliffs from which a rope ladder is falling out'.

The German garrison on the cliff top tried to fire down at their attackers and drop grenades on them, but close support from the destroyers USS *Satterlee* and HMS *Talybont* forced them to keep their heads down in the early stage. The *Satterlee* remained with the Rangers all day, ready to support them. The bravery and skill of the first Rangers climbing the cliff enabled them to seize a foothold at the top. They were soon reinforced by others. To their surprise, they found that there were no large guns mounted in the battery. The guns were lying a little way inland and were soon dealt with.

Rudder's radio operator tried to send off the success signal 'Praise the Lord', but the radios were not working due to sea water. In any case it was too late. The delay in getting to their objective meant that the 5th Battalion of the Rangers, which had been waiting offshore ready to come in to reinforce them, assumed that the attack had failed. As a result they resorted to their alternative plan and landed on Omaha in support of the 116th Infantry, where Brigadier General Cota soon sent them forward to attack the bluffs.

The battalion of the German 916th Grenadier-Regiment on the Pointe du Hoc took even longer to communicate. The 352nd Infanterie-Division heard only at 08.19 hours that the Rangers had succeeded in scaling the cliffs. The fighting was to continue all that day and most of the next, as the 916th counter-attacked Rudder's force again and again. The Rangers ran out of ammunition and armed themselves with German weapons taken from those they had killed. This was to prove a dangerous measure when a relief force eventually arrived.

Not far from the first large landing craft, which was still ablaze, Cota chose a section of the sea wall with a mound five yards beyond. He told a soldier with a Browning automatic rifle to keep German heads down on the bluff above. He then supervised the placing of Bangalore torpedoes under the barbed-wire entanglement. Cota had also told Lieutenant Colonel Max Snyder of the 5th Rangers to blow similar gaps, advance inland and then swing round westwards to attack the German fortifications at Pointe et Raz de la Percée.

With the wire blown and smoke from the seagrass set on fire by naval shells, Cota decided the time had come to make a rush across the stretch of marshy grassland which led to the base of the bluff. The first soldier through the wire, however, was hit by a burst of machine-gun fire. 'Medico!' he yelled. 'Medico I'm hit. Help me!' He moaned and cried for a few minutes. 'Finally he died after sobbing "Mama", several times.' The other men were so shaken that Cota led the way to get them moving. Soon a single file of riflemen from the 116th were through to the bluff and making their way to the top. The smoke from the burning grass was so thick that those who had not thrown away their gas masks put them on.

At 08.30 hours Cota returned to join Canham at his improvised command post under the bluff. Attention turned to an American soldier marching five German prisoners in front of him, their hands above their heads. But a burst of German machine-gun fire from above killed the first two prisoners. The others knelt pleading in the direction of the machine-gun nest not to fire at them, but another prisoner was hit full in the chest.

The Germans, suddenly realizing that most American soldiers were sheltering out of sight under the sea wall, began to use their mortars to target them. Exploding rounds sent pebbles flying like grapeshot. A mortar bomb landed by Canham's group, killing two men next to Cota and blasting his radio operator twenty feet up the hill. They moved the command post rapidly, but still had no contact with the 1st Division on the left. Communications had collapsed. To compound the problem of radios wrecked by sea water, German riflemen had targeted the heavily burdened signallers as they lumbered up the beach with their ninety-pound packs.

Lack of contact with the shore disturbed General Gerow as he waited for news on the bridge of the command ship, the USS *Ancon*, ten miles offshore. He was already alarmed by the sight of the choppy seas tossing landing craft around and sinking several of them. Confused reports were coming in, mainly from the crews of landing craft returning to collect their next load. At 09.15 hours he received a message from the control vessel off the Easy Red sector of Omaha. 'Boats and vehicles piled on beach. Troops dug in on beach. Enemy holds fire until craft beaches.' Gerow also heard that the engineers were unable to clear paths through the minefields and that 'enemy snipers and machineguns appear to concentrate fire on officers and non-commissioned officers'.

Gerow informed Bradley aboard the USS *Augusta* of the position. They were deeply worried. Bradley even began to consider the possibility of abandoning Omaha and switching following waves either to Utah beach or to the British sector. The situation on many parts of Omaha, especially round the Vierville exit, was indeed horrific. Yet despite the impression of universal chaos, some troops were landing almost unopposed and breaking through to the ridge with comparatively few casualties, as the 1st Division had already shown near Colleville. Even in the 29th Division's second wave, C Company of the 116th had experienced a relatively easy landing at 07.10 hours, 1,000 yards to the left of their objective. Having lost only twenty out of 194 men crossing to the sea wall, they too were helped when climbing the bluff by smoke from the seagrass set alight during the naval bombardment.

Major S. V. Bingham, the Texan commanding officer of the 2nd

Battalion, 116th Infantry, reported that from his batch of landing craft 'everyone got ashore safely' on Dog Red. One of his officers observed that 'enemy fire was not as bad as I had imagined it would be'. One of Bingham's companies which landed further down the beach, however, suffered heavily. Bingham led about fifty men across the sea wall and wire towards a three-storey house below the bluff surrounded by trenches. 'No one had weapons which would function,' he reported, so they dropped into the trenches to clean them. They cleared the house, even though the staircase had been destroyed by the shelling. Once it was secure, Bingham led his men straight up the bluff to their front. They pushed inland another 400 yards, then turned west towards Saint-Laurent-sur-Mer, but encountered a German strongpoint in a farmhouse on the edge of the village. Captain Cawthorn, in battalion headquarters, was shouting an order when a piece of shrapnel hit him. It entered one cheek and went out the other without damaging his jaws, purely because his mouth was open at the moment of impact. An officer who arrived soon afterwards noted that 'he spouted blood as he talked but did not seem to mind'.

The scenes of chaos on the beach and offshore had hardly improved by 09.30 hours. 'It was just one big mass of junk, of men and materials,' an officer reported later. There were burnt-out and still-burning vehicles, corpses, and discarded equipment scattered in all directions. Bodies continued to wash up, rolling like logs in the surf, parallel with the water's edge. One soldier said, 'They looked like Madame Tussaud's. Like wax. None of it seemed real.' The water's edge was blocked in places by damaged and destroyed landing craft. Further out, the chaos was even greater. Colonel Benjamin B. Talley, Gerow's assistant chief of staff, reported that the landing craft were milling around offshore like 'a stampeded herd of cattle'. The navy could not decide which craft should go in and which should be held back. But although many unsuitable vehicles had been landed, the tank reinforcements were at last starting to make a difference, even though a number of them threw a track when manoeuvring on the beach. Replacing the track in the open under mortar and machine-gun fire required extraordinary courage.

The course of the battle against the emplacements gradually turned against the defenders. In one case combat engineers managed to place a truck loaded with TNT beside a pillbox. 'They lit the fuse and blew it up. Going in, they found German bodies all untouched by the explosives, blood pouring out of their noses and mouths. They had been killed by concussion.' The most effective weapons were the guns of the destroyers, eight American and three British, which sailed in parallel to the shore and dangerously close to bombard German positions. Their guns became so hot that teams of sailors had to play hoses on them to cool them down. Many soldiers on Omaha later believed, with a good deal of truth, that these front-line destroyers saved the day. Most infantry officers afterwards felt that the naval support would have been much more effective if destroyers close in had targeted strongpoints from the start, rather than battleships firing blind from a great distance.

Tanks also played an important part. One German survivor of the 2nd Battalion of the 726th Grenadier Regiment remembered the farewell message from one bunker as Shermans attacked – '*Lebt wohl, Kameraden!*' – 'Farewell, comrades!' – then the connection was broken. He also claimed that 'the survivors of the "resistance nest" were brutally executed in defiance of the Geneva Convention, except for 66 prisoners, of whom half were wounded'.

Although there is no confirmation of this incident in any of the American accounts, there were cases of illegal killings, mainly prompted by the violence of repressed fear and a desire for revenge after so many fellow soldiers had been killed. 'There was a German, I don't know what his rank was, who was dying,' wrote a reporter with the *Baltimore Sun* who came across this scene late in the day. 'He was completely unconscious at the time but I remember a bunch of GIs standing around watching this guy and finally one guy just picked up his carbine and put a bullet in his head and said, "That'll take care of the bastard", and of course it did.'

Some American soldiers became convinced that Frenchmen and even women had taken part in the fighting on the German side. One of the rangers at Pointe du Hoc reported just after the battle, 'We came across civilians who were shooting at us with German rifles and serving as artillery observers. We shot them.' American soldiers also shot German prisoners of war who moved in an unexpected way, because in their nervous state they half expected some trick. But there were also moments of humanity. A signaller with the 5th Rangers who was ordered to take all the papers off prisoners separated the family photos they carried and slipped them back into their pockets. The German prisoners murmured, '*Danke schön*.' Another ranger, escorting prisoners of war back to the beach, stumbled and fell into a large shell hole. Three of the prisoners jumped in after him. His instinctive thought was that they were about to kill him. But they helped him up, dusted him down, picked up his rifle and returned it to him. Clearly they did not want to go back to their unit to continue fighting.

At 10.46 hours, Colonel Talley radioed back to the USS *Ancon*, 'Things look better.' But the landing system was still in a hopeless mess. There was a huge backlog, and often the wrong sort of vehicle or equipment arrived when far more necessary loads were held back. Many officers reported afterwards that until the beach was secured only infantry, tanks and armoured bulldozers should have gone in.

Brigadier General Cota was understandably impatient. He went up on to the bluff to see how the riflemen he had sent ahead were advancing. He found them on the flat stretch above, pinned down by machine-gun fire. Cota, with his .45 Colt automatic in his hand, moved among the men and said, 'OK, now let's see what you're made of.' He led them in a charge, having instructed them to fire on the move at hedgerows and houses. They reached a small road 300 yards inland. One officer came across 'a dead German, who had been killed with a half-smoked cigar still clutched in his teeth'. Almost every soldier seemed to remember the sight of their first dead German. A ranger was 'struck by the gray, waxy appearance' of the first one he saw. One soldier in the 1st Division even remembered the name of his first corpse: 'His helmet was off and I could see Schlitz printed [inside].'

The mixed group of men from the 29th Division and some of the 5th Ranger Battalion – with 'one helmetless Ranger proudly carrying a captured MG42' – worked their way westwards along both sides of this lane to Vierville-sur-Mer. There they found themselves above the Vierville exit. They were held up once more by machine-gun fire, so Cota again caught up with the front of the file and sent out a flanking group to force the Germans to withdraw.

It was around this time that C Company of the 116th appeared, having made their own way up after a comparatively easy landing thanks to the smoke from burning seagrass. As they turned along the escarpment towards Vierville, they met Brigadier General Cota, 'who was calmly twirling his pistol on his finger'. 'Where the hell have you been, boys?' he asked. They were ordered to join the advance to the west of Vierville.

Colonel Canham also appeared, having led another group up the bluff. Canham and Cota conferred and decided that these groups from the 1st Battalion of the 116th should push on with the Rangers to Pointe et Raz de la Percée. This mixed force became known as Cota's 'bastard brigade'. Men from the 116th said of the Rangers that 'individually they were the best fighting men we've ever worked with, but you couldn't get them together to work as a team'.

More and more groups of men made it up on to the bluff, but they had to contend with real as well as fake minefields. They tried to put their feet down on exactly the same places as the man in front. It concentrated the mind to encounter casualties along the way. A soldier in the 29th Division recorded how, as he climbed the hill through the seagrass, he came across a lieutenant with his leg blown off at the knee. 'Those jagged sharp bones sticking out from his knee were as white as could be. He said to me, "Soldier, be careful of these mines!"' This extraordinary sang-froid was not unique. A soldier in the 115th climbing the bluff came across a man lying down: 'As I drew near him I noticed why. He had stepped on a mine and it had blown off half of his right foot. He was arranged fairly comfortably and was smoking a cigarette. He warned almost everyone who came by about a mine that was embedded in the ground about a yard from him.'

Although Cota's 'bastard brigade' and other troops were inland by midday, no tanks had yet appeared up the Vierville draw from the beach. A US Navy warship had been bombarding the exit: 'Smoke, dust from the shattered concrete and the acrid tang of cordite from the exploded shells hung low.' Soon after 12.30 hours, when the shelling stopped, Cota led a patrol down the draw from above, taking the surrender of various dispirited Germans on the way. They also heard from French civilians in Vierville, whom they found drinking milk in a store, that 400 Germans had abandoned the village when the naval guns opened fire. At the bottom there was an anti tank wall and a small minefield. One of the German prisoners was forced to go through first, then everyone followed in his exact footsteps. Out on the promenade, they could see the bodies across the beach, the shot-up tanks and men still sheltering in the lee of seaside villas. Cota told their officers to get them moving and the engineers to blow the anti-tank wall.

Further down the beach he found more men cowering in the lee of the bluff. There was an abandoned tank with dozer blades nearby. He shouted at the soldiers that he had just come down the draw from above: 'There's nothing but a few riflemen on the cliff, and they're being cleaned up. Hasn't anyone got guts enough to drive it?' He finally found a man to take it down to the Vierville exit with its supply of urgently needed TNT. Cota carried on towards the next beach exit near Les Moulins, where his own headquarters staff had gathered. He issued a stream of orders.

Cota continued his eastward progression to find Brigadier General Weyman, the deputy commander of the 1st Division. Weyman cannot have looked very military, for he was huddled in a blanket after all his clothes had been soaked on landing. It was confirmed that the 116th would continue clearing the area to the west of Vierville towards Grandcamp and the 115th Regiment, the 29th Division's follow-up combat team, which had begun landing on Fox Green beach at 11.00 hours, would advance inland towards Longueville. Cota returned to his own command post. He was clearly not pleased by some of the sights: 'Some of the 6th Engineer Special Brigade troops who had dug themselves shallow trenches as protection from the artillery, were calmly eating K rations, while around them were bodies of the dead and dying.' But nobody could fault the medics, who were carrying back men wounded by anti-personnel mines on the bluff above.

The build-up of forces soon accelerated. By 12.30 hours the Americans had landed 18,772 men on Omaha. Half an hour later, a company from the 1st Division's 16th Infantry Regiment, supported by men from the 29th Division's 116th Infantry, began to attack Colleville-sur-Mer. A couple of accounts state that many of the Germans in Colleville were drunk, some finding it hilarious to shout orders in English. The

Americans fought their way in, but then found themselves bombarded by their own naval guns and suffered eight casualties. The cordite fumes became so intense that all of G Company, including the aid men attending the wounded, had to carry on in gas masks. Yellow signal flares failed to stop the fire, but eventually the warship ceased its bombardment. Not until some time afterwards did the headquarters of the German 352nd Infanterie-Division discover that the Americans had surrounded the village, having received a message that the 'wounded can no longer be sent back'.

The 1st Division's 18th Infantry came through, bypassing Colleville while the fighting there still continued. The 29th Division's 115th Infantry had also pushed inland and attacked Saint-Laurent. A short time later, at 14.15 hours, the first German prisoners from the 352nd Infanterie-Division were identified from their paybooks. 'I could not believe my eyes,' wrote the intelligence officer soon after the battle, shaken that they had not been informed of its presence.

Once most of the observed fire on the beach had been eliminated, the armoured bulldozers managed to clear patches to speed the arrival of more troops and vehicles. Burnt-out tanks were hauled or pushed aside; even damaged landing craft were towed out of the way. One engineer with the 1st Division said that the smell of burnt flesh made it hard to eat for several days afterwards. The demolition teams continued to blow the German beach obstacles. For items which might have been booby-trapped, they used grappling hooks on long ropes. Enemy artillery rounds were still coming in – the German artillery would continue to 'walk' its fire up and down the beach – but many of the explosions which looked like shellbursts were mines or obstacles being blown by clearance teams.

The medical teams were also working at frenetic speed. Many of the wounded, especially those suffering from shock, were doubly vulnerable to the cold. Soldiers were sent to salvage blankets from a wrecked landing craft and gather extra field dressings from the dead. Medics could often do little more than administer morphine and patch up flesh wounds, such as those in the buttocks caused by mortar fragments. Some of the wounded were beyond hope. 'I saw one young soldier, pale, crying and in obvious pain,' wrote a captain in the 60th Medical Battalion, 'with his intestines out under his uniform. There was nothing I could do except inject morphine and comfort him. He soon died.'

Doctors treated those suffering from combat trauma with Nembutal to knock them out. Plasma bags on drips were attached to those who had lost a lot of blood, a condition indicated by their hands going blue. Yet even with blankets and plasma, many were to die from shock and exposure during the night. Casualties of all sorts could now be sent back on empty landing craft to the ships, but the wounded on the more deserted stretches had a long time to wait. In the chaos of landing some sectors still lacked medical teams. The 1st Division's medical battalion had been so hard hit on landing that it had to concentrate on its own casualties first. Soldiers wounded in the minefields up on the bluffs had the longest wait of all, since engineers had to clear paths to get to them. Many lay there all through the night until they could be reached in daylight.

The wounded were taken out to the ships such as the *Samuel Chase* and the *Bayfield* or to LSTs, which had been prepared as temporary hospital ships for the return journey. From the landing craft, they were lifted by net litters on derricks. On board there was 'organized confusion' as doctors carried out triage. One wounded soldier suddenly realized that his right leg was missing. The aid men had to hold him down as he yelled, 'What am I going to do? My leg! I'm a farmer.'

Those who were going to die received morphine and plasma, and were then 'left alone to whatever fate would befall them'. Sailors carried the dead on litters to the ship's refrigerator, a solution which was not popular with the cooks. They were even more appalled when one of the surgeons began carrying out operations in their galley. The *Bayfield* had only one experienced army surgeon on board, assisted by navy surgeons unused to the work. Most of the medical orderlies had also never seen battle wounds before. One of them, faced with a ranger who had received terrible head wounds, did not realize that the man's brains were held in only by his helmet. When he removed the helmet, the brains started to fall out. He 'tried to push the brain back into the skull with very little success'. A doctor tried to reassure the horrified orderly that the man would have died anyway.

At 17.21 hours, Colonel Talley radioed the USS *Ancon* to say that the beach would permit 'wheeled and tracked vehicular traffic' over most of the area below the high-water mark. The relief for General Gerow was considerable. Gerow, determined to establish his corps headquarters on French soil before nightfall, went ashore. He crossed the beach in an armoured bulldozer sent by Colonel Talley to fetch him, and reached the corps command post at 20.30 hours. It was still within 500 yards of the front line.

Major General Charles H. Gerhardt, the diminutive martinet who commanded the 29th Division, had landed a little earlier. He set up his own headquarters, sitting on a box of C-Rations as he examined the map. Both generals had a great deal to reflect upon: their next moves and the casualties of that day. More than 2,000 men were reported killed, missing or wounded, and these figures are still not clear.* During his interviews with survivors, the official historian, Forrest C. Pogue, found they 'assumed that everyone else had been killed or captured. This kind of fog of war was responsible for terribly exaggerated casualty estimates, although those at their worst were still well under the pre-D-Day fears.' The only certain fact is that 3,000 French civilians died in the first twenty-four hours of the invasion, double the total number of American dead.

Even though Allied casualties on D-Day were far lighter than the planners' estimates, that did not in any way reduce the shock of the first wave's slaughter at Omaha. Company A of the 116th Infantry Regiment, a National Guard outfit, became a symbol of the sacrifice, albeit an unrepresentative one. One of the survivors of that company met Brigadier General Cota the next morning. Cota asked him what unit he was from. When he told him, Cota just shook his head in sadness. 'He knew better than I that Company A was practically . . . well, it was out of action.' Around 100 men out of 215 had been killed and many more wounded.†

Omaha became an American legend, but a crueller truth lay ahead

* V Corps gave the figures later of 1,190 casualties for the 1st Division, 743 for the 29th Division and 441 for corps troops. German losses amounted to around 1,200. The total number of American dead during the first twenty-four hours was 1,465.

† A myth has arisen that most of the dead in Company A came from the town of Bedford, Virginia. In fact only six came from Bedford, and there were just twenty-four from the whole of Bedford County serving in the company on 6 June.

in the fighting to come. The average losses per division on both sides in Normandy were to exceed those for Soviet and German divisions during an equivalent period on the eastern front.*

* German losses on the eastern front averaged just under 1,000 men per division per month. In Normandy they averaged 2,300 per division per month. The calculation of comparable figures for the Red Army is much more complicated, but it would appear to be well under 1,500 per division per month. Allied total losses in Normandy were close to an average of 2,000 per division per month.

8

Utah and the Airborne

The dawn of D-Day on the Cotentin peninsula brought only a little clarity to the scattered American airborne troops. The tall hedgerows of the Normandy fields made it hard to orientate themselves. For many, daylight meant that they could at last light a cigarette without giving their position away. Finding containers and equipment bundles also became easier. A French boy with a horse and cart helped an airborne staff officer gather them up. German soldiers also profited as a result of the manna from heaven which had rained down in containers during the night. They helped themselves to American K-Rations and cigarettes.

Those paratroopers who had survived the drop began to coalesce into mixed groups and attack their objectives, although they had no radio contact with their divisional headquarters. They were, however, aided by an even greater German confusion. The cutting of telephone wires by paratroopers and the Resistance had proved an invaluable tactic. German forces on the peninsula were also uncertain in their reactions. They had no idea where the main American paratroop forces were concentrated and they lacked leadership. Generalleutnant Falley of the 91st Luftlande-Division was dead from the ambush near his headquarters, and Generalleutnant Karl-Wilhelm Graf von Schlieben, the commander of the 709th Infanterie-Division, was still absent.

Schlieben had been asleep in a hotel in Rennes prior to the Seventh Army map exercise planned for that day. The telephone rang at 06.30 hours, waking him. 'The war game has been cancelled,' a staff officer informed him. 'You are requested to return to your unit.' Schlieben, realizing that the Allies had stolen a march on them, told his driver to take the road up the west coast of the peninsula. They drove as fast as possible and turned inland, stopping only to collect a wounded German soldier spotted in a hedgerow by the side of the road. Schlieben could hear heavy guns firing to the east.

When the curfew expired at 06.00 hours, French civilians emerged from their houses to find out what had been happening during the night. In Montebourg, north of the main drop zones, they went to the central square, where they saw 'American prisoners with blackened faces' guarded by German soldiers. The Americans winked at the French and made V for Victory signs. When the Ortskommandant appeared, the mayor could not resist asking him if he needed any workers that day for erecting the 'Rommel asparagus' poles against glider landings. 'It is not necessary,' he replied stiffly. The Germans, they noticed, were very nervous.

The 82nd Airborne Division had taken its chief objective of Sainte-Mère-Eglise, but it had landed close to the main units of the 91st Luftlande-Division and would suffer numerous counter-attacks. Its other task was to secure the line of the River Merderet in preparation for VII Corps to advance right across the peninsula. This proved hard, since its units were so scattered. Many small groups of paratroopers made their way to the La Fière crossing by following the railway embankment. Brigadier General James Gavin, the second in command of the division, took a large group further south to help the attack on Chef du Pont and the bridge there.

When a small bridgehead had been taken across the Merderet at Chef du Pont, the regimental surgeon of the 508th Parachute Infantry Regiment had to operate in the field with the barest equipment. All their medical bundles had been lost in the drop. 'A soldier had his leg blown off right by the knee and the only thing left attached was his patellar tendon. And I had him down there in this ditch and I said: "Son, I'm gonna have to cut the rest of your leg off and you're back to bullet-biting time because I don't have anything to use for an anesthetic." And he said: "Go ahead, Doc." I cut the patellar tendon and he didn't even whimper.'

Another medical officer in the same regiment, who had found himself having to hold up plasma bags while being shot at, was soon captured by the Germans. They took him to the 91st Luftlande-Division's Feldlazarett, or field hospital, set up in the Château de Hauteville, five miles west of Sainte-Mère-Eglise. The German medics treated him as a friend, and he went about his work tending wounded American paratroopers assisted by a German sergeant who was a Catholic priest in civilian life.

Although the Americans were superior in numbers, the capture of the bridge and causeway at La Fière proved very difficult. It was later taken and then lost again. The Germans had sited machine guns on the far side with excellent fields of fire. The river made it impossible to outflank them. The French family who had saved so many paratroopers with their rowing boat had told an airborne officer about a nearby ford across the Merderet, yet for some reason he never passed on the information. The ford was only put to good use later after it was discovered accidentally by another soldier.

Other widely scattered groups had dropped in the marshy area on the west side of the Merderet. They found the hedgerows thick with bramble and thorn, and small German detachments ensconced in Norman farms whose solid stone walls provided natural defensive positions. Once again, the lack of communication with the main American forces on the east of the river made it impossible to coordinate their efforts.

While the 82nd was responsible for holding the western flank, the 101st Airborne Division's task was to assist the landings at Utah on the east coast of the peninsula. This included suppressing German batteries and seizing causeways across the marshes just inland from the beach. Lieutenant Colonel Cole's group occupied the German battery position at Saint-Martin-de-Varreville, which they found abandoned. They then seized the western end of the causeway leading from Utah beach across the flooded area. Other groups, meanwhile, protected the northern flank by aggressive action, which convinced the isolated German defenders that they were heavily outnumbered. Attempts to seize the southern causeways from the beach to Saine-Marie-du-Mont and Pouppeville were, however, delayed by well-sited German machine guns.

Apart from securing the causeways ready for the 4th Infantry Division's advance from Utah beach, the other task of the 101st Airborne was to seize the lock on the River Douve at La Barquette and also take two bridges north-east of Carentan. This would later allow the American forces on the Cotentin and the 29th Division advancing from Omaha to link up. The biggest threat in the area was the unexpectedly large German force in Saint-Côme-du-Mont on the Carentan–Cherbourg road.

Major von der Heydte, a veteran of the German airborne invasion of Crete three years before, had pushed forward two battalions of his 6th Paratroop Regiment from Carentan. His men, among the most experienced of the Luftwaffe's Paratroop Army, were to prove formidable opponents. When dawn broke, they gazed in amazement at all the different coloured parachutes lying in the fields. They wondered at first whether they represented different units, but soon got out their knives to cut themselves silk scarves. Heydte himself went forward to Saint-Côme-du-Mont later in the morning and climbed the church tower. From there he could see the huge armada of ships lying offshore.

For American paratroopers, the sound of the naval bombardment of Utah beach provided the first reassurance that the invasion was proceeding according to plan. But with the loss of so much equipment and ammunition in the drop, and the increasing concentration of German forces against them, everything depended on how quickly the 4th Infantry Division would arrive.

The landings at Utah proved the most successful of all, largely due to good fortune. The naval bombardment force, commanded by Rear Admiral Alan G. Kirk in the heavy cruiser USS *Augusta*, was no less powerful than that at Omaha. Kirk had the battleship USS *Nevada*, the monitor HMS *Erebus*, the heavy cruisers USS *Quincy* and *Tuscaloosa*, the light cruiser HMS *Black Prince* and, for close-in support, the light cruiser HMS *Enterprise* with a dozen destroyers. As soon as the naval bombardment started, French civilians fled from their villages out into the countryside and awaited events in relative safety.

The gunfire, while failing to hit many of the German positions, cleared large parts of the minefields on which the enemy had relied. Meanwhile the medium bombers of the Ninth Air Force dropped their loads much closer to the target area at Utah than the Eighth had at Omaha, but even so the effect on German positions was negligible. The rocket ships were also inaccurate, but none of this seemed to matter.

Utah was the responsibility of VII Corps, commanded by Major

General J. Lawton Collins, a dynamic leader known to his men as 'Lightning Joe'. The assault was led by the 8th Infantry Regiment in Major General Raymond O. Barton's 4th Infantry Division. Luck certainly played a large part when the current pushed the landing craft towards the Vire estuary. Colonel Van Fleet's 8th Infantry came ashore 2,000 yards further south than planned, but on a stretch of beach which turned out to be far more lightly defended than where they were supposed to have landed.

The calmer waters meant also that none of the DD tanks were lost, except for four destroyed on a landing craft which struck a mine. One of the landing craft crewmen described them as 'odd-shaped sea-monsters depending upon huge, doughnut-like, canvas balloons for flotation, wallowing through heavy waves, and struggling to keep in formation as they followed us'. In fact the light resistance presented few targets for the tanks to attack. Even the artillery was landed without loss. Altogether, the 4th Infantry Division's 200 casualties on D-Day were far fewer than the 700 losses caused by an E-boat attack during Exercise Tiger off Slapton Sands in Devon that April.

The first senior officer ashore at Utah was the irrepressible Brigadier General Teddy Roosevelt Jr, son of a former president and a cousin of Franklin D. Roosevelt. Teddy Jr had named his Jeep 'Rough Rider' in his father's honour. On seeing that the 8th Infantry Regiment had landed in the wrong place, Roosevelt rightly decided that it would be stupid to try to redeploy. 'We'll start the war from here!' he announced.

Roosevelt, who stalked around fearlessly under fire with his walking stick, was loved by GIs for his constant jokes with them and his extraordinary courage. Many suspected that he secretly hoped to die in battle. A major who landed without his vehicle made for the beach, where he first sought cover and then 'met General Roosevelt, walking the beach wall oblivious to the fire'. 'General Teddy' was also known for preferring to wear the olive drab knitted cap and not a helmet, a habit for which he was often upbraided by more senior generals because it set a bad example.

The assault on Utah beach against isolated German riflemen and machine-gunners was 'more like guerrilla fighting', as an officer in the 4th Division put it. One young officer was amused when a colonel came over in the midst of heavy fire and said, 'Captain, how in the hell do you load this rifle?' In contrast to Omaha, the Germans had no 'observed fire'. Instead they just 'walked their fire up and down the beach, always maintaining a different pattern'. But the comparatively easy fighting did not mean that men were not ready for dirty tricks by the enemy. A soldier in the 8th Infantry Regiment recorded that their officers had ordered them to shoot any SS soldiers they captured on the grounds that 'they could not be trusted' and might be concealing a bomb or grenade. Another stated that 'during the briefings, we were informed that all civilians found along the beach area and for a certain distance inland were to be dealt with as enemy soldiers, shot or rounded up'.

The beaches were cleared of Germans in less than an hour, thus creating something of an anticlimax. 'There was little of the expected excitement and not much confusion.' Instead of opening fifty-yard channels through the obstacles, the engineers began to clear the whole beach at once. The contrast with Omaha could not have been greater.

The only factor the two beaches had in common was Allied air supremacy. The presence of Lightnings, Mustangs and Spitfires almost constantly overhead greatly boosted morale, but they found no Luftwaffe to attack. Only two German aircraft reached the beaches during daylight on D-Day, largely because of the huge Allied fighter umbrella inland, ready to attack any plane which took off. The wide-ranging sweeps inland of American Thunderbolt squadrons to attack German reinforcements and armour offered their pilots disappointingly few targets in the western sectors that first day.

Frustration and the inevitable tension of the historic day produced a trigger-happy mood. Allied aircraft shot up French *camionettes* run on charcoal. At Le Molay, due south of Omaha, US fighters riddled the water tower with cannon fire, perhaps thinking that it was an observation post. It became a huge shower, spraying water in all directions, until emptied of its 400,000 litres. Troops on the ground and at sea were also trigger-happy. A number of Allied aircraft were shot down by their own side, and on the following day an American pilot, shot down over Utah beach, was machine-gunned as he parachuted down by an over-excited combat engineer.

Beyond the western side of the Cotentin peninsula, an umbrella of Spitfires patrolled at 26,000 feet and P-47 Thunderbolts at 14,000 feet. Their task was to protect the anti-submarine patrols on the south-western approaches to the Channel from German fighters, thought to be based on the Brest peninsula. They did not know that the airfields had been destroyed by the Luftwaffe itself, fearing an invasion there. In any case, the RAF and US pilots were furious to be given this fruitless job, instead of what they had imagined to be direct combat over the beaches.

Another less than active duty was the dropping by medium bombers of leaflets to the French, to advise them to abandon towns and seek refuge in the countryside. Warnings had also been issued by the BBC, but many radios had been confiscated and most areas were without electricity.

The two leading battalions from the 4th Infantry Division began their advance inland as soon as the beach was secured. A Sherman from the 70th Tank Battalion fired at one strongpoint guarding the causeway and the Germans inside immediately came out to surrender. The company commander jumped down from his tank to approach them, but they began yelling at him. It took him a moment to work out that they were shouting, '*Achtung! Minen!*' at him. He retreated to the safety of his vehicle and called up the engineers. But he was to have less luck later in the day. After his tank company advanced south-west to Pouppeville, their attention was attracted by some wounded paratroopers from the 101st calling for help. The commander climbed down, taking their first-aid kit, but on the way over to them he stepped on an anti-personnel mine. He shouted to his crew not to come anywhere near, but they threw him a rope and towed him out with the tank. The remains of his left foot were amputated later.

Inevitably, civilians and their property suffered during the advance inland. A company of the 20th Field Artillery with the 4th Division came under fire from some farm buildings. The widow who lived in the farm told the Americans that the 'sniper' was a very young soldier in her barn who was drunk. The artillerymen turned one of their guns on the barn. The first round set it on fire and the young German inside shot himself.

One soldier's account was particularly revealing. 'French people, of course, lived there,' he recounted. 'Us being there was as big a surprise as anything in the world to those people. They didn't really know how to take us, I guess. One man started to run, and we hollered for him to halt. He didn't halt, and one of our men shot him and left him there. I remember one house a couple of us went into and hollered, trying to tell them to come out. We didn't know any French. Nobody came out. We took a rifle butt and knocked the door in. I threw a grenade in the door, stepped back and waited until it exploded. Then we went on in. There was a man, three or four women and two or three kids in that room. The only damage that was done was the old man had a cut on his cheek. It was just a piece of luck that they didn't all get killed.' He then went on to tell how they captured a small hill with the support of tank fire. 'It was pretty rough. And those guys [the Germans] were baffled and they were crazy. There were quite a few of them still in their foxholes. Then I saw quite a few of them shot right in the foxholes. We didn't take prisoners and there was nothing to do but kill them, and we did, and I had never shot one like that. Even our lieutenant did and some of the Non Coms.'

The French had to cope as best they could in the circumstances. A couple of American officers 'came across a little French farm cottage where a good sized French woman was dragging a dead German soldier out of her house. With one heave, she flung him across the road up next to the hedgerow. She waved to us indicating that she was glad to see us, but she went back into the house, I suppose to clean up the mess that had been made.' On the road to Sainte-Mère-Eglise another American saw 'a German soldier lying dead, stripped to the waist and shaving cream on his face'. He had been in the middle of a shave when paratroopers stormed the building and was shot down as he ran out. At the back, there was a field kitchen, or *Gulaschkanone* as the Germans called them, with its draught horses dead still in their traces.

The most extraordinary encounter of the 4th Division's advance to relieve the paratroopers was American infantry fighting a German cavalry unit made up of former Red Army prisoners. The horsemen had forced their mounts to the ground to take up firing positions behind them, a classic cavalry tactic. 'We had to kill most of the horses,' wrote a lieutenant unused to such warfare, 'because the Germans were using them for shelter.'

Other surprises came when talking to prisoners. One German captive spoke to an American soldier of German origin.

'There isn't much left of New York any more, is there?'

'What do you mean?'

'Well,' he said, 'you know it's been bombed by the Luftwaffe.'

Americans were to find that many German soldiers had swallowed the most outrageous lies of Nazi propaganda without question.

The paratroopers had managed to hold off German counter-attacks against their Chef du Pont bridgehead over the Merderet. They knocked out two light French tanks from the 100th Panzer-Battalion with bazookas. Elsewhere, particularly round Sainte-Mère-Eglise, they stalked them with Gammon grenades, which they found just as effective.

Generalleutnant von Schlieben, the commander of the 709th Infanterie-Division, had hoped that the sound of tanks would panic the Americans. He ordered this attached panzer battalion of Renault tanks, captured from the French in 1940, to drive around, but when they came to close quarters, the paratroopers found it comparatively easy to knock out these obsolete vehicles with their Gammon grenades. Yet the airborne commanders remained extremely concerned. Their men were low on ammunition and they had no idea how the seaborne invasion was progressing. French civilians were afraid that the landings might fail, like the raid on Dieppe in 1942, and that the Germans would return to take revenge on anyone who had assisted the Americans. Rumours even spread that the invasion had failed, so when the Shermans and leading elements of the 4th Infantry Division made contact with the 101st, the relief was considerable. The advance over the narrow causeways had been slow and came to a halt before nightfall, but at least the right flank between Sainte-Mère-Eglise and the marshes by the sea had been secured by the follow-up regiments of the 4th Division.

The area near Les Forges, south of Sainte-Mère-Eglise, where part of the 325th Glider Infantry Regiment was due to land at 21.00 hours, had still not been properly secured. An *Ost* battalion of Georgian troops held out just to the north. Spread between Turqueville and Fauville on the road from Carentan northwards, they prevented the reinforcement of the increasingly embattled force at Sainte-Mère-Eglise, which Schlieben was trying to recapture from the north. When the sixty gliders of the 325th Glider Regiment swooped in, fierce machine-gun fire opened up. They lost 160 men killed or injured on landing, but the

1. The Allied commanders before D–Day: (*front*) Tedder, Eisenhower and Montgomery; (*behind*) Bradley, Ramsay, Leigh-Mallory and Bedell Smith.

2. Generalfeldmarschall von Rundstedt visits the 12th SS Panzer-Division *Hitler Jugend*: (*left to right, standing*) Rundstedt, Kurt Meyer, Fritz Witt and Sepp Dietrich of 1 SS Panzer Corps.

3. Rommel inspects
the Atlantic Wall.

4. Eisenhower with members of the 101st Airborne at Greenham Common,
5 June, immediately before their take-off. His aide, Commander Harry
Butcher, is just behind.

5. Pathfinders of the 6th Airborne Division synchronize watches immediately before take-off.

6. A Royal Canadian Navy landing craft approaching Juno beach, 6 June.

8. A medic with wounded Rangers below the cliffs at Pointe du Hoc.

7. US medics tending a wounded soldier with plasma on Omaha beach.

9. Part of the 4th Infantry Division moves inland from Utah beach.

10. Major General Rod Keller and staff of the Canadian 3rd Infantry Division immediately after landing at Bernières-sur-Mer.

11. German prisoners of the Canadians carrying a wounded soldier back towards Juno beach.

12. A Sherman tank of the Second Army driving through Douvres-la–Délivrande, north of Caen.

13. Utah beach, 9 June.

14. Obersturmführer Michael Wittmann of the 101st SS Heavy Panzer Battalion (*left in black*) with his gunner from the eastern front, Balthazar Woll (*hands on hips*).

survivors had all their equipment and were fresh. They went into action that night, fording the Merderet, and swung left to secure the crossing at La Fière on the west side.

When the first American prisoners were marched through Carentan, the reserve battalion of Heydte's 6th Paratroop Regiment gazed at their tall, shaven-headed counterparts from across the Atlantic. 'They look as though they're from Sing Sing,' they joked. From Carentan, the prisoners were taken south to Saint-Lô to be interrogated at the Feldkommandantur, then on to a holding camp, which they dubbed 'starvation hill', because they received so little to eat. French civilians, having known since before dawn from the frantic activity of German troops that the invasion had begun, watched their arrival with sympathy.

Citizens of Saint-Lô had been reassured the day before by the precision of an American fighter-bomber strike against the railway station. One group playing cards had watched 'as if it were a movie' and applauded. 'These friendly pilots,' wrote one of them later, 'comforted us with the idea that the Allies did not blindly bomb targets where civilians were in danger.' But on the evening of 6 June at 20.00 hours, Allied bombers began to flatten the town systematically as part of a strategy to block major road junctions and thus delay German reinforcements rushing to the invasion area. The Allied warnings over the radio and by leaflet had either not been received or not been taken seriously.

'Windows and doors flew across rooms,' one citizen recalled, 'the grandfather clock fell flat, tables and chairs danced a ballet.' Terrorized families fled to their cellars and a number were buried alive. Old soldiers from the First World War refused to shelter underground. They had seen too many comrades suffocate under the earth of bombarded trenches. The air became choking with dust from smashed masonry. During this 'night of the great nightmare' they saw the double spires of their small cathedral silhouetted against the flames. Some burst into tears at the sight of their ruined town.

Four members of the Resistance from Cherbourg were killed in the prison. The headquarters of the Gendarmerie, the Caserne Bellevue, was completely destroyed. Well over half the houses in the town were razed to the ground. Doctors and aid workers could do little, so wounds were disinfected with Calvados. Accelerated by the vibration from the bombing, one heavily pregnant woman went straight into labour and a baby girl was 'born right in the apocalypse'. As soon as the air raid started, many had instinctively run out into the countryside, where they sought shelter in barns and farmyards. When they finally summoned the courage to return to Saint-Lô, they were horrified by the smell of corpses still buried beneath the ruins. Some 300 civilians had died. Normandy, they had discovered, was to be the sacrificial lamb for the liberation of France.

9

Gold and Juno

In the ancient Norman city of Caen, people were awake much earlier than usual. After the reports of paratroop drops had been confirmed, the headquarters of the 716th Infanterie-Division on the Avenue de Bagatelle came to life. A young member of the Resistance who lived nearby watched dispatch riders come and go. He knew very well what was afoot. His mother, who had pretended not to know about his activities, looked at him questioningly: 'Is this the landing?'* Her son did not reply. She turned away and began to fill bottles of water and to cook some potatoes in case the water and gas were shut off.

Neighbours emerging from apartments on to stairwells or calling to each other from their windows were confused.

'Do you think this is it?'

'Oh, not here.'

'The poor people on the coast, what will they be going through?'

'Don't worry. They'll be here this evening. The Fritzes are in a right panic.'

Marianne Daure, woken by aircraft in the early hours, also asked her husband if this was the landing. Pierre Daure, the rector of the university, who had been secretly appointed the new *préfet* of Calvados by de Gaulle, replied drily, 'Yes, it is indeed the landing.' Marianne Daure

---

* The French always said '*le débarquement*', never '*l'invasion*' when speaking of 6 June 1944. The word 'invasion' for them signified the German onslaught and occupation of 1940.

was also the sister of François Coulet, whom de Gaulle had chosen to be the *commissaire de la république* for Normandy, yet she had been told nothing. Despite SHAEF's fears, the Gaullists had kept the secret scrupulously.

By 06.00 hours, the *boulangeries* in Caen were besieged by housewives buying baguettes. But then German soldiers, spotting the crowds, rushed up to take the bread for themselves. They also seized bottles of alcohol from cafés.

In the excitement of the moment, some boys bicycled furiously north towards the beaches to see what was happening. They had to avoid German troops moving into defensive positions. When they returned, word spread quickly. One cyclist rode south out of Caen, shouting along the way, 'They're landing! The sea is black with ships! The Boches are screwed!'

Wild optimism became infectious. A newspaper seller climbed the tower of the Saint-Sauveur church and ran around afterwards claiming that he had seen the English advancing. It was not long before German loudspeaker vans toured the streets of Caen, telling the population to stay indoors. The military authorities gave the order that parts of the city were to be evacuated immediately. The inhabitants would not be allowed to take anything with them. Most, however, stayed put and did not answer the hammering on the door.

Generalfeldmarschall Rommel, meanwhile, was woken at home in Herrlingen, near Ulm, where he had gone to celebrate his wife's birthday. Generalleutnant Speidel rang him at 06.30 hours from La Roche-Guyon, as soon as reports of the huge invasion fleet anchored offshore were confirmed. Speidel told him of measures taken so far. Rommel rang the Berghof to cancel his visit to Hitler. His driver was waiting outside in the open Horch staff car and they drove back to France at top speed. Rommel would not reach his headquarters until nightfall.

Army Group B staff officers in the operations room at La Roche-Guyon worked feverishly as they tried to assess the situation from reports coming in from the Seventh Army. Speidel also had to deal with higher command: 'Continual telephone calls from OKW and OB West revealed the nervousness reigning at the highest levels.'

Outside Paris at Saint-Germain-en-Laye, the headquarters of OB

West was in a similar state, with teleprinters chattering and telephones ringing constantly. Rundstedt's chief of staff, General der Infanterie Günther Blumentritt, rang the OKW staff at the Berghof about the release of panzer divisions whose deployment Hitler had insisted on controlling. Shortly before 07.00 hours OKW rang back. It 'objected violently to OB West's arbitrary deployment of OKW reserves'. They were to be stopped immediately. Jodl then called Speidel to ensure that the order was carried out. Blumentritt also had to call the headquarters of the Luftwaffe Third Air Fleet, Naval Group West, even Otto Abetz, the German ambassador in Paris and the Vichy government, concerning pre-agreed proclamations, 'urging the population to keep the peace, with warnings against revolt, sabotage and obstruction of German counter-measures'.

Of the three British beaches, Gold in the west was the closest to Omaha. The landing there of the 50th (Northumbrian) Division was the one which took pressure off the Americans. Gold beach lay between Arromanches and La Rivière. H-Hour was at 07.30 hours, one hour after the Americans on their right, but the basic pattern remained the same, with bombing, shelling from the sea and then rocket ships firing close in. The cruisers HMS *Ajax* and *Argonaut* kept up a constant shelling of the German heavy coastal battery at Longues, which the bombers had failed to destroy.

Rough seas and vomiting affected the assault troops, just as at Omaha. The two armoured regiments launching their DD tanks rightly decided to ignore the order 'Floater five thousand'. The Sherwood Rangers Yeomanry on the left launched their two squadrons of swimming Shermans at only 1,000 yards out, yet still lost eight tanks. Officers in the 4th/7th Dragoon Guards had to argue forcefully with the commanders of their tank landing craft. In the end they lost even fewer tanks than the Sherwood Rangers.

The right-hand brigade group, led by the 1st Battalion of the Royal Hampshires and the 1st Dorsets, landed on the beach east of Le Hamel and the small seaside resort of Arromanches-les-Bains. The tanks of the Sherwood Rangers were delayed by the rough sea and the Hampshires suffered a bloody landing at Le Hamel. Their commanding officer and several of their headquarters officers became casualties almost

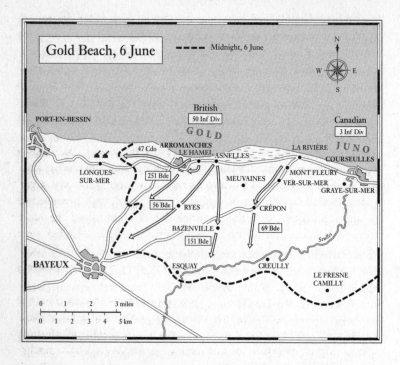

immediately. But the battalion fought on, backed up by the 2nd Devons. It took most of the day before German resistance was finally eliminated.

On the left the 69th Brigade group led by the 6th Battalion of the Green Howards wasted little time. Their huge second in command, Major George Young, had warned his men, 'Once you stop on the beach, you are never going to get up again.' As they pushed inland towards Mont Fleury, Germans emerged to surrender. The Green Howards simply turned to point towards the beach and said, *'Zurück!'* ('Back there!'), and the unescorted prisoners did as they were told.

The 5th Battalion of the East Yorkshire Regiment had a hard fight over on the extreme left-hand side of Gold beach at La Rivière, where the concrete defences had survived the shelling. After several armoured vehicles had been knocked out, an AVRE* tank appeared. The forty-

---

* Assault Vehicle Royal Engineers: this vehicle, based on a Churchill tank, had been developed by the 79th Armoured Division under Major General Percy Hobart to

pound petard bomb fired from its stubby barrel managed to destroy the emplacement containing the anti-tank gun which had inflicted so many losses. But the East Yorks, amid the dust and smoke from the bombardment, still needed several more hours to clear La Rivière, house by house. Flame-throwing Crocodile tanks also helped, while the flail tanks of the Westminster Dragoons soon cleared minefields. 'Hobart's funnies' had proved their worth in the face of British, but also American scepticism.

Under the direction of the Royal Navy beachmaster, the landing operation was soon in full swing. An American commander of an LST – a 'landing ship tank', known to its crew as a 'large stationary target' – described the traffic as 'a sort of aquatic turnpike', with 'a whole line of ships going one direction, a whole lot of ships going the other direction'. Three regiments of self-propelled artillery landed soon afterwards and the 50th Division began to push inland, with the independent 56th Brigade in the second wave, heading south-west towards Bayeux.

Having secured Le Hamel, the Hampshires advanced west along the coast towards Arromanches-les-Bains, where the Mulberry artificial harbour was to be sited. No. 47 Commando of the Royal Marines, which had lost three landing craft to mines, was to push even further west with the mission to take Port-en-Bessin. This was where the British right flank would join up with the American 1st Division spreading left from Omaha.

The Green Howards moved rapidly on Mont Fleury, where they forced the German defenders, shaken by the naval bombardment, to surrender. Company Sergeant Major Stanley Hollis first showed his quite selfless courage there. Hollis's company commander suddenly noticed that they had passed two pillboxes. He and Hollis went to investigate. A machine gun opened up on them. Hollis charged the pillbox, firing his Sten sub-machine gun, jumped on top to reload and threw grenades inside. Later, when the Green Howards advanced on the village of Crépon, his consistent bravery won him the only Victoria Cross awarded that day. In Crépon, his company encountered a German

---

destroy concrete emplacements. It had other roles, such as bridge-laying and filling anti-tank ditches with fascines.

position with a field gun and MG42 machine guns. Hollis mounted an attack from a house on the flank. The field gun was traversed on to them. Hollis led his men out, but on finding that two had been left behind, he mounted a diversionary attack armed with a Bren gun and rescued them.

In the centre, the advance continued along the ridge to Bazenville, where a furious battle was fought against Oberstleutnant Meyer's *Kampfgruppe* of the 352nd Division. As already mentioned, Meyer was killed and his force almost entirely wiped out. Just to the right, 56th Brigade Group, led by the 2nd Battalion of the Essex Regiment and the Sherwood Rangers, were given Bayeux as their objective. The Sherwood Rangers had already lost their commanding officer to a sniper, yet the tank commanders still kept their heads out of the turret (it was impossible to operate closed down). Major Stanley Christopherson, who commanded the squadron attached to the 2nd Essex, had not found their colonel at the rendezvous. Not wanting to go in search of him in his tank down narrow lanes encumbered with infantry, he left the squadron with his second in command, Keith Douglas, and decided to take a horse, which he found ready saddled outside a house. 'Never in my wildest dreams,' Christopherson wrote in his diary, 'did I ever anticipate that D-Day would find me dashing along the lanes of Normandy endeavouring, not very successfully, to control a very frightened horse with one hand, gripping a map case in the other, and wearing a tin hat and black overalls! The Essex colonel was somewhat startled when I eventually found him and reported that my Squadron was ready to support his battalion in the next phase of the attack.'

The battlegroup advanced, meeting only the lightest opposition, but stopped just short of Bayeux. 'Bayeux could have been attacked and captured that evening,' wrote Christopherson, 'as patrols reported that the town was very lightly held, but the commanding officer of the Essex preferred to remain on the outskirts for the night.'

Juno beach, the central sector for the Second British Army, extended from La Rivière to Saint-Aubin-sur-Mer. Juno was the objective of the 3rd Canadian Division. The Canadians were determined to take revenge for the Dieppe raid, the disastrous experiment from which fewer than half their men had returned. Dieppe had provided a cruel but vital lesson for the planning of D-Day: never attack a heavily defended port from the sea.

The 3rd Canadian Division was commanded by Major General Rod Keller, a large man with a round, florid face and military moustache. He was known as a compulsive raconteur with a penchant for whisky. The Canadians, despite their battledress uniform and regimental system inherited from the British Army, in many ways felt closer to the Americans than to their mother country. They cultivated a certain scepticism towards British Army conventions and referred to Overlord as 'Operation Overboard', after being smothered in instructions from British staff officers at Second Army headquarters. The strength of the Canadians lay in the quality of their junior officers, many of whom were borrowed eagerly by a British Army short of manpower.

Task Force J, which supported their landing, opened fire at 05.27 hours. The cruiser HMS *Belfast* was the flagship. One naval officer described her 'sitting like a broody hen with a swarm of landing craft round her'. This was an international squadron, with the cruiser HMS *Diadem* and five Royal Navy fleet destroyers, three Norwegian destroyers, the French destroyer *La Combattante*, which would bring de Gaulle to Normandy a week later, and two Canadian destroyers, HMCS *Algonquin* and *Sioux*.*

Allied warships continued to fire over the heads of the landing craft and the DD tanks of the 1st Hussars and the Fort Garry Horse. The rocket ships also fired their screaming salvoes just as the landing craft approached the beach. Then there was an eerie silence. The Canadian assault troops, also seasick and their battledress soaked with spray, were surprised that the German artillery had not opened fire.

Waiting until the landing craft dropped their ramps, the German defenders held their fire. As soon as the first men jumped down into the water at 07.49 hours, machine guns and field guns opened up on them. Canadian troops suffered a total of 961 casualties that day. Many ignored the order to leave those who had been hit and turned back to pull a comrade to safety.

The 7th Canadian Brigade landed either side of the River Seulles at Courseulles-sur-Mer. The Royal Winnipeg Rifles cleared the west bank,

---

* There were altogether 107 Canadian vessels involved in Overlord.

then, with the Canadian Scottish Regiment, pushed in towards Vaux and Graye-sur-Mer. The main part of the town on the east bank proved a much harder task for the Regina Rifles, which had suffered heavy losses on landing. Courseulles-sur-Mer had been partitioned into numbered blocks to be dealt with by designated companies. 'Nearly every foot of the town was known before it was ever entered,' said the commanding officer of the Regina Rifles. He described the performance of the supporting tank crews of the 1st Hussars as 'gallant rather than brilliant', and they learned the hard way. Even with support from the few remaining DD Shermans, it took until the afternoon to clear the town fully. The Canadians found that having chased the German defenders from some fortified houses, they then returned via tunnels and began shooting at them from behind.

Part of the 8th Canadian Brigade landing at Saint-Aubin-sur-Mer also faced fierce resistance. The North Shore Regiment suffered many losses from an extensive concrete bunker armed with an anti-tank gun, machine guns and 81 mm mortars. The squadron of DD tanks of the Fort Garry Horse, which had been delayed, finally arrived. In the confusion, as they charged around the beach, they ran over corpses and several of their own wounded soldiers. A sergeant in 48 Royal Marine Commando who witnessed this also saw a medical orderly in a state of complete shock, unable to face the wounded.

Only the arrival of an AVRE tank, firing its hefty petards on to the bunker system, brought resistance there to an end at 11.30 hours. Meanwhile another company from the North Shore Regiment, which had entered the town after blowing gaps in the wire with Bangalore torpedoes, continued to fight from house to house, with grenades, rifles and Bren guns. They too faced the danger of Germans re-emerging from tunnels behind them to fight on.

At Bernières-sur-Mer, the Queen's Own Rifles were reinforced by another squadron of Fort Garry Horse tanks, which, after landing 'dryshod', then lined up on the beach to blast defended houses. An AVRE tank blew a gap in the sea wall, then engineers prepared ramps for the tanks. Infantry and 'Priest' self-propelled artillery were soon streaming through, followed by the Shermans. The German defenders fled and civilians emerged from their cellars. By 09.00 hours, a bar was open for celebratory drinks. Officers had warned their men not to accept any food or drink from the French in case they were poisoned, but few took the idea seriously. The suspicion in official circles that the Normans had been won over by their German occupiers was contrary to what the Resistance and other sources had told them. In fact, considering the suffering of the French along the coast and in the main towns, the vast majority showed great understanding.

Although the leading infantry battalions pushed on inland, the advance was slowed by chaos on the beaches as the follow-up waves arrived. Tanks, self-propelled guns and Bren carriers became embroiled in traffic jams, to the intense frustration of beachmasters and the newly landed headquarter groups. Major General Keller was furious when he landed at Bernières accompanied by newspaper correspondents and photographers recording his arrival. On board, he had made a show in their presence of radioing through an optimistic report on progress to Lieutenant General Harry Crerar, the commander of Canadian troops in the invasion. The situation on the beach looked rather less encouraging.

French-Canadians of the Régiment de la Chaudière received a rapturous welcome from locals as soon as they spoke to them in French. Many rushed down to their cellar to fetch a keg of cider for the soldiers. But when the farming families began to pull the boots off dead Germans, the Canadians were clearly shocked. They had no idea that the Germans had commandeered all supplies of leather for the Wehrmacht until the French said to them, 'But what do you expect? It's war and we have no footwear.'

French civilians saw these 'cousins' from across the Atlantic as the next best thing to their own troops landing. They had no idea that one of the squadrons of Spitfires overhead covering the Canadians was piloted by Free French aviators. 'Les Cigognes' ('the Storks'), as 329 Squadron called itself, had been told by their wing commander, Christian Martell, 'I don't want to see pilots watching the ground. Today you've got to scan the sky.' But the heavens remained void of enemy fighters that day. The only danger was of collision with other aircraft.

The Chaudières took over the lead in the advance on Bény-sur-Mer, which, despite its name, lay three miles inland. Although the road south was straight, it ran between wheatfields in which the Germans had sited machine guns. Outflanking them became an arduous business, with infantry crawling through the standing corn on what had turned

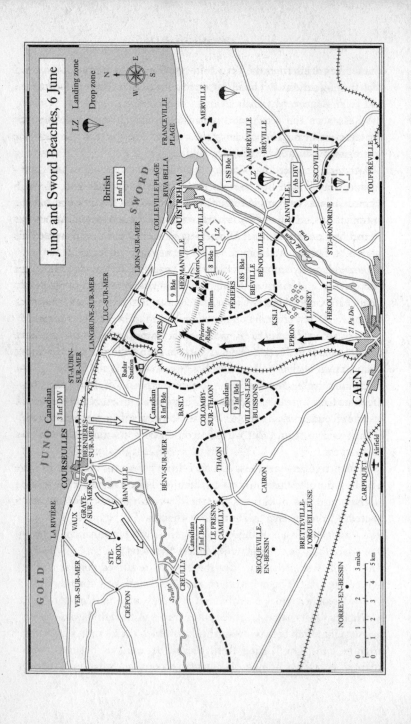

Juno and Sword Beaches, 6 June

LZ Landing zone

🪂 Drop zone

GOLD

JUNO Canadian 3 Inf DIV

SWORD British 3 Inf DIV

LA RIVIÈRE
VER-SUR-MER
CRÉPON
VAUX
STE-CROIX
GRAVE-SUR-MER
BANVILLE
BÉNY-SUR-MER
CRÉFULLY
CROUSEULLES
COURSEULLES
BERNIÈRES-SUR-MER
ST-AUBIN-SUR-MER
LANGRUNE-SUR-MER
LUC-SUR-MER
LION-SUR-MER
COLLEVILLE PLAGE
RIVA BELLA
OUISTREHAM
FRANCEVILLE PLAGE
MERVILLE
AMFRÉVILLE
BRÉVILLE
ESCOVILLE
TOUFFRÉVILLE

Radar Station
DOUVRES
BASLY
COLOMBY-SUR-THAON
THAON
CAIRON
SECQUEVILLE-EN-BESSIN
NORREY-EN-BESSIN
BRETTEVILLE-L'ORGUEILLEUSE
CARPIQUET
Airfield

CAEN

Canadian 8 Inf Bde
Canadian 9 Inf Bde
Canadian 7 Inf Bde
LE FRESNE-CAMILLY
VILLONS-LES-BUISSONS

9 Bde
8 Bde
185 Bde
1 SS Bde
6 Ab DIV

HERMANVILLE
COLLEVILLE
Morris
Hillman
PERIERS
Periers Ridge
BIÉVILLE
BÉNOUVILLE
LÉBISEY
HÉROUVILLE
BLAINVILLE
LE BISEY
EPRON
KSLI
RANVILLE
STE-HONORINE
21 Pz Div

Orne

Canal de Caen

Seulle

0   1   2   3 miles
0   1   2   3   4   5 km

into a sultry afternoon. After a battery of guns near Bény-sur-Mer had been knocked out by some very accurate gunfire from the destroyer HMCS *Algonquin*, the advance slowly continued.

Delays on the beach, and surprisingly strong resistance from the underestimated 716th Infanterie-Division, meant that the advance battlegroup of the 9th Canadian Infantry Brigade had too little time to reach its main objective. Carpiquet airfield lay just south of the Caen–Bayeux road. The flat ground ahead sloped upwards and, through binoculars, its hangars were tantalizingly visible in the distance, but the supporting tanks were low on ammunition. Major General Keller was expecting a counter-attack by the 21st Panzer-Division and wanted his advance elements to be in defensive positions by nightfall.

One certainly cannot criticize the Canadians for the way they went about it. The battlegroup of the North Nova Scotia Highlanders rightly used all the vehicles available – light Stuart tanks, Shermans, M10 tank destroyers, trucks and Bren gun carriers – to speed the advance. If Keller had known of the panic and chaos on the airfield, he might have pushed them on. The Third Luftflotte in Paris reported, 'At Carpiquet at 19.20 hours on 6 June, everybody lost their heads badly . . . the station commandant gave orders for evacuation.' The Luftwaffe's hurried attempts to destroy installations proved remarkably inept, as the 12th SS Panzer-Division *Hitler Jugend* observed two days later: 'Take-off runway at Carpiquet inefficiently blown up. Rest of taxiing area hardly damaged at all. Most of the fuel could still be saved.'

Over the next few weeks, the airfield and its surrounding area were to see some of the most bitter fighting of the whole battle for Normandy against the *Hitler Jugend* Division. It would take just over a month before Carpiquet was finally in Allied hands.

10

Sword

The landings of the British 3rd Infantry Division at the eastern end on
Sword beach, between Saint-Aubin-sur-Mer and the River Orne, had
heavy guns in support. The battleships HMS *Ramillies* and *Warspite*,
and the monitor HMS *Roberts*, were augmented by four cruisers,
including the Polish ship *Dragon*, and thirteen destroyers. The Overlord
planners had increased this naval support because of the many German
batteries in the sector. Birds in the Orne estuary were driven wild by
their gunfire. 'Widgeon and teal fly low over the sea and look like black
tracer,' wrote an observer in his diary.

The landing craft were lowered into the heavy sea at 05.30 hours
and, after circling, made their way inshore, vainly attempting to maintain formation. One company commander in the 2nd Battalion of the
East Yorkshire Regiment read extracts from Shakespeare's *Henry V* to
his men over the tannoy, but most of them were probably too seasick
to pay much attention. Many regretted the tot of navy rum with
breakfast.

The DD tank crews of the 13th/18th Hussars and the Staffordshire
Yeomanry felt a different form of nausea when they received the order
'Floater, 5,000!' The launch of the swimming tanks planned for 8,000
yards out had been reduced, but it was still a very long way to go in a
sea with waves up to five feet high. Surprisingly, only six out of forty
sank, two of them as a result of being rammed by landing craft out of
control. At 06.50 hours, the self-propelled guns of the 3rd Infantry

Division also opened fire from their landing craft at a range of 10,000 yards.

Just before landing, an officer with the 41st Royal Marine Commando observed those around him on the landing craft: 'Some were scared shitless, others fiercely proud just to be a part of it. Anticipation with nervous excitement showed everywhere.' The first wave of infantry, the 1st Battalion the South Lancashire Regiment and the 2nd East Yorkshires, arrived to find that the first DD tanks were already ashore and firing at strongpoints. The South Lancs immediately attacked the German position codenamed 'Cod' opposite the beach. Their commanding officer died ten feet from the top of the beach with the battalion medical officer wounded beside him. A Bren-gun platoon, landing in carriers, charged straight up the beach and the defenders surrendered. The 2nd Battalion of the Middlesex Regiment, which followed, was astonished to be welcomed by a man in a brass fireman's helmet 'like a Napoleonic dragoon'. This was the mayor of Colleville. He was accompanied by a young woman who wasted no time in starting to care for the wounded.

Other young Frenchwomen also showed extraordinary bravery, coming to the beaches to help. Purely by chance, a student nurse who had left her bathing dress in a beach hut the day before had arrived on a bicycle that morning to retrieve it. She ignored the wolf whistles of the amazed squaddies and set to work bandaging wounds. Her work lasted two days and during the course of it she met her future husband, a young English officer.

Flail tanks from the 22nd Dragoons and the Westminster Dragoons cleared paths through minefields, and exits from the beach were opened more quickly than on any other sector. The Royal Engineers also wasted no time. 'Every now and then there's a big flash and clouds of smoke and a noise as some part of the beach is cleared by sappers,' a naval officer noted in his diary.

A young officer landing in the second wave noticed near the beachmaster's post a fat German officer held prisoner with half a dozen of his men. They were crouching under the shelter of the sea wall as shells from their own artillery landed. The German officer suddenly protested to a sergeant with the beachmaster's team that under the Geneva

Convention they had the right to be taken to a place of safety. The sergeant threw a spade at him and yelled, 'Well, dig yourself a fucking hole then!'

The 2nd East Yorkshires pushed inland, turning left towards the River Orne to attack strongpoint 'Sole' and then take on 'Daimler', which had four 155 mm guns. A captain charged the bunker firing his Sten gun and entered. Unfortunately his batman, 'with misjudged enthusiasm', chose that moment to drop a grenade down the ventilation shaft. It was his gallant captain who received most of the blast. He emerged shaken but fortunately unwounded. The seventy defenders surrendered quickly. When soldiers of the East Yorks discovered a stock of beer and wine, their company sergeant major, concerned that discipline might collapse, threatened them with the penalty for looting. But then 'he relented a little', considering how agreeable some of it would be.

Lord Lovat's 1st Special Service Brigade also landed near Colleville. His commandos had thrown away their helmets at the last moment and wore their green berets instead, with their own regimental cap badges. Lovat had his personal piper, Bill Millin, from the Cameron Highlanders, with him. Millin was glad that Lovat led the way off the landing craft, since he was more than six feet tall and would show how deep the water was. The man just behind Lovat received a bullet in the face and collapsed. Millin jumped in and was shocked by the cold as his kilt spread around him. By the time he strode up out of the surf he was playing 'Highland Laddie'. Lovat turned round and gave him the thumbs up because it was a march of his old regiment, the Scots Guards. Amid the crump of mortars, shouting and small-arms fire, Millin could hardly believe it when Lovat then asked him if he would mind marching up and down playing 'The Road to the Isles' as the rest of the men disembarked. Most of the astonished soldiers on the beach loved it, but one or two almost lost their tempers at what they thought was insane behaviour.

Later than planned, Lovat led his force inland on a forced march towards the two bridges at Bénouville captured by John Howard's company early that morning. Lovat's conspicuous bravery had prompted his men to refer to him as 'the mad bastard'. Although a great fighter, he still retained, as 25th Chief of the Clan Fraser, a touch of the grand seigneur. As they advanced beside the Caen Canal towards Bénouville, a German rifleman shot at them from a tree. He then must have panicked. Jumping down to the ground, he tried to dash into a cornfield to hide. Lovat dropped to one knee and brought him down with a single shot from his deerstalking rifle. He sent off two men to retrieve the body, almost as if it were a stag.

Lovat turned to Millin: 'Right, Piper. Start the pipes again and keep playing as long as you can until we get to Bénouville. The Airborne are at the bridges there, and when they hear the pipes, they will know we are coming.' Millin played 'Blue Bonnets Over the Border' as they approached their objective. Lovat, with a great sense of occasion, shook hands with Howard and remarked that they had made history that day. He was clearly unaware that Howard's men had not only been relieved by Colonel Pine-Coffin's parachute battalion, but even that some of his own men had beaten him to the bridges.

Captain Alan Pyman, MC, had led 3 Troop of 6 Commando across half an hour earlier. This unit included Belgians, Dutch, Norwegians and Poles. Most striking of all was X Troop, which consisted almost entirely of German Jewish refugees. Most had transferred from the Pioneer Corps. They had all been given English names, with identity discs marking their religion as Church of England in case they were captured. As native German speakers, they were also extremely useful interrogating prisoners, as Lovat soon found. Pyman led his troop all the way to Bréville, which was still heavily defended. He was killed by a sniper and, without further support, his men were forced to pull back to Amfréville.

No. 4 Commando, with two troops of French *fusiliers marins* under Commandant Philippe Kieffer, had landed at 07.55 hours. Kieffer and his men, the first regular French troops to land in Normandy, headed east to the resort of Riva Bella and the port of Ouistreham at the mouth of the Orne. The Germans had fortified the casino at Riva Bella. Kieffer's commandos had a tough fight to reduce it and then silence the heavy gun battery, a massive concrete structure set among the seaside villas.

*

Hitler had finally gone to bed at three in the morning, after chatting with Eva Braun and Goebbels about the cinema and the world situation until two. Reports of the Allied parachute drops had still not reached Berchtesgaden. Accounts disagree on when Hitler was woken the next morning. Albert Speer wrote that he arrived at the Berghof at about ten to find that Hitler had not been woken before because the OKW considered the landings a diversionary attack. His adjutants had not wanted to disturb him with inaccurate information. But Hitler's personal adjutant, Hauptsturmführer Otto Günsche, stated that he entered the great hall of the Berghof at 08.00 hours. There he greeted Generalfeldmarschall Keitel and General Jodl with the words, 'Gentlemen, this is the invasion. I have said all along that this is where it would come.'

It would have been typical of Hitler to claim he had always been right, even though his prediction had in fact switched from Normandy back to the Pas-de-Calais. But Günsche's version must be treated with great caution. Others also testified to Hitler's late rising, and in any case Günsche's account still does not explain why Hitler would not allow the panzer divisions in the OKW reserve to be released until that afternoon if he really believed that Normandy was the main invasion area.* Everyone, however, seems to agree that he reacted with glee to the news, convinced that the enemy would be smashed on the beaches. And in the next few days he looked forward to crushing London with his V-1 flying bombs.

The closest armoured formation to the coast was the 21st Panzer-Division, distributed over a large area around Caen. Its commander, Generalmajor Edgar Feuchtinger, was an artilleryman with no experience of tank warfare. Described by his Canadian interrogator at the end of the war as 'a tall wiry, well-built man with a slightly bent nose, which gave him the appearance of a somewhat elderly pugilist', Feuchtinger did not arouse the admiration of his officers. He owed his appointment to his Nazi connections, and his dalliance in Paris on the night of 5 June, together with late arrival at his headquarters, added to the confusion already created by the complicated chain of command.

Generalmajor Richter of the 716th Infanterie-Division had tried as early as 01.20 hours to order part of the 21st Panzer to attack the para-

---

* A Nazi conspiracy theory connected with these events is discussed in Chapter 20.

chute landings of the 6th Airborne Division east of the Orne. But the absence of Feuchtinger and his chief of staff delayed any orders until 06.30 hours, and the panzer regiment under Oberst Hermann von Oppeln-Bronikowski did not move out until 08.00 hours. The British airborne forces faced only Oberstleutnant Hans von Luck's 125th Panzergrenadier-Regiment in the early hours of 6 June, and even then its attempts to counter-attack Bénouville betrayed a considerable uncertainty.

British paratroopers, hoping to prepare the Château de Bénouville for defence, discovered that it had been taken over as a maternity and paediatric hospital. An officer accompanied by a couple of men went in to warn them to take refuge. The woman in charge said that she must call the director. The paratroop officer, who was understandably tense, pointed his gun at her to stop her picking up the telephone. '*Non téléphonique!*' he ordered. Fortunately, Madame Vion, the director, appeared very soon. She showed great sang-froid and wasted no time. While the mothers were moved from their beds upstairs, the children were dispatched rapidly into the basement via the linen chute.

The massive armoured counter-attack which the airborne expected never materialized. After Oppeln-Bronikowski had assembled his force and set off down the east bank of the Orne, he received an order at 09.30 hours to turn around, go back through Caen, then attack the British beachhead west of the river. This long diversion on open roads exposed his force to fighter-bomber attacks. Having set out with 104 Mark IV panzers, the two battalions were reduced to no more than sixty serviceable vehicles by the time they reached the Périers ridge late in the afternoon.

General Marcks, the corps commander, was dismayed by the long diversion of Oppeln-Bronikowski's column of tanks. In a telephone call to Seventh Army headquarters at 09.25 hours, he attempted to obtain the immediate deployment of the much more formidable 12th SS Panzer-Division *Hitler Jugend*. But every headquarters involved in the fighting in Normandy – Seventh Army, Panzer Group West, Army Group B and OB West – was thwarted by the refusal of the OKW staff at the Berghof to make a decision. When an officer at OB West, Rundstedt's headquarters at Saint-Germain-en-Laye, protested, he was told that they were 'in no position to judge' and 'The main landing was going to come at an entirely different place.' OB West tried to argue that if that were the case 'it was all the more logical to destroy one landing so as to be able to meet a possible second one with all available forces. Moreover, the enemy would certainly concentrate on the successful landing.' Once again they were told that only the Führer could make the decision, and that did not happen until 15.00 hours.

This delay was doubly unfortunate for the Germans. Bad visibility persisted until late in the morning, which would have given the *Hitler Jugend* Division the opportunity to cover much of the ground between Lisieux and Caen without air attack. Apart from the reconnaissance battalion and the panzergrenadiers sent on ahead, the bulk of the division could not move until nightfall.

Although Sword beach, between Lion-sur-Mer and Ouistreham, was secured rapidly, the advance inland was unnecessarily sluggish. An astonishing number of soldiers, tired from wading in through the waves and relieved to have survived the landing, felt that they had earned the right to a cigarette and a mug of tea. Many started to brew up on the beach, even though it was still under fire. The naval staff yelled at them to get inland and chase the Germans off.

Both Canadians and Americans were bemused by the British Army's apparent inability to complete a task without a tea break. They also noticed a widespread reluctance to help other arms. Infantry refused to help 'fill a crater or get a vehicle out of difficulties', and when not engaged on an engineering task, sappers failed to fire at the enemy. Whether this demarcation mentality arose out of the trade union movement or the regimental system – both of which cultivated an ideal of collective loyalty – the basic fault often came from a lack of confidence among young officers.

The failure of the British 3rd Infantry Division to seize their objective of Caen on the first day soon proved critical. A vast amount of effort and ingenuity had been invested in planning the assault on the coast, but little thought had been put into the immediate follow-up phase. If Montgomery had intended to seize the city, as he stated, then he failed to put in place the equipment and organization of his forces to carry out such a daring stroke. One could well argue that as soon as the presence of the 21st Panzer-Division was established, his stated objective became far too optimistic.

In any case, to reach Caen in a single day, the 3rd Infantry Division would have needed to send forward at least two battlegroups, each with an armoured regiment and an infantry battalion. The infantry should ideally have been mounted in armoured personnel carriers, vehicles which the British Army took another twenty years to acquire. With only a few honourable exceptions, the British Army was woefully un-prepared for infantry-tank operations. Much of the problem stemmed from the regimental system and thus a reluctance to imitate the German panzergrenadier system, with closely knit armoured infantry and tank forces working together on a permanent basis.

The plan was for the 8th Infantry Brigade to seize the Périers ridge. Then the 185th Brigade, with three infantry battalions and only one armoured regiment, would pass through them and on to Caen. The 2nd Battalion of the King's Shropshire Light Infantry had been supposed to mount the tanks of the Staffordshire Yeomanry in the assembly area near Hermanville, then lead the advance south to Caen. They were to be supported by the 2nd Battalion of the Royal Warwickshire Regiment on the right and the 1st Battalion of the Royal Norfolk Regiment on the left.

The three infantry battalions were ready at Hermanville by 11.00 hours, but there was no sign of the Staffordshire Yeomanry. An un-usually high tide had reduced the depth of the beach to little more than ten yards, leaving no space for tanks to manoeuvre. And as German artillery was still shelling the routes south, traffic jams tailed back all the way to the beaches when vehicles were set ablaze. Minefields prevented the tanks from going across country. The brigade commander agonized over whether to launch the attack on foot and without tank support. After waiting an hour, he ordered the infantry to set off.

Meanwhile the 8th Brigade found the attack on the Périers ridge greatly hampered by two strongpoints codenamed 'Hillman' and 'Morris'. Morris, which had four 105 mm guns, was taken quite quickly, its dispirited defenders surrendering after an hour, but Hillman proved a far more formidable complex. Spread out over 400 yards by 600 yards, it had 'deep concrete pillboxes and steel cupolas with a complete system of connecting trenches'. Lacking the planned naval gunfire support, because the forward observation officer had been killed, the 1st Battalion of the Suffolk Regiment faced a terrible task crossing minefields and barbed wire covered by artillery and machine guns.

The Suffolks asked for tank support and a squadron of the badly needed Staffordshire Yeomanry was diverted to help them, reducing even more the weak armoured force assigned to the advance on Caen. With its wide fields of fire, the Hillman strongpoint made it hard for part of the 185th Brigade to bypass it on its advance, and the Norfolks lost 150 men. The Hillman strongpoint was also the headquarters of the 736th Grenadier Regiment. Its commander made sure that his men 'fought with determination to the bitter end'. In certain cases, the defenders had to be 'blown out of their emplacements by heavy explosive charges laid by the battalion pioneers'. The 3rd Infantry Division, although well aware of Hillman's existence – it was accurately marked on all their maps – had gravely underestimated its strength.

Although the British were suffering many casualties around Hillman, the 60,000 citizens of Caen endured far worse. The heavy bombers of the RAF, as part of the strategy to slow German reinforcements, had begun to bomb the city systematically at 13.45 hours. The leaflets dropped that morning with the 'Message Urgent du Commandement Suprême des Forces Expéditionnaires Alliées' warning them to disperse immediately into the countryside had little effect. Only a few hundred citizens left before the bombers arrived.

André Heintz, a young member of the Resistance, saw the formation of aircraft approach and the bombs drop, oscillating as they fell. Buildings shuddered with the explosions. Some seemed about to collapse and then settled back into place. Others crashed down, their façades falling into the narrow streets, blocking them. The smashed masonry produced huge clouds of dust, from which sometimes people emerged as if through a wall of smoke. Covered in a fine, pale powder, they had a spectral air, holding damaged arms or shoulders. Far more were buried in the rubble of their homes with their children, since school had been cancelled that morning. A doctor hurrying on his way to the hospital saw the main Monoprix department store in flames. Bombs severed the water mains, so the *sapeurs pompiers* of the fire service were extremely limited in what they could do.

Among the main buildings severely damaged or destroyed were the Abbaye aux Hommes, a huge, round-ended basilica with five spires, the Palais des Ducs, which dated back to the fourteenth century, a cloister dating from the period of William the Conqueror, the ornate Eglise Saint-Etienne, and the Gare Routière, a massive art deco terminus. Several bombers were shot down during the course of the operation. One, on fire, skimmed the roof of a manor house outside the city near Carpiquet and crashed in the park beyond. There was an immense fireball and ammunition began to explode. 'One could see the silhouettes of terrorized cattle galloping in front of the flames,' wrote a witness. 'It was a hallucinating sight.'

The youth of the city rapidly revealed considerable courage and dedication. Many were already members of the Défense Passive, the volunteer aid service, and many more immediately joined to help. Ambulances could not get through blocked streets, so the badly injured had to be taken on stretchers to the main emergency hospital set up in the convent of the Bon Sauveur. A very large man being carried across the ruined city by stretcher bearers, sweating under their load, could not stop apologizing: 'If only I was a little less fat,' he kept saying. Other volunteers began to shift rubble in an attempt to search for people who might be buried alive. One young man from the Défense Passive found a looter at work and threatened to arrest him. The looter laughed in his face because he was unarmed. The infuriated volunteer swung his spade at him and its blade happened to sever the man's jugular. In the looter's pockets were found a quantity of jewels, and – it is said – the severed hand of a woman with rings on the fingers.

The refuge of the Bon Sauveur itself had also suffered. A nun who leaped for shelter into one bomb crater was buried by another bomb exploding next to it. An outbuilding of the convent housed an asylum for the insane. Some of the last bombs to be dropped struck it, killing several of the inmates and driving the rest wild with fear, screaming as they held on to the bars. Heintz's sister was assisting one of the surgeons in the improvised operating theatre, so he decided to go there to help too. On seeing the pails of blood, he suddenly had the idea of soaking sheets in it and spreading them out on the lawn as a signal to the aircraft that this was a hospital. Once the blood dried, it was no longer scarlet, but another cross was improvised the next morning with red carpets and sheets dyed in mercurochrome.

Six surgical teams had been on standby since news of the invasion that morning. The Défense Passive organization for Caen had been based at the Bon Sauveur since the beginning of the year. The Lycée Malherbe was designated its subsidiary hospital, while on the other bank of the Orne, the Hospice des Petites Soeurs des Pauvres also acted as a casualty reception centre. The different organizations worked together with great effect. At the request of the surgeons, groups of police set out to seize supplies from pharmacies and clinics around the town. The medical profession in Caen was highly praised in an official report which recorded the 'magnificent attitude of the town's doctors who showed a boundless devotion'.

In the southern fringes of the city, some 15,000 people sought shelter in tunnels, recently rediscovered, which were part of the medieval stone quarries. They had packed suitcases with food and prayer books, not knowing that these damp, airless quarters were to be their squalid refuge for just over a month. With no sanitation or water, almost everyone suffered from lice, fleas and bedbugs.

A smaller but more intense tragedy had already taken place in Caen that morning. The Gestapo had gone to the Maison d'Arrêt, the city prison, and entered the section where French Resistance prisoners were held by German guards. The French warders on the civil side watched what happened through a hole in the canvas screen which had been erected to blank off the German military section. Altogether, eighty-seven members of the Resistance were taken out into the courtyard and shot that morning in batches of six. Victims of the massacre ranged across the political spectrum of the Resistance, from the ORA to Communists, and from a railway worker to the Marquis de Touchet. Another prisoner, who heard the shooting from a cell, recorded that none of them cried out except one man who, on entering the courtyard, perceived his fate. He began to shout, 'Oh, no! No! My wife, my children . . . my children!' He was silenced by the volley.

That night the German woman warder, who had previously behaved monstrously towards her charges, was 'pale and evidently terrified' by what had happened. She even returned to the surviving prisoners some of their possessions, insisting, 'The German army is honest.' Three weeks later, when the British had still not taken the city, the Gestapo came back and removed the bodies.*

The bitterness of many citizens over the destruction of Caen is not hard to imagine. 'With a bestial frenzy,' wrote one, 'the bombs eviscerated the city without pity.' Another described the bombing as 'useless as well as criminal'. There had never been more than 300 Germans in the town, he wrote, and even if the purpose was to disrupt transport communications, the bombers failed to hit a single bridge. Altogether some 800 people died in Caen as a result of the bombing and naval bombardments of the first two days. Many thousands more were wounded.

A number of other towns astride main routes to the invasion area suffered a similar fate. As well as Saint-Lô, Caen and Falaise, Lisieux to the east received two major bombing raids. 'The town is in flames and appears to be completely abandoned,' a report to Paris stated. It also demanded that the Commissaire of Police be punished for having fled his post during the night while the town burned. So many firemen were killed and so much equipment was lost during the first raid that it became impossible to fight the flames when more bombers returned. To the south, both Argentan and Ecouché were described as 'almost destroyed'. In Argentan 'all the gendarmes [were] killed or injured'. The bombing caused terrible panic as well as widespread destruction of homes. Altogether, some 100,000 residents of Calvados would become refugees. Caen's population of 60,000 was reduced to 17,000.

A curious contradiction lingers within this strategy of interdiction by bombing. If Montgomery really did intend to capture Caen on the first day, then why did he want the RAF to smash it so that its streets became impassable? That could help only the defender.

In London, meanwhile, everyone waited uncertainly for more news after the King's broadcast to the nation. Churchill later made a statement to a packed House of Commons. 'This is the first of a series of landings,'

---

* Dagmar Dreabeck, a young Dutchwoman whose bravery and kindness stirred the admiration of all – she was known as 'l'Ange de la prison' – was separated from the French prisoners and sent to Ravensbrück. She died less than a year later, the day the Red Army liberated the camp.

he said, bolstering Plan Fortitude, even if he was technically guilty of misleading the House of Commons. 'So far the commanders who are engaged report that everything is proceeding according to plan – and what a plan!'

Outside, London's streets and shops were empty, with taxis cruising about unable to find a customer. 'In Westminster Abbey,' wrote a woman journalist, 'typists in summer dresses and the usual elderly visitors in country-looking clothes came in to pray beside the tomb of the last war's Unknown Soldier, or to gaze rather vacantly at the tattered colours and the marble heroes of battles which no longer seemed remote.' Field Marshal Sir Alan Brooke was unable to get out of a lunch that day for the Maharajah of Kashmir with Mrs Churchill. 'It has been very hard to realize all day,' he wrote in his diary, 'that whilst London went on calmly with its job, a fierce conflict was being fought at a close distance on the French coast!'

Less than 200 miles to the south, the battle for Hillman was indeed still fierce. The unfortunate Suffolks were unfairly blamed for the delay and so was their brigadier. The main fault lay with the 3rd Division's lack of foresight to provide sufficient support, such as AVREs, which could have knocked out bunkers with their petards. And nobody can blame the King's Shropshire Light Infantry, which had pushed ahead bravely towards Caen with insufficient armoured support. Even taking into account the unpredictably high tide that day, the responsibility rested at higher levels. Neither General Sir Miles Dempsey, the commander-in-chief of the British Second Army, nor General Montgomery had thought through this vital part of the operation and allotted priorities clearly enough.

The Canadians also lacked the American half-track, but they had shown the right approach in their advance on Carpiquet by mounting infantry on tanks and rounding up every available Bren-gun carrier. But the British attempt to take Caen was bound to fail, even if there had not been delays at the start and congestion on the beaches when the second wave arrived. The advance of the King's Shropshire Light Infantry to Lebisey, less than a couple of miles from the centre of Caen, was a courageous achievement. Its battered remnants had to withdraw, lacking that vital armoured support.

On the other hand, their fate would have been far worse if the 21st Panzer-Division had received the decisive leadership which Feucht-inger so conspicuously failed to provide. By the time Oppeln-Bronikowski's panzer regiment had circumnavigated its way through Caen and was ready to attack the gap between the 3rd Division and the Canadians late in the afternoon, the British were ready to receive them. Lieutenant Colonel Eadie, the commanding officer of the Stafford-shire Yeomanry, had predicted their move. He had concentrated three troops of 'Firefly' Shermans armed with the seventeen-pounder gun, a main armament almost as effective as the Tiger's 88 mm, just west of Hermanville.* With their greatly superior range, these tanks of the Staffordshire Yeomanry knocked out thirteen of Oppeln-Bronikowski's Mark IV panzers in a matter of minutes. Only a small detachment of the 21st Panzer-Division slipped through to the coast, but they too withdrew rapidly.

By a happy coincidence for the British, the dramatic appearance at 20.30 hours of nearly 250 gliders bringing an air-landing brigade to reinforce the 6th Airborne Division, helped persuade Oppeln-Bronikowski to withdraw. The battlefield virtually froze as everyone stared in admiration at the sight. A subaltern in the 2nd Battalion Royal Ulster Rifles then overheard one of his soldiers comment on the arrival of their sister unit by air: 'I suppose that's what the 1st Battalion calls a fucking route march.' Suddenly the flak detachments and machine guns of the 21st Panzer opened up, firing furiously. They brought down fewer than a dozen gliders, although they claimed twenty-six.

Hillman was finally subdued at 20.15 hours. The Suffolks began to dig in for the night and their supporting tank squadron pulled back to reammunition. All work stopped as they too watched the gliders arrive. 'It equally impressed the German prisoners,' their commanding officer noted, 'but in a different way. They did not seem to think it was quite fair.'

A different sense of unreality still cocooned their supreme commander at the Berghof. Three hours before, General Günther Blumentritt, the

---

* Most British armoured regiments spread their precious Firefly tanks around, usually allocating one to each troop.

chief of staff of OB West, had to tell Seventh Army headquarters that Hitler wanted 'the enemy annihilated by the evening of 6 June since there exists a danger of additional sea and airborne landings. In accordance with an order from General Jodl, all units must be diverted to the point of penetration in Calvados. The beachhead there must be cleaned up by NOT later than tonight.' The chief of staff Seventh Army replied that that would be impossible. Hitler's Luftwaffe adjutant, Nicolaus von Below, who was with him at the Berghof, saw that he had not yet accepted the true might of Allied air power: 'He was still convinced that the ground forces could be thrown back.'

A striking example of Allied air supremacy took place that very evening. Together with the SS *Hitler Jugend* Division, Hitler was counting on another full-strength panzer division to drive the Allies back into the sea. Generalleutnant Fritz Bayerlein's Panzer Lehr Division had been ordered to make all speed for the coast. But even before Panzer Lehr moved out during the afternoon of 6 June, its units were bombed in their assembly area. Bayerlein reported to Generaloberst Dollmann at his headquarters at Le Mans. He wanted to keep his tank troops under cover during the day to avoid the Allied fighter-bombers, but Dollmann ordered him to keep moving. Bayerlein, 'a short, stocky, energetic man', who had been Rommel's chief of staff in North Africa, was almost speechless with rage at the long delay and then the stupid waste.

Rommel himself was not in a good mood when he returned to discover that the last remaining bridge over the lower Seine had been destroyed by Allied fighter-bombers. He went straight to the operations room in the Château de La Roche-Guyon and stared for a long time at the map. 'What's happened to our proud Luftwaffe?' he asked cynically. The answer was predictable. 'How goes the attack of the 21st Panzer-Division?' No details had arrived. 'Why were the Panzer Lehr Division and the 12th SS held up?' In reply, Speidel explained the refusal of OKW to come to a decision. 'Madness,' said Rommel. 'Of course, now they will arrive too late, but we must get them moving immediately.'

The Allies, although they had failed to secure key objectives, were at least ashore. Hitler's beloved panzer divisions were incapable of dislodging them now. But the fighting ahead would make the Allied casualties suffered on D-Day appear light in comparison. Those British formations which felt that they had 'done it all before' in North Africa were about to receive a nasty shock when they came up against the Waffen-SS. Allied air power could do comparatively little to help them when it came to fighting skilled and determined defenders, village by village in the cornfields round Caen and field by field in the Normandy *bocage*.*

* 21st Army Group headquarters had predicted 9,250 casualties out of the 70,000 soldiers landing on the first day. Some 3,000 of these – sailors, paratroopers landing in flooded areas and crews of DD tanks – were expected to suffer death by drowning. In the event, casualty figures are very hard to define for D-Day itself, since most formations' figures accounted for a longer period, never less than 6 to 10 June. In the confusion of the time, the high figure of missing had to be constantly recalculated, with some proved killed, some to have joined up with other units, some unaccounted wounded taken back to England, and others later found to have been taken prisoner. In very rough terms, British and Canadian casualties for D-Day itself were around 3,000 killed, missing and wounded. American losses were much higher because of Omaha and the two Airborne Divisions. General Bradley gave a figure of 4,649 US seaborne casualties, but this appears on the high side when compared with divisional returns. The only accurate figures one can give are those from 6 to 20 June inclusive. American First Army losses came to 24,162 (of whom 3,082 were killed, 13,121 wounded and 7,959 missing). British casualties over the same period totalled 13,572 (of whom 1,842 were killed, 8,599 wounded and 3,131 missing). Canadian casualties for the same period amounted to 2,815 (of whom 363 were killed, 1,359 wounded and 1,093 missing).

11

Securing the Beachheads

On the night following D-Day, few in the Omaha beachhead managed to sleep. In a quarry beside the Vierville draw, 29th Division staff officers bedded down on discarded lifebelts at their headquarters. Up on the bluffs and in apple orchards inland, farmhands and Pennsylvania coal miners from their division dug their foxholes with professional speed. They were to need them as protection from the indiscriminate firing that night. Nervous and exhausted men shot at any movement or silhouette, imagining it to be a German sniper. One young soldier shot a calf with his Thompson sub-machine gun.

Others tried to create an instant trench by exploding a charge of TNT in the ground, with the warning cry of 'Fire in the hole!' This only heightened the impression of fighting in all directions. Luftwaffe bombers arrived after nightfall to attack the ships at anchor, and the barrage of anti-aircraft tracer fire prompted many to compare it to a Fourth of July firework party. But the German air raid was too little and too late to help the defenders.

On 7 June, Oberstleutnant Ziegelmann of the 352nd Infanterie-Division looked out from the cliffs near Pointe et Raz de la Percée. He was less than 2,000 yards to the west of General Gerow's command post on Omaha beach. 'The sea was like the picture of "Kiel review of the fleet",' he noted angrily. 'Ships of all sorts were close together on the beach and in the water broadly echeloned in depth. And the entire agglomeration remained there intact without any real interference from the German side. I clearly understood the mood of the German soldier abandoned by the Luftwaffe.' The embittered cry of '*Wo ist die Luft-waffe?*' became a constant refrain of the German army's experience in Normandy.

Fragments of German battalions still held on in the sector, especially on the cliffs round the Pointe du Hoc, where they had counter-attacked Colonel Rudder's Rangers. The Americans had finally cleared Colleville-sur-Mer and Saint-Laurent-sur-Mer that morning. One soldier advancing through the village had turned to find a military policeman just a few yards behind him putting up 'out of bounds' signs. On the beach, the detritus of war defied description, with burnt-out vehicles, smashed landing craft, abandoned gas masks, Bangalore torpedoes and weapons. The scene did not stop that stickler for discipline General Gerhardt from yelling at a soldier for dropping orange peel on the ground.

Other isolated pockets of German resistance still had to be overcome. When a German soldier suddenly emerged from a hole to surrender, the troops who surrounded him found that he had 'a regular hotel underground' with a radio. They presumed that it was for calling down artillery fire on the beach. They summoned some military police. 'The MP Sergeant was from Czechoslovakia, and apparently his parents had been killed by the Nazis, so he shot him on the spot as a spy.'

Houses in Vierville were also placed out of bounds to American troops. French civilians were equally forbidden on the beach, to keep them out of the way. They felt that their presence even in their own village was unwelcome. American soldiers 'looked at us in a very suspicious way, those first days,' a French woman wrote later. The suspicion was mutual. An engineer sergeant with two of his men went into Saint-Laurent and entered the church, having seen a German slip in through the door. They found him spread-eagled and mortally wounded in front of the altar. The sergeant then noticed that the two soldiers with him, both from Alabama, were taking the coins from the poor box near the entrance. 'I guess they didn't know what a poor box was,' he said later. In fact, they just wanted a few coins as souvenirs, the obsession of almost all soldiers arriving in this very foreign land. But the priest entered at that moment and, taking in the scene, was scandalized. '*Pour les pauvres!*' he shouted at them.

The beach remained a dangerous place, and not just for civilians. Odd artillery rounds still fell and men from the 6th Engineer Special

Brigade were blowing up obstacles and mines. White tape marked the 'deloused' areas, but further on bodies could still be seen in minefields which had not yet been cleared. Bulldozer crews worked hard to open routes for the follow-up troops and vehicles landing. Bodies were stacked outside tented casualty clearing centres. A makeshift cemetery was cordoned off. Spare soldiers were assigned to grave registration. 'We all seemed in a trance,' noted one of them, 'removing dog tags and other morbid duties.' To speed the work, German prisoners were offered double rations if they volunteered to dig graves. Most shrugged and agreed. Later this harrowing work was passed to quartermaster companies of black soldiers.

An almost constant stream of prisoners arrived under escort on the beach to be searched by the military police. Many of them were Poles or Soviet *Hiwis* in German uniform with their hands up. 'Some were crying,' recorded the same engineer sergeant. 'They didn't know what to expect from us. Well they were lucky to have been taken on this front instead of having been taken on the Russian front where they would have been shot immediately as traitors.' The vast majority of them would be handed back by the Allies to the Soviet authorities later. Some were executed, but most were dispatched to slave labour camps. Many of the prisoners from Central Asia had such oriental features that American soldiers believed that they must be Japanese attached to the German army.

Just before dawn, General Gerhardt had received orders from his corps commander, General Gerow, to advance inland towards Isigny and the River Vire to link up with the 101st Airborne. Gerhardt wanted to use his reserve regiment, the 175th Infantry, which had not yet landed. Getting it ashore would take much of the day. A more urgent priority, however, was to relieve Colonel Rudder's 2nd Rangers on the Pointe du Hoc. Outnumbered by the German battalion of the 916th Grenadier-Regiment, they were also low on ammunition. Their only support came from the guns of the destroyer the USS *Harding*.

A mixed force of 116th Infantry and Rangers from the Omaha landing, strengthened with two Sherman tanks, attacked west along the coast towards Pointe du Hoc. But with a German strongpoint on the cliffs nearby (the one from which Ziegelmann observed the fleet), and other pockets of resistance, it took until the next day before they approached Rudder's embattled force.

Rudder's men, having run out of ammunition, were using captured German weapons. Their very distinctive noise confused the relief force and the Shermans from the 743rd Tank Battalion began firing on the Rangers, killing four and wounding another six. 'Again Colonel Rudder,' wrote an engineer with his group, 'displayed his great courage and leadership as he helped the men in his command post hold up an American flag as high as they could, so the troops advancing would know that we were Americans.' One report described their relief as a 'stumble-footed action', because another American force, coming in from the south-west, began firing at the original relief force approaching from the south-east.

Part of the 1st Infantry Division, the 'Big Red One', had meanwhile advanced east on 7 June along the coast road towards Port-en-Bessin, with infantry riding on the Shermans of the 745th Tank Battalion. There they met up with elements of the British 50th Division. Almost immediately bartering began, with English field gunners swapping eggs for American cigarettes.

Profiting from Allied air supremacy, American artillery had the great advantage of being able to use light spotter planes. That morning, an artillery officer with the 1st Division organized a makeshift runway on the bluffs overlooking Omaha beach. He went up to a bulldozer driver.

'Hey, I need a hedgerow knocked out,' he told him. 'Can you help me?'

'Sure,' came the reply.

So the operator brought his bulldozer over, knocked out the hedgerow and made them a runway a little more than fifty yards long, which was all the Piper Cub needed to take off. As the sea was much calmer, artillery ammunition for their guns was soon coming ashore in relays on pre-loaded DUKWs, which no longer risked sinking.

An air service squadron started to construct a proper landing strip for transport planes above Saint-Laurent-sur-Mer. Finished in record time, it was designated A-1. Soon olive drab C-47 Skytrains were landing ammunition in a constant stream, then taking off again filled with wounded strapped to litters. On her first trip, a flight nurse found that one of her patients had died. To prevent the others finding out, she pretended to check him every few minutes until they landed back in England.

While some things happened quickly, others seemed to take an interminable time. Nobody was more exasperated by the delays than the commander of the 29th Infantry Division, Major General Charles Hunter Gerhardt. Gerhardt was in some ways a miniature version of General Patton. A diminutive cavalryman with a large ego, he prided himself on his appearance, with highly polished riding boots and helmet correctly fastened under the chin. The 29th was a National Guard division and right from the start Gerhardt had intended to smarten it up in every way possible. He had no patience for paperwork and pushed his officers even harder than the men. In the process, he seems to have inspired admiration and loathing in equal quantities.

Gerhardt's determination to capture the town of Isigny in record time was frustrated by the delays in sending the 175th Infantry Regiment ashore. Then, to his fury, he heard that the navy had landed his men a mile and a half to the east. By the time they reached the Vierville draw, they were shaken by the bodies they passed and the occasional firing from a few German positions which had still not yet been suppressed by the 115th Regiment.

Mopping up was slow, dangerous work, because of isolated riflemen and machine guns. A lieutenant desperate to exert his authority soon fell victim. He had deliberately said to his platoon sergeant in front of everyone, 'Sergeant, I want you to understand that you have my permission to shoot any man who does not obey any order given from here on out.' When they came under fire, he took the sergeant's binoculars and rifle. Rejecting advice from his non-coms, he announced that he was going 'to get those bastards' and began to climb a prominent tree in a hedgerow. After firing a couple of rounds, he was hit, and fell mortally wounded on the far side of the hedge.

That evening, a German pioneer from the 352nd Infanterie-Division found a copy of the American operational plan on the body of a young officer from the 29th Division. He passed it to Oberst Ziegelmann, who could hardly believe his eyes. The key points were conveyed to General Marcks that night, but the documents did not reach Rommel and OB West for another two days. Rundstedt's chief of staff, Blumentritt, wrote that the plan clearly showed that this was '*Die* Invasion', but 'the Führer personally still expected a second cross-Channel invasion against the Fifteenth Army at any time up to the beginning of August'. Plan Fortitude's deception had proved more effective than the Allies had ever dared imagine.

On 8 June, the 115th Infantry, having secured the 29th Division's beachhead, advanced due south to the partly inundated valley of the River Aure. They faced little opposition because Generalmajor Kraiss had pulled back the remaining troops during the night. But once across the marshes, the regiment faced 'a tough learning period, with some successes and quite a few disasters'. With great bravery and skill, 'Lieutenant Kermit Miller of E Company crossed the inundated area just north of Colombières with his platoon and killed 46 Germans, knocked out two armored cars and one staff car, wrecked an enemy headquarters and returned with 12 prisoners.'

Providing a grim foretaste of fighting in the hedgerows of the *bocage*, the worst of the disasters took place during the night of 10 June. The 2nd Battalion had been warned by some locals that there were about 100 Germans ahead. 'It was nearly midnight now,' a report stated afterwards, 'and the men were so tired that they just fell down and started snoring where they lay. One of the men in O Company fell down, discharged his gun and killed the man ahead of him. The shot gave away their position and German machineguns opened up.' The battalion had halted in a small field, unaware that they were surrounded by a detachment from the 352nd Infanterie-Division. The adjutant and the headquarters company commander were killed and the communications officer captured. 'The assistant battalion surgeon went crazy and about 100 men were captured. Colonel Warfield was heard to say "I never thought my men would say *Kamerad*". The remaining men of the battalion were very jittery after this.' Lieutenant Colonel Warfield, the commanding officer, and Lieutenant Miller later died of their wounds. General Gerhardt exploded in anger when he heard that the battalion had not dug foxholes and simply dropped down to sleep.

The 115th became even more unnerved when they had 'trouble from those trigger happy [Texan] boys' in the 2nd Infantry Division, coming up from behind shooting at everything to their front. 'One battalion of the 115th Infantry attributed 3% of its casualties to the 2nd Division.'

Gerhardt, meanwhile, had been urging on his 175th Infantry Regiment towards Isigny, famous for its Normandy butter and Camembert cheese. Because radio communications had not improved, Gerhardt designated 'post-riders', who were officers in Jeeps, dashing back and forth, reporting on the progress and exact position of the leading troops. They needed to drive fast to avoid the fire of German stragglers. Gerhardt himself, wearing white gloves and a blue scarf round his neck (which matched the blue ribbon round the neck of his dog), wanted to be wherever there was action. And if there was no action, he wanted to know why. Gerhardt did not believe in making himself inconspicuous. He was driven around in a specially adapted Jeep named 'Vixen Tor', on which was mounted a red flashing light and siren.

Accompanied by Shermans of the 747th Tank Battalion, the 175th Infantry Regiment found the advance to be more of a fast route march. Norman farmers offered milk from churns to the thirsty men. There were a few delaying actions by German groups. More serious losses were then inflicted by a squadron of RAF Typhoons mistaking the lead battalion for retreating Germans. Six men were killed and eighteen wounded. 'John Doughfoot looked very much like Hans Kraut from the air,' wrote an artillery officer with them. The infantry were less forgiving. They promised in future to shoot at any aircraft of whatever nationality heading in their direction.

The commander of the 175th was reluctant to advance further without more artillery support, but Gerhardt did not take kindly to such excuses. He ordered the regiment to continue the advance through the night of 8 June and by midnight it was outside Isigny. Most of the prisoners taken were Polish or *Osttruppen*. The anti-tank company was astonished when 'an American on a white horse came down the road with about eleven prisoners'. He called out to them, ' "These are Polish, all but two. They're Germans." He then took out his pistol and shot both of them in the back of the head and we just stood there.'

Isigny, having been heavily bombarded by Allied warships, was ablaze in many places. Gerhardt had been right. There was little resistance. When a lone German rifleman fired at the column from a church steeple, one of the Shermans traversed its 75 mm main armament on to the target and 'that was the end of the German in the steeple'.

Brigadier General Cota pushed the tanks up to the bridge over the River Aure. There, they came under fire from machine guns on the far side. The twelve tanks lined up and their weight of fire forced a rapid retreat. Infantrymen from the 175th, accompanied by Cota, dashed across the bridge. Cota could hardly believe that the Germans had failed to blow it up. It was one of the few structures untouched. 'Rubble was everywhere,' an officer reported. 'The roads were all but impassable to motor traffic and I stood in the middle of what had been a church without realizing that there had even been a building on the site.' Isigny appeared to be abandoned, but some Frenchwomen emerged from the ruins. They began to strip dead German soldiers of their boots, socks and shirts.

On the Cotentin peninsula, meanwhile, the paratroopers of the 82nd and 101st Airborne Divisions had received no respite, even though units from the 4th Infantry Division had begun to reinforce them from Utah beach. Generalleutnant von Schlieben mounted even stronger counter-attacks against Sainte-Mère-Eglise with the 709th Infanterie-Division and other detachments. His chief priority was to thwart any American attempt to advance on Cherbourg.

The most serious attack reached the centre of Sainte-Mère-Eglise during the afternoon of 7 June. An artillery officer from the 4th Division, arriving by Jeep, reported on what he saw: '17.00 hours went into Sainte-Mère-Eglise by Jeep from the south. Tank battle going on. Flame throwers. Saw a German soldier, a "human torch", crawl to the center of the street from the side when a German [panzer] rolled right over him squashing him flat and extinguishing the flames at the same time. American tanks destroyed most of the German tanks, for the loss of three of their own. Fighting moved northwards. Saw a sunken road north of the town which the German tanks had used and also crushed some of their own dead. Part of 8th Infantry took this road and used it for their own defense that night. They had to pull the German bodies aside to dig their foxholes and several of them fell to pieces.'

Another force under Generalleutnant Hellmich concentrated near Montebourg that day, ready to attack the Americans' northern flank between Sainte-Mère-Eglise and the coast. A spotter aircraft and a naval fire-control party directed the guns of the battleship *Nevada* on to the target. Firing at a range of more than fifteen miles, the projected attack was broken up. But the town of Montebourg itself suffered badly on that Wednesday afternoon as the naval shells exploded, setting fire to a number of shops. In the main square, the statue of Jeanne d'Arc remained undamaged when all the buildings around were smashed. Since Montebourg sat astride the main road to Cherbourg, the Germans were busy fortifying the *abbaye* for a determined defence of the town. And at Valognes, to the north-west, one shell exploded in a dormitory of the convent and killed several nuns.

The front lines were at least becoming clearer after the confused fighting of the previous day. Paratroopers and the 4th Infantry Division forced the surrender of the 795th Ost-Bataillon of Georgians surrounded at Turqueville. And further south, Oberstleutnant von der Heydte's 6th Paratroop Regiment pulled back to Saint-Côme-du-Mont after one of its battalions was cut off and destroyed. Other pockets of resistance closer to Utah beach were also eliminated. At Saint-Martin-de-Varreville, the elaborate strongpoint included pillboxes linked by underground tunnels 'and Jerry went from one to another at will often returning to one we thought had been captured'.

The fighting on both sides remained just as vicious. An officer with the 4th Infantry Division stated that the bodies of four men from an airborne medical unit had been found: 'Their throats had been cut almost from ear to ear.' A trick frequently reported in the *bocage* fighting was for German soldiers to pretend to surrender. Then, as soon as Americans approached to take them prisoner, they would throw themselves to the ground as a hidden machine-gunner opened fire. The 4th Infantry first encountered this with German paratroopers from the 6th Paratroop Regiment, who apparently killed a lieutenant in this way.

Less reliable reports claimed that Germans were putting on American uniforms. This only became true later the following month, when German soldiers took combat jackets from American corpses when their own uniforms had started to disintegrate. A most unconvincing, although extraordinarily widespread belief developed among American, and sometimes British troops, that Frenchwomen, supposedly the lovers of German soldiers, acted as snipers. Near Saint-Marcouf on 7 June a sergeant reported on 'sniping coming from a building in the town. When investigated, [we] found a French woman and a man with

German rifles. Both denied sniping. Both were dead two seconds later.' The possibility that French civilians might have collected German weapons to give to the Resistance did not seem to have occurred to Allied soldiers at the time.

A number of American soldiers appear to have acquired a strong suspicion of the French before even setting foot in the country. 'France was like enemy country,' commented a captain in the 29th Infantry Division. Many had never been to another country where a foreign language was spoken and found it hard to see the difference between 'enemy-occupied' and just 'enemy'. Others said openly that they 'couldn't trust them in Normandy'. There is a story, perhaps true, perhaps apocryphal, of an American tank platoon pulling into a Norman farmyard. The farmer emerges with cider and Calvados and all the soldiers have a drink. Afterwards the Norman farmer says to the young American lieutenant that the drinks come to 100 francs. The lieutenant protests that they have just liberated him. 'But what are you complaining about?' the farmer replies. 'It's no more than I charged the Germans.'

The battlefield myth of female snipers spread with astonishing rapidity through 'latrine rumours', as they were known. But stories of young Frenchwomen staying with their German boyfriends were almost certainly true. Just inland from Omaha beach, a sergeant in the 6th Engineer Special Brigade recounted, 'we saw in the ditches French girls lying alongside their German soldiers. These girls had gone along with the [German] army as they retreated and they were killed by our planes and they were found lying side by side.'

On both sides, mercifully, there were also cases of unexpected humanity. On the northern flank near Sainte-Mère-Eglise, Sergeant Prybowski, a medical non-com, was searching hedgerows for wounded when he came across two injured paratroopers. As he sat there applying bandages to their wounds, one of them whispered to him, 'You'd better get down. There's an 88 back of you.' The sergeant laughingly turned round, only to stare down the barrel of a field gun. In the hedgerow a group of German artillerymen were watching them. But they allowed Prybowski to finish bandaging the two men and take them away.

To the west, at Chef du Pont and La Fière along the River Merderet, the 82nd Airborne could do little more than hang on to its positions until reinforced and resupplied with ammunition. To the west of the river, a force under Lieutenant Colonel Thomas Shanley was surrounded on a small feature known as Hill 30. With great courage and endurance, Shanley and his men held out for four days with no food apart from their original emergency rations. Many were wounded and had to be carried to the shelter of ditches and hedgerows, but the paratroopers were so weak from hunger and fatigue that four of them found it hard to carry one casualty. 'There were so many wounded along the ditches, they had them head to toe,' one soldier recounted. Shanley sent messengers to the main force east of the Merderet, begging for plasma. A small group of paratroopers tried to slip through with a supply, but they were all wounded.

Surrounded by part of the 1057th Grenadier-Regiment, Shanley's reduced force was heavily outnumbered. Then they found that the Germans were bringing up artillery. This development was spotted from across the river. A naval gunfire controller radioed back to the bombardment force offshore. Allied warships, at a range of more than twelve miles, proceeded to knock out the German artillery without inflicting serious casualties on the beleaguered paratroopers.

Many of Shanley's men kept going only with the help of Benzedrine. Lacking radio communications, they had no idea whether the invasion had succeeded or failed. But their prolonged resistance on Hill 30 greatly helped the establishment of a bridgehead over the Merderet by the time they were finally relieved. The newly landed 90th Infantry Division now had the task of increasing that bridgehead, prior to cutting off the peninsula for a general advance on Cherbourg. But due to a lack of leadership and discipline at many levels, the 90th started disastrously. Before the division reached the front, its point unit, on sighting a column of German prisoners being escorted back towards Utah, opened fire with every weapon available. Fighting the 91st Luftlande-Division among the hedgerows proved traumatic for these untested troops. Their performance was so lamentable that the divisional commander and two of his regimental commanders were sacked.

American generals were ruthless with subordinate commanders who 'could not get their troops to perform the task which a division or corps said had to be done'. Even that fire-eater General Patton felt the US Army resorted to sacking commanders before they had been given a proper chance. The combat historian Forrest Pogue talked with a colonel who had just been relieved of his command. 'He was sitting out along the road with his belongings beside him, waiting for a jeep to take him to the rear. The day before he had held the destiny of three thousand or more men in his hands; now he looked almost like a mendicant. He was dazed and uncertain whether he could control his voice.'*

For Overlord planners, one of the key items in their calculations had been the speed with which German reinforcements would reach the invasion front. Much depended on Allied efforts to seal off the battlefield by the bombing programme of 'Transportation', by Allied fighter-bombers and by the sabotage and attacks of the French Resistance groups trained by SOE and the Jedburgh teams. From 7 June, Rund-stedt's headquarters finally had permission to bring up reinforcements from Brittany and south of the Loire.

One of the first formations the Americans were to encounter in the battle for Carentan was the 17th SS Panzergrenadier-Division *Götz von Berlichingen*. This new division was named after an old warhorse of the sixteenth century who, after losing his right hand in combat, had a blacksmith make him an iron fist as a replacement. The iron fist became the divisional emblem. On 10 April, less than two months before D-Day, Himmler had inspected the division at Thouars, an event which had ended with them all singing together the SS anthem, the 'Treuelied'. Although the division contained many young soldiers (60 per cent were under twenty), the 17th SS was not nearly as well trained and armed as the SS *Hitler Jugend*. It had no modern tanks, just a regiment of assault guns, and the morale of its soldiers was not nearly as fanatical as in other Waffen-SS formations. 'Well, we don't know what's still ahead of us,' a soldier wrote home before reaching the front. 'There's a lot of news I could write to you about but it's better that I'm silent. One's known for a long time that it had to come to this. Maybe we will envy those who have already died.'

At dawn on 7 June, the first units of the 17th SS began to move out

---

* Patton felt that the sacking of commanders was becoming excessive. 'Collins and Bradley are too prone to cut off heads,' he wrote. 'This will make division commanders lose their confidence. A man should not be damned for an initial failure with a new division.'

from their bases just south of the River Loire. They crossed the river at Montsoreau and motored on towards Saint-Lô, through small towns with advertisements on the walls for Castrol and aperitifs such as Byrrh and Dubonnet. By the evening of 8 June, advance elements of the reconnaissance battalion had reached the eastern edge of the Forêt de Cerisy, unaware that the American 1st Infantry Division from Omaha was heading in their direction.

The next morning, SS-Untersturmführer Hoffmann of the division's 38th SS Panzergrenadier-Regiment was going forward west of Isigny to reconnoitre the positions his troops were to take up. A Kübelwagen, the German equivalent of the Jeep, came towards them at speed. There was an army major in the front and two dead soldiers in the back. 'Turn round!' he yelled. 'Ahead everything's lost. The Amis are just behind me.'

Hoffmann continued up to the top of the hill, halted the vehicle and went forward on foot. He did not need binoculars. He could see American infantry advancing just 400 yards away. Behind them were some motorized units and, to the east, he could see a column of tanks on a road. Hoffmann's driver shouted that they must turn back. He reversed at high speed, then swung round. Hoffmann had to leap behind a tree. The American soldiers had spotted him and opened fire. The two SS men drove back as quickly as possible. Hoffmann's commander asked him why he had returned so soon. 'Because our start-line is already occupied,' he replied. 'By the enemy.' Most of the 17th SS Division, however, was held back near Saint-Lô because of fuel shortages, before being allocated to a counter-attack planned against the American paratroopers attacking Carentan.

On 7 June at 11.00 hours, Generalleutnant Eugen Meindl of the II Paratroop Corps in Brittany ordered the 3rd Paratroop Division to move to the north-east of Saint-Lô 'and push the enemy to the north back into the sea in order to retake the coast'. Its commander, Generalleutnant Richard Schimpf, sent off his few motorized units that evening and two battalions in trucks via Avranches. The units on foot had to march twenty-five miles on each of the short June nights. They suffered 'a general exhaustion among troops who were unaccustomed to marching in their new parachute boots'. Some were so footsore that officers commandeered farm carts drawn by huge Percheron horses. It took them ten days to reach the south-west end of the Forêt de Cerisy.

Schimpf was given the remnants of the 352nd Infanterie-Division which had escaped from the Omaha front. He wanted to push forward into the forest along with the reconnaissance battalion of the 17th SS Panzergrenadiers, but his corps commander, Generalleutnant Meindl, refused. He told Schimpf to organize a front, but it was no more than 'a mere line of combat outposts', with his flak battalion as the only anti-tank defence. In fact, the order to hold back had come from Seventh Army headquarters, which felt that Schimpf had 'insufficient forces' and that they were 'poorly trained for attacks'. The strength of the division 'rested in defence'. But Schimpf was still convinced that 'if the Americans at that time had launched an energetic attack from the Forêt de Cerisy, Saint-Lô would have fallen'.

General Mahlmann's 353rd Infanterie-Division had even less motorized transport. His most mobile units were two battalions on bicycles designated the *Radfahrbeweglichemarschgruppe* (the Mobile Bicycle March Group). The rest of the division, following on foot, was delayed by Resistance attacks which inflicted a number of casualties, including a severely wounded company commander. The Germans also suffered from Allied air attacks, forcing them to hide in barns and orchards during daylight hours. Another divisional commander described these approach marches as a 'nocturnal game of hide-and-seek'. The journey, which cost the 353rd a tenth of its strength, took them eleven days.

Most notorious of all movements to the Normandy front was that of the 2nd SS Panzer-Division *Das Reich*. Its commander, SS-Brigadeführer Heinz Lammerding, had been chief of staff to the infamous Erich von dem Bach-Zelewski, who would soon be brought in to destroy the Warsaw uprising. The *Das Reich* Division revelled in its brutality. It had taken part in *Partisanenkrieg* in the Soviet Union and the mass murder of Jews with Einsatzgruppe B in the region around Minsk. When they moved from the eastern front to the area of Toulouse in April, its officers saw no reason why they should behave any differently. On 21 May, in the Lot, they had massacred fifteen people, including several women, as reprisals for some shots fired at one of their detachments. On the same day, all the males in another village were deported to Germany.

Inspired by Allied messages and de Gaulle's broadcast, the over-hasty rising of the Resistance in many parts of France alarmed all German commanders, not just the SS. Many saw it as 'the initiation of a Communist revolution'. There was an element of truth in this view. On 7 June, the Communist-led FTP took over Tulle, the departmental capital of Corrèze, and inflicted 122 casualties on the Germans, shooting a number of their prisoners and mutilating some corpses of the forty dead. Nothing could have been better calculated to provoke a violent reaction from the Waffen-SS.

On 8 June, the *Das Reich* began its long journey north from Montauban. Some of its units reached Tulle the following day. They hanged ninety-nine citizens of the town from trees in the streets. Another 200 were deported to Germany. On 10 June, the 3rd Company of the division's *Führer* Regiment surrounded the village of Oradour-sur-Glane, fourteen miles north-east of Limoges. Its officers and soldiers shot the male inhabitants and herded the women and children into the church, which they set on fire. The village also was burned to the ground. Altogether, 642 people died in this massacre. Some of the victims were not even locals, but refugee children from Paris and passengers from a train halted nearby. None of them were members of the Resistance.

The SS had even chosen the wrong Oradour. The company commander, whose death they were avenging, had in fact been killed in Oradour-sur-Vayres, fifteen miles away. The *Führer* Regiment was almost certainly responsible for another massacre of sixty-seven people at Argenton in the Indre *département*. The Vichy French authorities were also alarmed by reports of 'regions where a hideous civil war is breaking out', as some Resistance groups began a settling of accounts against political enemies. But even loyal Pétainists were appalled by the brutal reprisals of the *Das Reich* Division.

General Koenig in London had ordered the FFI to hold German divisions south of the Loire. The achievement of the Resistance in delaying the *Das Reich* Division was one of its greatest contributions to the battle for Normandy. SOE networks had played a large part, destroying the *Das Reich*'s fuel dumps before they even started, sabotaging rolling stock, blowing railway lines and organizing sequences of small ambushes. In the Dordogne, twenty-eight members of the Resistance managed to hold up one column for forty-eight hours near Souillac.

Almost all were killed in this utterly courageous act of self-sacrifice. The delays inflicted, combined with reports radioed back to London, gave the RAF the opportunity to attack the division on several occasions, most notably in Angoulême. Altogether it took the *Das Reich* Division seventeen days to reach the front, fourteen more than expected.

While a detachment from the American 1st Infantry Division had advanced east along the coast to meet up with the British around Port-en-Bessin, the main part slowly advanced due south towards Caumont. The tanks supporting them provided 'spray jobs' with their machine guns on suspected sniper positions.

The newly landed 2nd Infantry Division, on its right, meanwhile headed towards the Fôret de Cerisy, midway between Saint-Lô and Bayeux. Neither division realized that they 'were in fact facing a gaping hole in the German lines more than ten miles broad'. Both the 17th SS and the 3rd Paratroop Division later argued that their opponents had missed the opportunity of capturing Saint-Lô in the first week of the invasion.

Rommel, however, was less concerned about this gap in the line than by the threat to Carentan. That was where he decided to launch a counter-attack to prevent the two American beachheads from joining up. Leaving the 17th SS reconnaissance battalion to face the 1st Division, he ordered the main part of the *Götz von Berlichingen* to Carentan, which was held by nothing more than the remnants of Heydte's 6th Paratroop Regiment.

Heydte's regiment, having lost a whole battalion near Côme-du-Mont, had been forced to retreat rapidly to avoid encirclement by the 101st Airborne. Many of his men had swum the River Douve to escape. By 10 June, Heydte was defending the northern edge of Carentan, an inland port with fine stone buildings. Lacking ammunition and out of touch with the LXXXIV Corps headquarters of General Marcks, Heydte gave the order for the 6th Paratroop Regiment to withdraw from Carentan during the night of 11 June. Their retreat was to be protected by a rearguard to hold back the American paratroopers until the next morning.

That evening, as the withdrawal was under way, Brigadeführer Ostendorff, the commander of the 17th SS Panzergrenadier Division

Götz von Berlichingen appeared at Heydte's command post. He informed Heydte that he was now under his command. They were to hold Carentan at any price. Heydte told him that he had already given the order to evacuate the town, not knowing that the 17th SS was on its way. If he had known, he would not have taken the decision. Ostendorff was a heavily built, genial-looking thug with a shaven head, but this news did not put him in an amiable mood. A furious row ensued, although little could be done except prepare a counter-attack to retake Carentan the next day.

On the following morning, 12 June, as the 101st Airborne moved into Carentan, General der Artillerie Marcks died in his vehicle after a low-flying attack by Allied fighters on a road north-west of Saint-Lô. Just before he set out, his chief of staff had asked him not to expose himself unnecessarily to danger. 'You people are always worried about your little bit of life,' Marcks replied. One or two of his colleagues suspected that the disillusioned Marcks wanted to die in battle, since two of his three sons had already been killed in the war. Marcks's death and various delays led to the counter-attack being postponed until 13 June. This was fortunate for the Allies. Ultra intercepts, including requests to the Luftwaffe to support the 17th SS Division in the attack, had revealed Rommel's plan. Bradley, forewarned, brought Brigadier General Maurice Rose's combat command from the 2nd Armored Division across from the 1st Infantry Division's Caumont sector.

On the eve of battle, Brigadeführer Ostendorff tried to raise his men's morale in a strange way. He warned of the enemy's phosphorus shells, which caused terrible burns, and the 101st Airborne's 'sly, underhand way of fighting', but then added that they had a 'poor fighting spirit'.

On 13 June at 05.30 hours, the 37th SS Panzergrenadier-Regiment advanced in the misty dawn, supported by artillery fire. When they came close to the barrage, they fired red flares to tell the batteries to increase their range. The advance appeared to be going to plan, but as they neared the Carentan–Domville road, they came under very accurate sniper fire. The panzergrenadiers found that American paratroopers had concealed themselves in trees all over the place. The accompanying flak platoon began blasting the hedgerows and trees with their quadruple 20 mm anti-aircraft guns, but this took time. Having suffered 'moderately high losses', the Germans pushed on as the Americans slipped back towards Carentan.

Ostendorff's men reached the south-west edge of Carentan at 09.00 hours, but soon his right wing was brought to a sudden halt. The commander called in vain for tank support. The Shermans of the 2nd Armored Division had appeared, commanded by Brigadier General Rose in his open half-track. The panzergrenadiers, lacking even light Panzerfaust anti-tank weapons, pulled back in confusion. Early in the afternoon, the Americans themselves attacked in full strength, with fighter-bomber support. The key position was a hill on the southern edge of Carentan. It had been occupied by *Osttruppen*, but they fled as soon as their German commander was killed. Ostendorff was furious that his new division had suffered a humiliating reverse. He blamed the Luftwaffe for failing to appear in any strength, and then Heydte for having given up Carentan in the first place.

Oberstleutnant von der Heydte, with his aquiline nose and sharp intelligence, was far too independent, if not high-handed, in the view of senior German officers. He certainly showed little respect towards Ostendorff, and did little to conceal his opinion that the newly formed *Götz von Berlichingen* had been trained more in SS ideology than in sound military principles. Heydte claimed that during the battle he even had to order his paratroopers to round up at gunpoint some of their fleeing panzergrenadiers. Ostendorff summoned him to the 17th SS headquarters to be interviewed by a military judge attached to the division about responsibility for the loss of Carentan. Although accused by Ostendorff of cowardice, Heydte avoided a court martial mainly because he had just been awarded the Oak Leaves to the Knight's Cross. Pemsel, the chief of staff of the Seventh Army, did not believe Heydte's version of events, but General Meindl, the commander of II Paratroop Corps, ordered his release. In any case, German commanders had rather more serious matters to consider. The next day, American advances linked up the Utah and Omaha beachheads.

12

Failure at Caen

At midnight on 6 June, Generalmajor Pemsel, the chief of staff of the Seventh Army, rang the commanders of the 21st Panzer-Division and 716th Infanterie-Division. He passed on the order from the OKW that the counter-attack next day must reach the coast 'without fail' to relieve those defenders of strongpoints still holding out. General Richter of the 716th told him that 'communications between division, regimental and battalion command posts no longer exist', so he had no idea which positions still held out and which had been taken. In fact, the 716th Infanterie-Division had virtually ceased to exist, and its 200 survivors were withdrawn two days later.

Although the British 3rd Division had captured most of the defensive positions which had held them up on D-Day, the most powerful of all still held out on their right flank. This was the Luftwaffe radar station near Douvres-la-Délivrande, which had been turned into a veritable underground fortress. It also possessed a buried landline back to Caen, so its defenders could act as artillery observers. The Canadians who tried to reduce it faced a hard fight. They also had to clear the woods near the heavily defended radar station, which were 'honeycombed with trenches, shelters and tunnels'.

The 21st Panzer-Division, following its unsuccessful attack on the late afternoon of D-Day, was put under the 1st SS Panzer Corps. Its commander was Obergruppenführer Sepp Dietrich. Dietrich had been an apprentice butcher, then a front-line soldier in the First World War. In the chaos after the Armistice, when Germany was on the edge of civil war, Dietrich joined the Freikorps. An early member of the Nazi Party, he became commander of Hitler's personal SS bodyguard in 1928. This later formed the basis for the 1st SS Panzer Division *Leibstandarte Adolf Hitler*, which fought under Dietrich in France, the Balkans and on the eastern front. Goebbels deliberately portrayed him as a hero for ordinary people to counterbalance the aristocracy in the regular army. Although more honest than most of his senior Waffen-SS comrades, Dietrich was a brutal and unintelligent field commander. According to General der Panzertruppen Heinz Eberbach, who replaced Geyr von Schweppenburg later, 'under his command the *Leibstandarte* killed thousands of Jews'.*

Dietrich had been in Brussels with I SS Panzer Corps headquarters early on the morning of 6 June when news of the landings arrived. Rundstedt immediately summoned him to Paris. Dietrich was to take under his command the 12th SS Panzer-Division *Hitler Jugend*, the Panzer Lehr Division, the 21st Panzer-Division and the remains of the 716th Infanterie-Division. The corps was then to attack the British around Caen at dawn the next day and sweep them into the sea. But the effectiveness of Allied air attacks, together with the delayed start of both the *Hitler Jugend* and the Panzer Lehr Divisions, played havoc with the plan.

Dietrich reached the headquarters of Feuchtinger's 21st Panzer-Division at Saint-Pierre-sur-Dives that night. Feuchtinger was away at the command post of the 716th Infanterie-Division in a tunnel on the edge of Caen. Dietrich exploded when he heard that Feuchtinger had forgotten to take a radio with him. In his place, the divisional chief of staff, Oberst Freiherr von Berlichingen, a descendant of the knight with the iron fist, ventured to suggest that two panzer divisions were not enough to throw the British and Canadians back. Surely they should wait for the Panzer Lehr Division to join them. Dietrich replied in no uncertain terms that only the two formations were available and he should liaise immediately with the *Hitler Jugend* Division to plan their attack.

Brigadeführer Fritz Witt, the commander of the *Hitler Jugend*, sent Standartenführer Kurt Meyer to see Feuchtinger and Richter in the

---

* This was probably at Taganrog in southern Russia. At the beginning of 1942, the division also murdered 4,000 Soviet prisoners.

headquarters tunnel on the edge of Caen. Meyer, the commander of the 25th SS Panzergrenadier-Regiment, was an utterly devoted Nazi and a ruthless fighter. Tall, blue-eyed and good-looking, he was the beau ideal of a Waffen-SS leader. His men called him 'Panzer Meyer' in admiration. He finally found the 716th's headquarters in the very early hours of 7 June. The entrance was crammed with wounded. He told Richter, 'It has taken about eight hours to reach you here. I spent more than four hours in road ditches because of air attacks. The march columns of the division are suffering heavy losses.' The *Hitler Jugend* referred to Allied fighter-bombers as 'meatflies'.

After studying the marked-up map during their briefing, Meyer arrogantly dismissed Feuchtinger's concerns about enemy strength. 'Little fish!' he said. 'We'll throw them back into the sea in the morning.' But the great counter-attack had to be postponed. The Panzer Lehr Division coming from the south continued to suffer even more from air strikes than the *Hitler Jugend*. The disastrous loss of fuel to Allied air attack also meant that it needed to take almost all of Richter's own reserves. In addition, Richter claimed that he had to move the division's field hospital back to near Falaise because, despite being 'clearly marked with red crosses', it was bombed and strafed constantly by Allied aircraft.

The complications of the German command structure added greatly to the confusion. The Seventh Army was responsible for the coast, yet I SS Panzer Corps became part of General Geyr von Schweppenburg's Panzer Group West. Geyr himself wrote later, 'At a moment when everything depended on rapid action, orders were issued to just two and three-quarter Panzer Divisions by the following headquarters: I SS Panzer Corps, Panzer Group West, Seventh Army at Le Mans, Army Group B, OB West and OKW.'

Geyr, who believed like Guderian in the importance of a massive panzer counter-attack, was shaken to find how effective the Allied bombing of key towns had been in blocking approach routes. Having strongly opposed the idea of deploying panzer divisions close to the coast, he still refused to acknowledge that Rommel's healthy respect for Allied air power had been more prescient. Geyr was to suffer for this hubris when Ultra intercepts identified the exact location of his headquarters a few days later.

*

At the end of D-Day, British commanders in the Sword beachhead had played down their failure to take Caen with the misplaced optimism that 'we can always take it tomorrow'. The repulse of the 21st Panzer-Division had raised exaggerated hopes. They had not yet come up against the *Hitler Jugend* and they also failed to appreciate that the most effective weapon in the 21st Panzer's armoury was not its tanks, but its twenty-four 88 mm anti-tank guns.

Whether it was the retreat of the 21st Panzer, the constant fighter-bomber attacks on the roads, or the naval guns taking on targets well inland, panic-stricken rumours that Caen had fallen spread among German rear troops. On 7 June, these 'fright reports', as the I SS Panzer Corps called them, prompted its chief of staff to send detachments of Feldgendarmerie to the roads leading into Falaise. Those fleeing in this 'faint-hearted rabble who, in the West, had grown unaccustomed to war' were rounded up. In any case, the I Panzer Corps despised the British for failing to strike while German forces were unable to bring up reinforcements quickly enough.

Apart from the problems created by the prolonged defence of 'Hillman' and insufficient armoured units to fight through to Caen, the British I Corps commander, Lieutenant General John Crocker, had made a grave error. On the afternoon of D-Day, fearing a major counter-attack east of the River Orne, he took the 9th Infantry Brigade away from its task of attacking between Caen and Carpiquet, and switched it to support the airborne division. This transfer also con-tributed to the dangerous gap between the Canadians and the British 3rd Division.

On 7 June, the attack towards Caen was renewed with fighting near its northern edge, around the village of Lebisey and its woods. But even with heavy artillery support, the 185th Brigade suffered heavy losses. The 21st Panzer-Division had sorted itself out and established effective positions on the higher ground in front of Caen and forward to Bénouville, where Major Hans von Luck's panzergrenadiers were still launching counter-attacks against the 6th Airborne.

Montgomery's old regiment, the 2nd Battalion of the Royal Warwicks, formed part of the attack near Lebisey. On their brigadier's orders, the anti-tank platoon, with six Bren-gun carriers towing their guns, charged up a sunken road with high banks. The firing went right over their heads and they could see little. Suddenly they found themselves in Lebisey in the middle of a 21st Panzer-Division grenadier regiment. They went past a Mark IV, drove right on through to their rear and halted in a wheatfield to deploy their anti-tank guns. 'Action rear!' the lieutenant yelled. His Birmingham lads swore merrily as they brought the guns to bear and fired. But then a shell blew up his carrier and the blast knocked them all flat.

They tried to slip back to their own lines but were captured and marched back to Lebisey wood. The panzergrenadiers were very non-chalant and 'elegant'. They asked their prisoners what they would like to drink, milk or wine. Then shells from HMS *Warspite* began roaring overhead. The German guarding them said to the lieutenant, 'I think we better dig a hole, don't you?' and the two of them began digging together. They sat in the trench side by side as the bombardment continued, both shrinking each time a shell came over. 'You will be back in the sea in a few days,' the German remarked. 'No, I am sorry,' Bannerman replied. 'We will be in Paris in a week.' Agreeing to disagree, the panzergrenadier showed a snapshot of his fiancée. The lieutenant repaid the compliment by producing a photograph of his wife. He could not help thinking that just half an hour before they had been trying to kill each other.

General Crocker had then moved the 9th Brigade back to its original sector, just to the right of the 185th Brigade. This area, like the Canadian sector, consisted of gently rolling country with wheatfields, stone farm-houses surrounded by an orchard, and copses which hid anti-tank guns. Farmers had brought in their cows and horses, hoping that they would be better protected in barns and yards. Some watched the fighting from a loft, while their family sheltered in the cellar. Yet much of the fighting and shelling was concentrated on buildings. In the hamlet of Gruchy, near Buron, nine out of ten houses were destroyed or badly damaged. Germans looted cider and Calvados from their cellars, several drinking themselves into a stupor.

The 2nd Battalion of the Royal Ulster Rifles made a brave charge across open cornfields towards the village of Cambes. They fought their way in, but a newly arrived detachment of the 12th SS *Hitler Jugend* forced them to retreat. The Ulster Rifles had to leave their wounded from D Company in a ditch outside the village. They were certain that the young soldiers from the *Hitler Jugend* shot them all as they lay there afterwards.

Further to the right of 9th Brigade, the Canadians also came up against detachments of the *Hitler Jugend* when they renewed their advance on Carpiquet airfield. After Standartenführer Meyer had set up his command post in the Abbaye d'Ardennes, his 25th Panzergrenadier-Regiment was due to attack at 16.00 hours to the west of the railway line from Caen to Saint-Luc-sur-Mer, while the 21st Panzer-Division were to advance on the east side. But the approach of the Canadians made him decide to attack immediately. The order was passed to the *Hitler Jugend* tank battalion: 'Panzer, March!' They took the Canadian armoured regiment, the Sherbrooke Fusiliers, unawares and rapidly recaptured the village of Authie. But in their triumphant rush forward, the *Hitler Jugend* tanks were surprised in their turn by well-sited Canadian anti-tank guns. Meyer soon sent the tanks which had withdrawn back into another firefight, this time concentrated on the village of Buron. The fighting that afternoon ended in a bloody draw, with British, Canadian and German attacks brought to a standstill.

The British had a much better day on the Bayeux front to the west. Patrols during the night had established that the small city had been almost entirely evacuated by the German administration. So the Essex Regiment and the South Wales Borderers, supported by the Sherwood Rangers, were able to liberate Bayeux on 7 June with little damage. 'We were the first troops into the town', wrote Stanley Christopherson, who commanded A Squadron of the Sherwood Rangers, 'and were most relieved to find that except for isolated strong-points in the town and the odd sniper no Germans were to be found, which prevented any damage to the beautiful and historic buildings. We were given a most enthusiastic and spontaneous reception by the inhabitants who appeared genuinely delighted to welcome us and demonstrated their joy by throwing flowers at the tanks and distributing cider and food among the men.'

In the south of the town, one enemy machine-gun post held out in a house, which caught fire when a Sherwood Ranger tank shelled it. 'After a very short time the clanging of a bell heralded the arrival of the Bayeux fire brigade, manned by a full team all wearing shiny helmets. Regardless of the machine gun fire, they held up the battle, entered the house, extinguished the fire and brought out the German machine gun section.'

The next day, 8 June, the Sherwood Rangers rejoined the 8th Armoured Brigade to advance south. Bypassing anti-tank guns, they occupied some high ground seven miles to the south-east of Bayeux known as Hill 103. It overlooked the villages of Tilly-sur-Seulles and Fontenay-le-Pesnel, which British squaddies dubbed 'Piss in the Fountain'. The main danger on the way had been the odd rifleman shooting at the heads of tank commanders. But on the next day the Sherwood Rangers and the 6th Durham Light Infantry suddenly came under attack.

The Panzer Lehr Division had finally arrived at the front. General-leutnant Fritz Bayerlein, its commander, was still furious after Generaloberst Dollmann's order to move during daylight hours. Rocket-firing Typhoons from the RAF and American Lightning squadrons had appeared overhead almost immediately on the afternoon of 6 June and destroyed a number of vehicles. Bayerlein's men pushed on through the cover of darkness, expecting to go into camouflaged positions before dawn, but General Dollmann ordered the division to keep going. The first air strike had hit them at 05.30 hours the next morning. Tanks and half-tracks, already camouflaged with leafy branches, sprinted for the cover of woods and orchards, but there were too many open spaces. According to Bayerlein, his men nicknamed the straight road north-east from Vire the 'fighter-bomber racecourse'. He claimed that by the end of the day the division had lost five tanks, eighty-four half-tracks and self-propelled guns, and 130 trucks, but this was almost certainly a gross exaggeration.*

When the advance elements of the Panzer Lehr Division attacked northwards from Tilly-sur-Seulles on the morning of 8 June, the Sherwood Rangers and the Durham Light Infantry towards Lingèvres received the full force. 'It was a terrible day for the regiment,' wrote Christopherson in his diary. His squadron on Hill 103 lost four tanks. One of his troop leaders was killed and also his second in command,

---

* The commander of Panzer Lehr's repair and maintenance company later wrote that the figure of eighty-four half-tracks lost applied to the whole month of June.

the poet Captain Keith Douglas. Douglas, who had been reconnoitring on foot, 'was hit in the head by a piece of mortar shell as he was running along a ditch towards his tank'. He died instantly. Douglas had been the odd man out in this yeomanry regiment. He did not hunt, ride or show any interest in countryside pursuits. In his poem about the regiment, entitled 'Aristocrats', he had written:

> How can I live among this gentle
> obsolescent breed of heroes, and not weep?

Yet the regiment always remembered Douglas for his bravery as well as his awkwardness. In North Africa, he had abandoned his post back in Cairo, risking a charge of desertion, to rejoin his squadron when the fighting was at its fiercest. 'I like you, sir,' said his soldier servant. 'You're shit or bust, you are.'

Christopherson wrote in his diary, 'In action he had undaunted courage and always showed initiative and complete disregard for his own personal safety. At times he appeared even to be somewhat foolhardy – maybe on account of his short-sightedness which compelled him to wear large thick-lensed glasses.' The regimental padre, Leslie Skinner, who remembered their conversation on the Sunday before D-Day, when the young captain had talked of his imminent death, buried Douglas by the hedge where he had died.

Three days later, the Sherwood Rangers, again close to Hill 103, suffered another disaster. An artillery shell exploded beside the regimental headquarters tank, named 'Robin Hood', just as an orders group was being held. The commanding officer, Michael Laycock, the brother of the commando leader, Major General Robert Laycock, was killed along with his adjutant and signals officer. The adjutant, George Jones, was the son of the head woodsman on the Laycock estate. Their recce troop leader and the signals sergeant were also badly wounded. The Sherwood Rangers had lost two commanding officers in under a week. Christopherson, as senior squadron leader, then took over.

Padre Skinner, their Methodist minister, seldom rested during those days from burying the dead, having selflessly recovered the bodies himself. Skinner, a small, dark man with a strong Yorkshire accent, was much loved. He did not want his soldiers to suffer the horrible task of scraping the carbonized remains of comrades off the inside of a 'brewed-up' tank. Shermans, which ran on gasoline, not diesel, were notorious for catching fire. The Americans gave them the nickname 'Ronsons' (after the lighter) and the Germans called them 'Tommy cookers'. For all tank troops, the thought of being trapped in a burning hull was their greatest fear. To conceal their anxiety, British tank commanders tended to assume a leisurely drawl over the radio.

The attack of the Panzer Lehr on 8 June was halted partly by the resistance north of Tilly-sur-Seulles, but also because, in mid-afternoon, Sepp Dietrich ordered the division to pull back and then advance north-west towards Bayeux instead. Confusion in the German command was fragmenting the immediate panzer counter-attack towards the coast which Geyr von Schweppenburg so wanted. He complained later that they 'missed the psychological moment . . . to deal the British a severe blow'. But he was still determined to carry it out.

The British and Canadians west of the Orne continued to attack on 9 June, trying to force their way forward, one fortified village at a time. The same day, a full battalion assault on Cambes was planned, supported by artillery and the guns of the cruiser HMS *Danae*. The 2nd Royal Ulster Rifles moved forward to their start line for the attack. They looked at the huge stretch of undulating wheatfield ahead, across which they would have to attack. A young platoon commander recorded his men's nervous jokes as they waited for the order to advance while the artillery and naval barrage went overhead.

'Last time I was in a cornfield it was with my bird, all quiet and peaceful.'

'Hope that bloody boat stops firing when we get there.'

'It looks a long way, sir. Do we stop for a brew-up halfway?'

The thigh-high green wheat gave an impression of cover, but they soon found that it offered no protection at all when the advance began. 'This became quite obvious,' the lieutenant wrote, 'as one saw the frightening number of men staggering and dropping into the corn.' One company lost all three platoon commanders.

The Ulster Rifles were supported by the Shermans of the East Riding Yeomanry, which knocked out a Mark IV panzer, but then a concealed German 88 mm gun hit one British tank after another. With great courage in the face of the machine-gun positions, the Ulster Rifles pushed on to take Cambes and dug in. But when they counted their casualties, they found that they had lost eleven officers and 182 NCOs and soldiers.

The King's Own Scottish Borderers came up at dusk to reinforce the depleted battalion just as a sudden mortar 'stonk' began. One of the Jocks, taking cover from the explosions, jumped down into the nearest trench, clapped the occupant on the back and said, 'Well, Paddy, you old bastard, we never expected to see you again.' He found that he had just greeted the Ulster Rifles' commanding officer.

During the previous night, the *Hitler Jugend*, led by Panzer Meyer on a motorcycle, attacked Norrey and Bretteville-l'Orgueilleuse with Panther tanks, reconnaissance troops and panzergrenadiers. The Regina Rifles were ready for them. By the dead light of magnesium parachute flares, their anti-tank guns had inflicted heavy casualties. The SS troops had been forced to withdraw.

Most attacks on 9 June, however, were repulsed as the I Panzer Corps pushed more tanks into the front line to assist the panzergrenadiers in seizing a start line for the attack towards the coast. British and Canadian artillery, supplemented by naval guns, proved extremely effective in breaking up the panzer detachments. And once again the anti-tank guns of the Regina Rifles smashed another attack by a company of Panthers. The panzer commander described how his tank lurched to a halt. 'When I looked to the left to check the situation, I happened to see the turret being torn off the panzer driving on the left flank. At the same moment, after another explosion, my vehicle began to burn. The machine-gun ammunition caught on fire and there was a crackling noise like dry wood burning.' He just managed to escape from his tank with severe burns. Only five tanks out of twelve returned. A *Hitler Jugend* officer watching the scene wrote afterwards: 'I could have cried for rage and sorrow.'

The *Hitler Jugend* were forced to recognize that these 'surprise raids' which had worked so well against the Red Army on the eastern front did not succeed in Normandy. Yet another frontal attack was made on Norrey before dawn on 10 June, this time with the Pioneer battalion thrown in with the panzergrenadiers. Again it was repulsed. The body of one Pioneer company commander, Otto Toll, was found afterwards.

'He had tried to make a tourniquet using the ribbon of his Knight's Cross and a flashlight, obviously to stop the bleeding from an artery.'

The fighting had been pitiless. Accusations of war crimes were made by both sides. At a tribunal after the war, officers from the 26th Panzergrenadier-Regiment of the *Hitler Jugend* claimed that they had shot three Canadian prisoners on 9 June in retaliation for an incident the day before. On 8 June south of Cristot, a detachment from the Inns of Court armoured reconnaissance regiment surprised a small party from a Panzer Lehr Division artillery regiment, including its commander. The British told their prisoners to climb on to the front of their vehicles as there was no room inside. The Germans refused, stating that it would make them a human shield. According to Hauptmann Graf Clary-Aldringen, two British officers beat up Oberst Luxenburger, a one-armed veteran of the First World War, and then tied him to one of their vehicles. As they left, they machine-gunned the others who still refused to mount. But the Inns of Court group ran into a German anti-tank position. Their two officers were killed and Oberst Luxenburger mortally wounded.

Apart from this incident, the *Hitler Jugend* also tried to justify its actions on the grounds that they had captured Canadian orders telling their soldiers not to take prisoners if it slowed down their advance. British and Canadian soldiers, especially those in armoured regiments who had no infantry to escort captives to the rear, did indeed shoot prisoners on occasion. But the *Hitler Jugend* argument sounds less than convincing, especially when a total of 187 Canadian soldiers are said to have been executed during the first days of the invasion, almost all by members of the 12th SS. And their first killings had taken place on 7 June, before the incident near Cristot. One Frenchwoman from Caen, who had walked to Authie to see if an old aunt was all right, discovered 'about thirty Canadian soldiers massacred and mutilated by the Germans'. The Royal Winnipeg Rifles later found that the SS had shot eighteen of their men, who had been taken prisoner and interrogated at Meyer's command post in the Abbaye d'Ardennes. One of them, Major Hodge, had apparently been decapitated.

The *Hitler Jugend* was probably the most indoctrinated of all Waffen-SS divisions. Many of its key commanders came from the 1st SS Panzer-Division *Leibstandarte Adolf Hitler*. They had been formed in the *Rassenkrieg*, or 'race war', of the eastern front. The worst appears to have been the reconnaissance battalion, whose commander, Bremer, was known within the division as a 'dare-devil'. Meyer himself was accused of shooting fifty Jews near Modlin in Poland in 1939 and during the invasion of the Soviet Union, he is said to have ordered the burning of a village near Kharkov. All its inhabitants were murdered. Nazi propaganda and fighting on the eastern front had brutalized them, and they saw the war in the west as no different. Killing Allied prisoners was considered their revenge for the 'terror bombing' of German cities. In any case, bitterness between Canadians and soldiers of the *Hitler Jugend* became a vicious circle throughout the battle for Normandy.

All German headquarters in Normandy soon found to their cost that they had to resort to the radio more and more. Bombing and shelling, to say nothing of the Resistance and airborne troops, had severed many of their landlines in the invasion area. This was the bonus which the decrypters at Bletchley Park had been anticipating. The head of the Secret Intelligence Service passed Churchill their first haul.* They intercepted a report from General Marcks on 8 June stating that the 716th Infanterie-Division had lost at least two-thirds of its strength and that 'the men show signs of nervous exhaustion'. There was also a warning, but received too late, of the *Hitler Jugend* attack on the night of 8 June. The next day, General Meindl of II Paratroop Corps complained that 'most of the land-line links are interrupted. Operations are greatly impeded by the considerable delay in the passing on of orders.' On 10 June, they intercepted a message saying that 'by order of commander-in-chief West at 10.30 hours, thorough destruction of Cherbourg harbour to begin forthwith'. They also discovered that fear of another invasion in Brittany had prompted the Luftwaffe to destroy four airfields immediately. The greatest coup, however, came with two messages giving the location of Panzer Group West's headquarters. To preserve the secret of Ultra, an aircraft was sent over the target area first.

---

* Churchill evidently could not deal with the twenty-four-hour clock or just hated it, so 'C', the head of the Secret Intelligence Service, used to cross out each timing and insert the more familiar twelve-hour version with a.m. or p.m.

Geyr von Schweppenburg was planning his major attack for dusk on 10 June. Soon after dawn that morning, he climbed the steeple of the Abbaye d'Ardennes on the west side of the city, which Meyer had established as the command post of the 25th SS Panzergrenadier-Regiment. Geyr examined the ground ahead through powerful binoculars. He knew the area well from the late summer of 1940, when he had been training the XXIV Corps ready for the invasion of England. While he was up there he watched British aircraft bomb the panzer regiment of the *Hitler Jugend* and it confirmed him in his decision that only a night attack was possible.

That afternoon, Rommel came to see him at his command post in the grounds of the Château de La Caine near Thury-Harcourt. Geyr told him his plan, and although both men would have preferred to attack more towards Bayeux, this change would cause too great a delay. Rommel also wanted to know the next step. Geyr quoted the Napoleonic principle of *'s'engager puis voir'*. Rommel agreed and took his leave. Geyr warned him about the danger of Allied fighter-bombers. Yet his own headquarters offered the most tempting target. Just after Rommel's departure reports came in from the Panzer Lehr Division that about sixty British tanks had broken through from Bretteville-l'Orgueilleuse towards Tilly-sur-Seulles. Geyr claimed that because he had no reserves available, he felt obliged to cancel the night attack near Caen. In fact, a far more pressing reason arose for cancelling the offensive that night.

Rocket-firing RAF Typhoon squadrons came in low, their pilots well briefed on their target. They were then followed by waves of Mitchell medium bombers. Astonishingly, Geyr's headquarters and its vehicles in the park of the château had not been properly camouflaged. The effect was devastating. His chief of staff died and 'all personnel of the operations section as well as most of the officers of the forward echelon were killed,' Geyr wrote later. His signals battalion was virtually wiped out. Geyr himself was wounded, but the psychological shock was far greater. He was incapable of resuming command of Panzer Group West before the end of the month.

There would be no more attempts to launch a major panzer counter-attack against the British Second Army until the II SS Panzer Corps arrived from the eastern front. The lack of infantry reinforcements, because of the time it took to march by night to the battlefront, meant that the panzer divisions had to be broken up into *Kampfgruppen*, or battlegroups, to hold the line. This completely disrupted German plans to concentrate its armoured forces to throw the Allies back into the sea. All they could do now was secure a front, especially against the British, to prevent a breakout towards Paris. British hopes of enlarging their beachhead were therefore dashed. The open country south-east of Caen remained beyond their reach, and any thought of pivoting on Caen, as Montgomery had claimed, had become impossible. Thus, in the first few days, the pattern of a battle of attrition became established.

Montgomery had to change his approach, although he refused to admit this later. On 10 June, accompanied by General Dempsey, he had a meeting with General Bradley in a field near Port-en-Bessin, where the British and American sectors had joined up. Using a map spread out on the bonnet of his Humber staff car, he explained his amended plan. Instead of a head-on assault on Caen, he would now create a pincer movement on the city. The 51st Highland Division and 4th Armoured Brigade would attack south out of the bridgehead east of the Orne to take Cagny. Meanwhile the 7th Armoured Division would launch a right-hook from inland of where they were standing to take Evrecy. They would start that very day.

The most daring part of his plan was to drop the 1st Airborne Division, his reserve back in England, around Evrecy. This idea ran into determined opposition from Leigh-Mallory. He said his transport aircraft could not risk a day drop because of German flak in the Caen area. A night drop was also out of the question because they would have to fly over the Allied ships offshore and the Royal Navy refused to provide a ceasefire because of the Luftwaffe attacks during darkness. An infuriated Montgomery wrote to Freddie de Guingand, his chief of staff at 21st Army Group rear headquarters back in England, declaring that Leigh-Mallory was 'a gutless bugger'.

This plan to envelop Caen was strikingly out of character. Montgomery was usually criticized for taking too long to mount an operation. Was he simply responding to the crisis with the best plan available in the circumstances? Or was there also an element of show, to divert attention from the way the Second Army had failed to achieve its objectives?* On 11 June, the day after the meeting with Bradley, Montgomery wrote to de Guingand that his general objective was to 'pull the Germans on to Second Army so that the [American] First Army can extend and expand'. This rather more modest assessment was hardly in keeping with his earlier pugnacious declarations. 'Inaction and a defensive mentality are criminal in any officer – however senior,' he had told senior officers two months before the invasion. 'Every officer and man must be enthusiastic for the fight and have the light of battle in his eyes.' They were 'to assault to the west of the River Orne and to develop operations to the south and south-east, in order to secure airfield sites and to protect the eastern flank of First US Army while the latter is capturing Cherbourg'.

The problem was that Montgomery, partly for reasons of morale and partly out of puerile pride, could not admit that any of his plans had gone wrong. He later created resentment and suspicion among his American colleagues by claiming that he still intended to break out towards Falaise, while insisting at the same time that he had always planned to pull the bulk of the German panzer divisions on to his front, to give the Americans the great chance of a breakout on theirs later. This, as his letter to de Guingand shows, was simply making a virtue out of a rather sore necessity.

It was not, of course, Montgomery who determined this state of affairs but the Germans who sent their panzer divisions against the British. Both Rundstedt and Rommel regarded the Second Army as the chief threat. This was partly because they considered the British more experienced soldiers (they later admitted to underestimating the Americans), but also because a south-easterly breakthrough towards Falaise opened the possibility of an Allied dash for Paris. Such a disaster, if it came about, would cut off all German forces in Normandy and Brittany. Even Hitler agreed with this analysis, if only because of the symbolic value of Paris. His obsessive desire to hold on to foreign capitals was described as 'a peevish imperialism' by the intelligence chief at Montgomery's 21st Army Group headquarters. Geyr was the only one who disagreed with the OKW's determination 'to block the

---

* Montgomery's 'Forecast of Operations' had predicted that the British Second Army would be five miles south-east of Caen by 14 June.

enemy's direct route to Paris', because it led to the 'unfortunate decision to employ on the inner flank the most powerful and mobile force'.

Equally serious for the British, the failure to expand the beachhead left them with far too little room to bring in and deploy more divisions during the build-up of forces. The RAF was furious, especially when Montgomery pretended that everything had gone according to plan. All air preparations had been calculated on establishing forward airbases for Spitfires and Typhoons within a few days. Now, because of the shallow depth of the beachhead, any airfield they built would be within the range of German artillery. There was also little room left for fuel depots, supply dumps, repair workshops, base camps, field hospitals and vehicle parks. Almost every orchard and field in the rear area was crammed. 'The British were so crowded that they overflowed into our area,' Bradley said later, a tactful remark concealing the degree of frustration that he felt. The Americans were even less impressed by Montgomery's grandiose statement that Caen was 'the key to Cherbourg'. General Collins, whose task it was to take Cherbourg, observed drily to Bradley, 'Why doesn't he just send us the key?'

German commanders were also dismayed by the way the battle had developed. 'By premature commitment in driblets,' the chief of staff of I Panzer Corps complained bitterly, 'the Germans missed their opportunity to stake everything on one card – to lose or win all'. In fact, the inability to launch a major counter-attack at this stage determined the manner of German deployment throughout most of the campaign. It also set the pattern for British tactics, despite Montgomery's great boast that he always made the enemy dance to his tune. To the despair of all panzer commanders, the constant pressure of Allied ground, air and artillery attack, while seldom adventurous, prevented Rommel from using his armoured divisions effectively. The emergency fire brigade approach, simply plugging gaps, led to their panzer divisions being divided up to reinforce infantry formations on the point of collapse.

The Germans could thus never hope to win a major victory, even though they retained an extraordinary ability to thwart their opponents and inflict heavy casualties. British commanders soon began to fear that they would run out of manpower in this battle of attrition.

13

Villers-Bocage

As the bloody stalemate in front of Caen became clear, Montgomery decided to send his two 'best batsmen' into play on 11 June. Both the 7th Armoured Division and the 51st Highland Division had distinguished themselves under his command in North Africa, but they were to receive a rude shock in Normandy. The 51st was diverted to the east of the River Orne to prepare the left-hook on Caen, while the Desert Rats of the 7th Armoured would mount a right-hook from the American flank near Tilly-sur-Seulles.

The Scots of the 51st Highland Division did not believe in hiding their light under a bushel. Other formations called them the 'Highway Decorators', because almost every road junction had a prominently displayed 'HD' and an arrow. The 51st moved over the Orne into the 6th Airborne's bridgehead. There, the heavily outnumbered and outgunned paratroopers had been forced back by relentless counter-attacks. With astonishing resilience, they faced Luck's *Kampfgruppe* from the 21st Panzer-Division, the 711th Infanterie-Division and the newly arrived 346th Infanterie-Division.

On 9 June, the paratroopers had fought off an attack by Luck's tanks and panzergrenadiers on Escoville. Another attack took place the following day as the 51st Highland Division began to take position. And on 11 June, when the 5th Black Watch found themselves in action, some of their men were taken prisoner and executed. The Highland Division, which had been supposed to advance all the way south to Cagny as part of Montgomery's pincer movement, made no headway at all. They seemed completely disorientated by the small, sharp actions and the sudden deadly mortar 'stonks' and artillery barrages at which the Germans were so efficient.

'The fury of artillery is a cold, mechanical fury,' wrote a Highlander, 'but its intent is personal. When you are under its fire you are the sole target. All of that shrieking, whining venom is directed at you and at no one else. You hunch in your hole in the ground, reduce yourself into as small a thing as you can become, and you harden your muscles in a pitiful attempt at defying the jagged, burning teeth of the shrapnel. Involuntarily you curl up into the foetal position except that your hands go down to protect your genitalia. This instinct to defend the place of generation against the forces of annihilation was universal.' Many resorted to a litany of repetitive swearing, a sort of profane mantra to dull their fear.

The same soldier went on to describe the psychological collapse of the most warlike member of their company. It took place in the cellar of a farmhouse. This battle-shock casualty was curled up on the floor, howling and sobbing. 'The smart, keen young soldier was now transformed into something that was at once pitiful and disgusting. The neatly-shaped, alert features had melted and blurred, the mouth was sagging and the whole face, dirty and stubbled, seemed swollen and was smeared with tears and snot.' He made bleating noises, crying for his mother. As well as a feeling of slightly sadistic contempt, the observer became 'aware of a kind of envy of the boy's shameless surrender to his terror'.

Paratroopers were contemptuous of the Scottish regiments involved. 'The thing that shocked me was 51st Highland Division,' wrote a major in the 1st Canadian Parachute Battalion. 'Three different times our division restored a situation for them. If you could have seen our lads come up to help them out on one occasion and call them yellow bastards when the Scotties threw their weapons and equipment away and fled.' On the left flank, Lieutenant Colonel Otway, who led the attack on the Merville battery, had to take a battalion of the Black Watch under command because its commanding officer 'broke down'. They had lost 200 men in their first attack.

General Gale, the 6th Airborne commander, realized that the village of Bréville had to be retaken at all costs. He sent in his own 12th Battalion of the Parachute Regiment. Suffering almost as many casualties as the

Black Watch, the 12th Battalion took the heavily defended village and the perimeter east of the Orne was saved. With the demoralized Highland Division unable to take even Sainte-Honorine, Montgomery's plan of striking through to Cagny, another five miles to the south, was quietly forgotten. In the circumstances, he should perhaps have been thankful that Leigh-Mallory had thwarted his plan. To have dropped the 1st Airborne Division on the Caen–Falaise plain and then failed to get to them would have achieved little more than a foretaste of the Arnhem disaster. General Bradley, although he said nothing at the time, clearly saw the danger of using airborne forces tactically and refused the opportunity later on during the great break-out.

Montgomery had higher hopes of his right-hook from the American 1st Division's flank. Lieutenant General Sir Miles Dempsey, the commander-in-chief of the British Second Army, was more sanguine. Dempsey was in many ways the opposite of Montgomery in character. Although he had the unfortunate nickname of 'Bimbo', he was a modest, quiet man, with a weather-beaten face and conventional military moustache. Patton, after meeting him for the first time, was dismissive in his diary: 'He is not very impressive looking, and I take him to be a yes-man.' The truth was that Montgomery insisted on running the Second Army as well as the 21st Army Group. Unable to delegate, Monty often gave orders to corps commanders over Dempsey's head. Dempsey had little choice but to accept his position as a glorified chief of staff. In many ways, the role suited him. He provided a steady pair of hands. His phenomenal memory combined effectively with an uncanny ability to visualize a landscape just from studying a map. In addition, he never complained when Montgomery took all the credit.

Dempsey had been the chief planner of the double-hook on Caen and the parachute operation. Even before the invasion, he had clearly not been convinced that Caen would fall on the first day, and doubted that they could capture it head on. Yet he was well aware of the danger if the front stagnated. Dempsey's plan was basically a sound one. Unfortunately, the 7th Armoured Division had landed later than expected because of bad weather. Then, the 50th Division and the 8th Armoured Brigade suffered a setback when advancing to secure the start line for the attack in the Seulles valley. A sudden advance by the

Panzer Lehr Division blocked the route, but it also presented a better opening. The 7th Armoured could outflank the Panzer Lehr by crossing into the American sector as their 1st Division advanced on Caumont, and then swing left. This would take it through a gap behind the Panzer Lehr while it was kept occupied by the 50th Division.

The commander of the 7th Armoured Division, Major General Erskine, expressed great confidence in the opportunity when Dempsey visited him at his headquarters on the morning of 12 June. 'Bobby' Erskine could not believe that anything would stop his division. The cavalry regiments of the famed 'Desert Rats' had brought their rather insouciant attitude with them to a very different battleground. Unlike the undulating cornfields of the Caen sector, this was *bocage* country, with sunken lanes and high hedges. 'You'll get a shock after the desert,' a trooper in the Sherwood Rangers warned a newly arrived friend. 'We could see the buggers in the desert and they could see us. Here they can see us, but I'll be buggered if we can see them.' Attacking through the leafy green tunnels, he added, 'gives you the bloody creeps'. Despite all the months of training for the invasion, both the British and the Americans were totally unprepared for this beautiful but claustrophobic terrain. The Normandy hedgerows, enclosing small fields and bordering every road and track, were at least three times the height of their English equivalent, heavily banked and far too dense for even a tank to smash through.

Dempsey told Erskine to push on to Villers-Bocage with the 11th Hussars, an armoured reconnaissance regiment, out in front. But Erskine switched them to the role of flank guards instead. This was to prove a very serious mistake. Erskine, who had wanted to attack twenty-four hours earlier, was impatient. He had good reason to be as things turned out. The delay was mainly the fault of his superior, Lieutenant General Gerard Bucknall, the commander of XXX Corps.

Although he had impressed Montgomery in Sicily and Italy, Bucknall had little experience of armour. He had certainly not impressed Field Marshal Brooke, who two months before the invasion wrote in his diary, 'Bucknall was very weak, and I am certain quite unfit to command a corps.' His reputation had been boosted by the capture of Bayeux, but he was not highly rated by those who knew him. Dempsey also had his doubts, but did nothing. As the American airborne commander

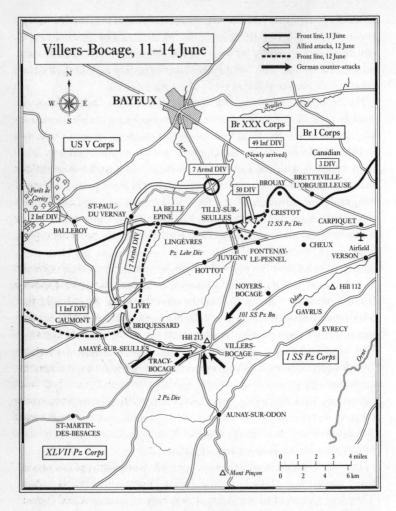

Villers–Bocage, 11–14 June

Front line, 11 June
Allied attacks, 12 June
Front line, 12 June
German counter-attacks

N
W — E
S

BAYEUX

Seulles

Br XXX Corps

49 Inf DIV
(Newly arrived)

Br I Corps

Canadian
3 DIV

US V Corps

Aure

7 Armd DIV

BROUAY

BRETTEVILLE-
L'ORGUEILLEUSE

*Forêt de
Cerisy*

2 Inf DIV

ST-PAUL-
DU VERNAY

LA BELLE
EPINE

TILLY-SUR-
SEULLES

CRISTOT

12 SS Pz Div

CARPIQUET

BALLEROY

7 Armd DIV

LINGÈVRES

Pz Lehr Div

JUVIGNY

FONTENAY-
LE-PESNEL

CHEUX

Airfield
VERSON

HOTTOT

NOYERS-
BOCAGE

Odon

Hill 112

1 Inf DIV
CAUMONT

LIVRY

BRIQUESSARD

101 SS Pz Bn

GAVRUS

EVRECY

AMAYÉ-SUR-SEULLES

Hill 213

TRACY-
BOCAGE

VILLERS-
BOCAGE

1 SS Pz Corps

Orne

2 Pz Div

AUNAY-SUR-ODON

ST-MARTIN-
DES-BESACES

XLVII Pz Corps

0 1 2 3 4 miles
0 2 4 6 km

△ *Mont Pinçon*

General Maxwell D. Taylor put it, British senior commanders never had the tradition of really pressing subordinates. American generals thought that their British counterparts were far too polite.

Erskine's failure to provide an armoured reconnaissance screen in front, rather than as a flank guard, led to one of the most devastating ambushes in British military history. The 22nd Armoured Brigade, led by its brave but eccentric commander, Brigadier 'Loony' Hinde, charged forward through the identified gap. By that evening his leading regiment, the 4th County of London Yeomanry (The Sharpshooters), had reached the Caumont road, just five miles short of Villers-Bocage. They leaguered for the night in all-round defence with their attached company of the 1st Battalion the Rifle Brigade.

At dawn, the Sharpshooters and their infantry trundled down the road to their objective. They entered Villers-Bocage at 08.00 hours on 13 June to an ecstatic reception from the local population. Gendarmes in their best uniforms held back the crowds, who threw flowers on to the Cromwell tanks and offered presents of cider and butter. In the exhilaration of the moment, the capture of this strategic town seemed too easy. Villers-Bocage, above the Seulles valley and just a mile from the River Odon, was a key position. Less than a dozen miles to the south stood Mont Pinçon, the dominating feature of the whole region, while Caen lay eight miles to the east.

The only enemy presence sighted had been a German eight-wheeled armoured car just before they entered the town, but it disappeared before the nearest Cromwell could traverse its turret. Brigadier Hinde, who accompanied them in a scout car, knew that to hold the town securely, they must occupy the feature on the north-east side known as Hill 213. The commanding officer of the Sharpshooters, Lieutenant Colonel the Viscount Cranley, wanted to carry out a thorough reconnaissance of the area, since more German armoured cars had been sighted, but 'Loony' Hinde would accept no delay. The reconnaissance troop of light Stuart tanks was not used. Cranley simply sent forward A Squadron and, leaving the rest of his tanks in the town, set off in a scout car to have a look himself at Hill 213.

In a small wood close to the road up which the Cromwells advanced, five Tiger tanks from the 101st SS Heavy Panzer Battalion lay hidden. They had just reached the front after a long and complicated journey from near Beauvais, north of Paris. Their commander was Obersturmführer Michael Wittmann, who was already famous as a 'panzer ace'. Credited with 137 tank 'kills' on the eastern front, he had received the Knight's Cross with Oak Leaves. Wittmann, enraged by the Allied bombing of German cities, had told his men, 'We have only one watchword and that is "revenge"!'

Wittmann's Tigers were the first reinforcements sent forward to fill the gap in the German line. Leading elements of the 2nd Panzer Division would also arrive in the area that day. In fact the 11th Hussars covering 22nd Armoured Brigade's flank identified their arrival from their first captive. A sergeant and trooper from the 11th had been stalking a sniper when they suddenly found themselves surrounded by a company of panzergrenadiers in half-tracks. They were marched off under guard towards the rear, but once out of sight, they jumped their escort, grabbed his rifle and brought him back as their prisoner instead. His paybook revealed that he was from the 304th Panzergrenadier-Regiment. Although Ultra had warned of the 2nd Panzer-Division's approach, this proof of its appearance on the southern flank seems to have come as a nasty shock for General Erskine.

Wittmann, seeing the squadron of Cromwells halt on this high-banked stretch of road, immediately recognized the opportunity. Some of the Sharpshooter crews had unwisely dismounted. This apparently prompted Wittmann's gunner to remark as he peered through his sight that they were behaving as if they had already won the war. Without waiting for his other Tigers to catch up, Wittmann emerged from the wood, swung parallel to the road and opened fire. The Tiger's 88 mm gun destroyed one Cromwell after another. The Cromwells, badly designed, under-armoured and under-gunned, did not stand a chance. They even found it hard to back out of danger, since their reverse speed was little more than two miles per hour.

Having caused havoc with A Squadron on the hill, Wittmann's Tiger lumbered down into the town of Villers-Bocage. It rammed aside a Bren-gun carrier of the Rifle Brigade and began to descend the main street. He dealt first with the tanks of the Sharpshooters' regimental headquarters, then attacked B Squadron. Many crews were dismounted and incapable of replying. But even those who managed to score direct hits on the Tiger found that their low-velocity 75 mm gun had little effect. Wittmann then returned to Hill 213 to finish the battle with A Squadron and the Rifle Brigade detachment.

That afternoon, Wittmann returned to Villers-Bocage with leading elements of the 2nd Panzer-Division. This time the Sharpshooters and the anti-tank guns of the Rifle Brigade were ready, and the attack was repulsed. But General Erskine, having failed to send forward sufficient support, was now worried that the 2nd Panzer-Division threatened his extended southern flank. He decided to withdraw the 22nd Armoured Brigade from its precarious position, rather than reinforce it. As they pulled out of the town that afternoon, British artillery fired a heavy barrage to cover the retreat. But many of the crews from knocked-out tanks had to escape on foot across country back to British lines.

Hinde withdrew the 22nd Armoured Brigade to a defensive position on Hill 174, between Tracy-Bocage and Amayé-sur-Seulles. Bucknall, the corps commander, agreed with the decision, but did little to help except order the 50th Division to continue their attacks on the Panzer Lehr Division. He failed to send infantry reinforcements to help the 22nd Armoured Brigade, isolated as it was between the Panzer Lehr and the 2nd Panzer.

On the afternoon of 14 June, Erskine felt compelled to withdraw his troops all the way back to the Caumont salient. Panzergrenadiers of the 2nd Panzer-Division attacked wherever they could. One British artillery regiment, finding itself in the front line, just managed to fight off an assault by firing airbursts with their twenty-five-pounders. The retreat of the 7th Armoured Division was greatly assisted by a devastating barrage from American artillery supporting their 1st Infantry Division. RAF bombers literally flattened Villers-Bocage that night. The townspeople who had welcomed the Sharpshooters so joyfully were now killed, injured or homeless. Most of the survivors sought shelter in the cellars of the nearby château, which belonged to local mayor, the Vicomte de Rugy.

Aunay-sur-Odon, an important crossroads four miles to the south, had also been smashed in a series of RAF bombing attacks. The first had taken place during Mass. The priest, the Abbé André Paul, recounted how the sound of aero engines overhead, rapidly followed by explosions which made the church shake, threw his congregation into panic. Many tried to crawl under an upturned prie-dieu for protection. As soon as it was over, the Abbé told them to leave quickly in small groups. As they emerged from the church, they were greeted by a vision of the Last Judgement. The bombs had disinterred many of the skeletons in the churchyard. Repeated raids killed 161 villagers and crushed the whole village to rubble. British troops were shocked by the scene when they finally reached the village just before the end of the battle for Normandy. The small town of Tilly-sur-Seulles had suffered almost as much. A local doctor tending the civilians said that even at Verdun he had not seen such terrible wounds.

On 15 June, the day after the British withdrawal, an Unteroffizier with the 2nd Panzer-Division found time to write home. 'The fighting in the west has now begun. You can imagine how much we are needed and that little time is left for writing. It is all or nothing now, it is about the existence or the end of our beloved Fatherland. How each of us soldiers will come through this is pretty irrelevant – the main thing is and remains that we will achieve a just and lasting peace ... we have learnt to do without everything regarding ourselves or the future and have often come to terms with our mortality. Yet repeatedly one catches oneself still having yearnings and they uphold our faith and our perseverance – but with the explosion of the next shell one's entire life could be extinguished in an eternal void. We have stepped up to the highest battle.'

The British attempt to break the deadlock in Normandy had failed humiliatingly. One can indulge in many fruitless arguments on the Villers-Bocage fiasco. Would everything have been different if, without the initial delay, the Sharpshooters had been established on Hill 213 before Wittmann arrived? Why did Bucknall not send reinforcements? And why was there no reconnaissance screen in front? The important point is that the operation was not just a major tactical setback. It was a devastating blow to the morale of the 7th Armoured Division and the rest of the British armoured regiments. An intelligence officer with 7th Armoured wrote in his diary a few days later that '131 Brigade were having a lot of cases of battle neurosis. 7th Armoured Division has a big reputation but neither 22 nor 131 Armoured Brigades are first class and they had too easy a time in Italy.'

Dempsey was furious with Erskine's performance and that of the division itself. The 7th Armoured, wrote Erskine's successor in August, made 'a very poor showing in Normandy'. But not all its regiments were going through a bad patch. 'The famous Desert Rats,' wrote the new commanding officer of the Sherwood Rangers, 'landed in Normandy with an outstanding reputation which, it must be admitted, it found difficult to retain. I think it is true to say that the only unit which had fought with this Division continually from its inception was the 11th Hussars, the most famous of all armoured reconnaissance regiments, which made for itself an unparalleled reputation which it never lost. When the 11th was out in front, no enemy could approach within miles without being seen and reported.'

The devastating ambush due to the lack of reconnaissance was certainly a shock. But the most unsettling aspect of the battle was the inability of the Cromwell to knock out a Tiger tank, even at point-blank range. There had been mutterings about the uselessness of British tanks before the invasion. Colonel Lord Cranley had felt obliged to address the Sharpshooters on the subject. He was quite aware of the faults in the tanks, but 'it was no good grousing as we would get no others so we must make the best of things'. The Cromwell was fast going forwards and had a low profile, but with its flat front it was vulnerable and it had an ineffective gun. Patton was dismissive of both the Churchill and the Cromwell, and even British generals were well aware of the Cromwell's 'design fault'.

Montgomery, in a letter to de Guingand on 12 June, hoped to stamp immediately on any idea of tank inferiority, however true. He did not want his armoured troops to develop 'a Tiger and Panther complex'. And yet Montgomery himself had criticized British tank design the previous August, when he said, 'We are outshot by the German tanks.' But to try to suppress the problem nearly a year later was flying in the face of reality. The German 88 mm gun, both on the Tiger and the flak gun in a ground role, could pick off Allied tanks before they were able to get within range. The diary of a British officer in Hinde's brigade was found in a shot-up tank near Tracy-Bocage. The penultimate entry on Sunday, 11 June, read, 'The squadron left to try to take a position and had to return rapidly having lost four tanks. After four years of preparation for the invasion why are our machines inferior?'

The Americans, proud of their technological sophistication, were shaken to find that even German small arms, especially their light machine gun the MG 42, were manifestly superior. Eisenhower's reaction on hearing how much better German tank guns were could not have been more different from Montgomery's attempt to suppress the issue. He wrote immediately to General Marshall and sent a senior tank expert back to the States to discuss what could be done to improve their armour-piercing ammunition. Montgomery should have written to Churchill demanding a massive increase in the production of Firefly tanks with the excellent seventeen-pounder gun. Churchill, an old cavalryman, would have done everything in his power to help.

Just before the Villers-Bocage operation, Churchill was in an ebullient mood. He was finally off to France for his first visit to the invasion area and had received encouraging news from Stalin. 'I have received the following from U.J. [Uncle Joe],' he cabled Roosevelt. 'It looks good. "The summer offensive of the Soviet forces, organised in accordance with the agreement at the Teheran conference, will begin towards the middle of June on one of the important sectors of the front".' This was confirmation of Operation Bagration, perhaps the most effective offensive of the whole war.

On 12 June, Churchill, having spent the night on his personal train, boarded the destroyer HMS *Kelvin* at Portsmouth accompanied by Field Marshal Smuts and Field Marshal Sir Alan Brooke. As they crossed the Channel, Brooke recorded that they 'passed convoys of landing craft, minesweepers, bits of floating breakwater (Phoenix) being towed out, parts of the floating piers (Whales) etc.' They came in sight of the coast at Courseulles-sur-Mer by 11.00 hours. 'The scene was beyond description,' Brooke wrote. 'Everywhere the sea was covered with ships of all sizes and shapes, and a continuous activity. We passed through rows of anchored LSTs and finally came to a "Gooseberry", namely a row of ships sunk in a half crescent to form a sort of harbour.'

They were met by Admiral Vian in his barge and then transferred to a DUKW, which drove them out of the water and right up the beach. 'It was a wonderful moment to find myself reentering France almost exactly 4 years after being thrown out,' Brooke continued. 'Floods of memories came back of my last trip of despair, and those long four years of work and anxiety.' General Montgomery was waiting for them with a small column of Jeeps. The large party climbed in and were driven off along the Bayeux road to 21st Army Group headquarters, in the grounds of the Château de Creully. After a typical Monty briefing, Churchill and his party set off to visit Dempsey at Second Army headquarters. Their route took them through countryside which had escaped destruction. Churchill turned to Brooke and said, 'We are surrounded by fat cattle lying in luscious pastures with their paws crossed.' But Brooke also noted that 'the French population did not seem in any way pleased to see us'. Churchill also heard the stories of French women snipers. 'There has been a recognizable amount of female sniping at us and the Americans by the women,' he wrote to Eden on his return.

When they finally returned to Courseulles, they watched an unsuccessful raid by German bombers and then re-embarked on Admiral Vian's barge for a trip along the coast. Churchill was entranced to see a monitor firing its fourteen-inch guns at targets inland. He announced that he had 'never been on one of His Majesty's ships engaging the enemy' and insisted on going aboard. Fortunately, Brooke noted, it was too difficult to climb up and the over-excited Prime Minister was denied his 'risky entertainment'. But Churchill was able to brag to Roosevelt, 'We went and had a plug at the Hun from our destroyer', because as they departed he persuaded the captain of HMS *Kelvin* and the accompanying HMS *Scourge* to open fire on German-held territory at a range of 6,000 yards. However, Churchill was not entirely out of the firing line, even when they reached England. That night, on their return to London, the first V1 flying bombs landed.

Royal Navy warships did not slacken in their gunfire. On 13 June, the battleship HMS *Ramillies* had to steam back to Portsmouth to replenish. And the next day a shell from HMS *Rodney* killed Brigadeführer Fritz Witt, the commander of the 12th SS *Hitler Jugend*, and one of his junior officers at their command post. The dynamic Meyer took over in his stead.

On that morning, 14 June, General de Gaulle, accompanied by a large entourage, drove down to Portsmouth from the Connaught Hotel in London in a convoy of six cars. The commander-in-chief Portsmouth greeted him even though they had arrived early for embarkation at the King's Stairs. The wait, with awkward small-talk – never de Gaulle's strong suit – was protracted because their ship, the Free French destroyer *La Combattante*, was late. This, the British liaison officer noted, provoked 'a slight display of ill-temper' in the General. The commander-in-chief had provided the admiral's barge, but it was not large enough to take all their luggage, an astonishing amount for what was supposed to be a one-day trip, so a picket boat had to be called up to ferry it all out. Clearly part of the retinue planned to stay on in France without informing the British. 'General de Gaulle's personal flag was broken at the main masthead as he went on board.'

As the French coast came in sight, one of the company said to their leader, 'Has it occurred to you, *mon Général*, that it is four years ago to the day since the Germans marched into Paris?'

'Well, they made a mistake,' came the inimitable reply.

They were met at the beach by officers of Montgomery's staff, who could not believe the size of the group and the quantity of luggage they were bringing ashore. Montgomery had asked that de Gaulle should bring no more than two people to lunch, but this request had been treated with monarchical disregard. In the event, only General de Gaulle, the French ambassador Viénot and Generals Koenig and Béthouart climbed into the Jeeps provided by 21st Army Group. The other fifteen members of the party and the luggage had to wait at the beach until transport could be found to send them on to Bayeux. De Gaulle even tried to insist at the last moment that the Jeeps should be driven by the French chauffeurs whom he had brought with him.

Montgomery's dislike of cigarettes was famous, but apparently de Gaulle and his companions filled Montgomery's caravan with smoke. This, according to the naval liaison officer accompanying the party, 'did little to ingratiate them with its tenant'. The lunch may have been a diplomatic ordeal for Montgomery, but it clearly gave de Gaulle little pleasure too. His companions noticed that he began to relax only afterwards, when the 21st Army Group Jeeps drove them on towards Bayeux, where they were to join up with the rest of the party. News of de Gaulle's appearance spread rapidly. The local *curé*, Father Paris, came cantering up on his horse. He reproved the General jovially for not having come to shake his hand. De Gaulle climbed out of the Jeep and, opening his seemingly endless arms, said, '*Monsieur le curé*, I do not shake your hand. I embrace you.'

In Bayeux, the General made his way to the Sous-Préfecture. There he was met by the *sous-préfet* standing self-importantly in his *tricolore* sash. The official then suddenly remembered to his horror that the portrait of Marshal Pétain still hung on the wall. De Gaulle, who was often so very thin-skinned, could also rise majestically above unintended insults. He continued talking to the embarrassed official as if nothing had happened. And also on that day he revealed his dry wit when an old woman in the crowd became confused in the cheering and cried out, '*Vive le Maréchal!*' He is said to have muttered to a companion, 'Another person who does not read the newspapers.' On the other hand, she might have been from a farming family outside the town. The historian Sergeant Forrest Pogue constantly found that the Normans in the countryside 'hated Laval, but not Pétain', and they harboured a certain distrust for de Gaulle.

In any case, there could be little doubt about the warmth of de Gaulle's reception in Bayeux itself. This was especially important, as he intended to install his own administration immediately. De Gaulle paid scant attention to Churchill's condition of the visit that there should be no public meetings. He mounted an improvised platform in the square outside the Sous-Préfecture and addressed the crowd. He finished his speech with the declaration, '*Le gouvernement français salue Bayeux – la première ville française libérée.*' There was no mention of the fact that the *gouvernement* was *provisoire*. He then led the crowd in singing the 'Marseillaise'. The only cloud on his horizon was that, according to a report Churchill had just received, the population seemed perfectly happy to accept the military currency issued by his Allies and denounced by the General as '*une fausse monnaie*'.

De Gaulle carried on to Isigny and Grandcamp, but arrived too late at the embarkation point for *La Combattante* to set sail that night. Even though he had been warned that no ship could leave the anchorage during the hours of darkness, due to the threat of German E-boats, de Gaulle was exasperated that the British naval authorities refused the French captain permission to weigh anchor, but he was in a very good humour after his reception. As the British liaison officer remarked, perhaps the fact that he had managed to 'post' four members of his party in France 'contributed to this feeling of satisfaction'. Montgomery, however, sent two signals to Churchill, the first saying that de Gaulle's visit to his headquarters 'was a great success', then another claiming without evidence that de Gaulle's reception in Bayeux and elsewhere had been 'definitely lukewarm'. He added that de Gaulle 'has left behind in Bayeux one civilian administrative officer and three colonels, but I have no idea what is their function'.*

* In fact the four men were Colonel de Chevigné (appointed regional military delegate), Commandant de Courcel (de Gaulle's personal aide since 1940), Monsieur François Coulet, whom de Gaulle had appointed the night before to be the Commissaire de la République for the region, and Commandant Laroque, who would be his chief of staff.

Roosevelt's attitude to the leader of the provisional government had certainly not changed. On the same day, he signalled to Churchill, 'In my opinion we should make full use of any organization of influence he may have in so far as is practicable without imposing him by force of our arms upon the French people as their government or giving recognition to his outfit as the Provisional Government of France.'

Churchill, who had been considering the recognition of de Gaulle as the leader of the provisional government, also remained in an unforgiving mood since the row about his refusal to send over French liaison officers. He had written to Eden just before his visit to France, 'There is not a scrap of generosity about this man, who only wishes to pose as the saviour of France in this operation.' The British press and most members of Parliament, on the other hand, strongly supported de Gaulle. *The Times* that morning had described Allied relations with the provisional government as 'intolerable'* – but for Churchill, relations with 'this wrong-headed, ambitious and detestable Anglophobe' had become a resigning matter. 'If the policy of the Government hitherto is attacked, I will unfold the story to Parliament. This may lead to the formation of a new Government, because I have every intention of telling the whole story and Parliament can then dismiss me if it wishes.'

De Gaulle, however, was to achieve more by covert means. The officials he had managed to leave behind in France as a 'Trojan horse', together with others already gathered there, turned Bayeux into the capital of Free France. Allied officers soon found it more practical to work with them and discreetly ignore outdated instructions from the politicians in London.

While Bayeux was a city of peace and plenty, Caen, the capital of Calvados, continued to suffer abominably from bombs and shelling. On the morning of 9 June, a favourite landmark, the bell tower of Saint-Pierre, was brought down by a shell from HMS *Rodney*. '*Le panorama est tout changé*,' wrote one citizen sadly. Buildings burned from further

---

* In stark contrast, part of the American press, incited by the White House, was saying that while American boys were dying for the liberation of France, de Gaulle was playing politics to gain power for himself.

air raids, and an impression of rain under a blue sky was in fact molten lead dripping from roofs.

The surgeons and doctors at the Bon Sauveur were exhausted from their work. The arrival of casualties by ambulance, stretcher or, in one case, on the back of a German tank was announced by whistles. As in a field hospital, a doctor was on hand to carry out an immediate triage and decide who should be operated on first. The strain on the surgeons was immense. One said, 'I simply cannot look at any more blood.' Another muttered, 'I've had it. I think if anyone brings me somebody who's injured I just couldn't operate.' They had no idea which day of the week it was.

In the first few days, three badly wounded Canadian paratroopers had been brought in from Troarn. One of them, a lieutenant, started yelling when he realized that the surgeon wanted to amputate his right arm. A translator was called for and the lieutenant explained that he was a painter. The surgeon agreed to do what he could to save the arm. The man nearly died during the operation, but he was saved by a nurse who offered herself in an arm-to-arm transfusion.

Another event which shook everyone in the Bon Sauveur occurred after a café owner was brought in with a bullet wound in the thigh. It transpired that, when drunk, he had shot at some soldiers from the *Hitler Jugend* who had been pillaging his café, a common event. While a surgeon was operating on him, an SS officer appeared armed with a sub-machine gun. The SS officer began hitting him as he lay on the operating table, asking whether he had fired at the soldiers. The café owner was speechless and did not reply. The SS officer fired a burst from his gun into his chest, killing him right there in front of all the medical staff.

Estimates of the number of people seeking shelter in the Bon Sauveur and the Abbaye aux Hommes vary greatly. There were well over 3,000. The Eglise Saint-Etienne was also crammed with refugees, sleeping on straw as if 'in the Middle Ages'. Ancient wells were opened up as the only source of water. Young men and women acted as foragers, seeking food in the larders of ruined houses or going out into the countryside, evading German patrols. Livestock killed by shells and bombs were butchered for meat. Dairy products were easy to come by since farmers could not send anything to market. In the city's main refuge south-east of the Orne, the convent of Les Petites Soeurs des Pauvres, the 500 refugees were tempted to complain that their bread was too thickly buttered. (In Paris, meanwhile, butter fetched astronomical prices on the black market.) Outside these havens, Caen was a sinister morgue. Rats grew fat on the corpses buried underground and stray dogs searched for an arm or leg sticking out of the rubble.

The Vichy authorities in Paris made an effort to help Caen. Two trucks loaded with food and blankets and a field kitchen were sent off by Secours National under the direction of Monsieur Gouineau. It was a hazardous journey. German soldiers in Lisieux were obsessed with 'terrorists' of the Resistance. They shot a policeman in the street simply because he carried a service pistol on his belt. Monsieur Gouineau, knowing that all the banks in Caen had been destroyed, had the authority to draw 100 million francs in Lisieux. There was no time to count the money, so he signed the receipt with his eyes closed and they drove on to Caen. When Allied fighters appeared overhead they waved a white flag frantically and the aircraft veered off.

After the money and supplies had been delivered, the return journey proved even more complicated. They obtained a laissez-passer from the German army Kommandantur in Caen, but were warned that the SS did not respect such pieces of paper. And beyond Lisieux a German patrol opened fire, suspecting that the trucks belonged to the Resistance. Monsieur Gouineau and several others were wounded. Nevertheless, a relay of supplies began and altogether some 250 tons were delivered.

For those French behind Allied lines, life was at least a little easier. In Lion-sur-Mer a local wrote, 'The English since their arrival distribute to left and right chocolate, sweets and cigarettes.' But there was no electricity or water, except from wells, and for food, most survived off their kitchen gardens. Rumour ran riot. Some believed that the swimming tanks had crossed the Channel all on their own, and a few convinced themselves that they had crossed on the bottom of the sea like tracked submarines. Often the sweets and cigarettes were not given but bartered for milk, eggs and meat from fallen livestock. An unofficial rate of exchange – '*le troc*' – rapidly established itself, with two eggs for a tin of corned beef.

Barter extended to other commodities with an astonishing rapidity.

A surgeon with the 2nd Field Dressing Station recorded that on 7 June 'a senior officer of the Military Police arrived in a Jeep loaded with medical comforts – army-issue chocolate, sweets and cigarettes for the wounded. Earlier that morning the police had raided a brothel set up on the beach in a wrecked landing craft by three ladies on the evening of D-Day and had confiscated the trading currency.' British sailors, sometimes drunk but still desperate for more alcohol, made a nuisance of themselves, going from house to house on the coast.

One of the very first temporary airfields constructed by the British with wire-mesh runways was B-5, outside Le Fresne-Camilly. Teenage boys, fascinated by all the military hardware, congregated to watch and make friends with the airmen and soldiers. On 15 June, a wing of Typhoons arrived to prepare a raid on a German panzer headquarters in a château near Villers-Bocage. The pilots landed to find the airfield under shellfire and they had to dive into slit trenches. The Typhoon aircrews knew how much they were hated by the Germans, so a number of them wore khaki battledress to avoid being lynched in case they were shot down. Considering the rather patronizing attitude of RAF pilots towards 'brown jobs', as they called the army, it was ironic that they borrowed their uniform.

Medical officers did all they could for wounded civilians. In a village near the fortified German radar station at La Délivrande, a shell had exploded in the schoolyard. The eighteen-year-old daughter of the schoolteacher lost her arm at the shoulder. There was no doctor available, but 'during the morning, the English occupied the village and their first concern was to take care of the injured'. The battalion doctor with his two assistants tended her. She was evacuated first to a casualty clearing station at Hermanville and then back across the Channel, to be cared for at Northwood, where other wounded French civilians were taken.

Dempsey's fears that the front would coagulate proved accurate. The Royal Ulster Rifles, having captured Cambes, stayed there for more than a month. Lieutenant Cyril Rand, a platoon commander, described it as a life of 'musical chairs', with gunfire and slit trenches replacing the stopped music and the chairs. Their padre, Father John O'Brien, used to visit the forward positions, with rum scrounged from the quartermaster, to play the odd hand of poker with soldiers in their dugouts. O'Brien was kept busy tending to the dead as well as the living. At one of the brief funeral services by an open grave, a newly arrived officer half-fainted beside him, dropped to his knees and began to slide into the hole. The padre caught him by his battledress, saying, 'Now there's no need to be in a hurry. All in good time.'

Black humour was just about the only amusement available. The Ulster Rifles had a forward observation officer from the Royal Artillery with them. He took a wicked pleasure in dropping a couple of shells on the German position whenever a *Landser* could be spied sneaking off to their latrine. The Ulsters, in their mud-encrusted battledress, longed for the chance to get clean. One day when in reserve, Lieutenant Rand slipped off to take an improvised bath in an abandoned house. He added a good measure of eau-de-Cologne from a bottle which he found there. On his return, he found the brigadier accompanied by the battalion second in command making an inspection. The brigadier moved on, apparently satisfied, but turned to give Rand a strange look. Rand's platoon sergeant murmured in his ear, 'I think they noticed, sir.'

'Noticed what?'

'Your smell, sir. You smell like a brothel.'

Their food, usually cooked over a biscuit tin filled with earth which had been soaked in petrol, was also monotonous. Compo rations came in a fourteen-day pack, with hard tack biscuits, margarine, jam, mixed vegetables, steak and kidney pudding, tins of M&V (meat and vegetables), plum pudding, latrine paper, soup, sweets, cigarettes (seven per man per day), matches and tea ready-mixed with milk powder and sugar for an instant brew-up. Oatmeal blocks could be crumbled into water to make porridge for breakfast as a change from the tins of over-salted and glutinous bacon and powdered egg. It was not surprising that barter for fresh produce became such an obsession.

Trench warfare and the quite arbitrary chance of death which went with it led to numerous superstitions. Few ever quite dared to risk fate by saying that they would do this or that 'when I get home'. For all but the most dedicated of soldiers, the hope of 'getting a Blighty one' – a wound which required evacuation back to Britain, but would not disable you – was akin to dreams of winning the lottery. A medal was all very well, but they preferred somebody else to play the role of hero, 'winning the war single-handed'. They just wanted to return home alive.

In almost every infantry platoon in most conscript armies there were seldom more than a handful of men prepared to take risks and attack. At the other end of the scale, there were usually a similar number who would do everything possible to avoid danger. The majority in the middle just followed the brave ones, but, faced with sudden disaster, they could equally run with the shirkers. The first study of behaviour under fire had been made in Sicily in 1943. A horrified Montgomery suppressed the report, fearing its effects on morale, and the career of the officer who wrote it suffered. More evidence emerged later to support his thesis.* Even in the Red Army officers were certain that six out of ten soldiers never fired their rifles in battle. This prompted one of their commanders to suggest that weapons should be inspected afterwards and anyone with a clean barrel should be treated as a deserter.

This platoon profile was probably reflected in below-average German infantry divisions, but almost certainly not in elite panzergrenadier and paratroop units or the highly indoctrinated Waffen-SS. They were convinced of Germany's rightful dominance and in 'final victory'. It was their duty to save the Fatherland from annihilation. The difference between the soldiers of a democracy and those of a dictatorship could hardly have been clearer. Yet the morale of the German *Landser* in Normandy was vulnerable. So much had been promised by the propaganda ministry and their own officers. Many had welcomed the invasion as an opportunity to settle scores over the Allied bombing and, by crushing it, to bring the war to an end.

'The whole world now anticipates the further course of the invasion,' wrote an Untersturmführer of the 9th SS Panzer-Division *Hohenstaufen* on 6 June. 'When I heard the news on the radio at noon today, I was honestly pleased, because by this measure we seem to be nearing the end of the war quite considerably.' The SS *Hohenstaufen* was part of II SS Panzer Corps, and about to leave the eastern front for Normandy to counter-attack the British. Four days later, when it was clear that

---

* For an excellent Ministry of Defence study of the question see David Rowland, *The Stress of Battle*, London, 2006, pp. 48–56. The best-known work on the subject, *Men Under Fire*, was written after the war by the American combat historian Brigadier General S. L. A. Marshall. Although Marshall's use of his source material has been challenged, notably by Professor Roger Spiller in the *RUSI Journal*, (Winter, 1988), his overall picture is undoubtedly accurate.

the Allies were safely ashore, the same Untersturmführer wrote, 'If the repulse of the invasion is not happening as swiftly as some believe, one may have some hope because things are moving. And we still have the retaliatory strike in store.'

Every time an assurance of the propaganda ministry proved false, another one quickly took its place. The Atlantic Wall was impregnable. The Allies would not dare to invade. The Luftwaffe and U-boats would smash the invasion fleet. A massive counter-attack would hurl the Allies back into the sea. The secret Vengeance weapons would bring Britain to her knees, begging for peace. New jet fighters would sweep the Allied aircraft from the sky. The more desperate the situation became, the more shameless the lie. The relentless inventions of Goebbels served as a form of morale-benzedrine for the soldier at the front, but when the effect wore off, he would be left truly exhausted. For SS soldiers especially, belief became nothing short of an addiction. Yet for many more ordinary German officers and soldiers, Normandy would prove the culmination of any private doubts they might have had about the outcome of the war.

14

The Americans on the Cotentin Peninsula

Like the British during the last seven days, the American First Army had also feared a major counter-attack from the south. Allied intelligence had not appreciated the success of its air forces and the Resistance in slowing the arrival of German reinforcements. Nor did they foresee that the German high command would throw the vast majority of its panzer divisions against the British Second Army.

Before the Villers-Bocage offensive, the American 1st Division, while establishing a deep salient around Caumont-l'Eventé, had feared an attack on its eastern flank. This was when the British 50th Division was fighting the Panzer Lehr Division round Tilly-sur-Seulles. General Huebner, the commander of the 1st Division, protested when Bradley took the tanks supporting them to smash the 17th SS Division's attack on Carentan. But Bradley had reassured him that Montgomery would be bringing the 7th Armoured Division in on that side.

The 2nd Division to the right, and the 29th Infantry Division now also forming part of the front advancing south towards Saint-Lô, had no idea how weak the German forces facing them were. By the time they did, the 275th Infanterie-Division and the German 3rd Paratroop Division had begun to arrive from Brittany. The American objective of Saint-Lô would not be taken for just over a month of bitter fighting through the hedgerows of the *bocage*.

To their west, Heydte's 6th Paratroop Regiment and the 17th SS Panzergrenadier-Division *Götz von Berlichingen* had established a defensive line on either side of the Carentan–Périers road. But the breakthrough the Germans feared there did not take place. The Allies had a much higher priority: the capture of the port of Cherbourg to speed their resupply.

The build-up of forces was already proceeding apace. In a triumph of American organization and industry, Omaha beach had been transformed. 'Within a week after D-Day,' wrote a naval officer, 'the beach resembled Coney Island on a hot Sunday. Thousands of men were at work, including Sea-Bees, Army engineers and French labourers. Big and little bulldozers were busy widening roads, levelling ground and hauling wreckage.' Before the end of June, Omaha beach command had a total strength of just over 20,000 officers and men, the bulk of them in the 5th and 6th Engineer Special Brigades. DUKWs ferried back and forth through the water with supplies and personnel. Once the beach was out of range of German artillery, then the landing ship tanks beached at low tide to disgorge more vehicles. When they opened their bow doors and dropped their ramps, according to one eyewitness, the strange grey vessel looked like a whale shark. 'Jeeps bearing staff officers were as common as yellow cabs in the heart of New York,' wrote the same naval officer. And 'large groups of German prisoners could be spotted here and there awaiting removal via LST'.

On the beach, a sergeant in the 6th Engineer Special Brigade recounted how, when they were escorting some prisoners to a stockade, paratroopers from the 101st Airborne started to yell, 'Turn those prisoners over to us. Turn them over to us! We know what to do with them!' A member of a naval combat demolition unit saw the same or a similar incident. 'Those wounded paratroopers were trying to do anything they could to get to those German prisoners. I guess they had been mistreated very badly in the rear or something. Bloody or not they were still ready to do more fighting if they could have gotten to those Germans.'

Unfortunately, wounded American airborne troops were evacuated on the same vessels as prisoners. An officer on LST 134 recorded, 'We had an incident where we had some paratroop soldiers and prisoners aboard, and I don't know what happened but I understand one or two Germans got killed.' On LST 44, a pharmacist's mate experienced a similarly tense encounter: 'One of our ship's officers started to herd these prisoners into the same area where I was helping tend some shell-shocked and wounded American soldiers. The immediate reaction of our troops was frightening and fierce. The situation was explosive. For the first and only time, I refused entry and demanded our officer stop sending the captured troops into this area. Our lieutenant looked surprised and extremely angry, but grudgingly complied.'

The LSTs were specially equipped for bringing wounded back to base hospitals in England. 'There were stretchers placed on brackets on the bulkheads of the tank deck,' noted the same pharmacist's mate, 'and they were several tiers high.' Some of the wounded prisoners of war were in a terrible state. 'A German prisoner brought aboard on a stretcher had a body cast extending from his ankles to his chest. He was pleading with me and our ship's doctor for help. He called us, "Comrade, comrade." Our ship's doctor, with my assistance, opened the cast, only to find this pitiful human being was being eaten by hordes of maggots. We removed the cast, cleaned him, bathed him, gave him pain killers. We were too late. He died peacefully that evening.'

Both at Utah and at Omaha, rear troops and sailors were as desperate as front-line soldiers to get their hands on war souvenirs. According to a Coast Guard officer on the USS *Bayfield*, souvenir hunters bartered away furiously for German medals and badges of rank. Many prisoners of war, still fearing execution as their commanders had warned them, handed them over with little protest. On land, the most eagerly sought trophies were Luger pistols. If anyone wanted a Luger, one officer remarked, he had to 'shoot the German himself and catch him before he fell'. Back at the beach sailors were paying $135 and there was talk of offers as high as $250, a great deal of money at the time. An enterprising sergeant from the 2nd Armored Division brought back to the beach a truck-load of captured weapons and bartered them for 100 pounds of instant coffee, a commodity which American tank troops regarded as body fuel.

As the officer in charge of Omaha admitted, a 'considerable laxity of discipline prevailed' in the beach area. Brigadier General William Hoge of the beach engineers did everything he could to stop the looting of local property, which, he declared in a conference, 'had been denounced by the French as worse now than when the Germans were there'. Many soldiers and beach personnel stole livestock to make a change from K- or C-Rations. Some frogmen with a naval combat demolition unit caught a pig, whom they nicknamed Hermann Göring. They tried to kill it with a sledgehammer, but it just screamed, so they shot it. They dug a pit in the sand and began to roast it. French civilians also looted, although paradoxically searching for US Army ration packs. This was, however, unsurprising, since the French ration was fixed at 720 grams of meat, 100 grams of butter and 50 grams of cheese per person per month.

Despite the looting, relations with the local population started to become a little more friendly. 'The [French] attitude is one of shrewd and watchful waiting,' a report stated. Many locals were still concerned that the Germans might return, although few would suffer as dramatically as the citizens of Villers-Bocage. The civil affairs department provided doctors with gasoline and the American medical corps did their best for injured civilians, especially since the hospital at Isigny was incapable of dealing with all the casualties.

Civil affairs officers were never short of work. Local farmers needed permits to travel to Bayeux to obtain veterinary supplies. They also asked for replacement fencing, because new military roads were bulldozed through their land, allowing their cattle to wander. The mayor of Saint-Laurent complained that American latrines were polluting the town's water supply. Civil affairs officers also had to recruit local labour. The Americans were clearly surprised at French working hours, which ran from seven in the morning to seven in the evening, but with an hour's break for lunch and two ten-minute breaks at nine and at four for a glass or two of wine. (Problems arose later in the eastern sector when news spread that the Americans paid far more than the cash-strapped British.) The wonderfully named Colonel Billion was responsible for requisitioning accommodation and had to negotiate with the Comtesse de Loy when taking over part of the Château de Vierville for senior officers.

The ingrained American suspicion of French collaborators assisting the Germans was also encouraged by the French themselves: 'The Mayor of Colleville reported [to the Counter Intelligence Corps detachment at Omaha] the presence of suspect women in that town and a suspicion that they may be in touch with Germans left behind in that area.' Stories of Frenchwomen acting as snipers continued to spread.

Even after the beachhead in the Cotentin peninsula increased to the point where Omaha was out of range of German artillery, nerves were still stretched, especially by German air raids at night. American sailors and beach personnel called the Luftwaffe 'Hermann's vermin' in honour of its commander-in-chief. But the wildly over-enthusiastic response of 'literally thousands' of anti-aircraft gunners on the ships anchored offshore created considerable problems when Allied aircraft arrived to intercept the attackers. One report stated that on the evening of 9 June, while it was still light, ships off Utah beach shot down four Mustangs, fired at four Spitfires, then fired again at another patrol of Spitfires, bringing one down, damaged two Typhoons and engaged another two Spitfires, all in the course of less than two hours. It became clear that US Navy warships were far more at fault than the merchantmen, who altogether had 800 trained air observers between them.

Air Chief Marshal Leigh-Mallory wrote that despite all the precautionary measures taken and 'despite undisputed air supremacy, flagrant instances of naval attack on friendly aircraft have occurred. If this continues, the fighter cover will be forced to fly so high that it can offer no protection against low-flying enemy aircraft . . . There is no foundation whatsoever in the rumour that enemy aircraft are imitating our own special markings.'* US warships did have a 'trained aircraft recognition officer' on board, 'but apparently they were only good at American types of aircraft'. The following night was almost as bad. Anti-aircraft fire from ships was so intense in reaction to a small Luftwaffe raid that six Allied fighters coming to intercept them were shot down. One of the pilots retrieved from the water could not stop cursing for four hours afterwards.

On 9 June, General Bradley told Major General J. Lawton Collins, the commander of VII Corps, to prepare to attack right across the Cotentin peninsula in readiness for the advance on Cherbourg. Two days later, Bradley had to cancel a meeting with Montgomery. He had heard that General George C. Marshall, Eisenhower and Admiral King were coming to visit him the next morning. They landed at Omaha early on 12 June, when part of the artificial harbour was already in position.

* He was, of course, referring to the prominent black and white stripes painted round the fuselage and wings of all Allied aircraft to prevent exactly this from happening.

Bradley took them on a tour to Isigny. They travelled in staff cars escorted by armoured cars and viewed the effect of naval gunfire on the town. Bradley, concerned about such an extraordinary concentration of senior commanders, remarked later that 'an enemy sniper could have won immortality as a hero of the Reich'. After seeing the big guns of the USS *Texas* firing its shells inland at the 17th SS Division south of Carentan, they lunched on C-Rations in a tent at First Army headquarters. There, Bradley briefed his visitors on the operation by Collins's VII Corps to take Cherbourg.

Major General Lawton Collins was only forty-eight years old. Quick and energetic, he was known as 'Lightning Joe', and had proved himself in the clearing of Guadalcanal in the Pacific. Bradley trusted him completely and the feeling was mutual.

The first attempt to expand the Merderet bridgehead by the 90th Division had been a disaster, as already mentioned. One of their soldiers acknowledged that men in the division were timid. They always wanted to check with a superior before they did anything, such as spotting a German observer and not shooting straight away. The 90th also learned the hard way that taking items from dead Germans was dangerous. A soldier from another division came across the body of a second lieutenant from the 90th with his hands tied behind his back, a German P-38 pistol thrust down his throat and the back of his head blown off. The second lieutenant was still wearing the German leather holster on his belt. 'When I saw that,' the soldier remarked, 'I said no souvenirs for me. But, of course, we did it too when we caught them with American cigarettes on them, or American wristwatches they had on their arms.'

Collins, realizing that the 90th Division's combat performance would not improve, brought in the newly arrived 9th Division to force its way across the Cotentin peninsula with the 82nd Airborne. They attacked on 14 June. Supported by Shermans and tank destroyers, the 9th Division forced aside the remnants of the 91st Luftlande-Division and reached the small seaside resort of Barneville four days later.

Hitler had given the strictest instruction that the maximum number of troops on the peninsula should fight in retreat towards Cherbourg. The commander of the 77th Infanterie-Division, however, decided to disobey the order. He saw no point in staying with the trapped and doomed forces, now under the command of General von Schlieben. He managed

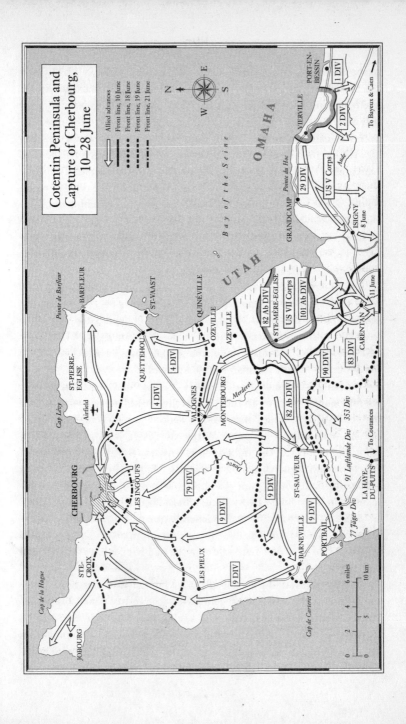

Cotentin Peninsula and
Capture of Cherbourg,
10–28 June

Allied advances
Front line, 10 June
Front line, 18 June
Front line, 19 June
Front line, 21 June

to slip through with part of his forces, just as the American 9th Division reached Barneville. The 91st Luftlande-Division also retreated to the south, having lost most of its equipment and nearly 3,000 men since 6 June.

'I was ordered to the supply train to help restock as we had lost everything in just a few days,' wrote an Obergefreiter in the 91st Luftlande. 'We had nothing but the clothes we stood up in. The worst thing continues to be the planes so everything has to be done at night. Those bastards strafe individuals with the onboard machine guns; we should have anti-aircraft artillery and planes here but they're nowhere in sight. You can imagine that this completely exhausts morale. Now we've been told that in the next few days there'll be a major air offensive with a great number of planes standing by.'

The American southern flank of the corridor became the responsibility of the 82nd Airborne and the hapless 90th Division. To oversee this sector, Bradley appointed Major General Troy H. Middleton, one of the most impressive commanders at his disposal, to command VIII Corps. Middleton, who had made his name in Italy, was said to look like 'a burly professor with his steel-rimmed glasses'.

Opposing Middleton, the LXXXIV Corps finally received its new commanding general on 18 June. Generalleutnant Dietrich von Choltitz may have been 'a pudgy man who looked like a night club comedian', but he had learned his skills in the ruthless school of the eastern front, especially in the fighting for Sebastopol. Choltitz had come from Seventh Army headquarters at Le Mans, where Generaloberst Dollmann had briefed him. Choltitz was not impressed. 'The commander-in-chief made a very tired, almost absent-minded impression,' he wrote at the end of the war. Generalleutnant Fritz Bayerlein of the Panzer Lehr Division was even more contemptuous of Dollmann. He regarded him as a *'Null'* and said that 'he had lived a life of luxury and had grown soft'.

Choltitz also found the staff of LXXXIV Corps demoralized. After the failure of the first panzer counter-attack west of Caen, his predecessor, General Marcks, had said openly that 'the war was lost', a treasonable offence. The casualty rate among divisional commanders also had an effect. As well as Falley of the 91st Luftlande and Marcks himself, General Helmlich had been killed on 10 June, and Ostendorff

of the 17th SS was seriously wounded on 16 June. To complicate matters even more, Choltitz found that with the American advance across the peninsula, his only contact with General von Schlieben was via the Channel Islands and Cherbourg.

As soon as the peninsula was cut off, Collins wanted to give the Germans no time to reorganize. General Manton Eddy, the commander of the 9th Division, had to turn his whole formation round in less than twenty-four hours to be ready to advance north up the west coast. Collins placed the 79th Infantry Division in the centre, while the 4th Division, still fighting hard round Montebourg and Valognes, would clear the eastern part and attack Cherbourg from the right. The 4th Division's commander, Major General Raymond O. Barton, may have lacked the flamboyance of some colleagues, but Liddell Hart had been impressed. He described him as 'refreshingly open-minded'.

Barton's 4th Division advanced against the concentration of forces to their north. Bombardments of naval and ground artillery had been battering the German defences around Montebourg and Valognes, along with the towns themselves. Montgomery's own reliance on artillery was revealed in a ghastly joke when he wrote to de Guingand 'Montebourg and Valognes have been "liberated" in the best 21st Army Group style, i.e. they are both completely destroyed!!!'

The three divisions advancing on Cherbourg also benefited from having their own air support party, ready to call in fighter-bomber attacks. At that stage, while this new liaison technique was being most emergency requests took at least three hours to accomplish there were exceptions. On 16 June, 'a Cub plane reported to artillery that a column of troops was crossing a bridge. Artillery it in. Corps contacted a squadron of fighter-bombers in the directed it onto the column. In 15 minutes they had a report strafed the column. Reports have come in that American being marched down the road by Germans escaped in th strafing by our planes.' This early attempt at ground–air was an important start in what would become a devastati combination later in the campaign.

But just as Collins's advance on Cherbourg was proce Allies were hit by an unforeseeable disaster. On 19

violent storm for forty years began to blow up in the Channel, combined with a spring tide. Locals had never seen anything like it. The gale force winds along the coast were, in the Norman saying, enough 'to take the horns off a cow'. Temperatures dropped to the equivalent of a cold November. The Mulberry artificial port at Omaha was destroyed beyond repair. One or two experts said that gaps in its construction had made it vulnerable, but it stood on the most exposed piece of coast. Its British counterpart at Arromanches was partly protected by a reef and rocks, and as a result could be rebuilt afterwards.

Landing craft were hurled by the waves high on to the beaches, smashing against each other. Flat Rhino ferries sliced into their sides. Even landing ship tanks were thrown ashore. 'The only chance we had of keeping our landing craft from being beaten to bits,' wrote a US Navy officer, 'was to anchor a long way off the beach out in the Channel and hope we could ride the storm out.' For ships en route to England, the crossing was unforgettable. 'It took us about four days to do the 80 nautical miles in very rough seas to Southampton,' wrote an officer on an LST. 'The seas were so rough that the skipper was afraid that the ship would crack in two; therefore he ordered the mooring cables to be strung fore and aft and tightened up on the winches to give extra support to two of the deck plates. That ship was strung like a mountaineer's fiddle.'

The storm continued until the evening of Thursday, 22 June. The destruction on the beaches defied belief. More ships and materiel had been lost than during the invasion itself. Yet those involved in the planning of D-Day could not help remembering with grateful relief the decision to go ahead taken on 5 June. If the invasion had been postponed for two weeks, as had been feared, the fleet would have sailed into one of the worst storms in Channel history. Eisenhower, after he had seen the damage on the beaches, took the time to write a note to Group Captain Stagg: 'I thank the gods of war we went when we did.'

Recovering from the effects afterwards took longer than the storm itself. To refloat an LST thrown up on to the beach required bulldozers to dig huge trenches around it in the hope that another high tide might float it off. The Americans, who 'never really believed in the Mulberry', cleared what they could, then proved that they could land

'an amazing tonnage with flat-bottomed barges and by beaching ships at low tide'.*

The storm badly delayed the build-up, hampered the return of casualties to England and forced the cancellation of air operations. This absence of Allied fighter-bombers from the sky allowed the Germans to accelerate their reinforcement of the Normandy front. At the same time, many Allied divisions, either already embarked for France or ready to cross, were delayed by a week or more. The most immediate effect was on supplies, especially artillery ammunition. General Bradley had a difficult choice, but decided to maintain full support for Collins's attack on Cherbourg. His other two corps – Gerow's V Corps to the south-east and Middleton's VIII Corps on the south side of the peninsula – would receive only a minimum of artillery shells, even though Bradley knew that this would allow the Germans time to prepare defences south of the Douve marshes.

Despite the fury of the storm, Collins had urged on his three divisions to encircle the tip of the peninsula. General von Schlieben, knowing that his fragmented forces could not hold the Americans in the open, had begun to withdraw to the forts around Cherbourg. His own division had taken under command a wide variety of units, including a Georgian battalion and a mounted regiment of Cossacks with five squadrons. Their Russian colonel when drunk confessed to wanting 'a bit of plunder'. 'It was a war of fun and games,' observed one of Schlieben's colonels sarcastically.

Although resistance on the advance to Cherbourg was mainly one of isolated actions, it was a testing time for the newly arrived 79th Division in the centre. 'The men were tired,' wrote one platoon commander, 'and the more tired they became the more they wanted to bunch, particularly during marching.' This failure to keep a safe distance led to many unnecessary casualties in the early days. Sometimes they encountered stragglers who claimed that their company had been

* Even after Cherbourg had been captured and made operational, the Americans managed to land much more over the beach than through the port. In the month of August they landed 266,804 tons and 817 vehicles at Cherbourg, 187,973 tons and 3,986 vehicles at Utah and 351,437 tons and 9,155 vehicles at Omaha. The British averaged 9,000 tons a day at Arromanches. They were also able to use small fishing ports which the Germans had not destroyed.

virtually wiped out, but it was never true. They were just disorientated by this first experience of hedgerow fighting. Platoon commanders felt vulnerable chasing around trying to find lost men or squads. Five miles east of Cherbourg, the 79th ran into an outpost line of scattered pillboxes and machine-gun nests: 'K Company [of the 314th Infantry] lost almost a full platoon, because of inexperience and a certain amount of panic, when the troops bunched and formed very profitable targets for enemy gunners.' But they found that if they encircled a pillbox and then fired a bazooka at the rear, the defenders surrendered rapidly.

On 22 June, the Americans launched a massive air raid on Cherbourg late in the morning. The alarms rang in the flak positions manned by German teenagers from the Reichsarbeitsdienst, recruits engaged on construction projects who were not yet proper soldiers. They ran to their guns as the first waves of fighter-bombers came in. 'We fired back like madmen,' wrote one of them. Then came a rumbling drone over the Channel as formations of American heavy bombers appeared, glinting in the sun. 'An inferno descended – roaring, shattering, shaking, crashing. Then quiet. Dust, ash and dirt made the sky gray. A horrific silence lay over our battery position.' There had been several direct hits. The boys' bodies were taken away in trucks later.

As the Americans closed in on Cherbourg they encountered a greater density of pillboxes and weapon pits, as well as major forts. Each position had to be dealt with individually. Colonel Bernard B. Mac-Mahon's 315th Infantry was faced with what seemed to be a major defence work at Les Ingoufs, with a garrison of several hundred. A Polish deserter led MacMahon and a reconnaissance party close to it. It looked as if the guns had been destroyed, either by air attack or by the Germans themselves. MacMahon ordered a newly arrived loudspeaker truck to be brought up. He then ordered forward some artillery and announced over the loudspeakers in German that a full divisional assault was about to be launched. They had ten minutes to surrender, then 'any part of the garrison not surrendering would be blasted out of existence'. He kept repeating the message, 'feeling rather foolish because his talking seemed to have produced no results'. Suddenly he heard yells: 'Here they come!' Large numbers of German soldiers could be seen advancing, some with white flags and the rest with their arms raised. But they represented only a portion of the garrison.

A group of five German officers appeared next, as delegates sent by the garrison commander. They asked MacMahon to have his guns fire one phosphorus shell at the position so that their commander could feel he 'had satisfied his obligation to the Führer and surrender'. MacMahon had to admit that he had no phosphorus shells. Would 'German honor be satisfied' if five phosphorus grenades were thrown? After discussion of this counter-proposal, the senior German officer agreed with more saluting. But only four grenades could be found in the whole company. There was more haggling, then these four grenades were thrown into a cornfield. The German officers inspected the results and agreed that they were indeed phosphorus, and returned to inform their commander that he could surrender the rest of the garrison and the field hospital attached.

MacMahon found that they had taken 2,000 prisoners. Later, when he and his divisional commander went to inspect the German field hospital, the senior officer there requested that they be allowed to keep eight rifles. Unless their Russian and Polish 'voluntary' helpers were held under guard, he explained, they would not work. The American divisional commander retorted that the Russians and Poles were now under American protection and the Germans could do the work themselves.

Cherbourg's most formidable defences were the coastal batteries. Because the heavy bombers had failed to smash their ferro-concrete emplacements, Bradley asked Admiral Kirk to help speed the capture of the port. Kirk felt that Bradley was becoming rather too fond of naval gunfire support, but agreed. A squadron including the battleships *Nevada*, *Texas* and several cruisers, sailed round the cape towards Cherbourg. Many regarded the operation as a pleasant excursion. 'At eight-thirty we went to General Quarters,' wrote the sky control officer on the cruiser USS *Quincy*. 'The sky was bright with a few pleasant flecks of cumulus. The air was like chilled wine.' According to Rear Admiral Carleton F. Bryant on the USS *Texas*, 'It was a beautiful sunny Sunday with just a bright ripple on the water and as we followed our mine-sweepers towards Cherbourg, we were lulled into a false sense of security.' They took their bombardment positions at about 13.00 hours.

Suddenly a coastal battery which they had failed to see opened fire.

A shell hit the conning tower of the *Texas*, severely damaging the captain's bridge and the flag bridge. 'Immediately we opened fire,' wrote an officer, 'we got salvos screaming over from [the coastal batteries] and the first salvo straddled us.' The *Nevada* also received near misses, while apart from the *Texas*, HMS *Glasgow* and several other ships were hit. None were crippled, but Rear Admiral Bryant rightly decided that discretion was the better part of valour and withdrew his task force behind a smoke screen.

On land, some of the infantry encountered strongpoints which would not give in rapidly. Great bravery was shown on a number of occasions. Armoured bulldozers were needed to bring up supplies under fire. Engineers and infantry used satchel charges and other explosive devices to drop down ventilation shafts. Occasionally, a display of strength would persuade a garrison commander to surrender. According to one extraordinary report, Private Smith in the 79th Infantry Division, who 'had drunk enough Calvados to make him reckless', captured one strongpoint single-handed.

Smith, armed only with a .45 automatic pistol and accompanied by a similarly inebriated friend who had no weapon at all, 'staggered up to the entrance of the fort'. Smith and his companion, on seeing that the steel doors were ajar, slipped inside and shot dead the German soldiers standing around in the entrance. Smith, 'who was in truth stewed to the ears', went from room to room, 'shooting and shouting, and as he appeared at each door, the Germans inside, thinking the whole American army was in the fort, gave up'. He herded his prisoners together and marched them out into the open, where they were handed over to his battalion. Smith then returned to the fort and discovered another room in which there were wounded Germans. 'Declaring to all and sundry that the only good German was a dead one, Smith made good Germans out of several of them before he could be stopped.'

After the main defence position, the Fort du Roule, had been taken, Generalleutnant von Schlieben knew that there was little point in continuing the agony. Virtually all his men were trapped below ground in their strongpoints, along with several thousand wounded. He decided to surrender after American engineers blew up the ventilation shafts to his subterranean headquarters. The wounded could hardly breathe, there was so little oxygen. One of his officers, Oberstleutnant Keil, who was lauded by the Nazi authorities for holding out until 30 June on the Jobourg peninsula, defended Schlieben's 'sound common sense'. Schlieben did not want to sacrifice his men's lives for no purpose, despite the fact that, as the commander of 'Fortress Cherbourg', Hitler had made him take an oath that he would fight to the death.

On 25 June, at 19.32 hours, an officer on his staff sent a message by radio: 'Final battle for Cherbourg has begun. General takes part in fighting. Long live the Führer and Germany.' Schlieben was embarrassed afterwards when he heard of it. The next day he surrendered with the 800 men in his position. 'Some of the boys,' wrote an officer in the 4th Infantry Division, 'could not understand why the Germans had given it up as quickly as they had.' Schlieben, who seemed to be something of an epicure, was not impressed by the K-Rations he received. One of Bradley's officers thought it highly amusing that he was about to face English cuisine as a prisoner when sent back across the Channel.

Cherbourg was a wreck, especially the port, which had been systematically destroyed by German engineers. American troops mopped up isolated pockets of resistance. Once again there were dubious reports of Frenchwomen with rifles. 'We saw a few women snipers,' stated a sergeant with the 4th Infantry Division, 'who were dressed in ordinary clothes. One day we brought in twenty Germans, including one woman.' Acts of revenge were also committed, especially after a US hospital had been hit by an artillery shell. American soldiers are said to have killed Organisation Todt workers who were non-combatants.

Over 600 German wounded were found in the Pasteur hospital. Captain Koehler, a battalion surgeon with the 22nd Infantry Regiment and a fluent German speaker, was put in charge. Although he had excellent cooperation from the German colonel and his medical staff, Koehler was appalled at the high death rate, largely due to the lack of preparation of patients before surgery. The unnecessary number of amputations also shocked him. 'The Teutonic tendency to operate on a surgical case and disregard the outcome on the life of the patient was very apparent,' he wrote.

Engineers from the 101st Airborne, who had been brought up to help with the reduction of strongpoints, joined in the general merriment of victory as the town returned to a version of normal life. 'That was quite an experience,' one of them wrote, 'because the houses of prostitution were open, the taverns were open, MPs were in there, military government, rangers, paratroopers, dog leg infantry, artillery officers, and we had our first experience of using sidewalk urinals.' The combat historian Sergeant Forrest Pogue saw nearly 100 soldiers queuing outside a former Wehrmacht brothel. A Frenchman warned him that they should be careful: 'The Germans have left much disease.'

Along with all American troops, they were amazed by the stores which the Germans had accumulated in their concrete bunkers. Bradley wrote of their defences as 'a massive underground wine cellar'. He ordered that the booty should be divided up among the front-line divisions, rather than allow it all to fall into the hands of rear troops and those working on reconstruction.

Hitler, when he heard of General von Schlieben's surrender, was furious. He had summoned all commanders of coastal ports to Berchtesgaden in April to look them over and assess their belief in victory. He had relieved several on the spot for lacking what he perceived as sufficient determination to fight to the last man, but not Schlieben. Afterwards, Hitler harped on about how pathetic Schlieben had been. He was almost as outraged as he had been over Paulus's capitulation at Stalingrad.

Two days after the surrender, Generaloberst Dollmann was found dead in his bathroom at Seventh Army headquarters near Le Mans. An official announcement stated that he had died from a heart attack. Most senior officers, however, believed that he had committed suicide in shame at the fall of Cherbourg.

15

Operation Epsom

Shortly before the fall of Cherbourg, Hitler made his last visit to France. He was in an unforgiving mood. His orders to sweep the Allies back into the sea had not been carried out and he regarded his senior commanders in the west as defeatist. Hitler complained openly at OKW headquarters that 'Field Marshal Rommel is a great and inspiring leader in victory, but as soon as there is the slightest difficulty, he becomes a complete pessimist.'

Rommel, on his side, did not conceal his dissatisfaction with the way Hitler interfered with his direction of the battle. Even senior officers at OKW were driven to distraction by Hitler's obsession with detail. He insisted that every emplacement should be marked on 1:25,000 maps. One day, he noticed in a report that the number of anti-aircraft guns in the Channel Islands had apparently been reduced by two. He demanded that the officer responsible should be punished for reducing the defences, but in fact somebody had miscounted the first time round. Hitler, without ever having visited the area of Caen in his life, continually pestered the OKW staff about the positioning of two units of multi-barrelled mortars: the 7th and 8th Nebelwerfer Brigades. He insisted that they would decide the outcome in the British sector if they were placed at a specific spot east of the River Orne.

Despite their earlier disagreements on tactics, both Rommel and General Geyr von Schweppenburg wanted to withdraw behind the line of the Orne. Geyr recognized that to launch a major panzer counter-attack within range of Allied naval guns was pointless. Instead, he wanted to adopt 'Jungle Tiger Tactics', with sudden armoured raids. This came just as the *Hitler Jugend* had started to have second thoughts after their battering at the hands of the Canadians. But Rommel's demands for 'flexibility of action', which meant having the right to pull back without reference to Führer headquarters, and the proposal to withdraw behind the Orne constituted a direct contradiction of Hitler's order that every inch of ground should be held.

Hitler, determined to have it out with both Rommel and Rundstedt, summoned them to a conference before the fall of Cherbourg. On 16 June, he flew from Berchtesgaden to Metz in his personal Focke-Wulf Condor. Accompanied by General Jodl and members of his military staff, he proceeded in convoy to Margival, near Soissons. The bunker complex at Margival had been prepared in 1940 as his head-quarters for the invasion of Britain. It had been set into a deep railway cutting near a tunnel where the Führer's special train could shelter.

The next morning, Rundstedt and Rommel arrived as instructed. '[Hitler] looked unhealthy and overtired,' noted Speidel, Rommel's chief of staff. 'He played nervously with his spectacles and the coloured pencils he held between his fingers. He sat on his chair bent forward while the Field Marshals remained standing. His former suggestive power seemed to have disappeared. After brief and cool greetings, Hitler, speaking in a loud voice, sharply expressed his displeasure over the success of the Allied landings, tried to find fault with the local commanders and ordered the holding of Fortress Cherbourg at any price.'

Rundstedt made a few introductory remarks, then asked Rommel to make his report. Rommel spoke of the 'hopelessness of fighting against tremendous enemy superiority in all three dimensions'. He spoke of the failure of air and naval reconnaissance, yet emphasized that his divisions along the coast had not been caught off guard and that 'the performance of officers and men in this unequal struggle had been superhuman'. He predicted the fall of Cherbourg and attacked the whole of Hitler's policy, which had designated some sixteen fortresses along the Channel and Brittany coasts to be held to the last. Altogether some 200,000 men and precious materiel were tied up in their defence and, in most cases, the Allies would simply bypass them. The Allies were landing two to three divisions a week, he continued, and even though they were slow and methodical, the three branches of the Wehrmacht simply would not be able to resist their overwhelming might. Rommel wanted to withdraw by six to ten miles east and south of the River Orne. This would enable him to pull out the panzer divisions to redeploy them for a major counter-attack. He also wanted to prepare the line of the River Seine for defence. Rundstedt supported these proposals. He wanted to pull back behind the Loire and the Seine, abandoning the whole of north-west France.

An outraged Hitler, refusing to face the facts, made 'a long auto-suggestive speech'. He predicted that the V-1, which had been used in quantity for the first time the day before, would 'have a decisive effect on the outcome of the war against England'. He then broke off the discussion to dictate an announcement about the V weapons to the representative of the Reich Press Chief. The two field marshals had to stand there listening to a frenzied Hitlerian monologue. Hitler refused to have the V weapons targeted at the beachheads or the south coast ports of Britain. He insisted that they must all be aimed at London, to bring the British to their knees. When Rommel criticized the lack of effective support from the Luftwaffe, Hitler acknowledged that he had been deceived by its leadership, but then claimed that 'swarms' of jet fighters would soon spell the end of Allied air superiority.

An increasingly angry Rommel demanded that representatives of the OKW should visit the front and discover the situation for themselves. 'You demand that we should have confidence,' he told Hitler, 'but we are not trusted ourselves!' Hitler apparently turned pale at this remark, but remained silent. As if to bear out Rommel's arguments about Allied superiority, an air raid warning at this point forced them to descend into the bomb shelter.

Once down there, Rommel outlined the wider picture, with Germany isolated, the western front about to collapse and the Wehrmacht facing defeat in Italy as well as on the eastern front. He urged Hitler to bring the war to an end as soon as possible. Hitler was furious. His Luftwaffe adjutant later observed, 'That was the last thing Hitler wanted to hear from the mouth of a field marshal.' He retorted that the Allies would not negotiate. In this he was right and Rommel and the July plotters hopelessly optimistic. But Hitler went on to insist that the destruction of Germany had been agreed upon. So 'everything would depend on a "fanatical resistance"'. As he dismissed Rommel, Hitler said, 'Do not concern yourself with the conduct of the war, but concentrate on the invasion front.'

Rundstedt and Rommel left Margival, having been told by Hitler's chief adjutant, General Schmundt, that the Führer would visit La Roche-Guyon to talk to field commanders himself in two days' time. But on returning to their respective headquarters, they heard that a V-1 missile, whose gyros had gone wrong, had exploded above the bunker soon after their departure. Hitler returned rapidly to Berchtesgaden that night. He never left the Reich again.

The first V-1 rockets, or 'Doodlebugs' as British civilians soon called them, landed on the night of 12 June. Four of them hit London. 'What principally bothers the southern English at this moment,' wrote a journalist, 'is a certain illogical, Wellsian creepiness about the idea of a robot skulking about overhead, in place of merely a young Nazi with his finger on the bomb button . . . Annoyance would seem to be the dominant public emotion, though lots of English might sneakingly admit that they don't feel displeased to be in it with the boys in Normandy, even in such a relatively minor way.' But the strain began to tell when the rhythm of attacks accelerated. The 'eerie howl of sirens' in London seemed to mark a revival of the Blitz. Thousands of people returned to sleeping in Underground stations.

Many discussions were held by the War Cabinet. On 16 June, Churchill and his ministers discussed whether to stop the anti-aircraft guns firing at night so that people could get some sleep. Fast fighter aircraft proved a better way of dealing with the threat of 'Divers', as they were codenamed. The most effective weapon of all on 'anti-Diver' operations was the wing of Tempests based at Dungeness. Brought to readiness on 16 June, they shot down 632 V-1s with their 20 mm cannon, more than a third of the total destroyed by Allied fighters during the next three months. A Belgian pilot, René van Learde, shot down forty-two. 'These things,' wrote their leader, Wing Commander R. Beamont, 'would be tearing across at night making noises like asthmatic motorbikes with streams of flame out of the back.' The Tempest was just faster than the V-1. Once, having run out of ammunition, Beamont flew alongside one. Applying the boundary layer of air over the wing of his Tempest on to the underside of the V-1's wing, he managed to lift it without even touching it. This rolled the V-1 over and sent it crashing to earth. But in the vast majority of cases, pilots continued to use their cannon, although the explosion of a ton of amitol just a few hundred yards ahead of their aircraft produced a terrifying blast.

V-1s were indeed volatile, as Hitler had discovered at Margival. The Director General of Gendarmerie's report to Vichy showed that many, up to five a day, crashed before even reaching the Channel. One came down north-east of Alençon, behind the lines of Panzer Group West. Yet despite their inaccuracy and the great achievement of Allied 'anti-Diver' squadrons, enough V-1s landed on London to cause great concern. One landed on the Guards Chapel, close to Buckingham Palace, during a Sunday service, killing 121 people. On 27 June, according to Field Marshal Brooke, a War Cabinet meeting finished 'with a pathetic wail from Herbert Morrison [the Home Secretary] who appears to be a real white-livered specimen! He was in a flat spin about the flying bombs and their effects on the population. After five years of war we could not ask them to stand such a strain etc etc!' Brooke noted in his diary that Morrison wanted the whole strategy in France to be changed. 'Our one and only objective should be to clear the north coast of France. It was a pathetic performance. There were no signs of London not being able to stand it, and if there had been it would only have been necessary to tell them that for the first time in history they could share the dangers their sons were running in France and that what fell on London was at any rate not falling on them. Thank heaven Winston very soon dealt with him.'

Since most of the rockets were falling short of London, the Double-Cross committee was told to find a way to encourage the Germans to maintain their present targeting. Using one of their tame agents, 'Lector', a message was passed via Madrid to his controllers in Berlin, 'Ludwig' and 'Herold'. 'Destructive effect of new German weapon devastating,' the signal stated. 'In spite of soft pedalling counter propaganda, the bombardment has created a feeling of panic among the population such as has never before existed ... The opinion had been expressed in governmental and military circles that if this and new weapons are intensively employed, they would find themselves sooner or later forced to come to a compromise peace with Germany ... In highly placed and influential circles, apparently serious peace tendencies are perceptible, in which connection the name of Rudolf Hess in the role of intermediary is mentioned.' This was perhaps a case of over-egging the pudding, since such news could only encourage the Germans to persist, but it was deemed justifiable in the circumstances. In any case, Hitler's blind belief that his new Vengeance weapon would knock Britain out of the war undoubtedly strengthened his determination not to give up any territory in Normandy. This obsessive obstinacy would lead to yet another clash with Rommel and Rundstedt before the end of the month. The two field marshals predicted that this inflexibility would destroy the German army in Normandy and lose France.

Montgomery, meanwhile, still tried to pretend that everything on his side was proceeding according to plan. On 14 June, the day after the disaster at Villers-Bocage, he wrote to Churchill, 'Battle is going well at junction of the two armies in the general area Caumont–Villers-Bocage–Tilly.' He also found it hard to acknowledge the true consequences of the great storm in the Channel which hit them less than a week later. The weather had not just halted the landing of supplies, it also put back the arrival of VIII Corps, the battering ram needed for a breakthrough. In the meantime, the Germans were reinforcing their front opposite the British with their most powerful panzer divisions. Ultra gave warning that the II SS Panzer Corps was on the way from the eastern front. For the moment only small attacks could be mounted because of the shortage of artillery ammunition. Although costly in lives and unrewarding in ground gained, they fitted Monty's new plan of tying down the Germans while the Americans took Cherbourg.

On 16 June, a battalion of the King's Own Yorkshire Light Infantry, supported by a depleted squadron of Shermans, attacked Cristot: 'We formed up in a lane near a farm with banks on either side.' The men's nostrils curled at the stench of rotting cows. They were to advance across another open cornfield. 'Suddenly, out of nowhere appeared the Padre and we all knelt down and prayed.' As they moved forward, their supporting artillery fired over their heads, but then the Germans played their trick of firing mortar shells into the leading troops to give the impression that their own artillery was falling short. Officers passed back orders for the barrage to stop and the German trick was revealed. But one soldier who had thrown himself flat during the mortar 'stonk' suffered a terrible fate. A piece of shrapnel ignited one of the phosphorus grenades in his pouch and 'he died terribly in minutes'.

Three days later, when the great storm was beginning, the rain was so heavy that fighting came to a halt. The infantry sat disconsolately in their trenches, the water dripping from their groundsheets worn as ponchos. Tank crews were luckier. They dug trenches to sleep in, then reversed their tank over the top to keep them dry.

On 22 June, the third anniversary of the German invasion of the Soviet Union, the first phase of Operation Bagration began. This was the massive Red Army attack in Belorussia to encircle the Wehrmacht's Army Group Centre. Having drawn German attention to a possible offensive in the Ukraine, with a brilliant exercise in *maskirovka* comparable to Plan Fortitude, the Soviet armies achieved surprise. Within three weeks they would kill or capture 350,000 Germans. Bagration would take the Red Army to the gates of Warsaw by the first week in August.

After several delays, mainly due to the weather, the major British offensive, Operation Epsom, was finally ready. Eisenhower was fuming with impatience, yet Montgomery refused to be hurried and 21st Army Group headquarters provided SHAEF with exasperatingly little information. Apparently Montgomery said to Dempsey on several occasions, 'There's no need to tell Ike.' Monty liked to keep his objectives vague, often with Delphic cricketing metaphors, so that if there was a breakout he could claim credit for it and if the operation ran into the sand he could say that they had simply been tying down German forces to help the Americans.

Altogether 60,000 men were to take part, mainly from VIII Corps, which included the 15th Scottish Division, the 43rd Wessex and the 11th Armoured Division. Most had never been in battle before, but they were determined to prove themselves alongside the Desert veterans. The plan was to attack to the west of Caen and establish a bridgehead south of the River Odon before advancing to the River Orne. This deep salient to the south-west of the city would then be used to threaten the whole German position. The key feature between the two rivers was Hill 112.

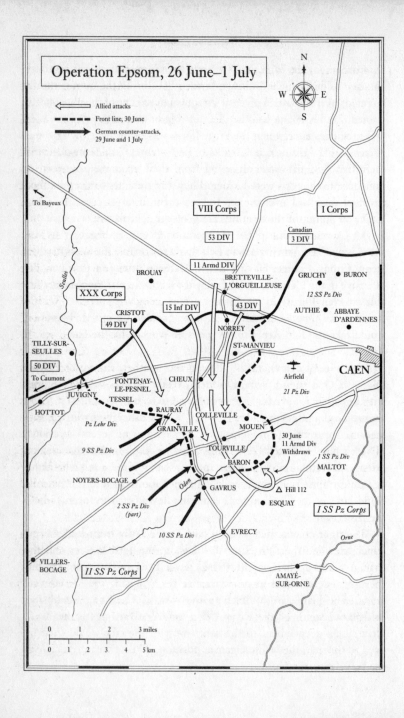

Operation Epsom, 26 June–1 July

N
W — E
S

Allied attacks
Front line, 30 June
German counter-attacks,
29 June and 1 July

To Bayeux

VIII Corps

I Corps

53 DIV

Canadian
3 DIV

11 Armd DIV

XXX Corps

BROUAY

BRETTEVILLE-
L'ORGUEILLEUSE

GRUCHY   BURON

12 SS Pz Div

15 Inf DIV

43 DIV

CRISTOT

NORREY

AUTHIE   ABBAYE
D'ARDENNES

49 DIV

ST-MANVIEU

Sceulles

TILLY-SUR-
SEULLES

FONTENAY-
LE-PESNEL

CHEUX

Airfield   CAEN

50 DIV

21 Pz Div

To Caumont

JUVIGNY

TESSEL   RAURAY

COLLEVILLE

HOTTOT

Pz Lehr Div

GRAINVILLE

MOUEN

9 SS Pz Div

TOURVILLE

30 June
11 Armd Div
Withdraws

1 SS Pz Div

BARON

MALTOT

NOYERS-BOCAGE

Odon

GAVRUS

Hill 112

I SS Pz Corps

2 SS Pz Div
(part)

ESQUAY

10 SS Pz Div

EVRECY

Orne

VILLERS-
BOCAGE

II SS Pz Corps

AMAYÉ-
SUR-ORNE

0   1   2   3 miles
0 1 2 3 4 5 km

On Sunday 25 June, XXX Corps on the right again attacked the Panzer Lehr Division. The 49th West Riding Division and the 8th Armoured Brigade forced them back, but although they inflicted heavy losses, the Germans held on to the village of Rauray. An armoured reconnaissance regiment was protecting their flank that day near Fontenay-le-Pesnel. 'The German trick,' wrote a Canadian officer with a British reconnaissance regiment, 'was to abandon their weapon pits and go into the corn when we approached.' Sometimes they crept back to their positions and opened fire again, but in most cases the 'Huns still pop up out of the corn but are no potential danger'.

The southern end of Fontenay was still held by the Panzer Lehr Division. The following morning, a Sherman of the Sherwood Rangers, 'on turning a corner in the centre of the village came face to face with a German Tiger tank trundling along the road. Fortunately [the Sherman commander] had an armour piercing shell in the breech of his 75 mm. gun which he released at 30 yards' range and then followed up with another six shells in quick succession, which brewed up the Tiger.' The next day, the Sherwood Rangers cleared Rauray, after losing several of their tanks. Their greatest prize was an abandoned Tiger tank in perfect running order. They even painted their brigade sign of a fox's mask on it, but orders came down from XXX Corps headquarters that it must be sent back to England. It was the first to be captured intact in Normandy.

That day, 26 June, the SS began clearing the French inhabitants of villages behind the lines. Their concern was spying, not the safety of civilians. This was not mere paranoia. The British 7th Armoured Division and other formations had been receiving very useful intelligence from Frenchmen and women slipping through the lines.

The fighting was also bitter round Tessel. There, a battalion from the 'Polar Bears', as the 49th Division was called from its shoulder badge, came up against the Panzer Lehr Division at close quarters. 'The order came to us while we were at Tessel Wood, "No Prisoners",' claimed a member of the King's Own Yorkshire Light Infantry. 'That is why we were called the Polar Bear butchers by Lord Haw-Haw.'*

---

* Lord Haw-Haw was the British name for William Joyce, who broadcast from Berlin like 'Axis Sally'.

An Ultra intercept picked up Panzer Lehr's report that it had suffered 'heavy losses' on the first day of the battle.

The main phase of what Montgomery called the 'show-down' began on 26 June, with a massive bombardment of field and naval artillery. After a night of heavy rain, the cloud was so low that few air sorties could be flown. The Scots of the 15th Division advanced rapidly. As men were shot down in the pale green wheat, comrades would mark their position for medical orderlies to find. They took the wounded man's rifle with fixed bayonet, rammed it upright into the ground and placed his helmet on top. One observer remarked that these markers looked 'like strange fungi sprouting up haphazardly through cornfields'.

Fierce fighting took place in several villages, especially in Cheux, where the Glasgow Highlanders lost a quarter of their strength in a single day. In Saint-Manvieu on the left flank, the 43rd Wessex Division and the 4th Armoured Brigade fought off the *Hitler Jugend*.* The Royal Scots Greys knocked out four Panthers as they emerged from a wood. The Greys, attached to a newly arrived brigade of the 43rd Division, 'were much amused over our infantry. This was evidently their first battle and they were doing everything according to the book: their faces were blackened; they had cut off all badges of rank; and they talked in whispers.' But the two fresh divisions were proving rather more effective than the veterans. By dusk, the 15th Scottish had almost reached the Odon in its thickly wooded valley. A Frenchman watching the battle that night from Fleury, on the southern edge of Caen, wrote, 'It's a vision out of Dante to see the whole horizon lighting up simultaneously.'

Congested roads, heavy rain and confusion slowed the attack, but the 2nd Argyll and Sutherland Highlanders seized a bridge over the Odon the following day. Showing unusual initiative, the Argylls infiltrated forward, rather than following conventional British infantry tactics. With great bravery, the 15th Scottish fought off a panzer counter-attack that day, and their capture of the bridge allowed the 11th Armoured to start crossing on the morning of 28 June. General O'Connor, the commander of VIII Corps, wanted to push forward to take a bridgehead over the River Orne beyond, but Dempsey, who knew from

---

* The commander of the 4th Armoured Brigade, Brigadier John Currie, was killed that day. He was replaced by Brigadier Michael Carver, aged only twenty-nine.

Ultra intercepts that the II SS Panzer Corps had just reached the front, became cautious. He preferred to establish a much firmer position south of the Odon before the next phase.

Obergruppenführer Sepp Dietrich wanted to throw the two divisions of the II SS Panzer Corps straight into the battle against the British bridgehead, but Rommel was reluctant. He had hoped to keep the 9th SS Panzer-Division *Hohenstaufen* and the 10th SS Panzer-Division *Frundsberg* back for the great armoured counter-attack which had so far failed to get off the ground. But on 28 June, Rommel was summoned to Berchtesgaden by Hitler, an extraordinary interruption in the middle of a battle. And a desperate Generaloberst Dollmann, just a few hours before he committed suicide, ordered the II SS Panzer Corps to attack north-westwards on either side of the River Odon to smash the western flank of the British salient. They were reinforced by a battlegroup from the 2nd SS Panzer-Division *Das Reich*. Meanwhile, because of Dollmann's sudden demise, Obergruppenführer Paul Hausser, who commanded the II SS Panzer Corps, was told that afternoon to proceed immediately to Le Mans to take command of the Seventh Army. He handed the corps over to Gruppenführer Bittrich.

The next day, 29 June, the 11th Armoured Division managed to get tanks on to the key position of Hill 112. They held off attacks by leading elements of the 1st SS Panzer-Division *Leibstandarte Adolf Hitler*, which was supported by the 7th Mortar Brigade with Nebelwerfer and a *Kampfgruppe* from the 21st Panzer-Division. At 11.00 hours, the unfortunate Bittrich, having taken command of the II SS Panzer Corps just the evening before, received orders to advance in one hour. Initially reluctant to mount such a hurried attack, he was then persuaded of the urgency. The 9th SS Panzer-Division *Hohenstaufen* received a signal stating the importance of the mission. Without the commitment of both panzer corps, it said, 'the enemy which has broken through to Baron could not be repulsed. They would break through to the Orne and Caen would be lost.' The Panzer Lehr Division was ordered to support the left flank of Bittrich's attack. But their opponents then had a great stroke of luck. The 15th Scottish captured an SS officer carrying the plan. Their forward battalions rapidly prepared defensive positions.

The onslaught of the II SS Panzer Corps began in earnest shortly after midday. At 16.05 hours, its headquarters reported to Panzer Group

West that they had destroyed eleven British tanks in front of Gavrus. Half an hour later they claimed to have taken Gavrus and knocked out twenty-three tanks. Geyr von Schweppenburg, who had returned the day before to assume command with his Panzer Group West head-quarters, urged on the two SS divisions at dusk. He told them that this attack offered '*die grosse Chance*'. But that night, the 15th Scottish Division, heavily supported by artillery and naval gunfire, fought off the 9th and 10th SS Divisions with spectacular success. Thirty-eight panzers were knocked out and the SS *Frundsberg* was forced back to its start line. The effect on the morale of the two SS panzer divisions was even greater. Unfortunately, Dempsey apparently never knew of the intelligence which revealed that this was the main counter-attack.* Fearing that a major assault would come on the other flank, he pulled back the 11th Armoured Division instead of reinforcing it. Hill 112 was then rapidly occupied by the Germans. It proved a disastrous mistake. To recapture Hill 112 would take far more time and lives than could ever have been saved by this withdrawal.

Montgomery halted the offensive the following day, after a renewed attack by the II Panzer Corps was driven off. VIII Corps had lost just over 4,000 men in five days. Over half the losses had been suffered by the 15th Scottish Division, which had proved its bravery beyond all doubt. That Dempsey missed a great opportunity through his caution is almost unquestionable. The delays in launching Epsom meant that VIII Corps ended up fighting the greatest concentration of SS panzer divisions which had been assembled since the Battle of Kursk. Yet the impressive performance of the British troops involved was let down at the last minute by the hesitation of their army commander. The only consolation was that the Germans never again managed to launch a major counter-attack against the British sector.

Eisenhower's frustration with Montgomery over strategy is not hard to understand. The confident messages Montgomery had been sending out about a 'show-down' simply did not tally with what he said in

---

* It is still not clear whether the warning of the attack of II SS Panzer Corps came from the captured plan or from two signals intercepted by Ultra on 29 June, one of which was communicated to the Second Army within four hours. But if the intelligence did come via Ultra, then it is hard to believe that Dempsey had not been told.

private. An intelligence officer with the 7th Armoured Division had recorded with amazement in his diary on 22 June what he heard from Major General Erskine on his return from a conference at 21st Army Group headquarters prior to Epsom. 'General talked about what Monty had said to him,' he wrote. 'Complete change so far as we are concerned as Monty doesn't want us to make ground. Satisfied Second Army has drawn all enemy panzer divisions, now wants Caen only on this front and Americans to press on for Brittany ports. So VIII Corps attack goes in but we have very limited objective. Monty reckons he lost the battle of the build-up – five days behind on account of weather.' So perhaps Dempsey's caution was dictated by Montgomery.

Rommel visited Geyr's headquarters on 1 July, the day after the battle ended. Both men were shaken by the effect of shelling from warships at a range of nearly twenty miles. Geyr demanded figures from both divisions on the number of tanks knocked out by naval gunfire. Even Hitler was persuaded that they could do no more than hold their present line for the moment. But Geyr was furious that every available panzer division had been thrown at the British offensive. This had caused huge disruption to his plans.

Above all, Geyr opposed the splitting of formations as an emergency measure, which also caused chaos in resupply. He told Rommel that the newly arrived infantry divisions should be used to hold the line while the panzer forces were withdrawn and reorganized for a proper blow. Rommel refused. 'The infantry cannot do this any more and is not prepared to do it,' was his reply. He did not believe that the newly arrived infantry divisions were capable of holding the British. This attitude happened to fit in with Hitler's obsession of not yielding any ground. Geyr railed against 'the armchair strategists of Berchtesgaden' and their 'lack of knowledge of panzer warfare'. He despised Jodl, an artilleryman: 'The artillery developed the unfortunate characteristic of the Bourbons – neither to learn nor to forget – and was in many respects more backward than the infantry.'

Geyr wrote a report in which he did not mince his words. He demanded a flexible defence and, as a result of Epsom, the withdrawal of panzer troops south of the Orne, out of the range of Allied naval gunfire. 'Decisions are taken directly by OKW itself,' he continued.

'As that headquarters is not in possession of first hand or personal knowledge of the situation at the front and is usually thinking very optimistically, its decisions are always wrong and arrive too late.' Rommel endorsed his conclusions and passed the report up to OKW. Hitler decided to relieve Geyr immediately. He replaced him with General der Panzertruppen Hans Eberbach.

Generalfeldmarschall von Rundstedt as well as Rommel had been summoned back to the Berghof on 28 June, at the height of the battle for the Odon crossing. Rundstedt 'returned in a vile humour', according to his chief of staff. Having driven over 600 miles from Saint-Germain-en-Laye to Berchtesgaden, he was kept waiting from three in the morning until eight the next evening, 'and then was given the opportunity to exchange only a few words with the Führer'. Just after his return, Rundstedt, with Blumentritt listening in, rang Keitel. He 'told him bluntly that the whole German position in Normandy was impossible'. Allied power was such that their troops could 'not withstand the Allied attacks, much less push them into the sea'.

'What should we do?'

'You should make an end to the whole war,' the old field marshal retorted.

Next day at noon, Keitel rang to say that he had reported their telephone conversation to the Führer. Another call from Jodl warned that Hitler was considering a change in command in the west. Rundstedt's endorsement of Geyr's report was a key factor. Hitler announced that Rundstedt was retiring for reasons of ill health and sent an officer to Paris to present him with a polite letter and the Knight's Cross with Oak Leaves. He would be replaced by Generalfeldmarschall Hans-Günter von Kluge.

Rommel was also furious. Without informing him, Hitler had appointed Obergruppenführer Hausser to take over the Seventh Army because he preferred to trust Waffen-SS commanders. His favourite remained Sepp Dietrich, yet Hitler did not know that Dietrich also believed that his interference was leading them to disaster in Normandy. Hitler would have sacked Rommel as well, but as Geyr's replacement Eberbach said, he was not relieved 'because of the effect his dismissal would have had on morale at the front and in Germany, as well as the impression it would have made abroad'.

On 30 June, Eberbach received the order to fly next day with Field Marshal von Kluge to the west to take over command of Panzer Group West. Kluge told him that OKW wanted them to stabilize the front and launch a counter-attack. Kluge reached Saint-Germain-en-Laye convinced that the reports from Normandy must be excessively pessimistic. He had spent eight days at the *Wolfsschanze* during the Soviet attack on Army Group Centre – Operation Bagration – and during this period, according to Blumentritt, he had 'become imbued with the unyielding spirit of the High Command'. As a result, he was not inclined to view the situation as hopeless when he assumed command in the west. Known as 'clever Hans' (a play on his family name, which means clever in German), he was not popular with his colleagues. Kluge, wrote Rommel's chief of staff, was 'energetic, quick-witted and unsparing toward himself. He was ruthless in his demands. The cold eyes in his sharply chiselled face concealed his suppressed emotions. He hated Hitler, but never ceased feeling bound to him, and this was due, perhaps, to his acceptance of the honors and favors bestowed on him.' Kluge, like Rundstedt, had accepted 250,000 Reichsmarks from Hitler as a present.

Kluge visited Rommel's headquarters at La Roche-Guyon on the afternoon of 5 July. 'After a rather frosty exchange of courtesies' with Rommel and Speidel, he addressed the Army Group staff in the *salle des gardes* of the château. He announced that the removal of Generalfeldmarschall von Rundstedt should be seen as an expression of the Führer's dissatisfaction with the leadership in the west. Hitler also considered Generalfeldmarschall Rommel to be too easily impressed by the 'allegedly overwhelming effect of enemy weapons', and thus to suffer from an over-pessimistic view of the situation. Kluge even went on to say to Rommel's face in front of the assembled staff officers that he had displayed an obstinate attitude and carried out Hitler's orders only half-heartedly. 'From now on,' Kluge concluded, 'you too, Generalfeldmarschall Rommel, will have to obey without reservations! I am giving you good advice.'

This provocation, not surprisingly, stirred Rommel into a sharp dispute, emphasizing the reality of the situation which they faced 'and the necessity of drawing the proper conclusions from it'. The row became so heated that Kluge asked the other staff officers to leave the room. Rommel demanded that Kluge should withdraw his accusations orally and in writing. He also warned him to talk to the army and divisional commanders and visit the front himself before laying down the law. Rommel was particularly taken aback because he knew that Kluge had been in touch with resistance circles in the army. He had expected Kluge of all people to be less under Hitler's sway.

Next day Kluge left La Roche-Guyon on a tour of the front. The reaction among all field commanders was so unanimous that he was converted to Rommel's point of view and apologized. He realized that, as with the eastern front, Hitler was out of touch with reality and, when his dreams failed to materialize, he looked for scapegoats.

Eberbach, meanwhile, had taken over from Geyr. He found that Panzer Group West lacked a proper army headquarters and staff. In his handover report, Geyr made several points. 'German tanks are superior to the English and American ones in armor and armament.' The morale of German troops was still 'comparatively good', due to 'efficient propaganda'. On the British sector, 'the ratio of forces is sufficient for defence under normal conditions,' and the terrain was favourable. They had 'created a centre of gravity against a probable enemy attack' by concentrating eight panzer divisions, a flak corps and two Nebelwerfer brigades. But an infantry division once committed was used up in two to four weeks. Even General Jodl admitted at the end of the war that 'the British attacks were a continual hindrance to quick relief of the panzer divisions by infantry divisions and continually thwarted our plan to move more forces to the west wing. These attacks did then contribute substantially to making the American breakthrough easier.'

Although Geyr insisted that the French were 'friendly' and that there were very few partisan attacks in Normandy, German military authorities had started to become very nervous. In an effort to awe the population of Paris, they marched 600 British and American prisoners of war through the city's streets. Some bystanders whispered encouragement to the Allied soldiers, while some yelled insults at them, perhaps influenced by German propaganda emphasizing the bombing raids. An American paratrooper who was kicked and spat at by a small group of German sympathizers 'jumped out of line to punch one' and received a jab in the buttocks from the guard's bayonet.

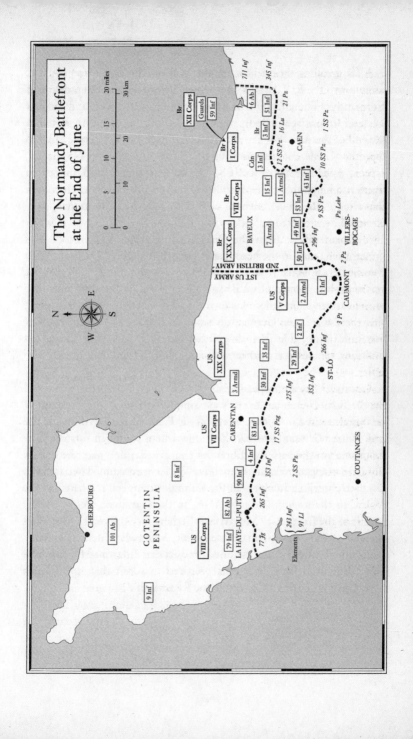

The Normandy Battlefront at the End of June

COTENTIN PENINSULA

CHERBOURG

9 Inf

101 Ab

8 Inf

79 Inf — **US VIII Corps**

82 Ab

90 Inf — **US VII Corps**

LA HAYE-DU-PUTS

4 Inf

CARENTAN

83 Inf

3 Armd — **US XIX Corps**

30 Inf

35 Inf

COUTANCES

77 Jg
265 Inf
353 Inf
2 SS Pz
17 SS Pzg
275 Inf
352 Inf
266 Inf

Elements
243 Inf
91 Ll

ST-LÔ

29 Inf

2 Inf — **US V Corps**

2 Armd

1 Inf

CAUMONT

3 Pz
2 Pz

1ST US ARMY
2ND BRITISH ARMY

50 Inf — **Br XXX Corps**

BAYEUX

7 Armd

49 Inf

296 Inf

VILLERS-BOCAGE

Pz Lehr
9 SS Pz

53 Inf

43 Inf

11 Armd — **Br VIII Corps**

15 Inf

3 Inf Cdn

10 SS Pz

12 SS Pz

CAEN

3 Inf — **Br I Corps**

16 Ln

1 SS Pz

21 Pz

51 Inf

6 Ab

59 Inf — **Br XII Corps**

Guards

711 Inf
345 Inf

N
W   E
S

20 miles
30 km

A far greater concern now for the Wehrmacht high command was coping with the Red Army's offensive in Belorussia and the pressure in Normandy. 'The effect of the major conflicts in the west and the east was reciprocal,' stated Jodl, when he was interrogated with Keitel at the end of the war. 'Each of the fronts felt itself neglected compared to the other.' The concentration of SS panzer divisions in Normandy, especially the transfer of the II SS Panzer Corps back from the eastern front, had highlighted their inability to respond effectively to Operation Bagration. 'The two-front war came into sight in all its rigour,' Jodl observed.

A liaison officer from the Red Army, Colonel Vassilievsky, was brought on a visit to the headquarters of 7th Armoured Division. With true Soviet diplomacy, he expressed the view that the British advance was very slow. Apparently a British officer asked him to show on a map of the eastern front where his own division was fighting. It transpired that there were nine German divisions on that sector, which was over 600 miles long. The British pointed out that they were facing ten divisions, including six panzer divisions, along a front of only sixty-two miles.

Claims by Soviet propagandists that Germany's best troops 'are still on the Soviet–German front' were simply untrue, as the presence of six SS armoured divisions, as well as the Panzer Lehr Division and the 2nd Panzer Division proved. 'We know where young and strong Germans are now,' wrote Ilya Ehrenburg in *Pravda*, decrying the quality of German formations in Normandy. 'We have accommodated them in the earth, in sand, in clay – in the Kalmuk steppe, on the banks of the Volga, in the swamps near Volkhov, in the Ukrainian steppe, in the woods of the Crimea, in Moldavia, in Rzhev, in Veliki-Luki. Our allies are now seeing the Germans whom we have nicknamed "Totalnik" [total mobilization], a prefabricated product that is destined for annihilation.' But even Ehrenburg was prepared to admit that 'the French frying pan is starting to resemble the Russian fire'.

16

The Battle of the Bocage

After the fall of Cherbourg at the end of June, Bradley's First US Army prepared to push south. In the west at the base of the peninsula, the 79th Infantry Division, the 82nd Airborne and the unhappy 90th Division stretched across marshland. They faced most of Choltitz's LXXXIV Corps, by now well entrenched on the wooded hills to their south. The 4th and 83rd Infantry Divisions south of Carentan were also in low-lying marshland. There they faced the 17th SS Panzergrenadier-Division *Götz von Berlichingen* and the 353rd Infanterie-Division.

To the east on the Saint-Lô front were the 30th, the 35th and the 29th Infantry Divisions already in *bocage* country. So were the 2nd and 1st Infantry Divisions around Caumont, running up to the British sector. They faced Meindl's II Paratroop Corps. Although Geyr and Guderian objected bitterly to the splitting of divisions, the Germans operated very effectively in defence, with their *Kampfgruppen*, or battlegroups of infantry, assault guns and engineers.

The American campaign began on 3 July, when VIII Corps, commanded by Major General Middleton, attacked on the west flank. In that unusually wet summer, they set off under a heavy downpour. American soldiers, sick of the chill and damp of British weather during their months of training, had expected the French climate to be more benign. Low cloud ruled out air support and the rain was too thick to allow accurate observation for the artillery. The 82nd Airborne seized its objective, Hill 131, north of La Haye-du-Puits, by early in the afternoon, but the rest of the offensive became bogged down. The 82nd waited with impatience for the other two divisions to come level. The Germans had different problems. A battalion of Volga Tartars 'immediately deserted to the enemy'. Another *Ost* battalion surrendered to the 82nd at the first opportunity and a third with the 243rd Infanterie-Division to the west also defected.

Next day, on the eastern side of the marshes around the River Sèves, the American VII Corps sent the 83rd Division into the attack on the Sainteny sector. To celebrate the Fourth of July, an order went out that every field gun along the front should open fire exactly at midday. Some units also fired red, white and blue smoke signals. The recently arrived 83rd had relieved the 101st Airborne at the end of June. They had been sent out on night patrols 'to gain experience and confidence' and reduce the effect of 'nervous and trigger happy' troops. But soldiers returning to their own lines found themselves being fired at 'promiscuously' by anxious sentries. The paratroopers of the 101st had saturated the newcomers 'with tall tales about the toughness and fighting ability of Jerry'. The fight for Sainteny proved a bloody baptism. The 83rd Infantry Division suffered 1,400 casualties. They had a lot to learn, as they heard from the few Germans they had taken. 'The prisoners we captured,' a sergeant reported, 'told us we were green troops, because they knew every move we were going to make. They saw us light cigarettes and heard us clanking metal against metal. If we use basic principles, we will live longer.' The Germans, on the other hand, were keen to take Allied prisoners if only to get hold of their excellent maps, which they themselves lacked.

Two days later, on 6 July, the 4th Infantry Division joined the attack south-westwards. After its hard fighting on the advance to Cherbourg, General Barton remarked, 'We no longer have the Division we brought ashore.' This was hardly an exaggeration. The division had suffered 5,400 casualties since coming ashore and had received 4,400 replacements. So many officers had fallen that divisional staff officers were sent back into combat units.

The American attack was hemmed in by the marshes along the River Sèves on the west and those along the River Taute to the east. This made it impossible to outflank German positions and much of the ground was too boggy for tanks. The 37th SS Panzergrenadier-Regiment from the *Götz von Berlichingen* had a perfect bottleneck to defend. But even the SS panzergrenadiers complained that with the rain and the high water table they were getting foot rot, with two feet of water in their foxholes.

The young SS panzergrenadiers were also unused to the food. There was plenty of milk, butter and steak, but no bread or noodles. Just over a week before the American attack started, they had received mail for the first time since the invasion. After the costly battle for Carentan, many letters had to be returned to families and sweethearts in Germany with the official stamp on the envelope: 'Fallen for Greater Germany'. That day also saw the arrival of leading detachments from the 2nd SS Panzer-Division *Das Reich*, battered from its protracted trek north.

Although the attack in the far west went slowly at first, the Germans suffered a war of attrition under the relentless battering of American artillery. Even a surprise attack on 6 July by part of the SS *Das Reich* against the American advance into the Forêt de Mont Castre was rapidly smashed by artillery. With every priority awarded to the Caen front, the German LXXXIV Corps received little in the way of reinforcements and equipment to replace their losses. Wehrmacht losses in Normandy up to 25 June had reached 47,070 men, including six generals. Yet their effectiveness in defence provoked a bitter admiration among their opponents. 'The Germans haven't much left,' one American officer said, 'but they sure as hell know how to use it.'

The constant pressure maintained by the Americans meant that Choltitz had no opportunity to pull units back to rest and reorganize. His only reserve was a single battlegroup made up of elements from the *Das Reich* and the 15th Paratroop Regiment. Choltitz estimated that his corps lost up to a battalion and a half of men per day from American artillery fire and air attack. He regarded the order from OKW that there should be no withdrawal as grotesque. So, with Hausser's agreement, he sent back false reports to conceal minor withdrawals. Hausser's Seventh Army headquarters warned Rommel that a collapse on the far western flank was becoming a distinct possibility due to American artillery and air power. Constant attacks on rail and road links made it very hard for the Germans to resupply their own forces on the Atlantic side with artillery shells.

Choltitz's men, most of whom had been in action for just over a month, were exhausted. 'After having been without sleep for three

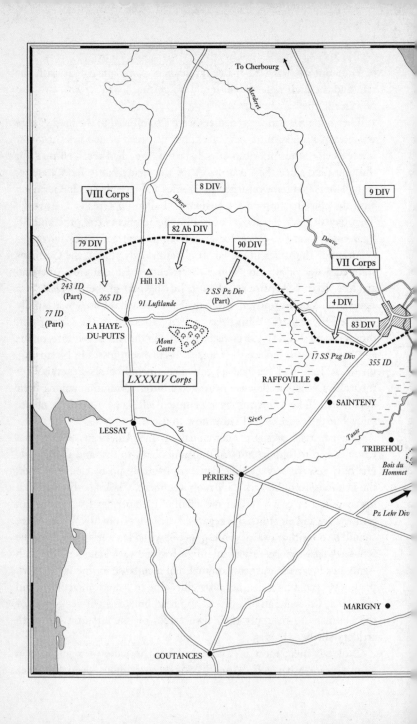

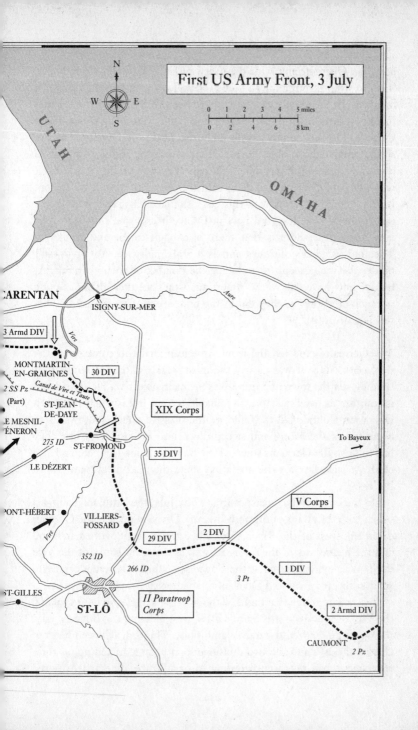

First US Army Front, 3 July

UTAH

OMAHA

CARENTAN

ISIGNY-SUR-MER

Aure

3 Armd DIV

Vire

MONTMARTIN-
EN-GRAIGNES

30 DIV

Canal de Vire et Taute

2 SS Pz

(Part)

ST-JEAN-
DE-DAYE

XIX Corps

LE MESNIL-
TÉNERON

275 ID

ST-FROMOND

35 DIV

To Bayeux

LE DÉZERT

PONT-HÉBERT

VILLIERS-
FOSSARD

V Corps

Vire

29 DIV

2 DIV

1 DIV

352 ID

266 ID

3 Pt

ST-GILLES

ST-LÔ

II Paratroop
Corps

2 Armd DIV

CAUMONT

2 Pz

days,' an Obergefreiter with the 91st Luftlande-Division wrote home, 'I could sleep through for 10 hours today. I am sitting in the ruins of a bombed-out farmhouse that must have been really large before it met its fate. It is a dreadful scene: cattle and poultry are lying about, killed by blast. The inhabitants have been buried next to it. Our Russians are sitting amidst the rubble, having found *Schnapps*, and are singing *Es geht alles vorüber* ("Everything will pass") as well as they can. Oh, if only this could be over and done with and humanity would see reason. I cannot come to terms with this confusion and this cruel war. In the east it affected me less, but here in France it just won't register. The only good thing here is that there is enough to eat and drink . . . The foul weather continues and is a real hindrance. Yet it doesn't hinder the war, except for reducing the number of enemy aircraft. At last we now have flak so the Americans won't see their flying as quite as much of a sport as they did in the first weeks of the invasion. That was just dreadful.'

The Germans expected the main American attack to come down the west coast, since it was clearly the most weakly defended sector. But Bradley saw the town of Saint-Lô as his main objective. He considered its capture as essential 'to gain suitable terrain from which to launch Operation Cobra'. Cobra would be the massive attack southwards to break out of the *bocage* and sweep down into Brittany. But first they had to push the Germans south of the Bayeux–Saint-Lô road, and also clear the start-line for the operation along the road from Saint-Lô to Périers.

On the foggy and overcast morning of 7 July, the battle for Saint-Lô began with the attack of the 30th Infantry Division to clear the German defenders west of the River Vire. They had to cope with marshland and the hedgerows of the *bocage* as well as the steep banks of the Vire itself. Bradley, frustrated at the slowness of their advance, decided to send in the 3rd Armored Division in an attempt to speed things up.

It went into action that night, with forty-five vehicles an hour crossing the Vire to attack towards Saint-Gilles, west of Saint-Lô. But next day, the operation proved to be over-ambitious. The 30th Division had not cleared the area and the two divisions soon became mixed up, as their movements had not been coordinated in advance. The 3rd Armored

Division's three task forces found themselves advancing field by field, rather than sweeping through in the manner which Bradley had envisaged. They had received a bloody introduction when twelve Shermans had been knocked out almost as soon as they emerged through a gap in a hedgerow. American tank ammunition, besides having less penetrative power, also gave off much more smoke than the German, which put them at a severe disadvantage in hedgerow fighting. Yet there was often the odd German soldier desperate to surrender. A combat engineer with the 3rd Armored began to urinate into a thick bush on the edge of an orchard. To his alarm, a soaked German emerged. He grabbed his rifle, which he had leaned against a tree trunk, but the German was extracting from his wallet photos of his wife and children in an attempt to persuade him not to shoot him. He kept saying, '*Meine Frau und meine Kinder!*'

Further German attacks from the west indicated that a *Kampfgruppe* of the 2nd SS Panzer-Division *Das Reich* had been diverted to the sector. Aerial reconnaissance also spotted a large armoured force approaching from Le Bény-Bocage, nearly twenty miles south-east of Saint-Lô. Ultra intercepts suggested that this was almost certainly part of the Panzer Lehr Division, transferred from the Caen front. Two squadrons of P-47 Thunderbolts were sent to intercept them.

On 9 July the intermittent rain continued, hampering air reconnaissance and fighter-bomber strikes. The hapless infantry was also soaked and covered in mud when it renewed the attack at 07.00 hours. It soon became clear, however, that the Germans were planning a counter-attack with the arrival of the Panzer Lehr. That morning reports went back that 'a lot of tanks' were coming up round the west side of Saint-Lô. Bazookas and anti-tank guns were rushed up to the forward troops and the corps artillery made ready, but the Americans did not halt their advance.

Chaos followed when the leading Shermans of Combat Command B reached Pont-Hébert and misread their maps. Instead of turning south, they turned north back up the main road to Saint-Jean-de-Daye. This brought them up against the advancing 30th Division, which had been warned to expect an attack by enemy tanks. In fact it was the 823rd Tank Destroyer Battalion and some self-propelled anti-aircraft guns which sighted the lost column and engaged them immediately. The two leading Shermans were knocked out and a fierce firefight developed, which caused panic among the untested infantry of the 30th Division as rumours spread of a major breakthrough by German panzers. It took some time to sort out the 'terrible mess', turn the 3rd Armored Division tanks south and bring up fresh troops to stabilize the line either side of the Pont-Hébert road.

The day had not gone well for the right flank either. The 120th Infantry Regiment and the 743rd Tank Battalion ran into a well-prepared ambush of Panther tanks and panzergrenadiers from the *Das Reich*. Waffen-SS grenadiers attacked the American tanks at close quarters, some even trying to climb aboard, as the commanders fought them off with heavy machine guns mounted on top of the turrets. A battalion of the 120th Infantry was almost surrounded and nearly broke 'because of the element of panic which began to sweep through relatively green troops'. The reserve and rear echelons gave way to their fear, which 'precipitated a frantic retreat northward by all kinds of vehicles, armored and otherwise'.

Only the energetic actions of officers and NCOs kept the front companies from running. The Americans had lost a total of thirteen Shermans. Their infantry had also suffered twice the losses of the Germans that day. Only prodigious support from their corps artillery, which had fired nearly 9,000 rounds since dawn, averted a complete disaster.

On 10 July, VII Corps, between the marshes and the River Taute, made another effort to advance south-west astride the Carentan–Périers road. Some local successes were achieved, but it was still impossible to break through the bottleneck. The 83rd Division had taken four days of hard fighting to advance about a mile. An officer in the 4th Division described it as a 'bitter week of pure grimness for the infantry' as they fought in the marshes from island to island 'in this abominable country', sometimes ankle deep, sometimes wading through water with their rifles above their heads. The men were exhausted: 'As soon as one of us sits down he falls asleep or drops into a stupor.' German military professionalism also made it hard for the Americans to estimate enemy casualties. The Germans pulled back their dead at night and took them with them whenever they retreated.

General Barton, the commander of the 4th Division, wrote, 'The Germans are staying in there just by the guts of their soldiers. We outnumber them 10 to 1 in infantry, 50 to 1 in artillery and an infinite number in the air.' He wanted unit commanders to convince their men 'that we have got to fight for our country just as hard as the Germans are fighting for theirs'.* One report on interviews with prisoners of war stated that the Germans 'have no regard for the fighting qualities of the average American'. Rangers and airborne troops were respected. The Germans were deeply indoctrinated by propaganda. One prisoner, a nineteen-year-old Hitler Youth from the 17th SS Panzergrenadier-Division, was convinced that the Americans were in a desperate state, that German forces had retaken Cherbourg and that Germany would destroy the western Allies and then defeat the Red Army.

To create hatred, the German equivalent of Soviet commissars, the National Socialist Leadership Officers, emphasized the destruction of German cities and the killing of German women and children by 'terror attacks'. Their basic theme was that the Allies intended to wipe out 'the German race'. Defeat would mean the annihilation of their Fatherland. Their propaganda leaflets addressed to Allied troops demanded, 'What do you want to do in Europe? To defend America? . . . To die for Stalin – and Israel?' This was all part of a basic Nazi theme that '*Amerikanismus*' allied the 'Jewish plutocrat' of the United States with the 'Jewish Bolshevik' of the Soviet Union.

Even German soldiers who wanted to give up were afraid to do so. Nazi propaganda persuaded them that they would not be safe in an England bombarded by the new secret weapons. 'Captivity is also a tricky matter,' wrote an Obergefreiter. 'Some would go, but they fear the V2 and V3.' Three days later he wrote home, still preoccupied by the dangers of surrender if Germany really were to win the war. 'I spoke to a veteran of the eastern front today. He said that it was hard

---

* One war correspondent on this front, Bob Miller of United Press, wrote, 'in comparing the average American, British or Canadian soldier with the average German soldier, it is difficult to deny that the German was by far, in most cases, a superior fighting man. He was better trained, better disciplined, and in most cases carried out his assignment with much greater efficiency than we did . . . The average American fighting in Europe today is discontented, he does not want to be here, he is not a soldier, he is a civilian in uniform.'

in the east, but it was never like it is here.' If a German soldier 'deserts
to the enemy . . . The family receives no support and if we were to win
the war, the *Landser* must be handed over and he will have to see what
will happen to him.'

As in all armies, the combat performance of American troops in every
battalion varied greatly. During the *bocage* battles, some GIs began to
get over their terror of German panzers. Private Hicks of the 22nd
Infantry with the 4th Division managed to destroy three Panthers over
three days with his bazooka. Although he was killed two days later,
confidence in the bazooka as an anti-tank weapon continued to increase.
Colonel Teague of the 22nd Infantry heard an account from one of his
bazooka men: 'Colonel, that was a great big son-of-a-bitch. It looked
like a whole road full of tank. It kept coming on and it looked like it
was going to destroy the whole world. I took three shots and the
son-of-a-bitch didn't stop.' He paused, and Teague asked him what he
did next. 'I ran round behind and took one shot. He stopped.' Some
junior officers became so excited by the idea of panzer hunts that they
had to be ordered to stop.

In five days of marsh and *bocage* fighting, however, the 22nd Infantry
suffered 729 casualties, including a battalion commander and five rifle
company commanders. 'Company G had only five non-coms left who
had been with the company more than two weeks. Four of these,
according to the First Sergeant, were battle exhaustion cases and would
not have been tolerated as non-coms if there had been anyone else
available. Due to the lack of effective non-coms, the company commander and the First Sergeant had to go around and boot every individual man out of his hole when under fire, only to have him hide again
as soon as they had passed.'

East of the Taute, the 9th and 30th Divisions of XIX Corps nervously
awaited the coming of the Panzer Lehr Division. A lack of air reconnaissance on 10 July due to bad visibility had allowed the Panzer Lehr to
move unhindered to its assembly areas that evening. The German plan
was to force the two divisions back over the Vire Canal and then attack
all the way up to Carentan. Panzer Lehr had started as the best equipped
and most highly trained of all German formations in Normandy, but it

had lost over two-thirds of its strength fighting the British on the Caen front.*

Bayerlein's men were also exhausted, having never been pulled out of the line for a rest. When he had protested to Seventh Army headquarters, he was told not to worry because the Americans were poor soldiers. Bayerlein then warned Choltitz that the Panzer Lehr 'was not in a position to make a counterattack'. Choltitz apparently retorted that he was a liar, 'like all panzer commanders', and that he must attack anyway.

Bayerlein was not exaggerating about the state of his division when it left the British sector. Geyr von Schweppenburg had written, 'Because of its exhausted condition, the division was regarded by I SS Panzer Corps as being in a critical situation'. Bayerlein had no option but to divide his remaining tanks, panzergrenadiers and artillery into three battlegroups. The strongest would attack from Pont-Hébert, the second up the road from Coutances towards Le Dézert, and the third from the Bois du Hommet towards Le Mesnil-Véneron.

During the night of 10 July, American infantry in forward positions reported the noise of tanks, and in the early hours of 11 July, Panzer Lehr units began to attack in the wooded hills south of Le Dézert and against a battalion of the 120th Infantry on Hill 90 near Le Rocher. Although individual Mark IV tanks broke into the American positions, bazooka teams dealt with them quite promptly in isolated actions.

The German attack from Pont-Hébert along the west bank of the Vire was also beaten off with bazookas and the assistance of tank destroyers. A task force from the 3rd Armored Division arrived to help, but six of its tanks were hit by German assault guns firing from the east bank of the River Vire. On the other flank, the 9th Division brought in reinforcements and tank destroyers. At 09.00 hours on 11 July, American fighter-bombers were diverted from another mission to attack Panzer Lehr armoured vehicles advancing north-east on the Le Dézert road.

* According to Bayerlein's own figures, his panzer regiment had been reduced from 2,200 men and 183 tanks down to just 400 men and sixty-five tanks by the time he reached the American sector in 7 July. The 901st Panzergrenadier-Regiment was reduced from 2,600 men to 600, and the 902nd Panzergrenadier-Regiment from 2,600 to 700.

A few miles to the west, other groups of tank destroyers managed to ambush Panthers as they approached. Even though several rounds were often needed to knock out a Panther completely, the tank destroyer crews fought with impressive self-control. Altogether, they destroyed twelve Panthers and one Mark IV. The Panzer Lehr offensive came to a complete halt after the central *Kampfgruppe* was sighted south of Le Dézert and then bombarded by 9th Division artillery and attacked by P-47 Thunderbolts and P-38 Lightnings. The Panzer Lehr had been badly mauled, losing twenty tanks and assault guns as well as nearly 700 men.

Bayerlein blamed his men's exhaustion and the unsuitability of the Panther Mark V among the hedgerows, which reduced its principal advantage of firing at long range. With its long barrel, the turret was also hard to traverse. Perhaps more to the point, the American troops involved had shown great courage and determination. There had been little sign of the panic which occurred two days earlier. At the same time, the weakened Panzer Lehr was nothing like the SS panzer divisions facing the British.

This brief outline cannot convey the reality of fighting in the *bocage*. The Germans described it as a *'schmutziger Buschkrieg'* – a 'dirty bush war' – but they acknowledged that the great advantage lay with them, the defenders. Fear aroused by fighting in the *bocage* produced a hatred which had never existed before the invasion. 'The only good Jerry soldiers are the dead ones,' a soldier in the 1st Infantry Division wrote home in a 'Dear Folks' letter to his family in Minnesota. 'I've never really hated anything quite as much. And it's not because of some blustery speech of a brass-hat. I guess I'm probably a little off my nut – but who isn't? Probably that's the best way to be.' Yet there were unspoken limits to the savagery of the fighting. Neither side made dum-dum bullets, knowing full well that the other would retaliate in kind.

The Americans were unprepared for the density of the *bocage*, with the height of the trees in the hedgerows and the solid high banks in which they grew. They had assumed when training that the hedgerows were like those in southern England. General Collins of VII Corps told Bradley that the *bocage* was as bad as anything he had encountered on Guadalcanal. And Bradley himself called it 'the damnedest country I've ever seen'. Even the British Army had failed to listen to Field Marshal Brooke's warnings. He had had experience of this countryside during the retreat of 1940 and foresaw the difficulties for the attacker.

Fresh troops especially were disorientated and spooked by the impossibility of sighting the enemy as they advanced across the small, enclosed fields. They forgot the basic lessons of infantry training. Their instinct, when bracketed by German artillery or mortar fire, was to throw themselves flat or run back to safety, rather than charge forwards, which was far less dangerous. A shot from a single German rifleman in a tree all too often prompted a whole platoon to drop to the ground, where they offered a much easier target. The Germans were adept at provoking this deliberately, then rapidly firing a barrage of mortar rounds on to them as they lay in the open. 'Keep moving if you want to live', was the slogan adopted by Bradley's headquarters in a general instruction. Officers and non-coms were told that they must not throw themselves to the ground, because the rest of the platoon would follow their example. Aggressive action led to fewer casualties because the Germans were rattled if you kept coming at them. And the importance of 'marching fire' was continually emphasized. This meant firing constantly at likely hiding places as you advanced, rather than waiting for an identifiable target.

Soldiers were advised to lie still if wounded by a sniper. He would not waste another round on a corpse, but would certainly fire again if they tried to crawl away. German snipers concealed in trees often tied themselves to the trunk so that they would not fall out if wounded. Quarter was never given to a sniper on either side. Another favourite hiding place in more open country was in a hayrick. That practice, however, was soon dropped when both American and British soldiers learned to fire tracer bullets to set the rick aflame, then gun down the hidden rifleman as he tried to escape.

German marksmanship was seldom good, mainly due to lack of practice on the ranges while they were working on the Atlantic Wall. But the fear inspired in American soldiers was out of all proportion to the number of casualties inflicted. Three times as many wounds and deaths were caused by mortars as by rifle or machine-gun fire. Most German units had very few trained snipers with telescopic sights, but that did not stop the conviction of frightened infantrymen that every concealed rifleman was a 'sniper'. 'The sniper menace ought not to be exaggerated,' the headquarters of the First US Army insisted in a circular. Snipers should be dealt with by snipers and not by 'indiscriminate fire'. Similar fears turned every German tank into a Tiger and every German field gun into an 88 mm.

Like the British on the Caen front, the Americans found that the Germans were brilliant at camouflage and concealment. Fresh branches were cut to hide guns and armoured vehicles from aircraft as well as on the ground. Their soldiers were made to cover up the tell-tale track marks of armoured vehicles, even by trying to make the flattened grass or corn stand up again. And the German infantry did not just dig foxholes. They dug themselves in like 'moles in the ground', with overhead cover against artillery treebursts and tunnels under the hedgerow. The small opening on to the field provided the ideal aperture from which to scythe down an advancing American platoon with the rapid fire of an MG 42.*

On the eastern front the Germans had learned from Soviet bombardments how to minimize their losses in defence. They applied these lessons to good effect in Normandy. Their front line was no more than a light screen of machine-gun positions. Several hundred yards further back, a rather more substantial line of positions was prepared. Then a third line, even further back, would include a force ready to counterattack immediately.

The Germans knew well that the best moment to catch British or American troops off guard was just after they had taken a position. More casualties were usually inflicted at this moment than during the original attack. Allied soldiers were slow to dig in afresh and often would just make use of the German foxholes or slit trenches. These would be booby-trapped in many cases, but always they would be pre-registered as targets by the supporting German artillery battalions, ready to fire the moment their own men pulled out. Time and again, Allied troops were caught out. Exhausted from the attack and com-

---

* The Maschinengewehr 42, known as the Spandau in Allied armies, fired 1,200 rounds a minute and was far superior to the British Bren gun or the American Browning Automatic Rifle. Distributed in great numbers within German units, it provided them with a volume of fire which the British and American infantry could never match.

placent from success, soldiers did not find the idea of frantically digging a new foxhole very appealing. It took a long time and many unnecessary deaths for British and American infantry to learn to follow the German Army dictum that 'sweat saves blood'.

Fighting against the Red Army had taught German veterans of the eastern front almost every trick imaginable. If there were shell holes on the approach to one of their positions, they would place anti-personnel mines at the bottom. An attacker's instinct would be to throw himself into it to take cover when under machine-gun or mortar fire. If the Germans abandoned a position, they not only prepared booby traps in their dugouts but left behind a box of grenades in which several had been tampered with to reduce the time delay to zero. They were also expert at concealing in a ditch beside a track an S-Mine, known to the Americans as a 'Bouncing Betty' or the 'castrator' mine, because it sprang up when released to explode shrapnel at crotch height. And wires were strung taut at neck height across roads used by Jeeps to behead their unwary occupants as they drove along. The Americans rapidly welded an inverted L-shaped rod to the front of their open vehicles to catch and cut these wires.

Another German trick when the Americans launched a night attack was for one machine gun to fire high with tracer over their attackers' heads. This encouraged them to remain upright, while the others fired low with ball ammunition. In all attacks, both British and American troops failed to follow their own artillery barrage closely enough. Newly arrived troops tended to hang back on the assumption that the enemy would be annihilated by the bombing or the shellfire, when in fact he was likely to be temporarily concussed or disorientated. The Germans recovered rapidly, so the moment needed to be seized.

Tanks supporting an attack were used to put down a heavy curtain of machine-gun fire at all likely machine-gun positions, especially in the far corners of each field. But they also caused a number of casualties to their own infantry, especially with the bow machine gun firing from a lower level. Infantry platoons often used to yell for tank support, but sometimes when their armour appeared uninvited, they were indignant. The presence of tanks almost always attracted German artillery or mortar fire.

The Sherman was a noisy beast. Germans claimed that they always knew from the sound of tank engines when an American attack was coming. Both American and British tank crews had many dangers to fear. The 88 mm anti-aircraft gun used in a ground role was terrifyingly accurate, even from a mile away. The Germans camouflaged them on a hill to the rear so that they could fire down over the hedgerows below. In the close country of the *bocage*, German tank-hunting groups with the shoulder-launched Panzerfaust would hide and wait for a column of American tanks to pass, then fire at them from behind at their vulnerable rear. Generalleutnant Richard Schimpf of the 3rd Paratroop Division on the Saint-Lô front noted how his men began rapidly to gain confidence and lose their *panzerschreck*, or fear of tanks, after disabling Shermans at close quarters. Others would creep up on tanks and throw a sticky bomb, like the Gammon grenade which the American paratroopers had used to such effect. Some would even climb on to the tank, if they could approach unseen, and try to drop a grenade into a hatch. Not surprisingly, companies of Shermans in the *bocage* did not like to move without a flank guard of infantry.

Germans often sited an assault gun or a tank at the end of a long straight lane to ambush any Shermans which tried to use it. This forced tanks out into the small fields. Unable to see much through the periscopes, the tank commander had to stick his head out of the turret hatch to have a look, and thus presented a target for a rifleman or a stay-behind machine gun.

The other danger was a German panzer concealed in a sunken track between hedgerows. Survival depended on very quick reactions. German tank turrets traversed slowly, so there was always the chance of getting at least one round off first. If they did not have an armour-piercing round ready in the breech, a hit with a white phosphorus shell could either blind the enemy tank or even panic its crew into abandoning their vehicle.

In the fields surrounded by hedgerows, tanks were at their most vulnerable when they entered or left a field by an obvious opening. Various methods were tried to avoid this. The accompanying infantry tried Bangalore torpedoes to make breaches in a hedgerow, but this was seldom effective because of the solidity of the mound and the time needed to dig the charge in. Engineers used explosive, but a huge quantity was required.

The perfect solution was finally discovered by Sergeant Curtis G. Culin of the 102nd Cavalry Reconnaissance with the 2nd Armored Division. Another soldier came up with the suggestion that steel prongs should be fitted to the front of the tank, then it could dig up the hedgerow. Most of those present laughed, but Culin went away and developed the idea by welding a pair of short steel girders to the front of a Sherman. General Bradley saw a demonstration. He immediately gave orders that the steel from German beach obstacles should be cut up for use. The 'rhino' tank was born. With a good driver, it took less than two and a half minutes to clear a hole through the bank and hedgerow.

One of the most important but least favourite pastimes in the *bocage* was patrolling at night. A sergeant usually led the patrol, whose task was either to try to capture a prisoner for interrogation, or simply to establish a presence out in front in case of surprise attacks. German paratroopers on the Saint-Lô front used to sneak up at night to lob grenades. Many stories were elaborated around night patrols. 'I talked to enough men,' wrote the combat historian Forrest Pogue, 'to believe the tale of a German and an American patrol which spent several days under a gentleman's agreement visiting a wine cellar in no-man's land at discreet intervals.' He also heard from one patrol leader that his group had 'reported itself cut off by the enemy for three days while they enjoyed the favors of two buxom French girls in a farmhouse'. But even if true, these were exceptions. Very few men, especially those from the city, liked leaving the reassuring company of their platoon. American units also used patrolling to give newly arrived 'replacements' a taste of the front line. But for a sergeant in command of some terrified recruits ready to shoot at anything in the dark, a night patrol was the worst task of all.

American military bureaucracy handled the whole 'replacement' system with a brutal lack of imagination. The word itself, which suggested the filling of dead men's shoes, was ill-chosen. It took several months before the term was changed to 'reinforcement'. But the basic problem remained. These new arrivals were poorly trained and totally unprepared for what lay ahead. 'Our younger men, especially the replacements who came up when I did,' reported a lieutenant in the 35th Division, 'were not real soldiers. They were too young to be killers and too soft to endure the hardships of battle.'

'Practically all of the replacements,' stated a report from the 4th Infantry Division, 'had come direct from replacement training centers.' They had received no unit or field training and, unlike those prepared in England for the invasion, they had never been put under overhead artillery fire. 'A great many of those furnished as specialists had never been trained in their official speciality. A good many of the infantry replacements had not been trained as combat infantry . . . I have found men trained as mail orderlies, cooks, officers' orderlies, truck drivers etc., for periods ranging from six months to a year, who had been sent over, assigned to a combat unit, and thrust into combat within 24 hours . . . These men were definitely inadequately prepared, both psychologically and militarily, for combat duty.' The only chance that the division had to train them was during the much needed periods of rest: less than six days out of the forty since it had landed on Utah. It was an impossible task. Having suffered 7,876 casualties since landing, the 4th had received 6,663 replacements.* The majority of suicides were committed by replacements. 'Just before they went across to France,' an American Red Cross woman recorded, 'belts and ties were removed from some of these young men. They were very, very young.'

Replacements joined their platoon usually at night, having no idea where they were. The old hands shunned them, partly because their arrival came just after they had lost buddies and they would not open up to newcomers. Also everyone knew that they would be the first to be killed and doomed men were seen as somehow contagious. It became a self-fulfilling prophecy, because replacements were often given the most dangerous tasks. A platoon did not want to waste experienced men.

Many replacements went into shock as soon as they came under fire. Aid men found themselves having to act as counsellors to replacements curled in terror at the bottom of their foxholes. These boys were convinced that they were under direct fire because of the intense vibrations in the earth from shells landing some distance away. The aid

---

* Only 14 per cent of US servicemen sent abroad during the Second World War were infantrymen, yet they suffered more than 70 per cent of the casualties. In Normandy the infantry suffered 85 per cent of the casualties.

men had to try to persuade them to stick their heads out of the hole to see that they were not in immediate danger.

Whenever the company advanced, a guide sergeant was placed in the rear of the platoon to grab any of them who panicked. Replacements were also the most likely to try to escape the front line by resorting to a self-inflicted wound. They usually shot themselves in the left foot or left hand. The cleverer ones used a sandbag or other material to prevent tell-tale cordite burns around the entry point, but the pattern of left foot and left hand was so obvious, as General George Patton observed, that there was 'a high probability that the wound was self-inflicted'. Those who took this way out were sectioned off in special wards in hospitals as if cowardice was infectious. As soon as they were discharged, they faced a sentence of six months in the stockade.

The real heroes of the *bocage* were the aid men. They had to tend the wounded in the open and try to evacuate them. Their only defence was a Red Cross brassard, which was usually respected, but often not by snipers. Aid men did not expect much help from the fighting soldiers, who were told to keep going even when a comrade was hit. 'Riflemen must leave first aid assistance to the medics,' stated an instruction from Bradley's headquarters, giving an example of a particular incident. 'Four replacements were killed and eight wounded in this company through attempting to render first aid to a fallen comrade.'

An aid man with the 30th Infantry Division recorded his experiences: 'To get down fast you needed to learn to buckle your knees and collapse rather than make a deliberate movement to the prone position.' He wrote of the 'light of hope' in the eyes of wounded men when he appeared. It was easy to spot those about to die with 'the grey-green color of death appearing beneath their eyes and fingernails. These we would only comfort. Those making the most noise were the lightest hit, and we would get them to bandage themselves using their own compresses and Sulfa [powder].' He concentrated on those in shock or with severe wounds and heavy bleeding. He hardly ever had to use tourniquets, 'since most wounds were puncture wounds and bled very little or were amputations or hits caused by hot and high velocity shell or mortar fragments which seared the wound shut'.

His main tools were bandage scissors to cut through uniform, Sulfa powder, compresses and morphine. He soon learned not to carry extra water for the wounded but cigarettes, since that was usually the first thing they wanted. They were also lighter to carry. Shellbursts in oak trees killed many, so he searched around for wounded and corpses whenever he saw branches on the ground. Work parties took the bodies back to Graves Registration. They were usually stiff and swollen, and sometimes infected with maggots. A limb might come off when they were lifted. The stench was unbearable, especially at the collection point. 'Here the smell was even worse, but most of the men working there were apparently so completely under the influence of alcohol that they no longer appeared to care.'

He once had to fill out 'Killed in Action' tags for a whole squad wiped out by a single German machine gun. And he never forgot an old sergeant who had died with a smile on his face. He wondered why. Had the sergeant been smiling at that instant of death, or had he thought of something while dying? Tall big men were the most vulnerable, however strong they might be. 'The combat men who really lasted were usually thin, smaller of stature and very quick in their movements.' Real hatred of the enemy came to soldiers, he noticed, when a buddy was killed. 'And this was often a total hatred; any German they encountered after that would be killed.' He even noted how sentimental GIs from farming communities would cover the open eyes of dead cows with twists of straw.

There was a marked divide between farm boys and city boys who had never been in the countryside. A soldier from a farm caught a cow, tied her to the hedgerow and began to milk her into his helmet. The city boys in his platoon came over and watched in amazement. They were also impressed when he put dried weed and branches out in front of their positions so that Germans could not creep up at night silently to throw grenades.

US Army medical services in Normandy were almost overwhelmed at times by cases of combat exhaustion, otherwise known as battle shock. At first, nobody really knew how to deal with this massive problem. The neuro-psychiatrist of the 29th Infantry Division, Major David Weintrob, recorded with cynical amusement that he was sent into action with 'a sphygmomanometer, a set of five tuning forks, a percussion hammer and an ophthalmoscope'.

By 18 June, all his tents had been filled with soldiers suffering combat exhaustion. The flow eased in a quieter period from 21 June to 10 July, with an average of only eight cases a day. But from the morning of 11 July, with the offensive to seize Saint-Lô, 'the rains came', as Weintrob put it. There were anything between thirty-five and eighty-nine admissions a day. He had to listen to 'visions of 88s to the right of him; 88s to the left of him; 88s on top of him'. Nearly half of the combat-exhaustion casualties were replacements who collapsed after less than forty-eight hours in the front line.

Weintrob had so many cases that he had to pass most on to the First Army Exhaustion Center, which soon became overwhelmed itself and 'bluntly refused to accept any but the very acute battle psychoneuroses'. This influx – 'the great majority of cases were those of extreme physical exhaustion with mild anxiety states' – enabled Weintrob to persuade their commander, General Gerhardt, to allow him to set up a new system. The diminutive but belligerent Gerhardt, who had invented the divisional battle-cry 'Twenty-nine, let's go!', was won over by Weintrob's argument that he could get many more men back into the firing line this way.

Weintrob had fifteen medical assistants covering ten large ward tents and eight pyramidal tents. Patients arrived from the forward casualty clearing stations. They received twenty-four hours' rest and light sedation. On the second day, they were cleaned up and given new uniforms. A psychiatric examination took place on the third. The most acute cases were evacuated rearwards. Weintrob divided the rest into three categories: fit for an immediate return to duty after a short rest, suitable for the new training programme, or to be classified as unfit for further combat duty. He recognized that there were some men who would never be able to cope with the stress of combat. They would simply be a danger and a hindrance to the rest.

Weintrob first set up what became known as the 'Hot Spot Spa', which was basically an 'out and out rest camp', with movies shown daily and ball games. But this became much too attractive, and soon many men who felt in need of a break started to fake combat-exhaustion symptoms. So he instituted a new programme with weapon training, target practice and road marches to rebuild military confidence. This was run by non-coms recovering from light wounds. The programme also helped him assess borderline cases. Out of 1,822 cases (an eighth of the total non-fatal battle casualties), 775 men were returned to duty. Just over half, 396 men, were still in combat after fourteen weeks. Weintrob estimated that 'a man who has broken down psychologically on two occasions is lost as an efficient combat soldier'.

Quite clearly the vulnerability of replacements was the most urgent problem to tackle. Weintrob and Major G. B. Hankins, who ran the training programme, urged Gerhardt to change the system. Instead of sending replacements forward to a platoon during darkness on the day they arrived, they should be held back and put into the training programme until the regiment to which they were allotted came back into reserve. This would allow the opportunity to train them with machine-gun and artillery fire going overhead and explosions set off around them to simulate shellbursts. Replacements also needed to be integrated better. They should be given the division's blue and grey patch to wear on their uniforms before they joined their platoons. Almost all of Weintrob's innovations were later brought into general use by the US Army by that autumn.

German officers, on the other hand, would have shaken their heads in amazement. Their hard-pressed divisions in Normandy never had the luxury of a few days' training behind the lines. New soldiers arrived at the point of a boot. And if they shot themselves through the hand or foot, they were executed. The Obergefreiter with the 91st Luftlande-Division wrote home on 15 July to say that 'Krammer, a capable and brave lad, stupidly shot himself through the hand. Now he is to be shot.' Their only hope was for 'a nice *Heimatschuss*', a wound severe enough for them to be sent home. Both British and American psychiatrists were struck by the 'apparently few cases of psychoneurosis' among German prisoners of war. They wondered whether this was because the German military authorities refused to acknowledge the condition or whether eleven years of Nazi propaganda had prepared their soldiers better for battle.

17

Caen and the Hill of Calvary

During the Epsom operation and after it, Montgomery continued his policy of telling Eisenhower as little as possible. 'Ike is considerably less than exuberant these days,' Eisenhower's aide wrote in his diary. The 'slowness of Monty's attack' was one his chief concerns, and Eisenhower had spoken to Churchill about it while the battle was in full swing.

Eisenhower's deputy, Air Chief Marshal Tedder, and Air Marshal Coningham even discussed the possibility of having Montgomery relieved. Coningham, who commanded the Tactical Air Force supporting 21st Army Group, had loathed Montgomery since the North African campaign. He had never been able to forgive Montgomery's compulsion to take all the credit. Now he was infuriated by Montgomery's pretence that his strategy was proceeding according to plan when he had manifestly failed to take the ground needed for airfields.

Senior American officers were becoming scornful of what they saw as inexcusable caution on the British front. By 30 June, the British Second Army had suffered 24,698 casualties since the invasion began, while the Americans had lost 34,034 men, nearly half as many again. (German losses for the same period were 80,783.) Casualties on D-Day itself had been much lighter than expected, but since then the situation had deteriorated rapidly. British infantry casualties were 80 per cent higher than estimated and there were fewer and fewer replacements to bring units back up to strength.*

* Carlo d'Este, however, argues that the British Army seems to have retained an abnormally large force of over 100,000 men for defence of the United Kingdom and other contingencies which could have been used in Normandy.

On top of an instinctive abhorrence of heavy losses from his experience in the First World War, Montgomery felt he had an even stronger
reason for caution in his attacks. Yet he did not discuss the manpower
crisis with Eisenhower. The British feared losing face as well as power.
Churchill was worried that such an admission of British weakness would
reduce his influence with Roosevelt when it came to deciding the
post-war future of Europe. It would not be long, however, before
Montgomery's 21st Army Group had to disband the 59th Division to
reinforce other formations. And in November, to Churchill's renewed
dismay, the 50th Division would also be split up.

Montgomery's reluctance to incur losses in Normandy has long been
a target for criticism. But the faults were perhaps more institutional
than merely personal. The disappointing performance of his three
veteran divisions from North Africa, the 7th Armoured, the 50th Northumbrian and the 51st Highland Division, revealed a war-weariness in
large parts of the British Army. An aversion to risk had become widespread and opportunities were seldom exploited. The repeated failures
to crack the German front round Caen inevitably blunted an aggressive
outlook. Increasingly, the Second Army in Normandy preferred to rely
on the excellent support provided by the Royal Artillery and on Allied
air power. The idea that high explosive saved British lives became
almost addictive. But it certainly did not save French lives, as Montgomery's next offensive showed in the most shocking way.

The battle for Caen began on 4 July with Operation Windsor, a preliminary attack by the Canadian 8th Infantry Brigade to seize the village
and airfield of Carpiquet to the west of the city. Carpiquet was defended
by a small detachment of their most hated enemy, the 12th SS Panzer-
Division *Hitler Jugend*. This battle, with the Régiment de la Chaudière,
the Queen's Own Rifles of Canada, the North Shore and the Winnipeg
Rifles out for revenge, was to be one of the most vicious of the whole
Normandy campaign.

The village and the airfield were held by fewer than 200 members of
the 26th SS Panzergrenadier-Regiment and five Mark IV tanks brought
up by night and hidden in the battered hangars at the southern end.
But their most powerful weapons consisted of a battery of 88 mm guns
sited to cover the eastern part of the airfield. They also had an artillery

battalion and some Nebelwerfer batteries from the 7th Mortar Brigade.

The Canadians attacked at 05.00 hours, supported by the heavy guns of HMS *Rodney* and the monitor HMS *Roberts* at a range of fifteen miles. The village was pounded to rubble. Many of the fifty-odd SS panzergrenadiers were buried alive. Coated in dust, some managed to struggle out from under the fallen beams and debris. They cleaned their weapons rapidly and fought back as the Régiment de la Chaudière attacked. Despite their small number, they inflicted heavy casualties on their attackers, but by 14.00 hours the remnants of the village were in Canadian hands. The few prisoners taken were treated roughly after the bitter fight.

Canadian artillery and the warships had also pounded the airfield itself. The SS artillery observer died, skewered with 'a twenty-five centimeter long fragment of a ship's artillery shell sticking in his back'. The Queen's Own Rifles, supported by the Shermans of the Fort Garry Horse, attacked the eastern end of the airfield, but the well-sited German 88s forced back the Canadian tanks. Those infantrymen who reached the hangars and the barracks faced a hard fight, since the fanatical young panzergrenadiers were installed in bunkers and tunnels. In many cases, Canadian infantry went past concealed positions without spotting them and were then shot in the back.

The Winnipeg Rifles advanced on the southern end of the airfield backed by another squadron and also some flame-throwing Crocodiles from the 79th Armoured Division. They too came under heavy fire. The Nebelwerfer 'Moaning Minnies' and the SS artillery battalion turned the airfield into a killing ground. The Winnipegs and their armour were forced to pull back to the cover of a small wood beyond the perimeter. They tried again in the afternoon, but by then the 12th SS had brought up more panzers. The Germans had been listening in to the Canadian radio net and knew their next move.

That night, after an unsuccessful attack by Allied fighter-bombers, the I SS Panzer Corps sent in the 1st SS Panzergrenadier-Regiment from the *Leibstandarte Adolf Hitler* to recapture the village of Carpiquet. The survivors from the 12th SS on the airfield were meanwhile told to withdraw with their wounded. But the attack of the 1st Panzer-grenadiers was hit initially by fire from their own artillery and then by a massive bombardment from Canadian guns and the warships.

According to one Canadian source, the French Canadians of the Régiment de la Chaudière went berserk around dawn, cutting the throats of any SS men they could find, 'wounded as well as dead'. Officers with drawn pistols eventually brought them back under control. An officer with the regiment wrote, 'No prisoners are taken this day on either side.'

The Canadians never managed to take Carpiquet with Operation Windsor. They blamed their failure on the British 43rd Division, which lost the village of Verson, just south of the airfield, when attacked by part of the 1st SS Panzer-Division *Leibstandarte Adolf Hitler*. Verson was not retaken until four days later, when the major attack on Caen itself took place.

Montgomery, well aware of the exasperation building up against him in Whitehall, SHAEF and at Bradley's First US Army headquarters, knew that he could not delay the capture of Caen any longer.* He would have to attack the city head on. The offensive would be called Operation Charnwood. On 6 July, to reduce British casualties, he decided to request a massive bombing attack by the RAF to hammer a way through, a possibility which Leigh-Mallory had suggested three weeks earlier. And on 25 June, Eisenhower had written to him, 'Please do not hesitate to make the maximum demands for any air assistance that can possibly be useful to you. Whenever there is any legitimate opportunity we must blast the enemy with everything we have.' On the same day, he also wrote to Tedder asking him to ensure that air support 'in maximum volume' was delivered.

On 7 July, Eisenhower himself went to a conference at Bentley Priory called by Leigh-Mallory to consider the plan. Even Air Chief Marshal Harris, the head of Bomber Command, did not object for once. It was agreed that 467 Lancasters and Halifaxes would attack the northern fringe of Caen that evening with delayed-action bombs. The two main sceptics, neither of whom was present at the meeting, were Eisenhower's deputy, Air Chief Marshal Tedder, and Montgomery's foe Air Marshal Coningham. They feared that the Second Army would keep asking for

---

* There are unsubstantiated rumours that Churchill had considered relieving Montgomery just before the capture of Caen, but the shock that this would have caused to British public opinion, as well as abroad, makes this unlikely.

Bomber Command every time it wanted to mount an offensive, but Eisenhower's support for the plan made them hold their peace.

When the massed formations of Lancasters and Halifaxes appeared that evening at 20.30 hours, British and Canadian infantry jumped out of their slit trenches to cheer. Tank crews climbed on to their turrets to get a better view. 'There was high cloud and the sun was reddening [the Lancasters] all across the sky,' wrote an artillery officer in his diary. 'An incredible barrage of flak' went up from German anti-aircraft batteries. British and Canadian artillery immediately began firing on their positions to help the RAF.

'We could see when the Lancasters released their bombs because they suddenly lifted several feet in the air,' a medical officer wrote. 'More and more bombers go in through the flak,' wrote the same artillery officer. 'A cloud of smoke starts to rise over the target, dirty grey white, blowing over to the north east.' 'Now and then, though pretty rarely, one of our planes comes down. A Lancaster spirals down to the north and crashes apparently into the sea. A number of parachutes open out and sail slowly down.' Then yet another wave of bombers appeared. 'The cloud over Caen covers the whole eastern and south eastern horizon. Now angry glows cover the same area as it gets dark. What could be more encouraging to our chaps?'

An officer in the Guards Armoured Division described the bombing of Caen as 'a magnificent spectacle'. Most spectators evidently assumed that French civilians had been evacuated. 'I sat smoking a cigarette beside a river watching 2,300 tons of bombs being dropped on Caen 6 or 7 miles away,' wrote a major in the Canadian parachute battalion east of the Orne. 'What an incredible sight it was – the poor bloody hun!'

While most cheered at the sight, a few had misgivings. 'The awful thing was,' wrote a captain in the Coldstream Guards, 'that as an infantry-man one was thinking: Why on earth are they knocking it to bits because it will be so easy to defend?' 'The sight was frightening,' wrote a member of the Somerset Light Infantry. 'Yellow tongues leapt up as the bombs burst on the stricken city and the rising smoke – combined with the dust from the devastated buildings – formed a blackened cloud which spread rapidly across the evening sky.' Throughout the raid some six miles away, they felt 'the ground beneath their feet tremble like jelly'.

*

If the ground shook six miles away, the effect within the city itself can hardly be imagined. One elderly man was asked later what it had felt like during the bombing raid of 7 July. He thought for some time before answering, 'Imagine a rat sewn up inside a football during an international match . . .'

The 15,000 inhabitants remaining in Caen despite German orders to leave could be forgiven for assuming that the bombers had targeted the centre of the city, rather than the northern outskirts. Many seemed to think that the ancient castle was the aiming point. Windows with any glass left in literally exploded from the concussion of the bombs. In the convent of Notre Dame de Bon Secours, the homeless seeking refuge there were blinded by dust and felt the bitter smoke in their throats: 'We had the impression of being thrown around on a ship in distress, beaten by a horrible storm and about to founder.' The only remaining candle was extinguished by shock waves. In a calm voice, the Mother Superior kept blessing them 'with a relic of the True Cross'.

As buildings collapsed all around, the sick lying in cots reacted to the noise and tremors with dilated eyes. Nuns offered sips of water with one hand while fingering their rosaries and praying rapidly. The housekeeper of the priest of Saint-Jean-Eudes cried out to him a hurried confession as she was being carried away on a stretcher: 'Monsieur le Curé, go into the garden. I buried for you a shirt and a dozen handker-chiefs. If I hadn't you would have given them all away.'

When the bombing finished, young civil defence volunteers arrived at the convent, urging them to depart immediately. They left by the only door which could be opened. The Mother Superior led the way along the Fossés Saint-Julien, carrying the sacred ciborium, 'a grandiose procession in an unforgettable setting under a magnificent sky dotted with stars, fires all around giving off a red glow, sparks falling all around and delayed action bombs still exploding'. They had to climb over great trees knocked down by the bombs as they made their way to the Bon Sauveur led by a member of the Défense Passive. One youth returned to the convent to guard it against looters and hide the large silver statue of Notre Dame de la Délivrande.

In Caen that evening, the university on the rue Pasteur was almost completely destroyed. Inhabitants sheltering in old cellars, who thought they were safe, were buried alive. In the rue de Geôle, over thirty died, and another fifty in a shelter in the rue de Vaugueux. British officers were horrified to hear from their own civil affairs division that 6,000 had died, but this would have represented nearly half of those left in the city. Another figure given at the time was 2,000. In fact the true number was close to 350 deaths,* which was still a terrible loss considering that over three-quarters of the population had left the city and that most of those who remained were sheltering in deep cellars.

Inhabitants of Caen had feared the worst, having heard German officers declare that the city would be the 'French Stalingrad'. Yet they were then encouraged by clear signs that the Wehrmacht was preparing to withdraw. On 26 June, rear troops began to pull out. The Gestapo returned to destroy evidence of their massacre of Resistance prisoners. And on 6 July, German engineers began to destroy the port installations in Caen along the ship canal. That day the Feldkommandantur also gave orders for the remaining civilians to evacuate the town, but once again that had little effect. Only a screen of SS *Hitler Jugend* panzer-grenadiers was left in Caen itself.

The bombing was a double disaster. It had failed to destroy most of the German positions around the northern fringe of Caen and instead inflicted massive damage on the city. The RAF's fear of hitting the British troops waiting to advance had shifted the bomb-line south towards the city centre, missing the German positions. The mistake was similar to the American failure to hit the beach defences at Omaha. Few except Montgomery ever believed that the bombing had been militarily effective. The only troops who appear to have been hit belonged to a detachment of the Luftwaffe 16th Feld-Division which had taken over from the 21st Panzer-Division near Lebisey, as well as two tanks and a mortar section of the *Hitler Jugend* in the villages just

---

* The Centre de Recherche d'Histoire Quantitative at the University of Caen arrived at a total of 1,150 deaths in Caen, 800 in the bombardments of 6–7 June, and 350 during the bombing of 7 July and the shelling and fighting of 8 July. Figures for injured are not available, except that the hospital at the Bon Sauveur cared for 1,734 injured between 6 June and the end of July, of whom 233 died. Lieutenant Colonel Kraminov, a Soviet war correspondent, claimed that more than 22,000 French were killed and buried in the destruction of Caen and that there were no Germans left in the town. This grotesque exaggeration was taken up as anti-British propaganda after the war by the French Communist Party.

north of Caen. Worst of all, the attack, like the German bombing of Stalingrad, turned much of the city into a mass of rubble which impeded the advance of vehicles and provided an ideal terrain for the defenders.* General Eberbach described the city as 'a heap of ruins which was hard to cross'.

The reason given for bombing on the evening which preceded the attack was said to have been a fear of bad weather the next day. But the meteorological reports for 8 July do not support this. And even allowing for the delayed-action bombs, the German defenders were given all the time they needed to reorganize. Losses suffered by British and Canadian units advancing into and around the city were far higher than expected, despite the heavy artillery bombardment. Lebisey wood was smashed to the point where it looked like something out of the First World War.

The *Hitler Jugend* emerged from their cellars and bunkers with Panzerfaust grenade launchers to take on the Shermans and Crocodile flame-throwers at close range. Riflemen climbed trees and tied themselves in. Their main target appears to have been the commanders of tanks which were 'shooting in' the infantry. The marksmanship of the SS panzergrenadiers was evidently far superior to that of ordinary German infantry divisions. On that day alone, the East Riding Yeomanry lost five crew commanders and a squadron leader from snipers.

Stretcher-bearers taking wounded to the rear became exhausted. 'There were all sorts of casualties,' recounted a member of 223rd Field Ambulance with the British 3rd Infantry Division. 'There were legs without feet, there were knees without kneecaps, there were shoulders without arms. I remember one sergeant major brought in with half of his head blown away, yet he was still conscious, and the MO said to me: "Give him two grains of morphia: it'll finish him quickly". But it didn't. And chest wounds, shocking chest wounds. On that one day we treated 466 British casualties and 40 Germans.'

In the advanced dressing station of 210th Field Ambulance, the doctors and staff also had to deal with a wide variety of battle casualties.

---

* One can only wonder with sympathy at the subsequent feelings of the French crews of two squadrons of Halifaxes involved, the 346th Guyenne Squadron and the 347th Tunisie Squadron, after they received messages of thanks and congratulations the next day from Air Marshal Harris, Dempsey and Montgomery.

They included 'a group of terrified, disorientated lads – battle shocked, jittering and yelling in a corner'. 'Several SS wounded came in – a tough and dirty bunch – some had been snipers up trees for days. One young Nazi had a broken jaw and was near death, but before he fainted he rolled his head over and murmured "Heil Hitler!".'

In field dressing stations, those doomed to die were taken away to another tent and injected with morphine. Medical staff became worried about the shortage of blood left for transfusions. They were also horrified by the ignorance of troops on how best to handle the wounded. Soldiers did far more damage moving those with severe fractures rather than leaving them where they were until trained stretcher-bearers could splint them up. 'All the lessons of the First World War seemed to have been forgotten,' wrote the same doctor with 210th Field Ambulance. Like the rest of his exhausted colleagues, he was afraid that his judgement was impaired by lack of sleep.

The 'Führer order' that Caen was to be held at all costs was followed for all of 8 July. Only that night did General Eberbach agree to Kurt Meyer's insistence that the mangled remains of his *Hitler Jugend* should pull back to the southern part of Caen across the Orne. Eberbach felt the withdrawal could be justified to OKW because they were virtually out of ammunition and it was impossible to send forward any more.

On 9 July, the city still lay under a pall of smoke and dust. André Heintz was woken at 05.30 hours by a companion in the Resistance. 'The Germans are leaving!' he told him. They watched the convoys pulling out through the town, yet no British guns fired. Their leader, Commandant Gilles, distributed the last few Sten guns and sent his members off northwards in pairs to act as guides for the Allied forces. Heintz put on his brassard, a tricolore with the Cross of Lorraine. Suddenly seeing a German soldier near what had been the university swimming pool, he snatched it off again. But the German was dead, frozen in position, having been killed by blast. The brassard was recognized by the first British soldiers he encountered, who gave him the thumbs-up sign.

So great was the destruction that, even with their maps, the British and Canadians found it impossible to work out where they were. Most routes were impassable and there were isolated snipers left behind. A column of Canadian armoured cars descended the rue Saint-Martin. The commander, whose orders were to cross the town as rapidly as possible to try to secure the bridges, asked a bystander, 'Where is the River Orne?' He climbed on to the armoured car to give directions, but a German defensive position further on opened up with machine-gun and anti-tank gun fire. The armoured car went into rapid reverse, and their French guide had to leap off and hide in a doorway.

The *Hitler Jugend*, having pulled back to the south of the Orne across the only bridge left standing, rapidly prepared it for demolition and established defensive positions. They forced locals at gunpoint to dig them trenches in the convent gardens of Les Petites Soeurs des Pauvres and cut down apple trees to improve the fields of fire for their machine guns. Cellar entrances were also sandbagged, ready for defence. The bridge was blown as soon as the leading Canadian platoon came into sight.

At the northern edge of Caen, the British civil affairs team under Lieutenant Colonel Usher had to abandon its vehicles. 'At last,' wrote one of his officers. 'Entered Caen with party of officers. The north end seems utterly devastated. Pile after pile of rubble and a deathly silence punctuated only by occasional bursts of machine gun fire.'

An officer from civil affairs told André Heintz that they intended to set up their headquarters in the Hôtel d'Angleterre. Heintz guided them to it, knowing that the only evidence of its former identity was a remnant of the royal arms with '*Honi soit qui mal y pense*'. He resisted the temptation to say that the British should not have destroyed it, but the officer himself recognized the black irony. He let Heintz lead him to the only area of the city where some buildings were relatively undamaged, but then asked if they would be able to have a bath. Heintz explained that Caen had been without water since the first bombing on 6 June. The liberators still seemed to have no idea what the city had suffered, despite the evidence around them. The following day, a Canadian captain asked for advice on a good restaurant in Caen, because he was sick of eating army rations.

Some Germans, who had been cut off, searched for civilian clothes in the ruins to help their escape. Others, especially some *Osttruppen*, began looting. Commandant Gilles and a couple of his men found two young SS soldiers trying to hide. They handed them over proudly to some Canadian troops on the rue de Bayeux. Care had to be taken in many places, as the SS had left behind booby-trapped grenades.

Civilians emerged, unable to believe that four years of German occupation was finally over and fearful that the SS might retake the town in a counter-attack. Some greeted the Allied soldiers with real warmth and joy, but far more were still numb from what they had been through. 'Most of the women were crying bitterly,' wrote a British sapper, 'griefstricken and anguished. They lingered by their shattered dwellings, perhaps for a last look at their own personal treasures. A child's book lay in the garden, its pages idly flipped by the wind. Inside the house, the doors hung creaking on their hinges, the tables lay where they had fallen from that first great concussion.'

Colonel Usher's groups set to work rapidly, clearing routes with bulldozers and trying to set up an emergency water supply. Most basic services were not restored until September. A convoy of army trucks with food had been prepared ready for the entry into Caen. Mine clearance was a slow and arduous task, and so was the recovery of bodies from under the rubble of ruined buildings. The stench from decomposing corpses was terrible. In fact, many people in Caen, however hungry, could not face a ripe Camembert for a long time because of the horrible memories evoked by the smell.

On 10 July, a ceremony to raise the tricolore on the façade of the Eglise Saint-Etienne was held in the presence of Monsieur Daure, the new *préfet* appointed by de Gaulle's provisional government. Tears ran down the cheeks of many of those present. Three days later, the British Second Army held what was supposed to be a victory parade in the Place Saint-Martin. A Scottish pipe band struck up, as another tricolore was raised. The bewilderment on the faces of the French crowd was plain. They had never heard the 'Marseillaise' played on bagpipes.

Operation Charnwood had been a very partial success, taking just the northern part of Caen. The Second Army had failed to secure enough ground to permit the build-up to continue. The bulk of what was to become the Canadian First Army had to wait behind in England. Exasperation at Bradley's headquarters and at SHAEF was now echoed loudly in Washington and in the American press. Many blamed Eisenhower for not adopting a firmer line with Montgomery.

On 10 July, Montgomery held a conference in his command caravan with Dempsey and Bradley. There was much to discuss, with the British blocked round Caen and the First US Army bogged down in the marshes and the *bocage* to the west. Montgomery suggested that Bradley was trying to attack on too wide a front. What he needed was a concentrated punch. Montgomery, as a result, later convinced himself that he was the original architect of what became Operation Cobra. Dempsey, that morning, decided that he also needed to mount a major offensive, aiming at a breakthrough towards Falaise. Since this was what the Germans feared most, it would also keep German panzer forces on the British front, as Montgomery wanted. This outline plan would become known as Operation Goodwood.

For the moment, however, another attempt was made to seize Hill 112, the key feature between the Odon and the Orne abandoned during Operation Epsom. The fighting for Hill 112 became pitiless. Germans of the 9th SS Panzer-Division *Hohenstaufen* soon called the place 'Kalvarienberg', the hill of Calvary. The name came from the Croix des Filandriers, a shrine of the crucifixion, which seemed to take on a new significance.

On 10 July, at 05.00 hours, the 43rd Wessex Division attacked from the Odon valley towards Hill 112 in Operation Jupiter. The divisional commander, Major General G. I. Thomas, was 'a small, fiery, very determined and grim gunner, without a spark of humour'. Thomas, who had just taken over, was determined to shake up his new command. He seems to have been generally disliked. Behind his back, officers called him 'von Thoma'. One brigade was to attack Hill 112, while the other on the left advanced on the village of Eterville.

The 129th Brigade heading for Hill 112 had to advance again across open cornfields sprinkled with poppies. Nebelwerfer rocket launchers opened fire. Sergeant Partridge with the 4th Battalion Somerset Light Infantry described how, on hearing the scream of the 'Moaning Minnies', 'eleven men dived into the corn for cover. Only one stood up again.' Whenever they encountered wounded Germans in the corn, there was little they could do except remove the bolt from their Mauser rifle and fling it far away.

After losing most of their men, they became pinned down by heavy machine-gun fire in the corn. The platoon commander ordered Partridge to hurl a smoke grenade so that they could advance again. Partridge thought it a stupid idea, but complied. As soon as he had thrown it, the platoon commander jumped to his feet before the smoke billowed and was shot. He gasped, 'Sarn't Partridge,' then expired. Partridge rounded up the other four survivors and crawled back through the corn some way, dug a pit and made a cup of tea, which they shared between them.

While the 129th Brigade struggled up Hill 112, the 130th Brigade on the left captured Eterville and then advanced towards the village of Maltot. The 7th Battalion of the Hampshire Regiment and the 5th Battalion of the Dorsets, with their supporting tanks of the 44th Royal Tank Regiment, had little idea of the shock awaiting them. The 502nd SS Heavy Panzer Battalion equipped with Mark VI Tiger tanks, the largest and most formidable fighting machine seen on the western front, was converging on the same spot. Unable to see what was ahead, the Tigers of one company smashed through the hedgerow in front and found themselves facing four Shermans. The Tigers' 88 mm guns turned three of them into blazing wrecks in a moment. The fourth escaped using high reverse. The Dorsets, unaware that the other battalion had withdrawn, were soon engaged in house-to-house fighting in the village. They learned the hard way that when clearing a building you had to go straight for the top rooms. If they went through a farmhouse and into the courtyard at the back, it was too easy for the Germans upstairs to throw down grenades or fire from the windows.

A mile and a half to the west, the British 129th Brigade almost reached the small road crossing the top of Hill 112, but the weight of German fire forced the battered 4th Somerset Light Infantry in the middle to go to ground again. At 17.00 hours, the 5th Duke of Cornwall's Light Infantry was sent on through the Somersets in another attempt to reach the top. Their advance just over the brow of the hill reached a small wood of chestnuts. There they were cut to pieces by machine-gun fire from the German positions on the reverse slope, then attacked by panzers. Part of the Cornwalls ran back in disorder. A wounded officer tried to halt this retreat: 'He had been hit in the jaw, so that part of his face had dropped, and he was waving a pistol and trying to shout, making terrible sounds.' Meanwhile the commanding officer of the Somersets and the brigade commander, trying to maintain an air of confidence in front of their men, sat on their shooting sticks in the open discussing the situation.

Despite the mortar and sniper fire, the Somersets held on in 'slit trenches scraped out of the bare open slope'. With Nebelwerfer mortar shells exploding continuously, the crews of their supporting armour remained closed down. But one officer was so desperate to relieve himself that he jumped out of his Sherman, grabbed a shovel off the back and raced across to a knocked-out tank nearby, where he proceeded to drop his trousers. Meanwhile, British artillery continued to hammer the summit. 'Not a metre of ground escaped being ploughed up by shells,' a member of the SS *Hohenstaufen* wrote. After nightfall, each company colour sergeant brought up hot food in containers and supplies of cigarettes for the infantry in the forward positions. For once there was more than enough to go around, because 'no allowance had been made for casualties'. Their only complaint was that the tea tasted of petrol.

Dawn on 11 July did not improve visibility because of a thick mist – '*eine Milchsuppe*', as the *Hohenstaufen* described it. But high overhead a British artillery spotter plane appeared just as the 19th and 20th SS Panzergrenadier-Regiments were about to attack. The crews of the Tiger tanks with them feared the worst. They quickly realized that the safest place would be in among their enemy. They charged the British positions, rolling over trenches. With an ironic admiration, they saw British anti-tank crews trying to bring their ineffective guns to bear. 'They're brave, the Anglo-Saxons!' one of them noted.

The monster panzers suddenly emerged from the bank of mist. 'We had a scene in front of us of which every Tiger dreams,' a crew member wrote. Barely a hundred yards away was a forward replenishment point with ammunition trucks and other vehicles, including tanks. 'Our commander called out: "Armour-piercing! Open fire!".' Two Churchill tanks in front of them were traversing their turrets towards them, but the Tigers blasted them at close range and they both exploded into flames.

That day, General Eberbach told II SS Panzer Corps that Hill 112 must not be lost under any circumstances. It was a '*Schlüsselstellung*' – a key position. Frantic telephone calls followed in an attempt to secure replacements of both men and materiel. The panzergrenadiers supported by the Tiger companies held the ridge all day.

After dusk, D Company of the Somersets received orders to 'infiltrate the enemy position'. 'The despair I felt when this order reached me can be imagined,' wrote Sergeant Partridge, who had taken over command of his platoon after the death of their lieutenant the day before. Weapons were cleaned and ammunition distributed. At 01.00 hours, they rose out of their slit trenches and advanced silently. But as soon as they reached the barbed wire on the summit which the SS panzergrenadiers had erected, a murderous fire opened. The platoons threw themselves flat. 'The tracer bullets,' wrote Sergeant Partridge, 'were arcing their way almost lazily through the air, winging their way to pre-selected targets chosen during daylight, and now being fired on "fixed lines".'

Any attempt to breach the wire ended when a section commander attempted to scramble through. A German bullet hit a phosphorus grenade in his ammunition pouch. 'Struggling in desperation,' wrote a corporal watching, 'he became entangled in the barbed wire and hung there, a living screaming human beacon.' Sergeant Partridge heard the man's 'anguished cries of "Shoot me, shoot me!"'. 'A single well-aimed bullet from a compassionate but no doubt appalled officer,' the corporal continued, 'put the lad out of his blazing hell. Even in death the horror continued as the phosphorus burned into the now mercifully lifeless body.' Everyone who witnessed the scene was determined never again to carry a phosphorus grenade in their webbing pouches.

An order was given to pull back, but that was not the end of the horror. Some men became lost in the dark on their way down the hill and were shot as they reached the positions of other companies who did not know who they were. The corporal noted that 18 Platoon of D Company had only nine men left out of thirty-six. One of the survivors then shot himself in the foot, because he could not take any more.

The nightmare of Hill 112 continued. The British recaptured it the next day, then the SS seized it back in another counter-attack with Tigers. After the rains of the week before, the temperature had now risen to thirty degrees centigrade and every explosion created clouds of dust. The small wood of chestnut trees was shredded by the British artillery firing airbursts. These were intended to rain splinters down on the defenders. Very soon the wood was reduced to smashed stumps and broken branches, a 'moon landscape' as one of the SS put it. On 15 July, the artillery fire was so intense that the panzergrenadiers were forced to withdraw, leaving the Tigers there alone.

All this time, the artillery of the II SS Panzer Corps resorted to the German tactic of sudden intense barrages on the British positions on the north slope of the ridge. The SS gunners, being much further back, did not suffer the same privations as the panzergrenadiers. One battery of the 9th SS Artillerie-Regiment with the *Hohenstaufen* Division appears to have been adopted by a young Frenchwoman, whom they knew as 'Mademoiselle Jeanette'. Each day, she used to bring food to the soldiers in the gun line.

Further to the east, German artillery now bombarded the liberated capital of Caen. On 14 July, the Lycée Malherbe and the quarter of Saint-Etienne were hit. People who had refused the British offer of evacuation a few days earlier now rushed for the trucks. An ancient Benedictine nun, who had never stepped outside the convent since her novitiate at the beginning of the century, was astonished to see trucks for the first time in her life, and even more thrilled to ride in one. But civilians trapped behind German lines, who had been sheltering in the damp caves by the village of Fleury, were in a terrible state. SS troops would not allow them out. Their chance of rescue would not come until later in the month.

In Caen, the French authorities and British civil affairs section became increasingly concerned about the danger of cholera. After the destruction of the city, the task of reconnecting the water supply was far harder than even the most pessimistic had imagined. Starving dogs had also become a menace and the *préfet* issued orders to shoot any found in the streets.

Disturbed by the lack of progress, the Second Army had at last started to sack incompetent or unenergetic commanders. After Epsom, General 'Pip' Roberts, the commander of the 11th Armoured Division, replaced a brigade commander and two commanding officers.

On 15 July, Montgomery wrote to Brooke about one of his favourite divisions from North Africa: 'Regret to report it is considered opinion Crocker, Dempsey and myself that 51st [Highland] Division is at present not – NOT – battleworthy. It does not fight with determination and has failed in every operation it has been given to do.' Montgomery sacked the commander for weakness and even considered ordering the whole division back to Britain for retraining. Word of their disgrace rapidly spread round the Second Army and soon a letter was sent out instructing officers 'not to criticise the 51st Highland Division'. Fortunately the new commander, Major General T. G. Rennie, rapidly turned the 51st Highland Division round and restored its morale.

Many more commanders had been battle casualties. The 50th Division had lost two brigadiers, twelve commanding officers and a very high proportion of company officers. Command of 4th Armoured Brigade was given to Brigadier Michael Carver at the age of only twenty-nine, after his predecessor was wounded. Officer casualties were very high. German snipers could identify them easily from their map boards, which gleamed in the sun. Their losses became a vicious circle. While most of the best NCOs had been promoted to command platoons, the rest often showed a lack of initiative. This forced officers to take extra risks to get their men to attack, or they had to stand up conspicuously to stop a panic.

Perhaps the most extreme example of this pattern affected the 6th Battalion of the Duke of Wellington's Regiment. In just over two weeks, the battalion had lost twenty-three officers and 350 NCOs and soldiers. The new commanding officer reported at the end of June that three-quarters of the battalion were 'jumpy' as a result of shelling, there were cases of self-inflicted wounds and a high number of shell-shock casualties. 'The situation has got worse each day as more key personnel have become casualties . . . NCO leadership is weak in most cases and the newly drafted officers are in consequence having to expose themselves unduly to try and get anything done.' Appalled by the report, Montgomery sacked the new commanding officer, who had been too honest, and disbanded the battalion.

Normandy proved what had hitherto been suspected. Troops bogged down in beachhead and bridgehead battles of attrition suffer a far higher rate of psychological breakdown than in one of movement. Even the retreat of a defeated army seemed to produce fewer cases. On 13 July, 21st Light Field Ambulance reported to General Richard O'Connor, the commander of VIII Corps, that 'during the 54 hours commencing

1800 hours 10 July 1944, 280 cases of exhaustion were transferred to this unit from the forward area, and it is felt that about 70% of them should not have been evacuated from their units.' They were no more physically tired than other walking wounded, 'while their anxiety was not above a normal apprehension of participating in battle'.

Major General G. H. A. Macmillan, the commander of the 15th Scottish Division, reported to O'Connor shortly afterwards: 'I have now organised a Divisional Exhaustion Centre.' Altogether 151 had been admitted, of whom forty-one came from a single battalion, 'which shows that something is wrong in that quarter'. His headquarters issued an instruction to medical officers warning them 'to be very careful not to send men down the line unless they are absolutely satisfied that the cases are genuine'. He suspected that medical officers, 'under pressure of work', had been sending them back 'merely to get them out of the way'. Any NCO sent back to an exhaustion centre was to be reduced to private soldier automatically. Commanders were also furious at the huge losses of equipment due to demoralized soldiers throwing away their weapons. Desertions and absence without leave increased. No fewer than 150 soldiers from the 50th (Northumberland) Division were convicted of desertion in Normandy, as many as in the whole of the rest of the Second Army.

The formation worst affected by combat fatigue was the 43rd Wessex Division, commanded by Major General Thomas, which had been involved in the battles for Maltot and Hill 112. Tank crews, on the other hand, were much less likely to collapse. 'The Corps psychiatrist and commander 21 Light Field Ambulance confirm that cases of feigned battle exhaustion by soldiers of Armd Divs are negligible. The main offenders are infantry units. The greatest number of cases come from 43 Division. During 3 or 4 days about 10 July some 360 cases came from that formation. Units particularly affected were 4 Dorsets and 7 Hamps.' General O'Connor wrote to Thomas about this 'most serious offence', ordering him to make it 'quite clear that anyone found guilty of feigning illness under this heading will be tried by [Field General Court Martial] for desertion'.

Infantrymen appear to have suffered the most because of the effects of German mortars and Nebelwerfer batteries firing concentrated sal- voes at unexpected moments. A close miss sent many men into shock.

At 129th Infantry Brigade headquarters, three men, including a sergeant major, suffered from battle shock from Nebelwerfer bombardments. 'Two of them during an attack did not stay in their slit trenches, but just ran around wildly screaming "Get me out of here!".' Another contributing factor to the sense of helplessness and disorientation was the lack of information. In the words of one soldier, they suffered from 'ignorance, stupefying, brutalizing ignorance. You never knew where you were or where the enemy was, or what you were supposed to be attempting to achieve.'

Tank crews appear to have been much less susceptible to combat fatigue, not just because of the protection offered by their armoured vehicle, but also because they were part of closely knit groups. British infantry, just like their American counterparts, suffered from the vulnerability of their replacements. The British system was no more imaginative than the American. A subaltern sent as replacement to the Somerset Light Infantry after its mauling on Hill 112 described how a moustached major at their reinforcement camp near Bayeux addressed the new officers: 'Gentlemen, your life expectancy from the day you join your battalion, will be precisely three weeks.'

18

The Final Battle for Saint-Lô

On 6 July, while the Americans were still bogged down in the general advance south towards Saint-Lô, General George S. Patton arrived in France. He was to command the Third US Army as soon as it was activated on Eisenhower's order.

Stuck in England for a month since the invasion, he had been 'awfully restless'. 'It is Hell to be on the side lines and see all the glory eluding me,' he had written to his wife on D-Day. He started wearing his shoulder holster 'so as to get myself into the spirit of the part', then packed for France even though there was no immediate prospect of being called over. For the time being, he had to play his part as commander-in-chief of the fictitious First US Army Group, that vital part of Plan Fortitude. The Germans were still convinced that he would command a second invasion around the Pas-de-Calais.

Patton was grateful to Eisenhower for having twice given him another chance. The first time was after he had slapped a soldier suffering from combat exhaustion in Sicily, the second being his gaffe in a speech in England, saying that the Americans and the British were destined to rule the world. But he never respected Ike 'as a soldier'. When he accompanied the supreme commander on a tour of divisions in the south-west of England, he described his friendly manner with the troops as that of 'an office seeker rather than that of a soldier'. 'His theory is that by this method one gets on a level with the men. A commander cannot command and be on the same level. At least that is my opinion. I try to arouse fighting emotion – he tries for votes – for what? However he was very pleasant [to me].'

Patton also despised Montgomery, whom he called 'the little monkey'. But he had felt a certain gratitude on 1 June, just before the invasion, when Montgomery insisted twice to Bradley that 'Patton should take over for the Brittany, and possibly the Rennes operation'. The next morning, he noted in his diary, 'I have a better impression of Monty than I had.' Patton, who followed events in Normandy with intense frustration, felt that Bradley's attempt to advance on a broad front was wrong. Constant minor attacks to win ground, in his view, led to far more casualties in the long run than a concentrated offensive.

German commanders agreed. 'I cannot follow the reasoning,' wrote Generalleutnant Schimpf of the 3rd Paratroop Division, 'that these tactics were supposed to have helped avoid bloodshed, as I was told by captured American officers. For although losses on the day of attack could be kept comparatively low, on the other hand the total losses suffered through the continuous minor attacks launched over a long period, were surely much heavier than would have been the case if a forceful attack had been conducted.' Elsewhere he wrote of American battalion attacks: 'For our troops, this type of defence against continual assaults was an excellent training and acclimatisation to the fighting ways of the enemy.' With impressive foresight, Patton wrote on 2 July that they should be attacking down the west coast towards Avranches with 'one or two armored divisions abreast', supported by air power.

At last on 4 July, his Third Army headquarters began to embark. Patton himself flew over two days later in a C-47 to the landing strip above Omaha beach. His plane was escorted by four P-47 Thunderbolts, the fighter-bomber which would later support his astonishing advance across France. As soon as he reached French soil, Patton was on exuberant form. News of his arrival spread instantly among the soldiers and sailors of Omaha beach command. His presence was supposed to be a closely guarded secret, but they crowded around with cameras, taking photographs as if he were a movie star. Patton stood up in the Jeep sent for him and addressed them in his inimitable style: 'I'm proud to be here to fight beside you. Now let's cut the guts out of those Krauts and get the hell on to Berlin. And when we get to Berlin, I am going to personally shoot that paper-hanging son of a bitch, just like I would a snake.' His audience loved it, cheering and whooping wildly. Patton and Eisenhower were indeed unalike.

The next day he had lunch with Bradley, Montgomery and his chief of staff, the charming General Freddie de Guingand. 'After lunch, Montgomery, Bradley and I went to the war tent,' Patton wrote in his diary. 'Here Montgomery went to great lengths explaining why the British had done nothing.' Despite his earlier support for Patton, Montgomery now did not want the Third Army to become operational until after Avranches had been captured. This, the Americans suspected, was an attempt to keep Bradley under the command of his own 21st Army Group for longer. Bradley studiously refused to answer. As soon as Patton's Third Army was activated, he would in practice become independent from Montgomery, since he would then command the US 12th Army Group, with Hodges and Patton as his two army commanders.

Bradley and his staff were beginning to thrash out ideas for Operation Cobra, which became the great breakthrough towards Avranches and Brittany. But in the meantime Bradley insisted on continuing the general advance to take Saint-Lô and the road west to Périers. Lying beyond the Cotentin and Bessin marshlands and *bocage*, the Saint-Lô–Périers road would provide their start-line for Cobra. But there was still a long and bloody fight in front of them to get there.

At the same time as the Panzer Lehr offensive in the early hours of 11 July, the German 5th and 9th Paratroop Regiments east of the River Vire had attacked the 29th Division and its neighbour, the 2nd Division. But while the Panzer Lehr assault against the 30th Division had disrupted its preparation for the general advance on Saint-Lô, the 35th, the 29th and the 2nd Infantry Divisions were still able to start their operation at 06.00 hours.

The overall American plan consisted of an advance on a broad front. While XIX Corps attacked south with the 30th, the 35th and the 29th Divisions, V Corps to the east was to help by sending the 2nd Infantry Division to take Hill 192, the main feature along the long ridge overlooking the road from Saint-Lô to Bayeux. The topography of rolling countryside, with small fields and orchards, bordered by impenetrable

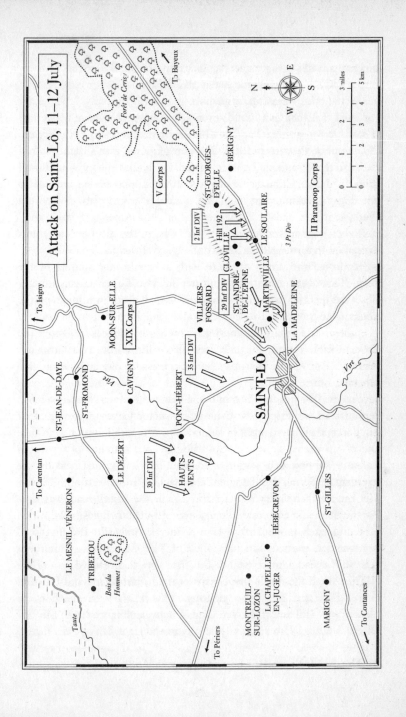

Attack on Saint-Lô, 11–12 July

To Bayeux

Forêt de Cerisy

V Corps

ST-GEORGES-D'ELLE

BÉRIGNY

2 Inf DIV

Hill 192

CLOVILLE

LE SOULAIRE

ST-ANDRÉ-DE-L'EPINE

MARTINVILLE

3 Pt Div

29 Inf DIV

II Paratroop Corps

LA MADELEINE

Vire

To Isigny

MOON-SUR-ELLE

XIX Corps

VILLIERS-FOSSARD

35 Inf DIV

ST-JEAN-DE-DAYE

ST-FROMOND

CAVIGNY

Vire

PONT-HÉBERT

SAINT-LÔ

To Carentan

LE DÉZERT

30 Inf DIV

HAUTS-VENTS

HÉBÉCREVON

ST-GILLES

LE MESNIL-VÉNERON

TRIBEHOU

Bois du Hommet

Taute

MONTREUIL-SUR-LOZON

LA CHAPELLE-EN-JUGER

MARIGNY

To Périers

To Coutances

N E S W

0 1 2 3 miles
0 1 2 3 4 5 km

hedgerows and sunken tracks, was horribly familiar to all except replacements and the newly operational 35th Division.

For the graves registration teams it was a grisly business. A lieutenant reported that they had found seventy bodies along a single hedgerow. 'I saw US troops who had been mined by the Germans,' he went on. 'They put boobytraps in the hollow part of a dead man's back. We had to blow those cases and that mangled the bodies, but we could still identify them.' Germans sometimes attached a concealed grenade to the dog-tag chain, so anyone who yanked at an identity disc would detonate it.

Bodies became swollen in the heat. One of the 4th Division teams explained that you had 'to relieve the body of the gas' by rolling it on to its front, and apply pressure with a knee in the middle of the back. 'One develops a strong stomach quickly,' he remarked. Another observed that the 'sickening stench' of 'human death' was tough on the cooks, who were used to collect bodies and then had to go back to prepare meat. Perhaps the most gruesome job of all was to remove the unidentifiable remains of tank crews from the insides of a burnt-out turret. 'As gruesome as it may sound, a mess kit cup and spoon were the tools of the trade.'

The weather was equally familiar in that wet summer. It was overcast, with drizzle and intermittent showers, which once again prevented air support and hindered artillery observation. The 29th Division's advance picked up after a slow start. Spearheaded by a battalion of the 116th Infantry supported by tanks, it found a gap in the line held by the German 9th Paratroop Regiment and reached Saint-André-de-l'Epine. But the 115th Infantry on its right, astride the Isigny road, was slow off the mark and then came up against well-defended positions, which it found hard to outflank. Major General Gerhardt, the divisional commander, warned General Corlett of XIX Corps that evening that 'the stuff ahead is pretty stout'. But the 116th had reached part of the Martinville ridge, while the Texans of the neighbouring 2nd Division seized Hill 192 after heavy fighting. This was a great relief to the Americans. Hill 192 had given the Germans a clear view into the rear of the V Corps sector and all the way to the right flank of the British front.

The 2nd Division had been planning this operation since 16 June.

On 1 July, taking advantage of the German tendency to withdraw the bulk of its front-line strength at night to avoid casualties from an early-morning bombardment, one of its battalions slipped forward during darkness and occupied all the German trenches. This was a calculated risk, because the Germans always had their own front-line positions registered as mortar and artillery targets. But it proved well worthwhile. This sudden advance provided the division with a good line of departure for the operation which they had been forced to postpone on several occasions. Time had not been wasted during the long wait. Battalions were withdrawn from the line in rotation for intensive tank–infantry training with engineer groups attached. They knew that they needed all the expertise and help they could get. They were up against part of the German 3rd Paratroop Division, which had been honeycombing the hedgerows on the hillside with concealed fire positions, tunnels and earth bunkers. German 50 mm mortars were targeted on every approaching hedgerow and 20 mm anti-aircraft guns commanded the road below. Heavy artillery and tanks to the rear on the south side of the Bayeux road were always ready to provide support.

The 2nd Division put the harsh lessons learned so far in the *bocage* to good use. Their supporting tanks all had telephones mounted on the rear of the vehicle so that infantry platoon commanders could indicate targets to the crew inside without having to climb on to the turret, exposing themselves dangerously. And the whole attacking force was divided into infantry–armour teams, each with its own engineer explosives group ready to blow holes in the hedgerows. The Shermans would bombard each hedgerow intersection with their 75 mm main armament, then spray the hedges in between with machine-gun fire, while the infantry advanced. All this was combined with a more flexible rolling barrage, which could be adapted to unexpected delays in the rate of advance. Each hedgerow when taken was to be treated as a new line of departure.

Perhaps more than any previous *bocage* operation, the 2nd Division's advance went according to plan, but it remained a 'grim job'. Even when it seemed that a hedgerow system had been thoroughly cleared, German paratroops would again emerge from hidden entrances to shoot at their backs. The western shoulder of Hill 192 was the most fiercely defended and was dubbed 'Kraut Corner'. It was finally outflanked after an hour and fifteen prisoners were taken. 'Three enemy paratroopers who still held out were eliminated by a tank dozer which buried them under five feet of dirt.'

Nearby, the hamlet of Cloville was cleared by house-to-house fighting amid the ruins from the artillery bombardment which had failed to destroy an assault gun and a tank supporting the German paratroops. A Sherman managed to knock out the two armoured vehicles to secure the objective. The advance continued shortly before 1200 hours. To avoid being slowed down again, the hamlet of Le Soulaire, half a mile further on, was bypassed, and by 1700 hours the leading platoons began to leapfrog across the Bayeux road in tiny groups. Their tank support could not stay with them because of anti-tank guns still concealed in the rough woodland on the reverse side of Hill 192.

While they were under fire, an unknown senior officer appeared, inspecting their positions. A GI called out to him to get down immediately or he would be killed. 'Mind your Goddam business, soldier!' the officer roared back. It was General George Patton, conducting a personal reconnaissance to familiarize himself with the terrain.

In the centre, the Shermans kept up with the infantry. They were even able to enter the woods on the side of the crest because the saturation of white phosphorus shells in the opening bombardment had almost burned it to the ground. They met only 'scattered opposition' and advanced down the southern slope. Although unable to cross the Bayeux road by nightfall, they were firmly dug in just north of it.

On the left flank of the attack, the 23rd Infantry had a very hard fight, sustaining many casualties near a re-entrant dubbed 'Purple Heart Draw' on the north-eastern slope of the feature. This had proved impassable for tanks, and far too exposed for infantry on their own, because German artillery and mortar batteries had registered every target in the area. Germans in houses a few hundred yards to the left, which should have been hit in the American bombardment, also contributed a withering automatic fire until two Shermans from the 741st Tank Battalion advanced to within thirty yards and blasted the foundations, causing the buildings to collapse on to the German machine-gun teams inside.

Closer in towards the summit, the right-hand company of the battalion perfected a technique of firing fragmentation rifle grenades to explode as airbursts over German machine-gun pits. By the end of the day, the battalion had advanced 1,500 yards and had reached the ridge, but it was still 400 yards short of the Bayeux road. One of the most unexpected achievements of the day's infantry–tank cooperation had been that not a single Sherman was lost. And on 12 July, the advance continued in the centre and east, so that the 2nd Division held all its objectives north of the Bayeux road. With the capture of Hill 192, the Americans now had observation posts with a clear view over Saint-Lô and its surrounding area.

Just to the east on the 1st Division's sector south of Caumont, an interesting contrast to the bitter fighting for the Bayeux road had just taken place. The Americans arranged a truce on 9 July with the 2nd Panzer-Division to hand over a second group of German nurses captured in Cherbourg. 'This second transfer and the chivalrous treatment of these nurses,' wrote their commander, Generalleutnant Freiherr von Lüttwitz, 'made at that time a deep impression upon the entire division.' Lüttwitz informed Rommel, who then decided that this would be the place to make contact with the Americans to negotiate a ceasefire in Normandy should Hitler continue to refuse to end the war. Rommel's discussions with his commanders on taking unilateral action against the regime was running in parallel, but separately from preparations for the assassination of Hitler at Rastenburg.

The unblooded 35th Division on the east bank of the Vire had to begin the 11 July offensive with a complicated manoeuvre, because of the L-shaped line it was holding. Then, almost immediately, the commander of its leading regiment, the 137th Infantry, was wounded by machine-gun fire. The Germans had fortified both a château and a church near Saint-Gilles in that sector, which held out despite a heavy battering from the divisional artillery. Machine-gun emplacements in the cemetery walls and in the church itself pinned down the battalion trying to attack it. When it was finally stormed the next day after another bombardment, 'only three prisoners, two of them wounded, were taken on this hotly contested ground'.

Yet according to General Bayerlein, the 17th SS Panzergrenadier-Division *Götz von Berlichingen* was 'in a poor state and had no will to fight'. Only the paratroopers and the *Das Reich Kampfgruppe* were dependable. This was perhaps helped by the way a *Das Reich* commander, Obersturmbahnführer Wisliczeny – 'a giant, brutal man', according to Bayerlein – stood behind the line with a stick and beat anyone who tried to run back.

West of the Vire, the 30th Division, recovering from the Panzer Lehr attack, advanced with Combat Command B of the 3rd Armored Division, supported by the divisional and corps artillery firing 14,000 rounds. They reached the northern edge of Pont-Hébert and Hauts-Vents at the cost of another 367 casualties.

Bradley's general advance on 11 July extended along almost all of the First US Army front. Towards the Atlantic coast of the Cotentin, in the VIII Corps sector, the 79th Division, aided by heavy air attacks, pushed forward west of La Haye-du-Puits and took the high ground near Montgardon. The 8th Division captured Hill 92 and carried on another mile south.

The 90th Division, having finally taken the Mont Castre ridge the day before, began to clear the forest on its reverse slopes. Its men were terrified of advancing against the well-camouflaged 15th Paratroop Regiment in thick underbrush with no more than ten yards' visibility. Contact between platoons, even between individuals in the same squad, became very hard. Their officers described it as 'more like jungle fighting'. The advance progressed only because of the courage of a few individuals outflanking machine-gun positions. The high proportion of dead to wounded showed how most engagements were fought at close quarters. The experience proved a considerable strain for a division which had not yet found its feet. By the next day, one battalion in the 358th Infantry had lost so many men that three companies had to be merged into one. Fortunately, the 90th then found that the German paratroops had slipped away in the night.

German Seventh Army headquarters was already extremely concerned at the situation on that western sector, because General von Choltitz lacked any reserves and the Mahlmann defence line had now been outflanked. Oberstgruppenführer Hausser had spoken to Rommel on the evening of 10 July, insisting that he must shorten that part of the front. Army Group B only gave its agreement late in the afternoon of 11 July. Choltitz ordered a general withdrawal back to the line of the River Ay and the town of Lessay.

'The population has to evacuate now and it's a complete mass migration,' wrote the Obergefreiter in the 91st Luftlande-Division. 'The fat nuns sweat profusely as they push their carts. It is hard to watch this and to go along with this accursed war. To continue to believe in victory is very hard since the USA is gaining more and more of a foothold.'

Allied fighter-bombers continued to attack not only front-line positions, but also any supply trucks coming up behind with food, ammunition and fuel. The almost total absence of the Luftwaffe to contest the enemy's air supremacy continued to provoke anger among German troops, although they often resorted to black humour. 'If you can see silver aircraft, they are American,' went one joke. 'If you can see khaki planes, they are British, and if you can't see any planes, then they're German.' The other version of this went, 'If British planes appear, we duck. If American planes come over, everyone ducks. And if the Luftwaffe appears, nobody ducks.' American forces had a different problem. Their trigger-happy soldiers were always opening fire at aircraft despite orders not to because they were far more likely to be shooting at an Allied plane than an enemy one.

In the VII Corps sector, the 4th and 83rd Divisions pushed down either side of the Carentan–Périers road, but the 9th Division, severely disrupted by the Panzer Lehr attack, was unable to join in that day. One of their battalion command posts received a direct hit. Convinced that the only possible German observation post was in a church tower, their divisional artillery brought it down. Church towers and steeples were always suspect. A few days later, on the slow advance towards Périers, soldiers from the division claimed to have found a German artillery observation officer dressed as a priest in a church tower with a radio. He was shot. But even in the more experienced 9th Division, officers reported that unnecessary casualties were sustained because their soldiers failed to shoot when advancing. 'The men said they held their fire because they could not see the enemy.'

General Meindl of II Paratroop Corps was rightly convinced that the Americans would use the Martinville ridge east of Saint-Lô for their assault on the town, but he did not have the strength to retake Hill 192.

With the 2nd Division firmly ensconced south of Hill 192, the main American effort was concentrated in the sector of the 29th Division towards the western part of the ridge. Another assault was launched that night, but it achieved little success in the face of German mortar and artillery fire, and was halted in the evening of 12 July. It was to take the 29th Division another five days at the cost of heavy casualties to clear the ridge and establish positions south of the Bayeux road. Thursday, 13 July, did not see much fighting and the medical staff finally had a rest. The surgeons of the 3rd Armored Division were able to enjoy 'poker and mint juleps in the evening – until midnight', as one of them noted in his diary. On 14 July, the weather was so bad that the American attack halted and for the first time the Germans found it 'possible to relieve units during daylight'. But XIX Corps was planning an attack for the next day. General Corlett called it his 'Sunday punch'.

Corlett's XIX Corps headquarters was made more colourful by its British liaison officer, Viscount Weymouth (soon to become the 6th Marquess of Bath), 'a tall Britisher who had gained a reputation for eccentricity because of some of his trips through the German lines and his habit of leading two ducks around on a leash'.

On 14 July, at nightfall, the funeral took place of Brigadier General Teddy Roosevelt, who sadly for him had died of a heart attack rather than in battle. Generals Bradley, Hodges, Collins, Patton, Barton and Huebner were the pall-bearers, an eloquent tribute in the middle of an offensive to Roosevelt's extraordinary courage and popularity. Patton, who had a great taste for military ceremonial, was, however, rather disappointed by the occasion. The guard of honour was too far away and formed up in column, not in line. He was particularly irritated by 'two preachers of uncertain denominations', who 'made orations which they concealed under the form of prayers'. In fact, the only fitting touch in his view came towards the end of the service, when 'our antiaircraft guns opened on some German planes and gave an appropriate requiem to the funeral of a really gallant man'. Yet even such a solemn occasion could not rest untouched by military prima-donnaship. 'Brad says he will put me in as soon as he can,' Patton added in his diary. 'He could do it now with much benefit to himself, if he had any backbone. Of course, Monty does not want me as he fears I will steal the show, which I will.'

*

In the far western sector, the German withdrawal carried out secretly by Choltitz had permitted VIII Corps to advance all the way to the River Ay. Next to it, VII Corps found that its artillery was now finally in range of Périers. The heavy mortars of the chemical battalions concentrated on firing white phosphorus, and more and more German dead were found with terrible burns.

Amid the high hedgerows of the *bocage*, observing the fall of mortar and artillery rounds was extremely difficult. The Americans learned to use high explosive when opening fire, as it threw up much more dirt. But their greatest advantage lay with their Piper Cub spotter planes and the bravery of their artillery observation pilots correcting bombardments. Airbursts proved very effective in an assault, for it forced the Germans to remain deep in their foxholes while infantry supported by tanks rushed a position. The 83rd Division reported how they trapped many Germans this way and then hauled them out. Occasionally a *Landser* would shoot himself, refusing to surrender. The spotter pilots could also drop red smoke canisters on a target less than 800 yards in front of their own troops, as a marker for fighter-bombers.

French families who refused to leave their farms remained at great risk during these battles. 'I remember one poignant scene that hurt all of us there,' recorded an officer with a chemical battalion. 'A family came through our position carrying a door on which was the body of a young boy. We did not know how he was killed. The pain on the faces of the innocent family affected each of us and made us feel for the people of the area and what they must be suffering.'

Sometimes French farmers and their families, on finding a dead soldier, would lay the body by a roadside crucifix and place flowers on it, even though they were trapped in an increasingly pitiless battle. Near Périers, a small American patrol was captured. According to a battalion surgeon with the 4th Division, a German officer demanded to know the whereabouts of the nearest American signals unit. Receiving no answer, he shot one of the prisoners in the leg. 'Then, he shot the commander of the patrol through the head when he refused to talk.'

Occasionally it seems that the Red Cross symbol offered no protection from reprisals. 'I saw medical aid men and medical officers who had been killed outright by the Germans,' reported a surgeon with the 2nd Armored Division. 'One medical man was stripped and hung from rafters and bayoneted in the stomach.' The Germans, on the other hand, complained that Allied fighters frequently attacked their ambulances despite the Red Cross markings.

In field hospitals well behind the lines, the chief danger was stress. Inevitably some surgeons broke down under the physical and psychological pressure. The screams, the stench of gangrene, the blood, the severed limbs, the terrible burns of armoured troops were bound to have a cumulative effect. What is astonishingly impressive is how the vast majority stayed the course. A captain in the 100th Evacuation Hospital calculated that in three and a half months he performed over 6,000 operations: 'I got so I can tell from the type of wound whether our troops are advancing, falling back or stationary. I can also detect self-inflicted wounds.' Green troops were more likely to suffer from booby-traps and mines. 'Self-inflicted wounds generally roll in just as a battle starts. On the advance it's mortar, machinegun and small arms. After breakthrough or capture of a position we get mine and booby trap cases. When stationary, all claim it's an 88 that hit them.' Yet the chief of the X-Ray department of the 2nd Evacuation Hospital expressed amazement at how uncomplaining the wounded usually were: 'It's such a paradox, this war,' he wrote, 'which produces the worst in man, and also raises him to the summits of self-sacrifice, self-denial and altruism.'

Psychological injury still constituted a large minority of their caseload. US Army medical services had to deal with 30,000 cases of combat exhaustion in Normandy. By late July, there were two 1,000-bed centres in operation. Doctors had initially been shocked by commanders talking of the need to get green troops 'blooded' in action, but a gradual introduction was clearly better than a sudden shock.

Nothing, however, seemed to reduce the flow of cases where men under artillery fire would go 'wide-eyed and jittery', or 'start running around in circles and crying', or 'curl up into little balls', or even wander out in a trance in an open field and start picking flowers as the shells exploded. Others cracked under the strain of patrols, suddenly crying, 'We're going to get killed! We're going to get killed!' Young officers had to try to deal with 'men suddenly whimpering, cringing, refusing to get up or get out of a foxhole and go forward under fire'. While some soldiers resorted to self-inflicted wounds, a smaller, unknown number committed suicide.

Military doctors also had to cope with the mundane. Flea bites from farmyards and barns could become infected. Many needless accidents were caused by a combination of exhaustion and raw Calvados, which GIs called 'applejack' or sometimes 'white lightning' because of its strength. The number of cases of diarrhoea rose alarmingly, but constipation was also a problem, especially among armoured crews. The over-salted contents of K-Rations were hated. Even the lemonade powder with Vitamin C was used instead for cleaning and scouring. A running joke developed that German prisoners of war were claiming that forcing them to eat K-Rations was a breach of the Geneva Convention. Men dreamed of ice cream, hot dogs and milkshakes. Their only hope of such comforts came when they were in reserve and the American Red Cross doughnut wagon turned up, run by young women volunteers. Its appearance also added the promise of a chat with a girl from back home. But when resting, soldiers resorted to more masculine pursuits. Paydays would see every form of gambling, with dice or seven-card stud. And if they had no money, they played for cigarettes, like before when waiting for D-Day.

Personal cleanliness in that humid summer was also hard to maintain when there were few opportunities for washing. Some French women clearly could not restrain their curiosity, to the discomfort of American modesty. 'I find it a bit hard getting used to women here looking at the men taking a bath,' wrote a medical officer in his diary. 'There were scores of GIs bare as the day they were born washing and swimming in the water round the mill house – and two women sat around quite nonchalantly, at times standing, overlooking the scene.'

To preserve anything from the rain that July required ingenuity. A sergeant in the 1st Infantry Division recounted that he always kept a dry pair of socks and some toilet paper in the top of his helmet liner. Soldiers also needed to hang on to their kit, because fascinated children were often trying to make off with their own souvenirs. Little French boys pestered them, requesting '*cigarettes pour Papa*', only to go off and smoke them themselves. They were constantly hanging around the mess tents in rear areas, despite orders to clear them away. But American soldiers always indulged them: 'French kids used to come around, with their little tin pails and stand at the mess line, and we always made sure we had extra food to give them.'

A *gendarme* in Caumont, behind the 1st Division's lines, was persuaded to try a piece of chewing gum. One of his main tasks was to cope with soldiers searching cellars for wine and Calvados. He and his men had the idea of scrawling 'Mines' on the walls by the entrance. But while he was ready to forgive soldiers who felt a desperate need for alcohol, he was deeply shocked, on finding his first dead Allied soldier, to see that someone had already stolen his boots. 'I know we lack everything, but even so!' he wrote. Looting by the townsfolk made him look at his fellow citizens afresh. 'It was a great surprise to find it in all classes of society. The war has awakened atavistic instincts and transformed a number of law-abiding individuals into delinquents.'

While the German Seventh Army feared that Périers would be the immediate focus of the next American offensive, Bradley was still determined to take Saint-Lô from the Martinville ridge, just to the north-east of the town.

German commanders were concerned about the Martinville ridge sector because Schimpf's 3rd Paratroop Division was being ground down. An Ultra intercept provided Bradley with the information that Meindl's II Paratroop Corps had lost 6,000 men. Rommel had been left in no doubt about the gravity of the situation when he visited General Meindl at II Paratroop Corps headquarters on the evening of 14 July. (On that day of foul weather, Rommel had been able to drive around without fear of Allied fighters.) Meindl warned him that Hitler's demand to hold the present front line at all costs could well prove disastrous. Less than a week later, Meindl complained to General Kurt Student, the commander-in-chief of the paratroop army, that two requests for reinforcements had not been answered. Those who arrived were often unfit for battle and became casualties immediately, as both the Americans and British had found. Some of these paratroop replacements had been trainee pilots unable to complete their flying courses back in Germany due to the critical shortage of fuel.

Rommel was well aware of the dangers. He had been warned that the boundary between the Seventh Army and Panzer Group West (which corresponded with the British–American boundary) might well 'burst a seam'. In fact, reserves were desperately needed all along the line, especially when a full-strength formation, such as the 353rd

Infanterie-Division, was reduced to under 700 men after eleven days of fighting. And this had been during a period when the weather had grounded the US Air Force for most of the time.

The Americans were also worried about heavy casualties, as well as the slowness of their advance. Along the east bank of the Vire, the 35th Division had attempted to push forward, while the 30th Division on the far side of the river had also tried to break through with little success. The earlier disruption to the 9th Division, slowing it down, had left the 30th with an exposed right flank. The 30th found that it was also facing groups from the 2nd SS Panzer-Division *Das Reich*.

The situation only began to improve on 15 July, the day of Corlett's 'Sunday punch'. XIX Corps was at last able to profit from air support with P-47 Thunderbolts strafing and bombing German positions. Unfortunately, a pair of Thunderbolts misidentified a detachment of Combat Command B and knocked out an American tank and a half-track. But the 35th Division, using a well-prepared feint that morning, managed to break the German line and force a retreat. Pressure all along the XIX Corps front, with powerful counter-battery fire from its artillery, had forced the Germans to use up almost all their ammunition. The 30th Division's commander described the day as a 'slugfest'.*

All eyes in the American command structure were on the 29th Division, responsible for the sector which was the key to Saint-Lô. Its flamboyant commander, General Gerhardt, was determined to make the most of the opportunity. Gerhardt did not attract universal respect. Bradley Holbrook, a war correspondent from the *Baltimore Sun*, attached to the 29th Division, had observed Gerhardt's longing for publicity as the battle for Saint-Lô progressed. 'I remember going up there one morning where he was standing,' he recounted later. 'The casualties were mounting and it just seemed useless as hell to me. And I asked him why are we taking so many casualties when we can just go around this place and go on. And he turned and looked at me and said, "Because that's a name everybody is going to remember." And I thought, "Oh, shit, what kind of a war are we fighting?".'

---

* The 30th Division had suffered over 2,300 casualties since 7 July, 961 in the last two days.

Gerhardt, like Patton, was also a stickler for correct turnout in the field. He could do little about the unkempt state of his men, because opportunities for shaving came only when a battalion was in reserve. But with more justification, he was exasperated that most soldiers fastened the strap of their steel helmet round the back and not under the chin. This came from the misplaced fear that a nearby explosion would pull their head off if the helmet was securely fastened. Gerhardt himself always wore his steel helmet correctly buckled, and was hardly ever seen in other headgear, apparently because he wished to hide his baldness.

His division's immediate objective was the hamlet of Martinville on top of the key ridge. It consisted of no more than a handful of Norman stone farmhouses, with walled yards either side of the unpaved road which ran from west to east along the ridge. The hedgerows were as thick and as high as elsewhere in the region, and the densely planted apple orchards provided complete cover for vehicles and enclosed gun pits from air observation. The German paratroops had again dug themselves in deeply and cleverly in bunkers covered with logs and earth, which would survive almost anything except a direct hit from a large-calibre shell or bomb. They had been reinforced with combat engineers as well as other companies from their division, plus remnants of the 30th Mobile Brigade with machine guns and mortars, some remnants of the 352nd Infantry Division and well-camouflaged assault guns sited to fire down hedgerows.

The American attack was supported by thirteen battalions of artillery, together with P-47 Thunderbolts dropping 500-pound bombs on 88 mm batteries. But on almost all axes of advance, German fire inflicted heavy casualties. At 19.30 hours, General Gerhardt ordered another last push before dark, with the call, 'Fix bayonets! Twenty-nine, let's go!' The 116th Infantry struck along the ridge from the east with three battalions almost abreast. After several hours of heavy losses, Gerhardt reluctantly halted them with instructions to dig in and hold the ground they had won. But the order took a long time to reach Major Bingham, commanding the 2nd Battalion. By the time it did and he had rushed forward on foot to catch up with his leading company, they had reached their objective of La Capelle on the Bayeux road. Bingham never considered retreat. He immediately ordered his battalion to dig foxholes in all-round defence. Martinville itself on the ridge above had been cleared, but German paratroops, following their practice, had infiltrated back in again so his force was out on a limb.

Gerhardt was astonished to hear that the 2nd Battalion had got through. He did not want to pull them back, yet they were in a very exposed position with the ridge still partly in German hands. He ordered the 115th Infantry on the right to advance at dawn the next day, 16 July, as rapidly as possible down the road from Isigny to Saint-Lô. If they got through, then the Germans on the ridge would probably be forced to withdraw. But the 115th came up against such heavy fire from mortars, machine guns and assault guns that it was forced to go to ground.

Bingham's beleaguered force down by the Bayeux road managed to repel a counter-attack, but it was running short of ammunition and supplies. Water was not a problem, as there were two wells, but the battalion had thirty-five wounded and only three inexperienced aid men to tend them. An artillery spotter plane dropped plasma to them, but several men died who would have survived if they could have been evacuated. Bingham's battalion was nevertheless extremely lucky. Bad communications on the German side meant that their position had not been clearly identified by German artillery, which during that day, to the delight of American observers, had been shelling their own troops almost as much as their enemy.

The 1st Battalion up on the ridge, a quarter of a mile to the east of Martinville, suffered ferocious counter-attacks from German paratroops armed with flame-throwers and supported by three tanks. The American infantrymen emerged from their foxholes to make sure that they shot down the heavily laden flame-thrower teams before they came within range to use their devices. A Company of the 1st Battalion, which was on the right, had lost all its officers on the previous day. It was now commanded by Private Harold E. Peterson, because the survivors had elected him commander. A young lieutenant was sent across to take over, but since he was new to combat, he sensibly did what Peterson told him.

The Germans attacked yet again from Martinville. This sortie had a tank in support, which blasted the hedgerow in which Peterson's men were concealed. The bazooka team was knocked out and others who took over the weapon were targeted. The survivors had to run for it, dragging wounded men behind them 'like a sled'. But they rallied under the leadership of Peterson and another soldier, a full-blooded Native American 'known simply as "Chief"'. Peterson then stalked the tank with rifle grenades, which were hardly armour-piercing. He scored six hits on the exterior, and the noise alone must have convinced the crew of the tank that it was better to turn around and scuttle back to Martinville. Peterson's skeleton company then reoccupied their positions.

That night, Peterson gave the order that one soldier in each two-man foxhole should stay awake while the other slept. Early next morning, he crept off to check on the other foxholes. In some of those where both men had fallen asleep, he found that their throats had been cut. The enemy raiding party of paratroopers, some fifteen strong, was still nearby and Peterson attacked with grenades. He was forced back, but then managed to site two light machine guns and a bazooka to keep the German paratroops pinned down. In fact their fire cut the enemy, in some cases quite literally, to pieces. Every German was killed. During all of this time, battalion headquarters had no idea that Peterson was in command.

During the night of 15 July, General Gerhardt ordered his deputy, Brigadier General Norman Cota, to assemble a task force 'on three hours' notice to complete the occupation of Saint-Lô'. This was perhaps a little premature, considering the ferocious battle on the ridge and the division's shortage of artillery ammunition. Also that night, 269 replacements arrived, and were instantly sent forward to strengthen the 1st Battalion of the 116th Infantry on the ridge. This was a brutally abrupt baptism of fire, contrary to the recommendations of the divisional psychiatrist, but Gerhardt did not want to lose the initiative.

The 3rd Battalion, commanded by Major Thomas D. Howie, was also seriously under-strength, but it received only a handful of new officers. Howie's battalion was to attack westwards before dawn, along the southern slope of the ridge, to join up with Bingham's men and then advance together into Saint-Lô. To maintain surprise, he ordered his men to rely on the bayonet. Only two men per platoon were authorized to shoot in an emergency.

Howie's battalion 'jumped off' on 16 July when there was only a pre-dawn glimmer of light. It advanced rapidly in column of companies.

They were lucky to be shrouded by an early-morning summer mist, but, presumably reacting to sound, German machine-gunners opened fire in their direction. As instructed, Howie's soldiers did not fire back. Good discipline and rapid footwork took them through to their objective next to Bingham's battalion by 06.00 hours. Howie reported to their regimental commander by radio. He was told that their task was to push on immediately to the edge of Saint-Lô, little more than half a mile to the west. 'Will do,' he answered. His men rapidly shared their rations with the famished 2nd Battalion, though they could not spare any ammunition. But just after Major Howie gave the order to advance on Saint-Lô, a German mortar shell exploded among his headquarters group. Howie was killed instantly. Captain H. Puntenney, the executive officer, took command and tried to push the attack forward. German artillery and mortar batteries, however, had finally identified their position and also began shelling that stretch of the Bayeux–Saint-Lô road.

The 3rd Battalion dug foxholes rapidly to shelter from the bombardment and prepared to receive a counter-attack. One eventually came in at the end of the afternoon, but they fought it off. German tanks could be heard in the distance, so an air strike was requested before dark fell. The 506th Fighter Bomber Squadron was scrambled and zeroed in on the armour concentration. The results were demoralizing for the Germans, but provided a great boost for American morale. Some of Puntenney's men discovered a German ammunition dump nearby. This was a relief, as the force had only one bazooka round left. Teller mines were taken and planted along the Bayeux road and on the minor north–south route which crossed the highway at La Madeleine. It was an anxious night. Puntenney felt that they were only holding on through bluff. But the next morning, 17 July, they received a miraculous surprise. An Austrian doctor suddenly appeared, wanting to surrender. He was able to save the lives of several of the wounded by using the plasma dropped the day before.

On the ridge above them, the 1st Battalion continued its attack on Martinville, using a small force with an anti-tank gun and a tank destroyer to take up position on the eastern side of the hamlet. The 29th Division's other two regiments, the 175th further up the Bayeux road and the 115th still trying to push down the road from Isigny, made little progress that day. One battalion of the 115th managed to veer off to attack the Martinville feature on the north side, but that afternoon it was hit heavily by a German mortar concentration, and many wounded men died that evening without medical attention. The shortage of aid men right along the front had become critical, mainly due to heavy casualties and a lack of trained replacements.

The battalion of the 115th, shaken by its casualties, had begun to dig in that night east of Martinville when the regimental commander arrived. To their disbelief, they were ordered to continue the advance without delay. 'This order caused great consternation in the battalion,' remarked their regimental commander. But once the grumbling was over, they moved on again at midnight. To their even greater surprise, they found themselves advancing forward along the western slope of the ridge towards Saint-Lô without encountering heavy resistance. The Germans seemed to have melted away in the night.*

The two battalions, Bingham's and Puntenney's, isolated at the bottom of the ridge near La Madeleine, could now be supplied by a lifeline over the saddle from the north. But this supply route remained a hazardous enterprise under the deadly fire from guns sited south of the Bayeux road. Private Peterson's company was reinforced with eighty-five replacements and a new commander, Captain Rabbitt. New arrivals were mixed in with veterans so that they would not panic. This company then manned the lifeline down from the ridge, with small groups in every field armed with machine guns. To their astonishment, they suddenly sighted a column of German soldiers being marched down in the open past them. The machine guns opened up and they mowed them down.

During the night of 17 July, the Germans evacuated the ridge and the withdrawal proved even more widespread. Outflanked on the Bayeux road and the Martinville ridge, they had to pull back on the sector facing the 35th Division, even abandoning a considerable amount of equipment and weapons. General Corlett told Gerhardt on the

---

* The commanding officer of the 115th Regiment, Colonel Ordway, who had less than an hour and a half's sleep, returned to his headquarters exhausted. General Gerhardt rang him at 05.30 hours. Ordway was not very tactful. Gerhardt rang back at 6.15 to tell him he was to be relieved. Considering that his first battalion had already started to probe into the outskirts of Saint-Lô, Ordway was angry, as he felt his tactics had achieved success while Gerhardt's had been disastrous.

morning of 18 July to take Saint-Lô, which American troops now called 'Stilo'. Brigadier General Cota's task force, with reconnaissance elements, Shermans, tank destroyers and engineers, was ready to move. 'Looks like we're all set,' Gerhardt reported to Corps headquarters. At 14.30 hours, Cota sent the message, 'Ready to roll.' His column began to move down the Isigny road into Saint-Lô, where they were joined by a battalion of the 115th Infantry. After the heavy fighting of the last few weeks, German resistance seemed comparatively light. There was harassing fire from German artillery positions south of Saint-Lô and groups from the 30th Mobile Brigade fought a rearguard action in parts of the town.

Cota's task force entered 'a shell of a town', smashed both by the original Allied bombing of 6 June and by artillery fire during the recent battle. Sky could be seen through the upper windows of the roofless buildings. The streets were blocked with wrecked vehicles and rubble, and this brought most traffic to a halt. Different groups were assigned to seize key points and fight house-to-house battles against the stay-behind groups from the 30th Mobile Brigade. By 19.00 hours, Gerhardt was able to claim that the place was secured. The engineers and dozer tanks got to work clearing streets to allow free movement, but the harassing fire did not stop. A forward controller of the divisional artillery was planning to use one of the twin spires of Saint-Lô's small cathedral as an observation post, but before he and his men could get into position German artillery had brought down both towers. Brigadier General 'Dutch' Cota was wounded by shell fragments, having shown as much disregard for his personal safety as he had on Omaha beach. 'Cota was hit by a shell fragment in his arm,' wrote a lieutenant with the cavalry reconnaissance troop. 'I can remember the blood running from his sleeve and dripping off his fingers. Not a bad wound but he just stood there talking. It didn't bother him in the least.'

Saint-Lô's capture provoked a measure of over-confidence. When the 25th Cavalry Squadron relieved the 29th's reconnaissance troop the next day, they charged ahead, despite warnings of German anti-tank guns, and lost several Jeeps and armoured cars.

The general advance from 7 to 20 July had cost the Americans some 40,000 casualties. But in Bradley's view, it had finally secured the left flank for Cobra and ground down the German forces to such a point that the breakthrough being planned stood a far greater chance of success. General Gerhardt wished to mark the 29th Division's victory with a symbolic act. He ordered that the body of Major Howie, the battalion commander killed just before the final assault on the town, should be brought into the ruined city. The corpse, wrapped in an American flag, arrived on a Jeep. It was placed on a pile of rubble by the episcopal church of Notre Dame. Howie became known as the 'Major of Saint-Lô'. His death came to represent the sacrifice of all those whom General Montgomery, in his tribute, called 'the magnificent American troops who took Saint-Lô'. Yet German commanders, even after the war, still regarded the huge American effort to take the town as unnecessary. Saint-Lô would have been outflanked immediately once the great American attack, Operation Cobra, opened to the west just over a week later.

19

Operation Goodwood

After the costly battle for northern Caen, Montgomery was even more concerned about infantry shortages. British and Canadian losses had now risen to 37,563. The Adjutant-General, Sir Ronald Adam, had come over to Normandy to warn Montgomery and Dempsey that replacements would run out in the next few weeks.

Dempsey's Second Army was not, however, short of tanks. He now had three armoured divisions, five independent armoured brigades and three tank brigades. While Montgomery remained wedded to his idea of holding down the German panzer formations on his front to allow the Americans to break out, Dempsey was determined to break the bloody stalemate. The bridgehead east of the Orne appeared to offer a good opportunity for a major armoured attack over open country south-east towards Falaise. Dempsey had been deeply impressed by the destructive power of the heavy bombers in their attack of 7 July. He seems, however, to have been strangely misguided about its lack of military effectiveness.

On 12 July, Dempsey persuaded Montgomery that he should mass the three armoured divisions into General Richard O'Connor's VIII Corps. Montgomery was extremely reluctant. He did not like the idea of tank formations 'swanning about' as they had in the Western Desert, occasionally with disastrous consequences. But he felt he had no option in the circumstances. He did not want to risk another major infantry battle, yet he had to do something to head off the criticism building in London and at SHAEF headquarters. The attack on Caen had failed to gain the territory needed for airfields and to deploy the Canadian First Army.

Most important of all, in Montgomery's thinking, this offensive represented a major blow on the Caen front just before the Americans launched Operation Cobra in the west. If nothing else, this would prevent the Germans from transferring panzer divisions to face Bradley's First Army. Yet Montgomery's true feelings are still not clear. Either he had suddenly convinced himself that the operation must achieve a major breakthrough, or else he felt compelled to mislead his superiors to be sure of obtaining the heavy bombers to smash open the German lines. Politically, this was a very unwise course of action.

On 12 July, he sold Dempsey's plan to Eisenhower on the basis that it offered the possibility of a decisive breakthrough. The supreme commander, who had despaired of Montgomery's caution, replied exuberantly two days later, 'I am viewing the prospects with the most tremendous optimism and enthusiasm. I would not be at all surprised to see you gaining a victory that will make some of the "old classics" look like a skirmish between patrols.' Also on 14 July, Montgomery wrote to Field Marshal Brooke, saying that 'the time has come to have a real "showdown" on the eastern flank'. Then, the very next day, Montgomery gave Dempsey and O'Connor a revised directive. This was more modest in its objectives. He wanted to advance only a third of the way to Falaise and then see how things stood. This may well have been a more realistic assessment of what was possible, yet Montgomery never told Eisenhower and he never even informed his own 21st Army Group headquarters. The consequences would be disastrous for Montgomery's reputation and credibility.

The Guards Armoured Division, originally delayed by the great storm, was by now ready to take part. Its officers were urged to visit the different fronts in Jeeps to pick up what they could in battle knowledge. But the experience was not exactly encouraging. 'I came upon a line of six or seven British Sherman tanks,' wrote a member of the Irish Guards, 'each of which had a neat hole in the side. Most had been burnt out. They had obviously been hit in quick succession, probably by the same gun.' On their return, when briefed for Operation Goodwood, they were told that they were 'going to break right through'.

Goodwood, named like Epsom after a racecourse, prompted the joke that it would be a 'day at the races'.

Montgomery, using his strategy of 'alternate thrusts' to throw the Germans off balance before the main offensive, persuaded Dempsey to begin with diversionary attacks further west. Shortly before midnight on 15 July, the British attacked near Esquay, Hill 112 and Maltot with flame-throwing Crocodile tanks. In the dark, they must have appeared like armoured dragons. Even further west, XXX Corps mounted a limited push. 'There is a nice cool breeze now moving the ripening corn,' wrote a captain near Fontenay-le-Pesnel. 'Amongst the corn one can just see the tops of guns and tanks, the spurts of flame and clouds of dust as they fire . . . another gloriously hot day. Dusty, hazy, with gunfire smoke hanging low over the corn like a November fog.'

Once again, Hill 112, the 'hill of Calvary', saw the most bitter fighting. The commander of the 9th SS Panzer-Division *Hohenstaufen* recorded that, on the evening of 16 July, the British laid such a heavy smokescreen on this high ground that his defending troops felt sick and thought it was a gas attack. British tanks broke through at about 21.00 hours and took sixty of his panzergrenadiers prisoner. But *Hohenstaufen* Panthers on the reverse slope of the hill counter-attacked and claimed to have knocked out fifteen tanks.

The German 277th Infanterie-Division had just reached the front near Evrecy from Béziers on the Mediterranean coast. A young gunner with the division, Eberhard Beck, travelled with his artillery regiment to the Loire by train, then marched from there by night. Even the draught horses pulling their 150 mm howitzers and limbers had been half asleep. When the column halted, which was often, the horses trudged on, and the soldiers dozing on the back of the gun carriage in front found a horse's muzzle in their face. The only high point of their journey had been the successful looting of a wine cellar in a château. Beck and his fellow soldiers had no idea what to expect in Normandy.

Closer to the front, they were joined by infantry, carrying Panzerfaust anti-tank grenade launchers over their shoulders. They could see ahead the sickly light of magnesium flares and 'the whole length of the front flashed and flickered like lightning'. Beck wanted to hide himself in the depths of a wood or forest. 'An unbelievable nervousness came over both soldiers and horses.' The sound of aircraft overhead became 'an endless, relentless roar'.

Their battery commander, Oberleutnant Freiherr von Stenglin, directed them to their first fire position west of Evrecy. Almost immediately, shells began to explode. The head of a driver named Pommer was taken off by a piece of shrapnel. Horses reared in terror and a container of hot food brought up from the field kitchen went flying, spilling goulash on the ground. Beck had two preoccupations, one of which was to sleep after the exhaustion of the march. The other was that, like most young soldiers, he did not want to die a virgin.

Fire missions against British tank concentrations round Evrecy were few, because of the shortage of ammunition. Often their battery was rationed to three rounds per day. With time on their hands, Beck and the other gunners played chess or skat when not under fire. Allied air attacks on their supply lines also reduced their rations. Beck was so hungry that he had the 'hare-brained idea' of slipping forward to dig up potatoes by the front line. But, like the British troops on the other side, they almost all suffered from dysentery, which had spread from insects feeding off corpses.

They soon encountered very young SS panzergrenadiers in camouflage uniforms, 'outstandingly well-equipped' in comparison to their own infantry. 'They were not, however, to be envied,' he felt. 'They were ambitious and were splendid soldiers. We all respected them.' But 'for us the war had been lost for some time. What counted was to survive.' That was certainly the opinion of the older soldiers. 'They were more mature, concerned, fatherly and humane. They did not want any heroics.' Beck and his comrades sometimes had to go forwards with a two-wheeled handcart to collect the wounded, who told them that, as artillerymen, they were lucky not to be in the front line: 'Up there it is hell.' The young gunners, when sheltering in their trenches from a bombardment, also discussed the right sort of *Heimatschuss* which would be just serious enough to have you sent back to a hospital in Germany. 'My thoughts,' wrote Beck, 'were wound, casualty clearing station, hospital, home, end of the war. I wanted only to get out of this misery.' But the British bombardment, including naval guns which made craters thirteen feet across and six and a half feet deep, provoked psychological as well as physical wounds. When a senior sergeant was blown up by a shell, a seventeen-year-old signaller next to him went completely to pieces.

German infantry losses were so great that a division was ground down within three weeks. Rommel's headquarters noted that on 16 July the 277th Infanterie-Division near Evrecy had lost thirty-three officers and 800 men in the last few days. They were now reinforced by part of the 9th SS Panzer-Division *Hohenstaufen*, but even they had lost so many men that they had to reorganize their two panzergrenadier regiments into three weak battalions.

During the night of 16 July, Ultra intercepted a signal from General-feldmarschall Hugo Sperrle, the commander-in-chief of the Third Air Fleet. In it he predicted a major attack 'decisive for the course of the war to take place south-eastwards from Caen about the night of 17–18th'. German air reconnaissance had for once penetrated Allied lines and overflown the Orne bridgehead to photograph preparations. In any case, the British knew that the Germans in the factory district of Colombelles, on the east bank of the Orne, would have observation posts on the top of tall chimneys and could see almost everything in the bridgehead. Yet this clear warning from Ultra that the Germans were well aware of the main British thrust did not make Dempsey re-examine his priorities. Without surprise, their only chance of success was to follow the bombing with a speedy and resolute attack.

General Eberbach of Panzer Group West did not believe that his forces, with 150 tanks, would manage to hold back the 800 British tanks massing against them. When Hausser's Seventh Army demanded the transfer of a panzer division from the Caen sector, because it had no reserves left to meet the American attack round Saint-Lô, Eberbach said it was 'out of the question'. Rommel backed him up.

On 17 July, Standartenführer Kurt Meyer, the commander of the SS *Hitler Jugend* Division, received an order to report to General-feldmarschall Rommel at the headquarters of Dietrich's I SS Panzer Corps. Most of the division had been withdrawn to rest and refit near Livarot after its battering in Caen. Rommel asked Meyer for his assessment of the impending British attack. 'The units will fight and the soldiers will continue to die in their positions,' Meyer said, 'but they will not prevent the British tanks from rolling over their bodies and marching on to Paris. The enemy's overwhelming air supremacy makes tactical manoeuvre virtually impossible. The fighter-bombers even attack individual dispatch riders.'

Rommel became impassioned on the subject. He vented his exasperation with the OKW, which still refused to listen to his warnings. 'They don't believe my reports any more. Something has to happen. The war in the West has to end . . . But what will happen in the East?' As Rommel took his leave, Sepp Dietrich urged him to avoid the main road on his return to La Roche-Guyon. Rommel apparently waved away the idea with a smile.

Less than an hour later, Rommel's open Horch was attacked by two Spitfires on the road near Sainte-Foy-de-Montgommery. He was thrown from the car and badly injured. A Frenchwoman on her way to buy meat had been forced to duck in panic as the fighters came in. She recounted that the locals found it ironic that the attack should have taken place next to a village with a name so similar to that of his opposing commander. Rommel was taken first to a pharmacy in Livarot and then to a hospital at Bernay. He was out of the war.

Eberbach, on receiving the news, set off immediately with an army doctor. At 21.30 hours, Speidel rang Panzer Group West to say that Hitler had ordered Generalfeldmarschall von Kluge to take command of Army Group B while continuing as Commander-in-Chief West. When Eberbach returned, a call came through from Kluge's staff ordering the transfer of a panzer division to the Seventh Army to help stop the American breakthrough at Saint-Lô. Although his side of the conversation is not included in the log, General Eberbach evidently refused. Within a matter of minutes Kluge himself was on the telephone. Eberbach explained 'that the Panzer Group was facing a major English attack'. He then went on to specify the threat. The only reserve available was the 12th SS Panzer-Division *Hitler Jugend*, which had just been removed from him. In what was clearly an ill-tempered conversation, Kluge rejected Eberbach's demands for reinforcements as out of the question. The record then adds that Kluge reminded him of the situation on the eastern front, with the onslaught of the Red Army's Operation Bagration. But Eberbach refused to be browbeaten. He returned to the charge over the threat facing his sector and the consequences of sending one of his panzer divisions to Saint-Lô.

That night, the first bombardments began in preparation for Operation Goodwood and also Operation Atlantic. The idea was to cover the sound of tanks moving into position, but it only confirmed what the Germans already knew. Operation Atlantic was the simultaneous Canadian offensive aimed in part at taking Vaucelles, the southern part of Caen and its outskirts. Canadian artillery hit a large fuel and ammunition dump in Vaucelles, causing a huge explosion.

Of all the offensives in Normandy, Operation Goodwood was the most obvious to the enemy. Attempts to conceal it with deception measures, including 'pre-recorded wireless traffic' to simulate an attack towards Caumont, were doomed to failure. Even if the Germans had not known in advance from photo-reconnaissance and their observation posts in Colombelles, the dust clouds in the unusually hot weather indicated the movement of tank formations. The signs by the side of the road warning that 'Dust Kills' (because it attracted German artillery fire) seemed no more than an ironic reminder as the military police in their white canvas gaiters and white gauntlets waved the vehicles on.

Goodwood also represented a failure in military intelligence. Even with RAF Mustangs flying photo-reconnaissance missions, Dempsey's staff assumed that Eberbach's defences had a depth of less than three miles. In fact there were five lines going all the way back to the rear of the Bourguébus ridge, over six miles away. And despite the identification of the 16th Luftwaffe Feld-Division, they had no knowledge of the number of 88 mm guns brought forward with Generalleutnant Pickert's Flak Corps. Cavalry regiments were later to curse the intelligence staff, whom they dubbed the 'crystal-gazers'.

The 11th Armoured Division led the way across the Orne bridges into the eastern bridgehead that night. Despite Montgomery's revision to the plan, Dempsey's headquarters had done nothing to cool the fever of expectation. 'We'll be moving into top gear!' the commander of a brigade in the 7th Armoured Division told his officers. 'We are undoubtedly on the eve of a battle much bigger than Alamein,' wrote a squadron commander of the 13th/18th Hussars in his diary. 'The crush east of the Orne has to be seen to be believed. There isn't an orchard

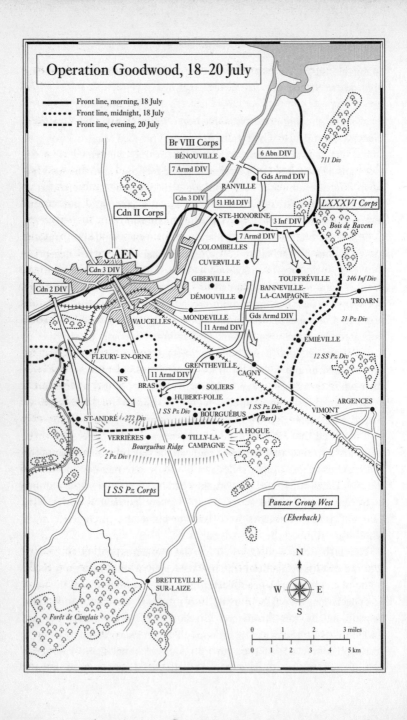

15. A sergeant in the East Yorkshires cleaning a sniper rifle while another soldier sleeps.

16. An American soldier and a dead German soldier on the outskirts of Cherbourg, 27 June.

17. 6th Royal Scots Fusiliers (15th Scottish Division) at the start of Operation Epsom, 26 June.

18. German panzergrenadier pioneers with a mine detector on a Panther tank.

19. Young Waffen-SS panzergrenadiers with a Mauser Model 98 rifle and shoulder-launched Panzerfaust on right.

20. American infantry advancing through a gap in a *bocage* hedgerow made by a Rhino tank.

21. American 105 mm howitzer gun crew in action in the *bocage*.

22. The great war correspondent Ernie Pyle heating up a meal on a Coleman stove given to him by the 90th Infantry Division in Normandy.

23. Two panzergrenadiers of the 12th SS Panzer-Division *Hitler Jugend* in the ruins of Caen.

24. Cromwell tanks waiting for Operation Goodwood to begin, 18 July.

25. Goodwood: 1st Battalion Welsh Guards in action near Cagny, 19 July.

26. French women accused of *collaboration horizontale* being paraded with their heads shaved through Cherbourg, 14 July.

27. Operation Cobra: effects of the bombing, 25 July. A dead German soldier has been thrown across the 75 mm barrel of a Sturmgeschutz III assault gun.

28. After the Roncey pocket: Robert Capa's shot of a 2nd Armored Division MP, Lt Paul Unger, searching an SS prisoner who had put on a civilian raincoat in an attempt to escape.

or a field empty.' Memories of the North African victory were perhaps in their minds also because of the great heat, the terrible dust, 'which we all agree is comparable to the desert', and the unrelenting swarms of mosquitoes. Soldiers complained that the army-issue insect repellent seemed to attract them even more.

Officers in the Guards Armoured Division were very conscious of the fact that they had not fought in North Africa and that this was their first battle. Rex Whistler, the painter and set designer, although fifteen years older than the other troop leaders in the armoured battalion of the Welsh Guards, had been determined to stay with his squadron. And just because they were at war, he saw no reason to stop painting. Back in England, Whistler had commissioned the local village blacksmith to make him a metal container to fix to the outside of his tank turret to take his paints, brushes and some small canvases. But as the senior subaltern, Whistler was made the battalion burial officer. His crew were unhappily superstitious about the twenty wooden crosses they had to carry on the tank.

Like the poet Keith Douglas, Whistler seems to have foreseen his own death. He told a friend that he did not want to be buried in a large military cemetery, but just where he had fallen. Shortly before their divisional commander, Major General Adair, briefed the officers, he wrote a last letter to his mother from the orchard where they were leaguered. He enclosed 'a bit of mistletoe from the tree above my bivvy', the tarpaulin stretched sideways from the tank under which the crew slept. At dusk on 17 July, Francis Portal, a fellow officer, talked to Whistler, while the tank engines were being tested and checked a last time. 'So we'll probably meet tomorrow evening,' Portal said as they parted. 'I hope so,' came the wistful answer.

Every senior commander on the Allied side was praying for Montgomery to make a breakthrough at last. Even his foes in the RAF, including 'Bomber' Harris, made no objection to his request for heavy bomber support. The commander of the tactical air force, Air Marshal Coningham, who loathed Montgomery most of all, was desperate for success so as to have room to build the forward airfields. Air Chief Marshal Tedder, who had privately been discussing with Coningham the possibility of Montgomery's dismissal, wrote to assure the commander-in-chief that all the air forces would be 'full out to support your far-reaching and decisive plan'.

At 05.30 hours on 18 July, the first wave of bombers flew in from the north to attack their targets. Over the next two and a half hours, 2,000 heavy and 600 medium bombers of the RAF and the USAAF dropped 7,567 tons of bombs on a frontage of 7,000 yards. It was the largest concentration of air power in support of a ground operation ever known. Warships of the Royal Navy off the coast also contributed a massive bombardment. The waiting tank crews climbed out to watch the spectacular dust clouds thrown up by the seemingly endless explosions. For those watching, it was unthinkable that anyone could survive such an onslaught.

Germans who endured the man-inflicted earthquake were stunned and deafened. The wounded and those driven mad screamed and screamed. Some, unable to bear the noise, the shock waves and the vibration of the ground, shot themselves. Heavy Tiger tanks were flipped over by the blast or half buried in huge craters. But with the target areas obscured by dust and smoke, the British could not see that the bombing had been far from accurate. And they still had no idea that Eberbach had formed five lines of defence. The most important of them, along the Bourguébus ridge, had to be taken if the Second Army were to advance towards Falaise. But this line received hardly any bombs at all.*

The 3rd Royal Tank Regiment moved forward to lead the 11th Armoured Division into battle. Ahead lay gently rolling country, mainly large fields full of ripening corn, dotted with hamlets of Norman stone farmhouses surrounded by orchards. The terrain sloped up towards the main objective, the Bourguébus ridge, rapidly dubbed Buggersbus by British soldiers.

Very soon a major drawback in the plan became apparent. The 51st

---

* The official RAF report later acknowledged the following faults. For the bombing of Area M round Cagny, the early markers overshot. Corrections were made, but smoke and dust soon obscured the target and they failed to destroy a battery of 88 mm guns. In Area I around Troarn on the left, only 18 per cent of the bombs fell within the target area. And for Area P, which covered Hubert-Folie, Soliers and the village of Bourguébus, only 40 per cent of the bombs fell within the target area.

Highland Division had laid an ill-mapped minefield across its front. General O'Connor decided that they could not lift the whole minefield without alerting the Germans (by then an unnecessary concern) so only a dozen narrow channels had been cleared during the night. This slowed the whole advance, with disastrous consequences.

There were also huge traffic jams behind while the Guards and 7th Armoured Division waited for 11th Armoured to clear the area so that they could cross the six Bailey bridges over the Orne. As the sun rose higher in the sky, tank crews ate or even stretched out to sleep at the edge of cornfields beside the road. Despite the dust and the petrol fumes, Rex Whistler and some fellow officers in the Welsh Guards passed the time playing piquet. Even when the columns began to move, the scene ahead was 'like cars crawling back to London from the coast on a summer Sunday, stationary as far as one could see, then shrugging forward'. Air Marshal Coningham, who was with Dempsey next to O'Connor's headquarters, was beside himself with frustration. The slow progress of the armoured brigades through the minefield meant that the shock effect of the bombing attack was going to waste.

On the west side of O'Connor's main thrust, the 3rd Canadian Division was advancing into Vaucelles, the southern part of Caen across the Orne. But heavy resistance halted the Régiment de la Chaudière at 10.30 hours. The Queen's Own Regiment of Canada swung left round the obstruction to take Giberville, and then the Regina Rifles crossed the Orne in Caen and took Vaucelles. Meanwhile, the Nova Scotia Highlanders went on to take the adjoining suburb of Mondeville. The North Shore Regiment attacked the factory buildings of Colombelles, where weakened infantrymen from the Luftwaffe's 16th Feld-Division were so shaken by the bombing that they were at first unable to walk. On the left side of the main advance, the British 3rd Infantry Division, supported by an armoured brigade, was advancing on Touffréville and then on towards Troarn.

For the first two hours of the battle, the attackers saw many encouraging signs. The 3rd Royal Tank Regiment encountered dazed German infantry, rising out of the corn with their hands up to surrender. Their tank crews directed them to the rear. B Squadron of the 11th Hussars came across a German dugout in which the men appeared to be asleep. Their bodies were untouched, but they were in fact dead, killed by shock waves. The 13th/18th Hussars, advancing on the east flank towards Touffréville with the 3rd Infantry Division, machine-gunned trenches until prisoners emerged with their hands up. 'Prisoners are streaming in past us, most of them paralysed by our bombing effort,' wrote a major with the 1st Canadian Parachute Battalion back in the Orne bridgehead. Even the commander-in-chief of Panzer Group West, General Eberbach, wrote that 'a breakthrough appeared unavoidable'.

Most of the 16th Feld-Division had been smashed by the bombing and was 'completely overrun'. The 21st Panzer-Division, reinforced by the 503rd Heavy Panzer Battalion with Tiger tanks, was the worst hit of the German armoured formations. 'Some tanks had received direct hits, others had turned over or had fallen into bomb craters. The tank turrets had been immobilised by the dirt which had been whirled up, the gunsights and radios had been incapacitated.' The 21st Panzer soon received orders from Eberbach to take part in a counter-attack with the 1st SS Panzer-Division *Leibstandarte Adolf Hitler*, but that was later postponed twice because of the state it was in. German artillery observers could still see little due to the dust and smoke and so their heavy batteries behind the Bourguébus ridge remained silent. 'At 10.00 hours,' wrote Eberbach, 'came the terrible news that the enemy had broken through to a depth of ten kilometres.'

The 3rd Royal Tank Regiment soon found, however, that Goodwood was not going to be 'a day at the races'. As they headed for Le Mesnil-Frémentel, a tiny hamlet of stone farmhouses near Cagny, they came under fire from German anti-tank guns. 'Suddenly a Sherman on my left rolled to a halt belching smoke,' wrote the squadron leader at the front. All the guns traversed on to the point where the shell had come from. They knocked out the German guns, but then they came under fire from another quarter. More Shermans were hit and the corn around them began to blaze.

The leading squadron of the 2nd Fife and Forfar Yeomanry on their left was hit by devastating fire from Cagny. This was where a battery of 88 mm guns from the 16th Feld-Division had escaped the bombing, along with two 105 mm assault guns. The squadron was almost entirely annihilated within minutes.

The 3rd Tanks received orders to bypass Le Mesnil and head south-west for Grentheville. Another major flaw in Dempsey's plan was becoming apparent. O'Connor had wanted to send in infantry with the armoured regiments to clear the defended villages and hamlets, but because of the constrictions caused by the minefield, Dempsey told him to hold back the infantry. For the tank crews, all the talk of breaking out into 'good tank country' now sounded like a sick joke. The range and accuracy of the German 88s meant that they were at even more of a disadvantage than they had been when attacking in the *bocage*.

There were anti-tank positions all round Grentheville and concealed assault guns. The 3rd Tanks had no option but to charge them like cavalry, and several tanks were set on fire. Burning crewmen rolled in agony on the ground, attempting to put out the flames. The regiment's losses were so heavy that they had to pull back and call in fire support from the 13th Royal Horse Artillery. The 11th Armoured Division had suffered an unexpected blow early in the battle when their RAF liaison officer was hit. They could not call in the Typhoons circling above, ready to attack a target when requested.

The Guards Armoured Division had meanwhile followed on to the rolling plain. Its officers, conscious of the fact that they were new to battle, tried to display an unnecessarily dangerous insouciance, such as not ducking inside the turret when under fire. The 2nd Armoured Battalion of the Grenadiers headed for Cagny, where the Fife and Forfar had received such a battering. They too lost nine Shermans to the 88s. This setback unaccountably held up the advance of the Guards Armoured, which should have pushed on to Vimont and not waited for their infantry to come up. General Eberbach could not believe his luck. With slight exaggeration, he wrote, 'What happened was incomprehensible to an armoured soldier: the enemy tanks remained stationary during the decisive hours of 10.00 to 15.00!'

On the right flank, Rex Whistler's squadron in their Cromwells were given the task of supporting the Canadian infantry moving into Giberville, two miles from the start-line. Whistler's troop circled Giberville on the east side to cut off any retreat. The village seemed deserted. One of his Cromwells ground to a halt, its sprocket entangled with wire. Whistler dismounted and went over with pliers to help free it. He should never have left his own tank. They came under fire. Whistler ran to his troop sergeant's tank to give him instructions to attack the village. But instead of staying in the lee of the sergeant's Cromwell as it moved forward, he ran back across open ground to his own tank. A mortar bomb exploded near his feet, hurling him into the air and breaking his neck. Having been appointed battalion burial officer, Whistler was their first casualty.

German anti-tank guns, not tanks, were mainly responsible for what was later called the 'death ride' of the British armoured divisions. The lack of infantry with the leading regiments had proved disastrous. Cagny was not taken until 16.00 hours, when the motorized 1st Battalion of the Grenadiers went in on foot. The 88s and the assault guns had no infantry protection and the Grenadiers overcame them rapidly.

At midday, General Eberbach had ordered a counter-attack with the remaining tanks of the 21st Panzer-Division and those of the 1st SS Panzer-Division, which had been held in reserve well behind the Bourguébus ridge. They were ordered to Hubert-Folie to concentrate against the approaching spearhead of the 11th Armoured Division. But the 21st Panzer, which had only five Tiger tanks and eight Mark IVs serviceable after the bombing, was still unable to move two hours later. The *Leibstandarte* panzer group set off on its own.

At 13.05 hours, Eberbach also demanded the remnants of the 12th SS Panzer-Division, which had been withdrawn on Hitler's personal order to recover near Lisieux. On the grounds that he had 'no more reserves', Eberbach's request was passed upwards from Army Group B at La Roche-Guyon to OB West in Saint-Germain-en-Laye, and then to the OKW, now at Hitler's *Wolfsschanze* headquarters in East Prussia. Just over two hours later, agreement was given.

The 1st SS Panzer-Division, now organized in three battlegroups, reached the area of Soliers, near the west end of the Bourguébus ridge, around 15.00 hours. They were in position by the time the 3rd Tanks and the rest of the 29th Armoured Brigade – the Fife and Forfar and the 23rd Hussars – pushed on to the hamlet of Ifs-Bras. There the 3rd Tanks came up against the *Leibstandarte* Panther tanks, which only the Firefly Shermans could hope to take on. The other Shermans concentrated on the anti-tank guns. Meanwhile, the Northamptonshire Yeomanry in their Cromwells swung round to the west to attack from the flank, but lost a dozen tanks in the process. The squadron leader with the 3rd Tanks escaped from a knocked-out Sherman for the second time that day and transferred to a third one. It took courage to get back into a tank after having just been 'brewed up'.

The 11th Armoured Division should have been supported by the 7th Armoured Division, but the traffic jams and delays caused by the minefield on the start-line meant that the Desert Rats played almost no part. O'Connor, well aware that the whole offensive had faltered, asked for a renewed bombing of the Bourguébus ridge, but this was refused. Yet even after the *Leibstandarte* entered the battle, Montgomery, with catastrophic bad timing, claimed success.

At 16.00 hours he signalled Field Marshal Brooke, 'Operations this morning a complete success. The effect of the bombing was decisive and the spectacle terrific . . . situation very promising and it is difficult to see what the enemy can do just at present. Few enemy tanks met so far and no (repeat) no mines.' He then went on to claim quite erroneously that the 11th Armoured had reached Tilly-la-Campagne, and that the Guards Armoured had taken Vimont. It was one thing to have misled Brooke, but he also issued a similar communiqué to the BBC and gave a press conference. According to one of Montgomery's own brigadiers, he talked to the assembled journalists 'like children'. This was to produce a bitter backlash.

The British had lost nearly 200 tanks that day. Fortunately, they had nearly 500 replacements in reserve. Many of these were brought forward to the Orne bridgehead during the night. The 29th Armoured Brigade – the 3rd Tanks, Fife and Forfar Yeomanry and the 23rd Hussars – received top priority having lost so many armoured vehicles. Although the British losses in tanks had been horrific, most crews escaped comparatively unharmed. They were assembled back in the Orne bridgehead to be reassigned to new tanks. But, in a terrible irony, the Luftwaffe finally made a daring raid and many who had survived that day were now killed or wounded.

German tank recovery teams, meanwhile, towed their damaged panzers back to workshops concealed in the Fôret de Cinglais. Knowing how few replacements they could expect, they worked with dedication and ingenuity, making as many vehicles serviceable as possible. 'We were fighting a poor man's war,' wrote Eberbach.

*

On the eastern flank, the British 3rd Infantry Division had been held up at Touffréville by a fiercer defence than they had expected because the bombers had missed the target. Yet part of the division pushed on through the southern edge of the Bois de Bavent to reach the edge of Troarn by nightfall. The German 346th Infanterie-Division had been so battered in the fighting that day that General Eberbach became deeply concerned. He was even more worried by the gap between Troarn and Emiéville, which, luckily for him, the British had not spotted: 'The enemy needed only to march in that direction, then there would have been a breakthrough. This was a bad moment for us.'

At 17.45 hours, he directed the 12th SS Panzer-Division *Hitler Jugend* to fill the gap in the line. But just fifteen minutes later, Eberbach heard that the *Hitler Jugend* had been attacked on their way by Allied fighter-bombers and lost ten tanks. Once darkness fell, according to Eberbach, 'the British continued to stay immobile, as if a miracle had happened'. The *Hitler Jugend* filled the gap and Eberbach had a continuous line again, albeit very thinly held.

On the following day, 19 July, the British divisions made more attacks, but none were in great strength. Rain began to fall and the sky was overcast, so there were no Typhoons overhead. A few more hamlets were taken, but most of the Bourguébus ridge remained in German hands. The 88 mm batteries positioned there continued to knock out tanks effortlessly. The Germans were bringing in rear troops to replace casualties and fresh divisions to reinforce the line. The 2nd Panzer-Division opposite the boundary between the British and American armies was brought eastwards to strengthen Panzer Group West's left flank and the 116th Panzer-Division began to move from Amiens. The only major benefit from Operation Goodwood was that Eberbach and Kluge became even more convinced that the major attack in Normandy would still come on the British front and head for Paris. This was confirmed by Ultra intercepts a few days later.

Field Marshal Brooke flew to France at midday, partly to sort out a ridiculous row with Churchill, who believed that Monty was trying to stop him visiting France. When he saw Montgomery after lunch, he 'found him in grand form and delighted with his success east of Caen'. Perhaps Montgomery was simply putting on a brave front. The gulf between the claims made before the operation began and the reality of the situation revealed after his press conference was becoming a major embarrassment.

On the eve of battle, war correspondents had been told of a 'Russian style' breakthrough, which might take the Second Army forward by 100 miles or more. Several of the journalists present pointed out that that meant all the way to Paris. When two days later the same colonel had to admit that the offensive had come to a halt, he faced tumultuous heckling. He tried to explain that Tiger and Panther tanks had appeared, and that General Montgomery had received a formal order from above not to risk a failure. This statement was openly disbelieved.

The next day Brigadier Alfred Neville from 21st Army Group was brought in to soothe the furious journalists. He tried to put a positive gloss on what had been achieved. The Second Army had taken the southern part of Caen and now controlled an important communications network. But then he claimed that the objective had not been to break through the German positions, but simply to penetrate them. Journalists threw back at him what they had been told before the offensive. Next day, Dempsey's chief of staff made another attempt to explain away the situation using impenetrable military jargon. An American correspondent caused roars of laughter by demanding a translation.

The heat became oppressive on the morning of 20 July and then the rains came again. Under an almighty downpour, the dust turned to sludge and slit trenches filled with water. Tracks were eighteen inches deep in mud. The conditions were so terrible that they provided an excuse to call off Goodwood officially.

For the troops who had taken part, the situation was a bitter disappointment after all the promises. An infantry officer with the 7th Armoured Division was bivouacked with his battalion near Démouville in 'a field strewn with German dead'. 'Countless flies swarmed over the corpses. Maggots seethed in open gash wounds. It was revolting, yet I could not take my eyes off a lad who could not have been much more than sixteen years of age; only fluff on his chin. His dead eyes seemingly stared into infinity, his teeth bared in the agony of death. He would not have hesitated to kill me, yet I was saddened.'

For some the strain had been too great. The squadron leader with the 3rd Tanks recorded that three senior sergeants asked to be relieved from tank duties. 'There comes a time when the bank of courage runs out,' he observed. Tank crews in other formations were also shaken by the losses inflicted on 11th Armoured Division. 'Either it was just gross bad handling on the part of senior commanders,' Major Julius Neave in the 13th/18th Hussars wrote in his diary, 'or else very bad "crystal gazing". They may have thought there was only a thin crust and once through it they could bum on. However, I feel it is monstrous that a division trained for three years – very highly – should lose two thirds of its tanks in its second battle.'

Their only consolation during the deluge of rain was to stay relatively dry inside their tank or under a bivvy alongside it. 'Thank God I am not an infanteer who has to choose between keeping "dry" above ground or dodging the mortars by jumping into a trench with three foot of water in it,' noted Major Neave.

The 3rd Infantry Division's field ambulance was established in Escoville, next to the troublesome minefield. 'It rained and there were mosquitoes, and you'd wake up in the morning with your face all puffy,' wrote a medic with them. 'It was here that we had a tremendous number of [combat] exhaustion cases. Some of our own men went down with it which was rather disturbing. Then at this point it seemed as though there was a jinx because casualties would arrive in quite good shape and then for no reason whatever they would begin to fail and flicker. And more died under our hand there than in any other place.'

The British and Canadians had suffered 5,537 casualties during the brief operation. This took their losses in Normandy to a total of 52,165. Goodwood had failed for a combination of reasons. There had been a lack of clarity in the thinking behind the operation and a lack of frankness in the briefing. While Dempsey still dreamed of a break-through, Montgomery had put pressure on O'Connor to be cautious. But a half-hearted charge was almost bound to lose more tanks than an all-out attack. O'Connor's biggest mistake was not to have accepted that they could never have hoped to hide the operation from the Germans. They should have cleared the whole minefield. Only then, with a greatly accelerated advance, could they have fully exploited the shock effect of the heavy bombers.

The bombing itself, in spite of its intensity, was also far less effective than had been imagined. Army officers complained to the RAF afterwards that more bombs should have been dropped on the Bourguébus ridge and fewer on the nearer targets, but this failure in priorities was largely the responsibility of the army intelligence staff. The RAF, on the other hand, was incandescent with rage. Tedder, Harris and Coningham felt that they had been badly misled by Montgomery. He had promised a dramatic breakthrough to secure the support of their heavy-bomber squadrons, yet secretly he was considering only a very limited offensive. The row continued long after the war was over. 'General Montgomery was reminded,' their version went, 'that the Air Forces were relying on the early capture of terrain beyond Caen, but after a few days he appeared to be accepting the situation with something like complacency.'

Liddell Hart, however, feared that the problem was more fundamental. He believed that there had been 'a national decline in boldness and initiative'. War-weariness had encouraged an attitude of 'let the machine win the battle'. The British were stubborn in defence, as the Germans acknowledged in their reports. But there was what Liddell Hart termed 'a growing reluctance to make sacrifices in attack'. 'When one goes deeply into the Normandy operations, it is disturbing and depressing to find how poor was the performance of the attacking force in many cases. Time after time they were checked or even induced to withdraw by boldly handled packets of Germans of greatly inferior strength. But for our air superiority, which hampered the Germans at every turn, the results would have been much worse. Our forces seem to have had too little initiative in infiltration, and also too little determination – with certain exceptions . . . Backing up was very poor and very slow.'

Although Liddell Hart's harsh criticisms contained important truths, they also revealed a lack of imagination. To put it mildly, it was dispiriting for tank crews to attack batteries of the dreaded 88 mm guns, knowing full well that they could be picked off long before their own inferior tanks could engage them. And once again, we should never forget that the essentially civilian soldiers of a democracy could not be expected to show the same level of self-sacrifice as indoctrinated members of the Waffen-SS, convinced that they were defending their country from annihilation.

In the main base hospital near Bayeux, Colonel Ian Fraser recounted how he used to make his rounds of the wounded German prisoners. They all smiled back when he greeted them. Then one morning they all turned their backs on him. The chief nursing sister told him that a wounded SS soldier had been brought in and they were now afraid of showing any friendliness to their enemy. Fraser examined this SS soldier, who was in such a serious condition that he needed a blood transfusion. 'But once the needle was in, the passionate young Nazi suddenly demanded: "Is this English blood?" When told that it was, he pulled it out, announcing: "I die for Hitler." Which is what in fact he did.' Fraser noted that the other German prisoners soon became friendly again.

Badly wounded prisoners from the 12th SS Panzer-Division *Hitler Jugend* behaved in a similar way. Churchill's aide, Jock Colville, serving as a Mustang photo-reconnaissance pilot, heard from a young British nurse about her experiences. 'One boy of about sixteen had torn off the bandage with which she had dressed his serious wound, shouting that he only wanted to die for the Führer. Another had flung in her face the food she had brought him. She had quelled a third by threatening to arrange for him to have a transfusion of Jewish blood.' One could hardly imagine a British or Canadian prisoner of war wanting to die for Churchill or King George VI. Their loyalty in battle was much more parochial. They did not want to let their comrades down.

Whatever the serious flaws in Goodwood and Montgomery's false claims at the time and later, there can be no doubt that the British and Canadians had kept the panzer divisions tied down at the crucial moment. The Canadians renewed the attack on 25 July to coincide with Operation Cobra, Bradley's great offensive in the west. This again convinced the Germans that the major Allied attack towards Paris was coming down the Falaise road. A breakthrough here was their greatest fear, because it would cut off the whole of the Seventh Army facing the Americans. Kluge and his commanders did not recognize the true point of danger until it was too late. So the 'death ride' of the British armoured divisions was not entirely in vain.

The Germans also were shaken by news of the assassination attempt on Hitler at the *Wolfsschanze* near Rastenburg on 20 July. In fact the threat of an Allied breakthrough in Normandy and Hitler's refusal to face reality had played a large part in the course of the plot.

20

The Plot against Hitler

There is a Nazi conspiracy theory to explain their defeat in Normandy, which begins with D-Day itself. Hitler loyalists still accuse Rommel's chief of staff, Generalleutnant Hans Speidel, of diverting panzer divisions from counter-attacking the British. This first 'stab-in-the-back' legend of 1944 pretends that Hitler had been awake early on 6 June, and that any delays in deploying the panzer divisions were not his fault. He was certain that Normandy was the site of the invasion from the first moment. But then Speidel, acting in Rommel's absence, managed all by himself to sabotage the German response. This preposterous version, which attempts to switch the blame from Hitler to 'treacherous' officers of the German general staff, is riddled with countless holes and contradictions.

There was indeed a long-standing conspiracy against Hitler within the army, but nothing was ready by 6 June. So to suggest that Speidel was trying to misdirect the 12th SS Panzer-Division *Hitler Jugend* and hold back the 2nd and 116th Panzer-Divisions ready for a coup d'état in France at that moment is sheer fantasy. Speidel was, however, a key figure in the plot which produced the unsuccessful bomb explosion in East Prussia over six weeks later.

There was another level of opposition to Hitler, which did not believe in killing the dictator. This centred on Rommel himself, who wanted to force Hitler to make peace with the western Allies.* If he refused,

---

* Rommel may well have swung round at the last moment to believe that assassination was the only way. According to General Eberbach, Rommel finally said to him

then they would bring him to trial. But the tyrannicides grouped round Generalmajor Henning von Tresckow and Colonel Claus Graf Schenk von Stauffenberg rejected that course as doomed to failure. The SS and the Nazi Party would resist all the way. It would risk a civil war. Only the sudden decapitation of the Nazi regime in a coup d'état would allow them to form an administration which they hoped, with deeply misplaced optimism, that the western Allies might recognize.

Speidel had known Rommel since the First World War, when they had served together in the same regiment. On Speidel's appointment as Rommel's chief of staff, he had been summoned on 1 April to Führer headquarters at the Berghof. Jodl had briefed him on the 'inflexible mission of defending the coast', and told him that Rommel was 'inclined to pessimism' as a result of the African campaign. His task was to give Rommel encouragement.

When Speidel reached La Roche-Guyon two weeks later, Rommel spoke with bitterness about his experiences in Africa 'and above all about Hitler's constant attempts at deceit'. He added that the war should be 'finished as quickly as possible'. Speidel then told him about his contacts with Generaloberst Ludwig Beck, a former chief of the army general staff, and the resistance movement in Berlin who were 'ready and determined to do away with the present regime'. In subsequent discussions, Rommel condemned 'the excesses of Hitler and the utter lawlessness of the regime', but he still opposed assassination.

On 15 May, Rommel attended a secret conference with his old friend General Karl-Heinrich von Stülpnagel, the military commander of Belgium and northern France. Although a member of the anti-Hitler conspiracy, Stülpnagel was 'a hardline anti-semite'. If he had not shot himself later, he would probably have faced a war crimes tribunal after the war for his activities on the eastern front and the persecution of Jews in France. The two men discussed 'measures to be taken immediately for the termination of the war and elimination of the Hitler-regime'. Stülpnagel knew that they could not count on Generalfeldmarschall von Rundstedt, even though the 'old Prussian' was well

---

during their meeting on 17 July, just before he was severely injured, 'The Führer must be killed. There's nothing else for it, the man really has been the driving force in everything.'

aware of 'the catastrophic situation' and loathed the 'Bohemian corporal'. Stülpnagel believed that in an uprising, 'Field Marshal Rommel would be the only person who possessed the undisputed respect of the German people and armed forces, and even the Allies'.

A series of sympathetic visitors came to La Roche-Guyon, which became an 'oasis' for the Resistance. Towards the end of the month, General Eduard Wagner of the OKH* briefed Rommel on the preparations of the resistance group within the army. The extreme nationalist writer Ernst Jünger, who was serving on Stülpnagel's staff in Paris, presented him with his thoughts on the peace which should be made with the Allies. Speidel returned to Germany at the end of May to meet the former foreign minister Konstantin Freiherr von Neurath and Dr Karl Strölin, the mayor of Stuttgart. Both believed that Rommel's involvement was essential to gain the confidence of the German people as well as that of the Allies. Speidel felt able to brief General Blumentritt, Rundstedt's chief of staff, on the discussions.

Rommel and Speidel had agreed on a list of possible parliamentaries to talk to Eisenhower and Montgomery. It was headed by Geyr von Schweppenburg, who spoke excellent English, but after his dismissal they had to consider others. They would propose a withdrawal to Germany from all occupied territories in the west, while the Wehrmacht held a reduced front in the east. Rommel insisted that Hitler should be tried by a German court. He did not want to be the leader of the new regime. That role he felt should be taken by Generaloberst Beck or Dr Carl Goerdler, the former mayor of Leipzig. Rommel was, however, prepared to take command of the armed forces.

Few of the plotters appear to have imagined for a moment that the western Allies would reject their offer, even if they had been in a position to make it. Their proposals included an Allied recognition of the German annexation of the Sudetenland and the *Anschluss* with Austria, as well as the restoration of Germany's 1914 borders. Alsace-Lorraine should be independent. They had no plans for the revival of a full parliamentary democracy, in fact their solution appeared to be

---

* OKH, the Oberkommando des Heeres, was the High Command of the Army, but its real responsibility was the eastern front, while the OKW, the Oberkommando der Wehrmacht, was responsible for the western and all other fronts.

basically a resurrection of the Second Reich, but without the Kaiser. Such a formula would have been greeted with incredulity by the American and British governments, as well as by the vast majority of the German people.

Speidel and Rommel began to sound out army, corps and divisional commanders. The two most obvious supporters in command of fighting troops were Generalleutnant Graf von Schwerin, the commander of 116th Panzer-Division, and Generalleutnant Freiherr von Lüttwitz of the 2nd Panzer-Division. It was Lüttwitz's division which had received the German nurses from Cherbourg handed over by the Americans. When Hitler later heard of this contact with the enemy, he was outraged. He had already begun to fear that his generals might make peace overtures to the Americans behind his back.

After Rommel's humiliating visit with Rundstedt on 29 June to Berchtesgaden, he came to the conclusion that they would have to act. Even Keitel, the worst Hitler lackey of them all, admitted to him in private, 'I also know that nothing can be done any more.' And two senior commanders, Hausser and Eberbach, seem to have come to the conclusion that some form of unilateral action was unavoidable. At the beginning of July, just before the fall of Caen, Hitler's favourite, Obergruppenführer Sepp Dietrich, the commander of I SS Panzer Corps, came to La Roche-Guyon to ask what the commander-in-chief was intending to do in view of the 'imminent catastrophe'. According to Speidel, Dietrich assured them that the SS units were 'firmly in his hands'. It is not clear how much Dietrich was told of the plans afoot. At the same time the new commander-in-chief of the Seventh Army, Obergruppenführer Hausser, also predicted collapse.

On 9 July, the day the British and Canadians moved into Caen, Oberstleutnant Cäsar von Hofacker, a cousin of Stauffenberg, was sent by General von Stülpnagel in Paris to see Generalfeldmarschall von Kluge. Kluge had been in contact with the German Army resistance group when on the eastern front, but now prevaricated. Hofacker was Stülpnagel's chief contact with the plotters in Berlin. He tried to persuade Kluge on behalf of the resistance to end the war in the west by 'independent action' as soon as possible. The Allies would never negotiate with Hitler or one of his 'paladins', such as Göring, Himmler or Ribbentrop, so a change of government and the removal of the Nazi leaders were essential. He asked Kluge how long the Normandy front could hold out, because the decisions taken by the resistance in Berlin depended on his answer. 'No longer than two to three weeks at best,' he replied, 'then a breakthrough must be expected which we will be unable to cope with.'

Rommel and Kluge met on 12 July to discuss the military situation and the political consequences. Rommel would also sound out his corps commanders one last time, then prepare an ultimatum to be presented to Hitler. While Rommel consulted corps commanders, Speidel went to see Stülpnagel, who was already preparing to eliminate the Gestapo and SS in France. Two days later, Hitler moved from Berchtesgaden to the *Wolfsschanze* in East Prussia. On the eastern front, the vast Red Army offensive now threatened the whole of Army Group Centre. New bunkers had been built and there were much stronger anti-aircraft defences in the forest around. But the work had not been fully completed, so there were Organisation Todt labourers still on site.

The next day, Rommel wrote an assessment of the western front for Hitler. This warned that the Allies would soon break through rapidly all the way to the German border. The paper ended with the words, 'I must request you, *mein Führer*, to draw the conclusions from this situation without delay. Rommel, Field Marshal.' After Rommel handed over the message for dispatch, he said to Speidel, 'I have given Hitler one more chance. If he does not draw the necessary conclusions, we shall act.'

On 17 July, during their meeting at the headquarters of Panzer Group West, Rommel asked Eberbach for his views on the situation when they were alone. 'We are experiencing the overwhelming disaster of a war on two fronts,' Eberbach replied. 'We have lost the war. But we must inflict on the western Allies the highest possible casualties to bring them to a ceasefire and then prevent the Red Army from breaking through to our Germany.'

'I agree,' Rommel replied, 'but can you imagine the enemy engaging in any negotiations with us so long as Hitler is our leader?' Eberbach had to accept the point. 'So things cannot continue as they are,' Rommel continued. 'Hitler must go.' The panzer divisions were desperately needed on the eastern front. In the west they would withdraw to the Siegfried Line while trying to negotiate.

'Would it not then lead to a civil war,' Eberbach asked, 'which is worse than anything else?' This was the great fear of most officers. It brought back memories of November 1918 and revolutionary uprisings in Berlin, Munich and the mutiny of the fleet in Wilhelmshaven. An hour later, Rommel suffered a fractured skull during the attack by Spitfires near Sainte-Foy-de-Montgommery. He had no idea that an assassination was planned for three days later.

Attempts on Hitler's life had been made before, but they had failed through bad luck.* Hitler had evaded death by changing his movements at the last moment, almost as if he had a feral sixth sense. Yet the plotters faced a more fundamental problem of which they seemed to be unaware: what would be the attitude of the Allies?

The British were far from convinced that removing Hitler would be an advantage. His direction of military affairs since just before the Battle of Stalingrad had been disastrous for the Wehrmacht. Six weeks before D-Day, 21st Army Group summed up the position: 'The longer Hitler remains in power now, the better are Allied chances.' Yet during June, there was a subtle shift. 'The Chiefs of Staff,' Churchill was informed, 'were unanimous that, from the strictly military point of view, it was almost an advantage that Hitler should remain in control of German strategy, having regard to the blunders that he has made, but that on the wider point of view, the sooner he was got out of the way the better.' Special Operations Executive took this pronouncement as a green light to start planning Operation Foxley, their own assassination attempt on Hitler. The idea was to ambush Hitler near the Berghof, but it was never seriously pursued. Hitler had in any case left Berchtesgaden, never to return, but, more importantly, Churchill became con-

---

* Resistance within the army and plans to remove Hitler began with the Sudeten crisis of 1938. Attempts to kill him also included a failed attempt by a Swiss theology student in 1938 and the Bürgerbräu-Keller explosion of 8 November 1939 by a left-wing Swabian joiner acting alone. Most attempts, however, involved the military resistance. Speidel was part of a plan to seize Hitler at Poltava in February 1943, just after the Stalingrad disaster. Another planned attack failed to take place a month later. Then a bomb was put on Hitler's Condor aircraft but failed to go off. A third attempt that month, with Gersdorff detonating a suicide bomb, again failed because Hitler changed his programme at the last moment. Another three plans in December 1943 and in the spring of 1944 also came to nothing.

vinced that this time Germany had to be utterly defeated in the field. The Armistice in November 1918, and the consequent failure to occupy Germany itself, had provided the opportunity for the stab-in-the-back myth among nationalists and Nazis. They had convinced themselves that the German Army had been betrayed at home by revolutionaries and Jews.

In 1943, Stalin had cancelled his own plans to assassinate Hitler, although for rather different reasons.* After Stalingrad, the Soviet Union no longer faced defeat, and he had suddenly begun to fear that if Hitler were removed, the western Allies might be tempted to come to a separate peace with Germany. There is absolutely no evidence that this was ever considered, but right up to the end of the war Stalin, who tended to judge others by himself, was haunted by the idea of a Wehrmacht rearmed by American industry, turning back the victorious advance of the Red Army. In fact, Churchill and Roosevelt were totally committed to the principle of forcing unconditional surrender on Germany.

Stauffenberg, Tresckow and most of their comrades might be considered naïve for expecting the western Allies to enter into negotiations on the death of Hitler. Their planning and preparation were also astonishingly amateur, when one considers their general staff training. A few had been early admirers of Hitler, until they were forced to face the criminal reality of the regime. Yet nobody can cast doubt on their courage and self-sacrifice. They longed somehow to preserve their idealized image of Germany, a high-minded, less nationalistic version of the pre-1914 Wilhelmine era. And they may have hoped to save family estates from Soviet destruction, although they probably recognized it was far too late. Their overriding motive, however, had become a moral compulsion. They knew that there would be very little popular support for this act, so they and their families would be treated as traitors by everyone, not just the Gestapo. The chances of success were slim. But, as Stauffenberg put it, 'Since the generals have up to now

---

* The NKVD directorate under General Sudoplatov planned several attempts to kill Hitler, including one at Vinnitsa in the Ukraine, and another in Germany with an ex-boxer called Igor Miklashevsky and the composer Lev Knipper, the brother of the actress Olga Chekhova. None of these ever came close to being activated.

managed nothing, the colonels have now to step in.' It was their duty to attempt to salvage the honour of Germany and the German Army, despite the danger of laying down another stab-in-the-back legend for the future.

During his interrogation by Allied intelligence officers at the end of the war, General Walter Warlimont described events in East Prussia on 20 July. The midday situation conference took place as usual in the long wooden hut. Hitler entered at about 12.30. The room was bare save for a few chairs and a heavy oak table twenty feet long which ran the length of the room. Among those present were Field Marshal Keitel, Generaloberst Jodl, General Warlimont, General Buhle, Gruppenführer Fegelein and Hitler's adjudants: General Schmundt, Admiral von Puttkamer and Oberstleutnant von Below.

General Heusinger, representing the chief of the army general staff, had begun his briefing when Stauffenberg entered. He was the chief of staff of the Replacement Army, the Ersatzheer. Stauffenberg, according to Warlimont, was carrying a 'strikingly large briefcase', which he placed under the oak table not far from Hitler, who had his back to the door. Because of the briefing, nobody noticed that Stauffenberg left the room a few minutes later.*

At 12.50 hours, 'There suddenly occurred a terrific explosion which seemed to fill the whole room in dust, smoke and fire, and throw everything in all directions.' When Warlimont recovered his senses, he saw Hitler being 'led backwards through the door, supported by several attendants'. Casualties were remarkably few, only because the blast was dissipated through the windows and the thin walls. Hitler had been saved by Stauffenberg's failure to arm the second bomb and by the heavy oak table support between the briefcase and him when the explosion took place.

At first, suspicion focused on the Organisation Todt workers, but

---

* The two bombs, only one of which Stauffenberg had time to arm, used British fuses. These had been dropped by SOE to a Resistance group in France, and later captured by the Germans. They had then been passed on to the conspirators by a supporter within the Abwehr in September 1943. Stauffenberg had gone with his bomb to Rastenburg twice before, on 6 July and 15 July, but the right opportunity did not arise.

during the early afternoon, a sergeant on the staff mentioned that Oberst von Stauffenberg had arrived with a briefcase and had been seen to leave without it. He had flown back to Berlin.

Stauffenberg, convinced that nobody could have survived the blast, had driven straight to the airfield. Meanwhile, a garbled message from a co-conspirator at the *Wolfsschanze* left the conspirator generals waiting in Berlin in a terrible state of uncertainty. They had congregated at the Bendlerblock, the headquarters of the Replacement Army in the Bendlerstrasse. Nobody knew for sure whether the bomb had gone off or not, or whether Hitler was alive or dead. Generaloberst Friedrich Fromm, the commander of the Replacement Army, refused to trigger the coup with the codeword 'Valkyrie' until he was sure that Hitler was dead. Without his certain elimination, a coup d'état stood virtually no chance of success.

To make matters worse, there was no car waiting at Tempelhof airfield to collect Stauffenberg, which delayed his return to the Bendler-block for a further hour. Stauffenberg's assistant rang through from the airfield to say that Hitler was dead. Stauffenberg also insisted that this must be true when he finally arrived, but Keitel had rung Fromm, demanding where Stauffenberg was. Keitel insisted that Hitler's injuries were not serious. Fromm refused to act as a result, but other officers in the conspiracy went ahead. They sent out signals to different head-quarters announcing that Hitler was dead.

The plan was to exploit an existing mechanism specifically designed to suppress a revolt in Berlin against the Hitler regime. The authorities feared an uprising, because there were 'over a million foreign workers in Berlin, and if any revolution did start, these people would be a very great menace'. The codeword to set this counter-insurgency plan in motion was '*Gneisenau*'. It appears that somebody in the Bendlerblock had already jumped the gun, perhaps as a result of the telephone call from Tempelhof airfield to say that Hitler was dead. Because at 15.00 hours, Major Otto Remer, the commander of the *Grossdeutschland* Guard Regiment, was summoned with the codeword '*Gneisenau*' to the offices of another senior member of the conspiracy, Generaloberst Paul von Hase, the military commander of Berlin.

At exactly the same time, the plot was triggered in Paris. General

Blumentritt, Kluge's chief of staff, was told by one of his own officers that Hitler had been killed in a 'Gestapo riot'. He rang La Roche-Guyon to speak to Kluge, but was told that he was visiting the front in Normandy. Generalmajor Speidel asked Blumentritt to come immediately, as Kluge would be back that evening. Blumentritt, however, had no idea that General von Stülpnagel, the military commander, was issuing orders for the arrest of all Gestapo and SS officers in Paris.

There were many senior officers involved in the plot and so little organization or effective communication that the uncertainty over Hitler's death was bound to cause delay and chaos. When Remer reached Hase's office he noticed that the atmosphere was very nervous. Remer was told that the Führer had died in an incident, that a revolution had broken out and that 'executive powers had been passed to the army'. Remer claimed later to have asked a series of questions. Was the Führer dead? Where was the revolution, as he had seen no sign of anything on his way? Were the revolutionists foreign workers? Why had executive power passed to the army rather than to the Wehrmacht? Who was to be Hitler's successor and who had signed the orders passing control to the army?

Evidently, the plotters had not prepared themselves for such questions. Their answers were evasive and lacked confidence. Remer was suspicious, but still confused. He returned to his headquarters and summoned his officers. He ordered them to set up a cordon round the government buildings right down the Wilhelmstrasse. Remer's suspicions were further aroused when he heard that a general who had been dismissed by Hitler had been sighted in Berlin. Then Remer received an order from General von Hase to arrest Goebbels. He refused, as Goebbels had been patron of the *Grossdeutschland* division. In the meantime, an officer, Leutnant Hans Hagen, who was even more suspicious than Remer of what was afoot, had been to see Goebbels to find out the truth. Hagen then convinced Remer that Goebbels, as Reich Commissioner of Defence for Berlin, was his direct superior. Even though General von Hase had specifically forbidden him to see Goebbels, Remer went to the propaganda ministry. He was still confused by the conflicting stories, and did not entirely trust Goebbels.

'What do you know about the situation?' Goebbels asked. Remer recounted what he had been told. Goebbels told him it was not true and put a call through to the *Wolfsschanze*. A few moments later, Remer found himself talking to Hitler. The voice was unmistakable.

'Now we have the criminals and saboteurs of the eastern front,' Hitler said to him. 'Only a few officers are involved and we will eliminate them by the roots. You have been placed in a historic position. It is your responsibility to use your head. You are under my command until Himmler arrives to take over the Replacement Army. Do you understand me?'

Reichsmarschall Hermann Göring had also arrived in the office and asked what Hitler had said. Remer told him. Göring said that they should call out the SS. Remer replied that it was an army matter and that they would finish the task. Remer went out to find that a panzer detachment, summoned by the conspirators from the tank training base at Döberitz, had arrived in the Berlinerplatz. He spoke to their officer and took them under his command. Remer lifted the cordon around the Wilhelmstrasse and moved his troops to the Bendlerstrasse. The conspiracy was now doomed in Berlin.

In France, meanwhile, Kluge had returned to La Roche-Guyon around 20.00 hours and immediately called a conference. Blumentritt suspected that Kluge was involved in the plot simply because there had been two anonymous calls for him from the Reich. One of them was from General Beck, who failed to win him over at the last moment. Kluge insisted privately to Blumentritt that he had known nothing about the 'outrage'. He did, however, admit that the previous year he had been contacted twice by the plotters, but 'in the end' he had refused.

At 20.10 hours, Ultra intercept stations picked up a signal from Generalfeldmarschall von Witzleben, ironically marked with the ultimate priority of 'Führer-Blitz'. It began, 'The Führer is dead. I have been appointed commander-in-chief of the Wehrmacht, and also . . .' At this point the text ceased. Thirty minutes later, Kluge received a signal from the OKW in East Prussia: 'Today at midday, a despicable assassination attempt against the Führer was committed. The Führer is perfectly well.' Kluge rapidly ordered Stülpnagel to release all the Gestapo and SS officers who had been arrested in Paris.

Confirmation that Hitler was alive made the waverers run for cover, even though it would not save them from the Gestapo later. News that Himmler had been appointed commander-in-chief of the Replacement Army was received with horror by army officers, who sometimes referred to him as the '*Unterweltsmarschall*', the marshal of the underworld. An order was issued that the conventional army salute now had to be replaced by the 'German salute' of the Nazi Party.

Unaware that Kluge had already ordered Stülpnagel to release his prisoners, Himmler told the chief directorate of the SS to ring Sepp Dietrich. He was ordered to prepare to march on Paris with the 1st SS Panzer-Division *Leibstandarte Adolf Hitler*. Himmler seems to have been unaware that the division had just been involved in a major battle and could not possibly abandon the Bourguébus ridge at such a moment. He was also unaware that Hitler's 'loyal disciple', Sepp Dietrich, had in Eberbach's words, 'almost turned revolutionary'.*

Back in Berlin, there was chaos in the Bendlerblock. Generaloberst Fromm, in a doomed attempt to save himself from suspicion, ordered the arrest and instant court martial of four of the other officers involved. He allowed Generaloberst Beck to keep his pistol, provided he used it immediately on himself. Presumably because his hand was shaking, Beck shot himself twice in the head. He grazed his scalp the first time, then inflicted a terrible wound with the second shot. An exasperated Fromm ordered a sergeant, some accounts say an officer, to finish him off.

The four, including Stauffenberg, who tried to take all the responsibility for the attempted assassination on himself, were executed in the courtyard of the Bendlerblock by the light of automobile headlights. A detachment of Remer's men, who had just arrived, provided the firing

---

* It is important to remember that a number of those who opposed Hitler on military grounds did not necessarily object to the 'final solution', except in certain details. Eberbach was recorded on tape to have said to his son in captivity in England that September, 'In my opinion, one can even go as far as to say that the killing of those million Jews, or however many it was, was necessary in the interests of our people. But to kill the women and children wasn't necessary. That is going too far.' His son, a naval officer, replied, 'Well, if you are going to kill off the Jews, then kill the women and children too, or the children at least. There is no need to do it publicly, but what good does it do me to kill off the old people?'

squad. When it was Stauffenberg's turn, illuminated by the headlights, he called out, 'Long live holy Germany!' Fromm, as desperate as ever to save himself, gave a grotesque speech over their bodies in praise of Hitler and ended with a triple '*Sieg Heil!*'

In France, Generalfeldmarschall von Kluge ordered the arrest of Stülpnagel at 01.25 hours on the morning of 21 July. That afternoon, Stülpnagel was put in a car to be taken back to Berlin for interrogation by the Gestapo. Because of his seniority, his escort had not taken away his pistol. When the car had stopped en route, presumably to give the occupants a chance to relieve themselves, Stülpnagel attempted to commit suicide, but managed only to shoot both his eyes out. He was taken to a hospital in Verdun to be patched up for the journey on to Berlin, where he would be tried and hanged. At 22.15 hours, it was announced that 'the Military Commander of France, General von Stülpnagel, has been ambushed and wounded by terrorists'.

News of the assassination attempt 'came like a bomb-shell', in the words of Generalleutnant Bodo Zimmermann, one of Kluge's senior staff officers. 'As in the case of any sudden, unexpected event, a certain paralysis set in at first.' For most officers the 'burning question' was, 'What are the men at the front saying and doing? Would the front still hold?' When word of the attempt reached a *Kampfgruppe* of the 21st Panzer-Division near Troarn, 'it spread like wild-fire down the column'. Yet 'the front kept on fighting as though nothing had happened'. The 'high emotional tension of battle' meant that the news only touched the average soldier 'on the fringe of his consciousness . . . the combat soldier was in another world'. General Eberbach, on the other hand, later said he was 'amazed' at the 'indignation and anger' that the attempted putsch had provoked 'not only among the SS Divisions but also among some of the infantry Divisions'. Most officers were appalled that the plotters could have broken their oath to the Führer.

Eberhard Beck with the 277th Infanterie-Division, recorded what happened when the news reached his artillery battery. 'Our signaller heard over the radio that an attempt at assassination had been made against Adolf Hitler. His death could have been a turning point for us and we hoped that this pointless war would find its end.' Their battery commander, Oberleutnant Freiherr von Stenglin, came over and announced that the attempt had failed. Hitler was alive. The order had been given that from now on every soldier must make the 'German greeting' (the Nazi salute), instead of the military one. Stenglin made his own sympathies very clear by promptly bringing 'his hand up to the peak of his cap in the military salute'. Beck recorded that all his comrades were disappointed at the unlucky outcome. A few days later, Allied aircraft came over the German lines dropping propaganda leaflets. These gave details of the bomb plot and also of the Nazis' new *Sippenhaft* decree, ordering reprisals against the families of those involved.

The reaction of Stenglin and Beck was far from universal. Most junior officers were shaken and confused, yet preferred not to dwell on the subject. Staff officers like Zimmermann, on the other hand, suffered a 'feeling of moral oppression and worry'. Some were curiously shocked that Stauffenberg had placed a bomb and then left the scene. An assassination by pistol, during which the assassin had been gunned down, seemed to them more in keeping with the honour of the German officer corps. What depressed them most, however, was that the failed attempt handed all power to the fanatics and eliminated any possibility of a compromise peace.* 'Those who were far-seeing,' wrote Zimmermann, 'thought this is the beginning of the end, a terrible signal. The die-hards thought: it is good that the treacherous reactionaries have been unmasked and that we can now make a clean sweep of them.'

In London, hopes were raised that the failed bomb plot 'might well be the proverbial pebble which starts the avalanche'. But Hitler's belief that providence had saved him made him even more convinced of his

---

* When Churchill met Roosevelt in Quebec for the Octagon conference that September, Field Marshal Brooke wrote a brief 'Explanation of Continued German Resistance': 'Continued German Resistance is chiefly due to the fanatical determination of Nazi Party leaders to fight to the end and to their possession of the necessary political and psychological control in Germany. This determination is based on the doctrine held by the Nazis that Germany surrendered too quickly in 1918; their fear for their own safety; a fanatical belief in their own capabilities which prevents them from accurately appraising the situation; and the lack of any alternative to continued resistance which would seem to offer opportunities for a later revival of their power.'

military genius, to the despair of his generals. He happened to be right, however, about one thing. He described the idea of a truce with the British and Americans, perhaps even persuading them to join the war against the Soviet Union, as 'an idiotic idea'. The plotters, he said, were 'unbelievably naïve' and their attempt to kill him was 'like a Wild West story'.

Conspiracy theories flourished in Nazi circles over the next few months, once the large numbers of officers involved in the plot and their sympathizers became clearer. Altogether some 5,000 were arrested. These theories extended beyond the idea that Speidel had deliberately misdirected the panzer divisions on 6 June. Once Plan Fortitude and the threat of a second landing in the Pas-de-Calais were finally seen to have been a brilliant hoax, the SS became convinced that there had been treason within Fremde Heere West, the military intelligence department dealing with the western Allies. The SS demanded how military intelligence could have swallowed a deception involving a whole army group which never existed. Staff officers were suspected of having inflated Allied strengths deliberately, and accused of the 'falsification of the enemy situation'.

Tensions between Waffen-SS and the German Army also grew rapidly in the field in Normandy over the coming month. As rations were drastically reduced because of Allied air attacks on supply transport, SS foraging parties looted without compunction and threatened any army soldiers trying to do the same.

The one thing on which army and Waffen-SS seemed to agree in Normandy was their continued exasperation with the Luftwaffe. General Bülowius, the commander of II Air Corps, regarded this as very unfair. Allied air supremacy meant his aircraft were intercepted as soon as they took off, and bombers were forced to drop their loads long before they reached the target area. He suffered from the army's 'daily reports which even reached Führer headquarters that their own Luftwaffe and own aircraft were nowhere to be seen'. As a result he received 'many unpleasant reproaches and accusations' from the highest quarters.

Luftwaffe aircrew in Normandy consisted of a surviving handful of aces, while the vast majority were cannon fodder straight out of flying school. Major Hans-Ekkehard Bob, a fighter group commander with fifty-nine victories, often found himself being pursued by eight or ten Mustangs. He survived only by using all his flying skills, twisting and turning almost at ground level round small woods and church towers. He claims he was helped greatly by the intense competition between American pilots, each desperate to shoot him down and thus getting in each other's way.

Since every known airfield was bombed and strafed by the Allied air forces on a regular basis, fighter squadrons deployed to woods close to a stretch of straight road, which they could use as a runway. They had to land and then turn off into the trees, where ground crews would be ready to cover the plane with camouflage nets. For this sort of work, the Focke-Wulf 190, with its wide undercarriage and robust construction, proved much more effective than the Messerschmitt 109.

As Rommel and Kluge had warned, the German forces in Normandy were close to breaking point. They had received only a very small number of men to replace their losses. 'Alarm units' of clerks and others known disparagingly as 'half-soldiers' were brought forward to fill some of the gaps in the front-line divisions. They were not just losing men to enemy action. The reduced rations due to Allied air attacks prompted desertions, both of Poles, *Osttruppen*,* Alsatians and Volksdeutsche, but also of Germans born in the Reich.†

Some were soldiers who did not believe in the Nazi regime or who just hated the war. A British doctor was suspicious at the enthusiastic help of a young German soldier who had surrendered. Sensing this distrust, the boy pulled out a snapshot of his girlfriend and showed it to him. 'No, no,' he said. 'I play no tricks. I want to live to see *her*!'

Generalleutnant von Lüttwitz, the commander of the 2nd Panzer-

---

* Some Soviet *Hiwi* volunteers with the German forces proved fanatically loyal. A member of the 272nd Infantry Division wrote that they 'had a really good relationship with them'. They also proved extremely effective at looting food for their German comrades. And 'Panzer' Meyer of the 12th SS Division had a cossack orderly who seems to have been devoted to him.

† Altogether 130,000 men were drafted into the Wehrmacht and Waffen-SS from Alsace, Lorraine and areas of southern Belgium. They were classified as 'Volksdeutsche', but reluctant Francophones described themselves as '*malgré-nous*', or 'despite ourselves'.

Division, was shocked when three of his Austrians deserted to the enemy. He warned that the names of any deserters would be published in their home towns so that measures could be taken against their relatives. 'If somebody betrays his own people,' he announced, 'then their family does not belong within the German national community.' Lüttwitz may have supported the idea of resisting Hitler, but he was still prepared to adopt measures of a Nazi character.

Treatment of SS soldiers was even harsher. According to a Führer decree, SS soldiers could be accused of high treason if they were taken prisoner by the enemy unwounded. They had been forcefully reminded of this just before the invasion. It was hardly surprising that the British and Canadians captured so few SS alive.* But perhaps the most horrific story of SS discipline came from an Alsatian drafted into the 1st SS Panzer-Division *Leibstandarte Adolf Hitler*. A fellow Alsatian in the 11th Company of the 1st SS Regiment of the *Leibstandarte*, who had also been forcibly recruited, deserted and tried to escape in a column of French refugees. He was spotted by members of their regiment and brought back. Their commander then ordered members of his own company to beat him to death. With every bone in his body broken, the corpse was thrown into a shell-hole. The captain declared that this was an example of '*Kameradenerziehung*', an 'education in comradeship'.

---

* The US Army carried out a careful examination of their German prisoners. A report recorded that their average age was twenty-eight, their average height was 5 foot 5¾ inches, and that their average weight was just under 150 pounds. The shortest were those born between 1919 and 1921, the 'starvation years' in Germany.

21

Operation Cobra – Breakthrough

On 21 July, the Germans intercepted a radio message summoning American commanders for an orders group. This confirmed their suspicions that the US First Army was preparing a large-scale offensive, but they still did not know where. After the heavy fighting for Saint-Lô, Oberstgruppenführer Hausser expected a thrust south-westwards down the Vire valley from Saint-Lô to Torigni. Generalfeldmarschall von Kluge, on the other hand, was convinced that the main attack in Normandy would again come from the British on the Caen front. In the shadow world of signal intercepts, the Allies enjoyed a vast advantage. General Bradley knew from Ultra that the overstretched German forces were close to collapse. The moment for the breakthrough had at last arrived.

Bradley's forces had finally reached the long, straight road running from Lessay on the west coast via Périers to Saint-Lô, the line from which Operation Cobra was to be launched. The only problems were in the Lessay sector. On 22 July, the Germans had launched a sudden attack and the hapless American 90th Division, which had continued its downward spiral due to officer casualties, received the brunt of it. 'One unit surrendered to the enemy,' the report stated, 'and most of the rest broke and withdrew in disorder.' Patton wrote in his diary that 'a battalion of the 90th Division behaved very shamefully today', and the divisional commander would have to be relieved.

Operation Cobra was delayed for several days because of the heavy rain which began on 20 July, followed by low cloud which lingered. The downpours had been so intense that the K-Ration boxes which soldiers used to line their foxholes disintegrated into a soggy mess. Like the British and Canadians, they too were tormented by mosquitoes. The delays weighed heavily on many. An officer in the 3rd Armored Division was more philosophical. 'War is about 90% waiting,' he wrote in his diary, 'which is not so bad as long as the reading material holds out.' But Brigadier General Maurice Rose, who proved to be one of the very finest armoured commanders in the US Army, did not waste the days of bad weather. He used them instead for intensive training of his tank infantry teams.

Bradley needed good visibility. He was determined to smash open the front with heavy bombers, but he wanted to avoid the great mistake made during Goodwood, when the advance had not followed rapidly enough to exploit the shock effect. Bradley flew back to England on 19 July to discuss the bombing plan with the air force commanders. He wanted only light bombs, to avoid deep craters which might slow his armoured forces. The target area for saturation bombing was to be a rectangle along the south side of the Périers–Saint-Lô road.

The air chiefs agreed with Bradley's requests, but they made it clear that they could not attack following the line of the road.* They would have to come in from the north over the waiting army, rather as they had at Omaha. They also felt that withdrawing the front-line troops by only half a mile, as Bradley suggested to ensure rapid exploitation, would not provide a sufficient safety margin. The army and the air force haggled over this and settled on 1,200 yards. Meteorological reports indicated that the sky would be sufficiently clear by midday on 24 July, and 13.00 hours was chosen as H-Hour.

Air Marshal Leigh-Mallory had flown out to Normandy to observe the operation in person. The skies had not cleared by midday as predicted. Leigh-Mallory then decided that visibility was not good enough. He sent a signal back to England to postpone the attack until the next day, but the bombers were already on their way. An order went out to abort the mission, but most of the troops waiting to attack were not told. Journalists and officers from Allied armies, including the

---

* A lateral bomb run would mean approaching the narrowest side of the target area. This required them to attack in a very restricted formation. It also exposed their aircraft to flak along the length of the German front.

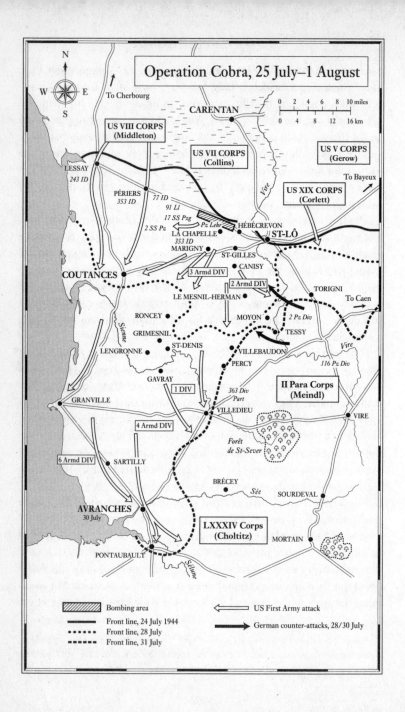

Operation Cobra, 25 July–1 August

N
W E
S

To Cherbourg

CARENTAN

0 2 4 6 8 10 miles
0 4 8 12 16 km

US VIII CORPS
(Middleton)

US VII CORPS
(Collins)

US V CORPS
(Gerow)

To Bayeux

LESSAY
243 ID

PÉRIERS
353 ID

77 ID
91 Ll
17 SS Pzg
2 SS Pz

Pz Lehr

HÉBÉCREVON

US XIX CORPS
(Corlett)

LA CHAPELLE
353 ID

MARIGNY

ST-GILLES

CANISY

ST-LÔ

COUTANCES

3 Armd DIV

LE MESNIL-HERMAN

2 Armd DIV

TORIGNI

To Caen

MOYON

2 Pz Div

RONCEY

GRIMESNIL

TESSY

LENGRONNE

ST-DENIS

VILLEBAUDON

PERCY

Vire

GAVRAY

*363 Div
Part*

II Para Corps
(Meindl)

GRANVILLE

VILLEDIEU

1 DIV

VIRE

4 Armd DIV

116 Pz Div

*Forêt
de St-Sever*

6 Armd DIV

SARTILLY

BRÉCEY

Sée

SOURDEVAL

AVRANCHES
30 July

LXXXIV Corps
(Choltitz)

MORTAIN

PONTAUBAULT

Sélune

	Bombing area	⟵	US First Army attack
	Front line, 24 July 1944		German counter-attacks, 28/30 July
	Front line, 28 July		
	Front line, 31 July		

Red Army, had been invited to forward command posts to watch the show. 'The observers hung around, fidgeted, cracked jokes, and waited,' an officer with the 4th Infantry Division noted.

Most aircraft received the order in time and turned back. Some dropped their bombs south of the road as planned, but in the lead aircraft of one formation, a bombardier who had trouble with the release mechanism, accidentally dropped his load a mile north of the Périers–Saint-Lô road. The rest of the formation, taking this to be the signal, promptly released theirs as well. The soldiers of the 30th Division right below were not in foxholes. Standing around or sitting on vehicles, they had been watching the bombers overhead. Then they heard that 'peculiar rustling in the sky' which signified that large numbers of bombs had been released. They ran in all directions, trying to find cover. Twenty-five men were killed and 131 were wounded. General Bradley was furious. He had convinced himself that the air chiefs would come round to his demand that the attack should be along the line of the road, not perpendicular to the target. A rapid decision had to be made if Cobra was to be launched the following day. The air force commanders insisted that they had to follow the same approach, otherwise there would be a delay. Bradley felt he had no choice but to agree.

An even larger number of observers gathered at Collins's VII Corps headquarters to watch 'the big show'. Journalists jostled impatiently as they waited. The Soviet war correspondent Colonel Kraminov, who had a spiteful word for almost everyone, described Ernest Hemingway, looking over everyone's head. 'The flamboyant, red-headed Knickerbocker,' he added, 'was recounting anecdotes as tedious as his numerous and superficial pieces.' After General Bradley briefed the correspondents, staff officers went further: 'This is no limited objective drive. This is it. This is the big breakthrough.' There was no mention of the casualties from their own bombs.

A Soviet military mission from London was also visiting the First US Army at this time. General Hodges arrived at Gerow's V Corps with a group of Soviet officers in red striped trousers and gold shoulderboards. The Red Army officers were interested in all that they saw and asked about the enemy soldiers captured. They 'stiffened perceptibly', however, when one of Gerow's staff replied, 'They weren't very good; they were Poles and Russians.' It was probably not so much the slight against their martial qualities which upset them, but this reminder of the fact that around a million former Red Army soldiers served in Wehrmacht uniform under varying degrees of duress.*

Lieutenant General Leslie J. McNair, the commander of ground forces, was another observer. His visit to the front had been kept highly secret, because he was to take over from Patton as the commander-in-chief of the fictitious 1st US Army Group, threatening the Pas-de-Calais.† McNair was at the headquarters of the 30th Division, then decided to go forward to the 120th Infantry Regiment to watch the bombing from the front line.

A sinister omen took place just before the attack. The Germans suddenly fired one of their short, sharp artillery salvoes. Two American soldiers in the 30th Division, who ran from different directions to leap into the same foxhole, bayoneted each other. An aid man rushed to help them and bandaged their wounds. Shortly afterwards, General McNair, who had heard of this freak accident, sought out the aid man to question him about the story. But this misfortune was about to be repeated on a far larger scale.

On that morning of 25 July, with H-Hour now set for 11.00 hours, the bombing process was repeated. The first fighter-bombers screamed in at 09.40 hours, right on time. Over the next twenty minutes waves consisting of a squadron at a time hit their targets between the front line and the Saint-Lô–Périers road with great accuracy. The soldiers sitting and standing on their vehicles waved and cheered. Then, even before the sound of the Thunderbolts' engines had died away, the steady roar of heavy bombers could be heard coming from behind, as more than a thousand B-17 Flying Fortresses and B-24 Liberators approached in formation.

---

* Stalin's government was extremely sensitive on this issue. The Soviet ambassador in Washington, DC, made an official complaint after stories about former Red Army soldiers fighting for the Germans were filed by Associated Press and United Press correspondents in Normandy.

† Three days later, on 28 July, the Germans became aware from some captured documents that the Third US Army had already moved to France, but the staff running Plan Fortitude had prepared for such a detail leaking out. Through their agents, they had topped up the dummy invasion force with a new Army Group headquarters and the so-called 'Fourteenth US Army'.

Nobody seemed to have imagined that things could go wrong a second time. General McNair had left his command car behind a tank and went forward on foot to see better. There was a breeze blowing from the south, whose effect had not been taken into account. The first bombs were dropped on target, but the wind blew the smoke and dust north across the Périers–Saint-Lô road, so subsequent waves began to drop their loads short. The forward companies, realizing the danger, threw orange smoke grenades as a warning, but the quantity of drifting smoke and dirt covered them. There was no radio link between the ground and heavy bombers.

Tank crews jumped back into their vehicles and closed the hatches, but the infantry and General McNair were left in the open. In the forward infantry regiments a total of 101 men were killed and 463 wounded. One of the medics who went to help was astonished to find that 'the faces of the dead were still pink'. This was presumably because they had been killed by blast rather than by shrapnel penetration.

McNair was one of those killed. His body was taken back to a field hospital and all the personnel there sworn to secrecy. Apart from the casualties, the effect on the men about to attack was devastating. A lieutenant recorded how his men were buried in their foxholes: 'Many of them only got an arm or leg up through the dirt and had to be dug out.' The 4th Infantry Division reported that 'all men and officers who were under the bombing testify to the terrific shock effect. A great number of the men were in a daze for a while, just staring blankly and unable to understand when spoken to.' In the 30th Division, 164 men were evacuated suffering from combat exhaustion as a result.

Companies hit by the bombing expected H-Hour to be postponed after what had happened, but Bradley insisted that the operation should start immediately. This was optimistic in the circumstances. Apart from the shock, the tanks due to accompany the advancing infantry had pulled back during the bombing and lost contact with them.

The Germans, who had received the full force of the bombing, were in a far worse state. Bayerlein's Panzer Lehr Division and the 275th Infanterie-Division were at the centre of the storm. Panzer Lehr had been hit hard the day before, even by the limited bombing, and the German artillery had used up a large proportion of their reduced supply of ammunition, assuming it was the main attack. Bayerlein had pulled back the bulk of his forces, which placed them right in the target area for 25 July. Some German commanders even believed that they had managed to repel the aborted attack the day before, so the postponement by a day had in fact confused the Germans and not revealed the American plan. Kluge thought that the bombing on 24 July might have been a diversion to conceal a major British offensive. He immediately visited the front of Panzer Group West and discussed the situation with General Eberbach.

His suspicions seemed to have been confirmed, because Montgomery, with perfect timing, launched Operation Spring the following dawn, just four hours before Cobra began in earnest. This was the attempt by II Canadian Corps to seize the Verrières ridge beside the Caen–Falaise road. Although the offensive failed dismally, the result could hardly have been better. Kluge became even more certain that Falaise was the key Allied objective. As a result, he did not agree to the transfer of two panzer divisions from the British to the American sector until over twenty-four hours after the launch of Cobra and they did not reach the front in strength for another two days.* Goodwood and Spring had thus achieved Montgomery's principal objective, even though they both failed to make a breakthrough.†

The full bombing on 25 July had a devastating effect on both German soldiers and vehicles. 'The whole place looked like a moon landscape; everything was burned and blasted,' wrote Bayerlein. 'It was impossible to bring up vehicles or recover the ones that were damaged. The survivors were like madmen and could not be used for anything. I don't believe hell could be as bad as what we experienced.' Bayerlein, who was prone to exaggeration, initially claimed that Panzer Lehr had lost thirty-five tanks, fifteen assault guns and 2,000 men. He later revised this to twenty-five tanks, ten assault guns and just under 1,000 men. A paratroop regiment in his sector was also annihilated. In any case, the

* Patton and even Bradley became convinced that the Germans had transferred two panzer divisions before Cobra started. German sources show that this is not the case.
† Montgomery's personal liaison officer with the First US Army observed later that 'the drawing off of German panzers and the launch of Cobra put an end to the attempts, mainly by Tedder, to get Churchill and Ike to replace Monty'.

shock effect cannot be doubted. An American doctor noted in his diary that 'many of [the prisoners taken] were actually babbling, knocked silly'.

An American infantry officer, advancing through the target area, observed, 'At the end of this great bombing action the earth was as if it had been plowed. Within an area of many square miles, scarcely a human being or an animal was alive and all kinds of trucks, guns and machines of every type were in twisted disorder over the deeply-scarred soil.' In some cases, Panther tanks had been flipped over on to their backs like turtles. Several days after the breakthrough, Patton flew over the Cobra sector at 300 feet in a spotter plane. Even at that altitude, he found the stench of dead cows overpowering.

Not all resistance had been eliminated, however. The 4th Infantry Division advanced while still waiting for their tanks to come up. After the first 700 yards, they came up against German positions, supported by tanks concealed in a sunken track between hedgerows. Bazooka teams knocked out the tanks, which may have been disabled already, and they shot up a group of Germans that came along the hedgerow just in front of them. 'The rest huddled in a corner of the hedgerow and yelled "*Kamerad!*".· One of the squad leaders stepped forward and motioned for them to come over. As he did so he was shot. The other squad leader stepped forward but they got him with a grenade. We could not see what part of the enemy position this fire was coming from and we couldn't risk anyone else so we shot down the Germans who wanted to surrender.'

The 4th Infantry Division did not manage to advance more than about a mile and a half. 'The result for the first day hardly constituted a real breakthrough,' its headquarters acknowledged. The 9th Division on their right and the 30th Division on their left did not achieve much more. A general feeling arose that the results of the bombing had been deeply disappointing. But both commanders and troops were being over-cautious, partly as a result of the weeks of *bocage* fighting. Their corps commander, General Collins, then made a bold decision. He decided on 26 July to throw in the armoured divisions ahead of schedule.

That day, the Germans sent their last remaining reserves towards La Chapelle-en-Juger, but they were hit by fighter-bomber attacks. Soon it became clear that the sector between the 4th and 9th Divisions lay virtually open. Choltitz and Hausser did not comprehend the full extent of the danger, mainly because the bombing had destroyed so many landlines.

In the centre, the 4th Infantry Division now advanced well. 'The effectiveness of the bombardment was still evident,' the division reported. 'Even though it was a day later many of the Germans still looked very shaky. A good many prisoners were taken and they looked beaten to a frazzle.' In one case, three Panther tanks were surrounded by infantry and their crews surrendered. One platoon was amused to discover in a tank abandoned by the Panzer Lehr 'quite a collection of women's clothes including silk stockings and step-ins'. The 30th Division on the east flank, having recovered remarkably well from the accidental bombing, faced hard fighting round Hébécrevon just north-west of Saint-Lô. But then German resistance began to collapse rapidly.

On that morning of 26 July, Collins had ordered the 1st Division with a combat command of the 3rd Armored Division to break through on the right. Meanwhile Brigadier General Rose's combat command of the 2nd Armored Division was to attack on the left, first with the 30th Division, then pushing on alone due south towards Saint-Gilles. Rose's intensive training beforehand to 'marry up' infantry and armour in combined tactics paid off. He had the 22nd Infantry from the 4th Division riding the tanks, eight men to a Sherman and four to a light tank. Their third battalion followed behind in trucks. Roads cratered by bombing and shelling held them up at times, and whenever they encountered resistance, the infantry dismounted. They would creep forward to locate any panzers, a task made easier by the German practice of keeping their engines running. The infantry would then indicate their position to their own tanks, which proceeded to engage them. Rose, well aware that the main problem would be resupply, had ordered extra rations, grenades and bandoliers of rifle ammunition for the infantry to be loaded on to the tanks.

The 2nd Armored Division, proudly known as 'Hell on Wheels', had been shaped by General Patton himself. It prided itself as a hard-drinking, hard-fighting formation. These 'tankers' were patronizing towards the infantry, whom they called the 'doughs', and the Patton spirit of recklessness was also reflected in their taste for gambling. One officer acknowledged that they went in for 'a lot of looting'. Tank troops in all armies tend to be the worst looters, if only because they are there first with the infantry, but have better opportunities to stow their booty. Another officer observed, however, that few of their men ran out of control in battle. 'The number of kill-lusty people is fortunately, very small,' he wrote. 'They are treacherous, unskillful and dangerous to have around.' In any case, the professionalism and the gung-ho attitude of the 2nd Armored were exactly what was needed in exploiting the opportunity provided by Operation Cobra.

Slowed by hedgerows and craters, the tanks with infantry mounted averaged only a mile an hour, but it was still an incomparably faster advance than those made during the previous periods of *bocage* fighting. The 22nd Infantry Regiment dismounted to clear the small town of Saint-Gilles, on the Coutances–Saint-Lô road. As the tanks moved on south out of the town, they passed 'Private De Castro, lying by the roadside badly wounded. His right foot had been nearly cut off above the ankle, and was just hanging by the tendon. He had a terrible gash on his right shoulder. As we passed, he tried to raise up a little, waved his good left arm, and said "Go get 'em, boys!".'

Once Rose's armoured column was out of the bombed area and past Saint-Gilles, the rate of advance increased, even though night had fallen. Rose saw no reason to halt during the hours of darkness. His armour bypassed German positions. Some German vehicles, thinking that the column must be one of their own units retreating, joined it and were promptly captured. On the road south to Canisy, Rose's Shermans blasted German half-tracks which had nothing heavier than a machine gun for defence.

Canisy was in flames, having been bombed by P-47 Thunderbolts. The armoured column took time to get through the rubble. In the local château, they found a German field hospital, where they captured wounded soldiers, doctors and nurses. Rose did not want to waste time. He pushed his men on towards Le Mesnil-Herman, over seven miles south of Saint-Lô.

On the right flank, the 1st Infantry Division and combat command A of the 3rd Armored Division, under Brigadier General Doyle O. Hickey, attacked south. They spotted an assault gun and a Mark IV tank at

Montreuil-sur-Lozon. They radioed a squadron of P-47 Thunderbolts, which came in low and destroyed the assault gun. The crew of the tank leaped out and ran away.

Each combat command had an air support party riding in tanks provided on Bradley's orders for air force liaison officers. An exceptionally effective working relationship had been established with Lieutenant General Elwood R. Quesada, the chief of IX Tactical Air Command. The forty-year-old 'Pete' Quesada, unlike most airmen, had a real enthusiasm for the ground-attack role. This was to provide the basis for 'armored column cover', in which fighter-bomber squadrons, working in relays, were constantly on hand to provide support, like the cab-rank system of Typhoons operating with the British Second Army. That day, Quesada's fighter-bombers were out in force. One German commander complained bitterly that they were 'overhead like hawks watching for any movement on the ground then swooping into the attack'.

Hickey's combat command and the 1st Division pushed on south to Marigny, nearly four miles beyond the Périers–Saint-Lô road. At 13.00 hours on 26 July, a Piper Cub pilot reported 'friendly tanks' in Marigny. But the town did not fall immediately. Roads were blocked with rubble and the walls of burning houses collapsed. The Americans took nearly 200 German prisoners, many of them replacements who had just arrived from training battalions. 'An old soldier,' remarked Leutnant Schneider, who was taken with them, 'is one who has been in this sector since Sunday.' By nightfall, Marigny was completely secured. American casualties had been very light. One battalion reported only a dozen wounded for the whole day.

Fortunately for American tank units, the Germans had begun to run out of 88 mm shells, as an Ultra intercept early on 26 July revealed. Another Ultra intercept that day showed that the Germans still believed that the main thrust would come from the Caen front and not in the west down the Atlantic coast. Choltitz, rather closer to the crisis, began to pull back his forces between Périers and the coast. Only a light screen was left behind, but it could do little as the American 6th Armored Division entered Lessay. 'We were riding along with people waving and throwing flowers at us,' reported a tank platoon commander, when the Germans opened up with machine guns and machine pistols. The

6th Armored pushed on through down the coast road, leaving the infantry to clean up behind them.

General Patton, waiting impatiently for his Third Army to become operational, received a call from Bradley, asking him to come to dinner wearing 'good clothes'. Patton was slightly taken aback. 'I always do,' commented the stickler for turnout. In fact, Bradley had not wanted to tell him the true reason for the summons over the telephone. They were to bury General McNair in total secrecy.

The decisive American breakthrough had a marked effect on German morale. Soldiers began speaking among themselves in a way they would not have dared before. A senior medical *Unteroffizier* called Klein described the night of 26 July, when they were told to abandon their dressing station south of Saint-Lô with seventy-eight severely wounded men, and fall back towards Vire. He recorded the conversation of the walking wounded.

A corporal with the German Cross in Gold for having destroyed five tanks on the eastern front said to him, 'I tell you one thing, Sani, this is no longer a war here in Normandy. The enemy is superior in men and materiel. We are simply being sent to our deaths with insufficient weapons. Our Highest Command [Hitler and the OKW] doesn't do anything to help us. No airplanes, not enough ammunition for the artillery . . . Well, for me the war is over.'

An infantryman wounded in the shoulder by shrapnel said, 'This piece of iron which hit me, should have hit the Führer's head on 20 July, and the war would be over already.' Another soldier who helped Klein carry the wounded said, 'I am beyond caring. Two of my brothers were sacrificed in Stalingrad and it was quite useless. And here we have the same.' Younger casualties asked 'whether their wound was sufficient'. They wanted to know if they were to be sent home or simply transferred to the main dressing station. The lightly wounded, such as those who had lost a finger or been shot through the leg without breaking a bone, were sent back to the front within five days.

At noon on 27 July, Bradley issued new orders. Cobra was going so well that he wanted a full-out advance to Avranches, the gateway to Brittany. The commander of British airborne forces, Lieutenant

General Sir Frederick 'Boy' Browning, had tried to sell Bradley the idea of a paratroop drop on Avranches in the German rear. But Bradley rejected the idea. An air drop would greatly reduce the flexibility he needed in this type of operation, because it would create a moral imperative to relieve the airborne force before anything else.

Bradley decided to give Patton unofficial command over VIII Corps in the west, even though the Third Army would not become operational until 1 August. 'Felt much happier over the war,' Patton noted in his diary. 'May get in yet.' Following firm Patton precepts, Wood's 4th Armored Division and Grow's 6th Armored Division became double spearheads for VIII Corps.

German commanders suddenly comprehended the enormity of the disaster which they faced. Their reactions had been slow largely due to the American tactic of cutting all cables and telephone lines. In many places, German troops had no idea that a breakthrough had occurred. They were often astonished when they found American troops far behind what they thought was the front line. Some officers in a VW Kübelwagen nearly crashed into one column, and on several occasions German motorcyclists drove up to American vehicles to discover what was happening, only to be shot down.

General Meindl signalled that II Paratroop Corps south of Saint-Lô in the Vire valley was now reduced to 3,400 men. 'Because of heavy losses [they were] no longer able to stand up to serious Allied pressure.' Kluge was finally forced to accept that the American offensive constituted the chief danger. He agreed to the panic-stricken request for panzer reinforcements from Hausser and ordered the transfer of the 2nd and 116th Panzer Divisions from the British front.

On the evening of 26 July, Lüttwitz went ahead to visit Meindl's headquarters, where he found 'a rather confused situation'. Meindl himself wrote that 'the din of shell-fire and tank engines was so great that it was impossible to talk over the telephone at all'. His command post was concealed in heaps of rubble, which at least provided good camouflage from American fighter-bombers. Meindl, who was irritated to find that Lüttwitz was not under his direct command, said that it was madness to launch an attack, especially during daylight. Things were so bad that they could barely hold on as it was.

'What are you thinking?' Lüttwitz retorted. 'All I want you to do is to see that my right flank is properly secured during the attack.' Meindl replied that they would hold the flank, but they could not keep up with the panzers.

Lüttwitz was then summoned to Hausser's Seventh Army command post, ten miles south of Percy. There he was briefed by his new corps commander, General von Funck. He was to cross the Vire around Tessy, then advance north-westward to block the road from Saint-Lô down to Percy. This was the route down which Brigadier General Rose's column was advancing. He would be followed by the 116th Panzer-Division as soon as it arrived.

Meindl, who was still feeling put out, decided to talk to General von Funck himself. So, even though his corps was in the middle of a desperate battle, he climbed into his Kübelwagen, which he had nick-named his '*Jaboflitzer*', or 'fighter-bomber dodger', and followed Lüttwitz to the Seventh Army command post to protest that the 2nd Panzer-Division had not been placed under his orders. The visit did him little good. During the journey back, he had to halt on several occasions and throw himself in the ditch as American fighters attacked.

On his return, he found Oberstleutnant von Kluge, the son of the field marshal, waiting impatiently at his headquarters along with Generaloberst Heinz Guderian, the new chief of the general staff. Kluge sent his son 'from staff to staff as what he called a "front traveller",' wrote Meindl, 'but what we in our manner of speaking called a spy, to collect his impressions for the old man'. Meindl, in a black mood, told the younger Kluge to inform his father that it was no longer possible to hold on in Normandy and that the attack by the two panzer divisions would achieve nothing. Instead the panzers should be used to build up an anti-tank defence, 'instead of throwing them away on imaginary goals as if in tank manoeuvres on a map'.

Meindl did not hide his disdain for panzer commanders – 'these superior people'. They never got out of their 'gasoline wagons' to reconnoitre on foot, because 'it was not pleasant going into the firing zone. It was much safer to bob down and close the lid. Only a few of the tank commanders had the insight to see – or could be convinced in discussion – that the moment of the great tank battles for us was past! They now had to wake up from a beautiful dream!'

Meindl went on, 'Those up at the top were apparently still waiting for a miracle to happen. In addition our propaganda announced the attempt of 20 July and its consequences. So it was up to us as paratroopers to see that *our* honour was not besmirched! The world was set on our destruction. Good! We would hold on to our blunderbusses.'

Although 27 July was overcast, which saved the 2nd Panzer-Division from air attack on their approach march to the Vire, they did not begin to cross the river at Tessy until that night, sixty hours after the start of Operation Cobra. By then they were far too late to stop the American advance.

On the west coast, when the 6th Armored Division reached Coutances on 27 July, they found that their reconnaissance unit had already taken the town. They bivouacked there that night, then 'just rushed on through', heading for Granville. German infantry were hiding in the hedgerows either side, so 6th Armored's light tanks advanced down the road at fifteen mph, spraying machine-gun fire right and left. Brigadier General Hickey's column of the 3rd Armored Division was also heading for Coutances. But General Collins, as well as Colonel Luckett of the 12th Infantry attached to it, criticized the 3rd Armored for advancing too cautiously.

The advance was more difficult on 27 July for the American formations in the centre of the breakthrough. Armoured divisions were delayed by the density of military traffic on the roads, with columns stretching back fifteen miles or so. The obstructions were usually due to knocked-out German vehicles blocking roads. Bradley, who had foreseen these problems, had assembled 15,000 engineers for Cobra. Their main task was 'opening and maintaining main supply routes' through the gap. This meant filling craters in roads, clearing wrecked German vehicles and even building bypasses round towns which had been destroyed.

On 28 July, visibility was better, to the relief of American commanders. Lüttwitz's attack with the 2nd Panzer-Division west of the River Vire was rapidly broken up by air attacks. The 116th Panzer-Division fared little better. In the west, Choltitz's Corps was in danger of encirclement and Seventh Army headquarters ordered it to pull back towards the centre near Roncey. Obersturmbannführer Tychsen, the new commander of the *Das Reich*, was killed near his command post by a US reconnaissance unit. And that evening, Standartenführer Baum of the 17th SS Panzergrenadier-Division *Götz von Berlichingen* took command of the remnants of both divisions.

The American advance accelerated down the coast road. With the sea on their right, the 6th Armored Division advanced nearly thirty miles. Whenever they reached a road block, the air liaison officer in his tank or half-track simply called in a squadron of P-47 Thunderbolts and the defensive position would be destroyed, usually within fifteen minutes.

The Germans suffered the downward spiral of sudden retreat and smashed communications. Few commanders knew where their troops were. Divisions were fragmented and there was chaos on the roads. Ammunition and fuel supplies could not get through, so panzers and vehicles had to be abandoned. Resistance was maintained only by small groups of soldiers, with an anti-tank gun or assault gun in support. Panzer Lehr Division reported that it had 'no forces fit for battle'. Its remnants were sent back towards Percy. On the same day, the headquarters of II Paratroop Corps reported that 'neither light nor medium field howitzer ammunition was available'.

Heavy fighting continued near Cerisy-la-Salle in the centre, but this was really a desperate attempt by a trapped German force to fight its way out, not a last-ditch stand. American field artillery and anti-aircraft guns were 'used to fire point-blank at the attackers'. P-47 Thunderbolts also screamed into the attack, but an unexpected sortie of Messerschmitt 109s also appeared, strafing American troops.

Part of the Kampfgruppe Heintz made its way behind hedges and avoiding villages to find a gap in the encirclement. Some of the men suggested that they should surrender, but their officers refused. 'For five days,' an *Unteroffizier* wrote, 'we had nothing to eat but unripe fruit and the iron rations we took from our dead comrades. Once more the Army was sacrificed in order to save the SS units from being made prisoners . . . we had to leave behind 178 wounded.' Surrendering was not always a safe option. An American officer with the 9th Division noted that 'when other elements of the enemy, such as Poles, tried to surrender, the SS shot them'. During the night marches to escape, morale began to deteriorate rapidly and tempers exploded. The paratroops blamed the

SS for their predicament and the SS in turn blamed them. Some officers collapsed from nervous strain and exhaustion.

On the eastern side of the breakthrough in the Vire valley, the 2nd Armored Division was beyond Villebaudon, level with Tessy. Rose's combat command was heading for Saint-Sever-Calvados, on the Villedieu–Vire road. Seventh Army headquarters suddenly feared that Choltitz's corps in the west would be completely isolated. Choltitz received an order from Generalmajor Pemsel, the chief of staff of Seventh Army, to counter-attack towards Percy to cut off the American spearhead. Choltitz knew that this would cause chaos and expose them to fighter-bomber attacks once dawn came. It would also leave the coastal route open all the way down to Avranches. But Hausser insisted that the order be obeyed.

That evening, when Kluge at La Roche-Guyon heard of the Seventh Army's decision to break out to the south-east, he lost his temper. He telephoned Oberstgruppenführer Hausser and ordered him to revoke the order immediately. Hausser replied that it was probably too late, but he would try. A message sent by an officer on a motorcycle finally reached Choltitz at midnight, but he had no communications with his divisions. They continued their attack towards the south-east, away from the coast.

Kluge, fearing to sack Hausser for this mistake because he belonged to the Waffen-SS, ordered that Pemsel should be replaced. General von Choltitz, who was summoned back to take over as commander of the Parisian region, was to hand over LXXXIV Corps to General Elfeldt. Hitler was also furious to hear that the road to Avranches, and thus to Brittany, lay exposed. OKW issued orders for a counter-attack immediately. Kluge demanded urgent reinforcements. He asked for the 9th Panzer-Division in the south of France and more infantry divisions. OKW accepted this request with unusual speed.

With many of the retreating German troops concentrated round Roncey, combat command B of the 2nd Armored Division started to establish blocking points along a line to the south. But during that night of 28 July, the US Army became a victim of its own profligate mechanization. Routes further north were so blocked in the breakthrough corridor that advance elements of the 4th Infantry Division's head-quarters were 'on the road all night'. Bottlenecks were caused in each case by 'a knocked out enemy vehicle standing partially across the road at a bad muddy spot'. Engineers could not find a way past to clear the obstacles. In one case, a staff officer commandeered a bulldozer and shifted a burnt-out vehicle himself. Some French, working furiously to help fill in craters, refused to accept any pay, insisting 'that they did it to help us shoot more Boches'.

Major General Huebner of 1st Infantry Division, the 'Big Red One', was determined not to allow anything to slow his advance. He insisted that 'only one-way traffic would prevail' along the narrow Norman roads. Not even ambulances would be allowed to return: 'Casualties would have to be cared for as best they could along the route of advance.' The armoured infantry of the 3rd Armored Division climbed on to the tanks so that their half-tracks could be filled with cans of gasoline, ammunition and other supplies. The 6th Armored Division on the coast had also decided that this was no time for supply dumps or distributing rations in bivouac areas. 'Hell, within a couple of days,' one officer remarked, 'we were passing out rations like Santa Claus on his sleigh, with both giver and receiver on the move.' The Sherman crews seldom halted to cook or relieve themselves. They kept going on boiled eggs and instant coffee. A medical officer said of their pudding-basin tank helmets, 'they crapped in them and cooked in them'. Another medical officer with the 2nd Armored Division noted an additional advantage of the rapid advance. There were very few casualties from mines and booby-traps. The Germans had had little time to leave behind any of their nasty surprises.

On 29 July, Rose's combat command A from the 2nd Armored Division had a hard fight on the road south to Villebaudon. They came up against a *Kampfgruppe* of Lüttwitz's 2nd Panzer-Division at the crossroads of La Denisière, with nearly twenty tanks and two companies of panzer-grenadiers in half-tracks. Lüttwitz's division and the newly arrived 116th Panzer-Division had been ordered to strike west to cut off the American advance, joining up with the amalgamated SS Division. But Lüttwitz perceived that this was impossible. He decided that it was more important to protect the flank along the River Vire, which was under pressure from the American 30th Infantry Division. American tank destroyers knocked out several panzers and forced the rest to withdraw eastwards to Moyon, where a much tougher battle took place.

A column of tanks from Rose's combat command, with their attached infantry from the 4th Infantry Division, advanced into the small town of Moyon, while Captain Reid led a patrol from his company round the east side. Reid's men shot down an anti-tank gun crew, then found themselves being fired at by a German tank. Private Sharkey, a 'bazooka hound', stalked it from the far side of a hedgerow and knocked it out with their second-last round. Another tank appeared close to the first one and began firing its machine gun. Captain Reid crept back along the hedgerow, stood up and lobbed a white phosphorus grenade on to the top of the tank and another underneath it. The tank was soon ablaze.

In Moyon itself, however, another German tank knocked out one of the Shermans. The tank battalion commander decided to pull out of the town and shell the place with high-explosive rounds. He told the infantry platoons in front to withdraw too. Just before they pulled back, Private Sharkey fired their last bazooka round at another German tank, the lead vehicle in a column with infantry approaching the town. He scored a direct hit on the turret ring. Captain Reid called out, 'Let's get out of here before they zero in on us!' But Sharkey's blood was clearly up. He remained standing at the hedgerow, firing with his carbine at the German infantry. A burst of machine-gun fire from one of the other tanks ripped off the side of his face, but Sharkey was able to retreat with the others, 'the flesh hanging down over his chest'. He walked standing upright, while the others crawled back.

They were cut off by another German column led by tanks. Reid had only two white phosphorus grenades left, but he managed to set the lead tank ablaze. The smoke acted as a screen and the patrol slipped back across the road. Sharkey collapsed from his terrible wound, but recovered after a rest and rejoined the rest of the company a little later, holding his two fingers up in a victory salute. 'Sharkey made the greatest display of guts I've ever seen,' Reid said later.

The infantry battalion commander, Major Latimer, heard about the tank commander's decision to pull out of the town too late to stop it. He was horrified for tactical reasons and also because of the effect on morale. It was one thing for tanks to pull back and have another go, but he believed that once infantry had moved in, they should hold what they had occupied. The German panzergrenadiers, who had been taken unawares by the initial assault, rapidly infiltrated back into the town. They brought up more tanks and artillery in addition to the column Reid's men had seen.

'A duel developed between the German tanks and ours with the infantry in between,' stated the report on the action. 'It was a terrible experience and losses were very high. Our forces were also under a great deal of artillery fire. In addition to the heavy physical casualties, both infantry and armor had a number of men who cracked up under the strain.' The task force was relieved late in the day by part of the 30th Division. The only satisfaction as they withdrew was to see German bombers come in and attack their own ground forces by mistake.

Further to the west, during that afternoon of 29 July, P-47 Thunderbolts of the 405th Fighter Group spotted a huge jam of German vehicles on the road east of Roncey. For six and a half hours they bombed and strafed in relays. The pilots claimed sixty-six tanks, 204 vehicles and eleven guns destroyed, as well as fifty-six tanks and fifty-five vehicles damaged. This was wildly optimistic, but the carnage was in any case considerable. The US Army also requested support from the RAF Typhoons of 121 Wing. They attacked another column south of Roncey and claimed seventeen tanks destroyed and another twenty-seven damaged. In fact operational research later showed that only four tanks and five half-tracks had been hit. Most vehicles had been abandoned and destroyed by their own crews. Nevertheless, the Typhoon's lack of precision was more than compensated by the psychological effect it had on German panzer crews.

Meanwhile combat command B of the 2nd Armored Division finished preparing their roadblocks and ambushes in the area of Grimesnil. The Germans in the Roncey pocket, under heavy pressure from the 3rd Armored Division to the north, were bound to try to escape past them.

Near Saint-Denis-le-Gast, a mile from Grimesnil, the 82nd Reconnaissance Battalion set up a block covered by anti-tank guns and the 92nd Field Artillery Battalion. They saw a column of vehicles approaching led by a couple of American armoured cars, but these had been captured and were being used as a *ruse de guerre*. As they passed, an anti-tank gunner spotted a German half-track immediately behind them and opened fire. The artillery also reacted quickly, firing over open sights, and the German column was destroyed.

Soon afterwards, the command post of the 2nd Armored's reserve was nearly overrun in a surprise attack, but the defenders, mostly clerks and rear-echelon personnel, held their nerve. With the help of a bright moon and the light from burning vehicles, they picked their targets at short range as the German infantry charged. This was clearly demonstrated later that morning when officers went out to examine the corpses of the attackers. The Germans had been killed 'by single rifle shots rather than machinegun bursts'.

Another report cited the bravery of Sergeant Bishop, whose body was found with seven dead Germans around him, and Staff Sergeant Barnes, who cut the throats of three German attackers with a trench knife. 'Action during the fight was so mixed up that an aid man looked up to find a German aid man sharing his slit trench. For a few minutes both men frantically pointed at their Red Cross armbands, then frisked each other for possible weapons.'

The same night, a couple of miles to the south-east, two companies of armoured infantry in the process of setting up a roadblock were taken by surprise when the Germans rolled 'their vehicles down the hill toward the Grimesnil road, with their engines off'. In the desperate fighting in the dark, the armoured infantry suffered heavy casualties not just from enemy fire, but also from their own artillery and tanks. When Lieutenant Colonel Crowley arrived at 07.00 hours on 30 July with the reserve company of his battalion, the battle was virtually over. The whole area was littered with burning vehicles. The roadblock itself had been overrun and Crowley could not contact one of the attacked companies by radio. But the Germans were exhausted and cowed by the artillery. His men picked up 300 prisoners in the area. The worst part of that morning was to be under consistent fire from the 4th Armored Division to their west: 'Even the use of yellow smoke failed to stop them until Colonel Crowley established radio communication with them.'

There were two main German columns trying to escape that night, one of which contained ninety-six vehicles, including 'tanks, 150 mm and 170 mm guns – towed and self-propelled – half-tracks, staff cars, motorcycles and trucks'. The troops came from three divisions, the

275th Infanterie-Division, the 17th SS Panzergrenadier-Division and the reconnaissance battalion of the 2nd SS Panzer-Division *Das Reich*. 'The mortars set the vehicles on fire, then the artillery of the 62nd and 78th [Armored Field Artillery] started firing at the crossroads, and without registering, continued to fire all the way down the road'.

A badly damaged M-10 tank destroyer had come to a halt by the side of the road from Saint-Denis to Lengronne. The crew inside played possum as the German column passed, then, as soon as the last half-track had gone by, they brought their three-inch gun to bear and began knocking them out, one by one, firing twenty-eight rounds altogether.

The main force at the crossroads had to pull back to higher ground, where infantry could protect the Shermans from German foot soldiers trying to stalk them with Panzerfaust launchers. The first vehicle in the German column, a Mark IV tank towing an 88 mm gun, advanced towards the defensive position and was destroyed by a tank shell. 'Then the organized slaughter started,' an officer reported. The mortar platoon began rapid fire down the line of the convoy, 'a ratio of one white phosphorus to three high explosive'. The vehicles set ablaze by the white phosphorus lit up the scene, aiding the tank gunners and mortar crews, who dropped high-explosive rounds into the open backs of the German half-tracks. While their gunners continued to engage targets, tank commanders were having to fight off German infantry with the .50 machine gun mounted over their hatch.

One officer recorded that 'as daylight broke, about 300 German infantrymen tried to advance through a swamp to the north of the Grimesnil road . . . the tanks went after them and killed nearly all. Close to 300 bodies were found in and around this swamp.' Another 600 dead were found along the road which had been shelled – 'a bloody mass of arms and legs and heads, [and] cremated corpses . . . at least three German women were found in various stages of decapitation'. One of them had been driving a major general's staff car. 'The major general was identified by his uniform, but when battalion officers returned later they found that souvenir hunters had taken all his clothes.'*

---

* The identity of this officer is not certain. It might have been Generalleutnant Dietrich Kraiss, the commander of the 352nd Infanterie-Division, although his death is recorded several days later on 2 August.

The American graves registration service retrieved 1,150 German dead from the convoy of ninety-six vehicles. 'The whole area was raw meat splattered on burned and ruined vehicles,' observed one officer. Another report stated that 'prisoners were coming in so fast that it became impossible to count them. Many stated that they had not eaten for two or three days.' Meanwhile the 82nd Reconnaissance Battalion slipped south to seize bridges over the River Sienne.

Brigadier General Hickey's combat command from the 3rd Armored Division, following the German retreat, found in Roncey that 'German equipment, abandoned and broken, cluttered the road to such an extent that progress through the main street was impossible, and the task force had to go through the back streets to get out of the town'. A tank dozer had to be brought up to clear the main road. So many German soldiers were surrendering that they had to send them to the rear without a guard. When the 3rd Armored reached the area of Grimesnil and Saint-Denis-le-Gast, a medical officer noted in his diary 'Carnage gruesome. Includes enemy dead smashed flat by our tanks.'

Generalmajor Rudolph-Christoff Freiherr von Gersdorff, the new chief of staff of the Seventh Army, who had reached their advanced command post three miles north-east of Avranches on the afternoon of 29 July, found a disastrous situation.* Nobody had issued orders to blow any of the bridges and no landline communications existed. As a result of the German retreat away from the coast, which had so infuriated Kluge, the American 6th and 4th Armored Divisions were now virtually unopposed.

In Granville, on the coast, the Germans began blowing up the port installations at 01.00 hours and it continued for five hours. The local *commissariat de police* reported that German soldiers were looting and stealing every vehicle they could find to make their escape south. One American tank platoon even passed within 100 yards of the Seventh Army command post without spotting it. At midnight, Oberstgruppen-führer Hausser and his staff pulled out to withdraw east to Mortain.

There was consternation at La Roche-Guyon and at the *Wolfsschanze*

---

* Hitler, who had approved his appointment, was unaware that Gersdorff had been ready to kill him with a suicide bomb on 21 March 1943 in Berlin.

in East Prussia. General Warlimont at Führer headquarters recorded that Kluge was given 'urgent orders to prevent any penetration into Avranches. Everybody saw that the whole front in Normandy was breaking up.' Hitler was also concerned about the fate of the 17th SS Panzergrenadier-Division *Götz von Berlichingen*, which appeared to have been 'virtually swallowed up' during the retreat. 'Nobody ever knew or could figure out what happened to it, despite frantic enquiries. Naturally we were especially interested in this division because the subject of the fighting qualities of an SS division was a "hot iron" – something you could not touch. Hitler was inclined to believe everything which was favourable about his SS troops. He never permitted any reproach against his "black guards".'

The bulk of the German forces had withdrawn in the direction of Percy. An American reconnaissance troop, trying to find an undefended route to Percy, searched the side roads, but found they were all blocked. On one small country lane, the sergeant in the lead Jeep spotted some German soldiers creeping behind a hedgerow. 'Pour it to them!' he yelled to the soldier standing in the back, manning the .50 machine gun. The gunner swept the line, killing most of them with 'incinerator' (tracer) bullets. He joked afterwards that the bullets were humane, as they sterilized the wound going in and the one going out the other side. Many soldiers saw it as payback time after all the hard fighting in the *bocage*.

The Germans had virtually no forces left to defend the coast road. A field replacement battalion on the south side of the River Sienne had rounded up stragglers who had managed to slip through the American screen. The 6th and 4th Armored Divisions, already under Patton's direction, were well on their way to Avranches. Patton did not accept any excuse for delay. 'The thing to do is to rush them off their feet before they get set,' he wrote in his diary on 29 July. He was in an exuberant mood. Breakthrough had been achieved. The breakout, which he felt belonged to him by divine right, was about to begin.

22

Operation Cobra – Breakout

On 30 July, when the 4th Armored Division was in striking distance of
Avranches, Montgomery launched Operation Bluecoat. He did not
usually mount an offensive in such a hurry. It seems that, once again,
the initiative had come from Dempsey, but that did not stop Montgomery from implying that it was his plan. He sent a signal to Eisenhower: 'I have ordered Dempsey to throw all caution overboard and to
take any risks he likes, and to accept any casualties, and to step on the
gas for Vire.'

The 13th/18th Hussars were in reserve, carrying out some much
needed maintenance work on their tanks, when their brigade commander 'grinds to a halt in his jeep' and tells one of their officers that
the regiment is due to take part in a battle on Sunday morning. They
were to move out at 06.00 hours the next morning. Their tank engines
were all in bits and they had to start reassembling them frantically.
Some units received only thirty-six hours' warning.

To move two corps from the Caen front to attack in the far west of
the British sector in less than forty-eight hours was a nightmare with
the narrow roads. Many units received their operational orders only as
they were approaching their start-lines. One of the 13th/18th's squadron leaders heard a rumour from headquarters and recorded it in his
diary: 'Monty is determined to make us catch up on the Yanks who are
doing magnificently. The only difference between us is (a) that their
army is twice as big and (b) that we have double the opposition against
us.' Although the proportions were a little exaggerated, British and

Canadian troops felt with some justification that they had been fighting the war of attrition against the panzer divisions and now the Americans were getting all the glory in the newspapers.

Bluecoat took place south of Caumont, where the British had taken over a part of the front from the Americans. One of the reasons for choosing this sector was that there were no SS panzer divisions there. O'Connor's VIII Corps was to be led by the 15th (Scottish) Division and the Guards 6th Tank Brigade. The 11th Armoured and the Guards Armoured Divisions were behind them, ready to break through. On their left, Bucknall's XXX Corps with the 7th Armoured Division was ordered to take Aunay-sur-Odon and then the Mont Pinçon massif. The idea was to seize the high ground there so as to control the roads to the south of the ridge, which the Germans would need for their retreat.

Sunday, 30 July was such a sweltering day that the infantry were allowed to attack in shirt-sleeve order, but at least the skies were clear for air support. Bluecoat was preceded by another bombing attack and a heavy artillery bombardment. The 15th Scottish got off to a good start, attacking on a narrow front. When their advance was slowed by the German 326th Infanterie-Division, the supporting tanks of the 4th Coldstream and the 3rd Scots Guards pushed on through. Their commanders told the infantry to follow their tracks. This was against British Army doctrine, but the commanders of the 6th Guards Brigade and the 15th Scottish had agreed before the battle to do this if necessary.

The steeply wooded slopes of the ridge would have defeated most tanks, but the Churchill, despite all its faults as a fighting machine, managed extraordinarily well. The Germans, not expecting British armour to get through, had no heavy anti-tank guns in their front line. They had kept their battalion of assault guns well back. As a result the Coldstream tanks reached their objective of Hill 309 by 16.00 hours. They had penetrated five miles behind the German lines. On their right the Scots Guards tanks had charged towards Hill 226 through hedgerows and orchards: 'The crews were shaken and bruised, commanders struck by low branches and pelted with small, hard cider apples which accumulated on the floors of tank turrets.' That evening, the Scottish battalions caught up with the two Guards tank battalions and prepared their hilltops for defence.

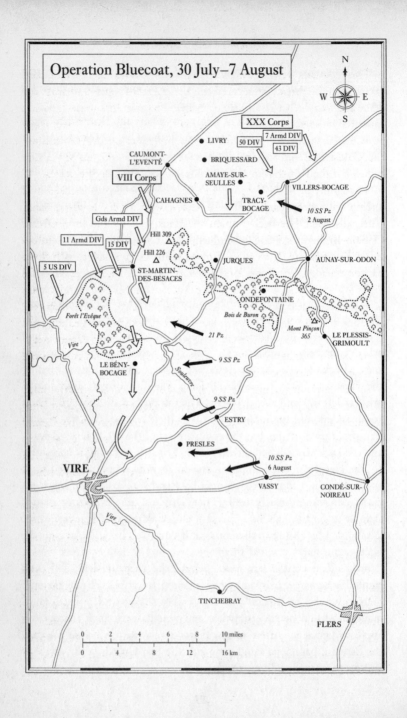

The Germans were unusually slow to react. When Eberbach finally recognized the threat, he ordered the 21st Panzer-Division to cross the Orne and join the battle. In the meantime, the 326th Infanterie-Division mounted desperate counter-attacks on the two hills and their commander, Generalmajor von Drabich-Wächter, was killed. They pushed the Coldstream and the 2nd Glasgow Highlanders off the hill at one point, but the British retook it in a counter-attack soon afterwards.

The failure of XXX Corps to advance on the left when blocked by a stream with steep banks left VIII Corps with a very exposed flank. This was what Eberbach wanted to attack, but by the time Oberst Oppeln-Bronikowski had assembled the 21st Panzer, their counter-attack was too late. It went in at 06.00 hours on 1 August, with three panzergrenadier battalions, each down to 200 men, the last 14 Mark IV tanks of the 1st Battalion of its panzer regiment and the last eight Tigers of the 503rd Heavy Panzer Battalion. The British counter-attacked, reaching the 21st Panzer's divisional command post. The headquarters staff had to flee, abandoning all their vehicles. The 21st Panzer withdrew, having lost almost a third of its strength. A furious row ensued at their corps headquarters over the failure.

British armour–infantry cooperation had improved greatly since Goodwood, but their Churchill and Cromwell tanks still stood little chance against the Tigers of the 503rd and the 502nd SS Heavy Panzer Battalion, as well as huge Ferdinand Jagdpanzer assault guns. One of the 3rd Scots Guards squadrons, having reached their objective after a wild ride across country, encountered three Ferdinands, which within moments knocked out twelve of their sixteen tanks. One of the Ferdinands passed close by a British artillery officer. He had a clear view of its commander, 'wearing only a vest presumably because of the heat, and laughing'. The II SS Panzer Corps was also diverted to block the British advance.

While the 15th Scottish and the 6th Guards Tank Brigade fought their battles, the Guards Armoured Division attacked Saint-Martin-des-Besaces, a large village from which roads extended in all directions. But the Germans defended it furiously, supported by assault guns.

On the right, the 11th Armoured Division had a stroke of luck, which it wasted no time in exploiting. On 31 July, an armoured car troop of the 2nd Household Cavalry Regiment managed to slip through German lines in the Forêt de l'Evêque. Six miles further on, they found that the bridge over the River Souleuvre was intact. They rapidly disposed of the only sentry. The bridge lay on the boundary between the German 326th Infanterie-Division and the 3rd Paratroop Division, which is probably why neither had taken proper responsibility for it. When they radioed through their discovery, the Household Cavalry commanding officer could hardly believe it and asked them to reconfirm their position. He immediately informed Major General 'Pip' Roberts of the 11th Armoured Division. Although the route lay to the west of their line of advance and in the American V Corps sector, Roberts sent the 29th Armoured Brigade at full speed, with infantry mounted on the tanks, to secure the crossing. It was already known as 'Dickie's Bridge', after the troop leader, Lieutenant D. B. Powle, who had taken it. Roberts subsequently sought O'Connor's approval to change his axis. This dramatic advance, which took 11th Armoured all the way to the high ground round Le Bény-Bocage, forced General Meindl to withdraw his 3rd Paratroop Division.

Just over thirty miles to the south-west, the first tanks from Wood's 4th Armored Division entered Avranches, the gateway to Brittany and central France, shortly before dusk on 30 July. The town was in chaos. On the west coast, the remaining German forces knew they were in a race to escape encirclement. The naval coastal battery near Granville had destroyed its guns and set off south behind the American spearhead. Oberst von Aulock and his *Kampfgruppe* were also trying to escape south through Avranches. Kluge was still hoping to hold on to this key position, but as the Americans advanced with four armoured divisions abreast – the 6th, 4th, 5th and 2nd – he had no reserves left to hold them.

Although American tanks were already in Avranches, groups of German stragglers were still trying to get through the town. A small pioneer detachment from the 256th Infanterie-Division sat for a long moment on the cliffs in their Soviet truck, captured on the eastern front, gazing at the 'unforgettable sight'. 'Below us the tidal shallows with Mont Saint-Michel in moonlight and in front of us Avranches in flames,' wrote Gefreiter Spiekerkötter. 'The Americans were already there and wanted to prevent us from breaking out. How we got through and over the bridge, I still do not know. I remember only that two [German] officers with drawn pistols tried to seize our truck from us.'

At 01.00 hours on 31 July, Feldmarschall von Kluge received a call from Generalleutnant Speidel, the chief of staff of Army Group B. Speidel warned the Commander-in-Chief West that the LXXXIV Corps had fallen back towards Villedieu, but they could not contact them: 'The situation is extraordinarily serious. The fighting strength of the troops has declined considerably.' The High Command, he added, should be informed that the left flank had collapsed. The threat to Brittany and the west coast ports was all too clear. Many officers and soldiers would have put it more strongly. They described the sense of disaster as '*Weltuntergangsstimmung*' – a feeling that their whole world was collapsing. On the left flank of the breakthrough, American divisions were forcing the Germans back over the River Vire.

Thirty-five minutes later, Kluge spoke to General Farmbacher, the commander of XXV Corps in the Brittany peninsula. Farmbacher told him of the scratch units he was trying to get together and requested 'a most forceful order to the Navy, whose co-operation is insufficient'. Kluge also rang Eberbach to ask whether Panzer Group West was in a position to hand over any more formations to the Seventh Army. He replied that it was impossible. The British double attack on Vire and towards Aunay-sur-Odon had begun. If any more panzer divisions were transferred, the British would at last break through to Falaise and Argentan, thus cutting off the whole of the Seventh Army as well.

At 02.00 Kluge issued an order that 'under all circumstances the Pontaubault bridge [south of Avranches] must remain in our hands. Avranches must be retaken.' Kluge was still furious with Hausser because the 'fatal decision of the Seventh Army to break out to the south-east has led to the collapse of the front'.

Although the 3rd Armored Division was criticized for its slow advance, Task Force X, commanded by Lieutenant Colonel Leander L. Doane, made an extraordinary dash forward. His column left the high ground south of Gavray at 16.07 hours, heading for Villedieu-les-Poêles. The weather was 'clear as a bell', and the twenty P-47 Thunderbolts flying air support for the column took out any German columns flushed out by Doane's rapid advance. Doane was in direct radio communication with them and could direct the pilots on to any target ahead. The soldiers in the armoured vehicles below were fascinated by the spray of empty cartridge cases as the Thunderbolts roared over them, strafing likely positions.

At 18.00 hours, they reached the edge of Villedieu. Despite having advanced ten miles in under two hours, Colonel Doane received the order, 'Do not stop on initial objective. Proceed to Sée river before halting for the night. Corps commander directs you to move with greater speed.' The Sée was just beyond Brécey, another sixteen miles further south. Doane ordered his men to bypass Villedieu and carry on at top speed. He also asked the Thunderbolts overhead to reconnoitre the road ahead.

The support from the P-47s was so close that one pilot radioed to Doane that he was going to bomb a German tank only fifty yards to his left and that he had better take cover. Air–tank cooperation could not have been closer. Another Thunderbolt pilot flying shotgun over Task Force Z 'facetiously suggested' to its commander 'that he had better draw in his antenna', because he was attacking right over their heads.

As they came to the outskirts of Brécey, Doane, who was in the lead tank, told the Thunderbolts to hold off, since there seemed to be no enemy present. But as his Sherman turned the corner into the main street of the town he saw 'crowds of German soldiers lounging along the curb'. Unable to fire at that moment because his radio operator was in the gunner's seat, Doane began taking potshots at the German infantry with his Colt .45 pistol. It was 'practically a Hollywood entry', the report stated. The following tanks, however, traversed their turrets left and right, raking the street and houses with machine-gun fire.

The main bridge over the Sée had been destroyed, so the column turned east to try another bridge just outside the town. They spotted a group of German infantry lying around in an orchard and sprayed them with machine-gun fire too. But when they reached the crossing, they found that the bridge there had also been destroyed. Doane radioed back and soon the engineer platoon came forward. Its commander decided that his men could construct a ford nearby, using one of the tank dozers. Crews dismounted to carry stones to give some sort of basis to the soft bed of the river, but only a few vehicles managed to get across before it became impassable.

Meanwhile the rear part of the column was approaching Brécey, but the German infantry had reorganized and was providing strong opposition. Doane pushed on with his leading tanks and reached the northern side of Hill 242 as night fell. In Brécey, the fighting was extremely confused. Captain Carlton Parish Russell of the 36th Armored Infantry left his half-track to stride back down the column to find out what was going on. He saw some Jeeps with their camouflage netting on fire. Then he saw a soldier trying to rip the burning material away. He shouted at him that if he did not get out of that camouflage uniform, he would be taken for a German. The man turned and he saw that he really was part of the Waffen-SS. This German detachment, which had been cut off, was trying to seize the vehicles they had ambushed for their escape. The SS soldier knocked the pistol from his hand and was bringing up his rifle when Russell seized it from him and knocked him out. He used it in the ensuing firefight with the Germans in the middle of the village.

Task Force Z, driving south from Gavray towards Avranches on 31 July, faced much more resistance, encountering roadblocks covered by tanks and anti-tank guns. But they also caught a German column in the open trying to escape across their route. They inflicted heavy damage on reconnaissance vehicles and half-tracks. General Doyle O. Hickey, in a command half-track near the front of the task force, saw one of his self-propelled 105 mm guns blast one of the half-tracks to pieces at a range of less than fifty yards.

When another column of the 3rd Armored Division also reached Avranches, Ernest Hemingway was just behind the spearhead. His accompanying officer, Lieutenant Stevenson, remarked that staying close to Hemingway was 'more dangerous than being [Brigadier General] Roosevelt's aide'. Hemingway, who had attached himself to General Barton's 4th Infantry Division, persuaded Stevenson to accompany him on risky trips in either a Mercedes convertible or a motorcycle with sidecar, both abandoned in the German retreat. He wrote to his next-in-line wife, Mary Welsh, describing 'a very jolly and gay life full of deads, German loot, much shooting, much fighting, hedges, small hills, dusty roads, green country, wheatfields, dead cows, dead horses, tanks, 88s, Kraftwagens, dead US guys'. He was soon joined by Robert Capa and nearly got him killed as well when they lost their way and ran into a German anti-tank gun. Hemingway, who had to shelter in a ditch under fire, afterwards accused Capa of failing to help in a crisis so that he could 'take the first picture of the famous writer's dead body'.

Behind the ill-defined lines of the front, the American breakthrough caused chaos of a different sort. In Granville, locals had begun to pillage the houses abandoned by the Germans. Even the most respectable of citizens were making off with furniture, from dining chairs to a cradle. A lynch mob of 300 to 400 people wanted to string up a collaborator. The police had a difficult time persuading them to calm down and hand over their prisoner for a proper trial. During the next few days, they also had to round up German stragglers attempting to hide, often dressed in civilian clothes which they had stolen. One woman on the Villedieu road had taken pity on a German soldier and hidden him herself. She was arrested and held at the local fire station, while her young children were handed over for safekeeping to Madame Roy, the keeper of the public gardens.

An elderly German *Unteroffizier* was captured in civilian clothes, hiding in a farm near Avranches. '*Ah, Monsieur*,' he said to the farmer who had called an American patrol to take him away, 'it's a great sadness for me. I am here and my son is a soldier in the American Army.' The farmer, who had heard that many young German emigrants were serving in the US forces, was inclined to believe him.

The 6th Armored Division was also pushing on ahead through the Avranches gap. In their first actions, the tank crews had been trigger-happy on spotting any group of Germans, however small. But when thirty Germans popped up from behind a hedge with their hands up, they had to take them with them, as they could not spare any men. They made them sit on the hoods of half-tracks and Jeeps. 'Our boys got their souvenirs that day,' an officer remarked. Their advance guard consisted of a company of tanks, a company of infantry in half-tracks, a battery of field artillery, a company of tank destroyers, a section of engineers in half-tracks ready to deal with mines, and a reconnaissance section. They moved at a steady fifteen mph and at times they would overtake 'unsuspecting Jerries bicycling or walking'. The Sherman crews loaded everything that was not essential on the outside of the tank so that they could stow '150 rounds of 75s and 12,000 rounds of .30 calibre', twice the normal load of ammunition.

To compound their problems, the Germans were suffering from increasingly audacious attacks by the Resistance further south. A train with sixty-nine wagons bringing urgently needed artillery ammunition had just been blown up in the Landes, while an armoured train was derailed in a tunnel north of Souillac. The British intercepted a signal calling for a construction train 'under strong military escort'.

On the evening of 31 July, Patton drove to the VIII Corps command post to see Middleton. Middleton's 4th Armored Division had secured the line of the River Sélune south of Avranches, as ordered, but he could not get in touch with Bradley to see what he should do next. Patton, apparently controlling his exasperation, told him that 'throughout history it had always been fatal not to cross a river'. Although he did not take over command officially until noon the next day, he made it very clear that VIII Corps was to cross immediately. Soon afterwards, a message came in to say that the bridge at Pontaubault had been captured. It was damaged but passable. Patton told Middleton to send the 4th and 6th Armored Divisions across as fast as possible.

South of Pontaubault, the road divided. One route led south and west towards Rennes and Brest. The other headed east towards the Seine and Paris. Patton went to bed at one in the morning of 1 August knowing that, eleven hours later, the Third Army would be fully operational under his command with four army corps, Middleton's VIII Corps, Haislip's XV Corps, Walker's XX Corps and Cook's XII Corps. The XV Corps immediately issued to its three divisions a warning order which clearly revealed the Patton style: 'As many troops as possible to be motorized and tanks to lead throughout.' Also at midday on 1 August, Bradley became commander-in-chief of 12th Army Group, with General Hodges taking over the First Army, which would continue the attack towards the line of the Vire and then on to Mortain.

On 1 August, Kluge was at Seventh Army forward headquarters with Hausser and his new chief of staff, Oberst von Gersdorff, when they heard of the American seizure of Avranches. According to his aide,

Oberleutnant Tangermann, he said, 'Gentlemen, this breakthrough means for us and the German people the beginning of a decisive and bitter end. I see no remaining possibility of halting this ongoing attack.' Some of his colleagues felt that the effects of his serious car crash in Russia the year before had started to show. He was losing the determination he had shown when he took over from Rundstedt.

As soon as the news reached the *Wolfsschanze* in East Prussia, Hitler issued an order to Kluge: 'The enemy is not under any circumstances to break out into the open. Army Group B will prepare a counter-attack with all panzer units to thrust as far as Avranches, cut off the units that have broken through and destroy them. All available panzer forces are to be released from their present positions without replacement and employed for this purpose under the command of General der Panzertruppen Eberbach. The future of the campaign in France depends upon this counter-attack.'

Kluge warned that the withdrawal of panzer divisions would lead to a collapse of the whole front, including the British sector. He proposed instead that German forces should be withdrawn behind the Seine, abandoning western France entirely. The panzer divisions could protect the retreat of the infantry divisions without motor transport. Hitler rejected this furiously and insisted that if his orders were carried out there would be 'certain victory in the end'. Kluge sensed that this would be a catastrophic decision, but there was nothing he could do. Hitler, obsessed with his maps but with no idea of the reality on the ground, had begun to plan Operation Lüttich, the great counter-attack from Mortain towards Avranches. But the enemy was breaking out into the open. By noon, the American 4th Armored Division was across the Sélune and 'round the corner into Brittany'.

The Americans found German resistance much tougher on the left, with heavy fighting round Percy and Villedieu, which the 3rd Armored Division had bypassed. The 4th Infantry Division called up four battalions of artillery to deal with German positions. The 155 mm 'Long Toms' fired a total of three 'serenades', the most intense bombardment on offer, and finally the German guns fell silent. Late in the afternoon, the 4th Division's reconnaissance squadron entered Villedieu.

Tessy was also captured that day after heavy and bitter fighting.

The Germans in retreat could resort to the brutality of the eastern front. According to Lieutenant Colonel Teague, commanding the 3rd Battalion of the 22nd Infantry Regiment, 'One of our trucks (an ambulance) was sent up the road north from the aid station near La Tilandière toward Villebaudon. The Jerries, attacking toward the highway, captured the truck, shot six wounded men in it, and made a road block out of the truck.'

Front-line troops adopted a very dismissive attitude towards the large numbers of prisoners they were taking. Middleton's VIII Corps had taken 7,000 prisoners in just three days, out of the whole First Army's bag of 20,000 in six days. When a battalion of the 8th Infantry Division captured a couple of hundred Germans, they sent them back with just one guard. Sometimes they returned weapons to Polish and Russian prisoners and told them to escort the Germans, which may well have led to several of the latter failing to reach the stockade alive. Empty supply trucks going back north were also used. 'We passed columns of prisoners, on foot and in trucks, but all under guard,' noted an officer with the 29th Infantry Division near Percy. 'They seemed low-spirited as to the older ones. The only defiant ones were the young.' Over-optimistic rumours had meanwhile begun to spread in German units that they were to be withdrawn behind the Seine.

On 2 August, fighting continued in the southern part of Villedieu after most of the town was cleared. American tanks drove a group of German infantry armed with Panzerfaust launchers into the railway station. The Shermans fired at the building with their 75 mm main armament until they had demolished the whole structure on top of them.

On the road towards the Forêt de Saint-Sever, where many German units were reorganizing, heavy fighting continued on the hills either side, especially Hill 213. Lieutenant Colonel Johnson was taking his battalion round the side of the ridge to outflank the Germans on the summit. 'As we came over the crest and saw the road I rubbed my eyes,' he wrote. 'I thought we must have got our directions mixed. The whole road was jammed with traffic of the 3rd Armored Division bumper to bumper – tanks, trucks, Jeeps and ambulances. I looked across the road and saw a medical station.' Nobody seemed to realize that a major battle was going on just 500 yards away. The 12th Infantry, one of their other officers observed, was 'so tired they could hardly walk up the hill, let alone attack up it'. German artillery fire from the Forêt de Saint-Sever to their east was very heavy and caused many casualties. This, combined with Luftwaffe attacks at night, kept men 'in a state of jitters', resulting in an increased rate of combat fatigue.

While some Germans fought ruthlessly in retreat, others respected the rules of war. Captain Ware, the battalion surgeon, reported that two men hit on patrol had not been found. Four medics, led by Corporal Baylor, set out in a Jeep with a large red cross flag to find them. 'One man stood on the hood and held the flag open so it could not be overlooked. The jeep rounded the bend of the road [and] reached the first casualty. He was dead. As the aid man was examining him the Germans fired a machinegun which hit Cpl Baylor in the chest. The other three crawled back under fire dragging the wounded man and leaving the two bodies and the jeep.' Captain Ware decided to abandon the attempt. 'But just as this decision was reached a German wearing a Geneva [Red Cross] brassard and carrying a white flag came round the bend of the road walking toward them. He was promptly covered. All the American weapons present were pointed at him but fortunately no shot was fired. As the German came up we could see that he was sweating profusely. But he did not falter. He handed me the attached note which no one present could read. A German speaking soldier of the anti-tank platoon was sent for. The German told him that he had been sent by his lieutenant to apologize for his soldiers firing on the American medics. The German was still sweating [and] kept removing his helmet to mop his brow. He said he had volunteered for this mission. He also told us that both the American casualties were dead. The German said that the note from his Lieutenant assured us that we might return and remove our casualties as well as the jeep and that the Germans would not fire again. We asked the German if he would like to stay with us now that he was across the lines. He laughed and said he supposed it made no difference which side he stayed with, but he pointed out that if he did stay it would look bad for the Americans since the Germans would think he had been detained by force.'

The American advance was still slowed by traffic jams on the narrow country roads and also by attacks from groups of German stragglers.

'The small number of Germans are causing us difficulty out of all proportion to their numbers,' the headquarters of the 4th Infantry Division recorded. 'However it is probably part of the plan to leave the enemy in position on our left flank in the hope of an encirclement.'

This assessment of Eisenhower's and Bradley's thinking was premature, but close to the mark. The original plan was to storm through the Avranches gap and seize ports in Brittany to speed the Allied supply lines for the advance to the Seine. But now a huge opening lay between the German Seventh Army and the Loire. On 3 August, Major General John Wood's 4th Armored Division swung round the west side of Rennes to the south. He was low on fuel and ammunition, so could not seize the city, but he had now sealed off the whole of the Brittany peninsula. Facing east, he sensed that the Germans had no reserves to block a charge straight towards Paris and the Seine. Eisenhower and Bradley both came to a similar conclusion. It offered an opportunity rare in war. German generals saw the implications with horror. The news that an American armoured division had reached Rennes, wrote Bayerlein, 'had a shattering effect, like a bomb-burst, upon us'.

23

Brittany and Operation Bluecoat

Brittany, as the Allies knew well, was one of the great centres of resistance in France. This was why the first Allied troops to drop in France had been the 2ème Régiment de Chasseurs Parachutistes just before midnight on 5 June. By the end of June the Gaullist-led Resistance in the FFI and the Communist-led FTP mustered a total of 19,500 men. By the end of July they had 31,500, of whom 13,750 had weapons.

On 4 July, General Koenig, who commanded the FFI from London, had summoned Colonel Eon to his offices in Upper Grosvenor Street. Eon was to command Resistance forces in Brittany. His second in command would be de Gaulle's chief intelligence officer, André de Wavrin, always known by his codename of Colonel 'Passy'. They would receive a staff of twenty officers and be supported by nine extra of the three-man Jedburgh teams to help train and direct their forces. Weapons would be provided for 30,000 men. But with the apparent stalemate on both the American and the British fronts at that time, the weapons drops did not receive a high priority.

The American capture of Avranches on 1 August took staffs in London by surprise. Two days later, at 18.00 hours, the BBC gave the coded message to launch guerrilla warfare throughout Brittany. On the morning of 4 August, Koenig took Eon on one side to ask if he would agree to his whole headquarters parachuting together en bloc, whether or not they had undergone parachute training. Eon, who had never made a parachute jump before, agreed and so did the other untrained officers and men. The British authorities, nevertheless, insisted that Eon, as he was being driven to the airfield, should sign 'a written declaration accepting all responsibility for making a parachute jump without training'. Fortunately, only parachutes attached to arms containers failed to open and the party landed safely. One of the containers held nine million francs. When it was found two miles from the drop zone, one million was already missing.

General Bradley, in contact with Koenig at SHAEF headquarters still back in England, issued an order that all Resistance groups in Brittany now came under the orders of General Patton's Third Army. They were to protect the railway along the north coast of the Brittany peninsula, to seize the high ground north of Vannes, to provide guides for US forces and to 'intensify general guerrilla activity, short of open warfare, in all Brittany'. By the time Eon and his party landed, 6,000 members of the FFI had occupied the area north of Vannes and seized the railway line. And on the night of 4 August, a reinforced squadron of 150 French SAS from the 3rd Régiment de Chasseurs Parachutistes dropped behind German lines to protect the railway lines east of Brest on the north side of the peninsula. In fact, the FFI and FTP were to do much more than Bradley asked of them.

Patton's charge into Brittany with the 6th and 4th Armored Divisions soon became confused, if not chaotic. This was due partly to bad communications. The radio sets were simply not good enough for the distances involved, while Patton and Middleton, the commander of VIII Corps, had utterly different approaches. Patton, the brash yet secretly thin-skinned cavalryman, believed in bold advance and the rapid exploitation of any opportunity. Middleton was an excellent corps commander, but he was an infantryman. Every advance in his book needed to be carefully planned. He was unprepared for Patton's style of warfare.

Patton's thinking was shared by General John Wood of the 4th Armored Division, 'a second General Patton if I ever saw one,' observed an officer in the 8th Infantry Division. Wood, 'a brawny, jovial type', was equally immune to indecision. From Pontaubault, he dashed south to the regional capital of Rennes. The city was too strongly held for him to take without infantry, so early on 3 August he circled it to the south, waiting for reinforcements and more fuel. His instinct was to head for Angers and then Paris, but he knew that that would alarm Middleton.

In Rennes itself, mixed groups of German troops, mainly remnants of the 91st Luftlande-Division, prepared their escape and destroyed equipment and files. Meanwhile the American 8th Infantry Division had arrived and began to bombard the city. Members of the French Resistance had slipped through the lines and told them of the exact position of Gestapo headquarters in Rennes. They did not say that it was just opposite the hospital where American and British prisoners of war were held, but fortunately there were few injuries. Other members of the Resistance, on spotting the hurried departure of the Gestapo, raided the headquarters and took the food there to feed the malnourished prisoners. That night, another FFI group blew up a German munitions dump just outside the town. A French doctor then reached the Americans outside the town with news of the prisoners and the 8th Division artillery ceased shelling.

The German troops slipped away during the night towards Saint-Nazaire, at the mouth of the Loire. The only ones who stayed behind were 'a handful of drunks'. They were easily rounded up by the American infantry on 4 August, 'but they had to be protected from the French'. The remaining population – some 60,000 out of 120,000 – surged on to the streets to welcome the Americans, who rushed medical units to the hospital. 'One paratrooper patient with a bad face wound came up and shook my hands and cried,' a captain reported. Soldiers immediately gave whatever they could, including their own combat kit, to those whose uniforms had fallen to pieces.

Middleton, back at VIII Corps headquarters, faced a difficult choice. He sympathized with Wood's desire to strike east, but his instructions remained to capture the ports on the coast of Brittany and he was not in contact with Patton. Middleton drove to see Wood and sent the 4th Armored Division back south-westwards to take Vannes and then Lorient. Vannes fell rapidly, but Lorient appeared impregnable.

On 4 August, Patton himself, escorted by an armoured car, drove down into Brittany. He was following the advance of the 6th Armored Division commanded by Major General Grow, whom he had ordered to rush for Brest, the main port of Brittany, bypassing all resistance. Patton whooped with joy every time they ran off a map and had to open a new one. This was warfare as he loved it. But Patton had not told Middleton the objective he had given the 6th Armored. Grow then received a signal from Middleton, ordering him not to bypass Saint-Malo, on the north coast of the peninsula, and to attack it the next day. Grow requested that the order should be cancelled, but Middleton was firm.

Grow was about to sit down with a cup of coffee outside his tent in a wheatfield, when Patton suddenly appeared. 'What in hell are you doing sitting here?' he demanded. 'I thought I told you to get to Brest.' Grow explained his order from Middleton and his chief of staff produced the written order. Patton read it, then folded it up. 'And he was a *good* doughboy, too,' Patton murmured to himself. 'I'll see Middleton,' he said to Grow. 'You go ahead where I told you to go.'

The confusion continued, but Patton settled the problem of communicating with divisions spread out over hundreds of miles. He allocated the 6th Cavalry Group to report on the exact position of all his divisions and armoured columns as well as on the enemy. Its thirteen reconnaissance platoons, each with six armoured cars and six quarter-ton trucks, had high-powered radios which could also act as a back-up if the Signal Corps network failed. The 6th Cavalry was soon known as 'General Patton's Household Cavalry'.

The advance of the 6th Armored Division towards Brest was hardly unopposed. Groups of German stragglers and improvised combat groups fought delaying actions. During daylight hours, the columns had support from Mustangs of the 363rd Fighter Group, but 'every night from 3 August to 6 August we had to fight for our bivouac areas,' reported Captain Donley from the 6th Armored. On 5 August, the town of Huelgoat was reported to be clear, so General Grow rode in with a tank and an armoured car. He was greeted with 'intense small arms fire from all directions'. Donley's company of armoured infantry was sent to get him out, supported by tanks. The German paratroopers in the town were now trapped. The armoured infantry accounted for many of them, but the FFI begged to be allowed to finish the rest off. They claimed that 'the paratroopers had cut off the hands of a woman' and the FFI 'was mighty anxious to mop them up'.

The 6th Armored put the FFI into reconnaissance Jeeps, known as 'Peeps', to lead the way. And the leading tank battalion placed sandbags on the front of their Shermans to absorb the blast of 50 mm anti-tank rounds. If a village was deserted, it usually meant that the Germans were there: 'The first thing we did was to blow off the church steeple in order to get rid of possible [observation posts] and sniper fire.'

With German stragglers roaming the countryside behind their advance, Jeeps had to dash through like the 'pony express'. Snipers and bands of Germans desperate for food tried to ambush supply vehicles. 'The trucks were like a band of stage-coaches making a run through Indian country.' Replacements coming forward to join their units found that they had to be ready to fight just to get there. The Americans asked the FFI to do what they could to guard their lines of communication.

Patton was faintly dismissive of the French Resistance. He later said that their help was 'better than expected and less than advertised'. Yet their contribution in Brittany was indeed considerable. 'They aided in loading heavy ammunition,' an officer with the 6th Armored reported, 'and they cleared snipers, while our columns kept going.' They also secured bridges, provided intelligence and harassed Germans at every turn. On 6 August, a German report to Kluge's headquarters complained that the American advance on Brest was carried out 'with the help of terrorists'. General Koenig back in London was labelled the '*Terroristenführer*', and the following day the Germans reported 'battles with terrorists everywhere'. German reprisals became predictably violent, with two massacres on the Finisterre peninsula near Brest. Twenty-five civilians were shot in St Pol-de-Léon on 4 August, and forty-two men, women and children in Gouesnou were killed by sailors of the 3rd Marineflakbrigade on 7 August.

On 6 August, Colonel Eon's force secured the surrender of a battalion of *Osttruppen* at Saint-Brieuc. But when Eon and Passy returned to their headquarters exhausted that evening, their camp was attacked by 250 Germans from the 2nd Paratroop Division. After six hours of fighting they managed to force them back. Passy and a small group were surrounded, but they eventually fought their way out. When they met up with the rest of the headquarters group they heard that their loss had been reported to London. But soon the FFI and FTP attacks forced the Germans to withdraw into coastal towns, which could be more easily defended. Further south, other FFI detachments helped Wood's 4th Armored Division, even clearing a minefield by hand.

Grow's leading troops approached Brest on 6 August. After some wildly excessive optimism that the city would surrender to a show of force, Grow soon had to accept that an armoured division was incapable of seizing a major fortified city. He did not know that the commander of 'Fortress Brest' was General der Fallschirmtruppen Hermann Ramcke, a ruthless paratroop veteran who had sworn to Hitler that he would defend the city to the last.* Grow then found he was being attacked from behind by the German 266th Infanterie-Division, which had been trying to join the large garrison in Brest. His forces soon dealt with them, but Brest proved far too great an obstacle, as Patton rapidly appreciated.

The 8th Infantry Division came up to help the 6th Armored. Their tasks included night patrols to prevent large German foraging parties, sometimes up to 150 strong, from seizing food from French farmers. The FFI came begging for arms and gasoline, but they were also bringing in prisoners. The 8th had to set up a stockade to hold 600 of them. One of their officers was very pleased 'to get a Hermann Goering ceremonial dagger off one of the paratroopers'. The 8th Infantry hardly knew what to expect in this very unconventional quarter of the war. At one moment a British special forces officer who had been dropped behind enemy lines turned up wanting fuel, the next they found themselves embroiled in French political rivalries. Two quite senior French officers turned up in uniform, offering their services, but the members of the Resistance who had been helping the Americans insisted angrily that they would never work with them. They were what they called 'moth-balls': those who had served under the Vichy regime and now brought their uniforms out of the closet as soon as the Allies appeared. The Americans 'courteously got rid of the old officers'.

Liberation also presented its two faces. 'The townspeople were so

---

* Ramcke systematically destroyed the city later by fire and with explosives. 'It was entirely wiped out!' he boasted to General von Choltitz later in British captivity. He claimed that he was following the example of Admiral Nelson burning Toulon in 1793.

nice to us that I had a hell of a time keeping my men sober,' a lieutenant reported. American troops found the civilians to be much more friendly in Brittany than in Normandy. But they also witnessed its much uglier side of vengeance against women accused of *collaboration horizontale* with the Germans. 'We had a hair-cutting party,' the lieutenant added. 'Several girls were in addition kicked in the stomach and had to be hospitalized.'

For the Americans, especially the 6th Armored Division, the Brittany campaign ended in anticlimax. They were left besieging Brest, Saint-Nazaire and Lorient, where the 6th took over from Wood's 4th Armored, but in fact there was little danger of a sally by any of the garrisons. The FFI battalions, with some American support, were quite capable of keeping the Germans bottled up. Meanwhile the 83rd Infantry Division, which had battered away at Saint-Malo because the force there threatened the rear of operations in Brittany, finally achieved its surrender.

Bradley was well aware of the frustrating situation, but the siege of Brest, although now pointless strategically, had become a matter of pride. 'I would not say this to anyone but you,' he confessed to Patton, 'and [I] have given different excuses to my staff and higher echelons, but we must take Brest in order to maintain the illusion of the fact that the US Army cannot be beaten.' Patton agreed strongly with this view. 'Any time we put our hand to a job we must finish it,' he noted in his diary. Yet both Patton and Bradley had their eyes on the open flank north of the River Loire which led all the way to Orléans and Paris.

Patton could see only too clearly that Brittany was going to be a backwater. He welcomed Bradley's new order to send Haislip's XV Corps south-east to Le Mans and Walker's XX Corps down towards Angers on the Loire, ready to protect their right flank when they turned east. Glory lay towards the Seine.

One of the divisions destined for Haislip's corps had only just landed on Utah beach. This was the French 2nd Armored Division, which would become famous in France as the Deuxième Division Blindée, or the 2ème DB. It was indeed an extraordinary formation commanded by a remarkable man.

General Comte Philippe de Hautecloque was better known by his nom de guerre of 'Leclerc' to avoid German reprisals against his family. He was a devout Catholic of the ancien régime. As chaplains, he had recruited a dozen members of the White Fathers, an order set up in the nineteenth century originally to take Christianity to the Tuaregs. Led by Père Houchet, they were dressed in white habits and wore flowing beards.

Leclerc, a tall, slim man, with crinkly eyes and a rectangular military moustache, was instantly recognizable to his men by the tank goggles round his kepi and the malacca cane he always carried. They revered him for his bravery, his determination and his skill in battle. An austere man, he was acutely patriotic. Like de Gaulle, he felt bitter that, since the disaster of 1940, the British had accumulated so much more power while France had declined dramatically. Both were inclined to suspect that the British took every opportunity to exploit this. In their resentment, they could not see that Britain, despite her apparent strength, had bankrupted herself, physically and economically, during five years of war. It was an unfortunate detail that part of the division had sailed to Britain from Mers-el-Kebir, where Admiral Somerville's battle squadron had sunk the French fleet in 1940 to prevent it falling into German hands. 'Even for us Gaullists,' wrote a young officer, 'it weighed heavily on our hearts.'

De Gaulle regarded Leclerc and his division as the incarnation of the spirit of Free France. Its ranks included officers and soldiers of every political opinion. Alongside arch-Catholics of *la vieille France*, Communists, monarchists, socialists, republicans and even some Spanish anarchists, all served well together. This encouraged de Gaulle to believe that somehow post-war France could achieve a similar solidarity, but he was to be sorely disappointed.

It was the Americans, with their military-industrial cornucopia, who had clothed, equipped, armed and trained the 2ème DB (Americans were later irritated when French civilians asked them why the US Army did not have 'a uniform different from ours'.) Leclerc, despite his old-fashioned views, was no reactionary when it came to warfare. He felt an immediate affinity with Patton and Wood. Patton was keen to help Leclerc, and the French armoured division would not disappoint him in the battles ahead. But de Gaulle's intention to use the 2ème DB to further French interests above Allied priorities would prove a source of conflict with other American generals.

For the soldiers of the division, the moment of landing in France on 1 August was intensely emotional. The sea had been rough and a few were sick into their helmets, like their American predecessors nearly two months before. British sailors, seeing the condoms on rifle muzzles, made predictable jokes about 'Free French letters'. Almost all of those coming ashore had not seen their country for four years or more. Some scooped up handfuls of sand on Utah beach to preserve in jars. News of the arrival of French troops spread quickly on the Cotentin peninsula, and soon 100 young men volunteered to serve in its ranks. In ten days, they would go into battle for the first time.

While Patton's two armoured divisions were charging into Brittany, the British continued with Operation Bluecoat. Roberts's 11th Armoured Division advanced brilliantly towards the town of Vire, with infantry mounted on tanks. Armoured cars of the 2nd Household Cavalry were halted at one village by the mayor running out, waving his arms. Ahead they saw the road covered with pieces of paper. The inhabitants had watched the Germans lay mines, then as soon as they left they had rushed out to mark each one.

The 11th Armoured still had to contend with the arrival of the II SS Panzer Corps on their left flank. As soon as enemy tanks were sighted, the infantry leaped off. Sergeant Kite of the 3rd Royal Tank Regiment later described the moment of death for his tank when he was severely wounded. 'Over in the next field the outlines of two Panthers appeared. The wheat had grown high and was almost ripe. Each time they fired the shells cut a narrow furrow through the ears of corn. One of [the Panthers] was knocked out. Suddenly the gun of the other turned and pointed in my direction. I saw the muzzle flash as it fired and the corn bending down along the line of flight of the shell that was about to hit us.'

On 2 August, 11th Armoured was poised to take Vire, when suddenly Montgomery ordered Roberts to turn his division east. Instead of taking Vire, he was to cut the road east from the town and occupy the Perrier ridge. The boundary between the British and American armies had been changed. Vire was to be an American objective. It is still not clear whether Montgomery feared that the division might be cut off by a German counter-attack or he was acceding to an American request.

In any case Meindl, alarmed by the threat to Vire which was virtually undefended, quickly brought up a newly arrived division to fill the gap. Then, because it was untried, he stiffened it with his 9th Para-troop Regiment and 12th Artillery Battalion. He also brought for-ward two batteries of 88 mm flak guns to deal with the British tanks turning east. The tragedy of Montgomery's decision, a subject which he tried to avoid after the war, was not just the lost opportunity. Meindl's reinforcements were in place by the time the Americans put in their attack on the town four days later and they suffered heavy casualties.

The American 5th Infantry Division, advancing just to the right of Roberts's division, had begun to be squeezed into a narrower sector when Roberts seized the opportunity offered by the capture of 'Dickie's bridge'. Like the British, they too had encountered difficult hilly country and woods. It was a curious advance, with bouts of intense fighting, then moments of uneasy calm. The commander of one com-pany described a strange experience as they advanced along a forest track. 'The woods seemed to cast an eerie spell over us as though we were the subjects of a fairy enchantment,' he wrote. He and his men suddenly heard a soft, gentle clapping. 'As we came closer we could see the shadowy forms of French men and women and children, lining the roadway, not talking, some crying softly, but most just gently clapping, extending for several hundred feet on both sides of the road. A little girl came alongside me. She was blonde, pretty and maybe all of five years old. She trustingly put her hand in mine and walked a short way with me, then stopped and waved until we were out of sight.' Even fifty years later he could still hear the sound of soft clapping in a wood.

The 5th and 35th Infantry Divisions were then transferred to Patton's Third Army, and Vire was left to the 29th Division from XIX Corps. The American attack did not begin until dusk on 6 August, four days after Montgomery turned Roberts's 11th Armoured away from the town. Vire, an ancient town on a rocky hill, had already been partly destroyed by bombing on D-Day itself. Meindl's reinforcements gave a menacing assurance to the civilians who remained: 'We'll defend your town house by house.' The American 29th Division faced a hard fight through the ruins.

While VIII Corps had advanced well on the right flank, Bucknall's XXX Corps's progress remained slow. Dempsey had warned Bucknall on the first evening of the offensive that he must push on faster for Aunay-sur-Odon. That section of the front was heavily mined, but this was not accepted as an excuse. On the following evening Dempsey sacked him, with Montgomery's full support. To replace Bucknall, Montgomery summoned from England Lieutenant General Sir Brian Horrocks, who had now recovered from wounds received in North Africa. Over the next two days, Dempsey also sacked Major General Erskine of the 7th Armoured Division and Brigadier 'Loony' Hinde. The 7th Armoured were shaken by the loss of their commander. 'Everyone very depressed,' a staff officer wrote in his diary. 'It didn't seem the way to treat the captor of Tripoli.' But most senior officers felt that Dempsey should have wielded the axe after the Villers-Bocage fiasco in June. In any event, the arrival of Horrocks was widely welcomed.

A large part of the problem with the XXX Corps attack lay with the 50th Northumbrian and the 43rd Wessex Divisions. Their men were exhausted. Many were weak from dysentery and suffering from boils. They were also suffering from dehydration, since water, brought up in bowsers at night, was severely rationed. When the British attacked across a ripe cornfield, the Germans would sometimes fire incendiary shells and 'the wretched wounded would get burned alive'. But the Allies could hardly complain, considering their use of white phosphorus and flame-throwing tanks.

Only a handful of experienced men were left in each platoon. The rest were all replacements. The padres were among the hardest-worked, evacuating the wounded and carrying out brief funeral services during the hours of darkness. 'I could not help thinking of the line of poetry from the Burial of Sir John Moore,' wrote the chaplain with the 4th Dorsets. '"We buried him darkly, at the dead of night".'

Under pressure from their commanders, the infantry battalions of XXX Corps kept pushing forward, taking a flattened Villers-Bocage, Jurques and Ondefontaine. Those August days were not pleasant for tank crews either. 'In the small fields of Normandy among the cider orchards,' wrote a tank commander, 'every move during the hot summer brought showers of small hard sour apples cascading into the turrets through the open hatches. After a few days there might be enough to jam the turret. Five men in close proximity, three in the turret and two below in the driving compartment, all in a thick metal oven, soon produced a foul smell: humanity, apples, cordite and heat.' Their heads throbbed with noise: 'the perpetual "mush" through the earphones twenty-four hours each day, and through it the machinery noises, the engine as background, with the whine of the turret [mechanism] and the thud and rattle of the guns as an accompaniment'.

Stanley Christopherson, commanding the Sherwood Rangers Yeomanry, was well aware of the strain on his men. 'To be the leading tank of the leading troop of the leading squadron of the leading regiment of the leading brigade, with an axis of advance along a narrow lane leading into a village known to be held by enemy armour and infantry was then, as at all times, a most unattractive position. It almost invariably resulted in your tank being brewed up by an anti-tank gun or enemy tank which had seen you first. It must have been equally unpleasant for the leading infantry, but they could at least dive into a ditch and make themselves small, but not even the Almighty could diminish the size of a Sherman tank waddling down a narrow lane.'

Yet often the Germans allowed the first tank through, or even several, before opening fire. 'It was a lovely morning and the sun was just about to break through and scatter the mist which surrounded the countryside,' Christopherson wrote of 3 August. 'We passed through the village of Jurques without meeting opposition, but the trouble started in La Bigne, a tiny village a little further on, when my two following tanks were knocked out.' A newly arrived troop leader was killed instantly in one of them. 'One of the burning tanks completely blocked the road and prevented any movement either way. However Sergeant Guy Saunders, displaying his usual calm and utter disregard for his own safety, jumped into the tank and drove it into the ditch, thus clearing the way. It was a most gallant action, especially as the shells in the fighting compartment had started to explode.'

Officers in the Guards Armoured Division did what they could to mitigate the discomforts of tank warfare, even if that meant taking a less than Guards-like attitude to dress regulations. With their pale brown tank suits, they began to wear silk scarves to mask their faces from the dust, and leather wellington boots from Gieves, 'because they slip on and off easily'. A number of officers, disliking the army-issue sleeping bags, obtained a more comfortable version from Fortnum & Mason. The headquarters of the 6th Guards Tank Brigade also benefited from the foresight of their catering officer, Terence O'Neill, later prime minister for Northern Ireland. He had brought a flock of poultry and cages over from England 'in the recesses of a LST'. His cousin, Jock Colville, who was Churchill's private secretary, had dined with them just before Goodwood. 'The Brigade of Guards,' he noted in his diary, 'as magnificent fighters as any in the world, saw no virtue in austerity on active service.'

Since Goodwood, the Guards Armoured had also greatly improved its infantry–tank cooperation. This had been helped by the installation of a handset on the back of a tank. The telephone allowed an infantry officer to talk directly to the tank commander, without having to climb on to the turret under enemy fire to direct the troop on to an enemy position. But a captain in the 5th Coldstream, who cranked the telephone wildly while bullets whistled around him, did not appreciate the compulsive flippancy of his brother officer from the 1st Battalion inside the Sherman: 'The tank commander would always say on picking up his handset: "Sloane 4929". Funny for him, but not so bloody funny for me.'

The Germans fought their deadly ambush battles with small combat teams, usually a scratch company of panzergrenadiers grouped around an assault gun. Yet German morale was suffering under the onslaught. Feldgendarmerie detachments at bridges seized stragglers and hanged them from trees nearby to act as a deterrent to others tempted by the idea of desertion.

The chaplain attached to the 4th Dorsets spoke to one of their prisoners called Willi, 'a little German stretcher-bearer, a studious looking lad with glasses'. He could not understand why the British did not break through with all their artillery and tanks. German soldiers, he said, were waiting for the chance to surrender, provided their officers and NCOs were not looking. 'Then it is a pity,' the chaplain replied, 'that several of your comrades came out with their hands up and then threw grenades at our men.' The young German's lip trembled, 'and he looked as if he were going break into childish tears at this betrayal by his fellow-countrymen'. Like other captured medical orderlies, Willi impressed British doctors with his skill and willingness, helping both British and German wounded while still under mortar fire. Yet despite the chaplain's lecture about German soldiers breaking the rules of war, the British frequently killed SS soldiers out of hand. 'Many of them probably deserve to be shot in any case and know it,' a XXX Corps report stated baldly.

While some parts of the countryside seemed to have been virtually untouched by war, in others the scenes of destruction were terrible. Almost everyone who saw the large village of Aunay-sur-Odon was shocked to the core. The place had been bombed several times from 11 June and was now smashed again by XXX Corps artillery. 'Apart from the church spire and three shells of houses it is razed to the ground,' a cavalry officer noted in his diary. An artillery officer was appalled by his own part in it. 'You really had to disassociate yourself from that because there was no way you could carry out your military duties,' he observed later. 'The only thing you could do was to shell and hope to God the French had gone away.'

The survival of civilians in towns ruined by bombing and shellfire always seemed a miracle. André Heintz, from the Resistance in Caen, had followed the mine-clearing teams to the ruins of Villers-Bocage. There he saw German and British tanks smashed into each other from the battle in June. He described them as an 'imbroglio of steel'. At the Château de Villers on the edge of the town, he found that the local mayor, the Vicomte de Rugy, had sheltered 200 people in a tunnel-like cellar under the building. They were in a 'pathetic' state. In another small town, a soldier from the 4th Somerset Light Infantry went off to relieve himself. His hobnailed army boots slipped when crossing a pile of rubble. As he fell, his hand encountered something soft. It was the severed hand of a girl. Just then came the call from their patrol commander: 'Fall in you lads, it's time to move on.' All he could do was scratch a cross on the slab and RIP.

. Soldiers, often sentimental about animals, were also touched by the plight of abandoned livestock. Unmilked cows were in agony. They stood still to avoid the pain of any movement which would make their udders swing. Those from farming backgrounds would milk them straight on to the ground to ease the pressure. A medical officer was also moved by a sad scene: 'a little foal walking in a small circle round his recently killed mother. He had worn a path in the grass and refused to leave her.'

While the 11th Armoured Division on the right continued to fight off the 10th SS Panzer-Division *Frundsberg* east of Vire on the Perrier ridge, and the Guards Armoured crushed in the shoulder of the German front, XXX Corps finally approached Mont Pinçon. The infantry mounted on tanks were nearly choked by the thick red dust which now coated the scrub.

The attack was scheduled for 6 August. Many soldiers and NCOs remarked on the fact that it was the Bank Holiday weekend back in England. The thought conjured up images of their families and the seaside, but they were given little time to daydream. The aggressive Major General Thomas of the 43rd Wessex Division continued to exert maximum pressure on his subordinates, as the commanding officer of one of their supporting armoured regiments noted: 'Brigade and battalion commanders in the 43rd Division were somewhat fearful of Von Thoma, who at the same time infuriated them, as he insisted on "fighting their battles" and would not leave them alone after the final operational orders had been issued.'

Julius Neave, commanding a squadron of the 13th/18th Hussars, was resigned to another hard battle: 'Our intention is to capture M[ont].P[inçon] – the biggest feature in Normandy – with a very depleted infantry brigade and a tired armoured regiment.' Even during their orders group at brigade headquarters they found themselves under a 'fierce stonk' from German mortars.

The infantry were even more depressed by the prospect. 'The nearer we got to our objective,' wrote Corporal Proctor, 'the more awesome our task appeared. The lower slopes were cultivated farmland divided into small fields by huge hedgerows. Higher up was woodland. The top appeared to be covered in gorse. Out of sight over the brow of the hill were German radar installations and these had to be destroyed. At the foot of the hill was a small stream we would have to cross.' The day was oppressively hot.

The artillery barrage began at 15.00 hours. The 4th Somersets advanced on the left and the 5th Battalion of the Wiltshire Regiment on the right. About 100 yards beyond the stream, they came under heavy machine-gun fire from the flanks and in front. All the leading companies were pinned down. Some broke back to seek shelter under the bank of the stream, but it became crowded. 'It was soon obvious that too many people were seeking too little protection,' wrote Sergeant Partridge with the Somersets. The Somersets and Wiltshires expected the Germans to run out of ammunition, but the rate of fire never seemed to slacken. The Wiltshires were hard hit and their commanding officer killed.

Partridge's company sergeant major had his nose shot off. As he staggered back holding a field dressing to his face, Partridge helped him to the regimental aid post near battalion headquarters. There he heard that Major Thomas, the commander of B Company, had been killed while single-handedly rushing a German machine gun. 'Very gallant,' observed Partridge, 'but I had long since learned that dead soldiers do not win battles, and my prime duty was to stay alive and preserve the lives of as many others as possible.'

A sharp order arrived from their commanding officer saying that there were too many NCOs back at the aid post. 'Please rejoin your troops.' Partridge acknowledged that it was a well-deserved rebuke. He returned to 17 Platoon to find 'four fellows in an abandoned trench crying their eyes out'. These newcomers were not striplings, but men in their late thirties – 'far too old to live our kind of life'. They came from a disbanded anti-aircraft unit and had been sent forward without infantry training as part of the desperate attempt to man front-line battalions.

Shortly before dusk, a Sherman of the 13th/18th managed to cross the stream and give covering fire, but the German machine-gun positions were well camouflaged. A different plan was adopted. Once darkness fell, the companies were reorganized. They began to move forward behind a smokescreen in single file as silently as possible. Each man's equipment was checked to make sure that nothing would rattle.

Never believing that they would get through unobserved or unheard, they continued to move up the slope. They could hear German voices on either side, but fortunately never stumbled on to one of the machine-gun positions. The first two companies of the 4th Somersets made it to the plateau and were soon followed by the other two. They tried to dig in, ready for the inevitable German counter-attack, but found the ground was rock hard.

Sergeant Partridge then heard what sounded like a Panther or Tiger tank. He sent a whispered message to the anti-tank man to bring over the PIAT launcher, but the soldier was apologetic. The PIAT had been too heavy to carry up the hill and he had left it behind. Partridge showed great self-control by not strangling him on the spot. In fact, the tank which caused them such alarm in the dark almost certainly belonged to the 13th/18th Hussars, one of whose squadrons had found a route up the side of Mont Pinçon earlier in the night. In the confusion, they do not seem to have known that the infantry had already arrived, and they were radioing for support. Their commanding officer sent up another squadron, while urgently demanding infantry reinforcements.

By the morning of 7 August, the most dominant feature in Normandy was finally in British hands. In fact, the Germans had melted away. Their withdrawal formed part of a desperately needed attempt to shorten their lines, partly to make up for the transfer of the 1st SS Panzer-Division for the counter-attack being prepared at Mortain.

Bluecoat had been the climax to a bitter battle on both sides. The 4th Somersets had lost 'more men in five weeks than in the following nine months' up to the end of the war. Further west towards Vire, the 10th SS Panzer-Division *Frundsberg* had been ground down by the 11th Armoured and the Guards Armoured. Eberbach's headquarters had reported the night before 'heavy enemy attacks along almost the whole front'. In a final effort, the *Frundsberg* had counter-attacked the 11th Armoured south of Presles, hoping to close the gap between the Seventh Army and Panzer Group West.

The next day, when on Hitler's order Panzer Group West officially became the Fifth Panzer Army, Eberbach reported that there were just 'three tanks still serviceable' in the 10th SS Panzer-Division. He had to withdraw it from the line. The 'fighting spirit' of his army was 'unsatisfactory' as a result of 'losses, withdrawals and exhaustion'. There was no question of the II Panzer Corps, or the 12th SS *Hitler Jugend*, or the 21st Panzer-Division being withdrawn for the counter-attack at Mortain. Even Kluge warned that 'it was already a grave decision to take away the 1st SS Panzer-Division'. That day, Army Group B reported that since the invasion they had suffered 151,487 casualties, dead, wounded and missing. They had received fewer than 20,000 replacements.

24

The Mortain Counter-attack

Just before midnight on 2 August, General der Artillerie Warlimont reached the Château de la Roche-Guyon from East Prussia. He had flown to Strasbourg, where a staff car awaited him. His instructions were to assess the American breakthrough, but that day Panzer Group West had been far more concerned about the British drive on Vire, combined with the attack by XXX Corps. 'Situation still more acute,' Eberbach reported. 'Allies trying to join up wedges of penetration on western flank and centre of front.'

The night before Warlimont left the *Wolfsschanze*, he and Jodl had been summoned by Hitler. They discussed the option of withdrawal to the lower Seine, but its twists and turns made it a difficult line to defend. Hitler was in two minds. He was extremely reluctant to lose contact with Spain and Portugal, dreading the consequent interruption to supplies of raw materials. Pulling back would also mean the end for the submarine bases on the Atlantic coast. Hitler showed himself more realistic than Warlimont had expected, yet he gave him the strictest instructions not to discuss the matter with Kluge. 'Whenever a line of defence is prepared to the rear of the front line,' Hitler remarked, 'my generals think of nothing but pulling back to that line.'

After talks with Kluge, Warlimont then visited various headquarters in the field. He saw General Eberbach of Panzer Group West and Sepp Dietrich of I SS Panzer Corps on the Caen front. The rumbustious Meindl appears to have been the most outspoken, especially when Warlimont gave a dramatic account of near misses from Allied fighters on the road. Afterwards, he said of Warlimont, 'He belonged to the set of toy soldiers into whose hands Fate had placed our fortune!' All the officers to whom Warlimont spoke were 'discouraged' by the overwhelming effect of Allied air power.

On the morning of 4 August, Warlimont returned to Kluge's headquarters at La Roche-Guyon. An order had just been received from Hitler to concentrate all the panzer divisions and attack towards Avranches to cut off Patton's lines of communication. It was to be called Operation Lüttich. Kluge had already considered a similar plan himself, but he feared that 'he could not hold the line and at the same time launch the counterattack'. Yet Kluge, suspected of complicity in the bomb plot, was in no position to oppose the Führer's will.

Since his meeting with Jodl and Warlimont, Hitler's mood had stiffened and he now rejected any idea of withdrawal. The gambler in him, combined with his taste for the dramatic, had inspired one of his map fantasies. He had been gazing at the divisional symbols on his map, while refusing to acknowledge that most were reduced to a fraction of their theoretical strength. For him, the idea of cutting off Patton's Third Army proved irresistible. He also justified his idea of holding on in Normandy on the grounds that almost all the infantry divisions were without mechanized transport. Retreat would leave them at the mercy of the American armoured divisions and the Allied air forces. At the same time he refused to take Allied air power into consideration when planning Operation Lüttich. This was typical of his compulsion to see only what suited him.

Time was against them, as Kluge knew better than Hitler. On the evening of 4 August, Patton returned from Brittany and conferred with Haislip, the commander of XV Corps. Bradley had issued orders for the Third Army to strike east along the Germans' open flank. Patton told Haislip to take Mayenne and Laval the following day. Less than two hours later, Haislip was briefing his divisional commanders for an attack the next morning. The 79th Infantry Division was to take Laval, while the 90th Infantry Division was to seize the town of Mayenne to the north.

Patton had been scathing about the 90th when he encountered them on the road east of Avranches just three days before. 'The division is bad, the discipline poor, the men filthy and the officers apathetic, many of them removing their insignia and covering the markings on helmets. I saw one artillery lieutenant jump out of his Peep and hide in a ditch when one plane flew over at high altitude firing a little.' But under its new commander, Major General Raymond McLain, the 90th rapidly showed how a formation with low morale could be turned round dramatically by good leadership and a change in circumstances. On 5 August, the 90th seized the town of Mayenne in just six hours. The main crossing over the river had been mined, but 'a fifteen-year-old French boy went out onto the bridge, and cut the wires'. The 79th took Laval the next morning. The American attack into Brittany, even though it failed to seize a major port, had at any rate distracted the Germans from the real threat to their southern flank. They never expected the Third Army to advance east so rapidly.

Patton also remained privately scornful of Bradley's concern that the Germans might launch a major counter-attack to his north around Mortain. 'Personally I do not give much credence to this,' he had written in his diary on 1 August, when Bradley broached the subject. He was then irritated the next day when Bradley ordered the corner of the front near Fougères to be strengthened. Patton felt that Bradley was being as cautious as the British. Yet Bradley's instinct was right, though at this point he had no intelligence to back up his hunch.*

For Patton, the most pressing problem was logistical. His armoured divisions were running out of fuel and his supply dumps were still north of Avranches. The roads to the rear were jammed with supply trucks and troops. Military police were overwhelmed as they tried to control the traffic passing through the Avranches bottleneck twenty-four hours a day. Even divisional and corps commanders tried to sort out the chaos. 'Approximately 13,000 trucks, tanks, jeeps, half-tracks and howitzers crossed over the Pontaubault bridge, averaging one vehicle every thirty seconds.' The Luftwaffe, ordered to make any sacrifice to attack the Avranches route, launched raids by day as well as

---

* The sole hint that the Germans might be planning something came on 2 August through Ultra. The signal said only that 2nd Panzer-Division had carried out 'withdrawal movements' on the fiercely contested sector south of Vire and the 1st SS Panzer-Division's position was unchanged.

by night with bombers and fighter-bombers. But the Americans, having overestimated their needs for anti-aircraft artillery battalions in Normandy, were able to concentrate a formidable firepower around the key bridges south of Avranches.

While Patton's Third Army began its advance east, Hodges's First Army continued to push back the Germans south of Vire. On the right, the American 1st Infantry Division was ordered to advance on Mortain and then forge a link with Patton's forces to the south. Huebner's 1st Division had an easier task than its neighbours to the north. By the morning of 4 August, the 1st Division had taken Mortain and secured the dominant feature above it, Hill 314, known as the Rochers de Montjoie. When his corps commander, General Collins, reminded him of its importance, Huebner was able to make the satisfying reply, 'Joe, I already have it.'

Mortain was a quiet town in dramatic countryside. Long and thin, it lay high on the west side of the Montjoie ridge, with the ravine of the River Cance below. At the north end of the town there were two waterfalls. Most houses had a magnificent view out over the ravine to the steep hills on the far side. Avranches lay less than twenty miles beyond as the crow flies.

French refugees escaping the battles to the north had sought refuge there. Most arrived on foot as German soldiers had seized their bicycles and carts to get away. The refugees envied its citizens, because the town had suffered no damage. Those who could afford it had a very pleasant lunch at the Hôtel Saint-Michel, and dreamed of peace to come. The only signs of war were Allied aircraft overhead. The Germans in the neighbourhood were mostly invisible during the day, emerging only after dark.

From behind curtains, others in the area watched the German retreat towards Domfront. 'Some of the troops held themselves well, others were in a terrible state, men on horses, in pony-traps, pushing handcarts. It reminded us of our own exodus in 1940.' When the Germans ordered villagers or townspeople to evacuate, the local mayor advised them simply to hide in barns out in the countryside. As the fighting came closer, mothers would check that their younger children had labels tied to their clothes with the address of a relative in case they themselves were killed.

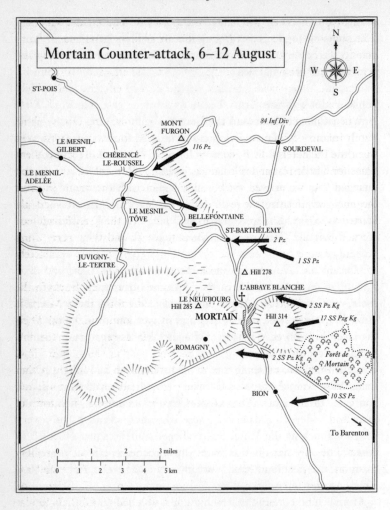

Mortain Counter-attack, 6–12 August

ST-POIS

MONT FURGON
△

84 Inf Div

LE MESNIL-GILBERT

116 Pz

CHÉRENCÉ-LE-ROUSSEL

SOURDEVAL

LE MESNIL-ADELÉE

LE MESNIL-TÓVE

BELLEFONTAINE

ST-BARTHÉLEMY

2 Pz

1 SS Pz

JUVIGNY-LE-TERTRE

△ Hill 278

L'ABBAYE BLANCHE
†

LE NEUFBOURG
Hill 285 △

MORTAIN

Hill 314
△

2 SS Pz Kg

17 SS Pzg Kg

2 SS Pz Kg

Forêt de Mortain

ROMAGNY

2 SS Pz Kg

BION

10 SS Pz

To Barenton

0   1   2   3 miles
0   1   2   3   4   5 km

On the evening of 5 August, Major General Huebner received orders to move the 1st Infantry Division towards Mayenne. At the same time, the 30th Infantry Division in reserve near Tessy-sur-Vire was to move to Mortain immediately in trucks to relieve Huebner's troops. But it took time to assemble the transport and then the roads were so packed that the 30th Division convoys averaged little more than three miles an hour. Their first troops did not reach Mortain until mid-morning on

6 August. Officers of the 1st Division briefed them on the situation. The sector was quiet, apart from a few artillery shells and some patrol activity on the flank of the Montjoie ridge. They admitted their surprise, however, that the night before the Luftwaffe had attacked Mortain with bombs and incendiaries. It had not been very effective, so nobody considered it significant.

When Colonel Hammond D. Birks, the commanding officer of the 120th Infantry Regiment, reached Mortain, he found that shops were open and the hotels full. To some of his men 'it seemed like an excellent place for a little rest and relaxation,' he noted. But suddenly the mood changed. 'As we arrived there,' an aid man with the 120th Infantry Regiment wrote later, 'the few French people left in the town suddenly started to vanish. The word was passed to us that the French had been warned that the Germans were about to attack and they were taking refuge in some caves near the town. This report seemed completely implausible and we continued to lie lazily on the grass.'

The 2nd Battalion of the 120th dismounted from their trucks in the main street of Mortain and trudged up the side of the rocky Montjoie ridge to take over the 1st Division's positions around Hill 314. Their commanding officer, Lieutenant Colonel Hardaway, made the unfortunate decision to set up his command post in the Grand Hôtel down in the town, rather than with his battalion up on Hill 314. Other companies manned roadblocks leading into the town from north and south. A battalion was also sent south-east to secure the small town of Barenton.

Most of the German divisions were already concealed in their assembly positions on the Sourdeval–Mortain sector. The *Das Reich* and the 116th Panzer-Division had withdrawn under cover of darkness on 3 August. The 1st SS Panzer-Division *Leibstandarte Adolf Hitler* also pulled out of the line south of Caen to join the attack, but it had far to go. The remnants of the 17th SS Panzergrenadier-Division *Götz von Berlichingen* were sent to strengthen the *Das Reich*, whose task was to cover the southern flank of the offensive and attack Mortain. In the centre, the main force was to consist of the 2nd Panzer-Division, which was to head straight for Juvigny-le-Tertre, just another fifteen miles away. On the northern flank, the 116th Panzer-Division was to attack from near Mont Furgon, west of Sourdeval. The 1st SS Panzer-Division *Leibstandarte Adolf Hitler*, once it arrived, would pass through the other divisions after they had broken the American line and race on to Avranches.

Jodl warned Kluge that Hitler wanted the attack to be made with the maximum force and told him that he should delay the offensive until 8 August. But Kluge, having just heard that the Americans were advancing from the River Mayenne towards Le Mans, felt he could not wait. Beyond Le Mans lay the Seventh Army's supply base at Alençon.

Kluge, Hausser and his chief of staff, Gersdorff, discussed this threat. An American map had been captured showing a thrust from Le Mans on towards Paris, but not north to cut them off. This encouraged them to think that the Allies were not aiming for encirclement. The heavy British attacks 'were the greatest obstacles in making the decision,' Gersdorff noted. Hitler showed little concern about the advance of the Third Army. In his view, it simply meant that the counter-attack would cut off even more American troops.

Kluge saw the Avranches offensive as a means of wrong-footing the Allies before withdrawing to the Loire in the south and the Seine in the east. Hitler, on the other hand, with his manic optimism, saw it as the first step towards re-establishing the front held in Normandy at the beginning of July. OKW promised 1,000 fighters in support of the operation, but none of the senior commanders believed this. 'They had been deceived so many times in the past and they felt that they would be deceived again,' Warlimont acknowledged after the war. Yet he himself had been one of Hitler's deceivers, convincing generals that the situation was better than it really was.

Operation Lüttich was to be led by General der Panzertruppen Hans Freiherr von Funck, the thoroughly disliked commander of XLVII Panzer Corps. Generalleutnant Gerhard Graf von Schwerin, the intellectually arrogant commander of the 116th Panzer-Division, had already had a series of furious rows with Funck over his handling of the counter-attack west of the Vire on 28 July. Funck had accused the 116th Panzer-Division of 'passive resistance, cowardice and incompetence'. Schwerin was now involved in another bitter argument with Funck over the fighting to maintain the start-line for Operation Lüttich. The newly arrived 84th Infanterie-Division on his right, which was supposed to take over his sector, was buckling under renewed American attacks. Then Funck believed wrongly that Schwerin had failed to transfer a Panther battalion to the 2nd Panzer-Division as ordered. He demanded that Schwerin should be relieved of his command. Since the attack was just about to start, Oberstgruppenführer Hausser refused. All the senior commanders were clearly in a very agitated state.

At 15.20 hours on 6 August, less than four hours before the offensive was due to begin, Generalfeldmarschall von Kluge received a signal which began in characteristic fashion: 'The Führer has ordered . . .' Operation Lüttich, it stated, was not to be led by General von Funck, but by General Eberbach. Hitler loathed Funck because he had been a personal staff officer of Generaloberst Werner Freiherr von Fritsch, whom Hitler had dismissed in 1938. In 1942, Funck had been destined to command the Afrika Korps, but Hitler appointed Rommel instead.

Kluge was appalled by this decision. He immediately rang the OKW in East Prussia to protest that a change of command a few hours before the attack was 'virtually impossible'. When told that the operation should be delayed as the Führer insisted, Kluge replied, 'The attack must be carried out this evening. If we wait any longer, we would have to deal with a grave deterioration in our position. The postponement by a day creates the danger that the enemy air forces would strike our assembly areas.'

Kluge managed to persuade OKW to postpone the transfer of command to Eberbach, but he had other worries. The advance elements of the 1st SS Panzer-Division *Leibstandarte Adolf Hitler* had only just reached Flers. Kluge rang Seventh Army headquarters to say that he was doubtful whether they would arrive in time. Although the *Leibstandarte* had started to pull out on the evening of 4 August, its move to the area of Mortain had been delayed by a sudden Canadian attack, then by traffic jams and the odd air strike.

In spite of Kluge's fears of bombing raids on their assembly areas, the day saw 'little air activity'. The 2nd SS Panzer-Division *Das Reich* lay well hidden under the beech and oak trees of the ancient Forêt de Mortain, a long wooded ridge to the south-east of the town. On the right it had the *Führer* Panzergrenadier-Regiment, in the middle the battlegroup of the 17th SS Panzergrenadier-Division *Götz von Berlichingen*, and on the left was the *Deutschland*-Regiment, supported by the 2nd SS Panzer-Regiment, ready to swing past Mortain to the south-west.

The American 30th Infantry Division in and around Mortain still had little idea of what was afoot. The 4th Infantry Division, which was in reserve, noted in its daily operations log, 'The war looks practically over.' This optimism was stimulated by the news of Turkey breaking off relations with Germany, the attempts by Finland, Bulgaria 'and possibly Hungary' to get out of the war, the American advances to Brest and Mayenne, and the Red Army reaching the outskirts of Warsaw and the edge of East Prussia. On 6 August, the division's 12th Infantry Regiment finally pulled back to rest in 'a beautiful bivouac near the picturesque little town of Brécey. Arrangements for showers, shows, movies and Red Cross "doughnut" girls have hurriedly been made. For the first time since D-Day the hollow-eyed, gaunt-cheeked men of the 12th combat team could relax.'

That afternoon and evening, the code-breakers at Bletchley Park began to work on a flurry of intercepts. The Luftwaffe was asked to provide night-fighter protection for the 2nd SS Panzer-Division for an attack on and beyond Mortain. The 2nd and 116th Panzer-Divisions and the *Leibstandarte* were also identified for an attack whose start-line was between Mortain and Sourdeval. Bradley, although more sceptical of Ultra intelligence than most commanders, was left in no doubt about the seriousness of the attack. He made sure that every artillery battalion available was rushed forward to the threatened sector between the rivers Sée and Sélune. A message was sent to the 30th Infantry Division to reinforce the battalion on Hill 314 above Mortain, but this does not appear to have been received in time. To the north-west, the mayor of Le Mesnil-Tôve warned a company commander of the 117th Infantry of the 30th Division that German troops with tanks were concealed in woods near Bellefontaine, which was behind American lines. When the company commander reported this, he was told by divisional head-quarters 'to stop spreading rumours'.

The start of the attack, originally scheduled for 18.00 hours, was delayed several times due to the SS *Leibstandarte*'s late arrival. Changes were also made to the formations at the last moment, mainly because other units to reinforce the operation failed to arrive as a result of Allied pressure on other parts of the front. Kluge, who wanted to make last-minute alterations to the plan, was persuaded to leave things as they were. Finally, at midnight, the advance began without any artillery preparation. The plan was to infiltrate as far as possible before daybreak.

The first clash took place on the northern flank even before Operation Lüttich officially began. At 22.30 hours on 6 August, two German half-track motorcycles charged through a roadblock of the 39th Infantry Regiment east of Chérencé-le-Roussel, but were knocked out by another company a little further down the road. Everything was then quiet, but around midnight tanks were heard on the road half a mile to their south which led from Bellefontaine to Le Mesnil-Tôve. Nobody made any connection with the mayor's earlier warning. They assumed that the tanks were American.

Two hours later, at 02.00 hours on the morning of Monday, 7 August, the battalion in the valley was attacked by German infantry coming from Mont Furgon, just to their north, and more infantry and tanks of the 116th Panzer-Division coming from the east. With the support of some Shermans from the 746th Tank Battalion, they fought them off. The Americans still assumed that this was just a local attack. But it soon became clear that the main German axis of advance lay on the smaller road to their south via Le Mesnil-Tôve. This was the northern column of the 2nd Panzer-Division and, by 05.00 hours, they had swarmed through the village and on to Le Mesnil-Adelée.

The advance of the 2nd Panzer-Division's southern column was delayed until 05.00 hours. Part of the 117th Infantry Regiment in Saint-Barthélemy could hear the ominous sound of panzers advancing, but the mist was so thick that visibility was reduced to little more than twenty yards. While some of the roadblocks outside the town were easily overrun, one anti-tank position managed to hold up a detachment of Panthers, knocking out two. Other groups of Panthers supported by infantry attacked from other directions, including an advance detachment from the 1st SS Panzer-Division. American infantrymen fought running battles, using bazookas. They resisted 'extraordinarily well,' as General von Lüttwitz of the 2nd Panzer-Division later acknowledged.

Eight Panthers entered Saint-Barthélemy and halted in the main street, just outside the advance headquarters of Lieutenant Colonel

Frankland of the 1st Battalion of the 117th Infantry. One of his officers looked out of the window to see a Panther just below. They then heard noises at the rear of the house. Frankland went to investigate and found two of his signallers being marched out with their hands above their heads. He shot down two of the SS troopers who had called them out and saw another Panther in the street at the back of the house. Astonishingly, Frankland's command group managed to escape out of a window and rejoin one of the companies. Under the onslaught of the SS panzergrenadiers, most of Frankland's battalion had to withdraw, jumping hedges and scuttling down ditches.

Although Frankland's battalion had been overrun, their fierce defence of Saint-Barthélemy had inflicted a crucial delay on the 2nd Panzer-Division's advance towards Juvigny-le-Tertre. The Panthers did not resume their advance until late in the morning. This gave the Americans time to rush in reinforcements, especially to block the northern column in Le Mesnil-Adelée, two miles west of Le Mesnil-Tôve.

Soon after midnight, the three *Kampfgruppen* of the *Das Reich* and *Götz von Berlichingen* had advanced on Mortain and Hill 314. They too were helped by the heavy mist, which muffled the noise of their engines.

At 01.25 hours on 7 August, the American battalion on Hill 314 stood to on hearing small-arms fire. The Germans had found a route past the roadblock down at the southern entry to the town. They were attacking up the hill and into Mortain itself. Colonel Hammond Birks, the commander of the 120th Infantry, sent a company into Mortain to clear it, but the Germans were already too well established. At 02.00 hours, the Germans also attacked Hill 314 from the north.

Birks had no more reserves and Lieutenant Colonel Hardaway, trapped in the Grand Hôtel in the centre of the town, could not rejoin the bulk of his battalion on the hill above. He and his group, including three other officers, tried to make their way from the Grand Hôtel across the town towards the hill, but patrols of SS panzergrenadiers forced them to seek shelter in an abandoned house.

While most of the roadblocks were quickly overrun, the defensive position near the Abbaye Blanche, just outside the northern edge of the town, inflicted heavy casualties on its SS *Das Reich* attackers. Lieutenant Springfield's tank destroyer platoon with its three-inch guns fired at comparatively close range as each German half-track emerged from the fog. 'A loud clang followed by a red glow announced each direct hit. As the occupants of the armored personnel carriers tumbled out of their stricken machines, they were sprayed with machinegun fire. Tracers ricocheted wildly off the road as well as the armored flanks of immobilized vehicles.' Colonel Birks, aware of the importance of the Abbaye Blanche position, reinforced it with two platoons. One of their commanders, Lieutenant Tom Andrew, soon took over the direction of the defensive battle there.

A company from Lieutenant Colonel Lockett's battalion of the 117th Infantry had been sent with four tank destroyers into Romagny, a mile south-west of Mortain, to block the road junction there. They received a nasty shock on finding that the Germans had already taken the place. Lockett's battalion was not only split into different detachments, they were facing in three directions and Germans were infiltrating their positions using captured American weapons. With the very distinctive sound that they made, American soldiers kept thinking that they were being fired on by their own side. Lockett had only about thirty men left under his direct control. Many of them were not riflemen, but they had to fight as such. The battalion aid station was almost overwhelmed by the number of casualties.

Across the valley on Hill 314, the situation for the 2nd Battalion of the 120th was already desperate. They were surrounded by the 17th SS Panzergrenadier *Kampfgruppe*. Their wounded lay in the open, vulnerable to mortar rounds. Company positions were isolated and short of ammunition because they could not reach their dump, which was now covered by sniper fire. As a result of Hardaway's absence, Captain Reynold C. Erichson was told to take command of the bulk of the 2nd Battalion on the hilltop position. Using boulders, foxholes and undergrowth for concealment, the 'Lost Battalion', as it became known, held out on Hill 314. Their greatest asset was a forward artillery observer who, once the mist began to lift, could call down fire and correct it from his commanding viewpoint.

In need of rapid support to halt the German panzers, General Bradley and General Hodges contacted General Quesada's headquarters. As soon as the mist lifted at around 11.00 hours, P-47 Thunderbolts went into action. But the Americans, accepting that the RAF's rocket-firing Typhoons offered the most effective weapon against tanks, contacted Air Marshal Coningham's 2nd Tactical Air Force. Coningham and Quesada agreed that the Typhoons 'should deal exclusively with the enemy armoured columns' while American fighters would provide a screen and American fighter-bombers would attack transport in the German rear areas.

Although it was a damp, misty morning at the airstrip of Le Fresne-Camilly, north of Caen, two Typhoons had been sent out on a reconnaissance mission. They spotted German armour moving in the Mortain area. On landing, the two pilots ran to the intelligence tent. A Jeep was sent over towards the aircrew tents beyond a tall hedge, the driver sounding his horn in warning. Ground crews rushed to prepare the Typhoons for take-off, while the pilots assembled in the briefing tent.

'This is the moment we have all been waiting for, Gentlemen,' Wing Commander Charles Green told them, having had confirmation of the mission from Coningham's headquarters a few moments before. 'The chance of getting at Panzers in the open. And there's lots of the bastards.' They were to attack in pairs, not in squadron formation. Flight time to target was no more than fifteen minutes. This meant that the whole wing could create a 'continuous cycle of Typhoon sorties'.

The pilots ran to their aircraft. One of them, out of a personal superstition, insisted on his usual practice of urinating against the tailplane before climbing into the cockpit. Pilots in 123 Wing came from many nations. It was almost an aerial foreign legion, with British pilots, Belgians, French, Canadians, Australians, New Zealanders, South Africans, Norwegians, Poles, an Argentinian and even a German Jew called Klaus Hugo Adam (later the film-maker, Sir Ken Adam).

The sun was burning off the mist as the eighteen squadrons of 83 Group scrambled. In addition to their 20 mm cannon, the Typhoons had underwing rails which carried eight rockets, each with a sixty-pound high-explosive warhead. Some pilots claimed that their salvo was the equivalent of a broadside from a light cruiser. Trials, however, had shown that the average pilot firing all eight rockets had 'roughly a four-per-cent chance of hitting a target the size of a German tank'. The plane at least had a 'brute strength and ruggedness' which stood up better than most aircraft to ground fire.

The first wave went into action against the 1st SS Panzer-Division *Leibstandarte Adolf Hitler* on the road running west from Saint-Barthélemy. Dun-coloured dust stirred up by the tracks of the armoured vehicles revealed their target as the Typhoons approached. New pilots tried to remember the training mantra 'Diving point – release point – Scram!', as well as the need to prevent the plane from sliding into a sideways 'skid'. The first target was the lead vehicle. The second was the last vehicle in the column. They either fired their rockets in salvoes of eight, or they 'rippled' them, firing in a sequence of pairs. Once their rockets were used up, pilots tried to bounce 20 mm cannon rounds off the road just short of their target so that they would hit the weaker underbelly of a tank or half-track. Soon the black smoke billowing from blazing panzers made it hard to see clearly, and the dangers of mid-air collision increased.

Within twenty minutes of take-off, the Typhoons were on their way back to rearm and refuel in a veritable production line. On the ground, the pilots sweated impatiently in the terrible heat of their cockpits under the bubble Perspex canopy. The propellers powered by the Typhoon's Sabre engine blasted dust in clouds everywhere, so ground-crew and armourers, stripped to the waist in the August heat, had to wear handkerchiefs tied over their face like bandits. As soon as the pilot received the thumbs-up sign, he could taxi round ready for take-off again. And so the shuttle went on. The 2nd Panzer-Division's advance on Juvigny-le-Tertre was also halted.

American fighter squadrons played their part superbly. Very few of the Luftwaffe's promised 300 fighters arrived within forty miles of Mortain. The Luftwaffe later rang Seventh Army headquarters to apologize: 'Our fighters have been engaged in aerial combat from the time of take-off and were unable to reach their actual target area. They hope, however, that their aerial engagements helped just the same.' The Seventh Army staff officer replied stiffly, 'There was no noticeable relief.' The main opposition to the Typhoons came from machine-gun fire. Three aircraft were lost and many damaged, but soon the *Leibstandarte* reported that their armoured vehicles were running low on ammunition.

Round Mortain, where the opposing forces were more mixed up and harder to differentiate, there were a number of cases of Typhoons attacking American positions by mistake. They destroyed several

American vehicles and inflicted some casualties. For example, at the Abbaye Blanche roadblock commanded by Lieutenant Andrew, they wounded two men from a tank destroyer crew. But 'the British were soon forgiven,' Lieutenant Andrew said afterwards, because 'they did a wonderful job against the Germans'.

American soldiers taken prisoner by the Germans in Mortain found it disorientating to shelter from Allied aircraft. An aid man hugging the ground during the attack found that he had to raise his chest from the earth to reduce the concussive effects from the explosions. After the Typhoons had left, their guards surveyed the burning vehicles, shook their heads and said, '*Alles kaputt!*' This time, the first things the Germans had taken from them were water purification tablets, morphine and other medical supplies for their own wounded. Usually, German captors were more interested in grabbing cigarettes or any candy from their prisoners to relieve a craving which their own rations seldom satisfied.

By 16.00 hours, smoke and dust over the target areas made further low-flying operations impossible. Most of the Typhoons were diverted to deal with a German counter-attack against the British 11th Armoured Division east of Vire. The eighteen Typhoon squadrons of 83 Group had flown 294 sorties. 'As the day developed,' Air Marshal Coningham wrote in his official report, 'it was obvious that air history was being made.' He then went on to record the score. 'During this day the rocket-firing Typhoons of the Second Tactical Air Force claimed to have destroyed 89 tanks, probably destroyed another 56 tracked vehicles and saw 47 motor vehicles smoking. These claims do not include 56 enemy tanks damaged and 81 motor vehicles damaged.'

Five months later Coningham was furious when he received the report of the Operational Research Section, which had examined the area immediately after the battle and studied the German vehicles left behind. In the Mortain area they found that out of seventy-eight German armoured vehicles destroyed, only nine were attributable to air attack. Clearly, some of the less seriously damaged had been recovered by the Germans before they retreated, but the general conclusion about the accuracy of the Typhoon came as a nasty shock to the Royal Air Force. Coningham seemed to consider the report somehow disloyal and rejected it, but a second report confirmed its findings.

German generals, on the other hand, were quick to attribute their reversal to Allied air power. 'Whether you realise it or not,' Geyr von Schweppenburg tactlessly told his American interrogators at the end of the war, 'it was British rocket-carrying planes that halted our counter-attack at Avranches, not your 30th Infantry Division.' In most cases their argument was based on sheer self-justification. And yet German sources are not alone in attributing their reversal at Mortain to these rocket attacks.

In many instances, fear of the Typhoon prompted panzer crews to abandon their tank in terror, even though they would have been safer inside it than out. An American sergeant observed, 'There is nothing but air attack that would make a crack panzer crew do that.' And an abandoned tank was almost as effective as a destroyed tank in blocking a column on a narrow road. In any case, the Typhoon operation on 7 August forced the 2nd Panzer-Division and the *Leibstandarte* off the roads and into cover, thus halting their advance. This gave the First US Army the chance to bring in artillery and armour to strengthen the line.

There were soon twelve and a half field artillery battalions firing in support of the 30th Infantry Division, including three battalions of 155 mm 'Long Toms'. Air observers in the Cub spotter planes could direct and adjust their fire, so that every major route was made virtually impassable. But although the German offensive had been thwarted, the position of American units around Mortain remained perilous.

Lieutenant Andrew's roadblock at the Abbaye Blanche suffered frequent Nebelwerfer salvoes, although fortunately they had taken over well-built German foxholes with overhead protection. A hazardous supply route to the west via Le Neufbourg was also kept open. But there was little chance of sending help to the 2nd Battalion of the 120th Infantry up on Hill 314. Captain Erichson's force was split between three positions. They had many wounded and were very short on ammunition. Only American artillery fire, directed by Lieutenant Robert Weiss, the forward observer with the 'Lost Battalion', had prevented the 17th SS Panzergrenadier *Kampfgruppe* from overrunning them. He had pre-registered all the likely attack routes and assembly areas below them, so that their field artillery could support them even through the hours of darkness.

At 19.00 hours, Lieutenant Colonel Lockett sent part of his battalion of the 117th Infantry (which had been attached to the 120th) into Le Neufbourg, the village at the north end of Mortain and next to the Abbaye Blanche. The idea was to clear Mortain, but as soon as the leading company entered the north-west edge of the town, German machine guns opened up from houses on both sides of the street and artillery and mortar shells soon began to rain down. They suffered seventy-three casualties in a very short time and the company was forced to withdraw. Colonel Lockett, realizing the impossibility of storming Mortain with such a reduced force and recognizing the importance of the Abbaye Blanche roadblock, told the remnants of the company to join the force there. But a number were severely traumatized by the firefight that they had just been in and took little part in the rest of the battle.

Meanwhile in Mortain itself, a group of about forty-five men from C Company of the 120th were trapped without food and water and with a number of wounded. They had inflicted heavy casualties on the SS panzergrenadiers trying to clear the town. Colonel Lockett wanted to get them out so that Mortain could be bombarded at will. A rescue patrol was assembled with several stragglers from the beleaguered company and a dozen litter-bearers to carry back the wounded. They were led by Sergeant Walter Stasko, who had reconnoitred the perilous route down into the gorge and up the far side. Covering fire was given by the mortar platoon, which had a clear view from its position on a hill west of the ravine. The patrol managed to reach most of the men and lead them out, but the steep descent was so difficult that they had to carry the wounded down the hill on their backs.

On 8 August, the main concern of the 30th Division was to preserve the position of the 'Lost Battalion' on Hill 314. They tried to drop supplies by Piper Cub spotter planes, but the *Das Reich* had brought in anti-aircraft guns to thwart this. The Lost Battalion was 'a thorn in the flesh', a German corps commander acknowledged. 'Its courageous commitment paralyzed all movements in the Mortain area.' But without water, ammunition, food or medical supplies, their hopes of holding out seemed to be diminishing rapidly.

That day, while fighting continued in and around Mortain, the

Americans launched a counter-attack against Romagny, to the south-west of the town. Meanwhile Bradley brought in the 2nd Armored Division and a regiment from the 35th Infantry Division to attack the German southern flanks round Mortain. The 2nd Armored, advancing from Barenton, ran into the remnants of the 10th SS Panzer-Division *Frundsberg*, which Eberbach had been forced to withdraw after its battering by the British 11th Armoured Division east of Vire. The increased strength of the Americans around Barenton ensured that the Germans were not able to relaunch their offensive further to the south, as they had hoped.

With Operation Lüttich thwarted by a much more robust American response than expected, the strain on German troops and their commanders increased dramatically. An American private who had been taken prisoner recorded how German officers and soldiers were steadying their nerves during American artillery barrages with bottles of cognac. And front-line units had started to hear from their supply troops that the advance of the American Third Army to the south threatened to cut them off.

In formation headquarters to the rear, the tension erupted in furious rows, most notably with General von Funck's vendetta against General von Schwerin of the 116th Panzer-Division. In the suspicious atmosphere following the bomb plot, Schwerin was vulnerable after all his anti-Nazi quips. Funck, falsely accusing the 116th of failing to take part in the operation, finally persuaded Oberstgruppenführer Hausser to relieve Schwerin, even while the battle continued.

Kluge was close to despair. The Canadian offensive, Operation Totalize, launched towards Falaise on the night of 7 August, meant that he could extract no more forces from the Fifth Panzer Army. He had also counted on the 9th Panzer-Division joining the attack on Avranches, but now found that it was desperately needed to their rear. The American Third Army had sent one of its corps north towards Alençon and the supply base of his own Seventh Army. 'It was quite clear,' wrote Gersdorff, Hausser's chief of staff, 'that this was to be the knockout blow and the end of the army and the whole of the western front.'

Encirclement was now a real threat, yet Hitler insisted that the

Avranches offensive should be renewed. On 9 August, General der Infanterie Walter Buhle from the OKW arrived at Seventh Army advance headquarters near Flers to ensure that this happened. 'He insisted on seeing General Hausser personally,' wrote Gersdorff, the chief of staff. 'He asked Hausser in a direct question on Hitler's orders whether he considered "that a continuation of the offensive could be of any success". Hausser answered in the affirmative.' He presumed that any other reply would lead to his instant dismissal. General-feldmarschall von Kluge, even though he knew that the operation was leading them to disaster, was also in no position to refuse. He ordered Hausser to relaunch the attack with what was now called Panzer Group Eberbach. Both men knew that even if their forces reached Avranches they would never have the strength to hold a position there.

In Mortain itself, Lieutenant Colonel Hardaway, the commanding officer of the 2nd Battalion of the 120th, managed to slip out of the town on the east side, but was captured trying to climb Hill 314 to rejoin his men.

At 18.20 hours, a Waffen-SS officer, accompanied by an SS trooper carrying a white flag, approached one of the battalion's perimeters. 'In formal manner', he stated that he was offering the Americans on the hill the chance of an honourable surrender. They were surrounded and their position was hopeless. If they did not surrender before 22.00 hours, his forces would 'blow them to bits'. The reply came back that they would not surrender as long as they possessed 'ammunition to kill Germans with, or a bayonet left to stick in a Boche belly'. The SS attacked with panzers that night, apparently shouting 'Surrender! Surrender!', but they were halted with anti-tank guns and bazookas. Only one tank broke through and took a single American soldier prisoner.

The Abbaye Blanche roadblock also fought off numerous attacks, including one with flame-throwers. In an attempt to help its defenders and to control the road north out of Mortain, efforts were made to seize the road junction on Hill 278, halfway between Mortain and Saint-Barthélemy. Part of the 12th Infantry Regiment brought down from its rest area in Brécey tried to force back the northern *Kampfgruppe* of the SS *Das Reich*. They were then to turn south into Mortain to relieve the beleaguered outposts of the 30th Division. The 2nd Battalion of the 12th Infantry had nearly reached the key crossroads when it was struck 'a stunning blow' by *Leibstandarte* panzers. They pulled back west of a stream and tried to bring up tanks and tank destroyers across the boggy ground, but it proved impossible.

On 9 August, the Germans attacked again in the early-morning mist south of Saint-Barthélemy. SS panzergrenadiers were seen wearing bits of American uniform and carrying American weapons. One group wore 'American shoes, leggings, field jackets and helmets'. At times the fighting consisted of close-quarter combat, with panzergrenadiers throwing themselves at the 12th Infantry in their foxholes. German artillery fire was unusually intense. 'For the first time we sustained heavier fire than we gave,' an officer observed afterwards. The strain of four days of desperate fighting told after so many weeks of combat: 'The Regiment had some 300 exhaustion cases during the period.'

The frenzy of the fighting is indicated by this extraordinary report from the 12th Infantry. Private Burik of E Company, 2nd Battalion, heard a tank approaching from the north. 'The tank he could see was coming down the road toward the orchard. Grabbing his bazooka he loaded it and stepped out onto the road. On his first attempt to fire the bazooka it did not go off. He found that the safety was stuck. While the tank continued to approach him, [Burik] released the safety and fired point-blank at the tank.' The tank then fired directly at him, knocking him down and seriously injuring him. He arose, loaded the bazooka, took direct aim and fired again. The tank fired another round, knocking him down again. 'Dragging himself up to a firing position, [Burik] loaded the bazooka a third time and from his shaky position fired at the tank. Jerry had had too much and withdrew up the hill. [Burik] with utter disregard for his own safety then tried to push another injured soldier into a foxhole.' Burik turned and called for more bazooka ammunition, then fell unconscious along the side of the road. Later he died from his wounds.

Another attempt to seize the road junction on Hill 278 was led by Lieutenant Colonel Samuel A. Hogan, with a battalion of the 119th Infantry riding on his tanks from the 3rd Armored Division. They took a circuitous route round to the west of Mortain and across the railway bridge near the Abbaye Blanche roadblock. Held up by the *Der Führer* Regiment of the *Das Reich*, they had to spend the night in all-round defence east of the road. Then, on 10 August, they were involved in furious fighting among high hedgerows which cost Hogan nine Shermans.

There was a particular hedgerow which the Shermans had to break through to continue the advance. After a 'rhino' tank made an opening, Lieutenant Wray, who had acknowledged that it was a suicide mission, led the charge through the gap. As his Sherman broke out into a wheatfield, a concealed German Panther scored a direct hit. Several of the crew died instantly. Wray himself jumped from the blazing tank, his body badly burned. He fell to his hands and knees, while the supporting infantry platoon, commanded by Lieutenant Edward Arn, watched in horror. 'Then he pulled himself to his feet,' Arn recounted, 'and started back towards the hedgerow he had just busted through. It seemed as if he remembered something because he went back to the tank. He helped get another man out and they both started to run, but the Jerries cut them down with a burst of machinegun fire.'

Arn's platoon had pulled back into the nearest hedgerow, but to their surprise they were able to exact a rapid revenge. A group of Germans walked up to inspect Wray's burning tank. 'They came out in a little bunch and stood around it,' said Arn. 'Curiosity, I guess.' Arn and his men 'mowed them down'.

Hogan's combat team was so short of men that Sergeant Kirkman went back to Le Neufbourg to fetch reinforcements. He returned with thirty-six inexperienced replacements through German artillery fire. Several were killed or wounded on the way. According to Kirkman, the man right next to him was hit with a splinter from a treeburst which entered the back of his head and came right out through his face. The new arrivals were severely shaken by the time they reached the combat team. Lieutenant Arn asked Kirkman where his replacements were.

'There, under that tank,' the sergeant replied.

Most of these replacements, 'suddenly placed under the heavy enemy artillery and machinegun fire, were frozen into immobility'. This, of course, made them doubly vulnerable. Arn recounted that he 'had to actually boot some of them in the tail to get them to move for their own protection. One man crouched in a foxhole with his hands clasped over his head and got a direct hit from an 88 that took his head clean off.' Out of the thirty-six new men, only four survived.

Hogan's reduced force, almost within striking distance of its objective, was attacked in the flank by a panzergrenadier battalion. The Americans fought them off, then as soon as the Germans had disappeared into their foxholes, they bombarded them with white phosphorus. The shower of burning particles forced them to jump out. The Americans then switched to high explosive to cut them down. Soon after night fell, German aircraft arrived to attack the American positions, 'but instead they bombed their own troops who frantically shot off green flares to stop this unexpected blow'. Colonel Hogan commented that the sight was 'very enjoyable'.

Before dawn on 10 August, the SS *Kampfgruppe* besieging the 'Lost Battalion' began the first of a series of attacks. Lieutenant Weiss again called down fire from their supporting artillery battalions. Communications, however, were becoming increasingly difficult as he could not recharge his radio batteries. Medical supplies were desperately needed. The battalion had no doctor and aid men cared for their wounded in deep slit trenches. All the soldiers felt weak from lack of food. Some of the more daring slipped out in foraging parties at night to fetch carrots, potatoes and radishes from allotment gardens down the hill. Two sergeants even managed to find some rabbits in cages being fattened for the pot by locals.

That afternoon C-47 transport planes, escorted by P-47 Thunderbolts, dropped seventy-one containers on Hill 314, but due to the breeze only a few fell within the American perimeters. Ammunition and rations were recovered, but no batteries or medical supplies. The 230th Field Artillery Battalion then tried to fire packs containing blood plasma, morphine, sulfa and bandages on to the hilltop using 105 mm smoke shells hollowed out. Only three packages were recovered and none of the plasma survived its explosive journey.

Although little could be done for the wounded on Hill 314, ambulances ferried casualties from the fighting elsewhere back for treatment. In addition to the usual battle injuries, there were many caused by rock fragments. The 128th Evacuation Hospital near Tessy-sur-Vire ran out of tentage. Ambulances waiting to unload were backed up for half a mile down the road.

*

By the evening of 11 August, the *Das Reich* had been forced to withdraw from their positions west of Mortain. And although the American counter-attacks from the south with the 35th Infantry Division and the 2nd Armored Division had been badly coordinated with the 30th Infantry Division, they were finally within reach of Hill 314.

That day, Kluge managed to persuade the OKW and Hitler that, as a temporary measure before resuming the Avranches offensive, part of Panzer Group Eberbach should counter-attack the American divisions threatening the supply base at Alençon. This was Kluge's only way of starting a retreat before they were encircled. 'Under cover of this operation, the Seventh Army was to withdraw,' one of his corps commanders observed.

That night, after firing off most of their artillery ammunition, German units began to pull back. They covered their traces well in most places, retiring behind an aggressive rearguard. The Americans were not sure of what was happening until after daylight on 12 August. The 1st Battalion of the 39th Infantry, as they advanced, found jocular thank-you notes from German panzergrenadiers for the chocolate, cigarettes and ammunition which had been dropped on them by mistake, instead of on Hill 314 above Mortain.

The withdrawal did not escape the attention of Lieutenant Weiss up on the Rochers de Montjoie. He called down fire on the troops and vehicles heading east and soon five artillery battalions were bombarding their exit. The 'Lost Battalion' was finally relieved. Trucks with food and medical supplies followed the troops as they trudged up the hill. The 2nd Battalion of the 120th Infantry on Hill 314 had suffered nearly 300 casualties out of 700 men. The battalion received a presidential citation for its outstanding resilience and bravery. Its heroic defence had been an essential element in the victory.

Colonel Birks, the commander of the 120th Infantry, had first hurried to the Abbaye Blanche roadblock, fearing to find only a few survivors. He was amazed to hear that just three men had been killed and twenty wounded out of this force. Birks walked up the different roads to survey all the burnt and smashed German vehicles. 'It was the best sight I had seen in the war,' he said afterwards. He proceeded down the hill and round the corner into Mortain.

The main street was impassable to vehicles. The centre of the town was little more than a heap of ruins, with just some walls and chimneys still standing. Most of the destruction had been wrought on the eve of its liberation. Almost unbelievably, the chief of staff of the 30th Division said, 'I want Mortain demolished . . . hammer that all night, burn it up so nothing can live in there.' This innocent French town had been destroyed in a terrifying fit of pique. Birks, to his astonishment, found himself being embraced by a small group of his officers and men in an emotional state, having been trapped there for several days and during its bombardment the night before.

Late on 13 August, the 12th Infantry Regiment and its 'incredibly weary troops' returned to the 4th Division to rest. It appears that their commander, Major General Barton, did not fully appreciate what his men had been through. He was more concerned about 'the attitude of "silent mutiny" which recently appeared among some men who up to now had been good soldiers. These men have decided that they're being pushed around, that nobody cares about them and they have decided that they are through and will quit trying.' The officers, he implied, were partly to blame for not keeping their men 'in fighting spirit'.

When Warlimont reported on the failure of Operation Lüttich, Hitler listened to him for almost an hour in the *Wolfsschanze* in East Prussia. 'Kluge did it deliberately,' was all he said when Warlimont had finished. 'He did it to prove that it was impossible to carry out my orders.'

25

Operation Totalize

While the American 30th Division fought desperately to hold on to Mortain, the newly constituted First Canadian Army launched another major attack down the road to Falaise. This was Operation Totalize. Montgomery did not think much of its commander, Lieutenant General Henry Crerar, and made it abundantly clear. He saw him as a gunner of the First World War, uninspiring and ponderous. Crerar's rigidity had not been admired by the Canadian 1st Infantry Division in Italy, who much preferred serving under experienced British commanders from the Eighth Army.

There was also a political dimension. Crerar was determined to defend Canadian interests. Monty saw this as a challenge to his command. Senior Canadian officers detected a supercilious attitude towards them, which was not helped when Montgomery sent some of his staff officers to Crerar's headquarters to supervise the operation. Montgomery also regarded Major General Rod Keller of the 3rd Canadian Division as 'quite unfit to command a division'. On the other hand, he greatly admired Lieutenant General Guy Simonds of II Canadian Corps, who planned and commanded Totalize.

Because of the shortage of Canadian troops, First Canadian Army was made up to strength with I British Corps and also the recently arrived 1st Polish Armoured Division. The attack was to begin just before midnight on 7 August. The 51st Highland Division, now returning to their earlier high standard, would advance down the east side of the Caen–Falaise road, while the 2nd Canadian Division advanced on the west side.

General Crerar, aware that stories of the SS killing Canadian prisoners had spread to his newly arrived troops, issued a strong order against committing excesses 'to avenge the death of our comrades'.

Simonds had learned from earlier British mistakes, especially those made during Goodwood. He decided to launch a night attack to reduce losses from the Germans' vastly superior 88 mm anti-tank guns. He also mounted leading infantry units in armoured vehicles. To obtain a sufficient quantity of carriers for them, the 105 mm artillery guns were removed from self-propelled 'Priests', which were dubbed 'defrocked Priests'. This would help the attacking formations to move forward with infantry immediately the bombers had finished saturating the German front-line positions.

Simonds, however, was misled by information gathered from a Yugoslav deserter who had slipped across the lines from the 89th Infanterie-Division to surrender. This man reported that his division had just replaced the 1st SS Panzer-Division. Simonds, not realizing that the *Leibstandarte* had been diverted to the Mortain counter-attack, assumed it had simply been withdrawn to stiffen the second line between Saint-Sylvain and Bretteville-sur-Laize. This influenced his view of the battle. He decided that the second phase, led by the Polish and Canadian armoured divisions, should not begin until after another bombing attack at 13.00 hours the following day.

The start-line for Totalize was along the Bourguébus ridge. The Canadians had already lost many men hammering away at the villages of Verrières, Tilly-la-Campagne and La Hogue, where their attack had in fact delayed the departure of the SS *Leibstandarte* for Mortain. The tank crews of the British 33rd Armoured Brigade with the 51st Highland Division had a 'last supper' of bully beef and hard-tack 'dog' biscuits, mugs of tea made foul with over-chlorinated water and a rum ration out of a large stoneware bottle. It was a hot night, so tank crews wore little more than a pair of shorts under their denim coveralls. Most felt the usual chill up the spine and an empty feeling in the guts at the prospect of battle.

At 23.00 hours on 7 August, a bombing raid on the flanks of the advance began with 1,000 Lancasters and Halifaxes. Without waiting, the offensive started with seven mobile columns of tanks and Priests carrying the infantry. An artillery bombardment, advancing at ninety yards a minute, preceded them. Each column – three British on the

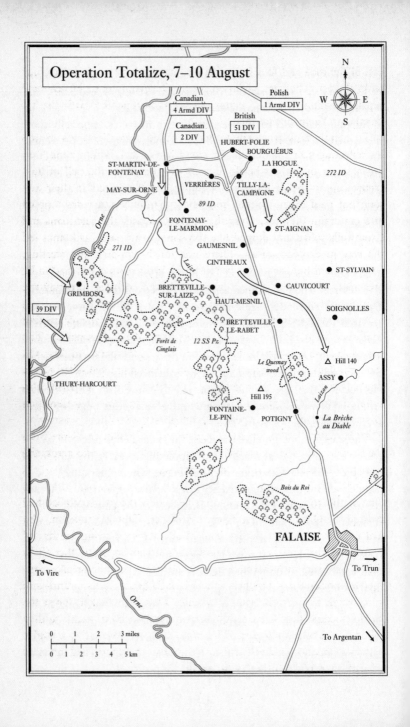

Operation Totalize, 7–10 August

N
W   E
S

Polish
1 Armd DIV

Canadian
4 Armd DIV

British
51 DIV

Canadian
2 DIV

HUBERT-FOLIE
BOURGUÉBUS

ST-MARTIN-DE-
FONTENAY

LA HOGUE

272 ID

VERRIÈRES

MAY-SUR-ORNE

TILLY-LA-
CAMPAGNE

89 ID

FONTENAY-
LE-MARMION

ST-AIGNAN

Orne

GAUMESNIL

271 ID

CINTHEAUX

ST-SYLVAIN

Laize

BRETTEVILLE-
SUR-LAIZE

CAUVICOURT

GRIMBOSQ

HAUT-MESNIL

SOIGNOLLES

59 DIV

BRETTEVILLE-
LE-RABET

*Forêt de
Cinglais*

12 SS Pz.

△ Hill 140

*Le Quesnay
wood*

ASSY

THURY-HARCOURT

△ Hill 195

Laison

FONTAINE-
LE-PIN

POTIGNY

*La Brèche
au Diable*

Bois du Roi

FALAISE

To Vire

To Trun

Orne

0 1 2 3 miles

0 1 2 3 4 5 km

To Argentan

east of the road and four Canadian on the west – proceeded with four tanks abreast. They had practised keeping formation at night. 'Blimey! Square-bashing in tanks,' commented a radio operator with the 1st Northants Yeomanry on the left.

To help the tank drivers in the dark, 'artificial moonlight' was created by reflecting searchlights off the cloud above and Bofors guns fired green tracer over their heads to point the way. But the pall of dust thrown up by the shelling and bombing, and the craters in their way soon put paid to the column formation. A number of tanks toppled into craters in the dark. Over the uneven ground, the Shermans and Cromwells rolled and dipped like ships in a heavy sea. Flail tanks led the way to explode mines. There was much stopping and starting, with frequent hold-ups usually caused by hedgerows which had to be breached in the dark, with a dismounted crew member directing the driver with the glow of a cigarette tip.

As ordered, the British columns forged on even though heavy fighting continued in their rear for La Hogue and Tilly-la-Campagne. The Canadians also had trouble finding their way in the dark and dust. On the right flank, the Calgary Highlanders encountered well-sited 88s as they advanced on May-sur-Orne, and the Black Watch of Canada also suffered in their attack on Fontenay-le-Marmion. The 2nd Canadian Division's lack of battle experience contributed to its heavy casualties. The Germans resisted fiercely. They were already under pressure from the British 59th Division, which had just gained bridgeheads across the river to their rear in the Forêt de Grimbosq.

One of the 59th Division's infantry battalions, the 7th Norfolks, had crossed the Orne, following a very tall officer, Captain Jamieson, who had marched in to see if they could wade across. During the day of 7 August, the 26th SS Panzergrenadier-Regiment from the *Hitler Jugend* had counter-attacked. Sergeant Courtman of the Norfolks managed to knock out two Panthers and a Mark III Panzer with his anti-tank gun, which had greatly boosted morale. That night in the forest the Norfolks could hear more tanks moving about ahead of them, so they called for artillery support. The rapid fire of twenty-five-pounder batteries convinced many German soldiers that the British had invented an artillery version of the machine gun.

The next morning, the panzergrenadiers launched another counter-attack on the Norfolks. Captain Jamieson, wounded in the right eye and left arm, won a Victoria Cross for leading the defence of D Company. As they were about to be overrun, he called down artillery fire on their own position. Fortunately, radio communications were working well and again their artillery support was excellent. It was also sympathetic. 'The artillery has an awfully easy job compared with the infantry,' a young gunner officer noted in his diary. A medical officer with the 59th Division described the battle from a hill west of the Orne: 'A magnificent view of the Orne valley running down to the small town of Thury-Harcourt. There were fires burning in the woods on the far side of the valley caused by shells or mortar bombs.'

The Orne sector continued to be a heavy slog after the capture of Mont Pinçon. 'Here on the British front,' wrote Myles Hildyard at 7th Armoured Division headquarters, '[the Germans] are slowly being driven back but [they] fight very hard, naturally, or we should encircle them. It is tiring, unexhilarating fighting, but it pins down Germans and kills them.' Throughout Operation Totalize, soldiers on field punishment from the 5th Wiltshires continued to bury their dead from the battle for Mont Pinçon. 'During these days, I seemed to be doing nothing but burials,' their padre wrote. But he was uplifted by the astonishing resilience of French civilians in the face of suffering. 'The further on we go,' he wrote, 'the more wonderful the spirit of the French, for whom "liberation" usually means loss of everything.'

Either side of the Falaise road, most of Simonds's columns had reached their objectives by dawn on 8 August. East of the road, the 1st Northants Yeomanry and the Black Watch had taken up positions in woods and orchards just south of Saint-Aignan-de-Cramesnil. They were very close to Gaumesnil, where Oberführer Kurt Meyer, the commander of the 12th SS Panzer-Division *Hitler Jugend*, had set up an observation post. This was the critical moment of the whole operation. Simonds, certain that the Germans had established a strong second line with the 1st SS Panzer-Division, had organized a second bombing raid for soon after midday. His two breakthrough armoured divisions were ready to move, but now had to wait for the bombers.

'Panzer' Meyer had driven forward, alarmed by inaccurate reports that the 89th Infanterie-Division had collapsed under the onslaught. Standing upright in his Kübelwagen, he was horrified to see soldiers from the 89th fleeing towards Falaise. He claims to have jumped out of his vehicle and stood alone on the road, armed with just a carbine to shame them into turning back to defend Cintheaux. General Eberbach, still commanding the Fifth Panzer Army before handing over to Sepp Dietrich, came forward to meet him. He promised to send in the 85th Infanterie-Division as soon as it arrived, but its leading elements were still a dozen miles away. Meyer had already received news of the 1st Polish Armoured Division on the east side of the road and the 4th Canadian Armoured Division to the west. They were halted in their assembly areas, waiting for a new phase of the offensive.

Meyer said that their only hope was to confuse the enemy with a sudden counter-attack. Eberbach agreed. They both knew that if the Canadians and British broke through to Falaise, the Seventh Army, still trying to relaunch the Avranches counter-attack, would be cut off. Meyer decided that he must pull the panzergrenadiers of the Kampfgruppe Wünsche out of the Forêt de Grimbosq to face the Canadians.

Meyer went to Cintheaux to brief Waldmüller, his other *Kampfgruppe* commander for the counter-attack, and the panzer ace Wittmann, who was to support him with his Tiger company. Meyer claims that as they were discussing the plan, they saw a single American bomber appear overhead and drop a marker. Knowing what that signified, they ran for their vehicles. If they advanced immediately, they would miss the worst of the bombing to come. From the northern edge of Cintheaux, Meyer watched Wittmann's Tigers roll forwards as fast as they could go towards Saint-Aignan, even though the Allied artillery had begun its bombardment. Waldmüller's panzergrenadiers followed rapidly in their half-tracks. A machine-gunner yelled to Meyer, pointing to the north. The American bombing force was approaching. Meyer claims that one of his young SS soldiers, a Berliner, called out, 'What an honour! Churchill is sending one bomber for each of us!'

Four Shermans from the 1st Northants Yeomanry were well concealed behind hedgerows and in an orchard south of Saint-Aignan. Suddenly they heard their troop leader over the radio. 'View Hallo! Three Tigers moving north, line ahead.' The armoured monsters were following a small lane parallel to the main road. The troop leader ordered them to hold their fire. At that range the Sherman's 75 mm gun against the armour of a fifty-six-ton Tiger 'would be like a pea-shooter against a concrete wall'. The Shermans needed to wait until the Tigers were closer. The three with 75 mm guns would smother them with fire, while the one Firefly tank with the powerful seventeen-pounder, would try to pick them off.

Knowing the oft-repeated statistic that a single Tiger usually accounted for three Shermans, the tank crews found their throats go dry in fearful anticipation. Each loader checked that they had an armour-piercing shell in the breech, not high explosive. The gunner, peering through the telescopic sight, traversed the motorized turret slowly, following their target which the troop leader had allocated. The first and last Tigers were the immediate priority.

After an unbearable wait, their prey came to within 800 yards. The troop leader gave the order over the radio. Wittmann and his Tiger crews, unable to see their ambushers, were taken by surprise. As they came under fire, the Tigers shot back, but they could not identify the concealed Shermans clearly. The first two Tigers were set ablaze, the third, the one in which Michael Wittmann probably was, blew up completely. The Sharpshooters ambushed at Villers-Bocage had finally been avenged by a fellow yeomanry regiment.

The Sherman tank crews from the Northants Yeomanry could hardly believe that they had managed to knock out three Tigers for no losses.* But there was no time for jubilation. Mark IV tanks and panzer-grenadiers from Kampfgruppe Waldmüller could be seen advancing through the cornfields ahead.

Troops of the Polish Armoured Division, wearing their distinctive berets on the centre of the head, were over to the left of the Northants Yeomanry, awaiting their turn to advance. Similarly, the 4th Canadian Armoured Division had moved forward to the west of the Falaise road

---

* Observers from the 12th SS Panzer-Division *Hitler Jugend* and the medical officer of the 101st SS Heavy Panzer Battalion were convinced that five Tigers had been knocked out. The other two may well have been knocked out by the 144th Regiment Royal Armoured Corps.

and halted. There then followed another 'friendly fire' disaster as the main American bombing force arrived.

Formations of over 500 B-17 bombers began to attack six target areas across the front. German sources claim that their flak hit one of the lead bombers, which dropped its load short and that others followed suit. A British artillery officer watching also saw the flak break up the bomber formation. 'Other aircraft could not find their target and dumped their bombs behind Allied lines causing many casualties,' he wrote. A doctor who had to deal with the casualties recorded in his diary, 'The American air force has a bad reputation. They are just as likely to mass bomb our own lines as the Jerries – numerous Canadian and Polish casualties as a result.'

The Canadian and Polish troops which found themselves under attack from their own side rapidly threw yellow smoke grenades to mark their positions. But due to an appalling case of bad liaison between ground and air forces, the Americans were using yellow markers for their bombing. As a result, 315 Canadians and Poles were killed or wounded. The Poles, with considerable self-restraint, described the incident as 'unfortunate support given by own aircraft'. But the blow to morale and the confusion were to slow the second phase of Simonds's offensive, with fatal effect. The bombing itself had achieved nothing save to handicap the subsequent advance. With the benefit of hindsight, Simonds should have done without it altogether so as to have maintained momentum. He should have sent in his two armoured divisions in the morning, while the Germans were still reeling from the night attack, rather than halting them to wait for the bombers.

Despite the destruction of Wittmann's group of Tigers, the counter-attack by Meyer's two *Kampfgruppen* took the two new Allied armoured divisions aback. Their subsequent performance was hesitant to say the least. After one disastrous cavalry charge in tanks, the Poles were cautious because they were very short of men. Most of their men had fought against the German invasion of Poland in 1939, then escaped across Europe in 1940 to defend France, and finally reached England to continue the battle. German soldiers called these exile volunteers 'the Sikorski tourists', after their commander-in-chief and their astonishing journeys.

Polish recruiting teams had even been scouring prisoner of war camps to find Wehrmacht soldiers of Polish origin to make up their numbers. Quite a few served as a result on both sides during the Normandy campaign. The Canadians were also short of men, after their very heavy losses south of Caen, especially around Verrières and on the Bourguébus ridge. Unlike the British, they could not produce reinforcements by disbanding a division.

It became clear during the afternoon of 8 August that the immense possibilities opened up by Totalize were rapidly lost. The Canadians to the west of the Falaise road suffered from bad communications and bad map-reading. Simonds became frantic at the lack of drive shown by the 4th Armoured Division, yet despite all his urging, few columns obtained any momentum. He ordered them to continue the advance during the night, but many units simply retired to all-round defence positions to await the next dawn.

The Germans, however, did not yet know how effective Meyer's counter-attack had been. Eberbach had been out of touch with Meyer since noon. At 21.10 hours that evening, Kluge, already desperate about the failure at Mortain, stated that the situation on the Falaise front was 'becoming very serious'. He thought that the 89th Infanterie-Division and the *Hitler Jugend* were 'practically destroyed' and that the bulk of the artillery was lost. He warned that a further Allied advance south towards Falaise would mean that their 'own attack towards Avranches would lose its purpose'. Kluge promised to send a Panther battalion of the 9th Panzer-Division and one from the SS *Hohenstaufen*, but neither was able to disengage from their own battles.

During the next day, 9 August, the panzergrenadiers of the *Hitler Jugend* continued to resist fiercely in small groups, holding off vastly superior Allied forces. But the greatest obstacle to the advance of the armoured divisions, as during Goodwood, remained the 88 mm guns, of both the SS and the Luftwaffe. The Luftwaffe's III Flak Corps had just moved another forty of them forward to the Falaise front.*

---

* The Luftwaffe III Flak Corps was commanded by Generalleutnant Wolfgang Pickert, who in November 1942 had pulled his 9th Flak Division at Stalingrad out during the Soviet encirclement of Paulus's Sixth Army.

Before dawn, Simonds ordered one column, known as Worthington Force, to advance south beside the Falaise road and seize Hill 195, north-east of Fontaine-le-Pin. This column, consisting of the British Columbia armoured regiment and two companies from the Algonquins, became hopelessly lost. They crossed the Falaise road south of Cintheaux and, instead of switching back to the west side, carried on and occupied Hill 140 instead of their real objective, four miles to the south-west. Convinced that they had seized the right hill, they reported back and waited.

Meyer's new observation post was just three miles to the south on another hill at La Brèche-au-Diable. As soon as the SS spotted this isolated detachment, Kampfgruppe Waldmüller prepared an attack. Worthington Force was surrounded for the rest of the day. When they called for artillery support, the 4th Canadian Armoured Division presumed that they were on Hill 195, as they claimed, and provided heavy interdiction fire there, which did no good at all. Worthington's ghastly mistake was discovered only in the afternoon. The Grenadier Guards of Canada, an armoured regiment, was sent to their aid, but they lost twenty-six Shermans in the open. Colonel Worthington was killed and his force virtually wiped out. Some of the survivors managed to slip through to join the Polish armoured division.

On the Orne flank, the German 271st Infanterie-Division received permission that evening from General Eberbach to pull back into the Forêt de Cinglais. Their commander, Generalleutnant Paul Dannhauser, recorded that they had lost half their officers and NCOs. He also noted that because German aircraft were seen so rarely, his own men opened fire at them immediately, assuming them to be Allied.

The British, now south of Mont Pinçon to the west of the River Orne, had encountered the new German defence line either side of Plessis Grimoult. British troops dubbed the place 'Bloody Village – a second and even worse Stonkville', because of the Nebelwerfer rockets raining down. Several tank commanders were killed by shellbursts in the crown of a tree.

Despite the pressure on the Orne flank, Kluge received reassuring news during the afternoon of 9 August. The German line forward of Falaise had been re-established far more rapidly than he had dared hope only twenty-four hours before. After a discussion with the OKW, he agreed to relaunch Operation Lüttich, the counter-attack towards Avranches. Eberbach took command of the panzer group on the Mortain front, while Sepp Dietrich replaced him as head of the Fifth Panzer Army.

This decision by the Germans to relaunch the Avranches offensive raises an intriguing but unanswerable question. Did the failure of Operation Totalize turn out to be an advantage for the Allies in the end? If the Canadians had reached Falaise and Kluge had decided to begin his withdrawal from Mortain on 9 August, would much more of the German Seventh Army, or much less, have managed to escape encirclement later?

Simonds, sorely disappointed, still tried to force forward the advance the next day, 10 August. He wanted to break through the woods at Le Quesnay and on across the River Laizon. But although I SS Panzer Corps was reduced to only forty tanks, most of its 88 mm guns were still in action and formed a powerful screen round Potigny. The Poles particularly felt that the 'crystal-gazers' had gravely underestimated German anti-tank defences. There was also little support from Typhoon squadrons, due to bad visibility, but the British and Canadians still do not appear to have improved ground–air cooperation to the degree which the Americans had achieved.

That evening, the *Hitler Jugend* claimed that they had knocked out 192 Allied tanks in the last two days. The OKW communiqué increased the figure to 278 Allied tanks destroyed on both sides of the River Orne. The Allies had in any case lost well over 150 tanks and General Simonds felt obliged to call off the offensive that night. He could only reflect bitterly on the loss of momentum on 8 August. The need to wait for the bombers in the second phase of his plan had given the Germans their chance.

The fight for the Falaise road appears to have been another savage battle. General Crerar's warning against retaliation does not seem to have had much effect, considering that there were only eight prisoners from the hated *Hitler Jugend* in the 1,327 prisoners of war taken to the rear by the II Canadian Corps. Of course, the young SS fanatics were the least likely to surrender even when surrounded, but the figure is nevertheless striking.

*

Unlike Simonds's forces attacking Falaise, General George Patton's Third Army, rampaging through the German rear seventy miles to the south, did not have to worry very much about 88 mm anti-tank guns. Patton's main concern was keeping his army replenished. 'The forces are so large,' he wrote, 'twelve divisions to me alone – that the supply system is colossal.' According to General John C. H. Lee, the chief of SHAEF's rear services, Patton tried to 'appropriate the whole of fuel resupply for his own army'. He flattered the truck drivers, handing them Third US Army patches, and sometimes he even commandeered the trucks to shift his infantry rapidly. This provoked exasperation and admiration in his colleagues.

The United States Army was the most mechanized force that the world had ever seen, but that brought its own problems. A single tank on average consumed 8,000 gallons of fuel a week. The 3rd Armored Division estimated that just following the road, the division required 60,000 gallons a day. If the division had to go across country, the figure soared. (One 3rd Armored quartermaster calculated 125,000 gallons for the whole division to move 100 yards.) On top of the fuel, an armoured division required thirty-five tons of rations per day for 21,000 men, including all those attached to it, and, depending on the intensity of the fighting, a far greater tonnage of ammunition.

The Americans met the challenge with ruthless prioritization. 'Supply trains' with fuel and oil received absolute priority. Each M-25 transporter carried 16,000 gallons. They even used ammunition trucks from the artillery to haul more gasoline. Military police and Piper Cubs were employed to monitor the progress of every convoy, and engineers worked round the clock to improve roads and bridges. At Le Mans, they built the biggest Bailey bridge so far in France and called it 'Miss America'. It was hardly surprising that the Germans were enviously amazed by what they called 'a rich man's war'.

On 8 August, while the battle for Mortain and Operation Totalize were at their height, Bradley became taken with the idea of trapping the Germans between Argentan and Falaise. Eisenhower, who was visiting his headquarters at the time, approved. Another visitor that day was Henry Morgenthau, the Secretary of the Treasury. Bradley, excitedly showing him the map, said, 'This is an opportunity that comes to a commander not more than once in a century. We're about to destroy an entire hostile army.'

Bradley rang Montgomery to outline the plan. Montgomery agreed somewhat hesitantly. He preferred a longer envelopment just short of the Seine. (If Bradley's idea had been proposed twenty-four hours later, once it was clear that Simonds's attack had stalled, Montgomery might well have rejected it.) Patton, who also preferred to catch the retreating Germans on the Seine, was even more dubious, but he agreed to divert Haislip's XV Corps north from Le Mans towards Alençon and Argentan, ready to meet up with the First Canadian Army coming south from Falaise. He felt that he could always set a second trap later.

Meanwhile, Patton's XX Corps was clearing his southern flank along the Loire valley. As they approached Angers, a company of Shermans cut off a small German convoy and found that they had captured 'the pay of an entire division'. On 9 August, part of the corps attacked Angers with three battalions abreast. They were held up by a large anti-tank ditch. Engineers with bulldozers filled in sections so that the tanks could cross and soon they were into the town. The three bridges over the River Mayenne had been blown, but the engineers managed to make one useable. On the night of 10 August, the Americans began crossing to the east bank. The 5th Division's 2nd Infantry Regiment set about clearing the town. 'The French beat up the collaborators,' reported one lieutenant, 'and although we took them away they would take them back and beat them up some more.'

German attempts to defend their southern flank seemed doomed to failure amid the chaos. The 9th Panzer-Division was badly mauled and the 708th Infanterie-Division completely smashed. Only sixty stragglers appeared later.* The local commander at Le Mans was accused of having 'lost his nerve', and faced a court martial.

---

* The unfortunate commander of the 708th Infanterie-Division, Generalmajor Edgar Arndt, was later taken prisoner by an FFI detachment commanded by Colonel 'Montcalm'. He was executed with two other officers on 25 August, the day of the Liberation of Paris, in reprisal for a massacre in Buchères carried out by the 51st SS Panzergrenadier-Brigade. They had shot sixty-six civilians, mostly women and children, and burned down forty-five houses.

Kluge and Eberbach had no clear idea where Patton's spearheads had reached. But on 10 August, the Germans intercepted a radio message of the 5th Armored Division. This confirmed their fears that the left flank of Patton's Third Army was swinging north towards Alençon, threatening both their rear and their main supply base. Scratch units were made up in the town from 'supply troops, maintenance platoons, and tanks under repair' from the remnants of the Panzer Lehr Division. Panzerfaust launchers were distributed to mechanics and cooks alike. But Alençon was doomed.

On 11 August at midday, Eberbach reached LXXXI Corps headquarters north-east of Alençon for a meeting with Kluge and Hausser. They heard that the 9th Panzer-Division had been badly battered and was retreating to the woods north of the town. The 9th Panzer, now reduced to little more than an infantry battalion, an artillery battalion and six tanks, would not be able to hold out much longer. The Americans would overrun the corps headquarters very soon. The senior officers present made preparations for a hurried departure to the east. There was now not even time for Eberbach's counter-attack on the southern flank with the panzer divisions withdrawn from Mortain. As soon as they arrived, they could do nothing but try to form a defence line. The German military order in France was collapsing around their heads, yet Hitler was still insisting, 'The counterattack against Avranches must be carried out!' Eberbach was almost speechless with rage. 'It was inconceivable that OKW could not see this trap, especially after Stalingrad, Tunis and the Crimea.'

Suddenly, tank guns could be heard nearby. 'Enemy shellfire began falling in the area,' wrote Eberbach. 'All around us smoke clouds were arising from burning cars. Not until darkness were we able to break camp. As we passed through Sées, I noticed a bakery company taking up defensive positions. All the streets were flooded with rear services streaming northwards.' Feldgendarmerie and roving courts martial to deal with deserters were deployed round road junctions. Most of the stragglers were formed into improvised combat teams.

Next day, on Eberbach's orders, the 116th Panzer-Division, the first to arrive from the Mortain sector, moved towards Sées, but it blundered into the French 2ème DB, which had just joined Haislip's corps. That evening, Eberbach heard that the division had been almost wiped out by artillery and tank fire and that the Americans were forcing their way towards Argentan. Eberbach's small staff escaped again, but it took them six hours to move twenty miles. The narrow roads were jammed with Wehrmacht vehicles which moved at walking pace. The loss of the supply base near Alençon meant that both the Seventh Army and Panzer Group Eberbach had to be supplied by the Fifth Panzer Army, which was itself dangerously short of fuel and ammunition.

News of the destruction of the 9th Panzer-Division had not yet spread among the divisions retreating east from the Mortain sector. They thought the southern flank was now protected. Allied fighter-bombers continued to target soft-skinned vehicles, especially supply trucks. It proved an effective tactic. The lack of fuel forced the 1st SS Panzer-Division *Leibstandarte Adolf Hitler* to abandon and destroy a number of its own tanks. Their troops were retreating with any vehicles to hand, usually with an air observer lying back on one of the front mudguards to watch for Allied fighters. One company still had a Fiat bus, spoils of war from Italy, but the tyres were so punctured that they had to be packed with hay instead of air.

Further south, Gefreiter Spiekerkötter and the small group of pioneers who had escaped through Avranches now headed east, just ahead of Patton's columns. In the back of their Soviet six-wheeler, the soldiers had hidden a small barrel of Calvados among the mines. Their commander, Leutnant Nowack, who found his men again in a small village square, unfortunately also discovered their hidden barrel of spirits. It was not long before he was drunk and making the ironic toast, 'Calvados still in German hands!'

Using mortar bombs or any other explosive, the pioneers continued to prepare bridges for demolition. In one small town, they had just finished their work when an SS assault gun, acting as rearguard, trundled over the bridge and ripped up all the wires with its tracks. Before the damage could be repaired, a Sherman tank appeared and started to turn on to the bridge. The SS assault gun hit it with the first shot and it burst into flames. The SS commander, an *Unteroffizier*, urged the pioneers to leave the town. They needed no further encouragement when American artillery shells began to fall a few moments later. By then their Soviet truck had finally broken down, so they seized a Citroën for their escape towards Paris. This may well have helped them avoid the attentions of Allied pilots and the Resistance.

Of the divisions withdrawing from the failed Avranches counter-attack, only General von Lüttwitz's 2nd Panzer-Division was in any sense battleworthy. It was given the task of holding the Ecouché sector, where it was to come up against the 2nd French Armoured Division – the 2ème DB – advancing north from Alençon, with the 5th US Armored Division on their right. Soon after dawn on 13 August, the 2ème DB received a shock when several Panthers, probably from the 116th Panzer-Division, blundered into their headquarters. French Shermans dealt with them at close range.

Leclerc's division continued that day to clear the Forêt d'Ecouves, nearly capturing General von Lüttwitz in the process. One detachment came across two 'badly disguised' civilians pushing a cart. On the cart were two sacks filled with their Wehrmacht uniforms. The French soldiers roared with laughter at their prisoners, who seemed to be relieved that the battle was over for them. '*Guerre kaputt!*' they said.

There was a considerable amount of confusion on the Allied side too as other divisions tried to fight their way north, only to find themselves blocked by a neighbour moving across their front. General Leclerc of the 2ème DB showed a lofty disregard of corps orders in the attack on the Forêt d'Ecouves. When he took over the main route to Argentan allotted to the 5th Armored Division, chaos ensued because it prevented the American division's fuel trucks getting through.

A deadly game of hide-and-seek developed in this forested area, with neither side clear where the enemy was. American recce groups would take up ambush positions round a crossroads and wait to see what turned up. On one occasion, a senior German officer who was clearly lost halted his staff car and climbed out with his map to study a signpost. The ambushers took great pleasure in making him jump by blowing up his staff car just behind him. When they ambushed a convoy and raked the trucks with fire, they would occasionally get a surprise themselves when one of the vehicles, carrying fuel and ammunition, went up in a massive explosion.

In the confused situation, the FFI and ordinary French civilians helped whenever they could with information. A tank battalion of the

5th Armored was warned just in time by a small boy about an 88 mm anti-tank gun concealed in the village they were about to enter. But the French were also taken aback by the casual manner of some American troops when it came to killing. In one small town, a French-woman asked what she should do about four Germans hiding in her house. 'There was no one to take care of them,' reported a lieutenant with the 10th Tank Battalion, 'so we put them up against a wall and shot them.'

The lead regiment of the newly arrived American 80th Division was held up both by the 2ème DB and then by the 90th Division of Haislip's corps. Colonel McHugh, its commander, went up in a Piper Cub spotter plane to try to see what was happening. A destroyed bridge proved another obstacle, and he needed to search for an alternative route. 'A Frenchman came up to me and in perfect English gave me proper directions to a bridge not far distant,' McHugh reported. 'I was so impressed that I took him along with me. Later, I found that he was an American serving in our Strategic Services [OSS] branch, and had been in that area for several months.'

McHugh had the usual problems with a green formation in combat. 'This was our first real fight and I had difficulty in getting the men to move forward. I had to literally kick the men up from the ground in order to get the attack started, and to encourage the men I walked across the road without any cover.' Then German tanks appeared. 'The commanding officer of my leading battalion panicked and the battalion took fright from him. It was necessary to replace his entire battalion to restore their nerve.' The 80th also suffered from the same mistakes in the replacement system. One regiment 'received seventeen cooks, when they had suffered no casualties in that department'. They could not send them back, so they had to send these unfortunate cooks into battle as infantrymen, despite their lack of training. Three days in action cost the regiment 523 casualties, of whom eighty-four were killed. On 13 August, McHugh, on hearing that part of the French 2ème DB was 'having a great tank battle near Carrouges', went up again in the Piper Cub to watch it from above. Armored Group D and the American 90th Division were fighting the 2nd Panzer-Division and part of the *Leibstandarte*.

Another armoured group of the 2ème DB then attacked a detachment of the 116th Panzer-Division in Ecouché. As the French Shermans entered the town, a priest leaned out of a window and shouted, '*Vive l'Amérique!*' '*C'est la France!*' a captain bellowed back to him. The *curé* came rushing out with a tricolore and yelled, '*Vive la France!*' The captain then insisted that he should also cry, '*Vive de Gaulle!*'

The 2ème DB had already suffered close to 600 casualties, including 129 from a bombing attack on 8 August before they had even got to grips with the enemy. As a result, they wasted no opportunity to pick recruits from among the hundreds of young Frenchmen who rushed to enlist. At Ecouché the division even enrolled an Alsatian deserter from the *Leibstandarte*, who ten days later took part in the Liberation of Paris in French uniform.*

On the afternoon of 13 August, a French fighting patrol entered Argentan, but was soon forced back. Another part of the 116th Panzer-Division had arrived, and the town's defences were now stiffened with the remnants of the 24th Panzer-Regiment, a flak regiment with quadruple 20 mm cannon and some 88 mm guns. The 116th had orders to hold Argentan at all costs to prevent a thrust up the road to Falaise. The 2ème DB remained in place to the south of the town acting as a 'solid cork'.

The evening before, Patton had just issued orders to Haislip to continue the advance north. 'Upon capture of Argentan push on slowly direction of Falaise . . . Upon arrival Falaise continue to push on slowly until you contact our Allies.' He had then spoken to Bradley by telephone from his advance headquarters near Laval, begging to be allowed to close the gap, but Bradley refused. Soon after midday on 13 August, Patton tried again, but was told categorically by Bradley's headquarters to halt Haislip's XV Corps at Argentan. 'This corps could easily advance to Falaise,' he wrote in his diary on 13 August, 'and completely close the gap, but we have been ordered to halt because the British sowed the area between with a large number of time bombs. I am sure that this halt is a great mistake as I am sure that the British

---

* Within a few days, the 2ème DB set up a recruiting centre in a barn near Sées to process those volunteers who lacked military training. Two weeks later, most of them were sent on by truck to Saint-Germain-en-Laye and billeted in the barracks formerly used by the guard for Generalfeldmarschall von Rundstedt's headquarters.

[*sic*] will not close on Falaise.' He later suspected it was due to 'British jealousy of the Americans or to utter ignorance of the situation or a combination of the two'.

An advance north might not have been quite as easy as Patton believed. The 5th Armored Division, like the 2ème DB, encountered well-sited 88 mm guns and lost many men and vehicles as it probed forward. But Bradley did not want to move his forces into an area allocated to Montgomery's 21st Army Group. Both he and Eisenhower were extremely concerned about American and Canadian forces bombarding or bombing each other as they advanced from opposite directions.

Bradley also feared that XV Corps was too weak to hold the Falaise–Argentan gap against the German divisions desperate to escape. And he worried about its open left flank towards Hodges's First Army, the one where Hitler expected Eberbach to launch his counter-attack. All one can say is that the decision to try for a short envelopment between Argentan and Falaise was a mistake. Yet Montgomery afterwards received far more criticism in many quarters for refusing to change the boundary between the British and American army groups to allow Patton to strike north.

The failure of Operation Totalize to take Falaise has generated more debate than almost any other aspect of the battle for Normandy. Montgomery made a major miscalculation when he expected the Canadians to reach Argentan before the Americans. He had assumed that the Germans would switch more formations to defend their southern flank against Patton. He had also underestimated once again the difficulties of sending untried armoured divisions against a strong screen of 88 mm guns. The Allied obsession with Tigers and Panthers obscured the fact, unrecognized at the time, that they lost rather more Shermans and Cromwells to German anti-tank weapons and *Jagdpanzer* tank destroyers.

Whatever the precise reasons which contributed to the failure to close the Falaise–Argentan gap, the fact remained that the Americans were furious, and none more so than General Patton. A killing ground for the retreating German armies now had to be found further east.

26

The Hammer and Anvil

On 12 August, Major Neave with the 13th/18th Hussars, still pushing forward in the Orne valley, noted in his diary, 'Very hot – not good fighting weather however – the infantry stream with sweat and dust, and we just roast inside our tanks'. But they consoled themselves that it would soon be over. 'The bigger picture is terrific, old "Blood and Guts" [Patton] is plugging on towards Paris and here in Normandy the Boche must be very nearly surrounded.'

The Germans, however, were not nearly surrounded. A gap of some twenty miles still existed between Simonds's Canadian corps north of Falaise and Haislip's XV Corps round Argentan. Attempts that day by the 59th Division to increase its bridgehead over the Orne near Thury-Harcourt were frustrated by the German 271st Infanterie-Division and the steep wooded hills either side of the river.

The next morning, 13 August, Simonds briefed his formation commanders for a fresh offensive, Operation Tractable. While the main Canadian forces attacked again towards Falaise on Montgomery's insistence, the Polish 1st Armoured Division on the left flank would head further east towards Trun. Montgomery does not appear to have discussed plans clearly with Bradley, despite a meeting with him that same day. He seems to have reverted to his earlier idea of encircling the Germans on the Seine. Instead of sending the 7th Armoured Division to reinforce the Canadian attack, he dispatched it east towards Lisieux. Montgomery was already starting to lobby Eisenhower to give him all the supplies and support, so that 21st Army Group could charge through to Berlin.

Simonds launched Tractable just at 11.00 hours on the morning of 14 August. Instead of using darkness to avoid losses from the German anti-tank defences, he organized a heavy smokescreen fired by the artillery. Bombers were also used, despite the mishaps during Totalize. This time most of the medium bomber force of 811 aircraft were accurate, although seventy-seven of them dropped their loads on Canadian and Polish troops to the rear, causing 391 casualties. Unbelievably, the same mistake was made of using yellow target markers from the air and yellow smoke grenades on the ground to identify their own troops.

The Canadians soon found that the River Laizon represented a more serious anti-tank ditch than they had imagined. Some of their armoured regiments suffered heavy losses that day. The Poles to their left advanced with great élan, led by their reconnaissance regiment, the 10th Mounted Rifles.

On 14 August, Panzer Group Eberbach received an order from Hitler, passed on over the radio. 'The attack ordered by me southward past Alençon is to be effected under all conditions immediately as a preparation for an attack on Avranches.' Eberbach, furious with Hitler's continuing fantasy, replied with the tank strengths of his divisions: the *Leibstandarte Adolf Hitler* had thirty, the 2nd Panzer twenty-five, the 116th Panzer had fifteen and the 9th Panzer was down to a company of panzergrenadiers.

'The fighting morale of the German troops had cracked,' wrote Eberbach. 'They were not just exhausted and weak from hunger. The propaganda promises had all proved false – the invincibility of the Atlantic Wall, the V weapons which would bring Britain to its knees, and the talk of new aircraft and submarines which assured final victory.' Eberbach became aware of machine guns being thrown away and tanks being abandoned without cause, or even without being blown up. 'Stragglers without arms were numerous. "Catch lines" to the rear of the front had to be inaugurated [to seize deserters and those fleeing without authorization]. Even the SS was no exception to this rule. The 1st SS Panzer-Division had never before fought so miserably as at that time.' The Germans also feared an airborne landing in their rear, a plan which the Allies had considered but rejected.

That same day Patton, who had become completely exasperated with the enforced inaction of XV Corps at Argentan, flew to see Bradley. He wanted to drive for the Seine without any further delay. He would send XV Corps to Dreux, XX Corps to Chartres and XII Corps towards Orléans. He was in an exuberant mood by the time he saw Bradley. 'It is really a great plan, wholly my own,' he wrote in his diary, 'and I made Bradley think he thought of it. I am very happy and elated. I got all the corps moving by 20.30 so that if Monty tries to be careful, it will be too late.' Major General Cook, at his XII Corps command post near Le Mans, received a typically terse message from Patton, delivered by a senior Third Army staff officer: 'Take Orléans at once.' Within a few hours, combat command A of the 4th Armored Division had moved out on the road from Saint-Calais to Orléans – a 'jump of 85 miles'.

Three of Haislip's divisions, the newly arrived 80th Division, the 90th and the French 2ème DB, were to stay at Argentan while the rest forced east towards Dreux, which lay no more than thirty miles from the Seine. The rapid advance was a huge boost to morale, Patton noted the next day: 'The number of cases of war-wearies (the new name for cowardice) and self-inflicted wounds have dropped materially since we got moving. People like to play on a winning team.'

The unshaven tank crews of the Third Army had become heroes to the supply troops and others in the rear. 'A few of the enlisted men even tried to raise beards emulating the combat outfits,' wrote a doctor with the 2nd Evacuation Hospital, 'but our commanding officer soon put a stop to that.'

Some people became too carried away by the air of excitement at the apparently unstoppable advance. An American war correspondent, determined to beat his rivals, turned up in Chartres so as to witness the capture of the city. Unfortunately, he was two days early. The German 6th Security Regiment promptly took him prisoner.

Gefreiter Spiekerkötter, still with the pioneer group from the 256th Infanterie-Division which had escaped Avranches, reached Chartres in their battered Citroën. While the garrison troops were organized to defend the town against the approaching Americans, Spiekerkötter and his comrades discovered a Wehrmacht supply depot. It had been abandoned by its staff, but not yet looted. They wandered around, gazing in amazement at the shelves laden with every sort of food, wine, spirits, cigarettes, even electric razors, suede gauntlets and large bottles of eau-de-Cologne: luxuries which the front-line soldier had never seen. 'We'd have been happy to stay here for the rest of the war,' Spieker-kötter observed. They loaded the Citroën with tins of food, cigarettes, the suede gloves and a bottle of eau-de-Cologne, and set off to cross the Seine at Melun. They were fortunate not to have been stopped by Feldgendarmerie and forced into a scratch unit to defend the city.

On 15 August, while the Canadians had a tough fight advancing on Falaise, the Poles broke through on the left. Fortunately for them, most of the Luftwaffe 88 mm guns had been withdrawn, but their advance, which took them to the River Dives near Jort, was still an impressive feat. Meanwhile east of Caen, the British I Corps, now part of the First Canadian Army, forced the Germans back to the line of the lower Dives. But as is so often the case in mid-August, the hot weather suddenly ended with heavy thunderstorms and torrential rain. The hard dusty ground turned to 'a slimy paste'.

Kluge's headquarters, all too aware of the dangers, wrote that the supply situation was becoming 'more critical by the hour'. Fifth Panzer Army described their ammunition shortages as 'catastrophic'. The 85th Infantry Division was reduced to one and a half battalions and the *Hitler Jugend* had only fifteen tanks left. Yet that day, while the remnants of the German armies in northern France were seeking to escape from the total disaster of encirclement, the end of the Nazi occupation of France was being sealed in the south.

The invasion of southern France, Operation Anvil, had been key to American planning ever since August 1943. Churchill had fought the idea with relentless obstinacy. He did not want to divert troops from the Italian front, mainly because he dreamed of invading Austria and the Balkans to prevent a post-war Soviet frontier running all the way down to the Adriatic.

President Roosevelt, irritated by what he saw as Churchill's excessive mistrust of Stalin, outmanoeuvred the British at the Teheran Conference in November 1943. Without warning Churchill, he told Stalin about the plan to invade southern France as well as Normandy. The British were appalled. Stalin approved the idea immediately. He even said that the Swiss were 'swine', and suggested that they 'invade the country on [their] way up the Rhône valley'. A lack of shipping and landing craft stopped the invasion of southern France from coinciding with Overlord, as the Americans had wanted, but they would not be blocked from launching it later.

To the exasperation of Roosevelt, Marshall and Eisenhower, the British never stopped trying to divert Anvil, renamed Operation Dragoon, away from southern France. The heated arguments did more to strain the Anglo-American relationship than almost any other disagreement on strategy. Eisenhower also believed that Dragoon, making use of French divisions from Italy and North Africa, would justify the huge American investment and also bring the French in as partners.

Churchill suddenly suggested to Roosevelt on 4 August that Dragoon should be switched to Brittany, even though none of the ports were in operation and the Allied supply system in northern France was stretched to breaking point. 'I cannot pretend to have worked out the details,' Churchill added lamely. Roosevelt firmly rejected the idea. Churchill tried again on 5 August when visiting Eisenhower. 'Ike said no,' wrote his aide, 'continued saying no all afternoon, and ended saying no in every form of the English language at his command.' Eisenhower was 'practically limp' by the time Churchill left.

Events proved the Americans resoundingly right. The landings of 151,000 Allied troops along the Côte d'Azur from Nice to Marseilles were practically unopposed, the major port of Marseilles was secured and the invasion provoked a rapid German withdrawal from central and south-western France. Even Hitler was forced to recognize the necessity, wrote General Warlimont, 'especially when the first paratroop and airborne operations proved immediately successful. This was the only occasion I can recall when Hitler did not hesitate too long before deciding to evacuate territory.' But the sudden German retreat produced a savage cycle of violence in France.

The Resistance, scenting victory, increased its attacks, and the Germans, especially the SS, responded with cruel and indiscriminate reprisals. Security police and the Gestapo in many places massacred their prisoners before pulling out. Altogether some 600 were shot, including almost all Jews in German custody. In some areas, the Resistance had tried to switch from guerrilla warfare to open insurrection, usually with catastrophic results.

In the Vercors, a high plateau between Grenoble and Valence, a large force of 3,200 *maquisards* had cleared the area of Germans by the end of June and raised the tricolore. General Cochet in Algiers had failed to tell them to wait for the landings in the south of France. Even so, their attempt to hold ground against regular troops was contrary to every rule of guerrilla warfare. The Americans dropped 1,000 containers of arms by parachute on 14 July, but by then the Germans had surrounded the plateau with 10,000 troops backed by artillery. A week later SS troops were landed by glider and soon the whole area was overrun. The Maquis should have dispersed to fight another day, but despite lacking heavy weapons they attempted to fight a conventional battle against overwhelming numbers. Their desperate heroism ended in a massacre. The reprisals were barbaric, as the British official history of SOE in France recorded: 'One woman was raped by seventeen men in succession while a German doctor held her pulse, ready to stop the soldiers when she fainted. Another was eviscerated and left to die with her guts round her neck.'

The Resistance targeted the Gestapo and SS wherever they could. On 6 August, Sturmbannführer Ludwig Kepplinger of the 17th SS Panzergrenadier-Division was ambushed at Villiers-Charlemagne, south of Laval. The next day, the head of the Gestapo in Châteauroux was gunned down. On the evening of 10 August, German authorities announced that '128 terrorists were eliminated in fighting on French territory' that day. Three days later at Tourouvre in the Orne, eighteen men were executed and the main street was set on fire, almost certainly by members of the *Hitler Jugend*. The artillery regiment of the *Hitler Jugend* Division issued an order stating that 'reprisals cannot be harsh enough'.

The massacres continued until almost the end of August, even after any hope of holding on to France had gone. Only a savage bitterness remained. In Buchères near Troyes (Aube), an SS unit killed sixty-eight civilians, including women, children and infants. On 25 August, following an FFI attack on a Wehrmacht truck in which three German soldiers were wounded, the SS murdered 124 people, including forty-two women and forty-four children, at Maillé (Indre-et-Loire) and the village was destroyed. In the Aisne at Tavaux and Plomion, members of the SS *Leibstandarte Adolf Hitler* and the *Hitler Jugend* killed a total of thirty-four civilians, of whom only one was a member of the Resistance. In the twenty-six worst massacres in France during 1944, 1,904 civilians were murdered.*

The breakthrough in Normandy combined with the 15 August landings in the south of France triggered a hasty withdrawal not only by the Germans, but also by Vichy's hated paramilitary force, the *Milice*. Over the next few days, Luftwaffe and naval personnel from ports in southern and western France, Organisation Todt officials, supply and clerical personnel from military depots, security police – in fact the whole apparatus of the German occupation built up over the last four years – pulled out. A running battle was fought across France against the *Milice*. Well aware of their fate if they stayed behind, these criminal paramilitaries sought safety in eastern France and then Germany. Vehicles, bicycles and horses were seized as well as food to help them on their way.

German forces in the south-west ordered their men to escape in 'march groups'. Few got through. Most succumbed to hunger and exhaustion and were forced to surrender to the FFI or the Americans. The Resistance killed relatively few of their German military prisoners. They handed them over proudly to the Allies or to regular French forces. But hardly any Gestapo, SS or Security Police survived capture.

As part of a scorched-earth policy during the retreat, German detachments were ordered to destroy bridges, telephone systems, railways and ports, as well as any establishments which might help repair them. SOE liaison groups at 21st Army Group and SHAEF advance headquarters passed 'counter-scorching' requests to the Resistance, which meant thwarting German attempts to wreck communications behind them.

The collapse of the German occupying power also signalled the collapse of the Vichy regime. In Normandy, a senior Vichy official reported

---

* Fewer than 2,000 German soldiers died at the hands of the Resistance before the retreat of August 1944. Figures during the retreat have proved impossible to establish. Yet up to the Liberation, the Germans and the Vichy *Milice* killed some 20,000 people. Another 61,000 were deported to concentration camps in Germany, of whom only 40 per cent returned alive. In addition, 76,000 French and foreign Jews were deported east to concentration camps. Very few returned.

during the American breakthrough that, 'military events having taken a new direction', he would withdraw to 'rejoin French territory according to the orders of the government'. He retreated with the local Feldkommandant, who provided him with fuel for his car. But every time he tried to set up a new *préfecture*, first at Gavray, then Saint-Pois and then Mortain, the rapidity of the American advance sent him hurrying on. Pierre Laval, Marshal Pétain's prime minister, tried to persuade the old marshal to seek refuge at Eisenhower's headquarters.*

The power vacuum in large areas of France, especially in the Dordogne, the Limousin, the Corrèze, the Massif Central and the southwest, meant that the different groups of the Maquis began to settle accounts. They took revenge on genuine collaborators, but also on those class enemies they considered collaborators. This was not hard to foresee once the invasion started. A Vichy report to Paris just after the invasion spoke of 'regions where hideous civil war will reign'. In July, an agent reported back to London on the situation in the Limousin created by Resistance attacks and ferocious German reprisals: 'In the face of these barbarous acts, the whole region trembles. The peasants hide in the woods and scouts signal the arrival of any German vehicles. The country experiences at one and the same time the violence of the enemy, of the Maquis, and of the *Milice*. There is no longer any legal authority.'

There was much to avenge, but the moral outrage of vengeance also concealed a degree of political and personal opportunism. Some private scores were settled and rivals for post-war power done away with. Resistance groups killed some 6,000 people before the German withdrawal. Then, in what became known as the *épuration sauvage*, or 'unofficial purges', at least 14,000 more were killed. A few British and American troops also killed French collaborators, but most preferred to look away, feeling that, having not experienced German occupation, they were in no position to judge. Perhaps the most shocking statistic is that in Brittany a third of those killed were women.

French people as well as Allied troops were sickened by the treatment

---

* That autumn, both Pierre Laval and Marshal Pétain, the latter under protest, would be taken back to Germany to the castle of Sigmaringen. In 1945, both would be tried in France, Laval receiving a death sentence and Pétain life imprisonment.

meted out to women accused of '*collaboration horizontale*' with German soldiers. Some of the victims were prostitutes who had plied their trade with Germans as well as Frenchmen. Some were silly young girls who had associated with German soldiers out of bravado or boredom. Many more were young mothers whose husbands were in German prisoner of war camps. They often had no means of support, and their only hope of obtaining food for themselves and their children in the hunger years had been to accept a liaison with a German soldier. As the German writer Ernst Jünger observed from the luxury of the Tour d'Argent restaurant in Paris, 'Food is power.'

After the humiliation of a public head-shaving, the *tondues* – 'the shorn women' – were usually paraded through the streets, occasionally to the sound of a drum, as if France was reliving the Revolution of 1789. Some were daubed with tar, some stripped half naked, some painted with swastikas. In Bayeux, Churchill's private secretary, Jock Colville, recorded his reactions to one such scene: 'I watched an open lorry drive past, to the accompaniment of boos and cat-calls from the French populace, with a dozen miserable women in the back, every hair on their heads shaved off. They were in tears, hanging their heads in shame. While disgusted by this cruelty, I reflected that we British had known no invasion or occupation for some nine hundred years. So we were not the best judges.' The American historian Forrest Pogue observed of the victims that 'their look, in the hands of their tormentors, was that of a hunted animal'. Colonel McHugh near Argentan reported, 'The French were rounding up collaborators, cutting their hair off and burning it in huge piles, which one could smell miles away. Also women collaborators were forced to run the gauntlet and were really beaten.'

It was indeed 'an ugly carnival', as one writer put it, but this had been the pattern since soon after D-Day. Once a city, town or even a village had been liberated by the Allies the shearers would get to work. In mid-June, on the market day following the 101st Airborne's capture of Carentan, a dozen women were shorn publicly. In Cherbourg on 14 July, a truck-load of young women, most of them teenagers, were driven through the streets. In Villedieu, one of the victims was a woman who had simply been a cleaner in the Kommandantur. In the *département* of the Manche alone, 621 women were arrested for '*collaboration sentimentale*'. Elsewhere some men who had volunteered to work in German factories had their heads shaved, but that was an exception. Women almost always were the first targets. It was jealousy masquerading as moral outrage. The jealousy was mainly provoked by the food they had received as a result of their conduct.* Quite simply, these young women were the easiest and most vulnerable scapegoats, particularly for men who wished to hide their own lack of Resistance credentials.

Moral confusion, if not outright hypocrisy, existed on the Allied side too. At his airfield near Bayeux, Jock Colville found it ironic when Montgomery ordered all brothels to be closed. 'Military police were posted to ensure that the order was obeyed. Undeterred and unabashed, several of the deprived ladies presented themselves in a field adjoining our orchard. Lines of airmen, including, I regret to say, the worthy Roman Catholic French Canadians, queued for their services, clutching such articles as tins of sardines for payment.' The French, meanwhile, were shocked by the attitude of American soldiers, who seemed to think that when it came to young French women 'everything can be bought'. After an evening's drinking, they would knock on farmhouse doors asking if there was a 'Mademoiselle' there for them. More enterprising soldiers had learned some French conversation from the language books produced by the army. Supposedly useful gambits were also provided in the daily lessons published by *Stars and Stripes*, such as the French for 'My wife doesn't understand me.'

Mutual incomprehension and the clash of very different cultures affected Franco–American relations perhaps even more than the joy of liberation. A woman in a town south-east of Mortain described their ecstasy, waving flags and singing the 'Marseillaise' when a column of the American 2nd Armored Division arrived. The French were amused

---

* When Arletty, the great actress and star of *Les enfants du Paradis*, died in 1992, she received admiring obituaries. These tended to pass over her controversial love affair conducted largely in the Hôtel Ritz with a Luftwaffe officer (who subsequently became a West German diplomat and was eaten by a crocodile when swimming in the River Congo). But then letters to some newspapers revealed a lingering bitterness nearly fifty years later. It was not the fact of her sleeping with the enemy that had angered them, but the way she had eaten well in the Ritz while the rest of France was hungry.

by the Creole accent of Cajuns from Louisiana, but in their turn were taken aback when they found that the Americans 'clearly considered us to be backward. One of them asked me in English if I had ever seen a cinema.' She replied that the cinema had been invented in France, and also the motorcar. 'He was left stunned, and not entirely convinced.'

Many American soldiers, who already saw France as almost an enemy country because of the German occupation, found their prejudices strengthened because so many people reported 'their neighbours as German sympathizers'. Even members of the OSS and the Counter Intelligence Corps had little grasp of French politics and the '*guerre franco-française*', which had simmered away ever since the Revolution and had now boiled up again. There was a widespread view, rooted in American history, that the problems of the Old World stemmed from a corrupt aristocracy and the evils of European colonialism.

Such ideas were encouraged by left-wingers in the Resistance who provided them with intelligence, especially the militant Communist-led FTP. They had good reason to loathe the Vichy regime after the executions of Communist Party members as hostages during the Occupation. They also believed that this was the time for a new revolution. So they tried to persuade American officers, often with some success, that the French aristocracy and bourgeoisie were all collaborators. For their own political purposes, they deliberately made no distinction between those people from all classes of society who had supported Marshal Pétain after the débâcle of 1940 and those who had actively helped the Germans.

The task of filtering the tens of thousands of Frenchmen and women arrested for collaboration in the summer of 1944 proved overwhelming for the nascent administration of de Gaulle's provisional government. That autumn, there were over 300,000 dossiers still outstanding. In Normandy, prisoners were brought to the camp at Sully near Bayeux by the *sécurité militaire*, the *gendarmerie* and sometimes by US military police. There were also large numbers of displaced foreigners, Russians, Italians and Spaniards, who were trying to survive by looting from farms.

The range of charges against French citizens was wide and often vague. They included 'supplying the enemy', 'relations with the Germans', denunciation of members of the Resistance or Allied paratroopers, 'an anti-national attitude during the Occupation', 'pro-German activity', 'providing civilian clothes to a German soldier', 'pillaging', even just 'suspicion from a national point of view'. Almost anybody who had encountered the Germans at any stage could be denounced and arrested.

Tensions between liberators and liberated arose with incidents both large and small. A major source of resentment came with hundreds of road accidents, mainly the killing of livestock but also civilians, due to the constant stream of heavy trucks rushing south to supply the fighting troops. At the other end of the scale, a woman who saw a British soldier give an orange to a German prisoner was furious because French children had never even tasted one. Yet army cooks and others were kind to children, whose eyes opened wide at the slices of white bread cut for them, although they were not quite so keen when they received marmalade sandwiches.

The historian Claude Quétel, then a small boy in Bernières-sur-Mer, remembers the Canadian troops and his astonishment at seeing a black man for the first time in his life among them. The young Claude could not stop himself from asking why he was black. 'It's because I don't wash enough,' he joked. Claude took him literally. He wanted to repay the generosity he had received from the soldiers, so he dashed home and stole his mother's precious cake of soap, then ran back to offer it to the black soldier just before they left for the front. On seeing the outstretched hand with the cake of soap, all the soldiers collapsed in laughter. As the column of trucks moved off, Claude was left there sobbing uncontrollably.

Allied troops, however, became exasperated with the constant pilfering of equipment. The French authorities delicately termed it '*réquisitions irrégulières*'. A black market based at first on American and British cigarettes then branched into stolen fuel and tyres. But Allied soldiers were far from innocent when it came to stealing. In Caen, an officer with the civil affairs team wrote that British troops 'pillaging shops and premises pose quite a problem, but offenders are heavily punished when caught'. In the chaos of war, many soldiers who would never have stolen at home were tempted by what they thought were easy pickings.

'Our soldiers have done some looting,' noted Myles Hildyard at 7th Armoured Division headquarters, 'including two military police of this division who held up two old countesses near here in a château.' Even British officers pocketed objects when billeted in country houses, prompting an increasing number of French to observe that 'the Germans were much more correct'.

Yet the greatest weight on Norman hearts was the terrible destruction wreaked upon their towns and countryside. An American doctor described the forests stripped of their leaves by artillery fire, livestock carcasses rotting in the fields and towns reduced to a mass of rubble, 'with occasionally a cynical touch such as an advertisement for Singer sewing machines stuck to a wall which had not been demolished, or a house whose façade has been blown away in front of the dining room, exposing like a theatre set, with the table and the chairs carefully positioned round it'. When French refugees from the fighting returned to their wrecked homes, some were traumatized by the unrecognizable scene, while others were bitterly resigned to the futile waste. Sometimes a tiny detail brought home to Allied troops the suffering of the French. For one British soldier, it was seeing a little house called 'Mon Repos' destroyed by shellfire.

Mines and unexploded shells, despite work by Allied and French teams, would continue to maim farmers and children for several years to come. Any work of reconstruction concentrated on improving supply facilities for the Allied armies. In Caen, 15,000 troops were put to work reopening the inland port at the head of the canal, but few could be spared to re-establish essential services for civilians.

Normandy had indeed been martyred, but its sacrifice saved the rest of France. Paradoxically, as a leading French historian has pointed out, the slowness of the Allied advance in the first two months, grinding down the German army, worked in favour of the French, 'whose liberation was more rapid and less destructive, outside the Normandy battlefields, than one might have feared'.

The battle for Normandy was reaching its climax. On 14 August, Kluge decided that his troops had to break out in a north-easterly direction, 'otherwise they must expect the loss of all their forces'. Artillery units lined up their guns and fired off all their remaining shells before retreating. On 16 August, Kluge ordered an immediate withdrawal to the line of the River Orne and the crossing began that night. Flak units were brought in to guard the bridges, but Allied air activity appears to have presented little threat over the next two vital days. No troops were allowed to stop or rest in the area. Vehicles were pushed off the road if they broke down and the Feldgendarmerie exerted a strict traffic discipline. Nothing was allowed to slow the withdrawal. Panzer troops aroused anger among the *Landser* of the infantry by the way they simply drove over corpses, crushing them flat with their tracks.

On 16 August, the Canadians fought their way into the ruined city of Falaise, where William the Conqueror had been born in the great castle. Again they faced their fanatical opponents in the *Hitler Jugend*. Sixty of these battle-hardened teenagers held out for three days. The only two taken alive were wounded.*

To the east of Falaise, the Polish 10th Mounted Rifles reconnaissance regiment, supported by the 12th Dragoons in Cromwell tanks, had secured crossings over the Dives on 15 August. Their success was a fitting celebration on the anniversary of their victory over the Red Army in the Battle of the Vistula in 1920. That night the Poles in their bridgehead fought off counter-attacks, while the reconnaissance troops pushed down the road towards Trun. On 16 August, Simonds wanted to send his 4th Armoured Division towards Trun as well, but the whole of the following day was lost as they pulled out and reorganized. Their divisional commander showed little initiative or drive. The consequent lack of support to the exposed Polish armoured division forced it to halt less than eight miles from Trun.

Ultra was still reporting that the Germans intended to counter-attack against the Americans in the south and break through between Argentan and Sées. This confirmed Montgomery in his view that they should revert to an envelopment on the Seine, rather than cut off the Germans south of Trun. As a result he made the mistake of failing to reinforce the Poles with the 7th Armoured Division, which he had ordered to advance on Lisieux. The critical lack of detailed liaison with the Americans at this stage was more Montgomery's fault than Bradley's. Between

---

* The Canadians at the end of Operation Tractable had suffered 18,444 casualties, including 5,021 killed.

them they had failed to decide clearly where to cut off the Germans. It was only on 16 August that Montgomery decided to revert to sealing the pocket between Trun and Chambois. But by then part of Haislip's corps had set off towards the Seine.

General Patton was far more interested in developments in that direction. On 16 August, Major General Kenner, SHAEF's chief medical officer, was invited along for the ride to visit Haislip's XV Corps, which had just taken Dreux. Patton was on exuberant form. He had just visited two evacuation hospitals that morning and found that 'for the first time our wounded wanted to go back and fight'.

They set off in two Jeeps, one of which carried a heavy machine gun. Patton's bodyguard Al had also brought a Browning automatic rifle. Kenner, clearly concerned for Patton's safety in this dash across wooded country full of retreating Germans, suggested that he should go in front. 'No, by God,' came the reply. 'No one rides in front of me.' According to Kenner, 'Haislip nearly had a fit' when he heard how they had come. He insisted on providing an escort for the return journey, but Patton swore at the idea. In any case, he wanted to see how things were progressing with XX Corps at Chartres.

When they reached the command post of the 7th Armored Division, Patton asked when they were going to take the town.* He was told that there were still Germans fighting in parts of it and it might take some time. According to Kenner, Patton retorted, 'There are no Germans. It is now three o'clock. I want Chartres at five or there will be a new commander.' Kenner was impressed by Patton's 'instinct about the enemy', but Patton was wrong. American intelligence sources had estimated the defenders as only 1,000 strong, but another German security regiment had been rushed into the town the day before. General der Infanterie Kurt von der Chevallerie, the commander-in-chief of the First Army south of the Loire, had been holding a conference there when the 7th Armored's tanks were sighted advancing on the city.

One task force had managed to clear most of the city three hours before Patton arrived, but the other task force had been compelled to

---

* Kenner in his account confused the 7th Armored Division with the 5th Armored Division, probably because the 5th Infantry Division was also joining the battle.

withdraw as the Germans resisted strongly in the outer part of the town. The Americans had brought up artillery, but it was instructed to fire only on targets in direct sight: 'All effort was made to spare the destruction of historic buildings.' The battle was, however, completed the following day, when the second task force attacked the Germans who had withdrawn into the wheatfields outside. This unequal battle turned into a massacre. Mortar platoóns dropped white phosphorus shells 'all over the place and as the fields burned, the Germans started running out like rats. While this was going on the tanks were having a field day killing dismounted Germans all over the place,' 7th Armored Division reported. 'The entire operation was a huge success: this small force knocking out numerous anti-tank guns, capturing around 400 of the enemy, and killing several thousand of the enemy at a cost of four tanks and 62 casualties of their own.'

In any event Wednesday, 16 August had indeed been a memorable day for Patton. Divisions from his Third Army had entered or captured the major towns of Dreux, Chartres, Châteaudun and Orléans. He was also to have full credit for his exploits after all the secrecy created for Operation Fortitude had been lifted. This security restriction had exasperated the war correspondents, who longed to write about Patton's exploits. Eisenhower had just publicly stated to a press conference that the drive to the Seine was led by the Third Army commanded by Patton himself. 'Old blood and guts' immediately became an international star. And finally on that day, Patton heard that he had been confirmed in the permanent rank of major general, backdated to the previous year.

While Patton's Third Army raced towards the Seine, the Americans suffered a day's delay from confusion when reorganizing their forces round Argentan. On the evening of 16 August, General Gerow, the commander of V Corps, received orders from General Hodges of the First US Army to take command of the three divisions – the 80th, the 90th and the 2ème DB – which Haislip had left round Argentan. The Ultra warning of a German counter-attack prompted him to drive through the night to Alençon, where he set up a temporary headquarters at the Hôtel de France. He could not find out where XV Corps headquarters were supposed to be. Finally, he heard from the commander of the 80th Division that Patton had sent his chief of staff, Major General Hugh Gaffey, to command the three divisions. He found

Gaffey at a temporary command post north of Sées and the two senior officers hammered out an agreement. Gaffey would carry out the attack north ordered by General Patton for 17 August, then Gerow would take command that evening. But after confusing messages between Hodges and Patton, General Bradley stepped in and told Gerow to take over immediately.

Patton flew to see Bradley on 17 August to sort out the muddle. He had left his Third Army staff with the instructions that the attack north to seal the pocket was to go in straight away under Gerow's command if he rang through with the phrase 'Change horses'. At 12.30 hours, Patton called from 12th Army Group headquarters with these words. He then added that once the original objective was taken, the three divisions should continue 'thence on'. His chief of staff asked what 'thence on' meant.

'Another Dunkirk,' Patton joked. This typically thoughtless remark was later picked up by war correspondents and reported far too freely as: 'Let me continue, and I'll drive the Limeys into the sea.' In fact the changes of command at this crucial moment succeeded only in allowing the Germans another twenty-four hours to extricate more men and vehicles from the pocket.

By chance on that same day, Thursday, 17 August, stories of Eisenhower and Bedell Smith's renewed irritation with Montgomery had filtered back to Downing Street and Buckingham Palace. Sir Alan Lascelles, King George VI's private secretary, had a long talk with general 'Pug' Ismay, Churchill's military adviser, and recorded his thoughts in his diary: 'Ismay takes a sane and broad-minded view of the Americans – they have won their spurs, and the days are past when we could treat them as green and untried soldiers; in fact he went so far as to say that we might well have something to learn from them, and that maybe we have been a bit too "staff collegey" in our conduct of the war.'

Tensions were also building up with another ally as American troops approached Paris. After General Philippe Leclerc had heard that the 2ème DB was to stay at Argentan while the rest of XV Corps advanced towards the Seine, he went to protest to Patton. 'Leclerc of the 2nd French Armored Division came in, very much excited,' Patton wrote in his diary. 'He said, among other things, that if he were not allowed to advance on Paris, he would resign. I told him in my best French that he was a baby, and I would not have division commanders tell me where they would fight, and that anyway I had left him in the most dangerous place. We parted friends.'

Leclerc, who got on well with Patton, was far from reassured. Both he and General de Gaulle, who was on his way to France, were deeply concerned that Bradley might want to bypass Paris. They both feared that a rising in the capital by the Resistance would be exploited by the Communists. And in the event of civil strife, the Americans would almost certainly try to enforce their own military government, as President Roosevelt wanted.

29. An exhausted GI sleeping in the street after the capture of Marigny, 28 July.

30. Elderly refugees in La-Haye-du-Puits, 28 July.

31. Operation Bluecoat: the advance with Bren-gun carriers and a flail tank, 30 July.

32. German prisoners sent back to Cherbourg for evacuation to England.

33. Patton, Bradley and Montgomery putting on smiles for the camera at 21st Army Group headquarters.

34. Refugees in Saint-Pois, 10 August.

5. Mortain after its destruction by 30th Division artillery. 'I want Mortain demolished . . . so that nothing can live in there,' the division's chief of staff had ordered on 11 August.

36. Two Canadians – the second one is a sniper – advancing into Falaise, 16 August.

37. A road cleared through the destruction of the Falaise pocket.

38. Patton's spearhead with tank destroyers crossing the Seine on a pontoon bridge.

39. Three Resistance fighters in the Latin Quarter descending the rue de la Montagne Sainte-Geneviève, 22 August.

40. The Liberation: a Parisienne kissing one of General Leclerc's Fusiliers Marins, 25 August.

41. General von Choltitz signing the surrender of Paris, 25 August.

42. General de Gaulle and Leclerc (without his kepi) at the 2ème DB's temporary headquarters in the Gare Montparnasse, 25 August.

27

The Killing Ground of the Falaise Pocket

While 16 August had been a great day for Patton, Hitler declared that 'the 15th August was the worst day of my life'. He had become convinced that Generalfeldmarschall von Kluge was entering into secret negotiations with the Allies in Normandy. 'Hitler suspected that Field Marshal von Kluge was guilty of such treachery,' General Warlimont recorded. Hitler already regarded Kluge as an accomplice of the July plotters. Now he had become convinced that the stab-in-the-back of the Second World War was coming not from Jews and revolutionaries, as in 1918, but from the aristocrats of the German general staff.

On the afternoon of 14 August, Kluge had left La Roche-Guyon. He spent the night at Fifth Panzer Army rear headquarters in the small château of Fontaine l'Abbé, east of Bernay. Soon after dawn on 15 August, Kluge set off westwards into the Falaise pocket for a meeting with the two army commanders, Generals Hausser and Eberbach. Kluge rode in his Kübelwagen, accompanied by his aide, Oberleutnant Tangermann, another officer on a motorbicycle and a signals vehicle.

This small convoy was soon spotted by RAF Typhoons, which swooped into the attack. Their cannon fire destroyed the signals vehicle, seriously wounding its occupants, one of them mortally. The numbers of Allied fighter-bombers overhead made any further movement by road extremely dangerous. Kluge, already in a state of nervous exhaustion, seems to have suffered some sort of breakdown. He was settled in the shade of a tree to rest. One can only speculate about his state of mind, except to say that he found it hard to accept that his name would forever be associated with the collapse of the German armies in the West. Oberleutnant Tangermann even believed that his venture into the *Kessel*, or encirclement, was to seek death in the face of the enemy.

When General Jodl telephoned that day from East Prussia to speak to Kluge and heard that he had been out of contact since the morning, Hitler's distrust flared into open suspicion that he was negotiating surrender terms. Jodl ordered Army Group B and General Eberbach to make every effort to establish Kluge's whereabouts and to report back every hour. At 21.00 hours, a KR-Blitz teleprinter message, the highest priority, arrived from East Prussia. It stated, 'The Führer has ordered: so long as Generalfeldmarschall von Kluge cannot be found while away from his command post, I entrust Generaloberst Hausser with the leadership of both the Fifth Panzer Army and Panzer Group Eberbach.'

Only after dark was it possible for Kluge and his surviving companions to continue. They finally reached Eberbach's command post at 22.00 hours. The fifty-mile journey had taken sixteen hours. Generalfeldmarschall Keitel insisted on speaking to Kluge as soon as he heard of his arrival. It seems that OKW believed Kluge's account of his movements, but Hitler, who had planned to replace Kluge in any case after the failure of the Avranches counter-attack, immediately ordered Generalfeldmarschall Model to fly to France and take over. Model, 'one of the harshest and most feared army commanders', was a devoted follower of Hitler, who had awarded him the Knight's Cross with Diamonds. Rather like Kluge himself before taking command, Model had been convinced that the disaster in Normandy was entirely due to bad leadership.

Leutnant Dankwart Graf von Arnim, a staff officer in Paris, was woken at 04.30 hours on 17 August to be told that Model had arrived. He was to go at once to the headquarters of Oberkommando West at Saint-Germain-en-Laye. The first thing he heard was that Model, finding only a drunken army doctor there, went berserk and had him shot on the spot. Arnim was to accompany Model to La Roche-Guyon. There was an early morning mist as they set off up the Seine valley in a convoy, with an escort troop of self-propelled 20 mm flak guns provided on Hitler's orders. Arnim was seated next to the driver in Model's armoured staff car. Model reprimanded him severely for wearing a uniform cap instead of a helmet.

When they drove up to the entrance of the château, Arnim spotted the faces of staff officers peering anxiously from windows. Speidel, the chief of staff, met them on the steps. Behind him was Kluge, who had received notice of his dismissal just an hour before by teleprinter. Model, according to Generalleutnant Bayerlein, who was present at the meeting, announced that the troops in Normandy 'were a pack of cowards, that it was much easier to fight the western Allies than the Russians, and that he would see that things changed'.

Kluge accepted his fate with dignity. Yet he clearly feared not only that he would be made responsible for all that had gone wrong but, in the atmosphere of suspicion, that he might also face trial and execution like the other senior generals involved in the July plot. He sat down to write a long letter to Hitler, which he asked Oberstgruppenführer Sepp Dietrich to deliver later. As well as an explanation of the impossibility of the task he had faced, he wrote, 'I cannot bear the reproach that I have sealed the fate of the West through faulty strategy, and I have no means of defending myself. I draw a conclusion from that, and am dispatching myself where thousands of my comrades already are.' The letter was respectful and avoided placing any blame on Hitler. No doubt Kluge wished to save his family from the *Sippenhaft* vengeance of the Nazis.

He finally argued, like Rommel before him, that with little chance of victory the war should be ended: 'The German people have borne such untold suffering that it is time to put an end to this frightfulness.' Although Kluge had finally come to see the terrible folly of this vast conflict, there was still no thought of the suffering they had caused by their invasions. That consideration simply did not register in the German army *Weltanschauung*, with its fundamental confusion of cause and effect.

A car and escort were sent to bring Kluge back to Berlin. They stopped for a midday break in the woods of the Argonne, just short of Verdun. It was not far from where General von Stülpnagel had so unsuccessfully shot himself. Kluge gave his aide another letter, this one for his brother, then went off behind some bushes where he swallowed a cyanide pill. After Kluge's suicide, Hitler ordered another investigation into his 'mysterious disappearance' in Normandy, but again no evidence could be found of a meeting with American officers.

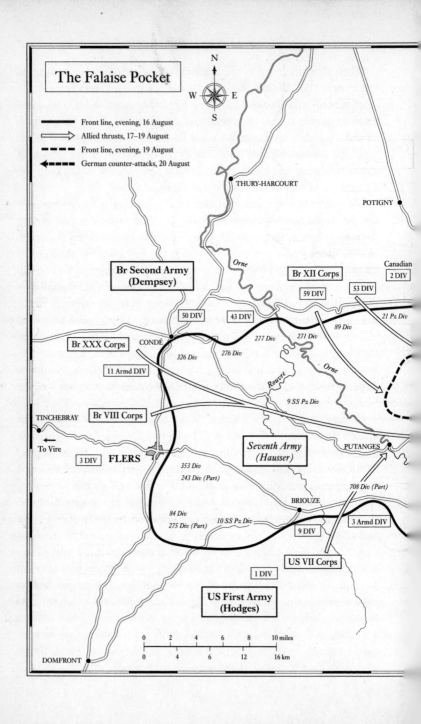

The Falaise Pocket

Legend:
- Front line, evening, 16 August
- Allied thrusts, 17–19 August
- Front line, evening, 19 August
- German counter-attacks, 20 August

N
W · E
S

THURY-HARCOURT

POTIGNY

Orne

Br Second Army (Dempsey)

Br XII Corps

Canadian 2 DIV

59 DIV | 53 DIV

50 DIV | 43 DIV

21 Pz Div

89 Div

Br XXX Corps

CONDÉ

277 Div | *271 Div*

326 Div | *276 Div*

Orne

11 Armd DIV

Rouvre

9 SS Pz Div

Br VIII Corps

TINCHEBRAY

→ To Vire

3 DIV | **FLERS**

Seventh Army (Hausser)

PUTANGES

353 Div
243 Div (Part)

708 Div (Part)

BRIOUZE

84 Div
275 Div (Part) | *10 SS Pz Div*

9 DIV | 3 Armd DIV

US VII Corps

1 DIV

US First Army (Hodges)

| 0 | 2 | 4 | 6 | 8 | 10 miles |
| 0 | 4 | 6 | 12 | 16 km |

DOMFRONT

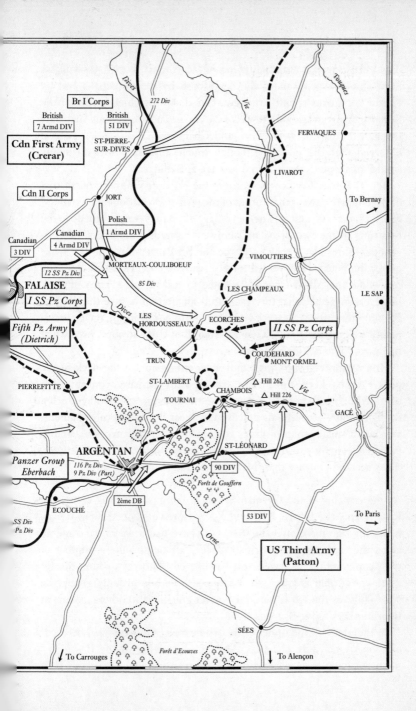

The Falaise pocket was tightening on 16 August, but it was still far from closed as a result of the delay both by the Canadians and by Gerow's V Corps round Argentan. Gersdorff, the chief of staff of the Seventh Army, was 'able to drive by car in both directions that day' through the gap between Trun and Chambois. One German general observed that the pocket, although much smaller, was disturbingly similar in shape to the battered lozenge at Stalingrad.

The II Panzer Corps was sent into the Forêt de Gouffern north-east of Argentan to defend that corner of the pocket, even though it mustered fewer than forty tanks. The next day, after they were refuelled, the remnants of the two divisions were sent towards Vimoutiers. Oberst-gruppenführer Hausser also sent the 2nd SS Panzer-Division *Das Reich* out of the pocket. He wanted a force ready to counter-attack from the rear when the Allied troops attempted to seal the gap. Army officers, however, suspected that this was purely an attempt to save the Waffen-SS. 'In other words *we* were good enough to be left inside the encircle-ment,' was the reaction of General Meindl of II Paratroop Corps when he heard. 'The SS look after their own.'

Other panzer groups were moved to either side of the neck of the pocket to help keep it open, but with a greatly increased concentration of Allied fighter-bombers overhead, vehicles had to stay hidden during daylight hours in orchards and woods. Near Trun, a local inhabitant watched a small group of tanks concealed under fruit trees. A soldier emerged from his turret with a violin and played some Viennese waltzes. They seemed to sense that this was the calm before the storm.

As the remains of the German Seventh Army pulled back across the River Orne, the British VIII and XXX Corps advanced rapidly east, liberating one town after another. 'We have had a warm welcome all along the route,' wrote a British officer, 'although quite a number of the people still seem dazed and bewildered. The very young do not quite know what is going on. I saw one little boy proudly giving the Nazi salute as though it were the correct greeting and others looking at their mothers to see if it was right to wave.'

In Putanges on the upper Orne, where many Germans had been cut off, the scenes were chaotic. 'While I was talking to the Brigadier,' wrote Major Neave in his diary, 'a German half-track – driven by a

Boche – and packed full of Boches passed by. Two civilian French – presumably Maquis – were sitting at the back with Sten guns, and a Frenchman on a motorcycle led the party. The Boche looked extremely unhappy and the French were shrieking with laughter.'

Meanwhile Hodges's First US Army was advancing from the south-west and the British XII Corps from the north-west. On 17 August, the Polish 1st Armoured Division received orders to push on to Chambois. But as the Poles were nearly five miles ahead of the Canadian 4th Armoured Division, they knew that they were in for a tough fight until support arrived. They reorganized rapidly. General Maczek sent the 24th Lancers and the 10th Dragoons towards Chambois, while the rest of the division took up positions around Mont Ormel. This was one of the dominant features along the high, wooded escarpment which overlooks the River Dives and seals the north-east end of the Falaise plain.

That day, the American 90th Division at Bourg-Saint-Léonard, south of Chambois, received a nasty shock when the *Das Reich* division and the remnants of the 17th SS Panzergrenadier-Division suddenly attacked, forcing them to withdraw rapidly. General Gerow sent them back that evening to recapture this vital high ground.

Generalfeldmarschall Model called a conference for 09.00 hours on 18 August at Fontaine l'Abbé. Eberbach, who had set out at 03.00 hours, still arrived two hours late because of the blocked roads. Oberstgruppenführer Hausser of the Seventh Army could not get through, so he was represented by Gersdorff, his chief of staff. Model gave them instructions for withdrawal to the line of the Seine. The panzer divisions were to hold open the bottleneck. But halfway through the meeting news came in that the Canadians had indeed taken Trun. Eberbach left immediately to organize a counter-attack by II Panzer Corps, now outside the pocket, but another shortage of fuel would delay them.

On the road to Vimoutiers, Eberbach's staff car was strafed by Allied fighters and the general had to shelter in a ditch. The RAF and Quesada's Ninth Tactical Air Force were out in strength on that day and the next. Flying conditions were almost perfect, and with the remains of two German armies packed into an area roughly twelve miles by five, there was no shortage of targets. Successful Typhoon rocket strikes on vehicles were marked by widening columns of oily smoke.

'The black mushrooms kept appearing,' wrote General Meindl, 'a sign that the enemy planes were having good hunting.' He felt dazed by what he called 'the flail of a fabulous air superiority'. He was also furious with the drivers, whose desperate attempts to escape sent up more clouds of dust, attracting the attention of fighter-bomber pilots. 'It was enough to make one tear one's hair and ask oneself if the drivers had gone off their heads completely and were hastening to place themselves in the view of the enemy planes until they went up in a blaze.' There was little anti-aircraft fire to deter the Allied aircrew. Few of the self-propelled flak vehicles had survived, and army units, unlike his paratroops, did not believe in using small arms against aircraft.

There was little sense of pity among the Allied pilots. 'We rippled the rockets,' wrote an Australian Typhoon pilot, 'then separately we did cannon attacks into the massed crowds of soldiers. We would commence firing, and then slowly pull the line of cannon fire through the crowd and then pull up and go around again and again until the ammunition ran out. After each run, which resulted in a large vacant path of chopped up soldiers, the space would be almost immediately filled with other escapees.' General von Lüttwitz of the 2nd Panzer-Division surveyed the scene that day with horror: 'On the road great heaps of vehicles, dead horses and dead soldiers were to be seen scattered everywhere, and their number increased from hour to hour.' Gunner Eberhard Beck of the 277th Infantry Division saw a soldier sitting motionless on a rock. He pulled him by the shoulder to get him out of danger, but the man rolled over. He was dead already.

On 18 August alone, the US Ninth Air Force estimated its tally at 400 vehicles, while the RAF claimed 1,159 vehicles destroyed and 1,700 damaged, as well as 124 tanks destroyed and 100 damaged. But these figures were preposterously high. Once again Air Marshal Coningham was furious when he received the Operational Research report later. Their teams had found only thirty-three armoured vehicles which had been destroyed by air attack. The report concluded that the random nature of the Allied air attacks had failed to achieve a decisive degree of destruction.* On the other hand, the Allied air attacks had once

---

* The RAF claimed that during the period of the encirclement they had destroyed 257 armoured vehicles and 3,340 soft-skinned vehicles, while the Americans esti-

again panicked German crews into abandoning their vehicles, and their destruction of fuel supplies had certainly contributed to the very high number of armoured vehicles which were left behind.

With so many RAF and American squadrons attacking targets at will on the ground, there were countless cases of 'friendly fire'. The ironic cry, 'Take cover, boys, they may be ours!' took on a new urgency. Bradley's 12th Army Group headquarters acknowledged that 'some British armored vehicles had been attacked inadvertently', but pointed out that British tank crews carried so much kit on the outside that their identifying white stars were often 'covered with paraphernalia'.

Because of the random air attacks, the Canadian 4th Armoured Division held back from occupying Trun until the afternoon of 18 August. The division was also hampered by the lethargy and incompetence of its commander, Major General George Kitching, and by Simonds's plan that its armoured brigade was about to break off to lead the advance to the Seine. On the evening of 18 August, a detachment from the division reached Saint-Lambert-sur-Dives, halfway between Trun and Chambois, but was too weak to take the village until reinforced.

The Polish battlegroup heading for Chambois made a serious mistake in map-reading and ended up six miles to the north. It was also short on ammunition and running out of fuel. The 10th Mounted Rifles reconnaissance regiment had reached the edge of Chambois, but did not have the strength to take it. Meanwhile, from the south, the American 90th Division, supported by part of Leclerc's 2ème DB, advanced to within a mile of Chambois. Both Montgomery and the American commanders seemed to think that the battle could be won with air power and artillery. Yet the screen of Canadian, Polish and American troops was far too thin both to hold back the waves of German forces

---

mated that they had accounted for 134 armoured vehicles and 2,520 soft-skinned. But the Operational Research Section could find only 133 armoured vehicles knocked out in the whole area. Of these only thirty-three had been hit by air attack. Almost all the rest had been abandoned and destroyed by their own crews. But of the 701 soft-skinned vehicles, the team found that half had been destroyed by air attack, most by cannon and machine-gun fire.

fighting to escape the pocket, and to face the threat of a counter-attack from behind by remnants of the SS panzer formations.

On 19 August, the Polish 10th Dragoons reinforced their reconnaissance regiment outside Trun and met up with the American 90th Division. Americans and Poles shook hands. 'They were excellent fighters and very cold-blooded,' an American lieutenant reported later. Chambois, soon known as 'Shambles', was in flames from the bombardment and filled with dead Germans and burnt-out vehicles. Reports of the scale of destruction certainly seem to have increased the sense of complacency among Allied commanders. Even the energetic Simonds, commanding the II Canadian Corps, spent the following morning 'tidying up official correspondence' instead of forcing forward his divisions.

Conditions within the pocket were, according to German sources, impossible to imagine if you had not seen it. 'The roads were blocked by two or three shot-up and burned-out vehicles standing side by side,' an officer with the 21st Panzer Division wrote. 'Ambulances packed with wounded were carbonized. Ammunition exploded, panzers blazed and horses lay on their backs kicking their legs in their death throes. The same chaos extended in the fields far and wide. Artillery and armour-piercing rounds came from either side into the milling crowd.'

Gunner Beck with the 277th Infanterie-Division saw teenage infantrymen stumble past: 'In their faces one could read the utter tragedy of this appalling experience, which they could not cope with.' Many men went to pieces after days without sleep. Some began to hide in the woods, preferring to be captured than continue such a hellish existence. He could not help feeling sorry for the horses, of whom even more was expected: 'The heads, backs and flanks of the horses were bathed in sweat, foaming white. We roamed around as if in a slaughter-house.'

During the day, men and vehicles hid in woods and orchards from Allied aircraft. At night, exhausted and famished German soldiers stumbled along, cursing their leaders, who became lost in the dark. Many used French two-wheeled handcarts to carry their equipment or heavy weapons. They found themselves mixed up with soldiers from rear services, including cobbler and tailoring detachments, all trying to escape but without any idea of where they were headed. Magnesium flares and 'Christmas tree' illuminations, descending slowly on parachutes, lit up the horizon. They revealed the silhouettes of ruined buildings and trees. There was a continual rumble of heavy guns as American and French artillery battalions continued to target the roads with harassing fire.

On 19 August, Oberstgruppenführer Hausser was urged by both General Meindl and Gersdorff to order a breakout that night east across the River Dives, which ran through Trun, Saint-Lambert and Chambois. The order was passed by radio and word of mouth. Hausser also requested II SS Panzer Corps to attack the Poles and Canadians from behind to open the gap.

At 22.00 hours, the remnants of the 277th Infantry Division received the order '*Fertigmachen zum Abmarsch*' – 'prepare to move out'. Hausser and the unwounded members of his staff joined the remains of the 3rd Paratroop Division to make the breakthrough on foot. Generalleutnant Schimpf, the commander of the division, who had been badly wounded, was put on the back of a tank along with other wounded. Breakout groups were led by the remaining Tiger and Panther tanks, which could push any vehicles blocking the track out of the way. Ordinary *Landser* and generals alike clambered on to half-tracks and other armoured vehicles, ready to jump off if needed to go into the attack. One officer claimed to have seen two generals whose divisions had been wiped out put on steel helmets and arm themselves with sub-machine guns.

An attack on Saint-Lambert began soon after midnight. The Argyll and Sutherland Highlanders of Canada were forced back out of the village. Lacking explosives, they had not blown the bridge. German troops were still streaming across after dawn.

General Meindl had assembled two groups of his paratroops during the night. He led them forward to the River Dives and they slipped into the water as silently as possible. The far bank was steep and covered in brambles. On the far side, when they reached the Trun–Chambois road, they could see the silhouettes of Allied tanks and hear the crews chatting. Every time a starshell was fired into the sky they threw themselves flat. They crept past the three tanks they had seen, but a fourth one spotted them and opened fire with its machine gun. Fortunately for them, it fired too high.

Further on, they passed a team of dead draught horses which had been machine-gunned in their traces by Allied fighter-bombers as they towed a broken-down Wehrmacht vehicle. After several hot August days, the swollen bodies gave off a deathly stench. They could hear bursts of firing behind them as other groups tried to break through the cordon. By then, they could see the first glimmer of the false dawn. Another group of paratroops who had also slipped through joined them. They heard tanks coming from the north-east. Meindl felt a surge of hope that they were from II SS Panzer Corps coming 'from outside' – from Vimoutiers to break the encirclement. But the profile of turret and hull was unmistakable. They were British Cromwell tanks. Three of them stopped near the dry ditch in which the German paratroops lay hidden by tall weeds. They heard the tank crew talking. After a few moments they realized that they were speaking Polish. 'So it was the Poles we had to thank!' Meindl commented ruefully. They had to lie there for an hour and a half, 'not daring to move a finger' in case they disturbed the tall weeds. By then it was 07.30 hours on 20 August.

A further disappointment came with the sound of enemy gunfire in the direction they were headed, the heights of Coudehard, the steep escarpment which ran roughly north to south. The mist lifted, the sun came out and, in the 'hothouse atmosphere' of their ditch, they steamed gently in their damp, ragged uniforms.

To the despair of the Germans who had not yet managed to cross the Dives and the Trun–Chambois road, the morning of 20 August dawned as 'clear and serene' as the previous days. As soon as the morning mist lifted, American artillery opened up and the fighter-bombers appeared overhead, coming in just above tree height with the heart-stopping scream of aero-engines.

Gersdorff, who had been wounded in the leg, arrived at dawn on 20 August in the village of Saint-Lambert in the middle of a convoy which included every sort of vehicle. But those who did not get through in the early-morning mist were soon blocked by American artillery fire and knocked-out vehicles. Improvised working parties tried to clear a way through, although they were under fire from American artillery and from the Canadians who had withdrawn.

Many more, including the last fifteen tanks of the 2nd Panzer Division, tried to cross the Dives by a small bridge between Saint-Lambert and Chambois which also came under heavy fire. 'People, horses, vehicles had fallen from the bridge into the depths of the Dives, and there formed a terrible heap,' wrote General von Lüttwitz. 'Without a break, columns of fire and smoke from burning tanks rose into the sky; ammunition exploded, horses lay all around on the ground, many of them severely wounded.' Lüttwitz, who had been wounded in the neck and back, led groups out on foot north-eastwards with members of his staff.

Finally, two tanks of the 2nd Panzer-Division knocked out the American tank destroyers covering the Trun–Chambois road and they managed to get across. 'This was the signal for a general exploitation of the break ... and a large number of scout cars, tanks, assault guns etc. appeared from every sort of cover.'

The American account of this day's action, viewed from the high ground to the south of Chambois, gives a slightly different picture. 'It was a gunner's dream from daylight to dark,' the 90th Division artillery reported, 'and we plastered the road, engaging targets as they appeared.' 'The Germans tried a desperate trick to cross this No Man's Land,' another American artillery report stated. 'In an area that was defiladed from our observation they massed their vehicles about six abreast, five or six deep and at a signal moved this square of transport into the open, depending upon speed to carry them through to safety across the zone of fire. It didn't work. The artillery had a prepared concentration that they could fire on call into the road that the Germans were trying to use. When the artillery observer saw the results of his call, he literally jumped up and down. Again and again the Huns attempted to send vehicles across this hell of fire, and again and again the artillery rained down on them ... We fired single batteries. We fired battalion concentrations. And when targets looked particularly interesting we dumped the whole division artillery or even the whole corps artillery on them. When evening came, the road was impassable and the fields on both sides of the road were littered with the junk that once was German equipment. Few Huns escaped by this route.'

In fact far more Germans than they believed had already got through in the early hours of the morning. Many others continued to slip across during the day, especially on the Canadian sector, which had not been properly reinforced, despite constant calls for help from those near Saint-Lambert. The 4th Armoured Division was supposed to be preparing to advance towards the Seine, but had not yet been relieved by the Canadian 3rd Infantry Division. This major flaw in the conduct of the battle again stemmed largely from Montgomery's indecision on whether to go for a long envelopment on the Seine or to seal the gap on the River Dives.

The main Polish force was by now established on the Mont Ormel escarpment to the north-east of Chambois. Short of fuel and ammunition, they received some supplies by parachute drop. The Poles, not surprisingly, saw the battle as an intensely symbolic contest between their white eagle and the black Nazi eagle. Poland's proud and tragic history was constantly in their thoughts. The 1st Armoured Division's insignia was the helmet and Husaria eagle wings worn upright on the shoulders of the Polish knights who saved Vienna from the Turks 300 years earlier. Their commander, General Maczek, declared with poignant pride, 'The Polish soldier fights for the freedom of other nations, but dies only for Poland.' Having heard of their compatriots' uprising in Warsaw as the Red Army approached the city, the Poles were doubly determined to kill as many Germans as possible.

For Maczek, who had commanded the 10th Cavalry Brigade in the defence of Lwow against the German 2nd Panzer-Division in September 1939, it seemed a heaven-sent coincidence that 'luck gave the 10th Cavalry Brigade the well-deserved revenge of surprising the same division' in this battle. That day, the 10th Mounted Infantry near Chambois also captured Generalleutnant Otto Elfeldt, the commander of LXXXIV Corps, with twenty-nine staff officers. But the real threat to the main Polish positions around Mont Ormel, as Ultra intercepts had warned, was about to come from the rear, as well as from the improvised battlegroups in front.

The Poles, fighting a desperate battle, also requested support from the Canadian 4th Armoured Division. Kitching's obstinate and unjustified refusal to help led to Simonds relieving him of his command the following day.

*

At 04.00 hours that morning, the remains of the *Der Führer* Regiment of 2nd SS Panzer-Division, which had been defending the line of the River Touques, was ordered south in their half-tracks towards Chambois to break open the pocket. At 10.00 hours, they sighted ten Allied tanks. All their guns were pointed in towards the pocket. Hauptmann Werner, who commanded the III Battalion, had just passed a broken-down Panther tank from another SS panzer division. He returned there rapidly. The soldier working on the tank implied that it could be moved, but added that its commander, an *Untersturmführer*, was in a house nearby. The *Untersturmführer* was reluctant to move, but Werner drew his pistol and forced him back to his tank. Werner climbed up on to the engine deck behind the turret and directed him back to where they had seen the Allied tanks. When they were close, Werner went forward on foot to reconnoitre the best firing position. By then the *Untersturmführer* was showing a good deal more enthusiasm. According to Werner, they took the enemy tanks entirely by surprise, knocking out five of them and damaging several others.[*]

Elements of the 9th SS Panzer-Division *Hohenstaufen* also counter-attacked from the direction of Vimoutiers, as Eberbach had planned. But their advance did not start until 10.00 hours, because of fuel shortages. A junior staff officer, reconnoitring the way in a motorcycle combination, ran straight into a large detachment of Polish troops. His driver was shot, and the Poles, seeing his SS uniform, were about to execute him. His life was saved by the intervention of a Canadian liaison officer, apparently a White Russian who had escaped to Canada in 1919.

Meindl and his paratroops, meanwhile, had been able to continue on towards the heights of Coudehard and Mont Ormel only after the detachment of Polish tanks set off for a new position. Meindl suddenly spotted another group of paratroops advancing in skirmishing order across an open field. He whistled. Their young commander recognized him and Meindl heard him mutter, 'Oh, it's the old man.' Meindl

---

[*] Werner's account states that the tanks were Shermans from the 4th Canadian Armoured Division, but the testimony of an officer from the 12th SS Panzer-Division *Hitler Jugend* holds that the Allied tanks were Polish, near the northern Hill 262, and the remainder withdrew rapidly.

briefed him rapidly and told him to take all the paratroops with him. The only way to get past the blocking detachments of tanks was by a flanking attack to the north. In return, the young officer told him that Oberstgruppenführer Hausser was not far away.

After a circuitous route, Meindl found the commander-in-chief of the Seventh Army sheltering in a bomb crater with men of the SS *Der Führer* Regiment. They collected other groups of infantry and two Panther tanks which appeared. Meindl, obsessively proud of his paratroops, was scathing about some of the army personnel who had joined them. Many had abandoned their weapons. He saw 'fear in their eyes and cowardice in their hearts' in the desperation to break out of the encirclement, rather than join in the battle to open the breach. 'Here one saw the communication zone troops from France, who had not known what war was for the past three years. It was a pitiful sight. Dissolution and panic. And in between them my paratroops, with contempt in their eyes, fulfilling their duty in an exemplary way.' His men, together with a handful from the SS and infantry, were prepared to make the sacrifice for the rest, while the 'toe-rags', as he called them, displayed nothing but 'crass egoism and cowardliness'. 'For the first time I now understood how war was the worst possible way of breeding the best type of human being . . . how the best blood was lost and the poorest retained.'

The improvised attack went forward, and, 'as if by a miracle', they seized the heights of Coudehard at 16.30 hours when the Waffen-SS panzers attacked from the other direction, thus breaking the encirclement and creating a gap nearly two miles wide. The few prisoners they took confirmed that they had been up against the 1st Polish Armoured Division.

In the meantime General Hausser, who had been badly wounded, was evacuated on the back of one of the very few tanks left. Meindl's main concern that afternoon was to send through the rest of the wounded in a column of clearly marked ambulances. 'Not a shot was fired at them,' wrote Meindl, 'and I recognised, with thankfulness in my heart, the chivalrous attitude of the enemy.' He waited a full half-hour after the column had disappeared before sending through any fighting troops, 'so that there should not be the slightest suspicion in the mind of the enemy that we had taken any unfair advantage'.

News had spread behind them that a gap had been opened at Coude-hard and that night a mass of stragglers hurried forward to take advantage of the opportunity. Meindl, however, was disgusted to hear from a senior officer who joined him that many more, including officers, had considered escape a hopeless project. As it grew light on 21 August, Meindl decided that they would not be able to hold open the gap for another day. He went round waking his men. It was not an easy task. Having organized a force to cover the retreat, he set off on foot eastwards towards the Seine. It began to rain steadily. That at least would help conceal the route of the long snaking column of exhausted men.

Although part of the 3rd Canadian Infantry Division finally arrived to strengthen the cordon between Trun and Saint-Lambert, small groups of Germans had continued to slip through all day. Some of them joined the SS combat teams fighting to keep open the gap, but a US spotter plane circling above them continued to direct artillery fire on the retreating troops. On the southern shoulder of the gap, a combat team from Leclerc's 2ème DB had taken up position on a hill, where they found themselves almost next to the main Polish force. And further round to the south-west, the Langlade battlegroup with the American 90th Division fought 'German attempts, more or less disorganized, to break through between Chambois and the Forêt de Gouffern'.

That day was also a significant one for the citizens of Caen. The very final shell, fired from the line of the River Touques, fell on the city: 'the sixty-sixth and last day of the martyrdom of Caen'.

On 21 August the Polish armoured division, cut off around Mont Ormel, was finally reinforced and resupplied by Canadian troops.* The gap was sealed. General Eberbach, accepting that hardly any more men would now escape, ordered the remains of II SS Panzer Corps to pull back to the Seine. The badly wounded Oberstgruppenführer Hausser was taken to the provisional Seventh Army command post at Le Sap, where he told General von Funck to take over. (General Eberbach assumed command two days later.) Staff officers began to collect and reorganize troops. To their surprise, they found that in

---

* In their Normandy battles, the Poles had lost 135 officers and 2,192 men.

many cases over 2,000 men per division had escaped, but this figure still seems high.

Those German troops left behind showed little resistance. It was time to round up prisoners. '[The] Yanks say they collected hundreds all day,' Major Julius Neave wrote in his diary. 'The 6th Durham Light infantry have just reported that they are in a wonderful position and can see hundreds more walking towards them.' Many units regarded flushing Germans out of the woods as a sport. But there were tragedies too. In Ecouché, the Germans had left hundreds of mines and booby-traps. 'A boy of about ten years stepped out of the church to meet us,' reported a young American officer with the 38th Cavalry Reconnaissance Squadron, 'and was blown up by one of these anti-personnel mines.' British sappers, who had just arrived, began to clear the town to try to prevent any more accidents. They dealt with 240 mines.

At first it was hard to enter the area of the pocket because the roads were blocked with burnt-out vehicles. Tanks and recovery vehicles had to work round the clock clearing a path. The scenes inside defied belief. 'The roads were choked with wreckage and the swollen bodies of men and horses,' wrote the commander of a Typhoon wing, interested in seeing the results of their work. He was clearly shaken. 'Bits of uniform were plastered to shattered tanks and trunks and human remains hung in grotesque shapes on the blackened hedgerows. Corpses lay in pools of dried blood, staring into space as if their eyes were being forced from their sockets. Two grey-clad bodies, both minus their legs, leaned against a clay bank as if in prayer.' Amid the skeletons of burnt trees, the detritus of war and of military bureaucracy lay all around, including typewriters and exploded mailbags. 'I picked up a photograph of a smiling German recruit standing between his parents, two solemn peasants who stared back at me in accusation.' It was a sharp reminder that 'each grey-clad body was a mother's son'.

The writer Kingsley Amis, who also witnessed the scene, was struck by the massive number of draught animals which the Germans had used in their attempts to escape: 'The horses seemed almost more pitiful, rigid in the shafts with their upper lips drawn above their teeth as if in continuing pain.'

American soldiers were drawn by the prospect of souvenirs to send home. A group from the 6th Engineer Special Brigade came across a whole cossack squadron lying beside their horses, as one of their number described: 'The Don cossacks, the Terek cossacks, all these wore their original cossack uniforms except for the German emblem on their breast, the eagle and swastika. They had the fur hats, and we found out later that the head of this squadron was named Captain Zagordny. His wife was killed right beside him. She rode along with him when they rode out. The French people I heard were terrified of the Russians.' The party of engineers eagerly collected up the long Russian sabres, 'which still had the hammer and sickle on them'. Some men even collected saddles as well as weapons, and they threw everything into the back of their trucks. They were later allowed to take all their booty home, but not the sabres, because they were marked with the Soviet symbol. American military authorities did not want to upset their great ally, who was so sensitive about all the former Red Army soldiers fighting on the German side.

As well as the large numbers of prisoners, there were also several thousand German wounded to look after. During the mopping up, a German field hospital with 250 wounded was discovered, hidden deep in the Forêt de Gouffern. Most of the injured left in the pocket had received no medical care at all.

British and American medical services were soon swamped. Their doctors were helped by hard-working German medical orderlies. 'On the collapse of the Falaise pocket,' wrote Lieutenant Colonel Snyder, '750 German wounded were brought in. Some of them were lightly wounded German officers, who complained that they had had to walk. One of the German orderlies, overhearing this, called back: "When I was in the German army, you officers told us we should march all day without grumbling".'

Many *Landser*, however, were in a pitiful condition, including twenty-five cases of gas gangrene. Two surgical teams operated in separate tents to prevent contamination. They did nothing but amputate gangrenous limbs. They had to keep changing the teams round because the stench from the gas gangrene was so terrible. 'Medical care during retreat is always difficult for any army,' Colonel Snyder observed.

British doctors with 6 General Hospital also had to deal with gas gangrene. They were in addition concerned with an epidemic of enteritis and the threat of typhus, when they discovered how many German prisoners were covered in lice: 'Their blankets have been segregated from the other patients and washed before being used on any other patient.'

The main fear of infection lay in the pocket itself. Dead horses and German corpses were covered in flies, and the plague of mosquitoes continued. The Americans brought in French workers to help deal with the problem. One of them recorded how he had to hold a handkerchief over his nose because of the pestilential stench as he surveyed the carbonized corpses and the grotesque grins of blackened skulls. They dragged bodies, both human and animal, to make funeral pyres, pouring gasoline over them. 'The air became unbreathable,' he wrote.

On 21 August, Montgomery issued a declaration to the 21st Army Group: 'The victory has been definite, complete and decisive. "The Lord mighty in battle" has given us the victory.' Many, however, did not agree that the victory had been 'definite, complete and decisive'. General Eberbach estimated that perhaps some 20,000 men, twenty-five tanks and fifty self-propelled guns had escaped the encirclement. 'The losses of tanks from lack of gasoline were greater than those due to all kinds of enemy armaments put together,' he wrote later. Gersdorff believed that between 20,000 and 30,000 managed to cross the Seine.* On the Allied side, Montgomery's strongest critics were British.

'One of Monty's great errors was at Falaise,' Air Chief Marshal Tedder said after the war. 'There he imperiously told US troops to stop and leave the British area alone. He didn't close the gap.' Predictably, Air Chief Marshal Coningham, who loathed Montgomery, was even harsher: 'Monty is supposed to have done a great job at Falaise. [But he] really helped the Germans get away. He still wanted to do the job by himself, and kept the Americans from coming up. We closed on Falaise too late.' Coningham attributed his actions to jealousy of Patton, which is not entirely true.

According to Montgomery's chief of staff, General Freddie de Guingand, Montgomery had been 'too tidy'. He thought the Americans

---

* The British and Americans between them took some 50,000 prisoners and estimated the enemy dead at 10,000.

should have been allowed to join the Poles at Trun. Monty regarded Bradley as under his command. Monty, said Brigadier Williams of the 21st Army Group, was 'the high cock on the dungheap'. When Montgomery told Bradley to hold back at Argentan, 'Bradley was indignant. We were indignant on Bradley's behalf.' According to Williams, Montgomery 'was fundamentally more interested in full envelopment than this inner envelopment. We fell between two stools. He missed his chance of closing at the Seine by doing the envelopment at Falaise. Monty changed his mind and went for a short hook too late, perhaps because he was afraid of the Americans taking all the credit.'

These strictures certainly indicate the frustration which boiled among both British and American officers at the missed opportunity to destroy the German armies in Normandy entirely. They are unfair in some respects. It was Bradley's decision to allow Patton to split Haislip's corps at Argentan, not Montgomery's. But there can be little doubt that Montgomery's failure to reinforce the Canadians at the crucial moment constituted a major factor in allowing so many German troops, especially those of the SS panzer divisions, to escape. The only chance of catching Model's battered remnants during the last ten days of August now lay on the River Seine.

28

The Paris Uprising and the Race for the Seine

Even before the battle of the Falaise encirclement had started, General Leclerc had been consumed with impatience. To have his whole force caught up in the fighting round Argentan while most of Patton's other divisions were sent towards the Seine had filled him with frustration. Then, on 17 August, when the 2ème DB was ordered to attack Trun, Leclerc at first refused. His American corps commander 'had to ask him categorically whether he would disobey a written order'. Leclerc eventually backed down. Eisenhower, on becoming Supreme Allied Commander had agreed to de Gaulle's request that French troops would be allowed to enter Paris first. In return, de Gaulle had promised that the French would do everything to support him. The political could not be separated from the military, especially when it came to symbolic gestures of vital importance to the French.

While Leclerc's division was stuck under General Gerow's V Corps, clearing up the south-east corner of the Falaise gap, Patton's Third Army had advanced much further than Bradley had realized. Patton, with his various corps spread over such a huge area, had to abandon his Jeep and take to the air. 'This Army covers so much ground that I have to fly in Cubs most places,' he wrote. 'I don't like it. I feel like a clay pigeon.'

Haislip's XV Corps had moved from Dreux to Mantes on the Seine, where one of his regiments would cross the river on the night of 19 August. Patton, after a flying visit, proudly announced to Bradley that he had 'pissed in the river that morning'. Meanwhile, XX Corps was advancing on Fontainebleau and Melun south of Paris. After Cook's XII Corps had taken Orléans and Châteaudun, General Patton, in inimitable fashion, simply told him, 'Go where you damn well please eastwards!' Cook said that he wanted to go straight for Koblenz on the Rhine. Patton was all in favour, Cook recorded, but Bradley was less certain. He thought that Montgomery would object because he needed to clear the rocket sites in the Pas-de-Calais as his top priority. But Patton was then forced to hold XII Corps at Orléans because of fuel shortages.

Montgomery was indeed objecting. On 19 August, he had discovered at a meeting with Bradley that Eisenhower wanted to advance with the American 12th Army Group straight across eastern France to the German border. The British and Canadians would clear the Pas-de-Calais, then go into Belgium and take the port of Antwerp, as Montgomery had proposed. But Montgomery despaired of a broad front advance. He wanted both army groups to proceed in a massed group together under a single field commander. This difference of opinion on strategy led to a major rift in the Allied command. It was a battle which the weakened British were now bound to lose.

Tensions between the Americans and the French also began to increase at an even higher level. Eisenhower was tipped off by the British commander-in-chief in the Mediterranean that General de Gaulle was about to fly from Algiers to France. De Gaulle, determined not to be beholden to the Allies in any way, refused to give detailed flight plans and rejected a fighter escort for his Lockheed Lodestar. The Americans, genuinely concerned for his safety, offered to provide a Flying Fortress. De Gaulle then insisted that it must bear French markings and have a French crew, but no French pilots were qualified to fly the aircraft.

On 19 August, de Gaulle arrived at Eisenhower's headquarters. He heard that the Americans had taken Chartres. 'We must march on Paris,' he said to Eisenhower. 'There must be an organized force there for internal order.' But Eisenhower wanted to bypass the city. Next day de Gaulle went to Rennes. News arrived that an insurrection had started in Paris. De Gaulle immediately sent General Alphonse Juin with a letter to Eisenhower insisting that it was 'absolutely necessary to have Leclerc sent into Paris'.* If this was not done, then he, de Gaulle, would order Leclerc into Paris.

The German commander of Gross-Paris – 'Greater Paris' – was now Generalleutnant von Choltitz, the former commander of LXXXIV Corps on the Cotentin coast. Hitler had summoned Choltitz to the *Wolfsschanze* on the morning of 7 August when the attack on Mortain was beginning. 'Hitler made me a speech for three-quarters of an hour, as though I were a public meeting,' he complained later. Hitler, looking sick and bloated, raged at the plotters of 20 July. He claimed that he had unmasked the opposition at one blow and would crush them all. Choltitz was convinced that he really had become deranged and that the war was lost. Hitler, having calmed down, then gave him his orders for Paris. Choltitz had full powers as the commander of a 'besieged fortress' over all Wehrmacht personnel in Greater Paris. The city was to be defended to the end.

Choltitz later portrayed himself as an anti-Nazi as well as the saviour of Paris, yet Hitler trusted him because of his performance in southern Russia. Choltitz had indeed carried out Nazi orders faithfully. In British captivity that autumn, Choltitz said to General Wilhelm Ritter von Thoma, 'The worst job I ever carried out – which however I carried out with great consistency – was the liquidation of the Jews. I carried out this order down to the very last detail.'† (Choltitz, however, never faced a war crimes tribunal for these acts.)

Choltitz reached Paris two days later when the Mortain counter-

---

* It appears that Juin was particularly disliked by senior officers at SHAEF. Juin, like Leclerc, appears to have been very critical of the Americans' indiscriminate use of artillery. According to Air Chief Marshal Sir James Robb, Eisenhower's chief of air staff, 'Bedell, Ike and all hands curse the French and say they can't depend on them. Bedell says that he has taken all he cares to from Juin, who thinks that the Americans don't know how to run a war. He says that if an American officer said to him what Juin had, he would have hit him in the face.' Forrest Pogue, who interviewed Juin later, thought him 'so like an American Chamber of Commerce secretary' that he could not understand why US Army generals distrusted him so much.

† Choltitz also railed in horror at Churchill's speech in the House of Commons on 28 September. 'Have you read Churchill's speech?' he exclaimed to General von Schlieben the next day. '*Appalling*, beyond all words! A Jewish brigade to go to Germany!'

attack had stalled. Leutnant Graf von Arnim met him at the Villa Coty, the residence of Generalleutnant Hans Freiherr von Boineburg-Lengsfeld, whom Choltitz was replacing. Arnim described the fifty-year-old general as 'short of stature and round in shape, with a rasping voice, wearing a monocle, and on his round head he had a small parting almost right in the middle. He spoke rapidly.' Arnim, who like many army officers in Paris had been linked to the July plot, was at first cautious with the new commander, purely because Hitler and the OKW evidently trusted him as 'a bold and experienced general'.

After a simple supper, Choltitz, Boineburg and the chief of staff, Oberst von Unger, went off for a quiet talk, which lasted over two hours. Choltitz told them of Hitler's instructions: 'His order was brief: to destroy Paris if the enemy advanced, and defend it from the ruins.' But Boineburg and Unger, both members of the army resistance, managed to persuade him that to destroy Paris served no useful military purpose. When the three men emerged, it was 'clear that Boineburg and Unger were on the very best of terms with Choltitz'. Late that night, Arnim accompanied Choltitz to the headquarters of Gross-Paris in the Hôtel Meurice. Choltitz asked him to stay on his staff instead of transferring to a panzer division as he had requested. Arnim, finding that they had many friends in common, agreed.

The Parisian region had several headquarters. The Supreme Command West was at Saint-Germain-en-Laye, while Generalfeldmarschall Sperrle's Luftwaffe headquarters were in the Palais Bourbon. There was also Admiral Krancke's Marinekommando West, as well as various SS and Gestapo staffs, Otto Abetz's embassy and numerous other German state and Nazi Party establishments. Hitler had told Choltitz to send the non-combatants back and form all rear troops into fighting units. Boineburg was returning to Berlin to take up another post. As the officer who had arrested the SS in Paris on 20 July, following Stülpnagel's orders, his survival was nothing short of miraculous. He had a farewell dinner with Unger and Arnim. They tried to forget the disastrous course of the war and Hitler's terrible revenge on the plotters by talking of their families, hunting and horses. Boineburg departed the next day from the Hôtel Majestic on the Avenue de Jéna in an armed convoy.

So far, there had been few attacks on German troops in Paris, but

German military intelligence warned that an uprising was bound to come as the Allies approached. On 14 August, the day before he had been trapped in the Falaise pocket, Generalfeldmarschall von Kluge had called a conference at Saint-Germain-en-Laye, with Luftwaffe, Kriegsmarine and army officers, to discuss the defence of Paris. The next day, Choltitz organized a display of force, including seventeen Panther tanks, to rumble through Paris in the hope of discouraging the Resistance. In theory, he had some 25,000 soldiers, but soon afterwards, many of the troops and most of the tanks were taken from him and sent to strengthen positions against Patton's spearheads.

Choltitz claims he was left with a security regiment of old soldiers, four tanks, two companies mounted on bicycles, some anti-aircraft detachments and a battalion with seventeen elderly French armoured cars. Whatever the exact number of troops remaining, they were of low quality. They included an 'interpreter battalion' which, perhaps unsurprisingly, 'did not show much fighting spirit', and another unit of 'frequently ill people who were only fit for office work'. Some were German civilians working in Paris, who had been called up at the last moment.

An outer ring of defence, strengthened with Luftwaffe flak batteries, was later put under the command of Generalmajor Hubertus von Aulock (the brother of the commander at Saint-Malo). Aulock, a hard-liner, believed that 'capitulation means treason'. Choltitz, however, felt that all he could do was to hold the western and southern suburbs as a route of withdrawal for the German troops still west of the Seine. Generalleutnant Bayerlein of the Panzer Lehr Division encountered him in civilian clothes on the Champs-Elysées. Choltitz immediately complained to him that he had no troops for the defence of Paris.

The insurrection, of which Choltitz had been warned, began to gather pace that week. Colonel Rol-Tanguy, the Communist commanding the FFI in the Parisian region and the Ile de France, had already issued an order to cut cables to German positions in the capital.

On 12 August, the railway workers went on strike. Three days later, the Parisian police force of 15,000 men, whom the Germans were attempting to disarm, refused to put on uniform. On that day of the landings in southern France, the Communist Party newspaper, *L'Humanité*, called for an *'insurrection populaire'*. The next day,

16 August, Jacques Chaban-Delmas, the Gaullist national military delegate, arrived from London. He had gone to England to warn General Koenig that an uprising was inevitable. Koenig told him to go back and stop it at all costs. The Allies did not want to take Paris before the beginning of September. That night Colonel Rol-Tanguy issued an instruction on how to attack tanks with Molotov cocktails, following the 'shining example of the *dinamiteros* of the Spanish Republican army'.*

On 17 August, the National Council of Resistance and its military wing held a meeting to debate the call to arms. The Communists, led by Rol, wanted to start immediately, even though the Resistance in Paris had little more than 400 weapons. Although the British had parachuted nearly 80,000 sub-machine guns to the Resistance in France, only just over 100 had reached Paris. The Gaullists were in a difficult position. In spite of Koenig's instruction, they knew that if they refused to act, the Communists would seize the initiative and perhaps power in the capital.

Hopes increased that day, which became know as '*la grande fuite des Fritz*', 'the great flight of the Fritzes'. The diarist Jean Galtier-Boissière, striding the streets of the capital, observed the departure of senior German officers and office staff with amusement as the Feldgendarmerie directed traffic with their discs on the end of a stick. 'Along the rue Lafayette,' he wrote, 'coming from the luxury hotels around the Etoile, sparkling torpedoes pass by containing purple-faced generals, accompanied by elegant blonde women, who look as if they are off to some fashionable resort.' The departure was accompanied by a great deal of last-minute looting. The contents of wine cellars were loaded on to Wehrmacht trucks, as well as rolls of carpet, Louis XVI furniture, bicycles and works of art. Parisians, who had tried to ignore their German occupiers during the last four years, now jeered them openly. Sylvia Beach, the founder of the bookshop Shakespeare & Company, described how a crowd of Parisians waved lavatory brushes at them, but then the angry and nervous soldiers opened fire.

---

* The French Communists seemed to overlook the fact that it was General Franco's foreign legionnaires who, in October 1936, had first invented what later became known as the Molotov cocktail, when they were attacked by Soviet T-26 tanks south of Madrid.

The next day, 18 August, Communist posters urging revolt appeared on walls. And early on the morning of 19 August, 3,000 members of the police in civilian clothes, but carrying their pistols, took over the Préfecture de Police. The tricolore was hoisted and they sang the 'Marseillaise'. Charles Luizet, appointed by de Gaulle as the new head of the Parisian police, slipped into the building on the Ile de la Cité. Amédée Bussière, his predecessor appointed by Vichy, was locked up in his apartment.

The Germans had no idea of events at the Préfecture de Police. 'A deceptive calm reigned in the city glowing from a hot August sun,' wrote Leutnant von Arnim later. Choltitz sent Arnim off in an open Kübelwagen with two sergeants as bodyguards on a tour of the city to find out what was happening. The streets were almost entirely empty. They drove along the Seine embankment on the north side and past the Palais de Justice, which was 'quiet as the grave'. They spotted nothing untoward at the Préfecture de Police. But when they reached the Place Saint-Michel on the left bank they suddenly came under fire. The NCO next to Arnim yelled out as he was hit in the upper arm. They grabbed their machine pistols and fired back blindly. A shot hit one of the front tyres. Arnim slapped the driver's back and shouted at him, 'Drive on! Drive on!' Fortunately for them, the firing came only from one building, and they were able to reach the Feldkommandantur. But the *Unteroffizier* who had been shot in the arm had also received a bullet in the chest and died that afternoon.

Choltitz, finally hearing of the revolt in the Préfecture de Police, sent infantry in trucks and two tanks to force a surrender. The Panthers had only armour-piercing rounds, which made holes right through the building but caused few casualties. Unable to achieve their objective, the small force withdrew. This caused ecstatic cheering and gave rise to a dangerous optimism. Following Rol-Tanguy's order to 'create a permanent state of insecurity among the enemy and to prevent all his movements', many attacks were carried out on isolated vehicles, but by that evening, the Resistance in Paris was almost out of ammunition.*

Over the next twenty-four hours, Parisians began to build barricades

---

* That day some forty Germans were killed and seventy wounded, while 125 Parisians died and nearly 500 were wounded.

to bottle up the Germans. The rue de Rivoli, on which the Hôtel Meurice stood, was blocked at numerous points all the way to the Faubourg Saint-Antoine. German officers watched from the hotel's balconies, but soon had to withdraw inside as bullets began to hit the hotel.

Two SS officers arrived at the Hôtel Meurice in an armoured vehicle. Arnim took them up to see Choltitz. They announced that on direct orders from the Führer they were to 'save' the Bayeux tapestry, which was in the cellars of the Louvre, by taking it back to Germany. By then the windows of the Meurice were under constant fire from the Louvre, because members of the FFI were shooting at the red and black Nazi banners hanging from the façade of the building. Choltitz pointed out the Louvre and told the two SS officers where the tapestry lay. He remarked that for the finest of the Führer's soldiers it would surely be a minor matter to take possession of it. The two of them did not dare object to his sarcasm. Persuaded of the impossibility of their task, they withdrew.

Clemens Graf Podewils, a well-known war reporter for the *Deutsche Allgemeine Zeitung*, was the next visitor. His assignment was 'to cover the heroic defence of Fortress Paris, and thus strengthen the determination of the homeland to resist'. But it did not take Podewils long to see that the German occupation of the French capital could now be counted in days. Arnim experienced 'an oppressive sense of paralysis', wondering what the end would bring.

The next morning, 20 August, a Gaullist group audaciously seized the Hôtel de Ville. It was part of their plan to take over as many key buildings and ministries as possible to install 'republican legality' and thwart the revolutionary aspirations of the Communist FTP. The sight of the French tricolore flying from public buildings once more stirred Parisians profoundly. Individuals followed this example and began to display the French flag from their balconies, even in the rue de Rivoli, close to Choltitz's headquarters. Long lines of Wehrmacht trucks were spotted hidden under the plane trees along the Boulevard de la Madeleine, ready to withdraw eastwards. Rumours began to spread that the Germans were about to pull out.

The Swedish consul-general, Raoul Nordling, then negotiated a truce with Choltitz. The German commander even agreed to recognize the FFI as regular troops and allow the Resistance to hold on to the public buildings in return for respecting German strongholds. The truce was endorsed at a meeting of the National Council for the Resistance, because only one of the Communist delegates was present. Rol-Tanguy was furious when he heard. In any case, sporadic fighting continued. Shirt-sleeved young men and women in summer dresses, some wearing old helmets from the First World War, continued to hold the barricades which had been constructed out of cobblestones, overturned vehicles, bedsteads, furniture and chopped-down trees. Many started to wear red, white and blue brassards with the initials FFI embroidered on them by wives and girlfriends.

On Monday, 21 August, the National Council met again. All of Chaban-Delmas's arguments to maintain the truce were violently rejected by the Communists, who regarded it as an act of treason. Eventually, a compromise was reached. The truce would not be rejected until the following day. The Communists prepared posters ordering '*Tous aux barricades!*' Skirmishes between the Germans and the FFI continued. In the Place de l'Odéon, just below the German strongpoint in the Palais de Luxembourg, a grenade was thrown into a German truck, setting it on fire. The Resistance in Paris was dismayed that the BBC still made no mention of the uprising.

That day, the British 11th Armoured Division relieved Leclerc's 2ème DB near Argentan, allowing them to be ready 'for new missions'. All the division's thoughts lay 'in the direction of Paris'. They heard over the radio that American reconnaissance patrols had already reached Rambouillet and the Forêt de Fontainebleau, while the 7th Armored Division was preparing to cross the Seine south of Paris at Melun, Montereau and Sens. 'What are we doing here?' was their dismayed reaction. 'The honor of relieving Paris is surely ours. We have been given a specific promise.'

Leclerc's troops knew that Paris was in a ferment, and their under-standably impatient commander felt that 'Paris cannot wait much longer for its solution'. As a Frenchman, and especially a conservative Catholic who feared some sort of Communist coup in the capital, he found it impossible to accept Eisenhower's argument that Paris must wait to allow a rapid advance towards the Rhine.

Without seeking General Gerow's permission, Leclerc ordered one of his officers, Jacques de Guillebon, with a squadron of light tanks and a platoon of infantry in half-tracks, to carry out a detailed reconnaissance towards Versailles and perhaps on to Paris. He also told Capitaine Alain de Boissieu (de Gaulle's future son-in-law) to take the American liaison officers off on a sightseeing trip to keep them out of the way. But the next day, one of them discovered what was happening and tipped off V Corps headquarters. Gerow was furious. He immediately ordered that the patrol should be called back, but Leclerc ignored his instruction. This marked the rapid deterioration of what had started as a good relationship. Gerow had previously acknowledged that Leclerc was not just the commander of a division, but the senior French officer with the Allied armies in Normandy. Now Gerow shared the suspicion of many senior American officers that the Gaullists were fighting their own war for France, not the Allies' war against Germany. He would have been even angrier if he had known that the 2ème DB had been secretly stockpiling fuel, through over-indenting and even stealing from gasoline dumps. The French troops were acutely aware that if Leclerc disobeyed orders by making an unauthorized dash for Paris, the Americans would cut off their supplies.

While Patton's divisions were crossing the Seine around Paris, the British and Canadians north of the Falaise gap slogged on eastwards towards Lisieux and the lower section of the river. Unlike the Americans to the south, they faced three unbroken infantry divisions which fought in retreat, from village to village and river to river. These small skirmishes cost a surprising number of lives. When a company from the Tyneside Scottish battalion with the 49th Infantry Division reached a village, a detachment of the 21st SS Panzergrenadier-Regiment which had just withdrawn promptly mortared the place. The British rapidly took shelter. A young soldier, Private Petrie, entered the house of a local scholar and climbed under a desk in the library. At that moment, a shell splinter from a mortar bomb came through the ceiling, through a book on top of the desk – it happened to be Kleist's *Prince of Homburg* – and finally skewered the unfortunate soldier's throat. He died rapidly and was buried by his comrades in a neighbouring garden as soon as the shelling ceased. The liberation of this one small village had cost eight dead and ten wounded.

In the woods and valleys of the Pays d'Auge, the Germans laid ambushes for tanks with their 88 mm flak guns. On 22 August, twenty-six Shermans were lost in a single attack. Disasters like this were even more of a shock when inflicted by a supposedly beaten enemy. The advance to the Seine was not very rapid as a result. A chaplain with the Wessex division wrote of the enemy, 'We all know he's lost the war, and feel all the more annoyed at any casualties.'

That same day near Lisieux, 'the infantry captured a pair of villainous looking SS men,' a gunner lieutenant noted in his diary, 'and I watched as they were interviewed at battalion headquarters. They were pretty arrogant, and after they were led off I had to wonder whether they even got as far as the PoW cage.'

In many places ordinary German soldiers paid for the crimes of the SS. South of Lisieux, near Livarot, a last group of retreating SS soldiers stopped at a large farm and asked for milk. The milkmaids told them that there was none left. They carried on a couple of hundred yards and rested in a ditch. Soon afterwards, they watched some Canadian scouts appear. The young women dashed out to cut flowers for their liberators. As soon as the Canadians moved on, the SS soldiers returned to the farm and wreaked their revenge on the young women with sub-machine guns and grenades, killing six of them. 'We took the same number of German prisoners as there had been victims at the farm at Le Mesnil-Bacley,' a member of the local Resistance wrote later, 'and made them dig their own graves . . . And once they had finished they were publicly executed.' He then added, 'To celebrate the liberation a few days later at Livarot, we paraded all the women who had had relations with the occupiers, after having shorn their heads.' Elsewhere, one woman noted cynically that when the Canadians arrived, the girls who had compromised themselves the most during the German occupation were the first to approach the victors, 'smiles on their lips and their arms full of flowers'. She also observed that when Allied troops threw chocolate and cigarettes to young women as they drove by, they waited until the truck had disappeared, then knelt down a little shamefacedly to pick them up.

Many Normans were cynical about members of the Resistance. 'The explosive growth of the FFI is incredible,' observed a local lawyer. 'All the village boys who chased girls and danced on Saturday nights appear with a brassard and a submachinegun.' Yet Allied troops greatly appreciated the help of the true Resistance fighters. 'The Maquis are doing an excellent job, we see more and more of them,' a Canadian major wrote home. And Myles Hildyard at 7th Armoured Division noted in his diary that, during the advance to the Seine, 'every 11th Hussar [armoured] car has a Maquis on it and they have been invaluable'.

Also near Livarot, a troop of the Inniskilling Dragoon Guards joined a company of the 1st/5th Queens soon after dawn. The company commander waved them to a halt. The troop leader, Lieutenant Woods, jumped down. 'Would you like a Panzer Mark IV for breakfast?' the infantry officer asked. He led him down a track to an orchard. 'Moving hesitantly in open ground on the next ridge about 800 yards away was the quarry, which had clearly no idea that he was observed.' Woods brought his tank through the apple orchard thick with foliage and fruit. They spent a seemingly endless time manoeuvring so that both the commander and the gunner could see the target, which drove Trooper Rose, the driver, to distraction as the tension mounted: 'The minutes ticked by; the dialogue in the turret verged on the acrimonious.' Finally, they had a clear shot. The first armour-piercing round hit the suspension towards the rear. The panzer's turret began to traverse round towards them. The second round also struck, but the gun continued to turn towards them. Only after the third strike did it stop. At first there was just a wisp of smoke, then flames appeared and the crew baled out frantically.

The Americans, having returned to the plan of a long envelopment of the Germans retreating to the Seine, sent first the 5th Armored Division and then Corlett's XIX Corps to swing left up the west bank of the river. But they too found it hard going and had a tough fight at Elbeuf, where Generalfeldmarschall Model had ordered his fragmented divisions to hold them off to protect the crossing places further downstream.

This manoeuvre also led to another row between the Americans and the British. Bradley, at his meeting with Montgomery and Dempsey on 19 August, had offered the British enough trucks to move two divisions to make this right-flanking move themselves. Dempsey declined on the grounds that he could not extricate them quickly enough.

'If you can't do it, Bimbo,' Bradley replied, 'have you any objection to our giving it a try? It'll mean cutting across your front.'

'Why no, not at all,' Dempsey said. 'We'd be delighted to have you do it.'

But when Dempsey was later questioned by British newspaper correspondents about the advance to the Seine, he replied that it would have been faster if they had not been held up by US Army traffic across their front. Monty apologized to Bradley afterwards, saying that Dempsey must have been misquoted, but Bradley was unconvinced. He never forgave Dempsey for that remark. Some years later, he described it as 'one of the greatest injustices ever done to the American army'.

On 21 August, the Canadian and British armies had reached a line running from Deauville on the coast to Lisieux and then Orbec. The Canadians were reinforced with the 1st Belgian Infantry Brigade, which took Deauville the next day, and the Royal Netherlands Brigade (Princess Irene's), which advanced towards Honfleur on the Seine estuary. A Czech armoured brigade also arrived right at the end of the battle. The roads leading to the Seine crossings were frequently blocked by German vehicles, some abandoned because of lack of fuel, others burned out from fighter-bomber attacks.

Once again Typhoon pilots made wildly excessive claims. They estimated that they had destroyed 222 armoured vehicles, but out of 150 abandoned by the Germans, only thirteen were found to have been destroyed by air attack. But there can be no doubt that their cannon accounted for a large proportion of the 3,468 German vehicles and guns. The Typhoons of 123 Wing also suffered a nasty shock over the Seine, losing four aircraft when 'bounced' by Messerschmitt 109s, which hardly ever managed to penetrate the protective screen of Mustang and Spitfire squadrons patrolling inland.

The Germans still on the west bank of the lower Seine crossed by night, using boats and even a pontoon bridge, which was disassembled at dawn to avoid air attacks. 'Ferry points for the Seine crossing were prepared and allotted to divisions,' wrote General Bayerlein. 'This allocation was not observed, and everyone crossed the river wherever he felt like it. Most of the ferries were confiscated by the SS, who generally did not allow members of other units to use them.' Artillery units had held on to their horses and some of them swam their animals across. On 23 August, when bad weather kept away the Allied fighter-bombers, the 21st Panzer Pioneer Battalion began to build a bridge at Rouen to get their tanks across. But the next day was sunny and the bridge was destroyed two hours after it was finished. The steep wooded sides of the twisting valley at least allowed the Germans to hide during daylight.

Model's headquarters at La Roche-Guyon had been abandoned on the approach of American forces. Fifth Panzer Army moved its command post first to Rouen and then to Amiens, where Eberbach and his chief of staff, Gersdorff, were later captured by the Guards Armoured Division, though Gersdorff managed to escape a few hours later.

South of Paris, the remains of the pioneer group from the 276th Infanterie-Division reached Melun on 22 August in their Citroën just before Patton's spearhead arrived. Gefreiter Spiekerkötter and his comrades thought that they had reached safety and could carry on to Metz. But as soon as they were identified as pioneers by the Feldgendarmerie they were ordered into Paris to prepare bridges over the Seine for demolition. Reunited with other members of their battalion, they received new Opel-Blitz trucks, but when they drove into the Place de la Concorde, they became increasingly aware of the empty streets and the threatening silence. Barricades manned by the FFI could be seen in side streets.

They were led to a fort used in 1871 during the Siege of Paris which was a naval depot for torpedo warheads. Kriegsmarine sailors helped them load the explosive into the trucks. Later, driving down the Champs-Elysées, they heard a shot. In a panic, all the pioneers opened fire in all directions. They discovered, shamefacedly, that one of their tyres had exploded. Fortunately nobody was killed.

On 22 August, the FFI ended the truce and went on to a general offensive with the order '*Tous aux barricades!*' On the same day, General von Choltitz received the clearest order from Hitler that Paris was to be destroyed. It was also the day on which Ralph Nordling, the brother of the Swedish consul-general in Paris, managed to reach Patton's headquarters at Dreux to ask him to save Paris. (He had been preceded by Commandant Roger Gallois, Colonel Rol-Tanguy's representative, with a similar plea.) Major General Gilbert Cook, the commander of XII Corps, was present and recorded the conversation.

'Paris should be declared an open city and spared,' Nordling said, having described conditions in the city in a perhaps over-apocalyptic manner.

'I can open it wide and fold it back in 24 hours,' Patton replied.

'The Germans there are in too great a force.'

'I am better informed', said Patton, presumably as a result of what Gallois had told him in the early hours of that morning.

He agreed to send Nordling and his companions on to Bradley's headquarters near Laval to plead their case there.

Both Nordling and Gallois, who had also been sent on to 12th Army Group, were assisted by urgent signals to Eisenhower from de Gaulle and General Koenig, who had learned of their arrival. Bradley, who was with Eisenhower at Granville, heard about their arguments from his chief of staff, Brigadier General Edwin L. Sibert. They had told him that 'between 4,000 and 5,000 children and old people were dying each day from starvation' and that the Metro and the sewage system had been mined.

Eisenhower had already been weakening in his resolve to bypass Paris. 'Well, what the hell, Brad,' he said, 'I guess we'll have to go in.' Bradley agreed that they had no option. Eisenhower had to sell the decision to General Marshall back in Washington as a purely military one to aid the Resistance. Roosevelt would be furious if he thought that the change in plan was an attempt to install de Gaulle in power.*

At 19.30 hours, Leclerc was waiting anxiously beside the landing strip at 12th Army Group headquarters for Bradley's return. Finally the Piper Cub appeared and taxied towards Leclerc's Jeep. 'Well, you

---

* Even before Eisenhower came to his decision, the supply side of SHAEF began to prepare for the relief of Paris. On 21 August, when the first news of the uprising in Paris arrived, a cable from Com Z (Communications Zone) Forward alerted General Rogers back in England to the likely need of feeding Paris. Rogers flew to France to start planning. The first convoy was on its way to Paris on 25 August, the day of its liberation.

win,' Bradley said to him as he climbed out. 'They've decided to send you to Paris.' Leclerc returned as quickly as possible to his divisional command post. Even before his Jeep came to a halt, Leclerc shouted to one of his staff officers, '*Mouvement immédiat sur Paris!*' The order brought tears of fierce joy. Even for those from the colonial army who had never seen Paris before, its freedom represented everything that they had fought for during the last few years.

General Gerow at V Corps had already been summoned to First US Army headquarters, where he was briefed on the uprising, the Resistance running out of ammunition and thousands supposedly dying each day from starvation. General Eisenhower, he was told, had given the order that a force of French, American and British troops start for Paris immediately.* 'The city was to be entered only if the resistance was such that it could be overcome with light forces. There was to be no severe fighting, air or artillery bombardment so as to avoid the destruction of the city.' As soon as Paris was secured, General Gerow was to hand over to General Koenig, who had been named as the military governor of the capital by de Gaulle. Gerow immediately issued a warning order to the 2ème DB and the 102nd Cavalry Group, to be on one-hour standby for a rapid move to the east.

Just after midnight, V Corps issued its orders. The 2ème DB with B Troop of the 102nd Cavalry Squadron was to cross the line of departure at midday, to 'gain control of Paris in coordination with the French Forces of the Interior, and be prepared to move east as ordered by the Corps Commander'. The American 4th Infantry Division, with the rest of 102nd Cavalry, was to take a more southerly route. But Leclerc had already issued his own orders before midnight. And as Gerow's staff noted, the 2ème DB did not wait: 'The march on Paris began that same night.'

On 23 August, the 2ème DB's three *groupements tactiques*, the equivalent of the American combat command, headed south-east in heavy rain with their seemingly endless columns of Staghound armoured cars,

* For reasons which are still unclear, Montgomery ignored Eisenhower's invitation to send a token British force and later refused to join Eisenhower and Bradley on their visit to Paris.

Stuart light tanks, half-tracks, Shermans, tank destroyers, Jeeps and trucks. Leclerc, preceding the main force, reached the Château de Rambouillet, the official country residence of French presidents. He sent a message back to de Gaulle, who replied that he would join him there. Leclerc then began to interview members of the local Resistance and *gendarmerie*, hoping to discover the least-defended route into the capital. It appeared from their information and from Commandant de Guillebon, commanding the reconnaissance patrol, that he should avoid Versailles and swing further round to the south of Paris. The fact that this might get in the way of the US 4th Infantry Division did not concern him.

In the town of Rambouillet, Leclerc's officers were surprised to find at the Hôtel du Grand Veneur a cast of characters worthy of an improbable play. Most were journalists, waiting impatiently for the liberation of Paris. Ernest Hemingway, officially a war correspondent for *Collier's* magazine, was far more interested in acting as an irregular soldier with the local Resistance. He openly carried a heavy automatic pistol, even though it was strictly illegal for a non-combatant. According to John Mowinckel, an American intelligence officer there, Hemingway wanted to interrogate a pathetic German prisoner hauled in by his new Resistance friends. 'I'll make him talk,' he boasted. 'Take his boots off. We'll grill his toes with a candle.' Mowinckel told Hemingway to go to hell and released the boy, who clearly knew nothing.

Others at Le Grand Veneur included David Bruce, then of the OSS and later American ambassador to Paris. There was also Major Airey Neave of MI9, the secret British organization to assist the escape of prisoners of war. Neave was in pursuit of a British sergeant who had betrayed a French Resistance network to the Germans. The combat historian Sam Marshall also turned up. He had to protect Hemingway afterwards with false testimony stating that he had never seen him carry a gun. Irwin Shaw, later author of *The Young Lions*, also appeared with a camera crew from the Signal Corps. This cannot have eased the atmosphere, since Hemingway was in the process of appropriating his lover, Mary Welsh, who later became the fourth Mrs Hemingway.

Shaw was followed by a group of American war correspondents, all no doubt longing to claim that they were the first to enter Paris. 'They looked like "50-mission fliers" with crushed hats to match,' wrote

Marshall's companion, Lieutenant John Westover. 'Among them were Ernie Pyle, and Bob Capa. Pyle was wearing a beret which made him look like Field Marshal Montgomery.' Some of them were irritated, although not entirely surprised, to find Hemingway acting as if he were the local military commander. When Bruce Grant of the *Chicago Daily News* made a sarcastic remark about 'General Hemingway and his Maquis', Hemingway walked over and punched him.

While so many could think only of Paris's liberation, senior American commanders were far more preoccupied with the advance on Germany. Patton flew that day to Laval to see Bradley before he left for a meeting with Montgomery and Eisenhower. Both Patton and Bradley were still worried that Eisenhower might give in to Montgomery's demand that both the 21st and the 12th Army Groups should turn north. According to Patton, 'Bradley was madder than I have ever seen him and wondered aloud "what the Supreme Commander amounted to".' Patton told him that the two of them and Hodges should offer to resign unless Eisenhower agreed to head east, instead of north into the Pas-de-Calais and Belgium, as Montgomery demanded. But Patton's fears were groundless. Eisenhower by this stage felt that Montgomery was disloyal and he refused to listen to his arguments.

When de Gaulle reached the Château de Rambouillet that evening, he was deeply concerned about the state of affairs in Paris. He feared that the Communist-led rising could lead to a disaster comparable to the Paris Commune of 1871. After de Gaulle had supped off cold C-Rations in the ornate surroundings of Rambouillet's state dining room, Leclerc briefed him on his plan of attack. De Gaulle approved. 'You are lucky,' he said to him after a long pause, thinking of the glory that awaited the liberator of Paris. Camped out beside their vehicles in the sodden park and forest, the soldiers of the 2ème DB cooked their rations, cleaned their weapons and shaved carefully in preparation for the welcome which awaited them.

29

The Liberation of Paris

When Colonel Rol-Tanguy gave the order '*Tous aux barricades!*' on 22 August, the plan was copied from the anarchists in Barcelona in July 1936. There, the rising of the right-wing Spanish generals in the city had been blocked by barricades erected by the working class. Rol wanted to bring all Wehrmacht traffic to a halt and besiege the Germans in their main strongpoints, which included Choltitz's headquarters in the Hôtel Meurice, the Palais de Luxembourg, the Ecole Militaire and Invalides, the Assemblée Nationale in the Palais Bourbon, and the Prinz Eugen barracks by the Place de la République.

The call to arms was relayed by posters, handbills and a new wireless station, Radiodiffusion de la Nation Française, which acted as the voice of the Resistance. Every time it played the forbidden 'Marseillaise', people opened their windows and turned up the volume so that those in the street outside could hear it. Very few barricades were erected in the fashionable 7th, 8th and 16th *arrondissements* of western Paris. The vast majority were in the north and eastern parts, which had voted overwhelmingly for the Popular Front in 1936.

The tension in Paris was palpable as rumours became even more exaggerated. Some said that the Americans were at the gates, others that two panzer divisions were approaching from the north and the city might be destroyed. Colonel Rol continued to issue calls to arms: 'Every barricade should be a recruiting centre recalling the "*Patrie en danger*" of the Revolution.' He instructed the FFI to move around the city through the Metro tunnels to avoid the tanks guarding key intersections. Appalled to hear that 'acts of looting seem to have taken on an unacceptable scale', he also ordered that anyone caught would be shot immediately and a notice stating 'Pillager' placed on the corpse.

Colette's husband, Maurice Goudeket, described those 'strange, indecisive days': 'The Germans held Paris only by little islands, and with a few tanks which made their way clumsily through the streets. Paris babbled the first words of a forgotten liberty, newspapers no larger than a leaflet began to appear, flags were made out of scraps of cloth. While waiting for an imminent settling of accounts, the Parisian rediscovered in his deepest memory the solidarity of the barricades, a heroic banter, a smell of gunpowder and sweat.'

Despite the rumours, both Communist and Gaullist leaders were now certain that the report of 150 Tiger tanks being sent to Paris was false. So the danger that the rising in Paris would be crushed like the Polish Home Army in Warsaw greatly diminished. The Gaullists were also prepared to join the fight, now that they had secured the ministries. One of the first and most satisfying tasks was to remove the official portraits and busts of Marshal Pétain. Alexandre Parodi, de Gaulle's representative, even held a symbolic council of ministers at the Hôtel Matignon, the official residence of the prime minister. For the Gaullist leaders in Paris, the arrival of the 2ème DB was vital to give substance to their skeleton administration.

The Communists, misled by their own propaganda, believed that power lay in street barricades and in the committees of the Resistance. Carried away by revolutionary exultation, they could not imagine that the last thing that Stalin wanted was a Communist uprising in France which would antagonize his American suppliers of Lend-Lease.

At dawn on 24 August, the 2ème DB moved out from the forest of Rambouillet. Leclerc sent a detachment of Spahis Marocains in their light Stuart tanks towards Versailles as a diversion to persuade the Germans that this was their main line of advance. The rest of Colonel Paul de Langlade's *groupement tactique*, accompanied by a squadron of the American 102nd Cavalry, was to advance across the Chevreuse valley, but they soon faced heavy opposition in the Bois de Meudon. The 12ème

Chasseurs d'Afrique lost three Shermans to anti-tank guns. Their ultimate objective was the Pont de Sèvres, on the western edge of Paris.

The day was grey and wet, to such a degree that it interfered with radio communications. Colonel Billotte's column headed for Arpajon and Longjumeau, while Colonel Dio's *groupement tactique* was kept in reserve. Billotte's force was headed by Commandant Putz's battalion of the 2ème Régiment de Marche du Tchad. Putz had been one of the most respected commanders in the International Brigades during the Spanish Civil War. His 9ème Compagnie was known as 'La Nueve' because it was manned almost entirely by Spanish Republicans. Their commander, Capitaine Raymond Dronne, a red-headed stalwart with a powerful paunch, had been chosen because he could keep his Spanish socialists, Communists and anarchists in order.

Putz's first major skirmish was in Longjumeau. Ten of his wounded were taken to the civilian hospital in the town and the bodies of eight men killed in the battle were placed in its morgue. One of the divisional chaplains, the Reverend Père Roger Fouquer, came across a terrible scene in a house partly demolished by a shell. He found two nuns kneeling by a young mother who, having just given birth, had been killed by a shell splinter through the chest. Her baby lay silently beside her dead body. Then the church bells rang out to celebrate liberation.

In many places it was a day of joy and horror. 'Slam' Marshall and his companion John Westover in their Jeep 'Sweet Eloise' joined one of Langlade's columns as it made its way through villages and towns on the south-western edges of the city. They attached an American flag to distinguish themselves from the tricolores all around. Advancing slowly, bumper to bumper, Westover described the scene as 'a big disordered picnic'. Vehicles were brought to a halt by rejoicing crowds, forcing kisses and bottles on the soldiers, who begged to be let through unhindered. 'We laughed so much at the insanity of the whole thing that we cried,' he wrote.

There were tragedies too that day. 'On one occasion a beautiful young woman approached a Sherman of the 501ème Régiment de Chars de Combat, raising her arms, certain of being pulled aboard, when a German machine gun opened up on them. The girl slipped back down to the ground, snagging on the tank's tracks, her best summer dress peppered with bloody bullet holes.'

By midday Putz's column had reached Antony, just south of Paris. On his right, another column had a lively encounter near Orly airfield, but then came up against 88 mm anti-tank guns outside Fresnes prison. The guns were manned by German soldiers who had been serving a sentence there. They still wore their canvas prison uniforms. Desert veterans of the 2ème DB thought that it made them look like their old adversaries, the Afrika Korps. After losing two Shermans, the remaining French tanks managed to knock out the guns. One charged straight into the courtyard of the prison. Some vehicles were still burning outside. Capitaine Dupont walked past one which was nearly burnt-out, but grenades in it suddenly exploded and killed him. Only three days before, he had told Father Fouquer that he knew he was going to die.

General Gerow, vainly hoping to keep the French division on a tight leash, had left his headquarters at Chartres that morning accompanied by his chief of staff, Brigadier General Charles Helmick. They could not find Leclerc anywhere. Gerow had to return to Chartres and told Helmick to seek him out 'and remain with him as senior United States Army representative'.

Irritated by the way Leclerc had pushed his advance round to the south without warning Corps headquarters, Gerow told his 4th Infantry Division to push on into Paris without waiting for the 2ème DB. Having no doubt seen the delays caused by welcoming crowds, he jumped to the conclusion that the 2ème DB was taking it easy. He is supposed to have claimed to Bradley that the French troops were doing little more than 'dance their way into Paris'. But the 12th Infantry Regiment of the 4th Division was also held up by 'over-enthusiastic French mademoiselles' who insisted on kissing the drivers.

Gerow was wrong. Nobody could have been more impatient that day than General Leclerc. To speed the advance he had already pushed his reserve, the *groupement tactique* Dio, into the battle for the industrial outer suburbs, but Antony was not taken until 16.00 hours. The line of advance via Arpajon had turned out to be more heavily defended than he had expected.

Leclerc, fearing that German reinforcements might reach the capital from the north, was desperate to have troops in the centre of Paris by nightfall. To encourage the Resistance to hold out, he sent orders to the senior pilot of his spotter planes to deliver a message packed in a weighted musette bag. It said simply, '*Tenez bon, nous arrivons*' – 'Hold on, we're coming.'

Capitaine Dronne's company had managed to bypass Fresnes and reached the Croix-de-Berny. They caught their first sight of the Eiffel Tower. The company then received orders to return to the Orléans road. They were intercepted by General Leclerc, his tank goggles round his kepi, tapping the ground impatiently with his malacca cane.

'Dronne!' Leclerc called to him. 'What are you doing there?'

'I'm returning to the axis [of advance] as ordered, *mon général*.'

Leclerc told him that that was idiotic. He took him by the sleeve and pointed to the capital. 'Slip straight into Paris, to the very heart of Paris.'

The unshaven Dronne, standing to attention, with his battered kepi and sweat-stained American uniform stretched over his belly, saluted. Leclerc, who had been questioning civilians, told him to take what other forces he could muster and avoid the main routes. He was to get to the centre of Paris and tell them to hold on and not lose courage. The rest of the division would be in the city the next day.

At 19.30 hours, Dronne's 'La Nueve', mustering fifteen vehicles including half-tracks bearing the names of Spanish Civil War battles, such as 'Madrid', 'Guadalajara' and 'Brunete', set off. This company of Spanish Republicans was reinforced at the last moment with a platoon of engineers and three Shermans from the 501ème Chars de Combat, a regiment of Gaullist loyalists. Their tanks bore the names of Napoleonic battles from 1814, 'Montmirail', 'Romilly' and 'Champaubert'. Their commander was Lieutenant Michard, a priest from the White Fathers.*

The half-track 'Guadalajara' led the way, guided by a local on an ancient motorcycle. He knew all the back streets and where the German roadblocks were, so Dronne's little column threaded its way safely through the remaining suburbs to the Porte d'Italie, the southernmost point of Paris. The men cheered as they passed the city boundary. The

---

* Dronne himself was mounted in his Jeep named 'Mort aux Cons!' – 'Death to Idiots!' When he first noticed this, Leclerc asked Dronne, 'Why do you want to kill everyone?'

column was frequently held up by ecstatic civilians, unable to believe that these were French troops arriving to save the capital. Another guide, an Armenian, presented himself on a moped. Dronne told him to take them to the Hôtel de Ville, but when he returned to his Jeep, he found that a heavily built woman from Alsace had planted herself on the front to act as the Republican symbol of 'Marianne'.

Dodging down back streets away from the Avenue d'Italie, they headed north to the Pont d'Austerlitz. As soon as the column reached the far bank of the Seine, they turned left along the *quais*. At 21.20 hours, the tanks and half-tracks rumbled into the Place de l'Hôtel de Ville.

At the other end of Paris, Colonel de Langlade's tanks finally reached their objective, the Pont de Sèvres. On the order of Commandant Massu, later famous for his pitiless role in the battle for Algiers, a Sherman of the Chasseurs d'Afrique began to cross the bridge, accompanied by four members of the FFI on foot. To their relief, they encountered no mines, but they were under intermittent fire from a German artillery battery sited on the racecourse at Longchamp.

At the Hôtel de Ville, Capitaine Dronne ordered his force to take up all-round defence. He entered the building and strode up the grand staircase to report. Leaders of the Resistance, led by Georges Bidault, embraced him. Bidault tried to make a speech, but the emotion of the moment was too much for him.

Outside, civilians crowded round the tanks and half-tracks. At first they were nervous, but when they saw the divisional symbol of a map of France with the Cross of Lorraine, they went wild, embracing and kissing the grizzled soldiers. Several people ran to nearby churches. Bells began to peal out and soon afterwards the great bell of Notre-Dame, 'Le Bourdon', began to sound across the city in the twilight. The housebound Colette, with tears of joy in her eyes, wrote of that momentous evening 'when the night rose like a dawn'.

It was the pealing of Le Bourdon which finally convinced the people of Paris. A woman refugee from Normandy was undressing for bed when she heard it. Then the street outside began to fill with people yelling, 'They're here!'

*

At the far end of the rue de Rivoli from the Hôtel de Ville, in the anteroom to his office, Choltitz and his staff officers were drinking champagne from the Meurice's cellar. On that humid August night, they were discussing the St Bartholomew's Eve massacre of Huguenots in Paris and whether there were any similarities to their own position. When they heard the bells, Choltitz stood up and went through to his desk. He rang Generalleutnant Speidel and, once he was through, he held the receiver towards the window. Speidel knew immediately what it signified. Choltitz, who knew that he would not see Germany again for a long time, asked him to look after his family.

While the bells rang out, the pioneer group from the 256th Infanterie-Division, with their truck-loads of torpedoes, were guarding the Alexandre III bridge opposite the Quai d'Orsay. Their officer, Leutnant Novick, had been summoned to an orders group. On his return, his men begged him to let them slip out of Paris. Novick replied firmly that they still had their duty to perform. The soldiers were less afraid of the prospect of fighting than of being lynched by the population when they surrendered.

Dronne's soldiers, on the other hand, received every kindness from civilians eager to be of service. They rang up the young men's relatives so that they could announce their arrival. Women brought mattresses and precious cakes of soap, and even took their filthy uniforms away to wash and press them.

The population of Paris rose early the next morning in an atmosphere of tense excitement. Many women had not slept, having stitched through the night to make flags and prepare dresses in patriotic colours to greet their liberators. One woman, who made an American flag, cut all the stars individually from an old dress.

After the days of rain, Friday, 25 August, the feast of France's patron saint, Saint-Louis, proved to be a beautiful sunny day once the morning mist evaporated. Crowds gathered in the south-west of the city to greet Langlade's troops. As news spread, others swarmed to the Porte d'Orléans and the Porte d'Italie, where Commandant Putz led Billotte's column into Paris. Leclerc followed, escorted by Spahis in Staghound armoured cars. He was met by the Gaullist Resistance leader, Chaban-Delmas, and they headed for the Gare Montparnasse, which Leclerc had designated as his divisional command post because of its good communications.

Ecstatic citizens surged forward waving improvised flags and holding their fingers up in V for victory signs. Streets cleared in a moment of panic when firing broke out, then filled again almost as quickly a short time later. The chaplain, Father Fouquer, described it as 'a noisy and lyrical carnival punctuated by shots'. Armoured columns were brought to a halt as young women in their best summer dresses clambered up to kiss the crew, while men proffered long-hoarded bottles to toast the Liberation. Fouquer, who was wearing the same combat kit and black tank beret of the 50ème Chars de Combat, complained good-naturedly that 'never in my life have I had cheeks so coloured by lipstick'. The soldiers called out to the women, 'Careful! Don't kiss him too much. He's our chaplain.'

Yet amid the singing of the 'Marseillaise' and the 'Internationale', Father Fouquer's thoughts were mixed. He could not stop thinking about the death of Capitaine Dupont at Fresnes the previous afternoon. He also eyed the crowd with a certain scepticism. 'In the spontaneous outpouring which accompanied the enthusiasm of the Liberation,' he wrote, 'it is hard to distinguish the real Resistance fighters from the parasites, that's to say the *miliciens* and the collaborators of the day before.'

For the Parisians in the streets, this was not an Allied victory, it was entirely French. The shame of 1940 and the Occupation seemed to have been obliterated. One young woman remembered glowing with pride at the sight of the Sherman tanks, with their French names: 'Victorious, Liberty advanced on their tracks. France delivered by France. It was exalting to be part of that nation.' The fact that the 2ème DB would never have reached France in its present form without American help was entirely overlooked in the delirious patriotism of the moment.

The leading American elements from the 38th Cavalry Reconnaissance Squadron and the 4th Infantry Division also entered Paris at 07.30 hours from the southern side. They found 'the people bewildered and afraid of us. They were not sure whether we were Americans or Germans.' But once they were convinced of the Americans' identity 'then the fun started'. Civilians helped pull aside the barricades to let them through. Within an hour, they were outside Notre-Dame. Having been told that the Parisians were starving, American soldiers thought that they looked healthy. 'French girls, beautiful girls, were climbing all over us and giving us flowers,' a staff sergeant wrote. 'Some of those girls had the most beautiful teeth. They must have been getting good food somewhere.'

Their progress had been slow through crowds shouting, *'Merci! Merci!* Sank you, sank you! *Vive l'Amérique!'* 'At every one of the numerous halts,' Colonel Luckett of the 12th Infantry Regiment recorded, 'mothers would hold up their children to be kissed, young girls would hug the grinning soldiers and cover them with kisses, old men saluted, and young men vigorously shook hands and patted the doughboys on the back.' Unlike General Gerow, their corps commander, Luckett and his men did not seem to mind that the 2ème DB were the stars of the show. The 4th Infantry Division freely recognized that 'Paris belonged to the French'.

General Gerow entered the city at 09.30 hours and also headed for the Montparnasse railway station to keep an eye on Leclerc. Gerow had the same reaction as his soldiers that the accounts of mass starvation had been somewhat exaggerated. 'The people of Paris were still well dressed and appeared well fed,' he reported at the time, but later amended this by saying that 'there were no signs of a long-standing malnutrition except in the poorer classes'. Americans simply did not appreciate how much physical survival during the Occupation had depended either on paying black-market prices or on having contacts in the countryside. Poorer Parisians had indeed suffered greatly.

The triumphal processions changed rapidly when columns approached the centres of German resistance. On the south-western side of Paris, Massu's men cleared the Bois de Boulogne, then Langlade's units advanced through the 16th *arrondissement* towards the Arc de Triomphe.

Colonel Dio's *groupement tactique* had some of the most heavily defended German strongpoints as their objectives – the Ecole Militaire, the Invalides and the Palais Bourbon of the Assemblée Nationale. Meanwhile, Capitaine Alain de Boissieu, with a squadron of Stuart light tanks and some Shermans from the 12ème Cuirassiers, headed towards the Boulevard Saint-Michel to tackle the German defences in and around the Palais de Luxembourg, which housed the Senate. The young cavalry officer was slightly surprised to find himself reinforced by the 'Fabien' battalion of the Communist FTP.

In the meantime some Staghound armoured cars manned by Spahis Marocains had already reached the Boulevard Saint-Michel, having come from the east via the rue Saint-Jacques. The diarist Jean Galtier-Boissière was in his bookshop near the Sorbonne when he heard that Leclerc's troops had arrived. He hurried out with his wife to see what was happening. 'A vibrant crowd,' he wrote, 'surrounds the French tanks draped in flags and covered in bouquets of flowers. On each tank, on each armoured car, next to crew members in khaki overalls and little red side-caps, there are clusters of girls, women, boys and *Fifis* wearing armbands. People lining the street applaud, blow kisses, shake their hands.'

Once Boissieu's force was in position, an officer blew a whistle. '*Allons, les femmes, descendez! On attaque le Sénat!*' The young women climbed down from the armoured vehicles, and gunners and loaders dropped back inside their turrets. German mortars in the Jardins du Luxembourg began to open fire, but the mass of civilians still followed the armoured vehicles towards the fighting. Boissieu, guessing that the Germans had an observation post on top of the palace's dome, ordered two of the Shermans to fire on it. They traversed their turrets, raising their guns to maximum elevation. A moment after they fired, he saw the German mortar controllers hurled into the air, then fall on the roof. But the large German force was too well entrenched in the park to force a rapid surrender.

Near the Arc de Triomphe, as Langlade's column advanced, a crowd including the actor Yves Montand and the singer Edith Piaf gathered to watch the surrender of the Germans in the Hôtel Majestic on the Avenue Kléber. They cheered as the prisoners were led out, but the head of the Protestant church in France, Pasteur Boegner, then looked on in horror when four bareheaded German soldiers, with their field-grey tunics unbuttoned, were dragged off to be shot. Edith Piaf managed to stop a young *Fifi* from throwing a grenade into a truck full of German prisoners.

Massu, who had taken the surrender, walked with Langlade up to the Arc de Triomphe to salute the Tomb of the Unknown Soldier. Above them, a huge tricolore, which had just been hoisted inside the arch by Paris firemen, moved gently in the breeze. But then a tank shell screamed over their heads. A Panther on the Place de la Concorde at the far end of the Champs-Elysées had spotted some of Langlade's tank destroyers move into position on either side of the Arc de Triomphe. Their commanders yelled their fire orders. One gave the range as 1,500 metres, but his gunner, a Parisian, suddenly remembered from his schooldays that the Champs-Elysées was 1,800 metres long. He made an adjustment and scored a first-round hit. The crowd surged forward and sang the 'Marseillaise'. Pasteur Boegner noted that the fighting and the impression of a Fourteenth of July celebration 'were mixed up in a hallucinating way'.

At 11.00 hours that morning, Colonel Billotte had sent an ultimatum via the Swedish consul-general, Raoul Nordling, to Generalleutnant von Choltitz. It demanded the surrender of the city by 12.15 hours. Choltitz sent back a message to say that the honour of a German officer prevented him from surrendering without a proper fight.

Fifteen minutes after the ultimatum expired, Choltitz and his staff officers assembled for their last lunch together in the large dining room of the Hôtel Meurice. 'Silent from the effort of showing no emotions, we gathered as usual,' wrote Leutnant Graf von Arnim. Instead of sitting at a table near the window to enjoy the view, as was the custom, they took their places further back in the room. Bullets fired from the Louvre riddled the windowpanes and sent chunks of wall flying around. 'But apart from that,' Arnim added, 'it was the same setting, the same waiter and the same food.'

Leclerc, having set up his headquarters alongside a railway platform in the Gare Montparnasse, left General Gerow there and went to the Préfecture de Police. This was where Choltitz would be brought as soon as he surrendered. Leclerc's impatient mood was not helped by the chaotic and noisy banquet which Charles Luizet had laid on. He swallowed a few mouthfuls hurriedly, then escaped to the Grand Salon. He had heard from Billotte that the attack on the Meurice would go in at 13.15 hours, with infantry and Shermans from the 501ème Chars de Combat advancing west along the rue de Rivoli.

As Choltitz and his officers finished their meal, the noise outside seemed to increase with more shooting. Arnim escorted Choltitz and Colonel von Unger back upstairs. On the way up, Choltitz paused to speak to an old soldier manning a machine gun by the elaborate wrought-iron balustrade of the staircase. He remarked to him that it would soon all be over and that one way or another he would be home before long. As they reached Choltitz's office, they heard explosions and the sound of shattered glass. Arnim saw Oberst von Unger, the chief of staff, go to his desk, open his briefcase and take out framed photographs of his wife, his children and his house on the Steinhuder Meer, a picture of peace and calm.

The explosions they had heard were tanks firing as the Shermans took on the few remaining Panthers in the Place de la Concorde and the Tuileries gardens. French infantry had been making their way down the rue de Rivoli, racing from pillar to pillar along the colonnade on the north side opposite the Louvre. Eventually, smoke grenades were thrown into the lobby of the Hôtel Meurice and there were bursts of automatic fire as French soldiers, led by Lieutenant Henri Karcher, surged into the building followed by members of the FFI.

Karcher raced upstairs to Choltitz's office, where he was joined by Commandant de la Horie, Billotte's chief of staff. 'After a short, correct conversation', according to Arnim, Choltitz stated that he surrendered with his staff and the occupation forces in Paris. Choltitz and Unger were then led downstairs. With smoke still swirling in most of the rooms, the Meurice was invaded by a crowd wanting to experience at first hand the capture of the German commander in Paris. The French officers hurried their two captives out of the rear door on the rue du Mont Thabor and drove them to the Préfecture de Police.

Some junior officers and soldiers of the headquarters staff were not so fortunate when they were escorted outside by the FFI. A screaming crowd rushed at them to seize what they could. Arnim's attaché case was wrenched from him. Hands searched their pockets, others grabbed spectacles and watches. German officers and soldiers were punched in the face and spat at. Finally, the prisoners were forced into three ranks and marched off. Their FFI escorts found it very hard to protect their prisoners and even themselves from the fury of the mob. Arnim saw 'a bearded giant in shirtsleeves' appear out of the crowd, put a pistol to the temple of his friend, Dr Kayser, who was in the row in front, and shoot him through the head. Arnim stumbled over the doctor's body as he fell. According to Arnim, unarmed members of the Kommandantur transport company were also shot down in the Tuileries gardens after they had surrendered. Father Fouquer of the 2ème DB was shocked by 'the crowd, often hateful when facing the enemy disarmed by others'.

Choltitz and Unger were led into the billiard room of the Préfecture de Police, where Leclerc awaited him with Chaban-Delmas and Colonel Billotte. General Barton of the 4th Infantry Division, who had also been present, retired to leave the honours to the French. Leclerc eyed his prisoner.

'I am General Leclerc,' he said. 'Are you General von Choltitz?'

Choltitz nodded.

Despite his German general's uniform, medals and the thick burgundy stripes of the general staff down his breeches, the squat Choltitz did not look impressive. His grey skin glistened from sweat. He was breathing heavily and soon swallowed a pill for his heart condition. When Choltitz sat down and adjusted his monocle to read the text of the surrender document, Oberst von Unger stood beside him, completely pale and with a vacant stare. Choltitz had just one comment to make. Only the garrison of Paris was under his orders. Other pockets of German resistance should not be declared outlaws if they did not obey his order. Leclerc accepted the point.

In an adjoining office, Colonel Rol-Tanguy and Kriegel-Valrimont, another senior Communist in the Resistance, protested to Luizet that the FFI should not be excluded from the surrender. Luizet slipped into the billiard room and told Chaban-Delmas, who in turn persuaded Leclerc to let Rol enter and sign the document too. Leclerc, who just wanted to get the ceremony over, agreed. But later, when de Gaulle saw that Rol had signed above Leclerc, he was deeply irritated.

After Choltitz was brought to the Gare Montparnasse from the Préfecture de Police, he was questioned by General Gerow. Choltitz stated that he had 'saved Paris'. He had 'only put up a sufficient fight to satisfy his government that the city was not capitulated without honour'. Gerow asked him when the Nazis would surrender. Choltitz replied that 'the Americans had something to go home to'. The Germans, on the other hand, had 'nothing to look forward to'.

Gerow believed that Choltitz, who had been their opponent in Normandy, should have 'surrendered Paris to V Corps'. This was certainly not a view shared by General de Gaulle. Gerow's revenge was a calculated insult. 'General Gerow, being in military command of Paris,' his report continued, 'set up the command post in the offices of Marshal Pétain in the Invalides.'

On that day of Paris's liberation, it was decided back in Britain that the dummy camps and signposts for the fictitious 1st US Army Group of Plan Fortitude could be dismantled. SHAEF insisted, however, that the false wireless traffic should be maintained to keep the Germans guessing about this phantom force.

The Allied victory was complete, yet elsewhere in France the savagery of the Occupation had not yet finished. At Maillé, south of Tours, trainee SS soldiers, bypassed by the Third Army's advance north of the Loire, carried out a terrible massacre in what had been an area of considerable Maquis activity. Following a clash with members of the Resistance the day before, they killed 124 civilians, ranging from a baby of three months to an eighty-nine-year-old woman. The troops involved were from a replacement battalion of the 17th SS Panzer-Division *Götz von Berlichingen* at Châtellerault. In their fury of defeat, they even used an anti-aircraft gun against their victims and gunned down livestock as well.

General von Choltitz, during the surrender, had also agreed to send several of his officers with French emissaries under a flag of truce to persuade the remaining strongpoints to give up the fight. So while intermittent firing echoed across the city and the burnt-out Panther tanks still smoked in the Jardins des Tuileries, these groups went off in Jeeps armed only with a piece of white cloth attached to a radio antenna.

German officers were terrified of being handed over to French 'terrorists'. Eventually they agreed to give in. But Gefreiter Spiekerkötter and the other pioneers from the 256th Infanterie-Division, who had become part of the Palais Bourbon garrison, soon suffered the same battering from the crowds as the soldiers outside the Hôtel Meurice. They were taken away in an old Parisian bus without windows, which stopped from time to time 'to give the crowd an opportunity to let off their anger'. By the time they reached the fire station, where they were to be locked up, most of their officers had blood pouring down their faces. Spiekerkötter found that their own heavy-drinking officer, Leutnant Nowack who had toasted 'Calvados still in German hands' as they left Normandy, now seized his bottle of eau-de-Cologne from the depot in Chartres and poured that down his throat.

Other surrender negotiations proved more dangerous for the emissaries. One German officer prisoner sent with a white flag was shot down along with an FFI officer. And a Luftwaffe flak officer killed himself by holding a grenade against his stomach and pulling out the pin. But by nightfall, the 2ème DB found itself responsible for over 12,000 prisoners who had to be lodged and fed amidst a hungry population who did not want any food to be given to the Germans. Later that night, infuriated Parisians tried to storm the fire station to kill the prisoners from the Palais Bourbon.

De Gaulle, after a meeting with Leclerc at the Gare Montparnasse, went to the ministry of war in the rue Saint-Dominique to make a symbolic visit to his old offices from 1940, when he was a junior minister. He was greeted by a guard of honour from the Garde Républicaine. He found that nothing had changed. Even the names alongside the buttons on the telephone were the same. The building had hardly been used during the four years of Occupation until the FFI took it over.

De Gaulle finally agreed to go to the Hôtel de Ville, where Georges Bidault and the National Council of the Resistance awaited him. Whatever the suspicions lingering between the two sides, their acclamation of the general who had refused to abandon the fight was overwhelming. There, in the great hall, their tall, awkward yet regal leader made one of the most famous speeches of his life: 'Paris. Paris outraged, Paris broken, Paris martyred, but Paris liberated! Liberated by herself, liberated by her people, with the help of the whole of France, that is to say of the France which fights, the true France, eternal France.'

Some members of the Resistance present still felt that he had not paid sufficient tribute to their work.* And when Bidault asked him to proclaim the Republic to the crowds waiting outside, de Gaulle refused. This was not a snub, as many people believed. De Gaulle in fact replied, 'But why should we proclaim the Republic? She has never ceased to exist.' Pétain's *Etat français*, in his view, was an aberration which should not be acknowledged. He agreed, however, to make an appearance to the crowd. De Gaulle simply raised those seemingly endless arms in a victory sign. The response was tumultuous.

When the fighting was over, most of the correspondents headed for the Hôtel Scribe, which they had known from before the war. Hemingway and David Bruce, surrounded by some of the writer's improvised militia, went straight to the Ritz, which Hemingway was determined to 'liberate'. But the most legendary part of the Liberation was what one young officer of the 2ème DB described as '*les délices d'une nuit dédiée à Vénus*'. The Parisiennes, who had greeted the troops with the heartfelt cry, 'We've waited for you for so long!', welcomed the Allies that night with unstinted generosity in their tents and armoured vehicles. Father Fouquer, when he returned to his unit after dining with some friends, found that most of the 2ème DB had moved to the Bois de Boulogne. 'I was providentially removed from the Bois de Boulogne and this night of madness,' he wrote. The American 4th Infantry Division, bivouacked in the Bois de Vincennes on the eastern edge of Paris and on the Ile de la Cité behind Notre-Dame, also enjoyed the generosity of young Frenchwomen.

The city seemed to suffer from a collective hangover the next morning. David Bruce recorded in his diary that the previous day they had drunk 'beer, cider, white and red Bordeaux, white and red Burgundy, Champagne, rum, Cognac, Armagnac and Calvados . . . the combination was enough to wreck one's constitution'.

'Slowly the tank hatches opened,' wrote an American officer, 'and

---

* The liberation of Paris cost the Germans 3,200 dead and 14,800 prisoners. The FFI probably accounted for at least 1,000 of the German casualties. The 2ème DB lost seventy-one men killed, 225 wounded and twenty-one missing in the advance on Paris and its capture. Altogether, 2,873 Parisians were killed in the month of August.

bedraggled women crawled stiffly out.' In the Bois de Boulogne, Capitaine Dronne went round pulling the young women out of his men's tents. One of them made advances to him. To roars of laughter from his men, he replied, 'Me, I don't give a damn. I'm homosexual.' The lovers of the night then breakfasted together on K-Rations round improvised campfires.

Saturday, 26 August was also a fine, sunny day. There were a few *miliciens* and isolated Germans who still held out, but the occasional bursts of shooting came mostly from over-excited members of the Resistance. Many of them charged around dangerously in commandeered black Citroëns with the letters FFI daubed all over them.

General Gerow, hearing the small-arms fire, persuaded himself that the 2ème DB was failing to carry out its primary duty of clearing the city. He still seethed at the way the French commanders flouted his authority. Hearing that General de Gaulle was planning a victory procession that afternoon, he sent the following signal at 12.55 hours to the 2ème DB: 'Direct General Leclerc that his command will not, repeat not, participate in parade this afternoon but will continue on present mission of clearing Paris and environs of enemy. He accepts orders only from me. Ack[nowledge] and report when directive delivered to Leclerc. Signed Gerow.'

Once again, Gerow was ignored. At 15.00 hours, de Gaulle took the salute of the Régiment de Marche du Tchad by the Arc de Triomphe. This uniquely French moment was in no way undermined by the international composition of the 2ème DB, with its Spaniards, Italians, German Jews, Poles, White Russians, Czechs and other nationalities.

When de Gaulle set off on foot down the Champs-Elysées on his way to Notre-Dame, he was guarded on either side by half-tracks of the division. Colonel Rol-Tanguy's headquarters had called for 6,000 members of the FFI to line the route of the procession, but their presence did little to reassure de Gaulle's entourage. He was followed by Generals Leclerc, Koenig and Juin. Behind them came the rather disgruntled members of the National Council of Resistance, who had not at first been invited. But the joy of the enormous crowds – lining the great avenue, perched on lamp posts, leaning out of windows and even standing on roofs – could not be doubted. Over a million people were estimated to have thronged central Paris that afternoon.

Shooting broke out on the Place de la Concorde, causing panic and chaos. Nobody knows how it started, but the first shot may well have come from a nervous or trigger-happy *Fifi*. Jean-Paul Sartre, watching from a balcony of the Hôtel du Louvre, came under fire and Jean Cocteau, watching from the Hôtel Crillon, claimed unconvincingly that the cigarette in his mouth was shot in half. But a senior official in the Ministry of Finance was shot dead at a window and at least half a dozen others died in the cross-fire.

De Gaulle was then taken by car to the cathedral of Notre-Dame. Cardinal Suhard was conspicuously absent. He had been prevented from attending because he had welcomed Pétain to Paris, and had recently presided over the memorial service in honour of Philippe Henriot, the Vichy minister of propaganda assassinated by the Resistance.

When de Gaulle entered Notre-Dame more fusillades broke out, both inside and outside the cathedral. But de Gaulle never flinched. As almost everyone threw themselves to the ground around him, he continued to march up the aisle, doubly determined to disarm the FFI, which he regarded as a far greater threat to order than any remaining *miliciens* or Germans. 'Public order is a matter of life and death,' he told Pasteur Boegner a few days later. 'If we do not re-establish it ourselves, foreigners will impose it upon us.' American and British forces now appeared to be seen as 'foreigners' rather than allies. France was truly liberated. As de Gaulle himself put it, France had no friends, only interests.

Although the French reluctance to acknowledge American help still rankled deeply, General Gerow subsequently accepted Leclerc's peace-making overture. His 2ème DB was ready to move on 27 August and went into action against the Germans round Le Bourget aerodrome. Also on that day, Eisenhower and Bradley paid 'an informal visit' to Paris. Eisenhower had invited Montgomery, but he refused on the grounds that he was too busy. Despite the informality of the event, General Gerow could not resist meeting his superiors at the Porte d'Orléans with a full armoured escort from the 38th Cavalry Reconnaissance Squadron to accompany them into the city. The following day, V Corps reported, 'General Gerow, as military commander of Paris, returned the capital city to the people of France.' When informed of this by Gerow, General Koenig replied that he had been in charge of Paris all along.

Gerow arranged for the 28th Infantry Division, newly attached to V Corps, to march through Paris the next day to create 'a parade of the might of the modern American Army for the populace'. Generals Bradley, Hodges and Gerow were joined by General de Gaulle at the Tomb of the Unknown Soldier at the Arc de Triomphe, where they laid a wreath. Then the four men reviewed the march-past from a stand erected by American engineers out of a Bailey bridge turned upside down on the Place de la Concorde. It was entirely fitting that Norman Cota, now the commander of the 28th Division, should lead the parade. Few men had demonstrated so clearly, as he had done at Omaha, the need for determined leadership in battle.

The ugly side of Liberation reared up almost immediately, with denunciations and revenge on women who had had liaisons with German soldiers. Marshall and Westover saw one woman scream '*collaboratrice!*' at another. The crowd turned on the accused woman and started to rip her clothes. Marshall and Westover, with a couple of American journalists, managed to save her. In Paris too the head-shaving began. On the balcony of a local *mairie*, barbers attacked the hair of women rounded up for '*collaboration horizontale*' with Germans. The crowd below yelled its approval and applauded. A young woman who had been present recorded afterwards how much she despised herself for having been part of that crowd. And a young officer with the 2ème DB wrote, 'We are sickened by these dregs who mistreat women with shaved heads for having slept with Germans.' Altogether some 20,000 Frenchwomen are estimated to have had their heads shaved in the summer of 1944.

Disillusionment between liberated and liberators also increased. Americans and British saw Paris not just as a symbol of Europe's freedom from Nazi oppression, but as a playground for their amusement. 'As we neared the city we were seized by a wild sort of excitement,' wrote Forrest Pogue. 'We began to giggle, to sing, yell and otherwise show exuberance.' American supply services, to Eisenhower's irritation, commandeered all the best hotels to lodge their senior officers in style. No French people were allowed to enter without an invitation. They were naturally jealous of the food. Simone de Beauvoir described the Hôtel Scribe, reserved for foreign journalists, as 'an American enclave in the heart of Paris: white bread, fresh eggs, jam, sugar and Spam'. In the centre of the city, US military police assumed full powers, often treating the local *gendarmerie* as auxiliaries. Soon the French Communist Party labelled the Americans 'the new occupying power'.

Pogue himself was shaken to find that the Petit Palais had been taken over, with a large sign announcing the distribution of free condoms to US troops. In Pigalle, rapidly dubbed 'Pig Alley' by GIs, prostitutes were coping with over 10,000 men a day. The French were also deeply shocked to see US Army soldiers lying drunk on the pavements of the Place Vendôme. The contrast with off-duty German troops, who had been forbidden even to smoke in the street, could hardly have been greater.

The problem was that many American soldiers, loaded with dollars of back-pay, believed that hardship at the front gave them the right to behave as they liked in the rear. And American deserters in Paris, combined with a few Milo Minderbenders in the supply services, fuelled a rampant black market. The capital of France became known as 'Chicago-sur-Seine'.

Sadly, the behaviour of a fairly unrepresentative minority soured Franco-American relations more profoundly and permanently than was understood at the time. It distorted the huge sacrifice of Allied soldiers and French civilians in the battle for Normandy, which had freed the country from the suffering and humiliation of the German Occupation. It also diverted attention away from the massive American aid. While combat engineers deactivated mines and booby traps, over 3,000 tons of supplies per day were rushed to Paris, bringing much of the Allied advance on Germany to a virtual halt.

'Paris had fallen very suddenly,' the Central Base Section reported. 'People thought that we had an inexhaustible supply of food and lots of clothing and plenty of gasoline for their cars. Our offices were as crowded as the Paris Metro.' There was an overwhelming demand for penicillin as well as morphine for civilian use. Major General Kenner, SHAEF's chief medical officer, organized a monthly allocation to be made to the French government. Meanwhile, the medical services of the American, British and Canadian armies did whatever they could for injured and sick civilians in their area.

The success of the Allied double invasion, first in Normandy and then on the Mediterranean coast, had at least spared most of France from a long-drawn-out battle of attrition.

30

Aftermath

News of the liberation of Paris had provoked almost as much emotion in the rest of France as in the capital itself. In Caen, Major Massey with the British civil affairs team wrote, 'I saw Frenchmen in the streets crying with joy as they took off their hats to the playing of the "Marseillaise".' But the citizens of Caen and other stricken towns and villages feared, with justification, that amidst the jubilation in Paris their suffering would be forgotten. This proved even more true as the war moved towards the German border. De Gaulle finally visited Caen in October and promised his support, but two months later the minister of reconstruction warned the region that it would be 'many years' before Calvados could be rebuilt.

The cruel martyrdom of Normandy had indeed saved the rest of France. Yet the debate about the overkill of Allied bombing and artillery is bound to continue. Altogether 19,890 French civilians were killed during the liberation of Normandy and an even larger number seriously injured. This was on top of the 15,000 French killed and 19,000 injured during the preparatory bombing for Overlord in the first five months of 1944. It is a sobering thought that 70,000 French civilians were killed by Allied action during the course of the war, a figure which exceeds the total number of British killed by German bombing.

Although some villages and areas of countryside had been miraculously spared during the battles, large tracts were devastated, with cratering from shells, trees stripped bare and orchards destroyed. A pestilential stench from the rotting corpses of bloated livestock still hung heavily in the air. Allied engineers had dealt with as many as they could, using bulldozers, or incinerated them with gasoline, but once the troops moved on, farmers had little but their own strength and a spade to bury the bodies. Casualties continued to rise from unexploded shells and mines after the Liberation. Around Troarn, more people are said to have been killed after the battle than during it. Many children died from playing with the grenades and ammunition they found abandoned by both sides.

As well as the towns and villages flattened by bombing, the hamlets and stone farmhouses, which the Germans had used as strongpoints, had been wrecked by artillery and mortar fire. In the *département* of Calvados alone, 76,000 people had lost their homes and virtually everything they possessed. The looting and unnecessary damage caused by Allied soldiers only added to the bitterness felt by many in the strongly mixed emotions of the Liberation. A number grumbled that they had been better off under the Germans. 'There are those who celebrate the landings,' said the wife of the Vichy mayor of Montebourg. 'As for me, I say that it was the start of our misfortunes. As you know, we were occupied, but at least we had what we needed.' Although most Normans would not have agreed with her political sentiments, the vast Allied presence in Normandy felt oppressive. In any case, as the more perceptive Allied soldiers understood, the local population had much to mourn, even beyond their own losses. Many were anxious about husbands and brothers still imprisoned or taken for forced labour in Germany. There were even greater fears for local members of the Resistance arrested by the Gestapo and transported to concentration camps.

Allied civil affairs teams, in cooperation with the French authorities, did what they could for food distribution, refugees and the restoration of essential services. Some towns, however, remained without water or electricity until well into the autumn. Sewerage systems were damaged and the infestation of rats became a major threat to public health. In Caen, only 8,000 homes were habitable for a population of 60,000. Few skylines remained recognizable after the spires of ancient churches had been blasted down by tank and gunfire to destroy possible German observation posts. A major source of resentment came about because German prisoners of war put to work by the Allies received regular army rations, according to the regulations of the International Red Cross. This meant that they were eating better than local civilians.

Despite the appalling strains placed upon the social fabric of Normandy, the population had discovered a *'camaraderie du malheur'*, a solidarity in suffering. The young had demonstrated an astonishing degree of bravery and self-sacrifice in the Défense Passive, while most Norman farmers, despite a reputation for independence and even tight fists, had displayed a great generosity to the thousands of refugees fleeing the bombarded towns. The Saingt family, who owned a brewery at Fleury, on the southern edge of Caen, had sheltered up to 900 people during the battle in their deep cellars, providing them with everything they could. Even amid the fear during the bombing of the city there had been remarkably few disputes in the refuges, with almost everyone showing a *'discipline exemplaire'* even over the distribution of food. The prolonged crisis, as many noted, had not only proved a great leveller, it had brought out the best in people.

Many British and American troops, overwhelmed by the joyous welcome they received as soon as they left the battle zones, could not help contrasting it with the sometimes cold reception they had received in Normandy. This showed a lack of imagination. The Normans could hardly be blamed for fearing that the invasion might fail and German reprisals would be harsh. And the local population, surveying the damage inflicted on their lives, were unlikely to be joyful even when it became clear that the Allied footing on the Continent was secure.

Considering the circumstances, most Normans were extraordinarily forgiving. The 195th Field Ambulance set up a dressing station near Honfleur beside a château overlooking the Seine. The officers' mess was in a small house nearby, where the doctors were most hospitably received by the elderly Frenchman living there alone. After a few days, as resistance had ceased south of the Seine and their only patients were local civilians who had been wounded in the fighting, the doctors decided to give a party. They 'invited the Countess and her relatives from the château'. She accepted but requested that the party be moved up to the château. Three days before their arrival, she explained, the wife of their host had been killed during an attack by an RAF aircraft on the retreating Germans. The medical officers were dazed when they thought of the courteous behaviour of the elderly Frenchman, 'so tragically bereaved on the eve of liberation', especially since it had been a British plane which caused his wife's death.

'Civil life will be mighty dull,' wrote the egocentric General Patton in his diary after the triumph of the Normandy campaign. 'No cheering crowds, no flowers, no private airplanes. I am convinced that the best end for an officer is the last bullet of the war.'* He would have done better to remember the Duke of Wellington's famous observation that 'next to a battle lost, the greatest misery is a battle gained'.

The ferocity of the fighting in north-west France can never be in doubt. And despite the sneers of Soviet propagandists, the battle for Normandy was certainly comparable to that of the eastern front. During the three summer months, the Wehrmacht suffered nearly 240,000 casualties and lost another 200,000 men to Allied captivity. The 21st Army Group of British, Canadians and Poles sustained 83,045 casualties and the Americans 125,847. In addition, the Allied air forces lost 16,714 men killed and missing.

The post-war squabble between Allied generals, claiming credit and apportioning blame in their reports and memoirs, was correspondingly ferocious. That keen observer of human frailty Field Marshal Sir Alan Brooke was presumably not surprised. He had once written about a row in June between senior naval officers: 'It is astonishing how petty and small men can be in connection with questions of command.'

Montgomery placed himself at the centre of the post-war storm mainly because of his preposterous assertions that everything had gone according to his master plan. He felt that he should be seen on a par with Marlborough and Wellington and implicitly denigrated his American colleagues. Almost single-handedly, he had managed in Normandy to make most senior American commanders anti-British at the very moment when Britain's power was waning dramatically. His behaviour thus constituted a diplomatic disaster of the first order. Whatever the merits of his arguments at the end of August 1944 about the planned thrust into Germany, Montgomery mishandled the situation badly. He had also provoked the higher ranks of the Royal Air

---

* Patton in fact died as a result of a traffic accident in Germany in December 1945.

Force, who were even more enraged than the Americans at his lack of frankness over operations in Normandy.

The usually tolerant Eisenhower refused to forgive Montgomery for the claims he made after the war. 'First of all he's a psychopath,' Eisenhower exploded in an interview in 1963. 'Don't forget that. He is such an egocentric that the man – everything he has done is perfect – has never made a mistake in his life.' It was tragic that Montgomery should have thus diverted attention away from his own undoubted qualities and from the sacrifice of his troops, who had held down the vast bulk of the German panzer formations and faced the greatest concentration of 88 mm anti-tank guns.

Montgomery's unplanned battle of attrition, as unplanned as the Americans' bloody slog through the *bocage*, had of course been handicapped by the delays caused by the appalling weather in mid-June. Yet British and American alike had gravely underestimated the tenacity and discipline of Wehrmacht troops. This was partly because they had failed to appreciate the effectiveness of Nazi propaganda in persuading its soldiers that defeat in Normandy meant the annihilation of their Fatherland. These soldiers, especially the SS, were bound to believe that they had everything to lose. Their armies had already provided so many reasons for Allied anger.

The battle for Normandy did not go as planned, but even the armchair critics could never dispute the eventual outcome, however imperfect. One must also consider what might have happened should the extraordinary undertaking of D-Day have failed: for example, if the invasion fleet had sailed into the great storm of mid-June. The post-war map and the history of Europe would have been very different indeed.

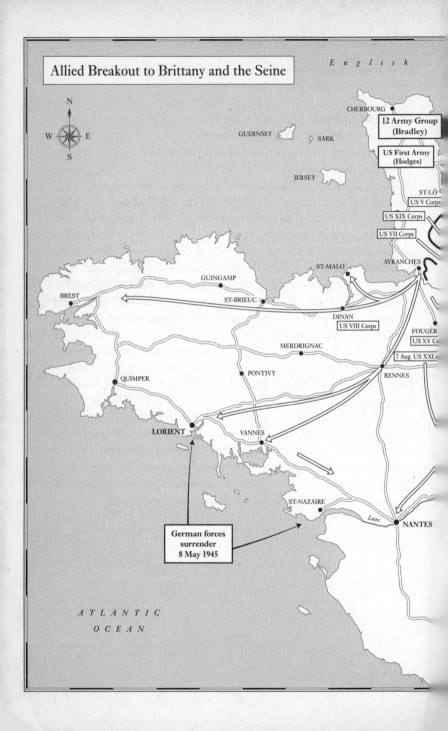

Allied Breakout to Brittany and the Seine

English

CHERBOURG

12 Army Group (Bradley)

US First Army (Hodges)

GUERNSEY

SARK

JERSEY

ST-LÔ
US V Corps

US XIX Corps

US VII Corps

AVRANCHES

ST-MALO

GUINGAMP

BREST

ST-BRIEUC

DINAN
US VIII Corps

FOUGÈR

US XV C

7 Aug. US XX C

MERDRIGNAC

RENNES

PONTIVY

QUIMPER

LORIENT

VANNES

ST-NAZAIRE

Loire

NANTES

German forces surrender 8 May 1945

ATLANTIC

OCEAN

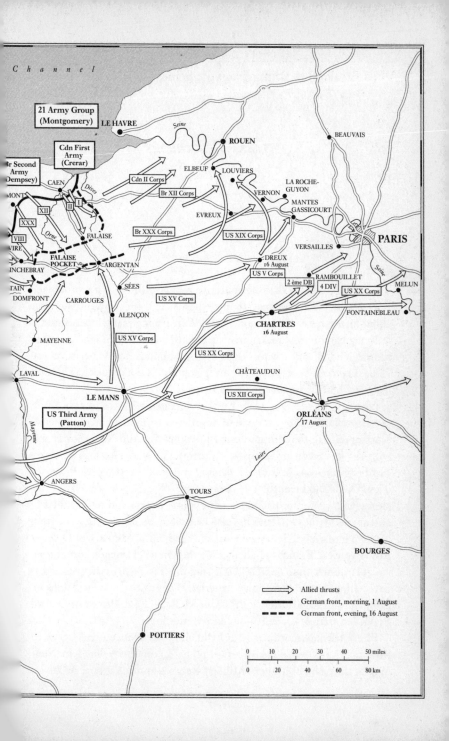

Channel

21 Army Group
(Montgomery)

LE HAVRE

Seine

BEAUVAIS

ROUEN

Cdn First
Army
(Crerar)

ELBEUF   LOUVIERS

LA ROCHE-
GUYON

Br Second
Army
(Dempsey)

CAEN   *Dives*   Cdn II Corps

VERNON

MONT

XII   II   I

Br XII Corps

MANTES
GASSICOURT

XXX

EVREUX

PARIS

VIII   Orne

Br XXX Corps

US XIX Corps

VIRE   FALAISE

VERSAILLES

INCHEBRAY   FALAISE
POCKET

ARGENTAN

DREUX
16 August

RAMBOUILLET

MELUN

TAIN

SÉES

US V Corps

DOMFRONT   CARROUGES

2 ème DB   4 DIV   US XX Corps

US XV Corps

ALENÇON

FONTAINEBLEAU

MAYENNE

CHARTRES
16 August

US XV Corps

LAVAL

CHÂTEAUDUN

US XX Corps

LE MANS

US XII Corps

US Third Army
(Patton)

Mayenne

ORLÉANS
17 August

ANGERS

TOURS

Loire

BOURGES

POITIERS

Allied thrusts

German front, morning, 1 August

German front, evening, 16 August

| 0 | 10 | 20 | 30 | 40 | 50 miles |

| 0 | 20 | 40 | 60 | 80 km |

Acknowledgements

There is an old joke that the collective noun for those in my profession is a 'mischief of historians'. In my experience, this is certainly not true about historians of the Second World War. Facing many lonely months in foreign archives, it makes an enormous difference to be able to discuss sources and theories with others whose opinions and experience you value. Over the years, the unstinting support of colleagues and friends has been both a comfort and a pleasure.

Nearly a decade ago, when I was still fixated with the eastern front, the late Martin Blumenson first urged me to take on the subject of Normandy. He too was interested in comparing the Nazi–Soviet war with the campaign in north-west Europe. Sir Max Hastings has been endlessly generous in loans of material and good suggestions. Professor Tami Davis Biddle of the US Army War College has given wise advice on the air war and provided me with books, papers and photocopies of documents. James Holland has also lent many books and material from his own interviews. Sebastian Cox, the head of the Ministry of Defence Air Historical Branch, is another in the circle of friends forming an irregular lunch-time *tertulia*, discussing the war. Many other historians have helped with advice and material. They include Rick Atkinson, Professor Michael Burleigh, Professor M. R. D. Foot, Professor Donald L. Miller, Claude Quétel and Niklas Zetterling.

I have been extraordinarily lucky in all the assistance I have received from archivists while researching this book, especially Dr Tim Nenninger, the Chief of Modern Military Records at the National Archives,

College Park, Maryland; Dr Conrad Crane, director of the US Army Military History Institute in Carlisle, Pennsylvania, and his staff; the staff of the National Archives at Kew; the Trustees and staff of the Liddell Hart Centre for Military Archives; Alain Talon at the Archives Départementales de la Manche; Frau Jana Brabant at the Bundesarchiv-Militärarchiv in Freiburg-im-Breisgau; and Frau Irina Renz of the Bibliothek für Zeitgeschichte in Stuttgart. As well as Sebastian Cox, I am also grateful to Clive Richards, the senior researcher at the Air Force Historical Branch, for his assistance.

At the National World War II Museum in New Orleans, Dr Gordon H. Mueller, Jeremy Collins and Seth Paridon could not have been more welcoming while I worked on the Eisenhower Center archive. I was also deeply touched by the kindness of everyone at the Mémorial de Caen: Stéphane Grimaldi, Stéphane Simonnet, Christophe Prime and Marie-Claude Berthelot, who put up with me for so long and so often.

I also owe a great deal to those who so kindly lent me their own diaries and letters or those of their parents. I am most grateful to David Christopherson, who sent me the diary of his father, Colonel Stanley Christopherson; Professor J. L. Cloudsley-Thompson; James Donald; L. B. Fiévet (the great-nephew of Raoul Nordling); Brigadier P. T. F. Gowans, OAM; Toby and Sarah Helm for the diary of their father, Dr Bill Helm; the late Myles Hildyard; and Charles Quest-Ritson for the collected letters of his father, Lieutenant T. T. Ritson, RHA. Others, such as Morten Malmø, Miles d'Arcy-Irvine and Philip Windsor-Aubrey, have offered leads and supplementary material, and William Mortimer Moore sent me his unpublished biography of General Leclerc. Dr Lyubov Vinogradova and Michelle Miles have helped with research and Angelica von Hase has again checked my translation and provided many useful details.

Once more, this whole project has been immeasurably assisted by Andrew Nurnberg, my literary agent for the last quarter of a century, by my editor Eleo Gordon at Penguin and by Lesley Levene, the copy-editor. But as always, my greatest thanks go to my wife, Artemis Cooper, who has edited, corrected and improved the text from start to finish.

Notes

ABBREVIATIONS

ADdC Archives départementales du Calvados, Caen

AdM Archives de la Manche, Saint-Lô

AFRHA Air Force Research Historical Agency, Maxwell Air Force Base, Alabama

AHB Air Historical Branch, Ministry of Defence, Northwood

AN Archives Nationales, Paris

AVP Archives de la Ville de Paris

AVPRF Arkhiv Vneshnoi Politiki Rossiiskii Federatsii (Foreign Policy Archives of the Russian Federation), Moscow

BA-MA Bundesarchiv-Militärarchiv, Freiburg-im-Breisgau

BD Bruce Diary, Papers of David Bruce, Virginia Historical Society, Richmond, Virginia

BfZ-SS Bibliothek für Zeitgeschichte, Sammlung Sterz, Stuttgart

CAC Churchill Archive Centre, Churchill College, Cambridge

CMH Center of Military History, Washington, DC

CRHQ Centre de Recherche d'Histoire Quantitative, University of Caen

CWM/MCG Canadian War Memorial/ Mémorial Canadien de la Guerre

DDEL Dwight D. Eisenhower Library, Abilene, Kansas

DTbA Deutsches Tagebucharchiv, Emmendingen

DWS Department of War Studies, Royal Military Academy Sandhurst

ETHINT European Theater Historical Interrogations, 1945, USAMHI

FMS Foreign Military Studies, USAMHI

HP Harris Papers, RAF Museum, Hendon

IfZ Archiv des Instituts für Zeitgeschichte, Munich

IHTP-CNRS Reports from the German Military Commander in France and the synthesis of the reports from the French prefects 1940–44, edited by the German Historical Institute Paris and the Institut d'Histoire du Temps Présent, revised by Regina Delacor, Jürgen Finger, Peter Lieb, Vincent Viet and Florent Brayard

IMT International Military Tribunal

IWM Imperial War Museum archives, London

LHCMA Liddell Hart Centre for Military Archives, London

LofC Library of Congress, The Veterans' History Project, Washington, DC

MdC Mémorial de Caen archives, Normandy

MHSA Montana Historical Society Archives

NA II National Archives II, College Park, Maryland

NAC/ANC National Archives of Canada/Archives Nationales du Canada

NWWIIM-EC National World War II Museum, Eisenhower Center archive, New Orleans

OCMH-FPP Office of the Chief of Military History, Forrest Pogue Papers, Forrest C. Pogue's interview notes for *Supreme Command*, Washington, 1954, now with USAMHI

PDDE *The Papers of Dwight David Eisenhower*, Vol. III, *The War Years*, edited by Alfred D. Chandler, Baltimore, MD, 1970

PP Portal Papers, Christ Church Library, Oxford

ROHA Rutgers Oral History Archive

SHD-DAT Service Historique de la Défense, Département de l'Armée de Terre, Vincennes

SODP Senior Officers' Debriefing Program, US Army War College, Carlisle, Pennsylvania

SWWEC Second World War Experience Centre archive, Horsforth, Leeds

TNA The National Archives (formerly the Public Record Office), Kew

USAMHI United States Army Military History Institute, US Army War College, Carlisle, Pennsylvania

WLHUM Wellcome Library for the History and Understanding of Medicine, London

WWII VS World War II Veterans' Survey, USAMHI

In addition the private diaries of the following people have been used:

Lieutenant Colonel Stanley Christopherson, Sherwood Rangers Yeomanry

Lieutenant William Helm, 210 Field Ambulance, 177th Brigade, 59th Infantry Division

Captain Myles Hildyard, intelligence officer with 7th Armoured Division

Lieutenant T. T. Ritson, RHA

FOREWORD

p. xviii 'The British had a much . . .', Colonel C. H. Bonesteel III, G-3 Plans, 12th Army Group, OCMH-FPP

'There was also a feeling . . .', NARA 407/427/24170

'The British Army couldn't fight . . .', Robert Elliott Rogge, Stormont, Dundas and Glengarry Highlanders, NWWIIM-EC

p. xix 'fill a crater. . .', NARA 407/427/24170

p. xx 'that we have got to fight . . .', NARA 407/427/6431

See Tom Ricks and Jörg Muth on *Auftragstaktik*, *Foreign Policy*, 11.9.2012

intelligence summary, 8 September 1944, TNA WO 171/287, quoted in Sönke Neitzel and Harald Welzer, *Soldaten – On Fighting, Killing and Dying: The Secret Second World War Tapes of German POWs*, New York, 2012, p. 316 and n. 843, p. 392.

p. xxi 'It is high time . . .', ibid., p. 319

p. xxii 'Die Einsatzfreudigen . . .', Dr Hans Mühle, 306th Infanterie-Division, 18.1.1943, BA-MA N241/42

I THE DECISION

p. 2 'For heaven's sake, Stagg', J. M. Stagg, *Forecast for Overlord*, London, 1971, p. 69

'pre-D-Day jitters', Harry C. Butcher, *Three Years with Eisenhower*, London, 1946, p. 479

p. 3 Plan Fortitude, TNA WO 219/5187

p. 4 'Garbo', TNA KV 2/39-2/42 and 2/63-2/71

Ironside, TNA KV 2/2098

'Bronx', TNA KV 2/2098

destruction of airfields, Luftgau West France, TNA HW 1/2927

Bletchley watch system, TNA HW 8/86

p. 5 'Latest evidence suggests . . .', TNA HW 40/6

'my circus wagon', Carlo D'Este, *Eisenhower*, New York, 2002, p. 518

'to establish a belt . . .', TNA WO 205/12

'There is no doubt . . .', Field Marshal Lord Alanbrooke, *War Diaries 1939–1945*, London, 2001, p. 575

p. 6 'Nice chap, no soldier', Cornelius Ryan interview, Ohio University Library Department of Archives and Special Collections

'national spectacles pervert . . .', Alanbrooke, p. 575

'My hat is worth . . .', Duff Hart-Davis (ed.), *King's Counsellor*, London, 2006, p. 196–7

'Monty is perhaps . . .', LHCMA Liddell Hart 11/1944/11

'The bloody Durhams . . .', Harry Moses, *The Faithful Sixth*, Durham, 1995, p. 270. I am most grateful to Miles d'Arcy-Irvine, Major Philip Windsor-Aubrey, Major C. Lawton, Harry Moses and Richard Atkinson for their help on this incident

p. 7 'unsatisfactory', NA II 407/427/24132

'hayseed expression . . . pragmatic . . .', Martin Blumenson, *The Battle of the Generals*, New York, 1993, p. 35

p. 8 'made everyone angry', Major General Kenner, chief medical officer, SHAEF, OCMH-FPP

'The landings in . . .', quoted in Butcher, p. 525

Omaha reconnaissance, Major General L. Scott-Bowden, SWWEC T2236

p. 9 'When we left . . .', Robert A. Wilkins, 149th Combat Engineers, NWWIIM-EC

'As we passed through . . .', Arthur Reddish, *A Tank Soldier's Story*, privately published, undated, p. 21

p. 10 'I've been fattened up . . .', quoted in Stuart Hills, *By Tank into Normandy*, London, 2002, p. 64

'All are tense . . .', LofC

'The women who have come . . .', Mollie Panter-Downes, *London War Notes*, London, 1971, p. 324

'One night . . . ,' Ernest A. Hilberg, 18th Infantry, 1st Division, NWWIIM-EC

p. 11 'Had it not been fraught . . .', Stagg, p. 86

'If I answered that . . .', ibid., p. 88

p. 12 'Good luck, Stagg . . .', ibid., p. 91

'Gentlemen . . . The fears . . .', ibid., pp. 97–8

'Eisenhower's forces are landing . . .', Butcher, p. 481

'the sky was almost clear . . .', Stagg, p. 99

2 BEARING THE CROSS OF LORRAINE

p. 14 'an empty feeling . . .', Field Marshal Lord Alanbrooke, *War Diaries 1939–1945*, London, 2001, pp. 553–4 (5 June)

'The British had a much . . .', Colonel C. H. Bonesteel III, G-3 Plans, 12th Army Group, OCMH-FPP

p. 15 'display some form of "reverse Dunkirk" . . .', TNA HW 1/12309

'My dear Winston . . .', CAC CHAR 20/136/004

'peevish', Butcher quoting Commander Thompson, Harry C. Butcher, *Three Years with Eisenhower*, London, 1946, p. 480

'Winston meanwhile . . .', Alanbrooke, p. 553

p. 16 'As I understand it . . .', Prime Minister to President, 23 February, in answer to telegram No. 457, TNA PREM 3/472

'an insurrectional government', quoted in Jean Lacouture, *De Gaulle*, New York, 1990, p. 511

De Gaulle and Waterloo, Robert and Isabelle Tombs, *That Sweet Enemy*, London, 2006, p. 569

'You might do him a great deal . . .', Prime Minister to President, 20 April, TNA PREM 3/472

p. 17 'I am unable at this time,' 13 May, TNA PREM 3/472

Eisenhower and CFLN, PDDE, p. 1592

'acute embarrassment', SCAF 24, 11 May, TNA PREM 3/345/1

'a working arrangement', Prime Minister to President, 12 May, TNA PREM 3/472

Joan of Arc mass, 14 May, SHD-DAT 11 P 218

p. 18 'Thanks to jokes . . .', quoted in Max Hastings, *Overlord*, London, 1984, p. 69

'all the faults . . .', Prime Minister to President, 26 May, TNA PREM 3/472

'the interest of security . . .', 13 May, TNA PREM 3/472

'This did not endear . . .', M. R. D. Foot, *SOE in France*, London, 1966, p. 241

'C' to Prime Minister, TNA PREM 3/345/1

p. 19 'Above all . . .', Duff Cooper diary, 2 June, John Julius Norwich (ed.), *The Duff Cooper Diaries*, London, 2005, p. 306

'My dear General de Gaulle . . .', TNA PREM 3/345/1

'absolutely unrecognized . . .', Charles de Gaulle, *Mémoires de Guerre*, Vol. II, Paris, 1959, pp. 223–4

p. 20 'We are going to liberate . . .' and 'To de Gaulle, who never accepted defeat', quoted in Lacouture, p. 522

'wished to suggest . . .', Bedell Smith to Churchill, 5 June, TNA PREM 3/339/6

p. 21 'Gentlemen, since I presented . . .', J. M. Stagg, *Forecast for Overlord*, London, 1971, p. 113

p. 22 'He always gets a lift . . .', Butcher, p. 482

cut-throat razors, Pfc Carl Cartledge, 501st Parachute Infantry Regiment, 101st Airborne, WWII VS

'to crawl through . . .', William True, NWWIIM-EC

p. 23 the paratrooper winning $2,500, Arthur B. 'Dutch' Schultz, C Company, 505th Parachute Infantry Regiment, 82nd Airborne Division, NWWIIM-EC

p. 24 'There was a great feeling . . .', Parker A. Alford, 26th Field Artillery, 9th Infantry Division, 501st Parachute Infantry Regiment, NWWIIM-EC

'he also said . . .', Don Malarkey, E Company of the 506th Parachute Infantry Regiment, 101st Airborne Division, NWWIIM-EC

'Men, what you're going . . .', Edward C. Boccafogli, 508th Parachute Infantry Regiment, 82nd Airborne Division, NWWIIM-EC

'Look to the right of you . . .', Major

General S. H. Matheson, Regimental Adjutant of the 506th Parachute Infantry Regiment, 101st Airborne Division, NWWIIM-EC

p. 25 '*übelste Untermenschentum amerikanischer Slums*', BA-MA RW 2/v.44, quoted in Peter Lieb, *Konventioneller Krieg oder Weltanschauungskrieg?*, Munich, 2007, p. 132

'one for pain . . .', Pfc Carl Cartledge, 501st Parachute Infantry Regiment, 101st Airborne, WWII VS

p. 26 'He was standing there . . .', Edward C. Boccafogli, 508th Parachute Infantry Regiment, 82nd Airborne Division, NWWIIM-EC

'informality and friendliness with troopers', Butcher, p. 485

'What's your name, soldier? . . .', Sherman Oyler, 502nd Parachute Infantry Regiment, 101st Airborne Division, NWWIIM-EC

p. 27 'We were surprised as dickens . . .', Edward J. Jeziorski, 507th Parachute Infantry Regiment, NWWIIM-EC

p. 28 'One trooper asked . . .', Tomaso William Porcella, 3rd Battalion, 508th Parachute Infantry Regiment, 82nd Airborne Division, NWWIIM-EC

'We ask you . . .', Prime Minister to Stalin, 14 April, TNA PREM 3/472

p. 29 'One should not forget . . .', Stalin to Prime Minister, TNA PREM 3/333/5

'We have heard from other sources . . .', Gusev diary, AVPRF 59a/7/p13/6, pp. 357–8

p. 30 Vishinsky, AVPRF 06/6/p2/d22, p. 147

'I have just returned . . .', Prime Minister to Stalin, 5 June, TNA PREM 3/346

3 WATCH ON THE CHANNEL

p. 31 'They are supposed . . .', Generalleutnant Fritz Bayerlein, Panzer Lehr Division, ETHINT 66

p. 32 Christmas boxes for the *Leibstandarte Adolf Hitler*, Traudl Junge, *Until the Final Hour*, London, 2002, p. 79

'just a bit of cheap bluff', General der Infanterie Blumentritt, debriefing 6 August 1945, NA II 407/427/24231

Rommel also wanting to abandon Italy, Generalleutnant Speidel, Chief of Staff Army Group B, FMS B-718–720

p. 33 'not favourably received', Shulman interview with Generalfeldmarschall Gerd von Rundstedt, October 1945, Milton Shulman, *Defeat in the West*, London, 1986, p. 107

'We considered the repulse . . .', Generalleutnant Fritz Bayerlein, Panzer Lehr Division, ETHINT 66

'The face of the war . . .', Leutnant Kurt Flume diary, 1 June 1944, BfZ-SS

p. 35 'When the Government . . .', Hans Speidel, *We Defended Normandy*, London, 1951, p. 88

p. 36 'If he does not do . . .', IfZ, NOKW-546, quoted in Peter Lieb, *Konventioneller Krieg oder Weltanschauungskrieg?*, Munich, 2007, p. 121

panzer army near Paris, Generaloberst Heinz Guderian, ETHINT 38

Rommel and Allied air supremacy, General der Infanterie Blumentritt, debriefing 6 August 1945, NA II 407/427/24231

identification of likely landing sites, General der Infanterie Blumentritt, debriefing 6 August 1945, NA II 407/427/24231

p. 37 dummy minefields, Lieutenant Cyril Rand, 2nd Battalion Royal Ulster Rifles, MdC TE 499

'ear and stomach battalions', Lieb, p. 106

'it is really sad . . .', Heinrich Böll, *Briefe aus dem Krieg 1939–1945*, Vol. II, Cologne, 2001, p. 918

'No good replacements . . .', Generalleutnant Fritz Bayerlein, Panzer Lehr Division, ETHINT 66

p. 38 'apprehensive impression . . .', BA-MA RH 19 iv/129, 28.12.1943, quoted in Lieb, p. 123

'*Plutokratenstaaten Amerika und England*', IfZ, MA-1024, quoted in Lieb, p. 120

'very different . . .', Fernand Louvoy, MdC TE 38

p. **39** 'You will be liberated . . .', Madame Richer, Bayeux, MdC TE 223

'With this division . . .', General-leutnant Fritz Bayerlein, Panzer Lehr Division, ETHINT 66

'could hardly understand . . .', General-leutnant Edgar Feuchtinger, FMS B-441

p. **40** 'He was of Spartan-like . . .', Oberst-leutnant Keil, FMS C-018

'a conqueror's paradise', interview with General der Infanterie Blumentritt, February 1946, Shulman, p. 60

'The enemy will certainly . . .', Truppen-ingenieur, Stab/Pz.Pi.Btl.86, 9.Pz.Div., BfZ-SS

p. **41** 'They had done nothing . . .', General-leutnant Fritz Bayerlein, Panzer Lehr Division, ETHINT 66

'King's Own German Grenadiers', Shulman interview with Generalfeldmar-schall Gerd von Rundstedt, October 1945, Shulman, p. 110

'the Canada Division', Speidel, p. 98

Bayeux Wehrmacht facilities, Franz Gockel, MdC TE 500

p. **42** 'I have here . . .', undated letter from Hauptfeldwebel Helmut Lichtenfels, Folder Newbold, Stefan, DDEL

'I will behave . . .', André Heintz diary, MdC TE 32 (1–4)

'Don't be too concerned . . .', Unter-offizier Leopold L., 5.Kp./Pz.Rgt.3, 2.Pz.Div., BfZ-SS

weather conditions, Admiral Friedrich Ruge, Admiral bei der Heeresgruppe B, FMS A-982; and Obserstleutnant Keil, FMS C-018

p. **43** 'Well, another false . . .', Hubert Meyer, *The 12th SS*, Vol. I, Mechanicsburg, Pa., 2005, p. 87

'Couriers and individual soldiers . . .', Generalleutnant Mahlmann, 353rd Infantry-Division, FMS A-983; and Oberst Cordes, Alfred Weißkopf, AdM 2 J 695

'made statements . . .', Oberstleutnant Fritz Ziegelmann, 352nd Infantry Division, FMS B-021

'Alert Stage II', Generalleutnant Bodo Zimmermann, OB West, FMS B-308; and Admiral Friedrich Ruge, FMS B 282

4 SEALING OFF THE INVASION AREA

p. **45** SOE estimates of the Resistance, William Mackenzie, *The Secret History of SOE*, London, 2000, p. 602

p. **46** 'Plan Vert' etc., SHD-DAT 13 P 33

p. **47** Resistance in the Orne, ADdC9W4/2

Resistance information gathering, André Heintz diary, MdC TE 32 (1–4)

'nothing more than . . .', First US Army headquarters, 10 March, NA II 407/427/24368/595

p. **48** SAS and Jedburghs, M. R. D. Foot, *SOE in France*, London, 1966, pp. 400–407

'We will undergo . . .', Generalleutnant Fritz Bayerlein, Panzer Lehr Division, ETHINT 66

'minimum diversions', letter of 24 March from Air Marshal Arthur Harris to Air Chief Marshal Sir Charles Portal, Chief of the Air Staff, HP, Folder H83

p. **49** Harris and Spaatz, Tami Davis Biddle, 'Bombing by the Square Yard: Sir Arthur Harris at War, 1942–1945', *International History Review*, XXI, 3, September 1999, pp. 569–852

'should be the main target', TNA PREM 3/4727

'However regrettable . . .', TNA PREM 3/4727

'The RAF was a house divided', Colonel C. H. Bonesteel III, G-3 Plans, 12th Army Group, OCMH-FPP

15,000 French killed and 19,000 injured, AN AJ 41/56

'You must get control . . .', Wing Commander Scarman, Tedder's aide, OCMH-FPP

Churchill's inability to see, Marshal of the RAF Viscount Portal, OCMH-FPP

p. **50** 'God, no!', Air Chief Marshal Sir James Robb, Chief of Staff (Air) to Eisenhower, OCMH-FPP

'insolent little sphinx . . .', anonymous, MdC TE 83

signals to the Resistance in Normandy, SHD-DAT 13 P 33

5 THE AIRBORNE ASSAULT

p. 51 'This is it', David Howarth, *Dawn of D-Day*, London, 1959, p. 13

p. 53 'Well, so far . . .', Garry Johnson and Christopher Dunphie, *Brightly Shone the Dawn*, London, 1980, p. 36

'Ham and Jam', Private Tappenden, NWWIIM-EC

p. 54 Generalleutnant Joseph Reichert, 711th Infanterie-Division, FMS B-403

p. 55 execution of paratroopers, Peter Lieb, *Konventioneller Krieg oder Weltanschauungskrieg?*, Munich, 2007, p. 173

'Gentlemen, in spite of . . .', Terry Copp, *Fields of Fire*, Toronto, 2003, p. 42

p. 57 Saint-Pair, Neville Smith, 9th Battalion Parachute Regiment, MdC TE 134

192 of Otway's men, Howarth, p. 61

'Shall we take . . .', ibid., p. 56

p. 58 Brigadier Hill's account, *Independent on Sunday*, 6 June 2004

'the means of mortal sin', Mark Zuehlke, *Juno Beach*, Vancouver, 2005, p. 129

p. 59 'The landing went . . .', NA II 407/427/24170

p. 60 'grossly overloaded . . .', Legrand Johnson, 101st Airborne Division, NWWIIM-EC

'by this time . . .', Lieutenant John R. Blackburn, Sky Control, USS *Quincy*, NWWIIM-EC

p. 61 'cocky unruly characters . . .', Roger L. Airgood, C-47 pilot, NWWIIM-EC

'two islands named . . .', Richard H. Denison, 437th Troop Carrier Group, NWWIIM-EC

p. 62 evasive action against orders, NA II 407/427/24137

'Often, a yellow . . .', Lieutenant John R. Blackburn, Sky Control, USS *Quincy*, NWWIIM-EC

p. 63 'Our plane never did slow . . .', Major Leland A. Baker, 502nd Parachute Infantry Regiment, 101st Airborne Division, NWWIIM-EC

'US parachute troops landed . . .', Obergefreiter Hans S., 9.Kp./Gren.Rgt.1058, 91.(LL.)Inf.Div., BfZ-SS

'watermelons falling off . . .', Sherman Oyler, 502nd Parachute Infantry Regiment, 101st Airborne Division, NWWIIM-EC

p. 64 'damn cricket', Parker A. Alford, attached to 501st Parachute Infantry Regiment, 101st Airborne, NWWIIM-EC

p. 66 'I had put it there . . .', John Fitzgerald, 502nd Parachute Infantry Regiment, NWWIIM-EC

Map of the Cotentin, Captain R. H. Brown, 506th Parachute Infantry Regiment, 101st Airborne, NA II 407/427/24242

'The Germans thought we were . . .', Fred C. Patheiger, 502nd Parachute Infantry Regiment, 101st Airborne Division, NWWIIM-EC

'Ou es Alamon?', Chris Courneotes Kanaras, 507th Parachute Infantry Regiment, 82nd Airborne Division, NWWIIM-EC

death of General Falley, Frank McKee, 82nd Airborne Division, NWWIIM-EC

p. 67 'Get to the drop zone . . .', Chris Courneotes Kanaras, 507th Parachute Infantry Regiment, 82nd Airborne Division, NWWIIM-EC

'They didn't come down to give us candies . . .', Rainer Hartmetz, NWWIIM-EC

p. 68 'nobody said a thing', Ken Cordry, 502nd Parachute Infantry Regiment, 101st Airborne, NWWIIM-EC

'you didn't dare trust him . . .', Don Malarkey, E Company, 506th Parachute Infantry Regiment, 101st Airborne Division, NWWIIM-EC

'with their privates cut off . . .', William Oatman, 506th Parachute Infantry Regiment, NWWIIM-EC

'I asked him where he got . . .', William M. Sawyer, 508th Parachute Infantry Regiment, NWWIIM-EC

'their bodies for bayonet practice', Briand

North Beaudin, Medical Officer, 508th Parachute Infantry Regiment, 82nd Airborne Division, NWWIIM-EC

German officer's ring, Lieutenant Eugen Brierre, 501st Parachute Infantry Regiment, 101st Airborne Division, NWWIIM-EC

p. 69 'Let's go and find some Krauts to kill!' and 'These people had gone ape', Sherman Oyler, 502nd Parachute Infantry Regiment, 101st Airborne Division, NWWIIM-EC

'Never before in the annals . . .', Parker A. Alford, attached to 501st Parachute Infantry Regiment, NWWIIM-EC

'They couldn't talk . . .', Rainer Hartmetz, NWWIIM-EC

p. 70 'We threw him in the cart . . .', Don Malarkey, E Company, 506th Parachute Infantry Regiment, 101st Airborne Division, NWWIIM-EC

'After a short march . . .', 'We could hear . . .' and 'We immediately tried to aid the injured . . .', John Fitzgerald, 502nd Parachute Infantry Regiment, NWWIIM-EC

p. 71 'The troop-carrying . . .', Obergefreiter Hans S., 9.Kp./Gren.Rgt.1058, 91.(LL.) Inf. Div., BfZ-SS

p. 72 'Upon landing, . . .', Charles E. Skidmore Jr, 439th Troop Carrier Squadron, NWWIIM-EC

'You've now seen . . .', Pfc Carl Cartledge, 501st Parachute Infantry Regiment, 101st Airborne, WWII VS

p. 73 'I am more thankful . . .', Leigh-Mallory, letter 7 June, quoted Carlo D'Este, *Eisenhower*, New York, 2002, p. 530

6 THE ARMADA CROSSES

p. 74 Royal Navy in Operation Neptune, Naval Plan TNA ADM 1/16259

'The Road to the Isles', Piper Bill Millin, SWWEC T654/666

'A-hunting We Will Go', A. D. E. Curtis, R Force, SWWEC 2000.384

'Marseillaise', Dr Ian Campbell, RAMC, 2nd Field Dressing Station, SWWEC 2000.477

'the traffic got thicker . . .', Admiral G. B. Middleton, HMS *Ramillies*, letter 12 June, IWM 01/2/1

p. 75 'a mixture of excitement . . .', Edwin Bramall, 'D-Day Plus One', in *More Tales from the Travellers*, Oxford, 2005, p. 147

memories of Dieppe, Rev. P. Symes, 4th County of London Yeomanry, SWWEC T563

'as a last reminder', Arthur Reddish, *A Tank Soldier's Story*, privately published, undated, p. 21

'The attempt to do . . .', V Corps, NA II 407/427/24235

p. 76 Operation Taxable and other diversions, TNA ADM 179/410

p. 77 'Although attendance was . . .', Ronald Seaborne, Royal Navy Forward Observer, 50th Division, NWWIIM-EC

gambling on USS *Samuel Chase*, Oscar Rich, 5th Field Artillery Battalion, 1st Infantry Division, NWWIIM-EC

'All are tense . . .', LofC

'Even though huddled . . .', Gardner Botsford, *A Life of Privilege, Mostly*, New York, 2003, p. 21

'who was going to . . .' and 'My thoughts turned to . . .', Everett P. Schultheis, 467th Anti-aircraft Artillery, NWWIIM-EC

'Anyone who has . . .', Harold Baumgarten, *Eyewitness on Omaha Beach*, Jacksonville, Fla., 1994, p. 7

'Don't worry . . .', K. G. Oakley, RN Beach Commando, Sword Beach, IWM 96/22/1

p. 78 'approaching a great abyss . . .', Cyrus C. Aydlett, USS *Bayfield*, NWWIIM-EC

USS *Shubrick*, Edward T. Duffy, US Navy, NWWIIM-EC

'dramatic announcement', William F. Rellstab Jr, 388th Bomber Group, 562nd Squadron, NWWIIM-EC

p. 79 'The preparations were staggering,' Desmond Scott, *Typhoon Pilot*, London, 1982, p. 99

Allied squadrons involved in D-Day operations, RAF-MoD

p. 80 'to provide shelter . . .', Weldon J. Allen, Pilot, 387th Bomb Group, diary, NWWIIM-EC

'as much steak, pork . . .', Theodore G. Aufort, 16th Infantry Regiment, 1st Infantry Division, NWWIIM-EC

'wieners, beans . . .', Sergeant Harry C. Bare, 116th Infantry, 29th Infantry Division, NWWIIM-EC

'as if it were Nelson's . . .', Major George Young, Green Howards, SWWEC T2452

'we might have been alongside . . .', Ludovic Kennedy, SWWEC T320

'skunk suits', Vincent Schlotterbeck, NWWIIM-EC

'nervously adjusting . . .', Cyrus C. Aydlett, USS *Bayfield*, NWWIIM-EC

p. 81 'We crept still further in . . .', Lieutenant J. G. Pelly, IWM 91/15/1

'Attention on deck! . . .', John Raaen, 5th Ranger Battalion, NWWIIM-EC

Seekommandant Normandie, Auszug aus dem Fernsprechmeldebuch der 352. I. D., Küstenverteidigungsabschnitt Bayeux, FMS B-388

p. 82 duffel coats and cocoa, Jean-Louis Salmon, MdC TE 213

'the whole horizon . . .', Generalleutnant Joseph Reichert, 711th Infanterie-Division, FMS B-403

smokescreen, Admiral G. B. Middleton, HMS *Ramillies*, letter 12 June, IWM 01/2/1

p. 83 'The screen was literally . . .', Anthony Drexel Duke, NWWIIM-EC

'Get your damn helmet on', Kenneth Romanski, 16th Infantry Regiment, 1st Infantry Division, NWWIIM-EC

'During this half-hour . . .', Major Dallas, 1st Battalion, 116th Infantry, 29th Infantry Division, NA II 407/427/24034

p. 84 'Good hunting, Rangers!', Lieutenant Francis W. Dawson, 5th Ranger Battalion, NWWIIM-EC

'the loneliest time . . .', Alfred F. Birra, 237th Engineers with 4th Infantry Division, Folder Birra, Alfred F., DDEL

'That, sirs . . .', John Raaen, 5th Ranger

Battalion, NWWIIM-EC

'The big guns . . .', Ludovic Kennedy, SWWEC T320

'It was a strange sight . . .', Robert L. Bogart, Staff Sergeant, 1st Division, NWWIIM-EC

'The other landing-craft . . .', Vernon Scannell, *Argument of Kings*, London, 1987, p. 145

p. 85 'started throwing up . . .', Kenneth Romanski, 16th Infantry Regiment, 1st Infantry Division, NWWIIM-EC

senior officer in Jeep, Ronald Seaborne, Royal Navy Forward Observer, 50th Division, NWWIIM-EC

'to be a bloody . . .', Stanley Christopherson diary

'Floater, five thousand!', Major Julius Neave, 13th/18th Hussars, diary, SWWEC T501

p. 86 'Off Asnelles . . .', 352nd Infanterie-Division, 6 June log, Bayeux Sector, FMS B-388

'Fancy having . . .', David Howarth, *Dawn of D-Day*, London, 1959, p. 185

rocket bombardment of Cabourg, conversation M. R. D. Foot

'missed the target entirely . . .', Combat Team, 16th Infantry, NA II 407/427/5927

p. 87 'Well, Ike . . .', PDDE pp. 1588–9

7 OMAHA

p. 88 description of Omaha, V Corps, NA II 407/427/24235

For Gerow and the planning of the Omaha operation see especially Adrian R. Lewis, *Omaha Beach – A Flawed Victory*, North Carolina, 2001

p. 90 'the greatest firepower . . .', Harry C. Butcher, *Three Years with Eisenhower*, London, 1946, p. 453

'about whether the importance . . .', LHCMA Liddell Hart 11/1944/7

'It's far too rough . . .', Major General L. Scott-Bowden, SWWEC T2236

DD tanks, 741st and 743rd Tank Battalions,

NA II 407/427/24235; and Dean Rockwell, US Navy, NWWIIM-EC

p. 91 'the Americans bungled . . .', LHCMA, Liddell Hart 11/1944/37

for the debate on DD tanks, see Lewis, pp. 307–18

'precision bombing', ibid., pp. 184–90

'The Air Corps might just . . .', NAII 407/427/5927

German gunnery practice, ADdC 6 W4

p. 92 shelling of Vierville, Michel Hardelay, MdC TE 59

'The invasion fleet was like . . .', Obergefreiter Alfred Sturm, 9. Kp., II Battalion, 726th Infanterie-Regiment, 716th Infanterie-Division, MdC TE 805

'stretching in front of our coast . . .', Franz Gockel, MdC TE 500

'heavy bombardment . . .', 352nd Infanterie-Division, 6 June log, FMS B-388

352nd Artillerie-Regiment and 716th Artillerie-Regiment, see Niklas Zetterling, *Normandy 1944*, Winnipeg, 2000, pp. 277–9 and 297–9

p. 93 Kraiss's dispositions, for an excellent summary see Joseph Balkoski, *Beyond the Beachhead*, Mechanicsburg, Pa., 1999, pp. 73–8

absence of fire from the beach, Sergeant Harry C. Bare, 116th Infantry, 29th Division, NWWIIM-EC

dead fish, Captain Joseph T. Dawson NA II 407/427/24011

'bucking like . . .', Edwin J. Best, First Lieutenant, 6th Engineer Special Brigade NWWIIM-EC

'reeked of vomit', John Raaen, 5th Ranger Battalion, WWII VS

navigation difficulties, Robert E. Adams, US Coast Guard, LCVP #22, USS *Samuel Chase*, NWWIIM-EC

p. 94 Royal Navy landing craft crews, I am grateful to Dr Kevan Elsby and Joseph Balkoski for information correcting the false impressions of earlier accounts.

'Soon we became conscious . . .', Lieutenant (MC) Alfred A. Schiller, USN, CWM/MCG 58A

'Make it look good, men . . .', First Lieutenant Donald S. Newbury, NA II 407/427/24242

experienced coxswains, E. Adams, US Coast Guard, LCVP #22, USS *Samuel Chase*, NWWIIM-EC

'As the ramp went down . . .', Pozek, 116th Regiment, 29th Division, NWWIIM-EC

'if you slipped . . .', J. Robert Slaughter, 116th Infantry, 29th Division, MdC TE 231

p. 95 'bullets were splashing . . .', William Huch, E Company, 16th Infantry, 1st Infantry Division, Folder Huch, William, DDEL

'had a gaping wound . . .', Harold Baumgarten, 1st Battalion, 116th Infantry, 29th Division, NWWIIM-EC

'I'm hit! I'm hit!', Private Elmer E. Matekintis, 16th Infantry, 1st Division, NA II 407/427/24242

'as it hit the wet sand . . .', Harry Parley, 2nd Battalion, 116th Infantry, 29th Division, NWWIIM-EC

'He screamed for a medic . . .', J. Robert Slaughter, 116th Infantry, 29th Division, MdC TE 231

p. 96 'frontal and enfilade', V Corps, NA II 407/427/24235

'fifty or sixty feet . . .', Staff Sergeant Robert L. Bogart, 1st Division, NWWIIM-EC

'We went to work . . .', William M. Jenkins, US Navy Reserve (Navy Combat Demolition Unit), MdC TE 438

'I've never in all my life . . .', William Huch, E Company, 16th Infantry, 1st Infantry Division, Folder Huch, William, DDEL

p. 97 121st Combat Engineer Battalion, Lieutenant P. W. J. Mallory, NA II 407/427/24242

'Some men were crying . . .', Second Lieutenant John T. Czuba, 116th Infantry, NA II 407/427/24242

'men were tumbling . . .', Alan Anderson, 467th Anti-aircraft Battalion, NWWIIM-EC

men trying to climb back on landing

craft, Robert V. Miller, US Navy, NWWIIM-EC

'Some of our boys said . . .', 116th Infantry, 29th Infantry Division, NA II 407/427/24241

'another miserable . . .', Lieutenant Ed R. McNabb Jr, H Company, 116th Infantry, 29th Division, NA II 407/427/24242

p. 98 'We talked to them . . .', NA II 407/427/24034

'yelled down at the troops . . .', John Raaen, 5th Ranger Battalion, NWWIIM-EC

'I saw a man coming . . .', Captain C. N. Hall, Assistant Surgeon, 16th Infantry, 1st Division, NA II 407/427/24242

p. 99 'started running . . .', Andrew A. Fellner, 112th Combat Engineers, Easy Red, NWWIIM-EC

tank on Fox Green, NA II 407/427/24034

'What saved us were . . .', Private Elmer E. Matekintis, 16th Infantry, 1st Division, NA II 407/427/24242

'were crowded . . .', V Corps, NA II 407/427/24235

p. 100 111th Field Artillery Battalion, NA II 407/427/24034

08.00 hours, timings taken from log kept by Major Thomas D. Howie, the RCT 116's S-3, NA II 407/427/24151

'He was catapulted . . .', NA II 407/427/24034

'Old Hatchetface . . .', J. Robert Slaughter, 116th Infantry, 29th Division, MdC TE 231

p. 101 'We've got to get off . . .', Captain C. N. Hall, Assistant Surgeon, 16th Infantry, 1st Division, NA II 407/427/24242

'The only people . . .', after action report, Headquarters Company, 16th Infantry, NA II 407/427/24011; confirmed by Major General Albert H. Smith Jr, 16th Infantry Regiment, 1st Infantry Division, NWWIIM-EC

'North-east of Colleville . . .', Ia, 352nd Infanterie-Division to Chief of Staff LXXXIV Corps, 6 June log, FMS B-388

'the gravest immediate threat . . .', Gordon A. Harrison, *US Army in World War II*, Washington, DC, 1951, pp. 320 and 330–31

p. 102 'from warships on the high seas . . .', 11.10 hours, 352nd Infantry Division, 6 June log, Bayeux Sector, FMS B-388

'Praise the Lord', Pfc Harold F. Plank, 2nd Ranger Battalion, WWII VS

p. 103 08.19 hours, telephone log, 352nd Infanterie-Division, FMS B-388

'Medico! . . .', NA II 407/427/24034

Cota and Canham, NA II 407/427/24235

p. 104 mortars, Franz Gockel, MdC TE 500, and NA II 407/427/24034

'Boats and vehicles . . .', V Corps, NA II 407/427/24235

C Company, 1st Battalion, 116th Infantry, NA II 407/427/24034

C Company losses, Captain Berthie B. Hawks, C Company, 1st Battalion, 116th Infantry, 29th Division, NA II 407/427/24242

p. 105 'everyone got ashore safely', NA II 407/427/24034

'enemy fire was not as bad . . .', Second Lieutenant George Athanasakos, 2nd Battalion, 116th Infantry, NA II 407/427/24242

'he spouted . . .', NA II 407/427/24034

'It was just one big mass . . .', NA II 407/427/24241

'They looked like . . .', NA II 07/427/24034

'a stampeded herd . . .', quoted in Harrison, p. 334

p. 106 'They lit the fuse . . .', Barnett Hoffner, 6th Engineer Special Brigade, NWWIIM-EC

destroyers at Omaha, Harrison, p. 322

'the survivors . . .', Obergefreiter Alfred Sturm, 9. Kp., II Battalion, 726 Inf Rgt, 716 ID, MdC TE 805

'There was a German . . .', Bradley Holbrook, NWWIIM-EC

'We came across . . .', Pfc Charles M. Bulap, 2nd Ranger Battalion, NA II 407/427/24241

p. 107 signaller, John Raaen, 5th Ranger Battalion, WWII VS

ranger helped up by prisoners, Nicholas Butrico, 5th Ranger Battalion, NWWIIM-EC

'Things look better', NA II 407/427/24235

'struck by the gray . . .', Gale B. Beccue, 5th Ranger Battalion, NWWIIM-EC

'His helmet was off . . .', Brugger, 16th Infantry, 1st Infantry Division, NWWIIM-EC

p. 108 'who was calmly . . .', NA II 407/427/24034

'individually they were . . .', NA II 407/427/24034

'Those jagged sharp bones . . .', Herbert Zafft, 29th Infantry Division, NWWIIM-EC

'As I drew near him . . .', Colin H. McLaurin, 115th Infantry, 29th Division, NWWIIM-EC

'Smoke, dust from . . .', NA II 407/427/24034

French civilians in Vierville, Howie journal, NA II 407/427/24151

p. 109 Cota and Vierville exit, NA II 407/427/24034

landed 18,772 men, NA II 407/427/24235

p. 110 'wounded can no longer . . .', telephone log, 352. I.D., 17.10 hours, FMS B-388

identifying the presence of the 352nd Infanterie-Division, letter from Captain Fred Gercke, 27 June, NA II 407/427/24011

smell of burnt flesh, Roy Arnn, 146th Combat Engineer Battalion attached to 1st Infantry Division, NWWIIM-EC

'I saw one young soldier . . .', Captain Benjamin A. Payson, 60th Medical Battalion, MdC TE 291

p. 111 treatment on Omaha, Lieutenant (MC) Alfred A. Schiller, USN, CWM/MCG 58A

'What am I going to do? . . .', Frank Feduik, pharmacist on LST, NWWIIM-EC

'left alone to whatever . . .', Vincent J. del Giudice, pharmacist, USS *Bayfield*, NWWIIM-EC

p. 112 Gerow landing, NA II 407/427/24235

29th Infantry Division command post, NA II 407/427/24034

'assumed that everyone . . .', Forrest C. Pogue, *Pogue's War*, Lexington, Kentucky, 2001, p. 83

Casualty figures, see Harrison, p. 330; and NA II 407/427/5919

'He knew better . . .', George Roach, Company A, 116th Infantry, 29th Division, NWWIIM-EC

Bedford casualties, see James W. Morrison, *Bedford Goes to War: The Heroic Story of a Small Virginia Community in World War II*, Lynchburg, Va., 2006; and George D. Salaita, 'Embellishing Omaha Beach', *Journal of Military History*, April 2008, pp. 531–4

p. 113 German losses on the eastern front and in Normandy, Niklas Zetterling, *Normandy 1944*, Winnipeg, 2000, p. 434

8 UTAH AND THE AIRBORNE

p. 114 German soldiers and American containers, Rainer Hartmetz, NWWIIM-EC

'The war game has . . .', Generalleutnant Karl-Wilhelm Graf von Schlieben, 709th Infanterie-Division, FMS B-845

p. 115 'American prisoners with . . .', Montebourg, Fernand Louvoy, MdC TE 38

'A soldier had his leg . . .', Brigadier General David E. Thomas, NWWIIM-EC

p. 116 Château de Hauteville, Briand N. Beaudin, 508th Parachute Infantry Regiment, 82nd Airborne Division, NWWIIM-EC

discovery of ford, NA II 407/427/24206

p. 118 'odd-shaped sea-monsters . . .', Howard van der Beek, USS LCC 60a, NWWIIM-EC

'met General Roosevelt . . .', NA II 407/427/24204

'more like guerrilla fighting', NA II 407/427/24242

'Captain, how in the hell . . .', Folder Birra, Alfred F., DDEL

p. 119 'walked their fire . . .', NA II 407/427/24240

'they could not be trusted', John Capell, 8th Infantry, 4th Infantry Division, NWWIIM-EC

'during the briefings . . .', NA II 407/427/24242

Le Molay, Danièle Höfler, MdC, TE 71

patrols over south-western approaches,

R. L. Delashaw, 405th Fighter Group, USAAC, NWWIIM-EC

p. 120 *'Achtung! Minen!'*, John L. Ahearn, 70th Tank Battalion, NWWIIM-EC

20th Field Artillery, 4th Infantry Division, Staff Sergeant Alfred Donald Allred, NWWIIM-EC

'French people, of course . . .', William E. Jones, 4th Infantry Division, NWWIIM-EC

p. 121 'came across a little . . .', Captain Carroll W. Wright, 33rd Chemical Company, NWWIIM-EC

'a German soldier lying dead . . .', John A. Beck, 87th Chemical Mortar Battalion with 4th Infantry Division, NWWIIM-EC

'We had to kill most . . .', Lieutenant John A. Le Trent, 8th Infantry, 4th Infantry Division, NA II 407/427/24242

p. 122 'There isn't much left . . .', R. R. Hughart, 2nd Battalion, 505th Parachute Infantry Regiment, 82nd Airborne Division, NWWIIM-EC

325th Glider Infantry Regiment, NA II 407/427/24206

p. 123 'They look as though they're from Sing Sing', Heinz Puschmann, 6th Paratroop Regiment, private account

'as if it were a movie . . .', Jean Roger, Saint-Lô, MdC TE 316

'Windows and doors . . .', MdC TE 285

p. 124 escape into the countryside, Michèle Chapron, MdC TE 278

9 GOLD AND JUNO

p. 125 'Is this the landing?', André Heintz diary, MdC TE 32 (1–4)

'Do you think . . .', MdC TE 149

'Yes, it is indeed . . .', Marianne Daure, MdC TE 48

p. 126 *boulangeries* in Caen, Marcel Ehly, MdC TE 11

Germans 'requisitioning' alcohol, Madeleine Betts-Quintaine, MdC TE 25

'They're landing! . . .', Marianne Daure, MdC TE 48

evacuation orders, Nadine Speck, MdC TE 2

'Continual telephone calls . . .', Generalleutnant Speidel, FMS B-718

p. 127 Blumentritt's calls, FMS B-284

p. 128 'Once you stop on the beach . . .', Major George Young, Green Howards, SWWEC T2452

p. 129 'a sort of aquatic turnpike . . .', Clifford H. Sinnett, USNR, LST 530, NWWIIM-EC

p. 130 'Never in my wildest dreams . . .', Stanley Christopherson diary

p. 131 Keller, Mark Zuehlke, *Juno Beach*, Toronto, 2005, pp. 31–2

'Operation Overboard', ibid., p. 84; and Papers of Frank A. Osmanski, G-4 SHAEF, USAMHI

HMS *Belfast*, Tony Hugill diary, CAC HUGL 1

Canadian vessels in Overlord, NA II 407/427/24200

p. 132 'Nearly every foot . . .', NA II 407/427/24200; and Terry Copp, *Fields of Fire*, Toronto, 2003, p. 48

Fort Garry Horse tanks, Sergeant Bill Hudson, A Troop, 48 Royal Marine Commando, MdC TE 84; and Zuehlke, p. 202

Bernières-sur-Mer, NA II 407/427/24200; Zuehlke, p. 219; and Copp, p. 52

p. 133 'But what do you expect? . . .', Louise Hamelin, MdC TE 222

'I don't want to see . . .', J. Kyle, SWWEC T1094

p. 135 'At Carpiquet . . .', Ultra intercept passed by 'C' to Churchill on 11 June, Luftflotte 3, TNA HW 1/2927

10 SWORD

p. 136 'Widgeon and teal . . .', Tony Hugill diary, CAC HUGL 1

'Floater, 5,000!', Major Julius Neave, 13th/18th Hussars, SWWEC T501

p. 137 'Some were scared . . .', N. G. Marshall, H Troop Armoured Support

Group with 41st RM Commando, SWWEC 2000.407

'like a Napoleonic dragoon', Lieutenant Ken Baxter, 2nd Battalion Middlesex Regiment, 3rd Infantry Division, MdC TE 164

John and Jacqueline Thornton, NWWIIM-EC

'Every now and then . . .', Tony Hugill diary, CAC HUGL 1

p. 138 'Well, dig yourself . . .', Lieutenant Cyril Rand, 2nd Battalion Royal Ulster Rifles, MdC TE 499

'with misjudged enthusiasm' and 'he relented a little', Lionel Roebuck, 2nd Battalion, East Yorkshire Regiment, MdC TE 199

Piper Bill Millin piping on the beach, SWWEC T654/666 and K. G. Oakley, IWM 96/22/1

p. 139 'Right, Piper . . .', Piper Bill Millin, SWWEC T654/666

3 Troop of 6 Commando, TNA DEFE 2/43; and Philip Biggerton Pritchard, *Soldiering in the British Forces in World War II*, privately published, undated

X Troop, Harry Nomburg, NWWIIM-EC, and Peter Masters, NWWIIM-EC

Kieffer, MdC TE 131

p. 140 'Gentlemen, this is the invasion . . .', letter from Otto Günsche, 2 October 1981, quoted in Hubert Meyer, *The 12th SS*, Vol. I, Mechanicsburg, Pa., 2005, p. 97

'a tall wiry . . .', Milton Shulman, *Defeat in the West*, London, 1988, pp. 118–19

p. 141 Château de Bénouville, Louise Moulin, MdC TE 350

Oppeln-Bronikowski's change of orders, Generalmajor Wilhelm Richter, 716th Infantry Division, FMS B-621

Marcks, Seventh Army telephone records captured in August by 1st Polish Armored Division, NA II 407/427/6431

'in no position to judge' and 'The main landing . . .', Generalleutnant Bodo Zimmermann, OB West, FMS B-308

p. 142 'fill a crater . . .', NA II 407/427/24170

p. 143 'deep concrete pillboxes . . .', 'fought with determination . . .' and 'blown out of

their emplacements . . .', Current Reports from Overseas, No. 56, NA II 407/427/24170

p. 144 André Heintz, diary, MdC, TE 32 (1–4); and Dr Robert Chaperon, MdC TE 42

p. 145 destruction in Caen, MdC TE 283

'One could see . . .', Félix Drougard, MdC TE 3

'If only I was a little less fat', MdC TE 149

looter, MdC TE 149

p. 146 Défense Passive etc., MdC TE 193

'magnificent attitude . . .', SIPEG (Service interministériel de protection contres les évènements de guerre) report of 10 June, AN AJ/41/56

executions in Caen prison, Jean-Baptiste Pierre (Surveillant-Chef Adjoint de la Maison d'Arrêt de Caen), MdC TE 521

'Oh, no! . . .', 'pale and evidently terrified' and 'The German army is honest', Madame Blanche Néel, MdC TE 201

p. 147 'With a bestial frenzy . . .', Nadine Speck MdC TE 2

'useless as well as criminal', Max Maurin, MdC TE 77 (2)

800 deaths in Caen, 600 on 6 June and 200 on 7 June, CRHQ

'The town is in flames . . .', 'almost destroyed' and 'all the gendarmes . . .', SIPEG report of 10 June, AN AJ/41/56

p. 148 'In Westminster Abbey . . .', Mollie Panter-Downes, *London War Notes*, London, 1971, p. 328

'It has been very hard . . .', Field Marshal Lord Alanbrooke, *War Diaries 1939–1945*, London, 2001, p. 555 (6 June)

p. 149 Eadie and 'Fireflies', see Carlo D'Este, *Decision in Normandy*, New York, 1983

'I suppose that's what . . .', Lieutenant Cyril Rand, 2nd Battalion Royal Ulster Rifles, MdC TE 499

'It equally impressed . . .', NA II 407/427/24170

p. 150 'the enemy annihilated . . .', Seventh Army telephone records, NA II 407/427/6431

'He was still convinced . . .', Nicolaus von

Below, *Als Hitlers Adjutant, 1937–1945*, Mainz, 1980, p. 374

Panzer Lehr Division, Generalleutnant Fritz Bayerlein, Panzer Lehr Division, ETHINT 66

'What's happened to . . .', BA-MA MSg2/5025

p. 151 4,649 US seaborne casualties, Omar Bradley, *A Soldier's Story*, New York, 1951, p. 242

11 SECURING THE BEACHHEADS

p. 152 29th Division headquarters, NA II 407/427/24034

farmhands and Pennsylvania coal miners, 29th Division, WWII VS

'The sea was like . . .', Oberstleutnant Ziegelmann, 352nd Infanterie-Division, FMS B-489

p. 153 MP Sergeant, Melvin Asche, 1006th Seabee Detachment, MdC TE 126

'looked at us . . .', Madame Huet-Patry, Vierville-sur-Mer, MdC TE 22

'I guess they didn't know . . .', Barnett Hoffner, 6th Engineer Special Brigade, NWWIIM-EC

p. 154 'deloused' areas, Forrest C. Pogue, *Pogue's War*, Lexington, Kentucky, 2001, p. 63

USS *Harding*, Walter Vollrath Jr, USN, NWWIIM-EC

p. 155 'Again Colonel Rudder . . .', Elmer H. Vermeer, 2nd Engineer Battalion, 2nd Infantry Division, with 2nd Ranger Battalion, NWWIIM-EC; also Lieutenant Francis W. Dawson, 5th Ranger Battalion, NWWIIM-EC; and Lieutenant Rex F. Gibson, Headquarters Company, 116th Infantry, 29th Division, NA II 407/427/24242

'stumble-footed action', NA II 407/427/24034

bartering, Brugger, 16th Infantry, 1st Infantry Division, NWWIIM-EC

'Hey, I need a hedgerow . . .', Oscar Rich, 5th Field Artillery Battalion, 1st Infantry Division, NWWIIM-EC

A-1 landing strip, W. G. Schuler, 382nd Air Service Squadron, 84th Group, NWWIIM-EC

evacuation of wounded by air, Louise Anthony de Flon, 816th Medical Air Evacuation, MdC TE 177

p. 156 Gerhardt, see Joseph Balkoski, *Beyond the Beachhead*, Mechanicsburg, Pa., 1999, pp. 44–50

'Sergeant, I want you . . .', John Hooper, 115th Infantry Regiment, 29th Division, NWWIIM-EC

V Corps plan, Oberst Ziegelmann, 352nd Infanterie-Division, FMS B-489 and B-636

p. 157 'the Führer personally . . .', General Günther Blumentritt, OB West, FMS B-637, p. 263

'a tough learning period . . .', Lieutenant Cameron K. Brooks, 115th Infantry, 29th Division, NA II 407/427/24242

'Lieutenant Kermit Miller . . .', NA II 407/427/24240; and Captain S. S. Suntag, 115th Infantry, NA II 407/427/24242

'It was nearly midnight . . .', NA II 407/427/24240

'trouble from those . . .', Captain Otto Grass, Headquarters Company, 29th Division, NA II 407/427/24241

p. 158 Gerhardt and 'Vixen Tor', Staff Sergeant Lester Zick, Anti-tank Company, 175th Infantry Regiment, 29th Division, NWWIIM-EC

'John Doughfoot looked . . .', Lieutenant George Wash, 224th Field Artillery Battalion, 29th Infantry Division, NA II 407/427/24242

'an American on a white horse . . .', Staff Sergeant Lester Zick, Anti-tank Company, 175th Infantry Regiment, 29th Division, NWWIIM-EC

Isigny, Edwin R. Schwartz, 747th Tank Battalion, NWWIIM-EC; Staff Sergeant Lester Zick, Anti-tank Company, 175th Infantry Regiment, 29th Division, NWWIIM-EC; and Balkoski, pp. 170–74

p. 159 'Rubble was everywhere . . .', Lieutenant George Wash, 224th Field Artillery Battalion, 29th Infantry Division, NA II 407/427/24242

Generalleutnant von Schlieben, FMS B-845

'17.00 hours went into . . .', Captain Claude J. Mercer, 29th Field Artillery Battalion, 4th Infantry Division, NA II 407/427/24242

p. 160 Montebourg, Louis Lucet, MdC TE 107; and Valognes, MdC TE 111

Georgians at Turqueville, Captain Le Grand K. Johnson, 502nd Parachute Infantry Regiment, NA II 407/427/24242

'and Jerry went from one to another . . .', Lieutenant George W. Goodridge, 44th Field Artillery Battalion, 4th Division, NA II 407/427/24240

'Their throats had been cut . . .', Captain Claude J. Mercer, 29th Field Artillery Battalion, 4th Infantry Division, NA II 407/427/24242

'sniping coming from a building . . .', Sergeant W. C. Cowards, 22nd Infantry, 4th Division, NA II 407/427/24242

p. 161 'France was like . . .', Captain Robert E. Walker, 19th Infantry Division, WWII VS

'couldn't trust them in Normandy', Pfc Robert Boyce, 502nd Parachute Infantry Regiment, WWII VS

'we saw in the ditches . . .', Barnett Hoffner, 6th Engineer Special Brigade, NWWIIM-EC

Sgt Prybowski, Captain Elmer G. Koehler, Battalion Surgeon, 12th Infantry, 4th Infantry Division, NA II 407/427/24242

p. 162 Hill 30, Tomaso William Porcella, 3rd Battalion, 508th Parachute Infantry Regiment, 82nd Airborne Division; and Kenneth J. Merritt, 508th Parachute Infantry Regiment, NWWIIM-EC

'There were so many . . .', Edward C. Boccafogli, 508th Parachute Infantry Regiment, 82nd Airborne Division, NWWIIM-EC

90th Division firing at prisoners, Max Hastings, *Overlord*, London, 1989, p. 154

p. 163 'He was sitting out . . .', Pogue, pp. 111–12

'Collins and Bradley . . .', Martin

Blumenson (ed.), *The Patton Papers, 1940–1945*, New York, 1974, p. 479

the 'Treuelied', Jean-Claude Perrigault and Rolf Meister, *Götz von Berlichingen*, Bayeux, 2005, p. 77

'Well, we don't know . . .', SS-Mann Johann H., 36 380 D = 3.Kp./SS-Pi.Btl.17 17.SS-Pz.Gren.Div. 8 June, BfZ-SS

p. 164 'Turn round!', Perrigault and Meister, p. 203

'and push the enemy . . .', Generalleutnant Richard Schimpf, 3rd Paratroop Division, FMS B-020

p. 165 'insufficient forces', Generalmajor Max Pemsel commentary, FMS B-541

353rd Infanterie-Division, General Mahlmann, FMS A-983

hiding in barns and orchards, AdM 2 J 695

'nocturnal game . . .', Generalleutnant Kurt Badinski 276th Infanterie-Division, FMS B-526

SS *Das Reich* in France, Peter Lieb, *Konventioneller Krieg oder Weltanschauungskrieg?*, Munich, 2007, p. 361

p. 166 'the initiation of . . .', IMT, Vol. XXXVII, quoted in Lieb, p. 364

For these and other killings, see Lieb, pp. 374–5 and AN AJ/41/56. According to one report, 108 were hanged in Tulle, AN AJ/41/56

Oradour, M. R. D. Foot, *SOE in France*, London, 1966, pp. 398–9

'regions where a hideous . . .', AN AJ/41/56

p. 167 'spray jobs', Technical Sergeant Donald J. Walworth, 3rd Battalion, 26th Infantry, 1st Division, NA II 407/427/24242

'were in fact facing . . .', Gordon A. Harrison, *US Army in World War II*, Washington, DC, 1951 p. 370

p. 168 'You people are always . . .', Oberstleutnant Keil, FMS C-018

'sly, underhand . . .', Perrigault and Meister, p. 245

'moderately high losses', ibid., p. 247

p. 169 accusation against Heydte, FMS B-839; and Perrigault and Meister, p. 248

12 FAILURE AT CAEN

p. 170 'communications between division . . .', Generalmajor Wilhelm Richter, 716th Infanterie-Division, FMS B-621

'honeycombed with trenches . . .', NA II 407/427/24200

p. 171 'under his command . . .', TNA WO 208/4363

1st SS Panzer-Division *Leibstandarte Adolf Hitler*, Taganrog, Sönke Neitzel (ed.), *Tapping Hitler's Generals*, St Paul, Mn, 2007, p. 344, n. 93

p. 172 'It has taken . . .', Generalmajor Wilhelm Richter, 716th Infanterie-Division, FMS B-621

'Little fish!', Shulman interview with Generalleutnant Edgar Feuchtinger, August 1945, Milton Shulman, *Defeat in the West*, London, 1988, p. 121

'At a moment when . . .', General Geyr von Schweppenburg, FMS B-466

p. 173 'Fright reports', Generalmajor Fritz Krämer, I SS Panzer Corps, FMS C-024

p. 174 'Action rear', etc., Alastair Bannerman, 2nd Battalion Royal Warwicks, SWWEC 2001–819

Gruchy, Raymond Pouchin, MdC TE 86

Hitler Jugend in Cambes, Lieutenant Cyril Rand, 2nd Battalion Royal Ulster Rifles, MdC TE 499

p. 175 'We were the first troops . . .' and 'After a very short time . . .', Stanley Christopherson diary

p. 176 'fighter-bomber racecourse', Generalleutnant Fritz Bayerlein, Panzer Lehr Division, ETHINT 66

Panzer Lehr losses, see H. Ritgen, *Die Geschichte der Panzer-Lehr Division im Westen, 1944–1945*, Stuttgart, 1979, p. 100, quoted in Niklas Zetterling, *Normandy 1944*, Winnipeg, 2000, p. 386

p. 177 'How can I live . . .', 'Aristocrats', Keith Douglas, *The Complete Poems*, London, 2000, p. 117

'I like you, sir', Stuart Hills, *By Tank into Normandy*, London, 2002, p. 54

p. 178 'missed the psychological moment . . .', General Geyr von Schweppenburg, FMS B-466

'Last time I was . . .', Lieutenant Cyril Rand, 2nd Battalion Royal Ulster Rifles, MdC TE 499

p. 179 'When I looked to the left . . .', Unterscharführer Alois Morawetz, 3. Panzerkompanie, SS Panzer-Regiment 12, Hubert Meyer, *The 12th SS: The History of the Hitler Youth Panzer Division*, Vol. I, Mechanicsburg, Pa., 2005, p. 188

'I could have cried . . .', ibid., p.191

p. 180 'He had tried to make . . .', ibid., p.197

killing of prisoners in Normandy, TNA TS 26/856

'about thirty Canadian . . .', Nelly Quidot, MdC TE 228

killings at Abbaye d'Ardennes, Sergeant Frank Geoffrey, Royal Winnipeg Rifles, NWWIIM-EC

p. 181 'dare-devil', Peter Lieb, *Konventioneller Krieg oder Weltanschauungskrieg?*, Munich, 2007, p. 163

Kurt Meyer executing Jews in Poland, ibid., p. 159

'the men show signs . . .', Ultra intercepts passed by 'C' to Churchill on 11 June, TNA HW 1/2927

location of headquarters of Panzer Group West, TNA KV 7171 and KV 7225

p. 182 'all personnel . . .', General Geyr von Schweppenburg, FMS B-466

p. 183 'a gutless bugger', TNA WO 205/5D

p. 184 'pull the Germans . . .', TNA WO 205/5B

'Inaction and a defensive mentality . . .', TNA PREM 3/339/1, p. 6

'to assault to the west . . .', LHCMA De Guingand 2/1/1–6

'a peevish imperialism', Army Group intelligence summary, 23 April 1944, TNA WO 205/532 (2)

'to block the enemy's . . .', General Geyr von Schweppenburg, FMS B-466

p. 185 'the key to Cherbourg', General Omar Bradley, OCMH-FPP

'By premature commitment . . .', General-major Fritz Krämer, I SS Panzer Corps, FMS C-024

13 VILLERS-BOCAGE

p. 187 'The fury of artillery . . .', Vernon Scannell, *Argument of Kings*, London, 1987, p. 165

'The smart, keen . . .', ibid., p. 156

'The thing that shocked . . .', Major Peter Griffin, 1st Canadian Parachute Battalion, NAC/ANC R5067-0-0-E

'broke down', Lieutenant Colonel Terence Otway, SWWEC T689

p. 188 'He is not very impressive . . .', Martin Blumenson (ed.), *The Patton Papers, 1940–1945*, New York, 1974, p. 461

Dempsey, see Carlo D'Este, *Decision in Normandy*, New York, 1983, p. 60

p. 189 'You'll get a shock . . .', Arthur Reddish, *A Tank Soldier's Story*, privately printed, undated, p. 29

'Bucknall was very weak', Field Marshal Lord Alanbrooke, *War Diaries 1939–1945*, London, 2001, p. 538 (7 April)

Bucknall and Bayeux, LHCMA, Liddell Hart 11/1944/36

p. 190 General Maxwell D. Taylor, SODP

p. 191 entry into Villers-Bocage, M. Diguet, MdC TE 220

'We have only one . . .', Patrick Agte, *Michael Wittmann*, Vol. I, Mechanicsburg, Pa., 2006, p. 354

p. 192 11th Hussars and prisoner from 2nd Panzer-Division, Dudley Clarke, *The Eleventh at War*, London, 1952, p. 339; and Myles Hildyard, who says in his diary that they strangled one guard and seized the other

Ultra on 2nd Panzer-Division, TNA KV 7707

p. 193 artillery regiment firing airbursts, NA II 407/427/24170

Aunay-sur-Odon, Abbé André Paul, MdC TE 21

p. 194 'The fighting in the west . . .', 15 June, Unteroffizier Leopold L., 25 644 = 5.Kp./ Pz.Rgt.3, 2.Pz.Div., BfZ-SS

'131 Brigade . . .', Myles Hildyard diary, 19 June

'a very poor showing . . .', Major General G. L. Verney diary, quoted in D'Este, pp. 272–4

'The famous Desert Rats . . .', Stanley Christopherson diary

p. 195 'it was no good grousing . . .', J. L. Cloudsley-Thompson, *Sharpshooter*, Fleet Hargate, 2006, p. 109

'design fault', Lieutenant General Richard O'Connor to Churchill, 5 May, LHCMA O'Connor 5/2/39

'a Tiger and Panther complex', letter, 12 June, TNA WO 205/5B

'We are outshot . . .', Algiers, 23 August 1943, Harry C. Butcher, *Three Years with Eisenhower*, London, 1946, p. 339

'The squadron left . . .', anonymous diary entry, 11 June, MdC TE 396

Eisenhower to Marshall, Brigadier Joseph A. Holly, 5 July, PDDE, p. 1973

p. 196 'I have received . . .', No. 695, Prime Minister to President, 9 June, TNA PREM 3/472

'passed convoys . . .', Alanbrooke, pp. 556–7 (12 June)

p. 197 'There has been a recognizable . . .', Churchill to Eden, 12 June, TNA PREM 3/339/7

'Plug at the Hun . . .', TNA PREM 3/339/7

HMS *Ramillies*, Admiral G. B. Middleton, IWM 01/2/1

'a slight display . . .' and 'General de Gaulle's personal flag . . .', report of British Naval Liaison Officer, 16 June, TNA ADM 1/16018

p. 198 'Has it occurred . . .', quoted in Henri Amouroux, *La grande histoire*, Vol. VIII, p. 546, and Robert Aron, *Histoire de la Libération de la France*, Paris, 1959, p. 78

'did little to ingratiate them . . .', report of British Naval Liaison Officer, TNA PREM 3/339/7

'*Monsieur le curé* . . .', Jean Lacouture, *De Gaulle – Le Rebelle*, Paris, 1984, p. 779

p. **199** 'hated Laval, but not Pétain', Forrest C. Pogue, *Pogue's War*, Lexington, Kentucky, 2006, p. 115

'has left behind in Bayeux . . .', Montgomery to Churchill, 14 June, TNA PREM 3/339/7

p. **200** 'In my opinion we should . . .', No. 561, President to Prime Minister, 14 June, TNA PREM 3/339/7

'There is not a scrap . . .', Churchill to Eden, 12 June, TNA PREM 3/339/7

'Trojan horse', Aron, p. 77

'*Le panorama* . . .', MdC TE 195

p. **201** 'I simply cannot . . .', André Heintz diary, MdC TE 32 (1–4)

Café owner, Dr Robert Chaperon, MdC TE 42

'in the Middle Ages', MdC TE 42

p. **202** Secours National, Céline Coantic-Dormoy, MdC TE 281

'The English since . . .' Le Dily diary, 11 June, MdC TE 143

'*le troc*', Claude Guillotin, 1944, 'L'aventure de mes quinze ans', Le Fresne-Camilly, MdC TE 397

p. **203** 'a senior officer of the Military Police . . .', Dr Ian Campbell, RAMC, 2nd Field Dressing Station, SWWEC 2000.477

'during the morning . . .', MdC TE 144

'musical chairs' and 'Now there's no need . . .', Lieutenant Cyril Rand, 2nd Battalion Royal Ulster Rifles, MdC TE 499

p. **205** Red Army, see Antony Beevor and Lyuba Vinogradova (eds.), *A Writer at War: Vasily Grossman with the Red Army, 1941–1945*, London, 2005, p. 109

'The whole world . . .', SS Untersturmführer Herbert E., 2.Kp./Nachr.Abt.SS.Pz.Div. '*Hohenstaufen*', 6 June and 10 June, 24 742C, BfZ-SS

14 THE AMERICANS ON THE COTENTIN PENINSULA

p. **208** 'Within a week . . .', Lieutenant (MC) Alfred A. Schiller, USN, CWM/MCG 58A

Omaha beach command, NA II 407/427/212

'Turn those prisoners . . .', Barnett Hoffner, 6th Engineer Special Brigade, NWWIIM-EC

'Those wounded paratroopers . . .', Orval Wakefield (Naval Combat Demolition Unit), NWWIIM-EC

'We had an incident . . .', Charles C. Zalewski, LST 134, NWWIIM-EC

'One of our ship's officers . . .', Ralph Crenshaw, LST 44, NWWIIM-EC

p. **209** trade in Lugers, Major John C. Geiglein, Forrest C. Pogue, *Pogue's War*, Lexington, Kentucky, 2006, pp. 127–8

bartering a truck-load of weapons, T/Sgt Eugene W. Griffin, 2nd Armored Division, WWII VS

'a considerable laxity . . .', Pogue, p. 87

pig roasting, Angelos Chatas (Naval Combat Demolition Unit), NWWIIM-EC

p. **210** 'The [French] attitude is . . .', NA II 407/427/212

'The Mayor of Colleville . . .', NA II 407/427/212

p. **211** 'Hermann's Vermin', Cyrus C. Aydlett, USS *Bayfield*, NWWIIM-EC

'despite undisputed air supremacy . . .', Leigh-Mallory, 1 July, Headquarters Allied Expeditionary Air Force, TNA ADM 1/16332

p. **212** 'an enemy sniper . . .', Omar Bradley, *A Soldier's Story*, New York, 1951, p. 292

'When I saw that . . .', John Troy, 8th Infantry, NWWIIM-EC

91st Luftlande-Division, Oberst Eugen König, FMS B-010

p. **214** 'I was ordered to . . .', Obergefreiter Hans S., 9.Kp./Gren.Rgt.1058, 91. (LL.) Inf. Div., 13 273 B, 7 July, BfZ-SS

'a burly professor . . .', Martin Blumenson, *The Duel for France*, New York, 2000, pp. 20–21

'a pudgy man . . .', ibid., p. 11

'The commander-in-chief . . .', Generalleutnant von Choltitz, LXXXIV Corps, FMS B-418

'he had lived a life . . .', Generalleutnant

Fritz Bayerlein, Panzer Lehr Division, ETHINT 66

'the war was lost', Generalleutnant von Choltitz, LXXXIV Corps, FMS B-418

p. 215 'refreshingly open-minded', LHCMA Liddell Hart 11/1944/7

'Montebourg and Valognes . . .', TNA WO 205/5B

'a Cub plane . . .', operation of air support parties, NA II 407/427/24204

p. 216 Mulberry and gale, 'Artificial Harbours in Operation Overlord', TNA ADM 1/17204

'The only chance . . .', Dean Rockwell, US Navy, NWWIIM-EC

'It took us about . . .', Werner Hugo Saenger, LST 27, NWWIIM-EC

'I thank the gods . . .', J. M. Stagg, *Forecast for Overlord*, London, 1971, p. 126

'never really believed . . .', Colonel Thomas Bigland, Montgomery's personal liaison officer to First US Army, then 12th Army Group, SWWEC 99–10

p. 217 tonnage and vehicles landed in August, Normandy Base Section Communications Zone, 8 September, Com Z, NA II 407/427/24133

'a bit of plunder', Oberst a.D. Dr Hans Kessler, BA-MA MSg 2/249

'The men were tired . . .', Lieutenant William Priestman, 315th Infantry, NA II 407/427/24242

p. 218 'K Company . . .', Lieutenant John E. Cunningham, 314th Infantry, 79th Infantry Division, NA II 407/427/24242

'We fired back . . .', Karl Hohmann, RAD, MdC TE 506

'any part of the garrison . . .', Colonel Bernard B. MacMahon, 315th Infantry, 79th Division, NA II 407/427/24242

p. 219 'At eight-thirty . . .', Lieutenant John R. Blackburn, Sky Control Officer, USS *Quincy*, NWWIIM-EC

'It was a beautiful . . .', Rear Admiral Carleton F. Bryant, USN, Commander Battleship Division 5, MdC TE 173

p. 220 'Immediately we opened fire', K. Jump, SWWEC T 1823

armoured bulldozers, Lieutenant Colonel

H. A. Delo, 346th Engineers, NA II 407/427/24242

display of strength, Lieutenant Ralph Powell, Cannon Company, 47th Infantry, 9th Division, NA II 407/427/24241

'had drunk enough . . .', NA II 407/427/24242

p. 221 'sound common sense', Oberstleutnant Keil, FMS C-018

'Final battle for Cherbourg . . .', Generalleutnant Karl-Wilhelm von Schlieben, 709th Infantry Division, FMS B-845

'Some of the boys . . .', Lieutenant John A. Le Trent, 8th Infantry, 4th Infantry Division, NA II 407/427/24242

'We saw a few women snipers . . .', Sergeant Walter M. Hedrick, 22nd Infantry, 4th Infantry Division, NA II 407/427/24242

Organisation Todt workers, BA-MA RH 19 iv/132, quoted in Peter Lieb, *Konventioneller Krieg oder Weltanschauungskrieg?*, Munich, 2007, p. 168

'The Teutonic tendency . . .', Captain Elmer G. Koehler, Battalion surgeon, 12th Infantry, 4th Infantry Division, NA II 407/427/24242

p. 220 'That was quite . . .', Clayton Storeby, 326th Airborne Engineer Battalion, NWWIIM-EC

'The Germans have left . . .', Pogue, p. 135

'a massive underground wine cellar', Bradley, p. 314

Hitler and Schlieben, General Warlimont, ETHINT 1

15 OPERATION EPSOM

p. 223 'Field Marshal Rommel is . . .', Wilhelm Ritter von Schramm, BA-MA MSg 2/247

Channel Islands and Nebelwerfer Brigades, General Warlimont, ETHINT 4

p. 224 'Jungle Tiger Tactics', General Geyr von Schweppenburg, FMS B-466

'[Hitler] looked unhealthy . . .', Speidel, FMS C-017. The description of this meeting is based on the accounts by Speidel, Rundstedt (FMS B-633), Blumentritt, chief of staff OB West (FMS B-284), and Hitler's Luftwaffe adjutant, Nicolaus von Below (*Als Hitlers Adjutant, 1937–1945*, Mainz, 1980)

p. 225 withdrawal of six to ten miles and 'a long auto-suggestive speech', General der Infanterie Blumentritt, debriefing 6 August 1945, NA II 407/427/24231

'That was the last thing . . .', Below, p. 375

'everything would depend . . .', Blumentritt, Chief of Staff OB West, FMS B-284

p. 226 'What principally bothers . . .', Mollie Panter-Downes, *London War Notes*, London, 1971, pp. 330–31

'eerie howl of sirens', Cyrus C. Aydlett, USS *Bayfield*, NWWIIM-EC

War Cabinet, 16 June, LHCMA Liddell Hart 11/1944/38

'These things . . .', Wing Commander R. Beamont, SWWEC T537

p. 227 Director General of Gendarmerie's report, General Martin, AN AJ/41/56

'with a pathetic wail . . .', Field Marshal Lord Alanbrooke, *War Diaries 1939–1945*, London, 2001, p. 562 (27 June)

Agent 'Lector', TNA HW 40/6

p. 228 'Battle is going well . . .', Montgomery to Churchill, 14 June, TNA PREM 3/339/8

'We formed up . . .', G. Steer, 1/4th King's Own Yorkshire Light Infantry, SWWEC 2002.1644

p. 229 'There's no need to tell Ike', LHCMA, LHP/1/230/22–23a

p. 231 'The German trick . . .', Peter Rubie, CWM/MCG 58A 1 40.7

'on turning a corner . . .', Stanley Christopherson diary

'The order came to us . . .', G. Steer 1/4th King's Own Yorkshire Light Infantry, SWWEC 2002.1644

p. 232 Ultra on Panzer Lehr, 27 June, TNA KV 9826

'like strange fungi . . .', John Keegan, *Six Armies in Normandy*, London, 1992, p. 174

'were much amused . . .', Aidan Sprot,

Swifter than Eagles, Edinburgh, 1998, p. 120

'It's a vision . . .', Félix Drougard, MdC TE 3

p. 233 'the enemy which has . . .', 9th SS Panzer-Division *Hohenstaufen*, BA-MA MSg 2/4831

p. 234 '*die grosse Chance*', Kriegstagebuch Panzer Group West, Fifth Panzer Army, BA-MA MSg 2/4831

Ultra, 29 June, XL 70, see Ralph Bennett, *Ultra in the West*, New York, 1979, p. 82

Operation Epsom, one of the best accounts is in Carlo D'Este, *Decision in Normandy*, New York, 1983

p. 235 'General talked about . . .', Myles Hildyard diary, 22 June

'the armchair strategists . . .', General Geyr von Schweppenburg, FMS B-466

p. 236 'returned in a vile humour', Blumentritt, Chief of Staff OB West, FMS B-284

'told him bluntly . . .', Blumentritt, ETHINT 73

'because of the effect . . .', General der Panzertruppen Eberbach, FMS A-922

p. 237 'become imbued . . .', Blumentritt, Chief of Staff OB West, FMS B-284

'energetic, quick-witted . . .', Speidel, FMS C-017

'After a rather frosty . . .', Speidel, FMS C-017

p. 238 'German tanks are superior . . .', Eberbach, BA-MA MSg 1/106

'the British attacks . . .', General Alfred Jodl, FMS A-913

'jumped out of line . . .', William Oatman, 506th Parachute Infantry Regiment, NWWIIM-EC

p. 240 'The effect of the major conflicts . . .', Keitel and Jodl, FMS A-915

visit of Colonel Vassilievsky, Arthur Reddish, *A Tank Soldier's Story*, privately published, undated, p. 56

'are still on the Soviet–German front', Major General Galaktionov, *Pravda*, 23 June

'We know where . . .', Ilya Ehrenburg, 'The West Wind', *Pravda*, 11 June

16 THE BATTLE OF THE *BOCAGE*

p. 242 'immediately deserted to the enemy', Generalleutnant Dietrich von Choltitz, LXXXIV Corps, FMS B-418; and Oberst Eugen König, 91st Luftlande-Division, FMS B-010

'to gain experience . . .', NA II 407/427/24203

'The prisoners we captured', T/Sergeant Laurence E. Ousley, 330th Infantry, 83rd Division, NA II 407/427/24242

'We no longer have . . .', NA II 407/427/6431

p. 243 'Fallen for Greater Germany', Jean-Claude Perrigault and Rolf Meister, *Götz von Berlichingen – Normandie*, Bayeux, 2005, p. 267

'The Germans haven't much left . . .', Martin Blumenson, *The Duel for France 1944*, New York, 2000, p. 23

LXXXIV Corps daily losses, General Dietrich von Choltitz, *De Sebastopol à Paris*, Paris, 1964, p. 184

'After having been . . .', Obergefreiter Hans S., 10 July, 9.Kp./Gren.Rgt. 1058, 91.(LL.) Inf.Div., 13 273 B, BfZ-SS

p. 246 'to gain suitable terrain . . .', NA II 407/427/24232

attack of 30th Infantry Division, 7 July, NA II 407/427/24232

p. 247 twelve Shermans knocked out, Pfc Bertrand J. Close, 3rd Battalion, 32nd Armored Regiment, 3rd Armored Division, WWII VS

'*Meine Frau und* . . .', Robert T. Gravelin, 23rd Combat Engineer Battalion, 3rd Armored Division, WWII VS

p. 248 'terrible mess', NA II 407/427/24232

'because of the element . . .', 120th Infantry Regiment, 30th Infantry Division, NA II 407/427/24037

4th Division in marshland fighting, Major Yarborough, NA II 407/427/6431

p. 249 'The Germans are staying . . .', General Barton, 4th Infantry Division, NA II 407/427/6431

'in comparing the average American . . .', NA II 407/427/24242

'have no regard . . .', NA II 407/427/24242

'What do you want to do in Europe?' TNA WO 171/337

'Captivity is . . .', Obergefreiter Hans S., 17 July, 9.Kp./Gren.Rgt.1058, 91.(LL.) Inf. Div., BfZ-SS

p. 250 'Colonel, that was . . .', 22nd Infantry, 4th Infantry Division, NA II 407/427/6431

'Company G had . . .', NA II 407/427/6431

p. 251 Panzer Lehr losses against British, Generalleutnant Fritz Bayerlein, FMS A-903

'was not in a position . . .', Generalleutnant Fritz Bayerlein, ETHINT 66

'Because of its exhausted condition . . .', Geyr von Schweppenburg, FMS B-466

p. 252 Panzer Lehr losses in American sector, Generalleutnant Fritz Bayerlein, ETHINT 66

Panzer Lehr offensive, NA II 407/427/24232; and Generalleutnant Fritz Bayerlein, ETHINT 67

'*schmutziger Buschkrieg*', Peter Lieb, *Konventioneller Krieg oder Weltanschauungskrieg?*, Munich, 2007, p. 176

'the only good Jerry soldiers . . .', E Company, 16th Infantry Regiment, 1st Infantry Division, Folder Huch, William, DDEL

p. 253 'Keep moving . . .', FUSAG 'Battle Experiences', NA II 407/427/24148

three times as many wounds, 9th Medical Battalion, NA II 407/427/7545

p. 254 'The sniper menace . . .', NA II 407/427/24170

'moles in the ground', NA II 407/427/24242

German rapid counter-attacks, Eberbach, BA-MA MSg 1/106

p. 256 Generalleutnant Richard Schimpf, 3rd Paratroop Division, FMS B-541

p. 257 rhino tanks, Lieutenant John M. Wilder, ADC to General Hickey, 3rd Armored Division, NA II 407/427/24242

'I talked to enough men . . .', Forrest C. Pogue, *Pogue's War*, Lexington, Kentucky, p. 105

'Our younger men . . .', Lieutenant Samuel E. Belk III, 320th Infantry, 35th Division, NA II 407/427/24242

p. 258 'Practically all of the replacements . . .', 4th Infantry Division, NA II 407/427/24021

'Just before they . . .', Paul Fussell, *The Boys' Crusade*, New York, 2003, p. 108

p. 259 'a high probability . . .', ibid., p. 110

'Riflemen must leave . . .', FUSAG 'Battle Experiences', NA II 407/427/24148

'To get down fast . . .', Robert B. Bradley, 120th Infantry Regiment, 30th Infantry Division, MdC TE 366

p. 260 'a sphygmomanometer . . .', 29th Infantry Division, Combat Exhaustion Survey, June–August, NA II 407/427/24035/84

p. 262 'Krammer, a capable . . .' and 'a nice *Heimatschuss*', Obergefreiter Hans S. 15.7.44, 9.Kp./Gren.Rgt.1058 91.(LL.)Inf.Div. 13 273 B, BfZ-SS

'apparently few . . .', L. B. Kalinowsky, *American Journal of Psychiatry*, Vol. 107, 1950; and TNA WO 177/316

17 CAEN AND THE HILL OF CALVARY

p. 263 'Ike is considerably less . . .', Harry C. Butcher, *Three Years with Eisenhower*, London, 1946, p. 512

Carlo D'Este, *Decision in Normandy*, New York, 1983, pp. 268–9

p. 265 'a twenty-five centimeter . . .', Erich Wohlgemut, quoted Hubert Meyer, *The 12th SS*, Vol. I, Mechanicsburg, Pa., 2005, p. 463

1st SS Panzergrenadier-Regiment, Kriegstagebuch Panzer Group West/Fifth Panzer Army, BA-MA MSg 2/4831

p. 266 'wounded as well as dead' and 'No prisoners are taken . . .', Alexander McKee, *Caen: Anvil of Victory*, London, 1965, pp. 199 and 197

Canadians and 43rd Infantry Division, NA II 407/427/24200

'Please do not hesitate . . .', 25 June, PDDE, p. 1949

'in maximum volume', 25 June, ibid., p. 1952

p. 267 'There was high cloud . . .', Lieutenant T. T. Ritson, RHA, diary

'We could see . . .', William Helm, 'The Normandy Field Diary of a Junior Medical Officer in 210 Field Ambulance', 177th Brigade, 59th Infantry Division

'a magnificent spectacle', W. Kingsley, IWM P424

'I sat smoking a cigarette . . .', Major Peter Griffin, 1st Canadian Parachute Battalion, letter 8 July, NAC/ANC R5067-0-0-E

'The awful thing was . . .', Captain Michael Bendix, Coldstream Guards, SWWEC 2000-356

'The sight was frightening . . .', Robert Thornburrow, 4th Somerset Light Infantry, 43rd Wessex Division, MdC TE 120

p. 268 'Imagine a rat . . .', MdC TE 149

'We had the impression . . .', MdC TE 145

'Monsieur le Curé . . .', MdC TE 149

'a grandiose procession . . .', MdC TE 145

p. 269 6,000 casualties, Robert Thornburrow, 4th Somerset Light Infantry, 43rd Wessex Division, MdC TE 120

350 deaths, CRHQ

Lieutenant Colonel Kraminov, MdC TE 246

bombing of Caen, 'Observations on Bomber Command Attack on Caen, 7 July 1944', TNA AIR 37/1255, quoted in D'Este, p. 315

p. 270 'a heap of ruins . . .', Eberbach, BA-MA MSg 1/106

French squadrons, logbook of Roger Piroutet, MdC TE 262

'There were all sorts of casualties . . .', Rev. Jim Wisewell, 223 Field Ambulance, SWWEC T1141

p. 271 'a group of terrified . . .', William Helm, 'The Normandy Field Diary of a Junior Medical Officer in 210 Field Ambulance', 177th Brigade, 59th Infantry Division

'The Germans are leaving!', André Heintz diary, MdC TE 32 (1–4)

p. 272 'Where is the River Orne?', Max Maurin, MdC TE 77 (2)

Les Petites Soeurs des Pauvres, Mme Laberthe, MdC TE 74

'At last . . .', Major L. J. Massey, civil affairs team, MdC TE 167

Canadian captain and restaurant, Mme Lucie Corbasson, MdC TE 49

p. 273 'Most of the women . . .', Sapper Douglas Waite, Royal Engineers, MdC TE 182

10 July parade, Place Saint-Martin, Henriette Guibé, MdC TE 237

p. 274 'Kalvarienberg', 9th SS Panzer-Division *Hohenstaufen*, BA-MA MSg 2/4832

'a small, fiery . . .', Michael Carver, *Out of Step*, London, 1989, p. 193

Sergeant W. Partridge, 4th Somerset Light Infantry, SWWEC 2006.419

p. 275 Maltot, Schwere Panzer-Abteilung 502, BA-MA MSg 2/4832

'He had been hit . . .', Corporal Jones, quoted in McKee, p. 230

p. 276 'slit trenches scraped . . .', Corporal D. Proctor, 'Section Commander', DWS

'Not a metre . . .', 9th SS Panzer-Division *Hohenstaufen*, BA-MA MSg 2/4832

'einer Milchsuppe', 9th SS Panzer-Division *Hohenstaufen*, BA-MA MSg 2/4832

'They're brave . . .', 9th SS Panzer-Division *Hohenstaufen*, BA-MA MSg 2/4832

'We had a scene . . .', 9th SS Panzer-Division *Hohenstaufen*, BA-MA MSg 2/4832

'Schlüsselstellung', Hubert Meyer, BA-MA MSg 2/4832

p. 277 'infiltrate the enemy position . . .', Sergeant W. Partridge, SWWEC 2006.419

'Struggling in desperation . . .', Corporal D. Proctor, 'Section Commander', DWS

'anguished cries . . .', Sergeant Partridge, SWWEC 2006.419

'A single well-aimed . . .', Corporal D. Proctor, 'Section Commander', DWS

p. 278 'moon landscape', 9th SS Panzer-Division *Hohenstaufen*, BA-MA MSg 2/4832

'Mademoiselle Jeanette', Ludwig Horlebein, 9th SS Panzer-Division, BA-MA MSg 2/4832

civilians in the caves of Fleury, MdC TE 149

cholera and dogs, Major L. J. Massey, MdC TE 167

'Regret to report . . .', TNA CAB 106/1092, quoted in D'Este, p. 274

p. 279 'not to criticise . . .', diary of Major Julius Neave, 13th/18th Hussars, SWWEC T2150

6th Duke of Wellington's Regiment, 49th Division, TNA WO 205/5G, quoted in D'Este, p. 282

'during the 54 hours . . .', 21st Light Field Ambulance, 13 July, LHCMA O'Connor 5/3/18

p. 280 15th Scottish Division, 22 July, LHCMA O'Connor 5/4/14

desertions in 50th Division, Stephen A. Hart, *Montgomery and 'Colossal Cracks'*, Westport, Conn., 2000, p. 31

'The Corps psychiatrist . . .', 21 July, LHCMA O'Connor 5/3/18

'most serious offence . . .', 21 July, LHCMA O'Connor 5/3/18

p. 281 'Two of them during . . .', 129th Infantry Brigade Headquarters, Robert Thornburrow, 4th Somerset Light Infantry, 43rd Wessex Division, MdC TE120

'ignorance, stupefying, brutalizing ignorance . . .', Vernon Scannell, *Argument of Kings*, London, 1987, p. 152

'Gentlemen, your life expectancy . . .', Sydney Jary, *18 Platoon*, Bristol, 1998

18 THE FINAL BATTLE FOR SAINT-LÔ

p. 282 'awfully restless', diary, 4 June, Martin Blumenson (ed.), *The Patton Papers, 1940–1945*, New York, 1974, p. 462

'It is Hell . . .', ibid., p. 464

'an office seeker . . .', ibid., pp. 468–9

p. 283 'I cannot follow the reasoning . . .', Generalleutnant Richard Schimpf, 3rd Paratroop Division, FMS B-541 and FMS B-020 'one or two armored . . .', Blumenson (ed.), p. 470

p. 284 'After lunch . . .', ibid., p. 479

p. 286 I saw U.S. troops . . .', 2nd Lieutenant Morton Kligerman, Graves Registration, 320th Infantry, 35th Infantry Division, NA II 407/427/24242

'to relieve the body . . .', John Capell, 8th Infantry, 4th Infantry Division, NWWIIM-EC

'sickening stench' and 'As gruesome . . .', Sergeant Charles D. Butte, 603rd Quartermaster, Graves Registration Company, VII Corps, First US Army, NWWIIM-EC

p. 287 'Three enemy paratroopers . . .', NA II 407/427/24232

p. 288 'Mind your Goddam business . . .', Max Feldman, 2nd Infantry Division, NWWIIM-EC

'scattered opposition', 2nd Infantry Division, NA II 407/427/24232

p. 289 'This second transfer . . .', Generalleutnant Freiherr von Lüttwitz, 2nd Panzer-Division, FMS B-257

'in a poor state . . .' and 'a giant, brutal man', Generalleutnant Fritz Bayerlein, ETHINT 66

p. 290 'more like jungle fighting', NA II 407/427/24206

358th Infantry, Lieutenant George W. Godfrey, 90th Division, NA II 407/427/24240

p. 291 'The population has to evacuate . . .', Obergefreiter Hans S., 17 July, 9.Kp./Gren. Rgt.1058, 91. (LL.) Inf.Div., BfZ-SS

German artillery observation officer dressed as a priest, Lieutenant James J. Williams, 47th Infantry, 9th Division, NA II 407/427/24241

'The men said they held . . .', Lieutenant James J. Williams, 47th Infantry, 9th Division, NA II 407/427/24241

p. 292 'poker and mint juleps . . .', diary of Captain Thomas P. Jacobs, MD, 45th Armored Medical Battalion, 3rd Armored Division, WWII VS

'Sunday punch', NA II 407/427/24232

'a tall Britisher . . .', Forrest C. Pogue, *Pogue's War*, Lexington, Kentucky, 2001, p. 130

'two preachers . . .', Blumenson (ed.), p. 481

p. 293 Artillery airbursts, 331st Infantry, 83rd Division, NA II 407/427/24203

'I remember one poignant . . .', James H. Watts, Chemical Battalion, NWWIIM-EC

'Then, he shot . . .', Captain Elmer G. Koehler, Battalion surgeon, 12th Infantry, 4th Infantry Division, NA II 407/427/24242

'I saw medical aid men . . .', Captain William Pola, Medical Detachment, 66th Armored Regiment, 2nd Armored Division, NA II 407/427/24242

p. 294 'I got so I can tell . . .', Captain William L. Johnston, 100th Evacuation Hospital, NA II 407/427/24240

'It's such a paradox . . .', George Silverton, Chief of X Ray Department, 2nd Evacuation Hospital, MdC TE 710

'blooded', diary of Captain Thomas P. Jacobs, MD, 45th Armored Medical Battalion, 3rd Armored Division, WWII VS

p. 295 K-Rations, WWII VS

'I find it a bit hard . . .', diary of Captain Jack H. Welch, 54th Armored Medical, 3rd Armored Division, WWII VS

sergeant in 1st Infantry Division, Sergeant Leroy N. Stewart, 26th Infantry Regiment, WWII VS

'French kids . . .', Vernon W. Tart, 618th Ordinance Ammunition Company, NWWIIM-EC

p. 296 'I know we lack . . .', J. Le Gal, 'Un Gendarme à Caumont l'Eventé', MdC TE 398

30th Division casualties, NA II 407/427/24232

p. 297 'I remember going up . . .', Bradley Holbrook, NWWIIM-EC

p. 298 'Fix bayonets! Twenty-nine, let's go!', NA II 407/427/24232

p. 300 'like a sled' and 'known simply as "Chief"', NA II 407/427/24232

p. 302 29th Division, night of 15 July, NA II 407/427/24232

Interview Colonel Godwin Ordway Jr, Commanding Officer, 115th Infantry, 20 July, NA II 407/427/24034

p. 303 'Cota was hit . . .', Lieutenant Edward

G. Jones, Cavalry Reconnaissance Troop, 29th Infantry Division, WWII VS

25th Cavalry Squadron, Lieutenant Edward G. Jones, Cavalry Reconnaissance Troop, 29th Infantry Division, WWII VS

p. 304 'the magnificent American troops . . .', Montgomery tribute, NA II 407/427/24232

19 OPERATION GOODWOOD

p. 306 'I am viewing the prospects . . .', 14 July, PDDE, p. 2004

'I came upon a line . . .', Brigadier M. J. P. O'Cock, 2nd Battalion Irish Guards, SWWEC 2003.2287

p. 307 'alternate thrusts', Stephen A. Hart, *Montgomery and 'Colossal Cracks'*, Westport, Conn., 2000, p. 103

Crocodile tanks, Kriegstagebuch Panzer Group West/Fifth Panzer Army, BA-MA MSg 2/4831

'There is a nice cool breeze . . .', Captain S. Beck, MdC TE 570

9th SS Panzer-Division *Hohenstaufen*, General Sylvester Stadler, FMS B-470

'the whole length . . .', Eberhard Beck, 277th Artillerie-Regiment, 277th Infanterie-Division, BA-MA MSg 2/3242

p. 309 277th Infanterie-Division, Heeresgruppe B, BA-MA RH 19 ix/86

'decisive for the course of the war . . .', XL 2287, quoted in Ralph Bennett, *Ultra in the West*, New York: 1979, p. 106

'out of the question', Heeresgruppe B, BA-MA RH 19 ix/86

'The units will fight . . .', Kurt Meyer, *Grenadiers*, Mechanicsburg, Pa., 2005, p. 270

p. 310 Frenchwoman at Sainte-Foy-de-Montgommery, Simone Grieux-Isabelle, MdC TE 419

'that the Panzer Group . . .', Kriegstagebuch Panzer Group West/Fifth Panzer Army, BA-MA MSg 2/4831

p. 311 Operations Goodwood and Atlantic, NA II 407/427/24200

'pre-recorded wireless traffic', A. D. E. Curtis, R Force, SWWEC 2000.384

'We'll be moving into top gear!', N. F. Burrell, 1/7th Queens, 131st Infantry Brigade, 7th Armoured Division, SWWEC LEEWW 2004.2680

'We are undoubtedly . . .', diary of Major Julius Neave, 13th/18th Hussars, SWWEC T2150

p. 313 'a bit of mistletoe . . .', quoted in Laurence Whistler, *The Laughter and the Urn: The Life of Rex Whistler*, London, 1985, p. 287

Tedder and Coningham on Goodwood, Air Publication 3235, Air Ministry, 1955, p. 151, AHB

p. 314 RAF report on Goodwood bombing, Air Support, Air Publication 3235, Air Ministry, 1955, AHB

p. 315 'like cars crawling . . .', Whistler, p. 289

p. 316 'Prisoners are streaming in . . .', Major Peter Griffin, 1st Canadian Parachute Battalion, NAC/ANC R5067-0-0-E

'a breakthrough appeared unavoidable', Eberbach, Panzer Group West, FMS B-840

'completely overrun' and 'Some tanks had received direct hits . . .', Heeresgruppe B, BA-MA RH 19 ix/86

'At 10.00 hours . . .', Eberbach, BA-MA MSg 1/106

'Suddenly a Sherman . . .', W. H. Close, 3rd Royal Tank Regiment, SWWEC 2002.1713

p. 317 'What happened was incomprehensible . . .', Eberbach, BA-MA MSg 1/106

p. 318 'death ride', Alexander McKee, *Caen: Anvil of Victory*, London, 1965, p. 263

five Tiger tanks and eight Mark IVs, Generalleutnant Edgar Feuchtinger, FMS B-441

'no more reserves', Heeresgruppe B, BA-MA RH 19 ix/86; and Kriegstagebuch Panzer Group West, BA-MA MSg 2/4831

1st SS Panzer-Division at Ifs-Bras, Heeresgruppe B, BA-MA RH 19 ix/86

p. 319 'Operations this morning . . .', quoted in L. F. Ellis, *Victory in the West*, London, 1962, Vol. I, pp. 344–5

'like children', Brigadier E. T. Williams, G-2, 21st Army Group, OCMH-FPP

'We were fighting . . .', Eberbach, Panzer Group West, FMS B-840

p. 320 'The enemy needed only . . .', Eberbach, BA-MA MSg 1/106

Hitler Jugend tank losses to fighter-bombers, Tagesmeldungen, Heeresgruppe B, BA-MA RH 19 ix/86

'the British continued to stay immobile . . .', Eberbach, Panzer Group West, FMS B-840

'found him in grand form . . .', 19 July, Field Marshal Lord Alanbrooke, *War Diaries 1939–1945*, London, 2001, p. 571

p. 321 'Russian style' breakthrough and press conferences, Lieutenant Colonel Kraminov, MdC TE 246

'a field strewn . . .', N. F. Burrell, 1/7th Queens, SWWEC LEEWW 2004.2680

p. 322 'There comes a time . . .', Bill Close, *A View from the Turret*, Tewkesbury, 1998, p. 130

'Either it was just gross . . .', diary of Major Julius Neave, 13th/18th Hussars, SWWEC T2150

'It rained and there were mosquitoes . . .', Rev. Jim Wisewell, 223rd Field Ambulance, 3rd Infantry Division, SWWEC T1141

British and Canadian losses in Normandy, TNA WO 171/139

p. 323 army complaints about the lack of bombs on Bourguébus ridge, *Air Support*, Air Publication 3235, Air Ministry, 1955, p. 158, AHB

'General Montgomery was reminded . . .', Royal Air Force Narrative, Vol. III, p. 81, AHB; and 2nd TAF Operations Report by Air Marshal Sir Arthur Coningham, TNA AIR 20/1593

'a national decline in boldness and initiative', LHCMA Liddell Hart 11/1944/45

p. 324 'But once the needle . . .', Brigadier Sir Ian Fraser, MdC TE 160

'One boy of about sixteen . . .', John Colville, *The Fringes of Power*, London, 1985, p. 474

20 THE PLOT AGAINST HITLER

p. 326 'inflexible mission of defending . . .', Generalleutnant Hans Speidel, FMS B-721

'The Führer must be killed . . .', TNA WO 208/4363

'and above all about . . .', Hans Speidel, *We Defended Normandy*, London, 1951, p. 132

'a hardline anti-semite', Richard J. Evans, *The Third Reich at War*, London, 2008, p. 379

'measures to be taken immediately . . .', Generalleutnant Hans Speidel, FMS B-721

p. 327 'oasis' for the Resistance, Wilhelm Ritter von Schramm, BA-MA MSg 2/247

for an excellent analysis of the Allies and the German opposition to Hitler, see Michael Howard, *Liberation or Catastrophe?*, London, 2007, pp. 80–93

p. 329 move of Führer headquarters on 14 July to *Wolfsschanze*, General Warlimont, ETHINT 5

I must request you . . .', Generalleutnant Hans Speidel, FMS B-721

'We are experiencing the overwhelming . . .', Eberbach, BA-MA MSg 1/1079

p. 330 'The longer Hitler . . .', 21st Army Group Intelligence Summary, 23 April 1944, TNA WO 205/532 (2)

'The Chiefs of Staff . . .', Ismay to Churchill, 21 June, TNA HS 6/623

Operation Foxley, TNA HS 6/624; and Mark Seaman (ed.), *Operation Foxley*, Kew, 1998

Churchill's views on Hitler and unconditional surrender, TNA HS 6/625; and Churchill's speech in House of Commons 2 August 1944

p. 331 'Since the generals have . . .', quoted in Ian Kershaw, *Hitler: 1936–1945, Nemesis*, London, 2000, p. 656

p. 332 'strikingly large briefcase', General Warlimont, ETHINT 5

British fuses used in bomb, M. R. D. Foot, *SOE in France*, London, 1966, p. 331 n. 5

p. 333 'over a million foreign workers . . .', Otto Remer, Commander Guard Regiment

Grossdeutschland, ETHINT 63

p. 334 'Gestapo riot', Blumentritt, FMS B-284

'executive powers had been passed . . .', Otto Remer, Commander Guard Regiment *Grossdeutschland*, ETHINT 63

'What do you know about the situation?', Otto Remer, Commander Guard Regiment *Grossdeutschland*, ETHINT 63

p. 335 'The Führer is dead . . .', quoted in Ralph Bennett, *Ultra in the West*, New York, 1979, p. 110

'Today at midday . . .', 20.40 hours, 20 July, Tagesmeldungen, Heeresgruppe B, BA-MA RH 19 ix/86

p. 336 '*Unterweltsmarschall*', Blumentritt, FMS B-284

Dietrich and Himmler, Eberbach, BA-MA MSg 1/1079

'almost turned revolutionary', Eberbach, TNA WO 208/4363, quoted in Sönke Neitzel (ed.), *Tapping Hitler's Generals*, St Paul, Mn, 2007, p. 101

'In my opinion . . .', TNA WO 208/4363

p. 337 'Long live holy Germany!', quoted in Kershaw, p. 683

Kluge's order to arrest Stülpnagel, BA-MA RH19 ix/86

'the Military Commander . . .', BA-MA RH19 ix/86

'came like a bomb-shell', Generalleutnant Bodo Zimmermann, OB West, FMS B-308

'it spread like wild-fire . . .', Hans Höller, 21st Panzer-Division, MdC TE 98

'the front kept on fighting . . .', Generalleutnant Bodo Zimmermann, OB West, FMS B-308

'indignation and anger', Eberbach, 23 December tape, TNA WO 208/4364

'Our signaller heard . . .', Eberhard Beck, 277th Artillerie Regiment, 277th Infanterie-Division, BA-MA MSg 2/3242

p. 338 'feeling of moral oppression . . .', Generalleutnant Bodo Zimmermann, OB West, FMS B-308

'might well be the proverbial . . .', Duff

Hart-Davis (ed.), *King's Counsellor*, London, 2006, p. 245

'Explanation of Continued German Resistance', 8 September 1944, LHCMA Alanbrooke 6/1/5

p. 339 'an idiotic idea', Wilhelm Ritter von Schramm, BA-MA MSg 2/247

'falsification of the enemy situation', Hubert Meyer, *The 12th SS*, Vol. I, Mechanicsburg Pa., 2005, p. 36

'daily reports which even . . .', General Bülowius, II Flieger Corps, FMS B-620

p. 340 'had a really good relationship . . .', Günter Peuckert, 272th Infanterie-Division, BA-MA MSg 2/5424

'*malgré-nous*', Nicolas Fank, 116th Panzer-Division, MdC TE 531

'No, no. I play no tricks . . .', Aitken, Medical Officer, 24th Lancers, WLHUM RAMC 1668

p. 341 'If somebody betrays . . .', 1944, BA-MA RH 21–5/50, quoted in Peter Lieb, *Konventioneller Krieg oder Weltanschauungskrieg?*, Munich, 2007, p. 439

US Army report on German prisoners in Normandy, NA II 407/427/24242

'*Kameradenerziehung*', Eugène Finance, MdC TE 331

21 OPERATION COBRA – BREAKTHROUGH

p. 342 German radio intercepts, Oberstleutnant Ziegelmann, 352nd Infanterie-Division, FMS B-455

'One unit surrendered . . .', NA II 407/427/24242

'a battalion of the 90th . . .', Martin Blumenson (ed.), *The Patton Papers, 1940–1945*, New York, 1974, p. 486

p. 343 'War is about 90% waiting . . .', diary of Captain Jack H. Welch, 54th Armored Medical, 3rd Armored Division, WWII VS

p. 345 'The observers hung around . . .', 4th Infantry Division, NA II 407/427/6431 'the peculiar rustling in the sky', 4th Infantry Division, NA II 407/427/6431

bombing casualties on 24 July, NA II 407/427/24245

'The flamboyant, red-headed . . .', Colonel Kraminov, MdC TE 246

'stiffened perceptibly', Forrest C. Pogue, *Pogue's War*, Lexington, Kentucky, 2001, pp. 167–8

p. 346 Soviet complaint about reports of former Red Army soldiers fighting for the Germans, see Eisenhower letters 26 and 27 July, PDDE, pp. 2031 and 2032

'Fourteenth US Army', TNA HW 40/6

accident with bayonets, Robert B. Bradley, 120th Infantry Regiment, 30th Infantry Division, MdC TE 366

p. 347 'the faces of the dead . . .', Robert B. Bradley, MdC TE 366

'Many of them only . . .', NA II 407/427/24245

'all men and officers who were under the bombing . . .', NA II 407/427/6431

p. 348 Kluge and Operation Spring, Oberstgruppenführer Paul Hausser, Seventh Army, ETHINT 48

'The whole place . . .', Generalleutnant Fritz Bayerlein, Panzer Lehr Division, ETHINT 66

transfer of German panzer divisions to American sector, Omar Bradley, *A Soldier's Story*, New York, 1951, p. 341

'the drawing off of German panzers . . .', Colonel Thomas Bigland, liaison officer with First US Army, then 12th Army Group, SWWEC 99–10

Panzer Lehr losses, ETHINT 66, then FMS A-903

p. 349 'many of . . .', diary of Captain Jack H. Welch, 54th Armored Medical, 3rd Armored Division, WWII VS

'At the end of this great bombing . . .', NA II 407/427/24242

'The rest huddled in a corner . . .', Lieutenant Clyde Eddinger, 4th Infantry Division, NA II 407/427/24021

'The result for the first day . . .', 4th Infantry Division, NA II 407/427/24021

p. 350 'The effectiveness of the bombardment . . .', 4th Infantry Division, NA II 407/427/6431

'quite a collection . . .', Lieutenant Donald Dickinson, Company B, 22nd Infantry, 4th Infantry Division, NA II 407/427/24021

p. 351 'a lot of looting', Lieutenant John B. Derden, 66th Armored Regiment, WWII VS

'The number of kill-lusty people . . .', Captain Jim R. Burt, 66th Armored Regiment, 2nd Armored Division, WWII VS

'Private De Castro . . . ,' E Company, 22nd Infantry, NA II 407/427/24021

p. 352 Montreuil-sur-Lozon, Brigadier General Doyle O. Hickey, Combat Command A, 3rd Armored Division, NA II 407/427/24088

'overhead like hawks . . .', General Schmidt, 275th Infanterie-Division, FMS A-973

'friendly tanks' and 'an old soldier . . .', NA II 407/427/6431

'We were riding along . . .', Lieutenant George O. Grant, 69th Tank Battalion, 6th Armored Division, NA II 407/427/24241

p. 353 'good clothes', Blumenson (ed.), p. 489

'I tell you one thing, Sani . . .', SanUffz Walter Klein, Kampfgruppe Heintz, FMS A-910

p. 354 Browning and air drop on Avranches, Wing Commander Scarman, Tedder's aide, OCMH-FPP

'Felt much happier over the war . . .', Blumenson (ed.), p. 490

'Because of heavy losses . . .', TNA DEFE 3/63

'a rather confused situation', General der Panzertruppen Freiherr von Lüttwitz, 2nd Panzer-Division, FMS A-903

'the din of shell-fire . . .', General Eugen Meindl, II Parachute Corps, FMS A-923

p. 355 'from staff to staff . . .', General Eugen Meindl, II Parachute Corps, FMS A-923

p. 356 'just rushed on through', Lieutenant George O. Grant, 69th Tank Battalion, 6th

Armored Division, NA II 407/427/24241

Collins's criticism of 3rd Armored Division, NA II 407/427/24235

p. 357 6th Armored Division on 28 July, 69th Tank Battalion, 6th Armored Division, NA II 407/427/24241

'no forces fit for battle' and 'neither light nor medium . . .', 28 July, TNA DEFE 3/63

'used to fire point-blank . . .', VII Corps, NA II 407/427/24235

'For five days . . .', SanUffz Walter Klein, Kampfgruppe Heintz, FMS A-910

'when other elements . . .', Lieutenant James J. Williams, 47th Infantry, 9th Division, NA II 407/427/24241

tension between SS and paratroops, Oberstleutnant Friedrich Freiherr von der Heydte, 6th Paratroop Regiment, FMS B-839

p. 358 the sacking of Generalmajor Pemsel, Generalmajor Freiherr von Gersdorff, Chief of Staff Seventh Army, FMS A-894

p. 359 'on the road all night' and 'that they did it . . .', 4th Infantry Division, NA II 407/427/6431

'a knocked out enemy vehicle standing . . .', NA II 407/427/24021

'only one-way traffic . . .', Major William A. Castille, Combat Command B, 3rd Armored Division, NA II 407/427/24088

'Hell, within a couple of days . . .', William M. King, 44th Armored Infantry Battalion, 6th Armored Division, NA II 407/427/24241

'they crapped in them and cooked in them', Captain Thomas P. Jacobs, MD, 45th Armored Medical Battalion, 3rd Armored Division, WWII VS

2nd Panzer-Division on 29 July, General der Panzertruppen Freiherr von Lüttwitz, FMS A-903

p. 360 Captain Reid and Private Sharkey, 22nd Infantry, 4th Infantry Division, NA II 407/427/24021

p. 361 Moyon engagement, Combat Command Rose, NA II 407/427/24021

82nd Reconnaissance Battalion, Major Willis T. Smith, 67th Armored Regiment,

2nd Armored Division, NA II 407/427/24242

p. 362 'by single rifle shots . . .', Lieutenant Colonel Briard P. Johnson, Executive Officer of Combat Command B, 2nd Armored Division, NA II 407/427/24082

Sergeant Bishop and 'Action during the fight . . .', Lieutenant Colonel Harry Hilliard, 3rd Battalion, 67th Armored Regiment, NA II 407/427/24082

'their vehicles down the hill . . .', NA II 407/427/24082

'Even the use . . .', Lieutenant Colonel Marshall L. Crowley, 41st Armored Infantry Regiment, 2nd Armored Division, 22 September, NA II 407/427/24082

p. 363 'The mortars set the vehicles . . .', Lieutenant Colonel John D. Wynne, 2nd Battalion, 67th Armored Regiment, NA II 407/427/24082

'Then the organized slaughter . . .', Captain James R. McCartney, 67th Armored Regiment, 2nd Armored Division, NA II 407/427/24082

'as daylight broke . . .', Lieutenant Colonel John D. Wynne, 2nd Battalion, 67th Armored Regiment, NA II 407/427/24082

Death of Generalleutnant Kraiss, Peter Lieb, *Konventioneller Krieg oder Weltanschauungskrieg?*, Munich, 2007, p. 548

p. 364 'The whole area . . .' and 'prisoners were coming . . .', NA II 407/427/24082

'German equipment, abandoned . . .', General Doyle O. Hickey, Combat Command A, 3rd Armored Division, NA II 407/427/24088

'Carnage gruesome . . .', diary of Captain Thomas P. Jacobs, MD, 45th Armored Medical Battalion, 3rd Armored Division, WWII VS

Generalmajor Freiherr von Gersdorff, Chief of Staff Seventh Army, FMS A-894

demolitions and looting in Granville, Commissariat de Police de Granville, AdM 1370 W 1

p. 365 'urgent orders to prevent . . .', General Warlimont, ETHINT 1

'Pour it to them!', Lieutenant Sancken,

4th Reconnaissance Troop, NA II 407/427/6431

'The thing to do . . .', Blumenson (ed.), p. 491

22 OPERATION COBRA – BREAKOUT

p. 366 'I have ordered Dempsey . . .', quoted in Carlo D'Este, *Decision in Normandy*, New York, 1983, p. 422

'grinds to a halt . . .', diary of Major Julius Neave, 13th/18th Hussars, SWWEC T2150

'Monty is determined to make us . . .', diary of Major Julius Neave, 13th/18th Hussars, SWWEC T2150

p. 367 'The crews were shaken . . .', Ian Daglish, 'Operation Bluecoat', in John Buckley (ed.), *The Normandy Campaign 1944*, London, 2006, p. 95

p. 369 326th Infanterie-Division, Eberbach, BA-MA MSg 1/106

21st Panzer-Division, FMS B-631

3rd Scots Guards, Major Charles Farrell, SWWEC 2001.960

'wearing only a vest . . .', Alexander McKee, *Caen*, London, 1965, p. 308

p. 370 Coastal battery at Granville and Aulock *Kampfgruppe*, BA-MA RH 19 ix/86

'unforgettable sight . . .', Gefreiter Spiekerkötter, 2nd Pionier Kompanie, 256th Infanterie-Division, BA-MA MSg 2/5526

p. 371 'The situation is extraordinarily . . .', BA-MA RH 19 ix/86

'a most forceful order . . .', Telephone Journal, Seventh Army, NA II 407/427/6431

Kluge to Eberbach, Eberbach, BA-MA MSg 1/106

'under all circumstances . . .', BA-MA RH 19 ix/86

p. 372 'Do not stop . . .' and 'facetiously suggested . . .', General Doyle O. Hickey, Combat Command A, 3rd Armored Division, NA II 407/427/24088

p. 373 action in Brécey, Captain Carlton

Parish Russell, 36th Armored Infantry Regiment, 3rd Armored Division, WWII VS

'more dangerous than . . .', Daily Operations, 4th Infantry Division, NA II 407/427/6431

'a very jolly . . .', Charles Whiting, *Papa Goes to War*, Marlborough, 1990, p. 66

p. 374 'take the first picture . . .', Robert Capa, *Slightly out of Focus*, New York, 1947, p. 168

looting and lynch mob in Granville, Commissariat de Police de Granville, AdM 1370 W 1

'*Ah, Monsieur* . . .', anon., MdC TE 388

'Our boys got their souvenirs . . .', Lieutenant D. S. Woodward, 69th Tank Battalion, 6th Armored Division, NA II 407/427/24241

p. 375 Resistance attack in the Landes, LCMHA Misc 24

armoured train derailed Souillac, TNA DEFE 3/62

'throughout history . . .', Martin Blumenson (ed.), *The Patton Papers, 1940–1945*, New York, 1974, p. 493

'As many troops as possible . . .', XV Corps, NA II 407/427/24203

p. 376 'Gentlemen, this breakthrough . . .', Wilhelm Ritter von Schramm, BA-MA MSg 2/247

'The enemy is not under any circumstances . . .', Hans Speidel, *We Defended Normandy*, London, 1951, p. 138

'round the corner into Brittany', NA II 407/427/6431

p. 377 'One of our trucks . . .', Lieutenant Colonel Teague, 22nd Infantry, NA II 407/427/24021

VIII Corps and First Army prisoners, Martin Blumenson, *The Duel for France*, New York, 2000, pp. 143–4 and 150

prisoners of 8th Division, Captain Graham V. Chamblee, 13th Infantry, 8th Division, NA II 407/427/24241

'We passed columns . . .', 29th Infantry Division, NA II 407/427/24034

rumours of German withdrawal to the

Seine, Oberstleutnant Friedrich Freiherr von der Heydte, 6th Paratroop Regiment, FMS B-839

'As we came over the crest . . .', Lieutenant Colonel Johnson and Captain Wright, 12th Infantry, 4th Infantry Division, NA II 407/427/24203

p. 378 'in a state of jitters', Captain Wright, NA II 407/427/24203

Captain Ware's account, NA II 407/427/24203

p. 379 'The small number of Germans . . .', 4th Infantry Division, NA II 407/427/6431

'had a shattering effect . . .', General-leutnant Fritz Bayerlein, ETHINT 66

23 BRITTANY AND OPERATION BLUECOAT

p. 381 'a written declaration . . .', SHD-DAT 13 P 33

'intensify general guerrilla activity . . .', SHD-DAT 13 P 33

'a second General Patton . . .', Lieutenant Harold H. Goodman, 13th Infantry, 8th Division, NA II 407/427/24241

'a brawny, jovial type', Martin Blumenson, *The Duel for France*, New York, 2000, p. 166

p. 382 French Resistance in Rennes, 2nd Lieutenant Edward W. Overman, 90th Division, NA II 407/427/24242

relief of prisoners of war, Lieutenant Harold H. Goodman, 8th Division, NA II 407/427/24241

'One paratrooper . . .', Captain Joseph Gray, 13th Infantry, 8th Division, NA II 407/427/24241

p. 383 'What in hell . . .', Blumenson, p. 176

'General Patton's Household Cavalry', Lieutenant Colonel Samuel Goodwin, 6th Cavalry Group, NA II 407/427/24242

'every night from . . .', Captain John C. Donley, 6th Armored Division, NA II 407/427/24241

p. 384 'The first thing we did . . .', Lieutenant

D. S. Woodward, 69th Tank Battalion, 6th Armored Division, NA II 407/427/24241

'pony express', William M. King, 44th Armored Infantry Battalion, 6th Armored Division, NA II 407/427/24241

replacements in Brittany, Captain John C. Donley, 44th Armored Infantry Battalion, 6th Armored Division, NA II 407/427/24241

'better than expected . . .', Martin Blumenson (ed.), *The Patton Papers, 1940–1945*, New York, 1974, p. 541

'They aided in loading . . .', William M. King, 44th Armored Infantry Battalion, 6th Armored Division, NA II 407/427/24241

'with the help of terrorists', 6 August, BA-MA RH 19 ix/87

'*Terroristenführer*', 6 August, Ob. West Tagesmeldungen, BA-MA RH 19 iv/45

'battles with terrorists . . .', BA-MA RH 19 ix/87

massacres in Finisterre, Peter Lieb, *Konventioneller Krieg oder Weltanschauungs-krieg?*, Munich, 2007, pp. 576 and 579

Eon and Passy, SHD-DAT 13 P 33

p. 385 Ramcke in Brest, see Lieb, pp. 483–4

'to get a Hermann Goering . . .', Lieutenant Harold H. Goodman, 8th Division, NA II 407/427/24241

'courteously got rid of . . .', Lieutenant Harold H. Goodman, 8th Division, NA II 407/427/24241

'It was entirely wiped out!', TNA WO 208/4364

'The townspeople were so nice . . .' and 'We had a hair-cutting party . . .', Lieutenant Harold H. Goodman, 8th Division, NA II 407/427/24241

p. 386 'I would not say this . . .', Blumenson (ed.), p. 532

p. 387 Leclerc's attitude to British, Christian Girard, *Journal de Guerre*, Paris, 2000, p. 80

'Even for us Gaullists . . .', Marc de Possesse, MdC TE 361

'a uniform different . . .', Forrest C. Pogue, *Pogue's War*, Lexington, Kentucky, 2001, p. 178

p. 388 2ème DB landing on Utah beach, Marc de Possesse, MdC TE 361

French villagers marking mines, Alexander McKee, *Caen*, London, 1965, p. 315

'Over in the next field . . .', Sergeant Kite, 3rd Royal Tank Regiment, BA-MA MSg 2/4837

p. 389 reinforcement of Vire, General Eugen Meindl, II Parachute Corps, FMS A-923

'The woods seemed to cast . . .', Colonel Tom Gilliam, B Company, 2nd Infantry, 5th Infantry Division, MdC TE 124

'We'll defend your town . . .', quoted in Blumenson, p. 215

p. 390 'Everyone very depressed . . .', Myles Hildyard diary, 3 August, and letter, 5 August

'the wretched wounded . . .', Captain Michael Bendix, Coldstream Guards, SWWEC 2000–356

'I could not help thinking . . .', Rev. A. R. C. Leaney, IWM PP/MCR/206

'In the small fields of Normandy . . .', quoted in Eversley Belfield and H. Essame, *The Battle for Normandy*, London, 1975, p. 206

p. 391 'To be the leading tank . . .', Stanley Christopherson diary

p. 392 'because they slip on . . .', Captain M. G. T. Webster, 2nd Battalion Grenadier Guards, IWM P 182

'in the recesses of a LST', John Colville, *The Fringes of Power*, London, 1985, p. 500

'The tank commander would . . .', Captain Michael Bendix, Coldstream Guards, SWWEC 2000–356

'a little German stretcher-bearer . . .', Rev. A. R. C. Leaney, attached to 4th Dorsets, 43rd Wessex Division, IWM PP/MCR/206

p. 393 'Many of them probably . . .', XXX Corps, TNA WO 171/342

'Apart from the church spire . . .', Major Julius Neave diary, SWWEC T2150

'You really had to disassociate . . .', Major Robert Kiln, 86th Field Artillery, SWWEC 99–63

'an imbroglio of steel', André Heintz diary, MdC TE 32 (1–4)

severed hand, Robert Thornburrow, 4th Somerset Light Infantry, 43rd Wessex Division, MdC TE120

p. 394 'a little foal walking . . .', William Helm, 'The Normandy Field Diary of a Junior Medical Officer in 210 Field Ambulance', 177th Brigade, 59th Infantry Division

'Brigade and battalion commanders . . .', Stanley Christopherson diary

'Our intention is to capture . . .', Major Julius Neave diary, SWWEC T2150

'The nearer we got . . .', Corporal D. Proctor, 4th Somerset Light Infantry, DWS

p. 395 'It was soon obvious . . .', Sergeant W. Partridge, 4th Somerset Light Infantry, SWWEC 2006.419

p. 396 'more men in five weeks . . .', Sergeant W. Partridge, 4th Somerset Light Infantry, SWWEC 2006.419

'heavy enemy attacks . . .', Heeresgruppe B, 6 August, BA-MA RH 19 ix/87

p. 397 German casualty figures to 7 August, Dieter Ose, *Entscheidung im Westen 1944*, Stuttgart, 1982, p. 266, quoted in Lieb, p. 422

24 THE MORTAIN COUNTER-ATTACK

p. 398 'Situation still more acute . . .', TNA DEFE 3/65

discussions Hitler, Jodl and Warlimont, Major Herbert Büchs, Luftwaffe aide to Generaloberst Jodl, ETHINT 36

'Whenever a line of defence . . .', General Warlimont, ETHINT 1

p. 399 'He belonged to the set . . .', General Eugen Meindl, II Parachute Corps, FMS A-923

'discouraged' and 'he could not hold . . .' General Warlimont, ETHINT 1

'The division is bad . . .', Martin Blumenson (ed.), *The Patton Papers, 1940–1945*, New York, 1974, p. 497

p. 400 'a fifteen-year-old French boy . . .', NA II 407/427/24242 strengthening of Fougères, Headquarters XV Corps, NA II 407/427/24203

'Approximately 13,000 trucks . . .', Mark J. Reardon, *Victory at Mortain*, Lawrence, Kansas, 2002, p. 39

'withdrawal movements', 2 August, TNA DEFE 3/65

p. 401 'Joe, I already have it', J. Lawton Collins, *Lightning Joe*, Novato, CA, 1994, p. 250

'Some of the troops held themselves well . . .', P. Peschet, MdC TE 215

p. 403 'it seemed like an excellent . . .', NA II 407/427/24037

'As we arrived there . . .', Robert B. Bradley, 120th Infantry Regiment, 30th Infantry Division, MdC TE 366

120th Infantry Regiment in Mortain, NA II 407/427/24037

p. 404 'were the greatest obstacles . . .', Generalmajor Freiherr Rudolf von Gersdorff, FMS A-918

'They had been deceived . . .', General Warlimont, ETHINT 1

'passive resistance . . .', Generalleutnant Graf von Schwerin, ETHINT 17

p. 405 'The Führer has ordered . . .', Heeresgruppe B, 6 August, BA-MA RH 19 ix/87

Hitler's opposition to General von Funck, General Warlimont, ETHINT 1

'virtually impossible', Heeresgruppe B, 6 August, BA-MA RH 19 ix/87

'little air activity', BA-MA RH 19 ix/87

p. 406 'The war looks practically over', 4th Infantry Division, NA II 407/427/6431

'a beautiful bivouac . . .', NA II 407/427/6431

Ultra intercepts, 6 August, TNA DEFE 3/65

Bradley's scepticism about Ultra, see Carlo D'Este, *Decision in Normandy*, New York, 1983, pp. 420–21

'to stop spreading rumours', NA II 407/427/24037

p. 407 German motorcyclists, Chérencé-le-Roussel, 39th Infantry Division, NA II 407/427/24037

'extraordinarily well', General der Panzertruppen Freiherr von Lüttwitz, FMS A-903

p. 408 fighting in Saint-Barthélemy, 30th Infantry Division, NA II 407/427/24037

120th Infantry in Mortain, NA II 407/427/24037

p. 409 'A loud clang followed . . .', Reardon, p. 100

p. 410 'should deal exclusively . . .', 2nd TAF Operations Report by Air Marshal Sir Arthur Coningham, TNA AIR 20/1593

'This is the moment . . .', John Golley, *The Day of the Typhoon*, Shrewsbury, 2000, p. 129

pilots in 123 Wing, Desmond Scott, *Typhoon Pilot*, London, 1982, p. 193

'roughly a four-per-cent chance . . .', Ian Gooderson, *Air Power at the Battlefront*, London, 1998, p. 76

p. 411 'Diving point . . .', 'The Rocket Racket', Air Ministry, AHB

Typhoon operations, 7 August, TNA AIR 25/704

'Our fighters have been engaged . . .', Telephone Journal, Seventh Army, 7 August, NA II 407/427/6431

p. 412 '*Alles kaputt!*', Robert B. Bradley, 30th Infantry Division, MdC TE 366

83 Group, Alfred Price, 'The Rocket-Firing Typhoons in Normandy', *Royal Air Force Air Power Review*, Vol. VIII, I, Spring 2005, pp. 78–88

'As the day developed . . .', 2nd Tactical Air Force Operations Report by Air Marshal Coningham, TNA AIR 20/1593

Operational Research Section reports: Joint Report No. 3, 'Rocket-firing Typhoons in Close Support of Military Operations', Operational Research in North-West Europe, TNA WO 291/1331; and No. 2 ORS, 2nd TAF, Report No.1, 'Investigations of the Operation of TAF Aircraft in the Mortain Area – 7th August 1944', TNA AIR 37/61

p. 413 'Whether you realise it or not', General der Panzertruppen Geyr von Schweppenburg, ETHINT 13

'There is nothing . . .', Operational Research Section, 'Investigation of the Operation of TAF Aircraft in the Mortain Area, 7th August 1944', dated 7 December 1944, AHB

field artillery in support of 30th Infantry Division, Brigadier General James M. Lewis, commanding 30th Division Artillery, NA II 407/427/24037

p. 414 'a thorn in the flesh . . .', General der Panzertruppen Walter Krüger, LVIII Panzer Corps, FMS B-445

p. 415 Germans with cognac, Pfc John Cole, 8th Infantry, NA II 407/427/6432

'It was quite clear . . .', comments on Seventh Army war diary, Generalmajor Rudolf Freiherr von Gersdorff, FMS A-918

p. 416 'In formal manner . . .', 30th Division, NA II 407/427/24242

12th Infantry, NA II 407/427/6431

p. 417 SS panzergrenadiers using American equipment, Captain Dunbar Whitman, 12th Infantry, 4th Infantry Division, NA II 407/427/24021

'For the first time . . .', 4th Infantry Division, NA II 407/427/24021

'The tank he could see . . .', NA II 407/427/6432 and Reardon, p. 256

p. 418 'Then he pulled himself to his feet . . .', 30th Infantry Division, NA II 407/427/24038

'There, under that tank . . .', NA II 407/427/24037

p. 419 air drop, Reardon, p. 201

smoke shells, Lieutenant Charles A. Bartz, 230th Field Artillery Battalion, 30th Division, NA II 407/427/24242; and Lieutenant Elmer Rohmiller, 120th Infantry, 30th Division, NA II 407/427/24242

128th Evacuation Hospital, Colonel John N. Snyder, MdC TE 648

p. 420 'Under cover of this operation . . .', General der Panzertruppen Walter Krüger, LVIII Panzer Corps, FMS B-445

1st Battalion, 39th Infantry, NA II 407/427/24037

Colonel Birks at Abbaye Blanche, NA II 407/427/24037

p. 421 'I want Mortain demolished . . .', 30th Division G-3 Journal, 11.05 hours, 11 August, quoted in Reardon, p. 267

'incredibly weary troops', NA II 407/427/6431

'the attitude of "silent mutiny" . . .', NA II 407/427/6432

'Kluge did it deliberately . . .', Wilhelm Ritter von Schramm, BA-MA MSg 2/247

25 OPERATION TOTALIZE

p. 422 Crerar as commander in Italy, see Terry Copp and Bill McAndrew, *Battle Exhaustion*, Montreal, 1990, pp. 66–8

Montgomery on Crerar and Keller, LCHMA AP/14/27; see also Stephen A. Hart, *Montgomery and 'Colossal Cracks'*, Westport, Conn., 2000

p. 423 'to avenge the death of our comrades', quoted in Howard Margolian, *Conduct Unbecoming*, Toronto, 1998, p. 29

p. 425 'Blimey! Square-bashing in tanks', Ken Tout, *Tank!*, London, 1985, p. 17

2nd Canadian Infantry Division in Operation Totalize, report by Canadian Military Headquarters, NA II 407/427/24200

7th Norfolks crossing the Orne, Lieutenant Colonel Freeland, 7th Battalion Norfolk Regiment, MdC TE 168

p. 426 'The artillery has an awfully easy job . . .', Lieutenant T. T. Ritson, RHA, diary, 6 August

'A magnificent view of the Orne valley . . .', William Helm, 'The Normandy Field Diary of a Junior Medical Officer in 210 Field Ambulance', 177th Brigade, 59th Infantry Division

'Here on the British front . . .', Myles Hildyard diary, 11 August

'During these days . . .', Rev. A. R. C. Leaney, IWM PP/MCR/206

p. 427 'What an honour!', Hubert Meyer, *The 12th SS*, Vol. II, Mechanicsburg, Pa., 2005, p. 25

'View Hallo! . . .', Tout, p. 111

p. 428 destruction of five Tiger tanks,

Hauptsturmführer Dr Wolfgang Rabe, quoted in Meyer, pp. 29 30; see also Stephen A. Hart, 'The Black Day Unrealised', in John Buckley (ed.), *The Normandy Campaign 1944*, London, 2006

p. 429 'Other aircraft could not . . .', Major Robert Kiln, Hertfordshire Yeomanry, 86th Field Artillery, SWWEC 99–63

'The American air force . . .', Aitken Hughes diary, 6 General Hospital, WLHUM RAMC 1771

'unfortunate support . . .', SHD-DAT 1 K 543 1

'the Sikorski tourists', SHD-DAT 1 K 543 1

p. 430 'becoming very serious . . .', Heeresgruppe B, BA-MA RH 19 ix/87

p. 431 Generalleutnant Paul Dannhauser, 271st Infantry Division, FMS B-256

Plessis Grimoult, diary of Major Julius Neave, 13th/18th Hussars, SWWEC T2150

p.434 intelligence failure over anti-tank defences, Captain A. Potozynski, 10th Polish Mounted Rifles, SWWEC LEEWW 2000.327

Hitler Jugend claim 192 tanks destroyed, 20.55 hours, Chief of Staff Fifth Panzer Army, BA-MA RH 19 ix/87

OKW communiqué, BA-MA MSg 2/3242

Hitler Jugend prisoners in Operation Totalize, Peter Lieb, *Konventioneller Krieg oder Weltanschauungskrieg?*, Munich, 2007, p. 165

p. 433 'The forces are so large . . .', Patton, letter 9 August, Martin Blumenson (ed.), *The Patton Papers, 1940–1945*, New York, 1974, p. 504

'appropriate the whole of fuel resupply . . .', General John C. H. Lee, head of Com Z (Communications Zone), OCMH-FPP

Patton commandeering supply trucks, Harry C. Butcher, *Three Years with Eisenhower*, London, 1946, p. 550

60,000 gallons a day, Lieutenant Colonel Eugene Orth, 3rd Armored Division, NA II 407/427/24088

125,000 gallons to move every 100 yards,

Captain Cecil Oppenheim, QM, 3rd Armored Division, NA II 407/427/24240

'Miss America', Lieutenant A. W. Loring, 133rd Engineer Combat Command, NA II 407/427/24242

'This is an opportunity . . .', Omar Bradley, *A Soldier's Story*, New York, 1951, p. 372

p. 434 'the pay of an entire division', 2nd Lieutenant A. Dominic Scialla, 735th Tank Battalion, 8 August, NA II 407/427/24242

5th Infantry Division in Angers, Lieutenant Anthony J. Miketinae, 11th Infantry, 5th Division, NA II 407/427/24241

'The French beat up the collaborators . . .', 2nd Lieutenant Derk van Raalte, 2nd Infantry, 5th Division, NA II 407/427/24241

'lost his nerve', Oberst Erich Helmdach, Ia Seventh Army, FMS B-822

p. 435 'supply troops, maintenance platoons . . .', Bayerlein, FMS A-901

'The counterattack against Avranches . . .', Gersdorff, Chief of Staff Seventh Army, FMS A-921

'It was inconceivable . . .', Eberbach, FMS A-922

'Enemy shellfire began falling . . .', Eberbach, FMS A-922

Feldgendarmerie and roving courts martial, Oberst Erich Helmdach, Ia Seventh Army, FMS B-822

p. 436 Retreat of 1st SS Panzer-Division from Sourdeval, Eugen Finanz, MdC TE 351

'Calvados still in German hands!', Gefreiter Spiekerkötter, 2nd Pionier Kompanie, 265th Infanterie-Division, BA-MA MSg 2/5526

p. 437 Panthers at 2ème DB headquarters, Service de Santé, 2ème DB, SHD-DAT 11 P 232

'badly disguised', Marc de Possesse, 2ème DB, MdC TE 361

p. 438 'There was no one to take care of them', 2nd Lieutenant R. W. Conger, 10th Tank Battalion, 5th Armored Division, NA II 407/427/24241

Colonel McHugh, 318th Infantry, 80th Division, NA II 407/427/24242

p. 439 *'Vive l'Amérique!'*, Rev. Père Roger Fouquer, Aumônier Divisionnaire, 2ème DB, MdC TE 825

129 casualties, 8 August, SHD-DAT 11 P 219

Alsatian deserter, MdC TE 351

116th Panzer-Division in Argentan, Generalmajor Gerhard Müller, 116th Panzer-Division, FMS B-162

'solid cork', 2nd French Armored Division, NA II 407/427/24205

'Upon capture . . .', USAMHI, quoted in Carlo D'Este, *Decision in Normandy*, New York, 1983, p. 428

'This corps could easily advance . . .', Blumenson (ed.), p. 508

p. 440 For the effectiveness of anti-tank guns in defence see David Rowland, *The Stress of Battle*, Norwich, 2006, pp. 106–41

26 THE HAMMER AND ANVIL

p. 441 'Very hot – not good . . .', diary of Major Julius Neave, 13th/18th Hussars, SWWEC T501

Montgomery and Berlin, Harry C. Butcher, *Three Years with Eisenhower*, London, 1946, p. 551

p. 442 Tractable bombing attack, Terry Copp, *Fields of Fire*, Toronto, 2003, p. 229

'The attack ordered by me . . .', Eberbach, FMS A-922

p. 443 'It is really a great plan . . .', Martin Blumenson (ed.), *The Patton Papers, 1940–1945*, New York, 1974, p. 510

'Take Orléans at once', Major General Gilbert Cook, commanding XII Corps, Third Army, NA II 07/427/24241

'The number of cases . . .', Blumenson (ed.), p. 510

'A few of the enlisted men . . .', George Silverton, Chief of X Ray Department, 2nd Evacuation Hospital, MdC TE 710

6th Security Regiment captures American war correspondent, Heeresgruppe B, 14 August, BA-MA RH 19 ix/87

p. 444 'We'd have been happy . . .', Gefreiter Spiekerkötter, 2nd Pionier Kompanie, 256th Infanterie-Division, BA-MA MSg 2/5526

'a slimy paste', Aitken Hughes diary, WLHUM RAMC 1771

'more critical by the hour', Heeresgruppe B, 14 August, BA-MA RH 19 ix/87

'catastrophic', Kriegstagebuch Panzer Group West, Fifth Panzer Army, BA-MA MSg 2/4831

'swine . . .', Marshal of the RAF Lord Portal, OCMH-FPP

p. 445 'I cannot pretend . . .', No. 742, Prime Minister to President, 4 August, TNA PREM 3/472

'Ike said no . . .', Butcher, p. 545

'especially when the first paratroops . . .' General Warlimont, ETHINT 1

p. 446 'One woman was raped . . .', M. R. D. Foot, *SOE in France*, London, 1966, p. 393

head of the Gestapo in Châteauroux killed, SHD-DAT 13 P 33

'128 terrorists . . .', BA-MA MSg 2/3242

'reprisals cannot be harsh enough', BA-MA M-854, quoted in Peter Lieb, *Konventioneller Krieg oder Weltanschauungskrieg?*, Munich, 2007, p. 463

p. 447 the twenty-six worst massacres, ibid., pp. 574–80

for a comprehensive and up-to-date discussion of French civilian casualty figures see ibid., pp. 412–15

'counter-scorching', Foot, p. 391

p. 448 'military events having taken . . .', Faugère, AN F/1cIII/1166

Laval and Pétain, AN F/1cIII/1166

'regions where hideous . . .', AN AJ/41/56

'In the face of these barbarous acts . . .', TNA WO 171/337, quoted in Lieb, p. 396

p. 449 'I watched an open lorry . . .', John Colville, *The Fringes of Power*, London, 1985, p. 475

'their look, in the hands . . .', Forrest C. Pogue, *Pogue's War*, Lexington, Kentucky, 2001, p. 199

'The French were rounding . . .', Colonel McHugh, 318th Infantry, 80th Division, NA II 407/427/24242

'an ugly carnival', Alain Brossat, *Les Tondues*, Paris, 1992

for the *département* of the Manche, see Michel Boivin, *Les Victimes civiles de la Manche*, Caen, 1994, p. 6

p. 450 'Military police were posted . . .', Colville, p. 499

'everything can be bought', Madame Richer, MdC TE 223

'My wife doesn't understand me', Pogue, p. 134

p. 451 'clearly considered us to be backward . . .', P. Peschet, MdC TE 215

'their neighbours as German sympathizers', NA II 407/427/24170

camp at Sully, ADdC 8 W 1/1 422

p. 452 'supplying the enemy', AdM 1380 W 236 and AdM 1380 W 254

'It's because I don't wash . . .', Claude Quétel, 'Avoir quatre ans et demi, le 6 juin 1944, à Bernières-sur-Mer', *Bulletin d'information de la Fondation canadienne de la Bataille de Normandie*, March 1993

'*réquisitions irrégulières*', AdM 158W 159–202

'pillaging shops . . .', Major L. J. Massey, MdC TE 167

p. 453 'Our soldiers have done some looting', Myles Hildyard diary, 19 June

'with occasionally a cynical touch . . .', George Silverton, Chief of X Ray Department, 2nd Evacuation Hospital, MdC TE 710

'Mon Repos', R. Makin, IWM 88/34/1

15,000 troops working on Port de Caen, Major L. J. Massey, MdC TE 167

'whose liberation was more rapid . . .', François Bédarida (ed.), *Normandie 44, du débarquement à la Libération*, Paris, 2004, p. 24

'otherwise they must expect . . .', Heeresgruppe B, 14 August, BA-MA RH 19 ix/87

p. 454 Kluge's order to cross the Orne, BA MA MSg 2/5117

panzers driving over bodies, Beck, 277th Artillerie Regiment, 277th Infanterie-Division, BA-MA MSg 2/3242

resistance of *Hitler Jugend* in Falaise, Copp, *Fields of Fire*, pp. 234–5

Canadian casualties at end of Tractable, Terry Copp, *Cinderella Army*, Toronto, 2007, p. 7

Polish crossing of the Dives, SHD-DAT 1 K 543 1

p. 455 'for the first time . . .', Blumenson (ed.), p. 513

'No, by God . . .', Major General Kenner, Chief Medical Officer, SHAEF, OCMH-FPP

p. 456 'All effort was made . . .', Combat Command B, 7th Armored Division, NA II 407/427/24096

p. 457 confusion with Gerow and Gaffey, NA II 407/427/24235

'Change horses', Blumenson (ed.), pp. 514–15

'Ismay takes a sane . . .', Duff Hart-Davis (ed.), *King's Counsellor*, London, 2006, p. 279

'Leclerc of the 2nd French Armored Division . . .', Blumenson (ed.), p. 510

27 THE KILLING GROUND OF THE FALAISE POCKET

p. 459 'the 15th August was . . .', Wilhelm Ritter von Schramm, BA-MA MSg 2/247

'Hitler suspected that . . .', General Warlimont, ETHINT 5

p. 460 'The Führer has ordered . . .', Wilhelm Ritter von Schramm, BA-MA MSg 2/247

'one of the harshest . . .', Leutnant Dankwart Graf von Arnim, MdC TE 819

p. 461 'were a pack of cowards . . .', Generalleutnant Fritz Bayerlein, ETHINT 66

Kluge's letter to Hitler, quoted in Milton

Shulman, *Defeat in the West*, London, 1986, pp. 174–7

p. 464 'able to drive by car . . .', General-major Rudolf Christoph Freiherr von Gersdorff, Chief of Staff Seventh Army, ETHINT 59

shape of Falaise pocket, General Mahlmann, 353rd Infantry Division, FMS A-984

II Panzer Corps in Forêt de Gouffern, Eberbach, FMS A-922

'In other words . . .', General Eugen Meindl, II Parachute Corps, FMS A-923

panzer soldier playing Viennese waltzes, Marcel Labussière, MdC TE 471

'We have had a warm welcome . . .', Captain S. Beck, 18 August, MdC TE 570

'While I was talking to the Brigadier . . .', diary of Major Julius Neave, 13th/18th Hussars, 19 August, SWWEC T501

p. 465 1st Polish Armoured Division reorganizes, SHD-DAT 1 K 543 1

Model's conference on 18 August, Eberbach, FMS A-922, and Generalmajor Freiherr von Gersdorff, written answers submitted October 1945, NA II 407/427/24231

p. 466 'The black mushrooms . . .', General Eugen Meindl, II Parachute Corps, FMS A-923

'We rippled the rockets . . .', Michael Veitch, *Tom Hall*, Sydney, 2006, p. 113

'On the road great heaps . . .', General der Panzertruppen Freiherr von Lüttwitz, FMS A-903

Eberhard Beck, 277th Artillerie-Regiment, 277th Infantry Division, BA-MA MSg 2/3242

Allied air claims on 18 August, Leigh-Mallory, TNA CAB 106/980

Operational Research Section, Report No. 15, 'Enemy Casualties in Vehicles and Equipment in the Retreat from Normandy to the Seine', AHB

p. 467 'Take cover, boys, they may be ours!' Rev. A. R. C. Leaney, IWM PP/MCR/206

'some British armored vehicles . . .', NA II 407/427/24143

p. 468 'They were excellent fighters . . .', Lieutenant George W. Godfrey, 358th

Infantry, 90th Division, NA II 407/427/24240

'tidying up official correspondence', quoted in Terry Copp, *Fields of Fire*, Toronto, 2003, p. 243

'The roads were blocked . . .', Hans Höller, 21st Panzer-Division, MdeC TE 98

'In their faces one could read . . .', Eberhard Beck, 277th Artillerie-Regiment, 277th Infantry Division, BA-MA MSg 2/3242

p. 469 '*Fertigmachen zum Abmarsch*', Eberhard Beck, 277th Artillerie-Regiment, 277th Infantry Division, BA-MA MSg 2/3242

escape of General Meindl and paratroops, General Eugen Meindl, II Parachute Corps, FMS A-923

p. 470 'clear and serene', Generalmajor Gerhard Müller, 116th Panzer-Division, FMS B-162

p. 471 'People, horses, vehicles . . .', General der Panzertruppen Freiherr von Lüttwitz, 2nd Panzer-Division, FMS A-903

'This was the signal . . .', Generalmajor Freiherr Rudolf von Gersdorff, FMS A-919

'It was a gunner's dream . . .', NA II 407/427/24242

p. 472 'The Polish soldier fights . . .', SHD-DAT 1 K 543 1

'luck gave the 10th Cavalry Brigade . . .', SHD-DAT 1 K 543 1

capture of General Elfeldt, Captain A. Potozynski, 10th Polish Mounted Rifles, SWWEC LEEWW 2000.327

Simonds and Kitching, Copp, pp. 249–50

p. 473 Hauptmann Werner, III Battalion, Regiment *Der Führer*, 2nd SS Panzer-Division *Das Reich*, MdC TE 158

SS officer saved by Canadian officer, Herbert Ronstedt, 9th SS Panzer-Division *Hohenstaufen*, BA-MA MSg 2/3225

Polish tanks near northern Hill 262, Hubert Meyer, BA-MA MSg 2/4832

'Oh it's the old man', General Eugen Meindl, II Parachute Corps, FMS A-923

p. 475 'German attempts, more or less . . .', SHD-DAT 11 P 221

'the sixty-sixth and last day . . .', MdC TE 149

Polish losses in Normandy, SHD-DAT 1 K 543 1

p. 476 over 2,000 men per division had escaped, Generalmajor Freiherr von Gersdorff, Chief of Staff Seventh Army, written answers submitted October 1945, NA II 407/427/24231

'[The] Yanks say . . .', diary of Major Julius Neave, 13th/18th Hussars, SWWEC 501T

'A boy of about ten years . . .', 2nd Lieutenant Roy J. Bolen, 38 Cavalry Reconnaissance Squadron, NA II 407/427/24240

'The roads were choked with wreckage . . .', Desmond Scott, *Typhoon Pilot*, London, 1982, p. 129

'The horses seemed almost more pitiful', Kingsley Amis, *Memoirs*, London, 1991, p. 221

p. 477 the cossack squadron, Barnett Hoffner, 6th Engineer Special Brigade, NWWIIM-EC

German field hospital in Forêt de Gouffern, NA II 407/427/24235

'On the collapse of the Falaise pocket . . .', Lieutenant Colonel John N. Snyder, MdC TE 648

p. 478 'Their blankets have been . . .', Aitken Hughes diary, WLHUM RAMC 1771

'The air became unbreathable', Jean Sorel, MdC TE 504

'The victory has been definite . . .', LHCMA De Guingand 3/1–27

Eberbach's estimate of those who escaped, Eberbach, FMS A-922

Gersdorff's estimate, Generalmajor Rudolf-Christoph Freiherr von Gersdorff, Chief of Staff Seventh Army, ETHINT 59

'One of Monty's great errors . . .', Air Chief Marshal Tedder, OCMH-FPP

'Monty is supposed to have done a great job . . .', Air Chief Marshal Coningham, OCMH-FPP

'too tidy', 'the high cock on the dungheap' and 'Bradley was indignant . . .', Brigadier E. T. Williams, G-2, 21st Army Group, OCMH-FPP

28 THE PARIS UPRISING AND THE RACE FOR THE SEINE

p. 480 'had to ask him categorically . . .', Martin Blumenson (ed.), *The Patton Papers, 1940–1945*, New York, 1974, p. 516

'This Army covers so much . . .', ibid., p. 517

p. 481 'pissed in the river that morning', ibid., pp. 521–2

'Go where you damn well . . .', Major General Gilbert Cook, commanding XII Corps, Third Army, NA II 407/427/24241

De Gaulle's unannounced journey, Wilson to SHAEF, 16 August, TNA ADM 1/16018

De Gaulle and the Flying Fortress, John Julius Norwich (ed.), *The Duff Cooper Diaries*, London, 2005, p. 318 (17 August)

'We must march on Paris . . .', Charles de Gaulle, OCMH-FPP

p. 482 Hitler and Choltitz, General Dietrich von Choltitz, *De Sebastopol à Paris*, Paris, 1964, pp. 203–9

'Bedell, Ike and all hands . . .', ACM Sir James Robb, OCMH-FPP

'The worst job . . .', TNA WO 208/4364, quoted in Sönke Neitzel (ed.), *Tapping Hitler's Generals*, St Paul, Mn., p. 192

'Have you read Churchill's . . .', TNA WO 208/4634

p. 483 'short of stature . . .', Leutnant Dankwart, Graf von Arnim, MdC TE 819

p. 484 25,000 soldiers, Generalleutnant Freiherr von Boineburg, FMS B-015

'interpreter battalion . . .', Oberst Professor Dr Kurt Hesse, FMS B-611

Bayerlein and Choltitz, Generalleutnant Fritz Bayerlein, Panzer Lehr Division, ETHINT 66

p. 485 'the shining example . . .', SHD-DAT 13 P 42 1

'Along the rue Lafayette . . .', Jean Galtier-Boissière, *Mon journal pendant l'Occupation*, Paris, 1944, p. 242

p. 486 'A deceptive calm reigned . . .', Leutnant Dankwart Graf von Arnim, MdC TE 819 'create a permanent state . . .', SHD-DAT 13 P 42 1

p. 487 'to cover the heroic defence . . .', Leutnant Dankwart Graf von Arnim, MdC TE 819

truce, SHD-DAT 13 P 42 1

p. 488 'for new missions', NA II 407/427/24205

'in the direction . . .', SHD-DAT 11 P 226

'What are we doing here?', NA II 407/427/24082

p. 489 American liaison officer warns V Corps, SHD-DAT 11 P 226

Private Petrie, Tyneside Scottish, MdC TE97

p. 490 'We all know he's lost the war . . .', Rev. A. R. C. Leaney, IWM PP/MCR/206

'the infantry captured . . .', Lieutenant T. T. Ritson, RHA, diary

'We took the same number . . .', Jean Marius Vesque, MdC TE 401

'smiles on their lips . . .', anon., MdC TE 83

'The explosive growth . . .', Maître Quairé, MdC TE 469

p. 491 'every 11th Hussar . . .', Myles Hildyard diary

'Would you like a Panzer . . .', Major General H. G. Woods, SWWEC LEEWW 2006.533

p. 492 'If you can't do it, Bimbo . . .', Omar Bradley, *A Soldier's Story*, New York, 1951, p. 377

'one of the greatest injustices . . .', General Omar Bradley, OCMH-FPP

only 13 armoured vehicles found to have been destroyed by air attack, Operational Research Section reports, Joint Report No. 3 'Rocket-firing Typhoons in Close Support of Military Operations', Operational Research in North-West Europe, TNA WO 291/1331

123 Wing, Desmond Scott, *Typhoon Pilot*, London, 1982, p. 129

'Ferry points for the Seine crossing . . .', Generalleutnant Fritz Bayerlein, ETHINT 66

p. 493 artillery horses swimming the Seine, Günter Peuckert, 272th Infanterie-Division, BA-MA MSg 2/5424

Fifth Panzer Army, Generalmajor Freiherr von Gersdorff, Chief of Staff Seventh Army, written answers submitted October 1945, NA II 407/427/24231

276th Infanterie-Division pioneers, Gefreiter Spiekerkötter, 2nd Pionier Kompanie, 256th Infantry Division, BA-MA MSg 2/5526

p. 494 'Paris should be declared . . .', Major General Gilbert Cook, commanding XII Corps, Third Army, NA II 407/427/24241

'between 4,000 and 5,000 . . .', NA II 407/427/24235

preparations to relieve Paris, Central Base Section, NA II 407/427/24201

p. 495 General Gerow's briefing, V Corps, NA II 407/427/24235

p. 496 'I'll make him talk . . .', John Mowinckel, quoted in Antony Beevor and Artemis Cooper, *Paris after the Liberation, 1944–1949*, London, 1994, p. 46

'They looked like . . .', John G. Westover, MdC TE 436 (2)

p. 497 'Bradley was madder than . . .', Blumenson (ed.), pp. 526–7

'You are lucky', Jean Lacouture, *De Gaulle*, New York, 1990, p. 568

29 THE LIBERATION OF PARIS

p. 498 'Every barricade . . .', Note de Service, 24 August, SHD-DAT 13 P 42 1

p. 499 'strange, indecisive days . . .', Maurice Goudeket, *Près de Colette*, Paris, 1955, pp. 216–17

102nd Cavalry attached to GTL, SHD-DAT 11 P 219

p. 500 rain interfering with radio traffic, NA II 407/427/24082

casualties in Longjumeau, SHD-DAT 11 P 230

Longjumeau, Rev. Père Roger Fouquer, Aumônier Divisionnaire, 2ème DB, MdC TE 825 'a big disordered picnic . . .', John G. Westover, MdC TE 436 (2)

'On one occasion . . .', William Mortimer Moore, *Leclerc – The Making of a French Legend*, unpublished MS

p. 501 battle outside Fresnes prison, SHD-DAT 11 P 226

Capitaine Dupont foretells his death, Rev. Père Roger Fouquer, Aumônier Divisionnaire, 2ème DB, MdC TE 825

'and remain with him . . .', NA II 407/427/242351349

'dance their way . . .', Martin Blumenson, *The Duel for France*, New York, 2000, p. 353

'over-enthusiastic French mademoiselles', NA II 407/427/6431

p. 502 '*Tenez bon, nous arrivons*', Journal de marche, 2ème DB, SHD-DAT 11 P 230

Dronne and Leclerc, SHD-DAT 11 P 226; Raymond Dronne, *La Libération de Paris*, Paris, 1970, pp. 280–81; and Marc de Possesse, 2e DB, MdC TE 361

'Mort aux Cons!', Moore, unpublished MS

p. 503 artillery fire from Longchamp, NA II 407/427/24021

Dronne's column reaches the Hôtel de Ville, Marc de Possesse, 2e DB, MdC TE 361; Dronne, pp. 284–5; Moore, *Leclerc – The Making of a French Legend*, unpublished MS

'when the night rose . . .', Goudeket, p. 217

'They're here!', Madeleine Betts-Quintaine, MdC TE 25

p. 504 2nd Pionier Kompanie of 256th Infanterie-Division, Gefreiter Spiekerkötter, BA-MA MSg 2/5526

p. 505 'a noisy and lyrical . . .', Rev. Père Roger Fouquer, Aumônier Divisionnaire, 2ème DB, MdC TE 825

'Victorious, Liberty advanced . . .', Madame Talbot, MdC TE 133

entry of American troops, NA II 407/427/242351349

'the people bewildered . . .', NA II 407/427/24240

p. 506 'French girls, beautiful girls . . .',

Alfred Donald Allred, Staff Sergeant, 20th Field Artillery, 4th Infantry Division. NWWIIM-EC

'*Merci! Merci!* . . .', Colonel J. S. Luckett, 12th Infantry, NA II 407/427/6431

'The people of Paris were . . .', NA II 407/427/242351349

p. 507 'A vibrant crowd . . .', Jean Galtier-Boissière, *Mon journal pendant l'Occupation*, Paris, 1944, pp. 275–6

p. 508 'were mixed up . . .', Philippe Boegner, *Carnets du Pasteur Boegner*, Paris, 1992, p. 287

ultimatum to Choltitz, SHD-DAT 11 P 218

'Silent also from the effort . . .', Leutnant Dankwart Graf von Arnim, MdC TE 819

p. 509 'After a short, correct conversation', Leutnant Dankwart, Graf von Arnim, MdC TE 819

'a bearded giant . . .', Leutnant Dankwart, Graf von Arnim, MdC TE 819

p. 510 'the crowd, often hateful . . .', Rev. Père Fouquer, MdC TE 825

Choltitz signing the surrender, SHD-DAT 11 P 226

'saved Paris . . .', NA II 407/427/24235

p. 511 'surrendered Paris to V Corps', NA II 407/427/24235

Plan Fortitude, TNA WO 199/1379

Maillé massacre, Fondation de la Résistance, Paris

'terrorists', SHD-DAT 13 P 42 1

p. 512 'to give the crowd an opportunity . . .', Gefreiter Spiekerkötter, BA-MA MSg 2/5526

p. 513 'But why should we proclaim . . .', Antony Beevor and Artemis Cooper, *Paris after the Liberation, 1944–1949*, London, 1994, p. 56

2ème DB casualties, SHD-DAT 11 P 218

2,873 Parisians killed in the month of August, AVP

'*les délices d'une nuit dédiée à Vénus*', Marc de Possesse, 2e DB, MdC TE 361

'I was providentially removed . . .', Rev. Père Roger Fouquer, Aumônier Divisionnaire, 2ème DB, MdC TE 825 'beer, cider . . .', BD

'Slowly the tank hatches . . .', John G. Westover, MdC TE 436 (2)

p. 514 'Me, I don't give a damn . . .', Marc de Possesse, 2e DB, MdC TE 361

'Direct General Leclerc that . . .', SHD-DAT 11 P 218

international composition of the 2ème DB, SHD-DAT 11 P 231

Rol-Tanguy's headquarters calls for 6,000 FFI, SHD-DAT 13 P 42 1

'members of the National Council of Resistance . . .', Robert Aron, *Historie de la Libération de la France*, Paris, 1959, p. 442

p. 515 'Public order is a matter . . .', Boegner, p. 301, quoted in Beevor and Cooper, p. 63

'an informal visit', NA II 407/427/24235

'General Gerow, as military . . .', NA II 407/427/24235

p. 516 '*collaboratrice!*' John G. Westover, MdC TE 436 (2)

head-shaving on balcony of Mairie, Madame Talbot, MdC TE 133

'We are sickened . . .', Marc de Possesse, 2e DB, MdC TE 361

20,000 Frenchwomen, Fabrice Virgili, *Shorn Women*, Oxford, 2002

'As we neared the city . . .', Forrest C. Pogue, *Pogue's War*, Lexington, Kentucky, 2001, p. 174

p. 517 'an American enclave . . .', Simone de Beauvoir, *La Force des Choses*, Paris, 1960, p. 29

'Pig Alley' and drunken soldiers in the Place Vendôme, Pogue, pp. 229–30

allocation of penicillin, Major General Kenner, SHAEF, OCMH-FPP

30 AFTERMATH

p. 519 'I saw Frenchmen in the streets . . .', Major L. J. Massey, MdC TE 167

De Gaulle's visit and minister for reconstruction, William I. Hitchcock, *Liberation*, London, 2008, p. 57

p. 520 76,000 people had lost their homes, TNA WO 219/3728, quoted in Hitchcock, p. 44

'There are those who . . .', Madame Ruet, Montebourg, MdC TE 63

p. 521 '*camaraderie du malheur*', MdC TE 149

Saingt family at Fleury, Georges Hebert, MdC TE 12

'*discipline exemplaire*', Bernard Goupil, MdC TE 191

195th Field Ambulance near Honfleur, J. C. Watts, *Surgeon at War*, London, 1955, p. 110

p. 522 'Civil life will be mighty dull', Martin Blumenson (ed.), *The Patton Papers, 1940–1945*, New York, 1974, p. 521

'It is astonishing . . .', 21 June, Field Marshal Lord Alanbrooke, *War Diaries 1939–1945*, London, 2001, p. 561

p. 523 'First of all he's a psychopath . . .', Cornelius Ryan papers, Ohio University Library Department of Archives and Special Collections, quoted in *The Times*, 9 November 2007

Select Bibliography

Agte, Patrick, *Michael Wittmann*, Mechanicsburg, Pa., 2006

Alanbrooke, Field Marshal Lord, *War Diaries 1939–1945*, London, 2001

Amouroux, Henri, *La grande histoire des Français sous l'Occupation*, Vol. VIII, Paris, 1988

Aron, Robert, *Histoire de la Libération de la France*, Paris, 1959

Balkoski, Joseph, *Beyond the Beachhead*, Mechanicsburg, Pa., 1999

Baumgarten, Harold, *Eyewitness on Omaha Beach*, Jacksonville, Fla., 1994

Bédarida, François (ed.), *Normandie 44, du débarquement à la Libération*, Paris, 2004

Beevor, Antony, and Cooper, Artemis, *Paris after the Liberation, 1944–1949*, London, 1994

Belfield, Eversley, and Essame, H., *The Battle for Normandy*, London, 1975

Below, Nicolaus von, *Als Hitlers Adjutant, 1937–1945*, Mainz, 1980

Bennett, Ralph, *Ultra in the West*, New York, 1979

Bidault, Georges, *D'une Résistance à l'autre*, Paris, 1965

Biddle, Tami Davis, 'Bombing by the Square Yard: Sir Arthur Harris at War, 1942–1945', *International History Review*, XXI, 3, September 1999

Blumenson, Martin, *Breakout and Pursuit*, Washington, DC, 1961

—— *The Battle of the Generals*, New York, 1993

—— *The Duel for France*, New York, 2000

Blumenson, Martin (ed.), *The Patton Papers, 1940–1945*, New York, 1974

Boegner, Philippe, *Carnets du Pasteur Boegner*, Paris, 1992

Boivin, Michel, *Les victimes civiles de la Manche dans la bataille de Normandie*, Caen, 1994

Böll, Heinrich, *Briefe aus dem Krieg 1939–1945*, Vol. II, Cologne, 2001

Botsford, Gardner, *A Life of Privilege, Mostly*, New York, 2003

Bradley, Omar, *A Soldier's Story*, New York, 1951

Bramall, Edwin, 'D-Day Plus One', in *More Tales from the Travellers*, Oxford, 2005

Brossat, Alain, *Les Tondues: un carnaval moche*, Paris, 1992

Buckley, John (ed.), *The Normandy Campaign 1944*, London, 2006

Butcher, Harry C., *Three Years with Eisenhower*, London, 1946

Butler, J. R. M., and Gwyer, M. A., *Grand Strategy*, Vol. III, London, 1964

Calmette, A., *Les Equipes Jedburgh dans la Bataille de France*, Paris, 1966

Capa, Robert, *Slightly out of Focus*, New York, 1947

Carver, Michael, *Out of Step*, London, 1989

Chandler, Alfred D. (ed.), *The Papers of Dwight David Eisenhower*, Vol. III, *The War Years*, Baltimore, MD, 1970

Choltitz, General Dietrich von, *De Sebastopol à Paris*, Paris, 1964

Clarke, Dudley, *The Eleventh at War*, London, 1952

Close, Bill, *A View from the Turret*, Tewkesbury, 1998

Cloudsley-Thompson, J. L., *Sharpshooter: Memories of Armoured Warfare, 1939–1945*, Fleet Hargate, 2006

Collins, J. Lawton, *Lightning Joe: An Autobiography*, Novato, CA, 1994

Colville, John, *The Fringes of Power: Downing Street Diaries 1939–1955*, London, 1985

Copp, Terry, *Fields of Fire*, Toronto, 2003

—— *Cinderella Army: The Canadians in Northwest Europe, 1944–1945*, Toronto, 2007

Copp, Terry, and McAndrew, Bill, *Battle Exhaustion: Soldiers and Psychiatrists in the Canadian Army, 1939–1945*, Montreal, 1990

Daglish, Ian, *Operation Bluecoat, The British Armoured Breakout*, 2003

—— 'Operation Bluecoat', in John Buckley (ed.), *The Normandy Campaign 1944*, London, 2006

Dansette, Adrien, *Histoire de la Libération de Paris*, Paris, 1946

De Beauvoir, Simone, *La Force des Choses*, Paris, 1960

De Gaulle, Charles, *Mémoires de Guerre*, Vol. II, Paris, 1959

D'Este, Carlo, *Decision in Normandy: The Unwritten Story of Montgomery and the Allied Campaign*, New York, 1983

—— *Eisenhower*, New York, 2002

Doubler, Michael D., *Closing with the Enemy: How GIs fought the War in Europe, 1944–1945*, Lawrence, Kansas, 1994

Douglas, Keith, *The Complete Poems*, London, 2000

Dronne, Raymond, *La Libération de Paris*, Paris, 1970

Select Bibliography

Ellis, L. F., *Victory in the West*, Vol. I, London, 1962

Evans, Richard J., *The Third Reich at War: How the Nazis led Germany from Conquest to Disaster*, London, 2008

Foot, M. R. D., *SOE in France*, London, 1966

Fussell, Paul, *The Boys' Crusade*, New York, 2003

Galtier-Boissière, Jean, *Mon journal pendant l'Occupation*, Paris, 1944

Girard, Christian, *Journal de Guerre: 1939–1945*, Paris, 2000

Golley, John, *The Day of the Typhoon*, Shrewsbury, 2000

Gooderson, Ian, *Air Power at the Battlefront: Allied Close Air Support in Europe 1943–1945*, London, 1998

Harrison, Gordon A., *The United States Army in World War II: Cross-Channel Attack*, Washington, DC, 1951

Hart, Stephen A., *Montgomery and 'Colossal Cracks': The 21st Army Group in Northwest Europe, 1944–1945*, Westport, Conn., 2000

—— 'The Black Day Unrealised', in John Buckley (ed.), *The Normandy Campaign 1944*, London, 2006

Hart-Davis, Duff (ed.), *King's Counsellor: Abdication and War, the Diaries of Sir Alan Lascelles*, London, 2006

Hastings, Max, *Overlord*, London, 1989

Hills, Stuart, *By Tank into Normandy*, London, 2002

Hitchcock, William I., *Liberation: Europe 1945*, London, 2008

Howard, Michael, *Liberation or Catastrophe? Reflections on the History of the Twentieth Century*, London, 2007

Howarth, David, *Dawn of D-Day*, London, 1959

Jary, Sydney, *18 Platoon*, Bristol, 1998

Johnson, Garry, and Dunphie, Christopher, *Brightly Shone the Dawn*, London, 1980

Keegan, John, *Six Armies in Normandy*, London, 1992

Kershaw, Ian, *Hitler: 1936–1945, Nemesis*, London, 2000

Lacouture, Jean, *De Gaulle: The Rebel 1890–1944*, New York, 1990

Lewis, Adrian R., *Omaha Beach: A Flawed Victory*, North Carolina, 2001

Lieb, Peter, *Konventioneller Krieg oder Weltanschauungskrieg? Kriegführung und Partisanenbekämpfung in Frankreich 1943/44*, Munich, 2007

McKee, Alexander, *Caen: Anvil of Victory*, London, 1965

Mackenzie, William, *The Secret History of SOE: Special Operations Executive 1940–1945*, London, 2000

Margolian, Howard, *Conduct Unbecoming: The Story of the Murder of Canadian Prisoners of War in Normandy*, Toronto, 1998

Meyer, Hubert, *The 12th SS: The History of the Hitler Youth Panzer Division*, Vol. I, Mechanicsburg, Pa., 2005

Meyer, Kurt, *Grenadiers*, Mechanicsburg, Pa., 2005

Moses, Harry, *The Faithful Sixth*, Durham, 1995

Neitzel, Sönke (ed.), *Tapping Hitler's Generals: Transcripts of Secret Conversations*, St Paul, Mn., 2007

Norwich, John Julius (ed.), *The Duff Cooper Diaries*, London, 2005

Ose, Dieter, *Entscheidung im Westen 1944: Der Oberbefehlshaber West und die Abwehr der alliierten Invasion*, Stuttgart, 1982

Panter-Downes, Mollie, *London War Notes*, London, 1971

Perrigault, Jean-Claude, and Meister, Rolf, *Götz von Berlichingen: Normandie*, Bayeux, 2005

Pogue, Forrest C., *The Supreme Command*, Washington, DC, 1954

—— *Pogue's War*, Lexington, Kentucky, 2001

Price, Alfred, 'The Rocket-Firing Typhoons in Normandy', *Royal Air Force Air Power Review*, VIII, I, Spring 2005

Quellien, Jean, and Garnier, Bernard, *Les victimes civiles du Calvados dans la bataille de Normandie, 1 mars 1944–31 décembre 1945*, Caen, 1995

Reardon, Mark J., *Victory at Mortain: Stopping Hitler's Panzer Counteroffensive*, Lawrence, Kansas, 2002

Ritgen, H., *Die Geschichte der Panzer-Lehr Division im Westen, 1944–1945*, Stuttgart, 1979

Rosse, Captain the Earl of, and Hill, Colonel E. R., *The Story of the Guards Armoured Division*, London, 1956

Rowland, David, *The Stress of Battle: Quantifying Human Performance in Battle*, Norwich, 2006

Salaita, George D., 'Embellishing Omaha Beach', *Journal of Military History*, April 2008

Scannell, Vernon, *Argument of Kings*, London, 1987

Scott, Desmond, *Typhoon Pilot*, London, 1982

Seaman, Mark (ed.), *Operation Foxley: The British Plan to Kill Hitler*, Kew, 1998

Sheffield, Gary, 'Dead Cows and Tigers: Some Aspects of the Experience of the British Soldier in Normandy, 1944', in John Buckley (ed.), *The Normandy Campaign 1944*, London, 2006

Shulman, Milton, *Defeat in the West*, London, 1986

Speidel, Hans, *We Defended Normandy*, London, 1951

Sprot, Aidan, *Swifter Than Eagles*, Edinburgh, 1998

Stagg, J. M., *Forecast for Overlord*, London, 1971

Tombs, Robert and Isabelle, *That Sweet Enemy*, London, 2006

Tout, Ken, *Tank! 40 Hours of Battle, August, 1944*, London, 1985

Virgili, Fabrice, *Shorn Women: Gender and Punishment in Liberation France*, Oxford, 2002

Vogel, Detlef, and Wette, Wolfram (eds.), *Andere Helme – Andere Menschen? Heimaterfahrung und Frontalltag im Zweiten Weltkrieg*, Essen, 1995

Watts, J. C., *Surgeon at War*, London, 1955

Weigley, Russell F., *Eisenhower's Lieutenants*, New York, 1981

Whistler, Laurence, *The Laughter and the Urn: The Life of Rex Whistler*, London, 1985

Wilmot, Chester, *The Struggle for Europe*, London, 1952

Zetterling, Niklas, *Normandy 1944: German Military Organization, Combat Power and Organizatonal Effectiveness*, Winnipeg, 2000

Zuehlke, Mark, *Juno Beach: Canada's D-Day Victory, June 6, 1944*, Vancouver, 2005

A more detailed bibliography is available at www.antonybeevor.com.

Index

Index

ANTONY BEEVOR

STALINGRAD

The classic international bestseller recounting the epic turning point of the Second World War.

'The colossal scale of Stalingrad, the megalomania, the utter absurdity, the sheer magnitude of the carnage, are marvellously captured in Beevor's history' Richard Bernstein, *New York Times*

'This superb work of narrative history (all of human despair, and also of heroism is there) chilled the marrow of my bones' Antonia Fraser, *Sunday Times*

'Magnificent' John Keegan, *Daily Telegraph*

'Brilliant' *The Times*

'A magnificent winter tapestry … reads like a novel rather than the superb history book it really is' *Daily Telegraph*

'Superb … a compelling tale of human tribulation' Max Hastings

ANTONY BEEVOR

BERLIN: THE DOWNFALL 1945

'Fascinating, extraordinary, gripping' Jeremy Paxman

'Recounts, in harrowing detail and with formidable skill, the brutal death throes of Hitler's Reich at the hands of the rampaging Red Army' Boyd Tonkin, *Independent*

'Makes us feel the chaos and the fear as if every drop of blood was our own … compellingly readable, deeply researched and beautifully written' Simon Sebag Montefiore, *Spectator*

'An irresistibly compelling narrative of events so terrible that they still have the power to provoke wonder and awe' Adam Sisman, *Observer*

'A masterpiece' Michael Burleigh, *Guardian*

He just wanted a decent book to read ...

Not too much to ask, is it? It was in 1935 when Allen Lane, Managing Director of Bodley Head Publishers, stood on a platform at Exeter railway station looking for something good to read on his journey back to London. His choice was limited to popular magazines and poor-quality paperbacks – the same choice faced every day by the vast majority of readers, few of whom could afford hardbacks. Lane's disappointment and subsequent anger at the range of books generally available led him to found a company – and change the world.

'We believed in the existence in this country of a vast reading public for intelligent books at a low price, and staked everything on it'
Sir Allen Lane, 1902–1970, founder of Penguin Books

The quality paperback had arrived – and not just in bookshops. Lane was adamant that his Penguins should appear in chain stores and tobacconists, and should cost no more than a packet of cigarettes.

Reading habits (and cigarette prices) have changed since 1935, but Penguin still believes in publishing the best books for everybody to enjoy. We still believe that good design costs no more than bad design, and we still believe that quality books published passionately and responsibly make the world a better place.

So wherever you see the little bird – whether it's on a piece of prize-winning literary fiction or a celebrity autobiography, political tour de force or historical masterpiece, a serial-killer thriller, reference book, world classic or a piece of pure escapism – you can bet that it represents the very best that the genre has to offer.

Whatever you like to read – trust Penguin.